EXPORTING THE FIRST AMENDMENT

LONGMAN SERIES IN
PUBLIC COMMUNICATION
Series Editor: Ray Eldon Hiebert

EXPORTING THE FIRST AMENDMENT
The Press-Government Crusade of 1945–1952

MARGARET A. BLANCHARD

University of North Carolina
at Chapel Hill

Longman
New York & London

Executive Editor: Gordon T. R. Anderson
Production Editor: Halley Gatenby
Cover Design: Steven August Krastin
Production Supervisor: Judith Stern
Compositor: Graphicraft Typesetters Ltd.
Printer and Binder: The Alpine Press, Inc.

Exporting the First Amendment

Longman Inc.
95 Church Street
White Plains, N.Y. 10601

Associated companies:
Longman Group Ltd., London
Longman Cheshire Pty., Melbourne
Longman Paul Pty., Auckland
Copp Clark Pitman, Toronto
Pitman Publishing Inc., Boston

Library of Congress Cataloging-in-Publication Data

Blanchard, Margaret A.
    Exporting the First Amendment.

    (Longman series in public communication)
    Bibliography: p.
    1. Freedom of the press.   2. Government and the
press.   3. Government and the press—United States.
4. United States—Relations—Foreign countries.
I. Title.   II. Series.
PN4735.B53   1985   323.44'5   86-109
ISBN 0-582-28430-9

86 87 88 89 9 8 7 6 5 4 3 2 1

For my parents

Contents

Acknowledgments

I would like to thank the University of North Carolina at Chapel Hill for awarding me a Junior Faculty Development Grant, without which the travel necessary for researching this book would have been impossible. My work at the National Archives in Washington, D.C., was greatly facilitated by Sally Marks and Kathy Nicastro of the Diplomatic Records Section, both of whom were helpful in tracking down elusive leads to pertinent documents. David Phieffer at the Washington National Records Center in Suitland, Maryland, provided similar assistance. Representatives of the Information and Privacy Staff of the Department of State also aided by processing Freedom of Information Acts requests.

Staff members in the Special Collections department of the Joseph Regenstein Library at the University of Chicago, the Special Collections department of the Robert Muldrow Cooper Library at Clemson University, Clemson, South Carolina, and the Manuscripts Department of the Alderman Library at the University of Virginia, Charlottesville, were extremely helpful when it came to working on the papers of William Benton, James F. Byrnes, and Edward R. Stettinius, Jr. Similar thanks must go to staff members of the Harry S. Truman Library in Independence, Missouri.

Without the help of Pat Langelier, international documents librarian at the Walter R. Davis Library at the University of North Carolina at Chapel Hill, the chapters of this book that deal with activities involving various United Nations bodies would have been much harder to research. Mrs. Langelier was tireless in her efforts to help me sort out the somewhat confusing hierarchical system of the United Nations and was very willing to assist in tracking down some of the more obscure references. Members of the Inter-Library Loan Department at Davis Library were also very helpful in obtaining several important professional journalism periodicals that were not in our collection.

Also invaluable in the researching of this book were the efforts of Betty Thorne Borthwick, a master's degree student in the School of Journalism at the University of North Carolina at Chapel Hill, who spent many hours in the library screening documents and following up information. She provided cheerful encouragement as we made our way through more pages of documents than either one of us was willing to count.

The book would not have been written without the support of Dr. John E. Semonche, professor of history at the University of North Carolina at Chapel Hill. This study began as a dissertation under his supervision and developed into this full-length work with his encouragement. This project taught me that an individual never stops learning about her profession. Fortunately, some teachers never stop teaching.

My fellow faculty members in the School of Journalism at the University of North Carolina at Chapel Hill, my friends, and my family have all bolstered my spirits and resolve during this research and writing process. Although I cannot name each one of them specifically, I do appreciate their interest, concern, and support.

Margaret A. Blanchard

Abbreviations Used in Notes

PRIVATE PAPERS

Benton Papers   William Benton Papers, University of Chicago, Chicago

Byrnes Papers   James F. Byrnes Papers, Clemson University, Clemson, South Carolina

Stettinius Papers   Edward R. Stettinius, Jr., Papers (#2723), Manuscripts Department, University of Virginia Library, Charlottesville, Virginia

Truman Papers   Harry S. Truman Papers, Truman Library, Independence, Missouri

PROFESSIONAL PUBLICATIONS

ASNE Bulletin   *The Bulletin of the American Society of Newspaper Editors*

E&P   *Editor & Publisher*

Problems of Journalism—xxxx   *Problems of Journalism, Proceedings of the xxxx Convention of the American Society of Newspaper Editors*

UNITED NATIONS PUBLICATIONS

A/AC.42/—   United Nations, General Assembly, Committee on the Draft Convention on Freedom of Information

A/C.3/—   United Nations, General Assembly, Third Committee

E/AC.7/—   United Nations, Economic and Social Council, Social Committee

E/AC.27/—   United Nations, Economic and Social Council, Human Rights Committee

E/AC.34/—   United Nations, Economic and Social Council, *Ad Hoc* Committee on the Organization and Operation of the Council and Its Commissions

ECOR	United Nations, Economic and Social Council Official Records
E/CN.4/—	United Nations, Economic and Social Council, Commission on Human Rights
E/CN.4/Sub.1/—	United Nations, Economic and Social Council, Commission on Human Rights, Subcommission on Freedom of Information and of the Press
E/CONF.6/—	United Nations, Economic and Social Council, Conference on Freedom of Information, Geneva, 1948
GAOR	United Nations, General Assembly Official Records
UNESCO Proceedings	UNESCO General Conference Proceedings

UNITED STATES GOVERNMENT PUBLICATIONS

FR	*Foreign Relations of the United States*
FR: Potsdam	*Foreign Relations: Conference of Berlin (Potsdam): 1945*
NA	National Archives, Washington, D.C.
SDR	State Department Records, Released through Freedom of Information Act
RG 43	Record Group 43, Records of International Conferences, Commissions, and Expositions, Records Relating to the United Nations Conference on Freedom of Information, 1948
RG 59	Record Group 59, General Records of the Department of State, Decimal file 1945–1949
RG 84	Record Group 84, Records of the Foreign Service Posts of the Department of State
RG 353	Record Group 353, Records of Interdepartmental and Intradepartmental Committees—State Department Washington National Records Center, Suitland, Maryland

EXPORTING THE FIRST AMENDMENT

Introduction

Leaders of the victorious allies failed to make the world safe for democracy immediately after World War I. Determined not to repeat the same mistakes, Americans began suggesting ways to ensure that the world would never war again even while World War II was raging. Supremely confident in the American system of government and way of life, Americans believed that the only sure means to save the world from future conflict was to convert the world to American ideals and values—to transform almost every country on earth into a miniature United States in form of government, traditions, and institutions. American journalists adopted this idea quickly, adapting the notion to the special needs of the institution they represented.

By the middle of the war, these journalists were advocating a campaign to export the First Amendment guarantee of freedom of the press to the rest of the world. If other nations adopted the American press system at war's end, the media of these countries would then be equipped to inform their audiences about their own governments and the rest of the world in much the same way that the press in America did. American journalists believed that their free-press system had prevented government leaders from propagandizing the country into war as Hitler and other World War II leaders had done in their respective countries. If journalists only could manage to export the blessings that the American free-press system brought to the United States then, indeed, the world would be assured of democracy and peace.

From the beginning, the free-press crusade encountered numerous difficulties. Many observers viewed the effort to export the American system of freedom of the press as little more than an attempt to open the world to reporters from American news agencies. In fact, news agency heads had spent much of the 1930s trying to convince other nations to allow correspondents from the United States into their territories to gather and report the news without interference. The free-press crusade of the 1940s rephrased the news agency endeavor in terms of opening all countries to all foreign correspondents and allowing journalists from all countries to operate freely throughout the world.

Another problem revealed by the free-press crusade centered on the inexperience of American journalists in the international arena. United States editors and reporters felt themselves competent to comment on and report on world affairs, but negotiating with the world's leaders on a topic that was both highly controversial and quite sensitive proved to be another matter entirely. With a firm conviction in their missionary dream, American press leaders had difficulty understanding the reluctance of journalists in other countries to enthusiastically embrace freedom of the press, American style. Complicating matters still further, American journalists seemed unable to grasp the basic fact that although freedom of the press worked well in the United States, the system's precepts simply did not mesh with practices and traditions in other countries. An impatient breed, American journalists also were poor candidates for diplomatic negotiations, where slowness, deliberation, and long debate were the keys to success. And international negotiations required a certain willingness to compromise, a characteristic impossible for a group so convinced of the moral rectitude of its position to accept. International negotiations also demanded consider- able commitment on the part of participants; throughout the crusade, observers questioned the depth of devotion to the international effort within the press community.

One reason the American press community was split over supporting the free-press crusade centered on the pivotal role played by the United States government in the campaign. When the press associations' chiefs tried to open the world to American correspondents in the 1930s, they worked primarily on their own, without a great deal of overt governmental help. When the free-press crusade of the post–World War II era took form, crusade leaders recognized immediately the essential nature of overt and active cooperation by the American government if the campaign was to succeed. Forming an alliance with the United States government, however, was difficult for the press, and vice versa.

Press relationships with the government traditionally are adversarial, and they were particularly so during the administrations of Franklin D. Roosevelt, when many press leaders stood in open opposition to the president's policies. Despite this ongoing conflict, the most ardent free-press advocates were at least one step removed from the New Deal battles. The American press establishment has three tiers, and the publishers—the top tier—were Roosevelt's main opponents. Leading backers of the international crusade were the editors, who, to a large extent, remained out of the New Deal controversies. The third tier of the press system, the reporters, generally was pro-Roosevelt but played a slightly lesser role in the interna- tional crusade. Thus, most of the crusade's participants were able to work with the government in order to gain this international goal. The coopera- tion between the two traditional adversaries was carefully circumscribed, however, for the government was expected to play only a limited role in the crusade. Through government help, international accords were to be negotiated. Those accords, though, were to call for no governmental interference in the activities of the press at home or abroad by participating nations. Once the government had served its purpose in arranging the pacts, its representatives were expected to abandon the field.

Cooperation between the press and American government during the crusade faced at least one more substantial obstacle. Even as American journalists worked with the State Department to promote international freedom of the press, journalists insisted on conducting business as usual on all other government-related matters. Here, business as usual meant prying loose as much information about various international problems and plans as possible and publishing that information, regardless of State Department entreaties for confidentiality. Business as usual also meant press opposition to State Department plans that the press felt unwise. On the State Department's side, diplomats struggled to preserve the sanctity of confidential negotiations and tried to fend off complaints from allies and adversaries about the overzealousness of the American press in reporting certain events. The press-government affiliation often seemed to be an uneasy alliance.

Members of the American press had other problems at home during the years of the crusade as well. Although most of the difficulties of the press during this period are beyond the scope of this study, the concerns were substantial. The prewar years, for instance, had featured increasing criticism of the organization and operation of the American press system from inside and outside of the profession. Many critics contended that the American press was an irresponsible institution more interested in making a profit than in serving the people of the United States. Similar charges continued after the war and dogged the crusade's progress. Nor could American journalists give their full attention to the international crusade due to the persistent nature of other domestic problems. As with many American industries during the postwar years, United States newspapers were plagued with rapidly escalating costs and with strikes that impaired their abilities to function. And, as with many other American industries, American journalism was undergoing massive changes brought on by new technology.

The free-press crusade is basically a story of newspaper journalists' efforts to establish worldwide freedom of the press, for the late 1940s and early 1950s were the last years of newspaper superiority in American journalism. By that time, radio broadcasters were commonplace, and most newspaper journalists had reluctantly accepted radio reporters as compatriots. The crusade also, ultimately, sought to protect the ability of newsreel camera operators to function. But the communication medium of the latter 1950s—television—was in its infancy during the free-press crusade. In fact, a Federal Communications Commission freeze on licenses, which lasted throughout the crusade, had temporarily halted television's progress pending evaluation of technical developments and the establishment of regulations for the new medium. Antagonism between the printed medium and the electronic media was apparent in American life, however, through skirmishes involving newspaper refusal to run radio program logs for free and repeated demands from broadcasters for equal treatment at important news events.

In addition, the international crusade had a "freedom to listen" aspect, even though the events are not a focal point of this story. During the years under consideration, freedom to listen meant freedom of people living behind the iron curtain to listen to Voice of America programming. Also included within the purview of the international crusade was freedom for American films, books, and magazines to circulate throughout the world, but these efforts digress from the primary thrust of this study. The crusade had a strong technical aspect as well, including discussions on access to cables for transmission of news, rates charged for transmission, and the ability to regulate news so dispatched. All these elements, too, save for the latter, are basically beyond the range of this study. This, then, is primarily a newspaper story seen through the last glory days of the newspaper's dominance as an information medium.

The crusade occurred during one of the most critical periods in American and world history—the postwar readjustment of nations into West, East, and nonaligned blocs. Indeed, most of the concerns voiced by diplomats and journalists alike during the crusade focused on how the Soviet bloc would react to certain moves or ideas. Few State Department planners or American journalists questioned whether allies within the Western nations were willing to abandon their own press systems in favor of the American system. Crusade leaders paid even less attention to how the newly independent, nonaligned nations felt about opening their territories to representatives of news agencies from other nations.

In general, the free-press crusade was part of a larger effort by American diplomats and business leaders to create a world safe for democracy by remodeling that world in the image of the United States. Although tinged with self-interest, the free-press effort was basically grounded in noble intentions. In fact, rhetoric surrounding the crusade often resembled that of a religious crusade designed to save the world from a press system unable to handle the delicate task of preserving the world's peace. The crusade was beset by problems, many of which arose from the inordinate naiveté displayed by free-press advocates. But the rise and fall of the free-press crusade shadows the pattern of other American philanthropic endeavors of the postwar years, many of which were lost in the deepening cold war. Regardless of any problems encountered, however, American journalists—full of missionary zeal and conviction—single-mindedly pursued the elusive goal of exporting the First Amendment.

CHAPTER 1

The Roots of the Crusade

When the American press and its allies within the United States government launched their great international free-press crusade at the end of World War II, the campaign's precepts had been incorporated into the nation's goals for peace. Leaders of the press establishment used their considerable power to promote the goal at home and abroad at every possible opportunity. The rhetoric surrounding the crusade was rousing, the fervor intense. But the worldwide free-press debate of the late 1940s and early 1950s was not a product of World War II. Indeed, free-press issues had troubled the relationships among press agencies in America and in other parts of the world since their foundings.

Actually, the free-press crusade began with the organized gathering of news itself during a fifteen-year span in the mid–nineteenth century when four organizations, soon known as news agencies, appeared in different parts of the world. In 1836, Charles Havas set up the Havas agency in France; in 1848, New York newspapers created the forerunner of the modern Associated Press; in 1849, Bernhard Wolff established the Wolff agency in Germany; and in 1851, Julius de Reuter founded Reuters in England. Although the first interest of the three European agencies was the distribution of commercial information, Havas, Reuter, and Wolff soon realized how profitable selling news could be. The years immediately after the agencies' founding were fiercely competitive, but the trio quickly decided that unbridled competition for customers throughout Europe meant lower profits for all. Consequently, in 1870 the three European agencies agreed to divide the world into three parts, with each agency obtaining a monopoly in its particular geographic area. Reuters served the British Empire, North America, certain states in the Middle East, and most of Asia. Havas had sole responsibility for the French Empire, southwestern Europe, South America, and parts of Africa. To Wolff went the remainder of Europe. The agreement granted the principals exclusive rights to gather and sell information in their territories. Cartel members also exchanged news of their geographic areas with other members, thus ensuring each of news from around the world.

Initially excluded from the international news cartel, the New York Associated Press gained the right to gather news in the United States for distribution abroad when Reuters agreed to share its North American territory. In 1887, the Associated Press became a cartel member, with its field of influence limited to the continental United States. After the turn of the century, Reuters allowed the Associated Press (AP) to venture into Canada. This international arrangement was highly prized by the American agency. In fact, when an intramural fight within the Associated Press resulted in a complete change in organization leadership in the 1890s, the new management quickly reaffirmed the agreement with the European agencies. Without the accord, the Associated Press had no European news to distribute to member newspapers. Sending Associated Press correspondents throughout the world to cover the news was not yet seen as a viable option. Some newspapers, including the *New York Herald* under James Gordon Bennett, Sr., had established a foreign correspondents' corps, but few publications saw the need to cover events abroad for themselves. The Associated Press did maintain bureaus in the major capitals of the world. These bureaus served as clearinghouses for the selection of news written by the European agencies for transmission to the United States rather than as headquarters for reporters collecting European news for the Associated Press.[1]

Associated Press participation in the cartel developed before the American agency faced any true competition in the United States. In fact, each member's monopoly on news gathering and distribution at home was the main reason for the cartel's success. The newspapers in France, for instance, received news of the world solely from Havas, which obtained news of places under others' supervision from the agencies in charge in those geographic locations. Once the news stories from the other agencies arrived in France, Havas employees chose from among the available information to compile a news report for distribution to French newspapers. Because of this control over the information circulated within various countries, Americans in the news business later charged that these cartel agencies provided a nationalistic slant to all information distributed to clients by careful selection and rewriting of incoming news items.

The foundation of the Associated Press's monopoly in the United States was its rigid membership requirements, which denied entrance to competitors of existing members. Once a newspaper won entry, the benefits of membership almost guaranteed success. But the turn of the century was a time of great growth for newspapers in America, particularly among afternoon publications. Due to membership restrictions, the Associated Press served few afternoon dailies. Also, its member newspapers tended to be older, entrenched publications, leaving no room for new publishers to gain access to the only wire service in the country. Although some entrepreneurs unsuccessfully had challenged the Associated Press in the late nineteenth century, the competitive situation changed dramatically in 1907, when E. W. Scripps set up the United Press Associations (UP) for his publications and others without Associated Press service.

Scripps's association was not a member of the international cartel; in fact, he saw nonmembership as a selling point to new clients. United Press correspondents eventually circled the globe, gathering news to sell to any American newspaper able to pay for it. Under aggressive management, the United Press captured overseas markets as well and soon sold news to newspapers in Tokyo and London. William Randolph Hearst, also denied Associated Press membership for many of his publications, started the International News Service (INS) about the same time. Operating on a smaller scale, Hearst also sent correspondents around the nation and world seeking news for publication in the United States. Consequently, the Associated Press faced strong competition for the first time in its history. The United Press was so successful in establishing an international news-gathering network that European cartel members and United Press leaders briefly discussed the possibility of the latter agency replacing the Associated Press as the American cartel member. The United Press, fiercely independent, rejected the offer.[2]

Quite naturally, these developments greatly upset the Associated Press. As a cooperative organization, Associated Press members shared the costs of news gathering. Corporate bylaws also prohibited members from purchasing news from other agencies. Thus, questions quickly arose as to whether members would continue to support the Associated Press when other American agencies obtained world news unavailable through the international cartel. Some Associated Press members began to feel restive about cartel arrangements that bound the news agency so tightly as the competition prospered, but no discussions of breaking the international agreement occurred before World War I. The outbreak of war brought a new challenge to the Associated Press, for the United Press repeatedly beat the other news agencies with stories and pushed that agency's client list to almost 500 American publications.[3]

Ultimately, American news agencies—the Associated Press included—criticized the European cartel on two major grounds. First, while news agencies in the United States dedicated themselves to honest and objective reporting, the Americans contended that the European agencies "saw news as something that might be bent or twisted as necessary to serve diplomatic or imperial interests."[4] Second, under the cartel agreement, the Associated Press gathered the news about America for distribution abroad, and then Reuters edited that news before distribution in Europe. Consequently, the news about America disseminated abroad—even in the early twentieth century—featured news about "Indians on the war path in the West, lynchings in the South and bizarre crimes in the North. The charge for decades was that nothing creditable to America ever was sent."[5] Despite cartel membership, the Associated Press considered itself untarnished by such criticisms because it was privately owned and rigidly nonpartisan.

THE APPROACH OF WAR BRINGS
COMPLAINTS OF SLANTED NEWS

Complaints about the European news cartel increased as World War I approached. The British, at the head of the transatlantic cable, cut the German cable to keep news from entering or leaving Germany, thus putting Great Britain and its ally, France, in control of all war news sent to the United States and the rest of the world. Such censorship was unforgivable, said Kent Cooper, leader of the developing free-press movement. Cooper, who was then a middle-level executive of the Associated Press, claimed that Reuters and Havas distorted news about the United States distributed in Europe before the war. The rewritten news made the Germans believe that the Americans were uninterested in Europe's plight and that they would not fight for the continent's freedom. These cartel shortcomings were costly for the United States as a whole, but correcting the image of the United States abroad was only one precipitant of the free-press crusade. The other factor was economic. This inextricable linkage between nobility of purpose and commercial advantage throughout the free-press campaign led to intense criticism of news agency efforts in later years.

Cooper, then traffic manager for the Associated Press, identified a plea for unadulterated news from *La Nación* of Buenos Aires, Argentina, as sparking the free-press crusade. Argentina was the suzerainty of the French agency, Havas, and that agency decided what the Argentines could know about the war. After the British cut the German cables, news from the German perspective, formerly hard to obtain, was now completely unavailable. The editors of *La Nación* wanted to print the texts of official German documents, but the French agency refused to transmit any material overseas that its leaders kept from the French people. Thus, the South American editors appealed to the Associated Press for the desired information. Cooper wanted to respond affirmatively, but he was told, apparently for the first time, of the cartel arrangement that made South America the territory of the French news agency and of the ban on American activity in Argentina.[6] Consequently, the editors of *La Nación* turned to the United Press for the desired news and, as a result, the United Press won entry to the lucrative South American market. The Associated Press moved into South America in 1918—after agreeing to compensate Havas for any revenues lost due to Associated Press competition.[7]

. About the same time, the United States government complicated the picture for the Associated Press by asking the news agency to break its cartel agreement and to serve South America, China, and Japan directly. President Woodrow Wilson was concerned that the foreign news services provided a warped view of America, and he was worried about the lack of understanding abroad of United States policies and intentions. Because American news agencies were privately owned, the president could only request assistance from the Associated Press. Wilson did add threats in 1915, however, when he said, "If private capital cannot soon enter upon the adventure of establishing these physical means of communication, the government must undertake to do so."[8] Requests and possible threats were unavailing, and the Associated Press refused to enter South America.

The Far Eastern request was harder to reject because several members of the Associated Press board of directors also wanted to increase the news agency's activities in the Far East. But that area was reserved for Reuters under the cartel agreement, and the board ultimately rejected the government's request. One reason for the refusal was the cartel agreement. Another reason for the board's response rested in the journalists' deeply ingrained suspicion of helping officials meet any goal that any government considered as desirable. Board members hoped that the end of the war would also end the cartel, thus opening up the world to Associated Press reporters.[9] Meanwhile, the United Press again benefited from the Associated Press's refusal to violate the cartel agreement. When Roy W. Howard of the United Press toured South America to sign up clients, he carried a letter of introduction from President Wilson and had the full support of the American diplomatic corps in his mission.[10]

But the cartel agreement did not fall under the weight of the war. Cooper was in Paris during the peace negotiations and argued for a treaty article that would ensure international freedom of the press. "The welfare of the people," he said, demanded that they have "true, unbiased news to read in their newspapers about either world or domestic affairs."[11] Associated Press General Manager Melville E. Stone had forbidden Cooper to attack the cartel directly. The campaign for a peace treaty provision guaranteeing freedom of the press throughout the world and free international exchange of news—meaning freedom for the Associated Press to operate within cartel territory—was Cooper's attempt to accomplish his goal indirectly.[12] Cooper hoped worldwide freedom of the press would prevail, for President Wilson had gone to Paris advocating "open covenants openly arrived at." American reporters covering the peace conference interpreted this statement to mean the emergence of a new diplomacy based on freedom of information as practiced in the United States. They would be sorely disappointed.[13]

No one knows whether peace conference delegates discussed Cooper's vision of international freedom of information.[14] Cooper believed the diplomats considered the topic, but as with most decisions made during the Versailles conference, free dissemination of news was caught up in diplomatic maneuvering. In any event, Reuters and Havas emerged from the war stronger than before. Wolff's position in the cartel diminished significantly as the English and French news agencies insulated Germany from the news of the world and the world from news of Germany just as their foreign ministries isolated Germany in other ways. This strengthening of the cartel occurred despite assurances from presidential adviser Edward M. House that the free-press guarantee issue "had been taken care of privately," a statement Cooper interpreted to mean that the heads of state had agreed to safeguard freedom of the press in the treaty. When the subject was omitted, Cooper admitted being disappointed and wondered if "the Associated Press would gain the freedom of action abroad that its chief competitor, the United Press, had always enjoyed."[15] Why was international freedom of the press left out of the treaty that ended World War I? One critic believed that diplomats ignored the subject because most negotiators thought the idea of the press watching their actions was "indecent."[16] Another observer felt that the ideal had fallen prey to "the machinations of European news agency heads who were bent on maintaining their monopoly on international news."[17]

International freedom of information had advocates within the official American delegation. For instance, Walter S. Rogers, the communications expert accompanying President Wilson to Paris and a former top aide to George Creel at the Committee on Public Information, argued that a growing closeness among all parts of the world led to the inescapable conclusion that "the ultimate basis of peace is common knowledge and understanding between the masses of the world."[18] The press associations and newspapers of the United States concurred. Looking at the propaganda that had surrounded World War I, the journalists worried about the lack of accurate information available to the people of the world about each other and themselves. Rogers agreed that "the ideal is a world-wide freedom for news, with important news going everywhere. The breaking-down of existing barriers resulting from selfishness, chauvinism, or a lack of vision is but a part of present-day needs." All the talents of the world's press organizations were needed "to develop the business of news gathering and distribution to the point where the individual newspaper reader in the remotest nook will have daily before him interesting items from all over the world." Such activity was necessary because more people in the world would be reading newspapers as a result of political power "passing to the common man."[19] Although American journalists endorsed almost everything that Rogers said, the notion of the government assisting to develop communications activities was difficult for many press representatives to accept.

Rogers, later investigating communications problems in the Far East, carried the question of governmental participation in communications even farther by questioning whether private enterprise could ever fill such extensive needs.[20] Indicating that such work was beyond the desires or abilities of private industry angered news agency personnel in the United States. In reality, however, the American news agencies required a sound financial base, and the information program that Rogers envisioned was far too expensive for private industry to undertake. An additional criticism noted that even if the American agencies did significantly increase the amount of news that they sent abroad, the data distributed would not necessarily improve anyone's understanding about the United States since only superficial news was sent overseas. And American newspapers, according to their critics, even had a poor record of publishing news of foreign countries designed to enlighten American readers about the rest of the world. Circulating information on the scale envisioned by Rogers required government participation in the operation[21] and that idea was an anathema to the press of the United States.

Some journalists already had contemplated a more limited ideal, one well within the reach of the American press and one that would gain in popularity over the years. Thus, the campaign began for spreading the American system of freedom of the press throughout the world. The plan called for making the presses of individual nations as free to operate without government interference or help as the press in America. Promotion of the campaign by journalists coincided with American entry into the war. Freedom of the press in America, wrote one of the crusade's earliest exponents, was the basis for informed opinion making and for running the United States government. Adoption of a similar system of press freedom worldwide meant freeing the peoples of other countries from the sway of dictatorship and from future wars. Free exchange of news among nations would obliterate international misunderstandings.[22] Clouding the horizon was the necessity of governmental assistance to establish this ideal. Kent Cooper's attempts to have a free-press guarantee written into the Treaty of Versailles already had revealed that relationship. Such governmental assistance, however, usually carried a price tag, but early advocates of the dream ignored that reality.

THE LEAGUE OF NATIONS ADDRESSES
FREEDOM OF INFORMATION QUESTIONS

The free-press idea lived on in the intrawar years as the League of Nations and other organizations sponsored international conferences on the topic.[23] The international sessions offered United States proponents of the ideal some valuable insights; the Americans regularly confronted advocates of different concepts on how the press of the world should operate.

Walter Williams tried to place press freedom on the world's agenda during a meeting of the nongovernmental Press Congress of the World in Geneva in 1926. Williams, the congress president and the dean of the University of Missouri School of Journalism, called for an international conference to study improving facilities for transmitting news throughout the world and for reducing the costs of that transmission. Reasonable transmission rates were critical, Williams explained, because the "lack of adequate and correct information makes impossible truthful interpretation and comment. It is useless to have liberty to publish and discuss facts unless there is unfettered opportunity to obtain these facts."[24] Williams termed each item vital to the existence of a free press and stressed that a free press was essential to the continuation of a free world. Williams realized that his goals were beyond the reach of journalists working alone: "Freedom to write the truth and freedom to obtain the truth necessitate government action. Laws, charters, treaties, have, in part at least, control." Since public opinion could force changes in such provisions, journalists must "aid in the creation of public opinion which will effectuate the desired changes." To accomplish this end, Williams urged the League of Nations to call a conference devoted specifically to press issues.[25]

A League-sponsored conference on press-related issues was planned for 1927. In fact, representatives of international news agencies met in Geneva shortly before the Press Congress of the World sessions to lay the groundwork for the upcoming conference. During those planning sessions, discussions included the now familiar concern for the cost of sending news cables from one part of the world to another. A new issue, one showing the importance of commercial concerns to American journalists, also surfaced. Under the prodding of Howard, now chairman of the board of Scripps-Howard Newspapers and representing the United Press, news agency representatives discussed property rights in news. The American wire services—including the Associated Press, which denounced the cartel agreement in 1927 in favor of a more liberal contractual accord[26]—worried about the pirating of their news stories by organizations not buying the stories.

The Americans wanted to obtain international agreement to the principles established by a 1918 United States Supreme Court decision determining that news had a commercial value; the decision denied use of that news by publications that were not customers of the originating agency until the expiration of its commercial value.[27] The Americans carefully explained that they wanted to protect the enterprise story that was the result of a reporter's ingenuity and hard work and the finished product. They denied any intentions of blockading government or official news, which would, of course, be equally available to all agencies and newspapers.[28] The equality of access to official news was critical to American correspondents who often found that governments favored their own domestic press agencies when releasing information. These problems were especially acute when the agency had ties to the regime in power. If the Americans won equal access to news, then their news would become even more valuable and would require even more protection.

When the International Conference of Press Experts convened in Geneva in August 1927, delegates faced an agenda crammed with controversial topics. For instance, should press messages receive priority treatment by cable companies and should these cables cost less than other messages? Should journalists carry international identity cards to simplify their foreign travels? Should journalists be protected from arbitrary expulsion from countries—and, if so, how? Should censorship in peacetime be strictly limited—and again, if so, how? Should governments practice absolute equality in distributing official news to all journalists and news agencies? Should a property right in news be created?[29]

United States journalists greeted the International Conference of Press Experts with great enthusiasm, and they went to Geneva ready to convince the world of the beneficial nature of American domestic news policies.[30] The conference attracted 120 delegates from thirty-six countries. The American delegation was the largest, with its membership including the heads of the three major American press agencies: Kent Cooper, Associated Press; Karl A. Bickel, United Press; and Moses Koenigsberg, International News Service. Delegates performed as expected in several areas. Without much debate, they approved resolutions calling for lower rates for press telegrams and for giving news cables priority over ordinary communications.[31] The conference also accepted the basic American proposal calling for protection of property rights in news,[32] approved a measure calling for limiting censorship in peacetime, and sanctioned the equality of news agencies in the receipt of official news. Conferees also passed a resolution calling on newspapers and news agencies to avoid publishing or distributing news "calculated to cause undesirable misunderstandings among nations and suspicions detrimental to international peace."[33]

Although the false-news proposal eventually would become a problem, the American delegates went home terming the session as "successful beyond the most hopeful expectations," with the less modest among them taking most of the responsibility for the business transacted and "the good feeling which marked the settlement of contentious questions."[34] The resolutions passed by the Geneva conference went to the League of Nations for disposition bearing the immodest preface that positive action on the suggestions would make the press more "effective in its responsible mission accurately and conscientiously to inform world public opinion and hence to contribute directly to the preservation of peace and the advancement of civilisation."[35]

Reactions of the American press to the accomplishments of the United States delegation were equally bold, with *Editor & Publisher* setting the tone. The resolution that established equality of access to the official news of foreign countries was "gratifying proof that the press in other lands is seeing its function in some slight degree as Thomas Jefferson saw it a century ago."[36] Blithely ignoring the non sequitur lurking in that statement, the trade journal added,

There is no vanity in asserting that the American ideal of the press is the highest and most beneficial to humanity that present civilization possesses, and, even though American practice does not always measure tip to tip with the criterion, the extension of the latter to places where it has not been known can result only for the welfare of their journalism and the people it is its privilege to serve.[37]

American journalists repeatedly displayed supreme confidence in their press system and in the potential efficacy of that system when applied to others, but this confidence was soon tested.

Recommendations from the Conference of Press Experts were filed in the League archives, with no official action being taken on the proposals. The topic of international freedom of the press disappeared for several years only to resurface in another time of international stress—1931—under a more ominous guise. The worldwide depression and the propagandistic rumblings emanating from Germany, Italy, and the Soviet Union frightened many individuals who dreaded the possibility of another war. Looking for a convenient scapegoat, League delegates decided that the press, which the Americans considered so instrumental in furthering world peace, actually promoted international disharmony. Thus, the League organized an international conference to investigate "the difficult problem of the spread of false information which may threaten to disturb the peace or the good understanding between nations." In 1932, representatives of government press bureaus, considered by American journalists to be propaganda organizations, met in Copenhagen, Denmark, to discuss the dissemination of allegedly false news. The League asked conferees to remember that the problem, "which is urgent in the interests of international relations," was "extremely delicate from the point of view of the maintenance of the liberty of the Press and the independence of journalists."[38] The impossibility of controlling the dissemination of false information without infringing on the rights of journalists apparently failed to occur to League diplomats. In fact, League leaders omitted representatives of the press from the delegate list. Nonetheless, many press agencies sent representatives to safeguard their interests. Although the United States never joined the League of Nations, Robert Pell, press adviser to the American ambassador in France, went to the conference as an observer.

A primary conference resolution reaffirmed the right of the press to operate and noted that one way to prevent the circulation of inaccurate reports was for government press departments to "furnish rapidly authentic information."[39] But American journalists worried about a proposal to enforce a professional code of honor designed to exclude persons guilty of serious infractions from membership in professional associations. The plan called for the use of an International Court of Honour, founded by the International Federation of Journalists, to adjudicate disputes.[40] American journalists, horrified by the proposal, claimed to be mystified about the organization designated to enforce the rules. Pell abstained from voting on the issue, terming the creation of a journalistic court of honor a prerogative of correspondents rather than directors of government press bureaus. American newspaper representatives at the conference labeled the international body as unnecessary because the reading public would "inevitably punish in its own effective way any professional dereliction."[41]

Another attempt "to restrict the activities of American and other foreign correspondents in Europe by . . . forcing them to send news 'compatible with the interests' of the country in which they are stationed" occurred in 1933. This time, the League summoned directors of government press bureaus to a meeting in Madrid, Spain, to discuss measures that would ensure the dissemination of true news. To American observers, the obvious targets of such efforts were United States correspondents, who transmitted unbiased stories and who could not be controlled "by the ordinary European means."[42] At this meeting, Germany was a leader in the effort to force foreign correspondents to carry international press cards, an idea termed acceptable in 1927, and to create an international court of honor for journalists, an idea sidetracked at the 1932 conference due to American opposition. The latter proposal suffered a similar fate in 1933. The administration of both operations was to rest in the hands of an International Association of Journalists, but American correspondents feared that both measures would fall under the control of governments, thus making possible the "'permanent elimination' of correspondents who would not submit to dictation."[43]

Once again the Americans fended off attempts to curtail the freedom of their correspondents to function. At the suggestion of United States delegate Pell, the conference skirted the false-news issue by proposing the creation of a commission "to study the false news problem by investigating the financial set-up and methods of news gathering agencies." This proposal underlined the American belief that European news agencies disseminated false news because of their close financial links to their home governments.[44] Problems with false news would end, American journalists reasoned, if foreign newspapers could build a financial base similar to the one enjoyed by United States publications. Even though they acknowledged the existence of a false-news problem, American journalists placed the responsibility for false reports squarely on news agencies operating under "the iron heels of dictators." Such systems polluted news for the rest of the world because false reports were spread in one country and then were transmitted around the world as news.[45] American news agencies refused to assume any responsibility for stopping the spread of false news. To Americans, the only solution consistent with the United States press system called for providing news in sufficient quantities to allow readers to sift the true from the false.

Although American news agencies traditionally rejected attempts to pry into their business operations, the fact-finding commission proposed in Madrid carried a possible benefit to the Americans, who were now united against the way European news agencies controlled access to information and convinced of the basic venality of the European press. The existing system discriminated against American correspondents in access both to the news and to the necessary facilities to transmit that information back to the United States. Under the current structure, American news agencies also had difficulty selling their services to European newspapers interested in purchasing the American product. Perhaps, the agency leaders thought, the League's study would lessen these obstacles. Hard pressed by numerous international problems, League delegates refused to act on the recommendation for the creation of a special commission, opting instead for more study and calling for another conference.[46] The world situation, however, was too unstable for another conference, and this battle was delayed until after World War II.

American journalists refused to let the topic of international freedom of the press disappear in the 1930s. For instance, Carl V. Ackerman, dean of the Columbia University Graduate School of Journalism and a close friend of Kent Cooper, reminded the American Society of Newspaper Editors (ASNE) of the importance of international freedom of the press in 1934: "The map of the world today is black with prohibitions upon freedom of speech, freedom of the press, freedom of assembly, of petition, or of religion." Believing in "a direct relationship between the freedom of the press and peace between nations," Ackerman suggested that "the time has come for the American Press to recommend and support a new American policy in foreign affairs." Only the British Commonwealth, a few small nations in Western Europe, and the United States advocated peace in the world. Each of these countries also advocated freedom of the press—which the journalism school dean termed as far from coincidental. "American newspaper correspondents abroad know from experience and as a result of daily contact with realities in every world capital that war follows the control of news as inevitably as darkness follows light."[47]

Therefore, Ackerman asked whether the American press should "demand freedom of the press in world affairs at least as far as every international conference or engagement of this country is concerned? Can we not insist that there must be a free flow of information to the American press?" Since freedom of the press was the greatest safeguard of international peace, "should not the press of America recommend that our own government refuse to participate in any international conference without complete freedom of information for our own press associations and newspapers?" If the American government took such a stand, "every other government in the world would be challenged by a new peace force."[48] ASNE members endorsed Ackerman's recommendation, but apparently they took no action to implement its suggestions at the time.

WORLD WAR II INCREASES FERVOR FOR INTERNATIONAL FREE-PRESS GUARANTEE

Once involved in World War II, American news agency personnel and others advocating international freedom of information as a bar to future wars picked up the crusade with greater vigor. Slowly, too slowly for some, the realization grew that in order "to lift the curse of war from mankind," everyone everywhere in the world "must have essentially the same honest, accurate, and adequate reports on events of world import." This world view, however, could come "only through a free and equal flow of the news, as reported by independent and competing press associations, among all nations."[49] Firmly believing in this fundamental freedom, Cooper again began his crusade to win worldwide freedom of the press.[50]

This time, the press associations had some powerful supporters within the United States government, who, from President Franklin D. Roosevelt on down, adopted freedom of information as a war aim.[51] Governmental support carried certain drawbacks; the main problem was that the president, and later the State Department, refused to speak solely of international freedom of the press. Instead, Roosevelt advocated freedom of information to achieve a stable world: people must have "freedom of knowledge, freedom of information" from all sources. People must also have freedom of expression, the president said, "so long as you don't advocate the overthrow of the Government."[52] As if to underline his support for international freedom of information, the president's Four Freedoms, announced in January 1941, began with "freedom of speech and expression."[53]

Coinciding with America's entry into the war was the establishment of two government agencies to control the flow of information: the Office of War Information, a propaganda agency charged with distributing information about the United States abroad, and the Office of Censorship, a news agency charged with establishing and enforcing voluntary codes of censorship to regulate the publication of war information within the United States. As the United States government again entered the propaganda realm, American journalists feared that this time these federal agencies might remain in existence after the war. Spurred on by such concerns, the effort to secure international freedom of the press increased in fervor. The adoption of the crusade's principles would surely prevent the continuation of propaganda anywhere in the world at the war's end.

The crusade had practical ramifications as well. As war clouds gathered in Europe and the Far East in 1941, Cooper worried about the safety of his correspondents, and he asked Secretary of State Cordell Hull to protect Associated Press reporters stranded abroad. If a United States ambassador or minister received safe transit out of a country, Cooper wanted Associated Press correspondents to be allowed to be taken along as part of the ambassador's entourage. Such security was the least the government could provide, Cooper said, considering that the correspondents "have done remarkably in serving their homeland in this time of stress."[54] Hull responded that although the government had "a thorough understanding and a sympathetic interest" in the problems of the press abroad, he could not protect reporters. Diplomats had a special immunity that allowed them to leave enemy lands, a privilege that could not be extended to nongovernment employees.[55]

Rebuffed on that particular point, Cooper remained undiscouraged. In 1943, Cooper urged Secretary Hull to make a speech "stressing the principles of (1) freedom of the press in every country, (2) equality of access by press agencies, native and foreign, to governmental and other news sources, (3) equality among newsmen in news transmission, and (4) freedom for all news agencies to make exchange arrangements of their own choosing."[56] The extent of Hull's open support for such a program came in a September 1944 news conference when the secretary admitted that the department had been studying the question of international freedom of information. He added, "I have consistently supported the cause of freedom of news and I would support any practical measure to give international recognition to this principle."[57] A special departmental committee was reviewing a wide range of options including placing specific free-press guarantees within peace treaties. "A minimum for the realization of this difficult principle," department personnel suggested, might be:

(1) A general agreement that reputable news reporters and commentators may be admitted to each country for the purpose of reporting events, and of sending these reports back to their country of origin; (2) A general understanding that no country will close its borders to the legitimate publications of other countries; and (3) A general understanding that where any news or communication is undertaken at the instance of a state or government, this fact shall appear in the text of the article.[58]

Even as the Department of State committee worked, the crusade for international freedom of the press assumed a higher profile among the leaders of American newspapers. Cooper was still the campaign's strongest advocate, but he no longer hinted at the commercial benefits that opening the world to all press associations would mean for the Associated Press. Such considerations remained, however, because during the early 1940s, an antitrust challenge to the Associated Press's restrictive membership policies was moving toward the United States Supreme Court. The Associated Press lost the case in 1945, and members of the news cooperative became free to buy other news services without violating their contracts,[59] thus creating even more competition among the American news agencies. Although Cooper's comments about the need for international freedom of the press contained some idealism, cynics saw within the remarks a public relations campaign designed to counter the impact of the antitrust case. Regardless of his other motivations, Cooper apparently truly believed, with many other journalists of his era, that permanent peace was impossible unless everyone everywhere could have "truthful, unbiased news of each other which shall be freely available at the source to all who seek it there, wherever that may be."[60]

To accomplish his goal, Cooper had a new idea: journalists must influence those individuals responsible for negotiating the peace treaties at the war's conclusion. Other interests were represented at the peace table, he said, so why not press interests? "Never at the end of any war in history has an organized effort of the newspaper men of any nation demanded that a peace treaty contain a clause affecting any element of the news business."[61] Now was time to rectify that oversight, and Cooper actively sought allies. This cause had become such a holy calling for Cooper that he even advocated exacting free-press guarantees from nations before granting United States economic aid for reconstruction after the war.[62]

The Associated Press's general manager was particularly eager to gain the support of the American Society of Newspaper Editors in this campaign because he believed that the ASNE was the only organization in the United States capable of sponsoring the movement. Cooper admitted that his proposal was a "stupendous undertaking" that called for the institution of "freedom of the press of the entire world as we know it here." In fact, the worldwide free-press campaign was "striving for the millennium," he said, but "it seems best to attempt that in order at least to gain acceptance of the second point of the program." His second, more achievable goal contained the now familiar demands that news be freely available to all correspondents at its source and that "no country shall give preferential transmission facilities to its own press against the press of any other country." The best press in the world existed in the United States, he added, and "it would be wonderful if the force that is available from that success would be directed altruistically toward the extension of the American accomplishments to the rest of the world."[63]

Hugh Baillie, head of Cooper's leading competitor, the United Press, had some doubts about extending the American system of freedom of the press abroad. To Baillie, the crusade did not "involve the establishment in all countries of what we in the U.S.A. term a free press. That is desirable, but not feasible, unless we wish to try to dictate our way of life to all the other countries of the world." Baillie saw the crusade as seeking something more limited—"equal access to news at its source in all countries, equal transmission rates, no peacetime censorship."[64] Members of the ASNE also voiced some initial concern about the propriety of changing the world's press systems, but they soon adopted the cause of international press freedom as their own.[65] As Cooper, entangled in an ongoing argument with the Department of State, pulled back to some extent, ASNE members became the campaign's primary exponents. Sigma Delta Chi, the society of professional journalists, also threw the considerable weight of working journalists behind the effort.[66]

Even though he disagreed with Cooper about the ultimate ends of the campaign, Baillie's proposed international program was similar to his rival's: news sources available to all equally, transmission facilities available to all equally, limited official interference with news flow, newspapers throughout the world free to purchase news from any available source. But every time Baillie talked of the crusade, he reminded his audience that his program was "based on the principle of free and fair competition in news gathering and distribution for which the U.P. has fought and campaigned in virtually every country of the world since the U.P. was founded in 1907."[67] At times, Baillie's criticisms of the Associated Press were quite direct, as when he noted the United Press's successes in gathering news abroad despite "the world-wide system of interlocking news monopolies," which other press associations—meaning the Associated Press—"chose to remain within."[68] Anticipating an effort by ASNE representatives, Baillie took his campaign overseas, where he met with leaders of the exiled governments of Belgium, the Netherlands, and Norway and won pledges from them to support his international free-press program.[69] Such competitiveness probably impeded the cause of international freedom of the press; indeed, the continuation of the rivalry was a contributing factor in the shift of impetus for the drive from the news associations to the American Society of Newspaper Editors.

As campaign leadership passed to the ASNE, so too did the stirring rhetoric used so effectively by the press associations' chiefs. In 1943, for instance, Roy Roberts, ASNE president and managing editor of the *Kansas City Star*, told members, "This present war was hastened, at least, because there was no free press the world over. Our people and other peoples did not know, nor did they understand, conditions that were developing in the various countries." ASNE members must ensure that similar conditions did not exist at the end of the current war. Acknowledging the concerns registered by his members who were, on the whole, more interested in problems closer to home than the press associations, Roberts stressed that the international effort to eradicate the conditions leading to World War II must be coupled with efforts to maintain and increase freedom of the press at home.[70]

The international free-press campaign carried an additional problem in that the crusade looked very much as if the American press wanted equal access to news sources and transmission facilities abroad to promote its own growth and prosperity. In fact, as Nelson Poynter, editor of the *St. Petersburg Times*, admitted, "our selfish interest in world-wide freedom of information is just as real, though less apparent than our interest in freedom of the seas and air." To support their international goals, newspaper leaders must pressure public officials into supporting worldwide freedom of the press. But, Poynter warned, "we should try for goals beyond the objectives which look to laymen like only newspaper industrial problems."[71] Without question, the press knew how to win the backing of political figures for the free-press crusade. This success soon became unmanageable, however, for the politicians and diplomats that the journalists attracted to the cause expanded the campaign beyond the narrow limits of freedom of the press.

Immediate results of the press's political efforts were spectacular.

Congress quickly passed a joint resolution backing international freedom of the press,[72] and both political parties adopted platform planks pledging to support the concept.[73] In each instance, the political body concerned called in some way for free interchange of news, equality of access to information and to facilities for transmission of news, and preservation of these rights by treaty. The points were exactly what the leaders of the press lobbying effort considered vital. Guaranteeing these rights by treaty, however, meant an alliance between the government and the press, for the press could not conclude treaties with foreign governments on its own. Even as the resolutions of support poured forth from the politicians, journalists and diplomats were warily negotiating with each other over the future of the crusade.

THE AMERICAN SOCIETY OF NEWSPAPER EDITORS ENTERS THE CAMPAIGN

Almost as soon as the editors had decided to support international freedom of the press, a special ASNE committee, chaired by Ralph McGill, editor of the *Atlanta Constitution*, talked with State Department officials and representatives of other appropriate agencies about incorporating free-press guarantees "in any general international organization or any peace settlement that may be established."[74] The ASNE "invited reciprocal declarations by the United States Government and all other governments, press, radio and other media of information, embracing the right of the people to read and hear news without censorship." Recent actions, including the president's declaration of the Four Freedoms, the congressional resolution, and the planks in the political platforms, encouraged the editors. But they vowed that "the ASNE never will relax in its campaign until freedom of information becomes a living reality everywhere in the world."[75] Nebulous plans grew more precise in late 1944, as John S. Knight, ASNE president and head of Knight Newspapers, named a three-man committee to visit various world capitals to discuss plans to establish international freedom of information after the war with governmental and press leaders.[76]

Plans for the trip around the world went forward rapidly. Wilbur Forrest, assistant editor of the *New York Herald Tribune* and ASNE vice president, headed the delegation, which consisted of McGill, chairman of the freedom of information committee, and Ackerman, who had a longtime interest in international freedom of the press. The delegation wanted to make its round-the-world trip as soon as possible, even though the war was still raging. Given statements by various State Department officials about their esteem for international freedom of information, the ASNE trio believed that American diplomats would welcome their mission.

After all, Secretary of State Hull had said in September 1944 that an international agreement guaranteeing freedom of information was under study. And Assistant Secretary of State Aldof A. Berle had assured the Foreign Press Association in June 1944 that "freedom of information is a major necessity if world organization is to succeed. With freedom of information there is a possibility of understanding between peoples. Without it the way is always open to build up misunderstandings, suspicion, fear, and finally, hatred."[77] Further support came from Sumner Welles, confidant of the president, who insisted that the charter of any new international organization must require member nations to prove that their citizens "are granted as inalienable rights freedom of worship, of expression, and of information."[78] Joining the chorus was James Lawrence Fly, chairman of the Federal Communications Commission, who said, "If nations are to live at peace with one another on the face of the earth, they must know and understand one another; and without freedom of communications, such knowledge and understanding is impossible."[79]

Such sterling testimonials, however, were not enough to entice support from the secretary of state when the ASNE delegation visited him on November 28, 1944. They met not twelve-year veteran Cordell Hull but the newly appointed Edward R. Stettinius, Jr.,[80] who had just spent several months fending off complaints from the press about the secrecy that surrounded the Dumbarton Oaks Conference[81] and requests that international freedom of information be part of the Dumbarton Oaks agreements.[82] Stettinius was in no mood to cope with new demands from representatives of the press, and he disliked the idea of journalists entering combat zones to promote an international goal not yet fully sanctioned by the Department of State. In addition, leaders of the free-press movement seemed unable to understand that United States diplomats could not mandate the internal policies of foreign lands.[83]

The initial session was somewhat tense. Stettinius pointed out that the department was studying the free-press matter, with an emerging consensus "that all persons and agencies responsible for getting and disseminating information should be free to do so and that all means of communication should be open to them without restrictions." Undoubtedly, he added, diplomats organizing the United Nations would discuss international freedom of information, and the State Department "would lose no opportunity" to support the ASNE request during those sessions. But, Stettinius concluded, the time was not yet propitious for advancing international freedom of the press. In fact, Michael J. McDermott, assistant to the secretary for press relations, suggested that any effort on the magnitude contemplated by the journalists might backfire because before the American government could discuss the matter with other governments, opponents of the measure already could have marshaled their arguments against efforts to institute international freedom of the press.[84]

Diplomatic problems, however, were unimportant to the ASNE members. The free-press crusade must go forward now, they said, to ensure support from the American people. In one last effort to dissuade the editors, McDermott said that arranging transportation for the trip might be difficult. The journalists quickly turned that problem aside by noting that "General Marshall might be able to help" with transportation. The State Department capitulated and set about facilitating the adventure.[85] A visit from delegation chief Forrest on December 14 finally convinced Stettinius that the trip might have some positive results. Partially responsible for the secretary's change of heart was his "frank talk" with Forrest about problems between the department and Forrest's employer, the *New York Herald Tribune*—"We discussed putting relations between that paper and the Department on a better footing." Stettinius asked Forrest to serve as his emissary to the newspaper's hierarchy,[86] a role that Forrest obviously saw as connected with smoothing the way for the ASNE mission. Within a day, Forrest reported that his employers intended "to give you all support consistent with honest and constructive editorial comment and I can assure you that there is not the slightest feudist tendency here and that all concerned wish you well."[87] The State Department placed no more obstacles in the way of the ASNE delegation, now popularly stylized as free-press missionaries.

Missionaries serve noble purposes, and, consequently, Forrest wanted no stigma of commercialism attached to the trip. In the past, Cooper's advocacy of international press freedom had drawn bitter attacks from abroad. *The Economist* of London, for instance, charged that Cooper's "ode to liberty" really meant the "huge financial resources of the American agencies might enable them to dominate the world." In fact, Cooper, "like most big business executives, experiences a peculiar moral glow in finding that his idea of freedom coincides with his commercial advantage . . . . Democracy does not necessarily mean making the whole world safe for the AP."[88] Forrest constantly reassured Stettinius that the delegation represented only the American Society of Newspaper Editors and that the trio wanted only to "make friendly contact with leading editors and with government officials." The goal was to tell these individuals about the ASNE's idea "that freedom of information internationally is a strong contribution to the future peace of the world. The Committee will in no way represent the American Press Associations which seek the same goal but on a commercial basis."[89]

Divorcing the free-press campaign from the possibility of financial gain won praise. Journalists noted that with few exceptions, the publications represented by ASNE members were "unlikely to enter the international field and have no prospect of financial gain, direct or indirect, from the translation of the ASNE declaration into reality."[90] Despite the truth of this statement, Forrest still feared that adverse commentary might prompt a skeptical secretary of state to withdraw support. Once more Forrest pledged: "The mission will not be a junket. I look upon it as a serious move to lay groundwork for official negotiations later and I sincerely hope that it will prove of value. We shall do our best."[91] Apparently basing his actions on Forrest's pledges, Stettinius notified diplomatic missions that the ASNE group was "embarking upon a very important mission,"[92] that he believed the journey could "achieve important results,"[93] and that American diplomats should give the three men all possible assistance.

The secretary of state was not the only person wishing the trio good luck. Their portfolios bulged with letters from President Roosevelt, Senate Foreign Relations Committee Chairman Tom Connally, House Foreign Affairs Committee Chairman Sol Bloom, Army Chief of Staff George C. Marshall, Army Air Forces Commanding General H. H. Arnold, and Secretary of the Navy James Forrestal. Most endorsements were similar to General Marshall's, which said that the Army would be "glad to facilitate your travel and take care of you while within our areas as well as we properly can." Marshall also asked for an "informal report on your return as to your observations and conclusions." General Arnold was somewhat more circumspect, saying that he was "glad to learn of this tour conducted in the interest of the freest and promptest dissemination of news compatible with the dictates of military security." Only Secretary of the Navy Forrestal was honest enough to state bluntly the reason for this outpouring of support: "We are indebted to the free press of America for our citizens' understanding of the Navy, and the facilitating of your journey will be a small installment in repayment."[94]

Armed with special passports from the State Department and War Department travel orders granting them priority seating on planes operated by the Army Transport Command, the trio visited editors and government leaders in London, Paris, Brussels, Rome, Athens, Cairo, Ankara, Istanbul, Teheran, Moscow, Chungking, New Delhi, Melbourne, Canberra, and Brisbane. The three emissaries canceled planned stops in South America after hearing that the Inter-American Conference on Problems of War and Peace had already endorsed hemispheric press freedom. The three men spent four months on the road, traveled 40,000 miles, and visited twenty-two major cities in eleven Allied and neutral countries. They found themselves caught in the beginnings of postwar problems ranging from crumbling colonial empires to growing distrust between the Soviet Union and the Western Allies—all, apparently, without benefit of any diplomatic briefing before embarkation.[95] The trip marked "the first time that a committee of editors from one country had traveled to gather at first hand the views and sentiments of other editors on the question of a free world press." And, perhaps, the excursion was also "the first time that an unofficial committee of Americans had conferred with officials of governments on the issue of press freedom."[96] But ASNE representatives felt welcomed abroad. They received statements of varying degrees of enthusiasm from the governmental and professional leaders with whom they talked. Many of the comments obviously were tailored to the American political situation. The possibility that the United States might require adherence to freedom of the press as a condition for reconstruction aid was quite real. Foreign diplomats, consequently, were loathe to offend American politicians by rebuffing the journalists who were able so demonstrably to influence politicians on the subject.

The three ASNE representatives seemed oblivious to the possible controversies and ulterior motives involved in their receptions. They returned home even more convinced of the efficacy of the campaign, telling ASNE members that one main point had been stressed repeatedly in many conferences: "Had not Fascist and Nazi forces in Italy and Germany seized and dominated the press and all communications facilities at the start, the growth of these poisonous dictatorships might well have been prevented and the indoctrination of national thought in the direction of hatred and mistrust might have been impossible." Preventing similar occurrences in the future would make the trip worthwhile. In addition to bringing home pledges of support from foreign leaders, the free-press missionaries brought home an obligation for the American press as well. To ensure foreign governments' adherence to treaty provisions establishing a "more liberal system of world communications and a freer exchange of news," the American press assumed a "new responsibility in promoting in every way international understanding."[97]

Although committee members might have misread the reactions of the foreign politicians they visited, they believed that a majority of journalists throughout the world would insist "that there be included in the peace treaties the elimination of peace-time censorship by governments, the elimination of press control by governments, and the establishment of a free flow of news between nations." The free-press missionaries, realistically, told fellow ASNE members that only time would tell how successful the trip had been. They felt the visits had shown that international freedom of the press would be "an important part of any enduring peace in the kind of a world we live in." Editors worldwide understood this and would "fight with words to accomplish it," and many world leaders also could be counted on to facilitate that goal. But, they warned, other leaders had given the goal "mere lip service" and would "seek to avoid it."[98]

The free-press missionaries returned home to a lukewarm reception. They were to report to the full ASNE membership, but on arriving home, the men discovered that the annual meeting had been canceled because of wartime travel restrictions. The board of directors received their report and commended Forrest, McGill, and Ackerman for making "an important contribution to the movement for world freedom of information."[99] Board members and the three free-press missionaries met with President Harry S. Truman, presented him with a copy of the report, and received a letter from Truman noting his hope that "freedom of the press may become a vehicle of more sympathetic understanding and therefore closer friendship among the nations of the world." Secretary of State Stettinius was in San Francisco at the Conference on International Organization when the group returned and thus was unable to receive the group's report in person.[100]

Only *Editor & Publisher* welcomed the trio back enthusiastically, commenting that the committee deserved "a vote of thanks from newspaper men everywhere for their exhaustive study." Realistically, however, these men would be rewarded "when the peace treaties are written with the guarantees we believe are so vital for future peace."[101] McGill, somewhat disheartened by the reception at home and by some of his experiences abroad, still believed in the concept of international freedom of the press. He stated that many journalists around the world, especially the younger ones, really wanted a free flow of news. Although a free-press clause in peace treaties would be an effective beginning for a longer-running campaign, he realized that such language would be unenforceable. After all, "one would not send bombers if a nation, pledged to free news, began to suppress it." That reality aside, any nation that suddenly started to suppress information "would be immediately suspected of violating some other, and more practically important, pledge of peace." Ultimately, "the moral weight of such a pledge would be far greater than is apparent at first thought."[102]

Years later, Forrest termed the excursion a failure, labeling the trio's report as "merely a recitation of experiences which proved nothing except that freedom exists only by permission of a prevailing government." The official ASNE historian likewise had a dismal evaluation of the missionary voyage, terming the trip an example of the editors' misguided desire to help build "something finer in the Brave New World the victorious war of the Allies would bring." The closing days of World War II were not "the hour or the place for a philosophic investigation of any of mankind's humanities. But the ASNE board felt an urgency about getting out in front, trusting its trio would find something or other that could be exhibited as proof of progress."[103]

Few newspapers in the country carried stories about the trip or the 18,000-word final report prepared by the trio. An official news release of 2,500 to 3,000 words was sent out; the news agencies distributed 600 words. Only *Editor & Publisher* and Tass, the Russian news agency, carried the whole report.[104] What better sign was needed to show the unimportance of international press freedom to American journalists? The reactions of both Forrest and the ASNE historian, coming some twenty years after the events being chronicled here, were tempered by the knowledge of what happened after the great missionary excursion. McGill's reaction was sounder given the times and what happened in the years immediately after the ASNE delegation's trip. The around-the-world adventure of the three men became the dramatic kickoff of an international campaign lasting into the early 1950s.

THE STATE DEPARTMENT JOINS
THE FREE-PRESS CRUSADE

While the three ASNE representatives traveled the world in search of souls committed to international freedom of the press, diplomats at the Department of State were making some inroads as well. Journalists later questioned the sincerity of the State Department's commitment to worldwide freedom of information, but initially, such doubts were highly inappropriate. According to State Department planners, worldwide freedom of the press was obviously "the one specific war aim which has been explicitly approved by the highest political bodies of our land, and which has been disapproved of by nobody." And, indeed, freedom of the press was "the one and only war aim which the U.S., officially or unofficially, is campaigning for regardless of whether or not the other 'United Nations' approve of it."[105] The Department of State actually promoted international freedom of information for reasons similar to those advanced by press leaders. For instance, Secretary of State Stettinius, in nominating an assistant secretary of state, told Congress that a secure peace required that "much fuller information about United States foreign policy should be made available through the established press, radio, and other media both to the people of this country and the people of other countries."[106] This perspective was slightly different from the press's, however, for the Department of State wanted freedom to send specific information about the United States around the world, whereas representatives of the press wanted freedom to gather and sell all information —not necessarily about the United States—throughout the world.

The impact of modern communications media on diplomacy also was more of a concern to the State Department than to press representatives. As Archibald MacLeish pointed out in his confirmation hearing for the post of assistant secretary of state for public affairs, "The foreign relations of a modern state are conducted quite as much through the instruments of public international communication as through diplomatic representatives and missions." Governments faced a new challenge, for "if the closer communications with each other of the peoples of the world are to result in mutual understanding, they must provide the full exchange of information and of knowledge upon which understanding rests." The government would not "supplant the existing instruments of international communication" but would make sure "that the job gets done and to help in every way it can to do it."[107] In fact, the government must realize that "instantaneous intercommunication between peoples—between peoples as peoples—is not something we can achieve or refuse to achieve as we wish. It is something which exists—which exists in all its potentialities—now," MacLeish later said. "Whether we like it or not we will find ourselves living at the war's end in a speaking, listening net of international intercommunication so sensitive and so delicately responsive that a whisper anywhere will be heard around the earth."[108] The impact of communications on diplomacy and the reliance on private industry to provide information necessary for that diplomacy were now facts of life. As the world situation grew tenser, the two became less complementary.

For now, however, the Department of State joined journalists in advocating an unrestricted freedom of information, with the responsibility for maintaining that freedom placed solely in the hands of private industry. The departmental support was not for freedom of the press but for freedom of information, which officials said was

> the right of all responsible persons and agencies engaged in gathering and disseminating information to the public of their own countries to discharge that duty in other countries where they may be stationed without restraint or hindrance, and to have unimpeded access to all means of communications in doing so. Conversely, we also believe that each nation should permit the reception within territories under its control of information so gathered in other countries, in order that its people may be adequately informed. You will readily see that if these principles were to embrace all modern forms of information, including the press, the radio, and the motion picture, a realistic foundation would be laid for peace through full knowledge and international understanding.[109]

The question debated within the State Department centered on how to implement this basic policy. For instance, should the United Nations Charter contain provisions that enforced freedom of information? Instead of placing the issue in the charter, should freedom of information be the topic discussed by the governments that were creating the United Nations? Or, should provisions guaranteeing freedom of information be written into peace treaties? On another level, should freedom of the press be the subject of bilateral treaties between allies? And a most basic question: How much international support for the idea was necessary before worldwide freedom of information could be instituted effectively? The questions were endless, and diplomatic decision-making was a slow process.

A complication arose when the State Department announced its interest in promoting freedom for all existing media—newspapers, news agencies, newsreels, radio, magazines, books, and motion pictures—rather than just for newspapers and news agencies. The department also was worried about the physical facilities for communications—cables and radio transmitters, for instance. The inclusiveness of the department's list of information-related topics was forward-looking, for in the mid-1940s, newspapers and news agencies considered themselves as almost the sole organs of information. Print representatives begrudgingly included radio journalists and newsreel camera operators within the fold as the crusade continued. Print media leaders still distrusted their electronic brethren, however, especially after they saw the impact of radio on the delivery of war news to America and on the spread of propaganda. The media were also highly competitive for advertising dollars, audiences, and news—and were destined to become more so. Newspaper leaders knew that radio was the reason why national boundaries now had "as much or as little meaning as the boundaries between the several states of our Union,"[110] and they knew that if peoples of other countries learned of America, radio and motion pictures probably would provide the lessons. The realities of technology did not make the situation any easier for print journalists to accept. The Department of State's increasing reliance on radio increased the tension between the department and some newspaper representatives.

Regardless of the possible causes of later tension, the State Department tried to promote international freedom of information as broadly as possible whenever possible. For instance, the peace treaty with Italy, the first signed with a defeated Axis power, contained a provision that required the new government to secure "the enjoyment of human rights and of the fundamental freedoms, including freedom of expression, of press and publication" for all countries. Treaties with Rumania, Hungary, and Finland likewise incorporated fundamental freedoms provisions. The German treaty guaranteed freedom of speech and press "in so far as consistent with military authority," and freedom of speech became a fundamental right in Japan as well.[111] The State Department also informally pressured the Chinese to relax their stringent censorship and encouraged the French Provisional Government in Algiers to abandon an attempt to establish a government monopoly on the news.[112]

A series of conferences beginning in 1945 tested the State Department's commitment to freedom of information. At the Chapultepec Conference, formally known as the Inter-American Conference on Problems of War and Peace, held at Mexico City, delegates from the American Republics adopted a series of statements on freedom of information. The resolution acknowledged the participating nations' "essential obligation to guarantee to their people, free and impartial access to sources of information." Signatory nations promised to abandon censorship as soon as possible, pledged to promote the free interchange of information among their peoples, and agreed to establish "the principle of free transmission and reception of information" at the war's end.[113] These accomplishments did not come without the admission, in private communications, that the watchful eyes of American journalists had influenced American diplomatic behavior. The sixty-five journalists from the United States assigned to cover the Chapultepec conference reacted favorably to the freedom of information resolution, and American diplomats believed the statement conformed "in principle and purposes with ideas advanced in recent months by Press Associations and publishers' groups."[114]

But the Chapultepec accords did not escape criticism. Representatives of the press quickly noted that, because the resolution was a recommendation only, the language ratified imposed no obligations on any nation.[115] Expressing concern about the inability of the Chapultepec accords to change restrictive practices in Argentina and other Latin American republics,[116] supporters of the free-press cause thought that United States diplomats were far too optimistic about the possible beneficial influence of the resolution. "It is an infelicitous as well as an unrealistic approach to assume that the 'dictator countries' will be willing to admit without further ado that our concept of what constitutes freedom of the press is the right concept, and theirs is wrong." Nor did the Chapultepec declaration ensure the rights of American journalists to gather news abroad.[117] Proponents of international freedom of information thus looked to later conferences for the desired binding policies.

WRITING FREE-PRESS GUARANTEES INTO EARLY INTERNATIONAL AGREEMENTS

State Department promotion of freedom of information often seemed to be more a means to an end than an end in itself during early international negotiations. Its ancillary nature was most obvious when, in planning American efforts to prevent Eastern Europe from falling under Soviet domination, State Department officials saw the free reporting of upcoming elections in newly liberated areas as essential to preserving democracy; this was especially true in Poland.[118] American diplomats making plans for the Conference of Berlin—Potsdam—in 1945, for instance, knew that the Russians expected the United States to present a strong stand on freedom of information at various conferences. The diplomats also expected firm Soviet opposition to the American position. But State Department planners believed that the American demands for reporters to enter Eastern Europe were justified "by our belief in the principle of the fullest possible freedom of information." The diplomats also thought that action on this issue of access to Eastern Europe was critical because American journalists knew that "important events are taking place in the Soviet-controlled countries and have urged the Department to obtain authorization for their representatives to go there." Obtaining permission for United States correspondents to work in Eastern bloc countries would satisfy several needs. Having American journalists on the scene would placate the United States press; through the correspondents' work, the American people would understand Soviet practices well enough to put the United States "in a position to exert its influence." If efforts to get the Soviets to lift their news blackout failed, American diplomats must tell their Russian counterparts that "we may be obliged to inform the American press that the Soviet Government insists on excluding American correspondents from Eastern Europe despite our earnest and firm requests, from which the press will undoubtedly conclude that the situation there is such that the Soviet authorities do not wish it brought to the attention of American and world opinion."[119] American diplomats planned to stress that the public relations fallout of such stories could be disastrous to any country seeking American reconstruction aid. These arguments were useless on the Russians, however, for the Soviets believed that the American press was incapable of swaying the nation's public opinion and that public opinion in America was very much overrated.[120]

American diplomats took their freedom of information proposals to the Potsdam Conference, where President Truman joined in advocating the insertion of free-press guarantees in peace treaties and in seeking to protect the right of correspondents to report on upcoming elections in Eastern Europe. The effort was quite unsuccessful. Marshal Joseph Stalin, as expected, strongly opposed placing any such guarantees on paper. On the issue of admitting correspondents to cover the elections in Eastern Europe, Stalin insisted the foreign correspondents already in those countries could do the necessary work. Referring specifically to Poland, Stalin said that any formal declaration about admitting additional correspondents to that country to report on elections would upset the "very touchy" Poles, who would "suspect us of accusing them of being unwilling to accord a free press." President Truman, however, refused to accept Stalin's objections and tried attacking the Soviet points from a pragmatic angle. After all, Truman said, he had a large Polish constituency in the United States, and "a free election in Poland reported to the United States by a free press would make it much easier to deal with these Polish people."[121] The American president's political problems did not sway the Russian leader, who strongly opposed British and American efforts to secure both freedom of movement and freedom from political censorship for their correspondents.[122]

Ultimately, the final Potsdam communiqué presented a compromise of sorts, saying, in general terms, that Great Britain, the United States, and the Soviet Union agreed "that representatives of the Allied press shall enjoy full freedom to report to the world upon developments in Poland before and during the elections."[123] Attempts to win access for the press to other areas of liberated Europe ended similarly; usually, the limited Allied success on free-press issues totally ignored the subject of freedom for the domestic press in the countries concerned.[124] An attempt to win permission for Allied press representatives to have radio facilities in Poland, Hungary, Rumania, Bulgaria, and Finland was equally unsuccessful[125] despite efforts by the Americans to convince the Russians that "there was no essential difference between a newspaperman reporting to his paper and a radioman reporting over the radio." The Russians contended, correctly, that in some countries the government controlled the broadcasting system; hence, a uniform rule was impossible.[126]

The Potsdam Conference exposed Western diplomats and journalists to the basic Soviet position on freedom of the press for the first time; that stance would become far too familiar to most American journalists in the years to come. The Soviets favored provisions for freedom of the press in peace treaties, Stalin told Harry L. Hopkins. But specialized guarantees "could only be applied in full in peace time, and even then with certain limitations." No country granted full freedom of expression during time of war, he added; even Great Britain, France, and the United States practiced wartime restrictions. Nor could certain groups, such as fascists, who intended to overthrow "democratic governments," have freedom of speech.[127]

One traditional press-government problem appeared at Potsdam—the confrontation between journalists and diplomats over access to information about the sessions. The initiative to exclude reporters from the conference site came from Prime Minister Winston Churchill,[128] but President Truman concurred.[129] When the delegates arrived in Berlin for the conference, however, they found journalists present. The meeting site was not as remote as Teheran or Yalta, Churchill complained, and journalists were everywhere. "They carry powerful weapons. They are making a great outcry." The British leader believed that secrecy was essential for negotiations, and he elicited pledges from the Americans and the Russians to deal with the press only through designated representatives.[130] Thus, the Potsdam conference, in which the Americans and the British promoted international freedom of information, followed the traditional rules of secret diplomatic negotiations. American journalists found something anomalous in promoting freedom of information under the shroud of confidentiality, but they were unable to secure any changes in policy.

While the State Department's promotion of freedom of the press abroad won accolades from American journalists, the department's news policies at home eroded press support. One complaint centered on the ability of American correspondents to obtain information about United States foreign policy abroad that was unavailable to them in Washington. The circumstances left "the impression that American foreign policy, instead of being indigenous to this country, was being planted, cultivated and marketed only in Europe," a situation that correspondents termed "disappointing and disheartening both for professional and policy reasons."[131] State Department officials realized that the department had a negative attitude toward the press and tended to release as little information as possible, while trying to discourage reporters' attempts to obtain clarification or elaboration on news stories. Also, the department seldom took the initiative in presenting information. Departmental press officers conceded that such longtime practices had created ill will among reporters. The department needed to develop a news policy designed to provide "complete answers to questions raised by reporters and the public" and to make an aggressive effort to release all possible news on foreign affairs. The reason behind the call for change was obvious: "The State Department has the biggest and most important story of our generation to tell. It also has the greatest educational job in its history to do." In order to fulfill its new responsibilities, the department had to realize that its "relations with the American people and the development of our foreign policy are largely shaped by the day-to-day reporting from the Department"; consequently, officials must avoid additional problems with reporters.[132]

Problems with press relations continued into the administration of James F. Byrnes, in which Assistant Secretary of State for Public Affairs William Benton attempted to revise departmental news practices. Again correspondents complained about "the confusion of the American people as to our foreign policy" and noted, "no policy can be successful that is not made known to and interpreted for the people. This means cooperation between officials and newsmen closer than has ever before existed."[133] Benton reported that he had received "letters, telegrams and phone calls from scores of responsible publishers and editors, most of them highly critical of the Department's news policies." Most of the journalists roundly condemned the department's "stupid secrecy." Benton quickly discovered that the problem rested in "the tradition of caution and secrecy, and failure to recognize that news is an opportunity, not a burden,"[134] adding, "this tradition is found in all foreign offices." American ambassadors "think they have learned something secret or confidential. They wire it in labelled 'secret' and it becomes secret within the Department. At the same time smart and capable foreign correspondents get the same story and write it better than the report submitted to us with the 'secret' label."[135] Suggested changes included liberalizing policies on the release of information and hiring a person to deal solely with the press.[136]

Straightening out the department's relationship with the press, however, was almost impossible. One factor working against solution of the department's press problems was the need for confidentiality that surrounded most State Department negotiations. Thus, not only did the department need to fend off journalists who were displeased with that confidentiality, but the diplomats also had to placate representatives of other governments who were deeply distressed when sensitive information appeared unexpectedly in the press.[137] The other major problem restricting State Department ability to reorganize press relations was demands by reporters to have exclusive access to the secretary of state. Complaints from Secretary of State Stettinius about the number of interviews requested by Time-Life correspondents resulted in Henry Luce ordering his reporters to clear requests for interviews with his Washington bureau chief to avoid taxing the secretary's patience.[138] In contrast, a complaint from Arthur Krock of *The New York Times* about his lack of access to Secretary of State Byrnes led to a recommendation from Byrnes's special assistant Walter Brown that the secretary invite Krock in for a talk. "I certainly do not think that you should make a habit of seeing him," Brown said, "but because of the great influence he wields, I do believe it would be well to let him drop in for a chat when things quiet down and you are not so terribly busy."[139]

Benton recognized the inequality among State Department correspondents when he suggested handling all reporters identically through press conferences while paying special attention to about "twenty men out of a group of over one hundred Department correspondents [who] are of key importance." Representatives of the departmental news office should pay special attention to these reporters. After all, "every capital in the world has favored correspondents." The State Department, however, must "avoid the stigma of this policy by making all official conferences open to everyone on an equal basis" while developing "personalized techniques that will give the ablest men the background material they need if the news they get is to be properly interpreted."[140] Although the policy had merit, Secretary of State Byrnes was, at times, criticized by reporters for having exclusive dinners with selected correspondents.[141]

AMERICAN CORRESPONDENTS ENCOUNTER PROBLEMS ABROAD

Obtaining information from the State Department was a traditional concern of American news organizations, but news-gathering problems in the United States were easily overcome when measured against difficulties involved in obtaining news elsewhere. As the war ended, getting correspondents into certain foreign countries, protecting them while they were there on assignment, and ensuring their ability to transmit stories from those countries were significant concerns for newspapers, news agencies, and broadcasting companies. Once again, the independently minded news organizations found themselves seeking State Department help when reporters ran into difficulty, especially in Russia, the Eastern European nations, and Argentina. In the early years of the free-press crusade, the State Department received numerous requests for aid for American correspondents who encountered difficulties abroad. Although the free-press crusade supposedly included a campaign for greater freedom for the domestic press of all nations, seldom did American journalists ask the department to intervene on behalf of a domestic press in trouble with its home government. Occasionally, however, American diplomats protested the mistreatment of domestic national press organs.[142]

Potentially explosive difficulties encountered by American correspondents in Argentina focused on the idiosyncratic personality of Juan Perón. Censorship of wire service dispatches was routine,[143] complaints about articles published in United States newspapers frequent,[144] threats against the safety of American correspondents commonplace,[145] and published attacks on the American ambassador regular.[146] The key issue there, however, was the safety of American correspondents. Ambassador Spruille Braden called on Vice President Perón to protest such attacks, only to hear Perón label American press representatives "liars and troublemakers making for bad relations with the U.S. as their despatches are telegraphed back here." The Argentine leader added, "So enraged are the people by these attacks that in their fanatical adoration for me they are entirely capable of murdering ... anyone who they think stands in my way."[147] The object of Perón's immediate hatred was Arnaldo Cortesi, correspondent for *The New York Times*, whose stories "had caused the Government great embarrassment." Perón added that Cortesi "should not be surprised at whatever might happen to him" and that Perón's government would not tolerate such articles in the future.[148] Braden warned Perón that if anything happened to Cortesi, "even an otherwise perfectly explicable accident," the American people would blame Perón and his followers. Despite Perón's threats, American correspondents, including Cortesi, stayed in Buenos Aires. Braden offered them refuge in the American Embassy and, if the department approved, permission to transmit their dispatches over embassy facilities.[149]

Back in Washington, the State Department pondered how to respond to Perón's antics. Quick public reaction was essential, Assistant Secretary for Public Affairs MacLeish argued, or else officials would be embarrassed when news stories filed by the affected correspondents reached the United States. Assistant Secretary of State Nelson Rockefeller counseled caution and delay; after all, Ambassador Braden's talk with the correspondents about Perón's threats had been off the record. Thus, the reporters should not have written stories about the problem for publication. Action should wait until Braden had a second meeting with Perón to confirm the threats.[150]

MacLeish also advocated helping American correspondents in Buenos Aires "transmit news stories which Argentine censorship attempts to block." By offering such help, the State Department would support its free-press position, MacLeish argued.[151] A session with the Argentine ambassador to the United States produced a warning for Perón: The American government expected the Argentine government "to guard the safety of American correspondents just as the lives of Argentine citizens are protected in this country."[152]

Perón responded to the American warnings by saying that his government "could no more be responsible for any fanatical attack on American journalists than it could were latter to get pneumonia," but he pledged that "no greater guarantees will be enjoyed by correspondents in any other country" than in Argentina. American journalists could even have police protection if they so desired, Perón said, adding that such concessions did not change his mind about the quality of American journalism. In fact, by the time Perón made such guarantees, he had already forbidden editors of major Argentine newspapers to publish news about developments in

Argentina originated by United States wire service correspondents in Buenos Aires. Perón's new attitude toward safeguarding American journalists was appreciated, Braden told the Argentine leader, but a new problem had developed. Buenos Aires newspapers now were "inferring that our correspondents were writing under instructions of Embassy." Braden tried to convince Perón that neither the American government nor its embassy in Buenos Aires controlled the reporters and "in point of fact we did not know what they were writing until we read it in press." On the other hand, the ambassador reported telling Perón that since the Argentine leader "had admitted an ability to control Argentine press," Braden was convinced that Perón could stop attacks on the American ambassador that then were occurring regularly in the Argentine newspapers.[153] The threat of physical harm befalling the American correspondents, however, seemed to be at an end for the moment, Braden said. But the ambassador warned, "in a fit of temper Perón is capable of taking revenge for any article which stings him too sharply."[154]

Although they may no longer have been in physical danger, the problems of American journalists in Argentina obviously were not over. For instance, Perón had a *Newsweek* correspondent deported for submitting a report "containing some incorrect though unimportant information."[155] Radio broadcasting facilities were denied a *New York Herald Tribune* correspondent, stories on particular topics were censored,[156] and *Time* magazine was barred from the mails.[157] Whenever any difficulty occurred, American diplomats protested without great success. Many of their complaints included reminders that Argentina was violating the agreements made at the Inter-American Conference on Problems of War and Peace, which pledged signatories to promote a free exchange of information and to guarantee their citizens access to impartial sources of information. Argentina refused to honor the agreements.[158]

The battle for freedom of the press in Eastern Europe centered on attempts to force the Soviet Union to abide by another diplomatic agreement—the Potsdam accords, which promised the world's press free entry into the liberated countries of Eastern Europe to cover the upcoming elections. Consequently, United States diplomats in Rumania, Hungary, Poland, and the Soviet Union sought clearances for American correspondents to enter these countries. In most instances, the Americans found themselves reiterating arguments made many times before with no avail. Still, acting Secretary of State Joseph Grew told Burton Y. Berry, the American representative in Rumania, to persevere in pursuing the issue because the American people and the world had to be informed of developments in Rumania. Thus, correspondents must be freely admitted into the country, and "their reports should be censored only on the basis of military considerations."[159] Despite Berry's efforts, only one correspondent obtained clearance to enter Rumania in the month after the Potsdam accords allegedly had opened Eastern countries for American correspondents; fourteen journalists had requested permission to enter.

Even if reporters entered Rumania, free reporting was far from certain. After repeated United States complaints about restricted access for American correspondents, in March 1945 the Russians brought four American journalists to Bucharest from Moscow. The correspondents were allowed to travel throughout the country; then, the Soviets flew them back to Moscow. The news stories resulting from the trip were disappointing, Berry said. "Such stories as they tried to send out from Bucharest were badly cut by the censor." As a result, no correspondent tried to send out a true story, and no important story from those journalists reached America until one reporter arrived in Rome two months later. Censorship in Rumania was so severe, Berry added, "that the last two journalists that came here said that they would not return and would advise against any of their colleagues coming here until American journalists were able to send out their stories without having them garbled by the Rumanian censor to the point where their context is changed."[160]

The inability or unwillingness of American correspondents to report the news of Rumania resulted in conditions that Berry termed intolerable. Rather than having independent American nationals report the news, leading American newspapers and news agencies relied on "local agents or 'stringers' and ... unreliable journalists willing to write material agreeable to the authorities instead of the facts." These individuals bent to governmental pressures and transmitted slanted copy. Even if Berry successfully lured an American correspondent from another Eastern European nation to Rumania for a visit, the need to preserve residency in a host country created additional problems. The correspondents visiting from Moscow, for instance, admitted that "in order to maintain their positions it would be necessary for them to write with extreme care" on what they found.[161]

In Hungary, American Representative H. F. Arthur Schoenfeld found American correspondents present without having obtained prior permission to enter the country from the Allied Control Commission (ACC). Although the Department of State did "not approve of these individuals having proceeded to Budapest without prior ACC clearance," officials in Washington hoped that, since their presence was in accord with the Potsdam agreement, the ACC would allow the reporters to remain in Hungary.[162] When American correspondents entered Hungary officially, Schoenfeld faced another problem, one becoming all too common as far as diplomats were concerned—the correspondents did superficial work. Hungary was just one brief stop for journalists making the grand tour of Eastern Europe. They were not well prepared, and their stories showed their lack of familiarity with local issues. Surely, Schoenfeld said, the department could ask press associations and newspapers with reporters in Hungary to tell their correspondents to send well-rounded stories back to the American public.

Perhaps the journalists understood the "serious need of reporting Hungarian situation adequately and with discernment but they may be assigned to cover too large an area and can devote but few hours to a single capital." If this was the case, the solution might lie in an appeal to the home offices. Most news about Hungary, Schoenfeld complained, came from Russian or British reporters. "This slanted news coupled with the lighter sometimes untrue largely human interest type of stories being despatched by American correspondents at present will result in unfortunate and mistaken opinions" being conveyed to the American people. Surely, the correspondents' employers wanted their reporters to do better work, he said in a lament many of his colleagues later joined.[163]

The records are silent on whether the State Department discussed the matter with the correspondents' employers. Given the utmost faith that most communications agencies had in their employees, however, department officials undertook such conversations only under the most urgent circumstances. Most likely, the correspondents' employers were well satisfied with the copy being transmitted from Hungary and other Eastern European nations, for the stories fit the mold of foreign news that the editors thought the American public desired. Even if American news agencies wanted to change approaches to news from Hungary, the Soviets denied them the opportunity to do so. A few days after Schoenfeld complained about the quality of work emanating from journalists assigned to Budapest, the Russians reimposed strict controls on the entrance of American correspondents into Hungary.[164]

When the few American correspondents in Hungary complained to Schoenfeld about censorship, the American representative made two unsuccessful attempts to alleviate the problem. The obligatory official protest before the Allied Control Commission based on the Potsdam pledges of freedom of movement for American correspondents was unavailing. The Russian representative responded routinely and promised that "censorship would hold up correspondents copy should they submit erroneous reports concerning conditions in Hungary."[165] A more imaginative approach called for allowing correspondents to use the radio and mail facilities of the American military outpost in Hungary to transmit dispatches because neither channel was subject to Soviet or Hungarian interference. This approach would circumvent foreign censorship, and, of course, attempts by the American authorities to impose censorship would be unthinkable.[166] As inspired as the suggestion was, the War Department soon notified American officials in Budapest that its facilities could not "be used to evade censorship." The correspondents then asked to use the State Department's communications channels for dispatches, a request that Schoenfeld endorsed.[167] The State Department traditionally refused such requests, arguing that such action would merely remove the issue "from the battlefield of freedom of the press to the battlefield of totalitarian competition. In such a competition we should certainly lose, since we cannot hope to beat a totalitarian state at its own game."[168]

The situation for correspondents in Poland was not much better, according to American Ambassador Arthur Bliss Lane. The Polish government contended that physical conditions in war-devastated Poland militated against early admission of correspondents; Lane pressured officials for a change in attitude.[169] When Polish officials finally agreed to open the country to correspondents, they wanted to admit only representatives of the three major American news agencies, allegedly because of problems with housing and transportation.[170] When the Department of State protested that in the five weeks since the Polish government had indicated a willingness to admit correspondents only one radio correspondent had entered the country,[171] the Polish government quickly responded that the government indeed welcomed foreign journalists. But the acting foreign minister added that the government "would of course reserve right to decline to issue visas to those who were regarded as Fascist supporters." Representatives of the Hearst press topped the list of correspondents that the Polish government wanted to exclude. Chargé Gerald Keith, on hearing this statement, lectured the Polish official about American press practices, suggesting that "it would be far better to let possible critics see what destruction and suffering had been experienced by Poland and what tremendous problems confront the country rather than to encourage criticism which would inevitably result from barring certain correspondents." The lecture had no effect; the government still reserved the right to bar certain correspondents.[172]

Repeated lectures on the role of American correspondents in the formulation of public opinion in the United States also failed to lessen the restrictions on journalists in Poland.[173] Polish leaders never understood the American system of freedom of the press, as Lane painfully learned after two Polish government representatives returned from a trip to the United States. The two men spent forty minutes complaining about "'lying' accounts from American correspondents in Poland," saying the "press in US was hostile and that this attitude could seriously affect relations between two countries." Lane tried to explain that the American government did not control the press and that the appearance of unfavorable articles was not an indication of official disfavor, as similar articles would be in countries where the government did control the press.[174] Lane's arguments won few converts. One problem that the free-press crusade consistently faced was the inability of people outside the United States to understand exactly how the American press operated. Without such an understanding, arguing for principles familiar to American diplomats and journalists was futile.

The American embassy in Moscow served as a clearinghouse for problems relating to the admission of United States correspondents to Eastern European countries, and State Department dispatches to Moscow stressed how strongly the American press desired to enter these countries.

Repeatedly, the department urged diplomats in the Soviet capital to vigorously pursue efforts to win admission visas because of "increasing concern in American press circles at the exclusion of American correspondents."[175] Ever mindful of the power of the American press, the State Department told its representatives in Moscow that the department "attaches considerable importance to this matter and hopes that some way may be found to end the news blackout in these countries which has occasioned much outspoken criticism in the American press and on which we may be obliged to make official comment."[176]

American newspapers noticed that Soviet correspondents accredited to allied headquarters had "every facility afforded" and simply wanted equal treatment, the department told diplomats in Moscow.[177] Despite the pressure exerted by the American press for visas for correspondents, Ambassador W. Averell Harriman reported little success: "I have used every way that I could in the past either by personal conversation or through officers of the Embassy to expedite applications for legitimate correspondents whose papers wished to send them to Moscow. I must confess that our efforts have not been very successful." While detailing his problems, the ambassador urged the State Department to keep the matter of admission of news correspondents to Eastern Europe in perspective. Every time Harriman used valuable audience time to discuss a visa matter, he had to set aside "some matter of importance to the US," and the ambassador wondered if the trade-off was worth it.[178]

Regardless of the value of the trade-off, American news organizations expected their diplomats to plead their causes before foreign governments. In that expectation, they were much as other business leaders who believed that the State Department should smooth the way for their endeavors. One significant difference between the press and other members of the business community, however, was the pressure that journalists could generate to force the department to behave as desired. As the crusade for worldwide freedom of information grew, the pressure on the department to implement its avowed belief in the campaign's goals increased.

NOTES

1. Oliver Boyd-Barrett, *The International News Agencies*, Beverly Hills, Calif., Sage, 1980, p. 158.
2. William H. Read, *America's Mass Media Merchants*, Baltimore, Md., Johns Hopkins University Press, 1976, pp. 110–11.
3. Ibid., p. 111. For details about the cartel arrangement and the positions of the Associated Press, the United Press, and International News Service, *see* Kent Cooper, *Barriers Down*, New York, Holt, Rinehart and Winston, 1942; Hugh Baillie, *High Tension*, New York, Harper & Row, 1959, pp. 283–85; Herbert

Brucker, *Freedom of Information*, New York, Macmillan, 1949, pp. 201–2; Llewellyn White and Robert D. Leigh, *Peoples Speaking to Peoples*, Chicago, University of Chicago Press, 1946, pp. 58–61; Oliver Gramling, *AP: The Story of News*, New York, Holt, Rinehart and Winston, 1940, pp. 93, 274; Joe Alex Morris, *Deadline Every Minute: The Story of the United Press*, Garden City, N.Y., Doubleday, 1957, pp. 53–57, 64, 72; John C. Merrill, Carter R. Bryan, and Marvin Alisky, *The Foreign Press*, Baton Rouge, Louisiana State University Press, 1975, pp. 35–36.

4. Brucker, *Freedom of Information*, p. 202.
5. Cooper, *Barriers Down*, p. 12.
6. Cooper's lack of knowledge about the cartel was not surprising since "little was said about the existence of the cartel during its life." Brucker, *Freedom of Information*, p. 204.
7. Cooper, *Barriers Down*, pp. 34–44, 79.
8. Emily S. Rosenberg, *Spreading the American Dream: American Economic and Cultural Expansion, 1890–1945*, New York, Hill & Wang, 1982, p. 88.
9. Cooper, *Barriers Down*, pp. 51–52.
10. Rosenberg, *Spreading the American Dream*, p. 98.
11. Cooper, *Barriers Down*, p. 88.
12. Cooper's plan called for
    > *press freedom in all countries, equality to news sources and transmission facilities, the prohibition of "intentional" biased international propaganda in any news service, the guarantee that at least one news agency in each country be owned and controlled mutually by the newspapers it serves, and the guarantee that each agency be permitted to make such international news arrangements as it chose.*

    William Reed, "50 Years of Resolutions Form Stage for UN Talks," *E&P*, April 12, 1947, p. 13.
13. George Juergens, *News from the White House*, Chicago, University of Chicago Press, 1981, pp. 205–47; Robert W. Desmond, *The Press and World Affairs*, Englewood Cliffs, N.J., Prentice-Hall, 1937, pp. 140–41.
14. American diplomatic representatives obviously felt that delegates had discussed and acted on the topic at the peace conference. In a compilation of American actions in support of international freedom of information published in 1948, the State Department listed as examples of such activities the portions of treaties that guaranteed freedom of communication by mail, telephone, and telegraph across the Polish Corridor and elsewhere, and efforts to secure freedom of religion and the right to use minority languages. "Freedom of Information in American Policy and Practice," Research Project 55, Division of Historical Policy Research, Office of Public Affairs, February 1948, RG 59, NA, Box 3, Research Projects 51–79, p. 10. This was not the kind of freedom of information Cooper had in mind.
15. Cooper, *Barriers Down*, pp. 90–91.
16. Brucker, *Freedom of Information*, p. 206.
17. "World-wide Free Press," *E&P*, July 10, 1943, p. 26.
18. Quoted in James P. Warburg, *Unwritten Treaty*, Orlando, Fla., Harcourt Brace Jovanovich, 1946, p. 3.

19. Walter S. Rogers to President Wilson, February 12, 1919, quoted in Report of the Dean of the Graduate School of Journalism, Columbia University, for the Academic Year Ending June 30, 1943, p. 12. Carl V. Ackerman Papers, Library of Congress, Washington, D.C., Container 191.

20. Walter S. Rogers, "Electrical Communications in the Pacific," *Annals of the American Academy of Political and Social Science* 122 (November 1925):78.

21. *See*, e.g., Admiral W. L. Rodgers, "The Effect of Cable and Radio Control on News and Commerce," Ibid. 112 (March 1924):245. In 1924, Admiral Rodgers argued for government aid in sending news to locations that private news agencies found fiscally impossible to serve. Ibid., p. 250.

22. David Lawrence, "International Freedom of the Press Essential to a Durable Peace," Ibid. 72 (July 1917):141 (emphasis in original).

23. The first World Press Conference on record met in Chicago in 1893 as part of the Columbian Exposition. Among the topics discussed by delegates was the international role of the press, including the idea that "the press has a right and obligation to dissipate misunderstandings between nations." *See* Reed, "50 Years of Resolutions," p. 13.

   A nongovernmental Press Congress of the World, organized in San Francisco in 1915, met in 1921 in Honolulu and again, in Geneva, Switzerland, in 1926. *See* "Williams Makes Plea for Crusading Press," *E&P*, September 18, 1926, p. 7. The Press Congress's goals included advancing "by conference, discussion and united effort the cause of journalism in every honourable way." Among the resolutions adopted in 1921 was one requiring that "all governments give the press means of access to avenues of information so as to enable the press to inform the world correctly and unreservedly on public matters." *See* E/CONF.6/4, *The Freedom of the Press: Some Historical Notes*, February 11, 1948, p. 15.

24. "Urges World Action on Exchange of News," *New York Times*, September 15, 1926, p. 19.

25. "Williams Makes Plea," p. 47.

26. By 1932, the Associated Press offered its service to other countries; by 1934, the final break with the European cartel occurred. Then, concerned that the United Press would pick up the cartel agreement, the Associated Press and the United Press signed a five-year contract binding both parties to independent news gathering abroad. *See* Cooper, *Barriers Down*, pp. 153, 203, 251–60.

27. *International News Service* v. *The Associated Press*, 248 U.S. 215 (1918).

28. "Property in News Heads Geneva Program," *E&P*, August 28, 1926, p. 5.

29. League of Nations, Conference of Press Experts, *Preparatory Documents* (C.231.M.93) (1927), *passim*. Formulating the agenda for the Conference of Press Experts were the committees of News Agencies, of Directors of Press Bureaux, and of Journalists. The Directors of Press Bureaux represented official government information agencies. The Committee of Journalists convened by the League Secretariat stressed that correspondents were not asking for "*favours*, but certain improvements which would enable them to present their information to the public with the greatest possible accuracy and speed." *See* Ibid., p. 28 (emphasis in original).

   Editor & Publisher, the newspaper trade journal, was not too optimistic about achieving many American goals at the upcoming conference, terming the establishment of a property right in news "a vain dream" but saying changes in cable rates and censorship practices would earn delegates the gratitude of the industry. The conference was important, however, because of the growing closeness of the world and the ability of the press to transmit "an impartial, yet interesting, record of events, or to be colored and polluted for the advantage of hidden national or commercial interests." *See* "At Geneva," *E&P*, August 20, 1927, p. 20.

30. Albin E. Johnson, "Geneva Conference Denounces Censorship," *E&P*, September 3, 1927, p. 3.

31. "Ask Priority for Press," *New York Times*, August 25, 1927, p. 5. Cable costs were particularly critical when newspapers wanted to obtain news from certain parts of the world. *The New York Times* reported costs of more than $200 per column for news from Japan and between $300 and $350 per column of news from China and labeled "transpacific news service . . . an expensive luxury. . . . As the number of ties which bind together the different continents continues to grow, the question of cable and radio communication becomes of world-wide interest." *See* "The Cost of Cables," *New York Times*, August 26, 1927, p. 16.

32. The notion of property rights in news had to be carefully explained, for some delegates considered the idea discriminatory. "In seeking to widen the legal recognition and protection of news as property, the American newspaper men at Geneva are simply attempting to secure for foreign publishers the rights they enjoy themselves," said *The New York Times*. *See* "Protecting World-wide News," *New York Times*, August 27, 1927, p. 12. Kent Cooper warned that without protection of the news as property he saw "no hope of a new and pretentious scale for the exchange of international news. . . . None of us should lie back and let others do the work and then appropriate it after the expense of transmission and the expense of gaining news at its source has been borne by others." *See* Wythe Williams, "News Experts Pass Protection Plans," *New York Times*, August 27, 1927, p. 13.

33. E/CONF.6/4, p. 10.

34. Johnson, "Geneva Conference," p. 3.

35. League of Nations, Conference of Press Experts, *Final Resolutions and Various Other Documents* (A.43) (1927), p. 9.

36. "Progress," *E&P*, August 27, 1927, p. 34.

37. "A New Day," *E&P*, September 3, 1927, p. 30.

38. League of Nations, *Official Journal*, July–December 1931, September 29, 1931, pp. 2294–95, 2294.

39. "World Press 'Tribunal of Honor' Shunned by U.S. Representatives," *E&P*, February 27, 1932, p. 26.

40. League of Nations, *Official Journal*, January–June 1932, "Collaboration of the Press in the Organisation of Peace. Letter from the Danish Government to the Secretary-General" (Annex 1352), pp. 793–94.

41. League of Nations, "Collaboration of the Press," p. 795.

42. Frank L. Kluckhohn, "Spain Asks World to Control News," *New York Times*, October 14, 1933, p. 2.

43. "Press Parley Sees Flurry over Arms," *New York Times*, November 9, 1933, p. 4.

44. John W. Perry, "Curb on False News Asked at Madrid," *E&P*, November 18,

1933, p. 5.
45. " 'True News'," *E&P*, November 18, 1933, p. 22.
46. League of Nations, *Official Journal*, July–December 1934, September 28, 1934, pp. 1473–74.
47. Carl V. Ackerman, Report, April 20, 1934, *Proceedings of the Twelfth Annual Convention of the American Society of Newspaper Editors*, pp. 139–41.
48. Ibid., pp. 141–42.
49. Brucker, *Freedom of Information*, p. 205.
50. Kent Cooper, *The Right to Know: An Exposition of the Evils of News Suppression and Propaganda*, New York, Farrar, Straus & Giroux, 1956, p. 156.
51. Some scholars find this press-government relationship somewhat contradictory because the arrangement violated traditional press association beliefs against governmental assistance of any kind. *See*, e.g., Jean-Luc Renaud-Komiya, "The U.S. Government's Assistance to the AP's World-Wide Expansion: 1912– 1948," paper presented at the Annual Convention of the Association for Education in Journalism and Mass Communication, Corvallis, Oreg., August 1983.
52. Statement Made in Presidential Press Conference of July 5, 1940, "American Policy toward Freedom of Information: A Selection of Official Papers, Statements of Policy, and Other Relevant Documents," Research Project 53, Division of Historical Policy Research, Office of Public Affairs, January 1948, RG 59, NA, Box 3, Research Projects 51–79, p. 11.
53. "Freedom of Information in American Policy and Practice," p. 19.
54. Kent Cooper to Cordell Hull, February 27, 1941, Decimal Classification 340.1115A/1866, NA.
55. Cordell Hull to Kent Cooper, March 15, 1941, Ibid.
56. "Freedom of Information in American Policy and Practice," pp. 21–22.
57. "American Policy toward Freedom of Information," p. 14a.
58. Unsigned Memorandum on the Status of Work on the Question of Freedom of Information, November 17, 1944, RG 353, NA, Box 97, File 13.2: Freedom of Information Committee, 1946, a. background materials, p. 2.
59. *Associated Press et al.* v. *United States*, 326 U.S. 1 (1945).
60. Cooper, *Barriers Down*, p. 9.
61. "World Press Freedom Crusade Urged by Cooper at AP Meeting," *E&P*, April 24, 1943, p. 12.
62. "Free News Exchange Put First in Crusade," *E&P*, January 27, 1945, p. 9.
63. "ASNE and Press Freedom—By Kent Cooper," *ASNE Bulletin*, September 1, 1943, p. 7.
64. Hugh Baillie, "Freedom of Information: Open Channels for News," *Free World*, November 1944, p. 433.
65. In 1943, ASNE members stressed that "freedom of expression and of communication, uncontrolled in any way by governments, is among the strongest safeguards of peace." *See* Arthur Robb, "ASNE Fights for Free Press against Federal Controls," *E&P*, February 20, 1943, p. 7. The debate among ASNE members about undertaking the campaign appeared in the July 1, August 1, and August 15, 1943, editions of the *ASNE Bulletin*.
66. In 1943, Palmer Hoyt, editor of the *Denver Post* and president of Sigma Delta Chi, said, "Our obligation is to extend freedom of the press to the entire world.

If we fail, then all fail." *See* "Sees Obligation to Extend Free Press around World," *E&P*, May 22, 1943, p. 9.

67. George A. Brandenburg, "Baillie Proposes Post-War News Plan," *E&P*, February 5, 1944, p. 12.

68. "Baillie Warns of Threat to Press Freedom," *E&P*, November 27, 1943, p. 20. Baillie was still conducting his campaign to win proper recognition for the United Press's efforts in 1949 when he protested to Secretary of State Dean Acheson that a State Department publication had given unwarranted credit to the Associated Press for the campaign. *See* Hugh Baillie to Secretary of State Dean Acheson, November 21, 1949, RG 59, NA, Box 4999, 811.918/11-2149.

69. "Baillie, Exiled Govts. Discuss Free Press," *E&P*, September 16, 1944, p. 8.

70. Roy A. Roberts, "Should ASNE Assume Leadership in Advocating World-wide Press Freedom?" *ASNE Bulletin*, July 1, 1943, p. 1.

71. Nelson Poynter, "Poynter Calls for Action Now toward Free World Expression," *E&P*, January 22, 1944, p. 6.

72. The congressional resolution read:
    Resolved by the Senate (the House of Representatives concurring), *That the Congress of the United States expresses its belief in the world-wide right of interchange of news by news gathering and distributing agencies, whether individual or associate, by any means, without discrimination as to sources, distribution, rates or charges; and that this right should be protected by international compact.*
    See U.S. Congress, Senate, S. Con. Res. 53, 78th Cong., 2nd sess., September 21, 1944, *Congressional Record*, 90:8123.

73. The Democrats pledged their belief "in the world right of all men to write, send and publish news at uniform communication rates and without interference by governmental or private monopoly, and that right should be protected by treaty." *See* Robert U. Brown, "Democrats Endorse World Press Freedom in Platform," *E&P*, July 22, 1944, p. 7.
    The Republicans noted that
    in times like these, when whole peoples have found themselves shackled by governments which denied the truth, or worse, dealt in half truths or withheld the facts from the public, it is imperative to the maintenance of a free America that the press and radio be free and that full and complete information be available to Americans. There must be no censorship except to the extent required by war necessity.
    The platform plank condemned "any tendency to regard the press or the radio as instruments of the administration and the use of government publicity agencies for partisan ends" and insisted that "all channels of news must be kept open with equality of access to information at the source. If agreement can be achieved with foreign nations to establish the same principles, it will be a valuable contribution to future peace." *See* Robert U. Brown, "GOP Endorses Principle of International Free Press," *E&P*, July 1, 1944, p. 7.

74. "Board Urges Plans on Free Press and Communications," *ASNE Bulletin*, July 1, 1944, p. 4.

75. "Resolution on World Freedom of Information," Ibid., January 1, 1945, p. 2.

76. "Overseas Conferences Are Next Step in Work Begun by McGill Group," Ibid., December 1, 1944, p. 1.

77. "American Policy toward Freedom of Information," p. 14.
78. Sumner Welles, "Freedom of Information: Pillar of Human Rights," *Free World*, September 1944, p. 220.
79. James Lawrence Fly, "A Free Flow of News Must Link the Nations," *Free World*, August 1944, p. 165.
80. "Editors Demand Uncensored Press," *New York Times*, November 29, 1944, p. 17; "President Accepts Hull's Resignation, Names Stettinius," *New York Times*, November 28, 1944, p. 1.
81. Edward R. Stettinius, Jr., *The Diaries of Edward R. Stettinius, Jr., 1943–1946*, ed. Thomas M. Campbell and George C. Herring, New York, New Viewpoints, 1975, pp. 107–9, 114, 121–22.
82. Unsigned Memorandum on the Status of Work on the Question of Freedom of Information, pp. 4–5.
83. "Free News Exchange Put First in Crusade," p. 9.
84. Memorandum of Conversation by Michael J. McDermott, November 28, 1944, Decimal Classification 800.918/11-2844, NA.
85. Ibid.
86. Memorandum of Conversation by Edward R. Stettinius, December 14, 1944, Decimal Classification FW 811.91200/12-2144, NA.
87. Wilbur Forrest to Edward R. Stettinius, December 15, 1944, Stettinius Papers, Box 691, Folder: F–Fo–Fz. Stettinius responded that Forrest's note was "a great comfort." *See* Edward R. Stettinius, Jr., to Wilbur Forrest, December 19, 1944, Ibid.
88. Quoted in "Charter for a Free Press," *Newsweek*, December 11, 1944, p. 88.
89. "Letter to Stettinius Outlines Mission," in "Complete Report of the ASNE World Freedom of Information Committee," *E&P*, June 18, 1945, p. 4 [hereinafter cited as "Complete Report"].
90. Ernest K. Lindley, "Freedom of Information," *Newsweek*, December 11, 1944, p. 47.
91. Wilbur Forrest to Edward R. Stettinius, Jr., January 2, 1945, Stettinius Papers, Box 722, Folder: Wilbur Forrest.
92. Edward R. Stettinius to All American Diplomatic and Consular Officers, December 18, 1944, Ibid.
93. Edward R. Stettinius to AME, Ankara, Turkey, December 20, 1944, Ibid.
94. "Complete Report," pp. 26, 25, 26.
95. George F. Kennan, Chargé in the Soviet Union, was especially critical of the lack of diplomatic sophistication shown in a speech that Wilbur Forrest made after returning to America. Based on conversations in Russia, the journalist said that the Soviets soon planned to lessen press restrictions. Kennan contended that the Soviets had used Forrest to spread Russian propaganda. *See* George F. Kennan, Chargé in the Soviet Union, to the Secretary of State, July 21, 1945, *FR: 1945*, V:871.
96. Wilbur Forrest, Report of the Committee on World Freedom of Information, April 19, 1946, *Problems of Journalism—1946*, p. 121.
97. "Complete Report," pp. 3, 5.
98. Ibid., pp. 5, 26.
99. "ASNE Board Endorses World Editors Meeting," *E&P*, June 16, 1945, p. 64.
100. "Complete Report," pp. 1, 2.

101. "ASNE Committee Report," *E&P*, June 16, 1945, p. 42.
102. Ralph McGill, "Reflections on World News Freedom Following the ASNE Tour," *Journalism Quarterly* 22 (September 1945):195.
103. Alice Fox Pitts, *Read All About It!*, Easton, Pa., American Society of Newspaper Editors, 1974, pp. 181, 174, 176.
104. Ibid., pp. 178–79.
105. "Crusade for Truth," *Fortune*, April 1945, p. 146.
106. "Edward Stettinius to Senate Foreign Relations Committee in Making Nominations for Assistant Secretary of State," *Department of State Bulletin*, December 10, 1944, p. 688.
107. "Statement by Archibald MacLeish before Senate Foreign Relations Committee Subject to His Nomination as Assistant Secretary of State in Charge of Public and Cultural Relations," Ibid., pp. 692–93.
108. Archibald MacLeish, "Popular Relations and the Press," Ibid., January 14, 1945, pp. 48–49.
109. Henry S. Villard, "The Positive Approach to an Enduring Peace," Ibid., January 28, 1945, p. 139.
110. Francis Colt de Wolf, "The International Control of Radiocommunications," Ibid., p. 136.
111. "Freedom of Information in American Policy and Practice," pp. 24–25.
112. "Crusade for Truth," p. 148.
113. "Free Access to Information," *Department of State Bulletin*, March 18, 1945, p. 451.
114. The American Delegation to the Chapultepec Conference to the Acting Secretary of State, March 6, 1945, *FR: 1945*, IX:144.
115. Jerry Walker, "Press and Radio Freedom Voted at Mexico City," *E&P*, March 10, 1945, p. 8.
116. "Freedom of Information," *E&P*, March 3, 1945, p. 40.
117. Warburg, *Unwritten Treaty*, p. 151.
118. Briefing Book Paper: Suggested United States Policy Regarding Poland, June 29, 1945, *FR: Potsdam*, I:716.
119. Briefing Book Paper: Admission of American Press Correspondents into Eastern Europe, June 29, 1945, Ibid., pp. 319–20.
120. American diplomats had been advised that the Soviets did not "appreciate the importance of public opinion in a democracy nor the importance of the press in the formation of public opinion." The Russians saw the American press as dominated by big business and as basically impotent, citing as proof the newspapers' inability to block Franklin Roosevelt's reelection as president "despite the strong opposition of the greater part of the American press." Consequently, threatening to use the press to mold an anti-Soviet public opinion was unlikely to be successful. *See* L. E. Thompson, Division of Eastern European Affairs, to James C. Dunn, Assistant Secretary of State, February 3, 1945, RG 59, NA, Box 4004, 761.00/2-345.
121. Fifth Plenary Meeting, July 21, 1945, *FR: Potsdam*, II:206. The British and American delegates proposed unlimited access for the press; the Soviets argued that because hostilities had just ended in Poland, such access would be impossible. To the Soviets, the absence of war automatically meant greater freedom of the press without the need for additional guarantees. Further

assurances constituted an internal Polish question beyond the reach of the Potsdam meeting. *See* Fourth Meeting of the Foreign Ministers, July 21, 1945, Ibid., p. 189.

122. Fifth Meeting of the Foreign Ministers, July 22, 1945, Ibid., pp. 228–31.

123. Communiqué, August 2, 1945, Ibid., p. 1508.

124. Third Meeting of the Subcommittee on Implementation of the Yalta Declaration on Liberated Europe, July 26, 1945, Ibid., p. 418.

125. Memorandum of the Executive Secretary of the Central Secretariat, August 7, 1945, Ibid., p. 605.

126. Eleventh Meeting of the Foreign Ministers, August 1, 1945, Ibid., p. 557.

127. Memorandum by Charles E. Bohlen, May 30, 1945, Ibid., I:55–56.

128. Prime Minister Churchill to President Truman, June 23, 1945, Ibid., p. 117.

129. President Truman to Prime Minister Churchill, June 23, 1945, Ibid., p. 118.

130. Second Plenary Meeting, July 18, 1945, Ibid., II:94–95. *Editor & Publisher*, while recognizing the need for secrecy, complained about what seemed to be an almost total blackout of news. *See* "Potsdam," *E&P*, July 21, 1945, p. 36.

131. John Hightower, Roland H. Shackford, Leon M. Pearson, Executive Committee, State Department Correspondents Association, to Secretary of State Edward Stettinius, Jr., February 15, 1945, Stettinius Papers, Box 220, Folder: A–M, 1944.

132. Unsigned Memorandum, January 10, 1945, Ibid., Box 738, Folder: Press Relations.

133. Roscoe Drummond, Bert Andrews, and Edgar Ansel Mowrer, to William Benton, October 23, 1945, Benton Papers, Box 375, Folder 9.

134. William Benton to Secretary of State James F. Byrnes, Memorandum on State Department News Policies, October 23, 1945, Ibid.

135. Draft of Memo on State Department News Policies, undated, Ibid., Box 376, Folder 3.

136. William Benton to Secretary of State James F. Byrnes, October 23, 1945, Ibid., Box 375, Folder 9.

137. For instance, Lord Halifax protested to Secretary of State Stettinius about some information that Drew Pearson planned to use. This led Stettinius to ask the attorney general to try to "persuade Pearson not to publish the piece." *See* Excerpt from Stettinius Record, Vol. III, sec. 5 and 6, Stettinius Papers, Box 467, Folder: Press.

The British press also complained about Pearson's leaks, commenting that "no government could hope to get anything done in the sphere of international relations if its confidential communications with its own servants and with other governments were published by any journalist who happened to get hold of them and think them good copy." *See* Ambassador John G. Winant to the Secretary of State, transcript of *News Chronicle* article, January 6, 1945, RG 59, NA, Box 4983, 811.911/1-645.

138. Henry R. Luce to Secretary of State Edward Stettinius, Jr., March 24, 1945, RG 59, NA, Box 4998, 811.917 TIME/3-2445.

139. Walter Brown, Special Assistant, to Secretary of State James F. Byrnes, October 9, 1945, Ibid., Box 4983, 811.91/10-945.

140. William Benton to Secretary of State James F. Byrnes, October 23, 1945, Benton Papers, Box 375, Folder 9.

141. Byrnes Press Conference, December 5, 1945, pp. 4–6, Byrnes Papers, Folder 555.
142. Arthur Bliss Lane, American Ambassador in Poland, was particularly vociferous about the need to protect the freedom of the domestic press. *See*, e.g., Arthur Bliss Lane, American Ambassador in Poland, to the Secretary of State, *FR: 1945*, V:370, 378–79, 415, 422–23.
143. Edward L. Reed, Counselor of Embassy, Buenos Aires, Argentina, to the Secretary of State, June 6, 1945, RG 59, NA, Box 5493, 835.918/6-645.
144. George H. Butler, Office of American Republic Affairs, to the Acting Secretary of State, Ibid., Box 4983, FW 811.91/6-1245.
145. Archibald MacLeish to Joseph Grew, Under Secretary of State, July 2, 1945, Ibid., Box 4986, 811.91235/7-245.
146. Unsigned Secretary's Staff Committee Memorandum on International Freedom of the Press, July 26, 1945, Byrnes Papers, File 588.
147. Spruille Braden, American Ambassador in Argentina, to the Secretary of State, June 30, 1945, *FR: 1945*, IX:509.
148. Spruille Braden, American Ambassador in Argentina, to the Secretary of State, June 5, 1945, RG 84, WNRC, Records of the American Embassy, Buenos Aires, Argentina, Confidential Box 68, File 891: Restrictions on the Press.
149. Spruille Braden, American Ambassador in Argentina, to the Secretary of State, June 30, 1945, *FR: 1945*, IX:510–11.
150. Archibald MacLeish to Joseph Grew, Under Secretary of State, July 2, 1945, RG 59, NA, Box 4986, 811.91235/7-245.
151. To prove his point, MacLeish attached a memo citing precedent for sending press dispatches in diplomatic pouches, in diplomatic code over commercial telegraph facilities, and in uncoded telegrams via American-owned transmitters abroad from immediately before World War II. *See* Archibald MacLeish to Joseph Grew, Under Secretary of State, Ibid. The secretary of state, however, told Braden that "American correspondents' messages should not be transmitted by Embassy without prior discussion with Department." *See* Secretary of State James Byrnes to the American Embassy, Buenos Aires, Argentina, July 4, 1945, RG 84, WNRC, Records of the American Embassy, Buenos Aires, Argentina, Confidential Box 68, File 891: Restrictions on the Press.
152. Joseph Grew, Acting Secretary of State, Memorandum of Conversation with Señor Oscar Ibarra García, Argentine Ambassador, July 10, 1945, RG 59, NA, Confidential Box 441, 811.91235/7-1045.
153. Spruille Braden, American Ambassador to Argentina, to the Secretary of State, July 5, 1945, *FR: 1945*, IX:514–15. The American government could do nothing about the attacks on Braden in the Argentine press because of the question of "whether a government committed to the policy of complete freedom of the press can protest press campaigns against itself or its representatives while at the same time maintaining the strength of its central position." *See* Unsigned Secretary's Staff Committee Memorandum on International Freedom of the Press, July 26, 1945, Byrnes Papers, File 588.
154. Spruille Braden, American Ambassador in Argentina, to the Secretary of State, July 7, 1945, *FR: 1945*, IX:517.
155. Ibid., July 15, 1945, pp. 519–20.
156. Ibid., September 29, 1945, p. 521.

157. Ibid., October 4, 1945, p. 522.
158. The American press also noted that Argentina was violating the Chapultepec accords. *See*, e.g., "Argentina," *E&P*, June 9, 1945, p. 38; "Argentina," *E&P*, July 14, 1945, p. 34; Ernie Hill, "Threat to Wreck La Prensa Caps Climax of Peron's Fight," *E&P*, July 21, 1945, pp. 9, 32.
159. Acting Secretary of State Joseph Grew to Burton Y. Berry, American Representative in Rumania, February 24, 1945, *FR: 1945*, V:479.
160. Burton Y. Berry, American Representative in Rumania, to the Secretary of State, September 10, 1945, Ibid., p. 612.
161. Burton Y. Berry, American Representative in Rumania, to the Secretary of State, April 17, 1945, RG 59, NA, Box 6855, 871.918/4-1745.
162. Secretary of State James Byrnes to H. F. Arthur Schoenfeld, American Representative in Hungary, August 17, 1945, Ibid., Box 4990, 811.91264/8-1745.
163. H. F. Arthur Schoenfeld, American Representative in Hungary, to the Secretary of State, August 31, 1945, Ibid., 811.91264/8-3145.
164. H. F. Arthur Schoenfeld, American Representative in Hungary, to the Secretary of State, September 7, 1945, Ibid., 811.91264/9-745.
165. H. F. Arthur Schoenfeld, American Representative in Hungary, to the Secretary of State, October 15, 1945, Ibid., Confidential Box 760, 864.918/10-1545.
166. H. F. Arthur Schoenfeld, American Representative in Hungary, to the Secretary of State, August 30, 1945, Ibid., Confidential Box 441, 811.91240/8-3045. Correspondents had used Signal Corps equipment for dispatches before the reestablishment of commercial service, according to Major General William S. Key, chief of the United States Representation on the Allied Control Commission for Hungary. General Key sought permission to reinstitute the practice from his superiors, but he warned Schoenfeld "that this may not be approved because the War Department may construe it as an attempt on the part of the correspondents to evade threatened censorship by the Russians." *See* Major General William S. Key, Chief of the United States Representation on the Allied Control Commission for Hungary, to H. F. Arthur Schoenfeld, American Representative in Hungary, October 11, 1945, RG 84, WNRC, Records of the American Legation in Budapest, Hungary, Box 153, File 891: News Censorship.
167. H. F. Arthur Schoenfeld, American Representative in Hungary, to the Secretary of State, October 18, 1945, RG 59, NA, Confidential Box 760, 864.918/10-1845.
168. Unsigned Secretary's Staff Committee Memorandum on International Freedom of the Press, Byrnes Papers. The memo's writer also worried lest "we should soon find ourselves in the position of having to decide which despatches we should transmit and which we should not: an untenable position for this Government at any time."
169. Arthur B. Lane, American Ambassador in Poland, to the Secretary of State, July 25, 1945, RG 59, NA, Confidential Box 441, 811.91260C/7-2545.
170. Arthur B. Lane, American Ambassador in Poland, to the Secretary of State, August 19, 1945, Ibid., 811.91260C/8-1945.
171. Dean Acheson, Acting Secretary of State, to the American Embassy in Warsaw, September 8, 1945, Ibid., 811.91260C/9-845.

172. Gerald Keith, Chargé in Poland, to the Secretary of State, September 14, 1945, Ibid., 811.91260C/9-1445.
173. Arthur B. Lane, American Ambassador in Poland, to the Secretary of State, November 13, 1945, *FR: 1945*, V:414.
174. Arthur B. Lane, American Ambassador in Poland, to the Secretary of State, November 20, 1945, RG 59, NA, Box 4987, 811.91260C/11-2045. Lane was equally unsuccessful in convincing Polish officials that the Potsdam agreement guaranteed uncensored reporting before the Polish elections. Polish officials retorted that since no election date had yet been set, correspondents obviously did not yet have the right to report freely. *See* Arthur B. Lane, American Ambassador in Poland, to the Secretary of State, September 26, 1945, *FR: 1945*, V:380-81.
175. Acting Secretary of State Joseph Grew to George F. Kennan, Chargé in the Soviet Union, February 10, 1945, *FR: 1945*, IV:158.
176. Acting Secretary of State Joseph Grew to the American Embassy, Moscow, March 23, 1945, RG 59, NA, Box 4988, 811.91261/2-1945.
177. Secretary of State Edward R. Stettinius to the American Embassy, Moscow, February 19, 1945, Ibid., 811.91261/2-1945.
178. Averell Harriman, American Ambassador in the Soviet Union, to the Secretary of State, June 4, 1945, Ibid., 811.91261/6-445.

CHAPTER 2

The Crusade Moves into the International Arena

The crusade for international freedom of the press had one primary goal: the placement of clauses guaranteeing that freedom into treaties and other covenants ending World War II. In early 1945, the possibilities of reaching that goal looked brighter than ever. With the groundwork for creating the United Nations established, organizers would soon meet in San Francisco to raise that body's superstructure.

Before taking the free-press campaign to the organizational conference, however, the American delegation faced the problem of reconciling proposals from various United States press groups. The plans had many similarities, especially in linking the freedom to gather news with the freedom to transmit the news from abroad. Kent Cooper of the Associated Press (AP) presented the most general proposal, asking for worldwide freedom of the press, a worldwide system of communications, and "facilities for newsmen to do their work everywhere without interference." The latter point, Cooper said, included a form of diplomatic immunity, which would allow reporters to work anywhere, write anything, and send news out of the country freely without fear of expulsion from the host country. Hugh Baillie of the United Press (UP) wanted all news sources, especially governmental sources, open competitively to all, transmission facilities equally available to all, minimal interference in the news flow by governments, and permission for newspapers throughout the world to buy their news from any source. Baillie's plan, while not calling specifically for international freedom of the press, assumed that the right would be built on the foundation established by his four principles.[1]

Members of the American Society of Newspaper Editors (ASNE) had a five-point program that called for direct communication between countries where feasible, eliminating impediments to the use of scientific advances in communications, removing commercial or political restrictions favoring the media of any particular nation, sharing available communications facilities equitably among correspondents of all nations, and fostering the unrestricted flow of news and information throughout the world.[2] Confusing the situation slightly were suggestions made by individuals on the fringes of the crusade, such as the proposals coming from a forum of journalists held at the

University of Pennsylvania. Session participants, including an assistant general manager of the Associated Press, added two points to the international free-press campaign: the establishment of an organization to ensure that reporters from all nations had free access to information throughout the world and the creation of a court of appeals to hear complaints from correspondents about alleged mistreatment.[3] The persons making these proposals obviously had forgotten objections to similar suggestions in 1932 and 1933. Opposition to suggestions for outside enforcement of journalistic values was no less vocal in 1945.

THE PRESS COVERS THE UNITED NATIONS ORGANIZING CONFERENCE

As journalists bombarded the State Department with proposals on freedom of information, they also laid plans for covering one of the biggest news events of the decade—the United Nations Conference on International Organization. According to preconference estimates, more journalists would be in San Francisco to cover the United Nations organizing session than had ever reported on any previous international meeting. In fact, more than a thousand representatives of broadcast and print media from all over the world were expected to record every event.[4] President Franklin D. Roosevelt, apparently responding to criticisms about the numerous closed meetings that laid the groundwork for the San Francisco conference, promised reporters that they would have full access to all information generated during the meetings.[5] Secretary of State Edward R. Stettinius, Jr., who headed the United States delegation, agreed with the principle of conducting sessions "with the greatest possible consideration for the wide-spread interest of the world in its deliberations" and promised journalists would have access to plenary and main conference committee meetings.[6] American journalists planned to use the organizing session to showcase the way in which a free press operated, but some editors worried about the negative influence that press misbehavior could have on the image of the profession and on the free-press crusade. Months of careful work promoting international freedom of the press could "go for nothing if San Francisco turns into an orgy of college-football-rivalry reporting," warned Erwin D. Canham, editor of the *Christian Science Monitor*, who soon became a leading international free-press spokesman.[7]

Journalistic behavior at San Francisco conformed to Canham's worst fears; the conference was far from a calm display of American freedom of the press in action. By the time the session opened, the almost 1,900 press correspondents on hand outnumbered 1,700 official delegates.[8] Among the American correspondents were "night club, Hollywood and humorous columnists," who "interrupted serious discussions where regular news correspondents were hard at work trying to get facts." The columnists behaved so poorly that *Editor & Publisher* suggested barring certain journalists from some news events in order to allow serious reporters to work without interruption. The trade journal's recommendation stemmed from entertainment columnist Earl Wilson's interruption of a serious news conference to question Soviet delegation head V. M. Molotov about the appropriate pronunciation of the word vodka and to ask if Molotov recommended the beverage for American consumption. After Wilson's question, Molotov abruptly ended the news conference. Before Wilson's inane query, Molotov was "adroitly answering well-phrased questions concerning the Polish situation."[9] Rather than displaying American press responsibility, that particular news conference and much of the coverage of the organizing session proved "that there are showoffs and crackpots, pests, pinheads and men of ill will among those who are supposed to inform and advise the public, as among the public itself." Press observers believed that responsible behavior by the majority of correspondents present and regular contact between the reporters and foreign diplomats must be relied on to compensate for the poor examples of a few journalists and to convince diplomats of the admirable qualities of freedom of the press, American style.[10]

The official American delegation took note of the antics of some representatives of the press as delegates tried to develop an equitable press policy. The basic question focused on how much information to release to the press and when to release it. For instance, should all statements to the press wait until the end of the preliminary discussions because of possible changes in the delegates' positions? Would the delegation be "better off if no evidence of division among various delegates were revealed"? Would leaks cause "difficulties in getting our ideas adopted at San Francisco"?[11] As an astute politician, United States Senator Arthur Vandenberg argued for openness, labeling good press relations vital. In fact, he added, the delegation's press contacts were "almost as important as what happened in the substantive discussions themselves."[12] The delegation ultimately authorized the chairman to make official announcements and allowed individual delegates to talk with journalists if they wished. The delegation also agreed to schedule regular background sessions for reporters, providing the number of correspondents attending the conference did not make the sessions physically impractical.[13]

Despite these arrangements, correspondents complained about a general lack of information regarding private negotiations and details of American positions on various issues. American delegation members reported that journalists had complained that they could "obtain all the background information they want from the British, but none from us." Secretary of State Stettinius conceded "that is not a desirable situation,"[14] but he grumbled that far too much information had been printed in the press already—

especially about sensitive negotiations—and pleaded for greater discretion when releasing materials to the press.[15] Obviously, no approach would satisfy reporters, politicians, and diplomats. Consequently, relationships between press and government representatives at the United Nations organizing session were on a fairly normal adversarial level. For the free-press crusade to succeed, however, closer cooperation was essential.

Journalists remained confident that the free-press issue would come up at the organizing conference and that the American delegation would strongly support a free-press clause for the United Nations Charter. Among the auspicious omens was an address by President Harry S. Truman to the opening session in which he discussed "the disaster which follows when freedom of thought is no longer tolerated."[16] The president's statement relieved the anxiety of some supporters of the free-press crusade, who worried about numerous rumors that the free-press issue would not be discussed in San Francisco. Another encouraging sign was the presence of Senator Tom Connally and Representative Sol Bloom on the United States delegation, for both were strong supporters of the congressional resolution favoring international freedom of information that was passed in 1944.[17]

Insertion of a free-press clause in the United Nations Charter, though, was far from guaranteed. The United States delegation strongly disagreed over not only the content of a free-press statement for the United Nations Charter but over whether the charter should mention that right at all. Any statement in the charter on international freedom of the press must either be "something real on this subject or a meaningless platitude," Leo Pasvolsky, special assistant to the secretary of state, said, as he argued for no provision at all. Although unsure about the exact direction that their free-press efforts would take, delegates agreed early that they would need to do "something" about freedom of information at San Francisco.[18]

Secretary of State Stettinius proclaimed his interest in guaranteeing freedom of worship and freedom of information somewhere in the United Nations Charter.[19] But if the United States suggested one or two specific guarantees—the ones dealing with worship and information—for the charter, representatives of all nations at the conference would want to add to the list of so-called fundamental freedoms. An uncontrolled recitation of basic rights could move the charter debate into areas that the United States delegation preferred to avoid. Ultimately, freedom of information provisions for the United Nations Charter fell before the objections of both the British and the Russians, neither of whom supported the proposal.[20] The unwillingness of the United States delegation to push for the inclusion of an international freedom of information provision in the United Nations Charter turned into a diplomatic plus for the Americans. Now, the delegation should have some leverage in negotiating other controversial matters because the Americans had not embarrassed other delegations on freedom of information questions.[21]

For public and free-press advocate consumption, Secretary Stettinius announced that obtaining an agreement enumerating fundamental rights acceptable to "more than two score nations of differing social systems, environments, and traditions" attending the conference would take too long. Delegates agreed to postpone making the list of fundamental rights until an appropriate commission within the United Nations bureaucracy could study the matter. One of the first tasks of this Human Rights Commission, which would operate under the Economic and Social Council, would be to write an international bill of rights, "which can be accepted by all the member nations as an integral part of their own systems of law." The Department of State, Stettinius promised, planned to "work actively and tirelessly" to protect and promote freedom of information through that and other United Nations documents.[22]

All that international free-press advocates won from the organizing conference was vague language in the United Nations Charter that called for the promotion of "universal respect for, and observance of, human rights and fundamental freedoms for all." Secretary of State Stettinius told Wilbur Forrest, chairman of the ASNE committee on world freedom of information, not to be discouraged because the American delegation regarded freedom of speech as "one of the fundamental freedoms referred to in this Charter." Furthermore, Stettinius assured Forrest, freedom of speech encompassed "freedom of the press, freedom of communication and freedom of exchange of information." Lest American newspaper editors consider the battle over, *Editor & Publisher* counseled that the work was only beginning. American diplomats needed vigorous support from editors at home to win insertion of their beliefs in international documents. In fact, editors must go beyond urging incorporation of freedom of the press into the United Nations framework. Editors must advocate inserting similar guarantees in peace treaties as well: "Constant hammering on the subject and vigilance will be required of all editors to keep these ideals in the foreground."[23]

The United Nations was not ready to consider any fundamental freedoms until early 1946. In the meantime, the State Department advanced international freedom of information wherever possible. At the Pan-American Radio Conference in Rio de Janeiro, Brazil, in September 1945, for instance, the United States suggested a resolution calling on the American states to recognize "the essential obligation to guarantee their peoples free and impartial access to sources of information" and to "develop unrestricted interchange of information between their peoples." The conference dealt with technical matters, so the resolution loosened restrictions on sending and receiving radio messages.[24] In December 1945, the British-American Telecommunications Conference in Bermuda resulted in additional gains for the "unimpeded flow of information among nations," including lower rates for press dispatches, greater speed in transmitting press cables, and more direct distribution of press association reports among clients.[25] Since access to communications facilities was a primary focus of the international freedom of information campaign, these efforts were an integral part of the overall crusade.

One person not very pleased with the delay in international negotiations was Cooper, general manager of the Associated Press. Never one to hide his feelings, Cooper sent a personal messenger to President Truman in September 1945 with a new list of priorities for the establishment of press freedom throughout the world. Now, Cooper wanted the United States to require that "the vanquished nations guarantee their peoples a free press as we know it." He also insisted that "any nation which requests help in reestablishing its economy guarantee its people a free press as we know it." Truman sent word back to Cooper that national policy precluded interference in the domestic affairs of these countries. "We will stay with them and help them get on their feet and establish a government we can recognize. Then, regardless of the government they may establish, provided it represents popular will, we will keep hands off."[26]

Cooper was incredulous. Surely, the president must "recognize press freedom as the sine qua non of enduring peace." If Truman abandoned the free-press crusade, the Associated Press executive warned, "we cannot withhold from the public the fact that nothing is to come of the declarations of policy in the party platforms last year and the concurrent resolutions of Congress." In fact, Cooper predicted, "the greatest opportunity of all time may be missed." Thus, "the public should understand that although this country is to furnish good will, money and patronage to the nations that tried to destroy us, there will be nothing imposed by us through the medium of a required press freedom to insure peace." State Department proposals on freedom of information attacked "the matter indifferently," Cooper maintained. And, although Cooper said he understood the problems of negotiating with Great Britain, China, and the Soviet Union, the journalist felt sure that "as respects the peace treaties with the aggressor nations, the Big Four would impose press freedom if you make it clear that the American public has expressed itself as demanding it." Supremely confident of his position, Cooper asked permission to make the president's comments public, thus placing the matter before the people in the hope that they would remind the president of their support of international freedom of the press.[27]

The president advised the Associated Press executive that he was "unduly agitated." Truman believed that several approaches for securing peace were feasible, and he stressed that his main desire was to obtain "a peace settlement that will work." But the president strongly opposed "cramming anything down the throat of an independent nation that will interfere with that peace settlement."[28] The president had heard the Associated Press's free-press complaints many times, including in a recent request from Senator Wayne Morse of Oregon for a favorable reception for the news agency's proposals.[29] Showing his irritation at the repeated requests, the president told Morse, "we have a sabotage press in this country whose principal aim in life has been to discredit the Roosevelt Administration and whose present approach is to smear him after he is dead." The press itself was "one of the principal causes for our inability to get a freer approach to Russia and other countries. Stalin takes the attitude that the press in Russia is Russia's business" and countering that stance was almost impossible. Truman thought that the United States might win concessions from a few friendly countries on free-press issues, but with those countries "with whom we are not on friendly terms and have not recognized there isn't very much chance of getting a free news service."[30]

THE PRESS SEEKS SUPPORT AT THE UNITED NATIONS

Despite political realities, press leaders refused to allow the crusade to die. As if to emphasize that international freedom of information was more than a passing fancy, the ASNE set up a permanent committee on the subject and installed Forrest, assistant editor of the *New York Herald Tribune* and former free-press missionary, as its head.[31] The United Nations Organization planned to meet in London in early 1946, and press leaders wanted the United States delegation to campaign for an international free-press guarantee during that session. Leaders of the American Society of Newspaper Editors pointedly asked Stettinius, now head of the United States delegation, to support treaties including such pledges. Hugh Baillie, president of the United Press, likewise petitioned the American delegation, claiming to have the backing of twelve nations for his plan to place the free-press issue before the Commission on Human Rights.[32]

Before too long, the head of the third American press association, Seymour Berkson, general manager of International News Service (INS), sent Stettinius his proposals. Although virtually duplicating suggestions from his colleagues, Berkson's proposals showed a marked sensitivity to the difficulties involved in implementing the ideas that was lacking in other recommendations. "We, who are accustomed in the United States to the highest standards of Freedom of the Press and who take it as much for granted as our daily bread, must not be deluded thereby into believing that this concept will be easy to establish throughout the world," he said. In fact, internationalization of freedom of the press "will be an evolutionary program. It will be an educational program. Foundation stones of Democracy must first be laid in many countries to provide the kind of fertile soil in which Freedom of the Press can be established and respected." And in a comment that some of his colleagues might have considered heretical, he suggested that "perhaps our pattern [of freedom of the press] cannot be transplanted totally to all countries."[33]

Most American supporters of the free-press ideal lacked Berkson's understanding. Toleration of differing approaches to freedom of the press, many journalists decided, was a bad idea. Contributing to this attitude in a perverse way was a collection of excerpts from the constitutions of the forty-seven members of the United Nations published by *Editor & Publisher*. Each fundamental document guaranteed freedom of the press in some way, but many nations did not honor their constitutional provisions. American journalists believed that other nations must live up to the letter of their constitutions and sought ways to enforce such conformity.[34]

Many journalists interested in international freedom of the press were restive; they wanted action. Polite correspondence with the American delegation had been insufficient to produce results at San Francisco, and alleged pledges of governmental support for free-press guarantees went unfulfilled. Now, journalists believed, the American press must intensify efforts for world freedom of information. With other countries regularly erecting roadblocks to the free flow of news, American journalists believed that trying to understand the reasons for the obstacles or trying to work around the barriers were no longer viable options. Instead, journalists must send "a man or a committee to do a sales job in London on delegations of other nations." Other issues could not be allowed to supersede freedom of information again.[35]

United States diplomats at the London meetings tried to advance freedom of information on various fronts, even though the purpose of the session was to create the United Nations bureaucracy rather than to deal with substantive issues. If possible, United States delegates planned to place freedom of information on the agendas of both the Commission on Human Rights and the United Nations Educational, Scientific, and Cultural Organization (UNESCO). Official instructions reminded American delegates that advancing freedom of information was considered "one of the most important tasks of the United Nations and its associated agencies." In fact, without freer international exchange of information, the delegates were told, establishing the level of understanding and confidence among nations necessary to preserve peace could be impossible. But establishing a formula for international interchange of information that would meet American standards would be most difficult. The phrase freedom of information had broad implications, departmental officials said, and "the problem of assuring such freedom raises grave political, economic and cultural problems, which can only be solved by prolonged and persistent efforts."[36]

American journalists, traditionally impatient, found the slowness of diplomacy maddeningly unappealing, and the American delegation at the first General Assembly session heard regularly from its frustrated journalistic constituency. Adding urgency to the free-press crusade was the depressing status of journalism around the world. Suppression of editors and newspapers opposing governments in power occurred far too often to suit the ASNE. The newspaper society's world freedom of information committee unhappily concluded that some nations "have evidently drawn no lessons from the most terrible and devastating struggle in history." The editors uncovered little evidence that world press conditions dismayed anyone other than American journalists and their supporters within the United States government. Consequently, any hope for international freedom of information agreements "uniquely depends for success upon the initiative of the American Delegation."[37] But the American delegation made little progress on what journalists back home thought was "a first order of business."[38]

Stettinius did pursue the matter with United Nations Secretary-General Trygve Lie, telling Lie that the United States expected the Commission on Human Rights to "undertake as promptly as possible a study of the problem of freedom of information with a view to preparing draft recommendations or a draft convention thereon." The earliest that the subject could come up, however, was at the May 1946 meeting of the Economic and Social Council in New York.[39] Assigning international freedom of information to the Human Rights Commission, which was under the Economic and Social Council, which in turn was under the General Assembly, displeased most American journalists, who believed that freedom of information was far too low on the United Nations' priority list. American journalists thought that free-press discussions should start in the General Assembly itself.[40] The journalists' disappointment and discouragement grew when Stettinius advised Cooper about the significant differences among the nations of the world on the subject, stressing, "the problem is so great in scope that we cannot expect to solve it immediately." American diplomats thought that placing the subject on the agenda was an acceptable first step. The possibilities were unlimited once discussion began.[41] Convincing American journalists of the future potential of United Nations debate was not easy; they believed solely in present realities.

One reason for freedom of information's fate at the first General Assembly session, according to United States delegate John Foster Dulles, was that the president had instructed the delegation to confine itself to organizational matters. Thus, strictly speaking, American representatives could not officially broach the subject of international freedom of information. Although the free-press issue was placed before the General Assembly through a Philippine proposal for an international press conference, Dulles deprecated the measure as being "poorly drawn" and considered it as having little potential.[42]

The Philippine proposal, however, became the one positive step taken to promote freedom of the press in the United Nations' first year of existence. Despite close ties between the United States and the Philippines, Filipino arguments brought a degree of international credence to the free-press crusade. Reasons in favor of convening the conference presented by

Philippine delegate Pedro López echoed the arguments in favor of world-wide press freedom offered by American newspaper representatives—except that the Filipino, with access to the floor of the United Nations, was able to plead for the cause in person. A free press, López argued, might be the world's only chance to save itself from the atom bomb. The world's press, he said, was the cause of "so much of the present misunderstanding, so much of the present irritation and suspicion being developed between one country and another country, between one people and another and between one government and another." Something must be done to coordinate the press's efforts to achieve world peace. United Nations members claimed to welcome the suggestion for an international press convocation, but they decided that the idea should be dealt with later in the United States. A postponement, López protested, was a mistake, for "now is the time to start laying the foundation of peace."[43]

Supporting the attempt to delay consideration was Senator Vandenberg, a member of the American delegation, who proclaimed himself a firm supporter of the idea that "international knowledge will disarm international suspicion." At the moment, however, Vandenberg argued, delegates must confine themselves "to the business of setting up our machinery, putting it in gear, and giving it a chance to get in running order before we attempt its substantive use."[44] Convinced that the United States would support the proposed conference at the next sitting of the assembly in New York, the Philippine delegate agreed to wait. The General Assembly passed the resolution calling for an international conference in December 1946.[45]

American policy planners, apparently caught off guard by the Philippine proposal, immediately began assessing the ramifications of an international press conference. Supporters of the proposal within the Department of State saw the session as a way "to mobilize the support of world opinion behind the effort to secure freedom of the press."[46] Members of the American press, however, had difficulty with the resolution's call for conference delegations to include only an "adequate representation" of press organizations.[47] American journalists wanted the conference delegations totally "composed of those actually engaged in the operation of the various channels of mass communication."[48] In fact, the ASNE world freedom of information committee wanted the statesmen and politicians to "stay out of it" because diplomats would taint and limit discussions among professionals. Admittedly, some governmental connection was necessary, if only for convenience. The United Nations had to call the conference, for instance; member states had to name delegations; and the United Nations had to provide the site and support facilities. After that, however, the ideal conference was for professionals only.[49] But a conference for professionals only neglected the role governments would play in implementing agreements. If the political experts were absent from the proposed conference, could delegates inexperienced in international diplomacy draft free-press documents capable of surviving debate within the United Nations? Ignoring such possible problems, American journalists continued to push for a professionals-only conference, and the United States government supported the journalists' demand.

To satisfy the press's demands and to eliminate as many problems connected with a professionals-only conference as possible, the State Department contemplated proposing an informal meeting rather than a full-blown international session. A less formal gathering, said former newspaperman J. Noel Macy, chairman of the department's freedom of information committee, might mobilize world opinion and dramatize "the need for such understanding between peoples." The conference, then, "might serve to counteract any accusation that this was merely a pet hobby of the United States." An informal session might also solve some of the problems expected when the United Nations began writing an international bill of rights. For instance, American diplomats knew that as soon as anyone proposed "the right of the people to get information" for inclusion in a bill of rights, a companion item—the "extreme necessity of self discipline on the part of an independent press"—would be introduced. If members of the working press, at an international conference, "set up their own set of controls" before the subject was brought up officially before the United Nations, some of the acrimony expected in later debates might be defused.[50]

State Department contemplation of possibilities and alternatives took a long time. Discouragement mounted among members of the American Society of Newspaper Editors, and Forrest found himself urging his colleagues not to abandon hope. Perhaps, Forrest told ASNE members meeting in April 1946, the delay was even beneficial. Plans now called for consideration of freedom of information at the September meeting of the United Nations, a session scheduled for the United States. Apparently forgetting the debacle of press coverage of the United Nations organizing session in San Francisco, Forrest noted, "foreign delegates called to negoti-ate here in the clear atmosphere of our American freedom of the press would be enabled better to understand its benefits." Intensified ASNE efforts to make United Nations delegates see the benefits of a free press while they visited America were critical, Forrest said, explaining that most of the delegates certainly never encountered a free press at home. To underline his point, Forrest told of a survey conducted by *Editor & Publisher* that revealed that only sixteen countries of the world enjoyed press freedom comparable to that in the United States. Twenty-one nations practiced partial repression of the press including "rationing and control of newsprint, subsidies, government licensing, visa restrictions for correspondents, domestic laws interpreted by government officials, checks on outgoing news, no criticism of the state permitted, etc." Another eight nations supported government news agencies or practiced "censorship of incoming dispatches against anything but favorable news, and other repressive controls." And nine countries enforced rigid government controls "without camouflage of any kind."[51]

On the brighter side, the ASNE was to play an even more important role in shaping international free-press guarantees, Forrest said. Copies of correspondence from the ASNE, the United Press, and the Associated Press to United Nations Secretary-General Lie about a free-press guarantee had been forwarded to Sir A. Ramaswami Mudaliar of India, president of the Economic and Social Council. Mudaliar wanted ASNE members to prepare a draft convention on the topic for council consideration. Forrest was excited by the possibilities raised by the request. Aside from the great honor being bestowed on the society, the organization could help frame international legislation or at least establish a basis for "agreements which can well be a major factor in a new world era of understanding between peoples."[52]

HOPES FOR PROGRESS AT THE UNITED NATIONS RISE AGAIN

The future then was quite rosy, even if the present was discouraging. Forrest saw no roadblocks to the adoption of a draft free-press convention by the General Assembly in the fall and its early ratification by United Nations members. ASNE members must be aware, however, that their proposal would be examined closely. Opposition to its provisions likely would appear as an attack "on the integrity and objectivity of the press," with assaults focusing on "irresponsible journalism and the dangers of an uncontrolled press." Suggestions would be made that self-discipline within the profession was necessary before entrusting journalists with the degree of freedom requested. "What this amounts to is the demand that world journalism raise its standards before freedom of the press is granted, or even the right to gather, write and transmit news freely between nations," Forrest said, adding, he hoped "this argument does not prevail."[53]

International freedom of the press finally came before a United Nations body when the Human Rights Commission convened in May 1946. Facing the commission, chaired by Eleanor Roosevelt, were five separate proposals on freedom of the press—one each from the American Society of Newspaper Editors, the Associated Press, the United Press, and from the delegates of Cuba and Panama.[54] The Human Rights Commission had numerous other issues—including the international bill of rights—to consider; the chances of worldwide freedom of the press receiving priority treatment were slim. Consequently, the crusade took a slight detour when Mrs. Roosevelt unveiled the United States government's proposal and suggested the creation of a special subcommission to deal solely with free-press issues.[55]

Although the Subcommission on Freedom of Information and of the

Press was quickly approved by the Commission on Human Rights, the brief debate surrounding its formation highlighted the difficulties that the American idea of worldwide freedom of information soon encountered. Even America's wartime allies were unwilling to support United States free-press proposals fully. In fact, allies raised the first questions about the crusade. For example, C. L. Hsia, the delegate from China, pointed out, "though America has done most of the thinking on this subject, the American people—forgive me for being frank—have a habit of looking at the world through an American point of view. In other countries, the press is not developed to the point it is in the United States." With the debate now in the United Nations, Hsia implied, American thinking would no longer prevail; amendments to United States proposals based on the needs of countries with lesser-developed press systems were necessary. Opposition also surfaced from allies who felt that the press needed greater supervision in the complicated postwar world. René Cassin, delegate from France, suggested the creation of an international organization to "regulate those who publish false information" because "national laws are no longer sufficient to govern the press, since the press itself is an international matter."[56]

Whether the United States government anticipated such disagreements is uncertain, but Mrs. Roosevelt tried to put the best face possible on the differences encountered. Early debates, she said, summarized two basic philosophies on the press. "Some people believe freedom of information implies that all kinds of information should be available and that the public can be relied on to sift the true from the false." The primary opposing view, thus far, showed that others believed "some kinds of information are deliberately falsified and slanted to give the public an incorrect impression of the facts, and that the average person because of lack of education, intelligence or knowledge about such matters is unable to tell the lie from the truth." Advocates of the latter theory "believe that freedom of information implies some kind of control over propaganda for protection of those who cannot recognize it." Far more divergent opinions on freedom of the press were likely before long. Reconciling the various views, Mrs. Roosevelt said, surpassed the abilities of mere diplomats. Consequently, the Commission on Human Rights suggested that members of the Subcommission on Freedom of Information and of the Press, which would handle this complicated issue, be experts in the field rather than representatives of governments as was customary for United Nations committees.[57]

As debate on establishing the subcommission moved into the Economic and Social Council, American journalists quickly learned that the rest of the world had quite different ideas about the place freedom of the press had in society. The very idea of placing the free-press issue before other, more important, human rights offended Soviet delegate Nikolai I. Fenov. On the other hand, Philip J. Noel-Baker, the British delegate, did not object to immediate discussion of freedom of the press, but he believed that debates must include consideration of ways to "restrain irresponsible perversion of or suppressions of the truth" in the press or on radio. Leo Mattes, the Yugoslav representative, agreed that the world must be protected from misuse of the press because "freedom which is not organized easily degenerates into anarchy."[58]

The proposed terms of reference for the subcommission worried State Department planners; under the suggested language, the panel was to "examine what rights, obligations and practices should be included in the concept of freedom of information." The idea that freedom of information carried obligations violated basic American thinking. If the terms of reference remained unchanged, United States representatives at the United Nations must insist that the subcommission also study existing obstacles to the free interchange of information such as "censorship of press and radio, control of correspondence, discriminatory cable rates, powers (beneficial and otherwise) of press agencies, customs and laws of different countries, and similar topics." Without such alterations, the American concept had no chance of receiving a fair hearing.[59]

UNESCO ENTERS THE FREE-PRESS DEBATE

While still fighting the free-press battle within the Economic and Social Council, State Department officials prepared for action on a second front. UNESCO soon would consider the place of mass communications in its operations. As a separate and autonomous specialized agency with its own members and hierarchy, UNESCO worked on projects of its own and cooperated with the United Nations on certain activities through the coordinating mechanism of the Economic and Social Council. No one doubted that UNESCO would help to determine the role of mass communications in the postwar world. Unlike the United Nations, which, thus far, had sidestepped the issue at every possible opportunity, the UNESCO constitution specifically required the organization to "collaborate in the work of advancing the mutual knowledge and understanding of peoples, through all means of mass communication and to that end recommend such international agreements as may be necessary to promote the free flow of ideas by word and image."[60] A specific resolution adopted at the UNESCO organizing conference in November 1945 authorized the study of the mass media in relation to maintaining "international peace and security by the spread of knowledge and understanding."[61]

Assistant Secretary of State William Benton, who headed the American delegation to the UNESCO conference in 1945, planted many of the seeds for future UNESCO mass communications activities. One of Benton's greatest contributions was putting Archibald MacLeish to work on the preamble to the UNESCO charter,[62] thus ensuring a poetic tone for almost all freedom of information arguments in succeeding years. MacLeish's preamble succinctly summarized American beliefs about the role of mass communications in the world by stating, "Since wars begin in the minds of men, it is in the minds of men that the defenses of peace must be constructed."[63] Freedom of information alone allowed the construction of the necessary defenses, and the United States Department of State and many American journalists vowed to work unstintingly to win the minds of men for peace.

American entrance into the UNESCO debates was in stark contrast to the seemingly haphazard approach to the United Nations effort. Before the UNESCO discussions, the State Department carefully established an American position on free-press issues. Citizen involvement was a key to UNESCO activities, and Benton quickly named a special committee on mass communications to study the American media and to prepare a report that would serve as the basis for United States proposals to UNESCO. The committee, headed by Edward W. Barrett, editorial director of *Newsweek*, met with leaders of the nation's newspapers, news agencies, radio, motion pictures, and other interested parties. Barrett promised no miracles, but he thought that UNESCO offered more hope for removing some of the obstacles to the free interchange of information than did the United Nations itself.[64]

Barrett committee consultations with American journalists, however, produced some proposals running so contrary to beliefs held sacred by the American press that the ideas were almost immediately condemned. Suggestions for equal access for national and foreign correspondents to sources of news, or for equal access to facilities for communication, or for keeping governmental censorship of news minimal raised no problems. But controversy immediately arose when the committee received a proposal for a system of international accreditation of journalists "preferably under criteria agreed on by the associations of foreign correspondents, whereby the travel, residence and working conditions of correspondents would be facilitated and standardized." Another suggestion called for accredited correspondents to "subscribe to a code of professional behavior, with assurance that so long as they observe it they shall be free from expulsion, restrictions, harassment or other impediments." Action against a journalist adhering to the code could be appealed "to the foreign correspondents' corps for judgment of the government's complaint."[65] The American press expected such suggestions from its international enemies—or from its domestic critics—but journalists refused to tolerate such proposals from a special committee assigned to develop a plan for advocating American ideas on freedom of the press before UNESCO. Accrediting correspondents, journalists told the State Department in no uncertain terms, "has no place in a peacetime world—unless that world is to be so regimented that even newspapers and press associations are to be told who they can send where and at what time."

If freedom of information was the goal, "let's stick to the letter of the word and steer clear of international authorities that will surely gum up the works."[66]

Press leaders did not abandon their international efforts because of these objectionable proposals, but the leaders' unbending attitude eliminated opportunities to achieve something close to the American dream through compromise with other nations. American journalists wanted their dream or nothing, and the State Department acceded to the journalists' wishes. Simply put, the American proposal demanded "freedom for the people of the world to read what they want, see what motion pictures they want, and hear what they will over the radio."[67] Specifically, the United States plan placed before UNESCO called for "broad freedom of information agreements among the nations," "free and equal access to news at its source in all countries," "elimination of censorship," "increased low-cost communication facilities," and "periodic consultation among mass media representatives."[68] State Department planners optimistically saw UNESCO as facilitating the "removal or diminution of such specific impediments by appropriate action, including ... the formulation and recommendation of international agreements."[69] The American UNESCO proposals were almost identical to the suggestions made at various United Nations meetings. Movement on free-press issues had almost stopped at the United Nations, but American diplomats hoped for action by UNESCO, primarily because UNESCO was "empowered to bring member nations into formal agreement on matters within its province." And international mass communication was definitely within UNESCO's province. Essentially, explained *Editor & Publisher*, the State Department was moving the "problem before a more powerful body, at the same time removing it from entanglement with the many other weighty matters involving the State Department and the UN."[70]

American journalists expected that difficulties would "beset the achievement of such a program," but they felt that if international agreements containing even half of their proposals were adopted and were "honestly adhered to by signatory nations," the world would enjoy greater freedom of information than ever before.[71] Whether UNESCO would live up to its billing was another matter. At the second meeting of the mass communication subcommission in December 1946, the Indian delegate, addressing himself primarily to American motion pictures, argued that one of UNESCO's first tasks should be "to correct the common tendency of organs of mass communication to distort the truth."[72] Ultimately, the UNESCO subcommission agreed to a United States proposal for a "survey of available facilities throughout the world for the printing of news, books and periodicals, and production and distribution of films, and the broadcasting and reception of radio programmes." But the subcommission also approved motions calling for a worldwide press conference for the "possible unification, by friendly negotiation, of rules and practices of the journalistic profession in various countries" and for the "formulation by journalists of a code of honour guiding their professional practices."[73]

Debates within various United Nations and UNESCO committees showed little support for the American free-press ideal, but the ASNE effort to win adherents continued unabated. Topping the group's agenda for the fall 1946 United Nations session was the publication of a twenty-eight page brochure on worldwide freedom of information to be distributed to members of the Economic and Social Council and the Human Rights Commission. The ASNE brochure detailed the history of the free-press crusade, contained comments from world leaders on the necessity for freer exchange of information, gently chided the United Nations for the delays encountered thus far, and pleaded for prompt action.[74] While soliciting a letter for the brochure from Secretary of State James F. Byrnes, Forrest, now ASNE president, discovered that a State Department committee planned to "crystallize" American free-press policy and "formulate it more clearly" in time for the upcoming United Nations sessions.[75] Despite this discovery and his public optimism, Forrest believed the chances of the brochure—or anything else—spurring United Nations action were slight. "Confidentially," Forrest told Benton, "I don't believe the document will do any good but I am satisfied that we have got to make the effort to keep the movement alive."[76]

THE ASNE PRESSURES THE STATE DEPARTMENT FOR ACTION

Despite his pessimism, Forrest continued to pressure the State Department for action. The international free-press crusade received some high-powered assistance when President Truman told the United Nations General Assembly session, "The United States believes a concerted effort must be made to break down the barriers to a free flow of information among the nations of the world." Furthermore, "we regard freedom of expression and freedom to receive information—the right of the people to know—as among the most important of those human rights and fundamental freedoms to which we are pledged under the United Nations Charter."[77] The president's public support was insufficient to satisfy ASNE leaders, and demands for action from Forrest and other free-press advocates occupied much of the time of the State Department's freedom of information committee. James P. Hendrick of the Office of International Organization Affairs wanted the ASNE leader told in no uncertain terms that introducing the subject of international freedom of the press at an early United Nations meeting would be unwise. In fact, Hendrick argued, "it might be embarrassing for the U.S. Delegation if pressure is brought to place the subject of freedom of information on the agenda prior to the formulation of the U.S. position." Macy, the committee chairman, defended Forrest's lobbying, noting that the ASNE leader was only "attempting to maintain public interest in freedom of information until some definite action is taken." But Macy agreed that the department had to develop its position on freedom of information before introducing the subject at the United Nations.[78]

State Department personnel assigned to developing a free-press policy, however, had encountered difficulties in drafting a universally acceptable statement of principles. Since the area was new in diplomatic circles, planners had to start by establishing basic definitions. The department needed to decide, for instance, what freedoms to place under the freedom of information umbrella. Consensus finally was established on two such freedoms: "the right to gather information in a country and to export it" and "the right to receive information and to utter it." But what subsidiary rights came under the main headings? American press leaders pushed for the freedom of movement, equality of access to sources of news and transmission facilities for information, limits on the ability of foreign governments to censor dispatches, and the right of any newspaper or radio station to buy the news service of its choice. But should the government's list mention something about the right of a government to declare a foreign correspondent persona non grata "if wrong on an important fact," with the complaining government carrying "the burden of proof that he is wrong"? Or should the State Department's position note that governments should publish texts of important documents? And what about the basic plank in free-press advocates' platforms calling for "non-discrimination between locals, locals working for foreigners and foreigners in the gathering of news"?[79]

Press leaders were likely to strongly disapprove of some of the proposed topics but were American journalists the primary audience for the proposals? And what would happen if a foreign government used the American proposals against United States journalists? The latter possibility was far from remote; even as the discussion about the rights encompassed in the concept of freedom of information occurred, the department received distressing news from negotiators of a free-press agreement between the United States and China. The Chinese, negotiators reported, were not opposed to the accord, but they wanted all correspondents equal on Chinese terms while the Americans wanted equality for reporters based on American standards. Basically, the Chinese offer meant a more limited range of freedom of action for foreign correspondents than that demanded by United States journalists.[80] Treating American journalists equally with reporters of a particular host nation obviously was not enough to satisfy representatives of the American press. But could that bias be stated bluntly in international negotiations?

Another question centered on whether the United States government should work toward enactment of broad ideals such as the adoption of the American system of freedom of the press internationally or whether the department should seek specific, limited goals such as the right to subscribe to any news service directly. Or, on an even more limited basis, should the government attack specified barriers to freedom of information—such as the inadequacy of physical facilities for transmission of information? And what should the government's position be about free-press problems in areas of the world where the primary barrier to freedom of information was illiteracy?[81] An entirely new series of questions arose when departmental planners began discussing whether the United States government should set an example by first establishing and abiding by the standards demanded of other governments. Could the American government lead by example in the free-press area?

Assistant Secretary of State Spruille Braden, while approving of the free-press crusade, pointed out that American practice fell short of reaching many of the suggested goals. For example, Braden was sure that the United States did not provide complete equality between foreigners and nationals seeking governmental news sources, and he doubted "that we could put this across."[82] Equal access to news and to facilities for transmission of the news, however, was a key to the entire free-press crusade. If problems in providing the requisite equality existed within the United States, how could journalists hope for improvement in the rest of the world?[83]

Realizing that such shortcomings might haunt American representatives in debates, the departmental committee decided "to ascertain the obstacles to free flow of information within the United States before it undertook a campaign to eliminate barriers in other countries."[84] After a thorough investigation, the department's legal adviser reported that "the former views of this Government militate against the contention that such a freedom is sanctioned as a matter of international law." In 1914, for instance, the department had decided that the exclusion of an American newspaper from the mails in Canada was a question for the Canadian government to decide. In 1931, the department had determined that "no government may question the right of another government to prevent within its territory the exhibition of any picture which the government concerned considers contrary to its interests." And as late as 1933, the department had said, "It is not the function of this Government to impose its precepts as to freedom of speech on other Governments of the world."[85]

On a more optimistic note, the legal adviser found that the United States government had reversed its position on the status of an international right of freedom of information, dating back at least to the congressional resolution of 1944, and that officials now approved of that international right. Nevertheless, the initial governmental approach was correct, for no legal basis for international freedom of information existed. American diplomats must create the right within the United Nations.[86] Efforts to create the international right to freedom of information ignored past departmental indiscretions, and the departmental historical division dutifully traced American support of freedom of information back to the Declaration of Independence, the Address to the Inhabitants of Quebec, and various statements affirming the rights of Americans to freedom of speech by secretaries of state in 1869, 1885, 1911, and 1935.[87]

One question still remained: What would the United States government get out of promoting international freedom of information? Assistant Secretary of State for Public Affairs Benton believed that the international freedom of information crusade had "caught popular fire" because Americans realized "that freedom of information and the spread of Soviet influence or any authoritarian ideology are antithetical" and "that the best immediate hope, meager as it may be, of modifying the authoritarian regimes in the Soviet Union and other countries—and thus of fostering peace and security—lies in getting news and information through the 'iron curtain.'" Therefore the State Department faced "a necessity and an opportunity. The necessity is to respond to the popular clamor for action that has reached our doorstep. The opportunity is to use freedom of information as a major instrument in furthering U.S. foreign policy."[88] Journalists, long aware of the potential dangers of government involvement in the free-press crusade, soon realized that the government might pervert the crusade into an instrument of foreign policy. As the awareness of this governmental aim increased so, too, did journalistic distrust and unease. For the moment, however, the problems facing the crusade were so great that possible governmental abuse of the campaign's aims was not high on the list of press concerns.

In fact, at the end of 1946, depression over the probable fate of worldwide freedom of the press was epidemic among the crusade's journalistic supporters. For example, only twenty-nine of the fifty-four countries belonging to the United Nations imposed no barriers to the free exchange of news, according to Berkson, the INS general manager. The other twenty-five nations imposed restrictions of some sort on their presses. The information almost demoralized *Editor & Publisher*, which lamented that within the United Nations—"supposedly the last remaining hope for world peace—the advocates of free expression are almost outnumbered by those governments which believe in some form of dictatorial control of information and thought." Given such circumstances, "How can we have One World if half is free and half slave, even if only in the products of the mind?"[89]

JOURNALISTS EXPLORE OTHER AVENUES FOR ADVANCING THE CRUSADE

Obviously, journalists believed, the time had come to seek action on free-press issues outside of the United Nations. Palmer Hoyt, editor of the

Denver Post, advocated negotiating bilateral treaties on freedom of information with allies, thus bypassing the United Nations structure temporarily, if not permanently. Berkson suggested using American "bargaining tools"—reconstruction assistance—to secure freedom of information. In dealing with Russia, for instance, the United States simply must insist on freedom of information guarantees before supplying requested aid.[90] Both proposals attracted interest, although bilateral treaties proved of more value than attaching restrictions to reconstruction aid. The State Department took the lead insofar as the bilateral treaties were concerned. Congress added free-press riders to the United Nations Relief and Rehabilitation Administration (UNRRA) monies.

The UNRRA effort began in 1945, when the House of Representatives forbade the distribution of reconstruction money to any government that "interferes with or refuses full and free access to the news" of UNRRA activities to American press and radio correspondents. The amendment also said that nations would forfeit financial assistance by maintaining "any barrier—technical, political, legal or economic—to obtaining, dispatching and disseminating the news of any and all activities," by discriminating "against the representatives of the press and radio of the United States in rates and charges for facilities used in collecting and dispatching such news," or by censoring or attempting to censor "in time of peace, news of any and all activities of the United Nations Relief and Rehabilitation Administration which may be prepared in or dispatched from such country by representatives of the press and radio of the United States."[91]

A "no free press, no relief" rule was distasteful to many, including such a staunch advocate of international press freedom as *Editor & Publisher*, which believed that the congressional rider sullied the ideal of freedom of information. International press freedom, said the trade journal, was "not something that can be bartered for or thrust upon a nation under threat."[92] The Senate refused to accept the amendment but joined the House in requesting that the president "facilitate the admission to recipient countries of properly accredited members of the American press and radio in order that they may be permitted to report without censorship" on the use of UNRRA monies.[93]

An effort to attach a free-press rider to UNRRA funding in 1946 was more successful; both houses of Congress agreed to require all countries receiving aid to allow a "reasonable number of properly accredited representatives of the American press to enter, observe and report on the distribution, and utilization of relief and rehabilitation supplies and services" without censorship. A supplemental appropriation approved in 1947 stipulated that any country receiving American assistance must convince the president that governmental and press representatives would be allowed to observe and report on the distribution and use of relief supplies. Similar language appeared in other relief appropriation measures throughout the period.[94]

Judging the effectiveness of these attempts to tie reconstruction aid to free-press guarantees is difficult. The best evaluation may rest in the lack of attention given the legislation by professional journals, almost all of which discussed the international free-press issues of the time. Also, although correspondents complained primarily about Soviet violations of UNRRA legislation, their complaints apparently were few. The Soviets, of course, immediately disputed any censorship charges.[95] The UNRRA riders might be classified more as attempts to curry favor with the press rather than as making any real difference in the free-press crusade. Tying monetary assistance to guaranteed access to information was a position that journalists such as Berkson discussed in times of deep frustration over the campaign's overall progress. Such provisos never were considered a truly viable option for pursuing the crusade. Humanitarian concerns generally overpowered even the driving force of the free-press crusade.

State Department planners had realized the potential power of reconstruction assistance in spurring interest in freedom of information causes abroad. But combining reconstruction money with the free-press crusade carried both benefits and dangers. Imposing such conditions before granting aid doubtlessly would be the fastest way to implement international freedom of information, but the restrictions inevitably would lead to resentment from the aid recipients. Earmarking rehabilitation funds for purchasing American books, magazines, and newspapers also left the United States "wide open to a charge of 'American cultural imperialism,' " especially if countries had to divert funds from reconstruction to make the mandated expenditures. State Department planners thought that the best way to link reconstruction money and freedom of information might be by requiring recipient countries to use part of the aid "to remedy deficiencies in the physical facilities of mass communications." The latter option was considered ideal because such language would prove "that we are trying to create a situation where peoples can speak to peoples, and not where America alone can speak to the rest of the world."[96]

Even more viable, however, were bilateral treaties between the United States and other nations securing freedom of the press between the two signatories without the manipulation of reconstruction aid. These specialized treaties built on the State Department practice of including freedom of information clauses in treaties of commerce and navigation, a policy in effect since 1944.[97] Although inserting such clauses in commercial treaties earned the praise of Assistant Secretary of State Benton, he doubted "that as part of general commercial treaty negotiations the freedom of information clause is likely to be very successful in cutting through barriers in countries where it is most needed." Benton favored bilateral agreements that focused solely on specific details designed to advance freedom of information and "carried on with great fanfare and all the pressure that the Department can muster."[98] As prospects for multilateral action through the United Nations dimmed in 1946 and 1947, journalists joined with the State Department to fine tune the bilateral treaty project.

A single agreement dealing solely with freedom of information had at least two points in its favor. First, Benton believed that work on international freedom of information at the United Nations had been retarded because the United States had "no experience, no precedents, no staff, no techniques, no clearly drafted principles, no knowledge on how far we can or ought to go" in the area. Bilateral agreements would allow the United States to develop the necessary expertise through limited negotiations. Second, Benton, a former advertising executive with many friends in the media, believed that the press had to change some of its practices before free-press treaty talks could succeed on any large scale. Negotiating with one country on a limited treaty that focused solely on freedom of the press would permit the department to "approach the information industry with some authority" about problems of concern to diplomats, including "industry responsibility for improving the quality and increasing the quantity of its product moving in international channels."[99]

After a period of reflection, Benton reversed his approach. Rather than negotiating with foreign emissaries first and then discussing treaty provisions with the industry, Benton asked media representatives to develop a draft treaty containing all the points that the various media considered vital to include in an international agreement. The industry thus became involved in planning the treaty venture, forcing its representatives to weigh demands and promises. On a more practical level, media involvement in the treaty-drafting process stemmed the tide of multiple industry proposals that had been flowing onto Benton's desk and halted the bombardment of United Nations officials with discrete proposals for worldwide freedom of information.[100]

Benton largely got the document he wanted from media representatives, for the draft treaty he released to the press in late 1946 was a carefully crafted proposal that considered several problems omitted from the itemized lists of freedoms termed as mandatory by the press associations and the American Society of Newspaper Editors. The proposed treaty—stylized the Finnegan draft after the man who supervised its writing, Richard J. Finnegan, editor and publisher of the *Chicago Times*—brought together the views of such stalwarts in the crusade as Cooper and Baillie, but the document bore little resemblance to the rhetoric of the press associations' chiefs.[101]

Under the terms of the Finnegan draft, signatories would allow correspondents, broadcasters, and photographers from each nation to enter and leave the other country freely and would grant visiting journalists access to sources of information equal to that provided to their own citizens. National security was a permissible exception to the freedom to travel and gather news. The proposed treaty also recognized that, at times, officials of the signatory nations might wish to talk solely to their own nationals about news events, much in the way United States government officials held background sessions for American correspondents. These special sessions would not violate the terms of the accord. If a correspondent became obnoxious to the host government, the correspondent's employer could replace the unwanted journalist without difficulty. News material, radio broadcasts, and photographs would leave each nation uncensored, with transmission on a nondiscriminatory basis. National laws governing libel, slander, and publication of obscene materials remained in effect against nationals of both signatories. And each nation signing the pact guaranteed its citizens the right to select their own sources of information.[102]

But the draft treaty ventured into one controversial area. To implement treaty provisions, the draft suggested the creation of an International Information Commission, made up of correspondents or executives of news agencies named by their respective governments.[103] American journalists had long rejected similar proposals, holding that a free press supervised itself, with public opinion being the press's only competent judge. Journalists accepted the Finnegan treaty's proposal, however, because the provision exerted only moral suasion against parties violating the agreement.[104] Thus, in the view of American journalists, regulation of a free press in the international arena would be identical to regulation of a free press in the United States. In fact, although subtler than the laundry lists of free-press requirements submitted earlier, the draft treaty intended to export the American system of the press just as the previous proposals did. Finnegan outlined the treaty's motivations quite bluntly: "Eventually the United States, under treaties, must try to secure for American correspondents wherever they may care to go overseas the freedom from government interference that they enjoy at home under our Bill of Rights."[105]

The emphasis on putting American press practice into effect in foreign countries became even clearer when Finnegan delivered his composite free-press plan to the State Department in September 1947. The document had weathered evaluation and approval by numerous American journalists. As submitted, the text was based on the idea that freedom of speech and press as practiced in the United States must exist throughout the world, that freedom of movement, observation, and transmission of facts and ideas must prevail, and that the ultimate judge of controversies between media and government must be public opinion. The treaty accomplished part of Benton's goal, for one proposal now was approved by most press leaders. But, although more sensitively written than other proposals, the draft treaty failed to indicate any willingness by American journalists to accommodate the press practices of other countries or to change objectionable American practices as Benton had desired. In fact, Finnegan stressed, American journalists believed that the United States should not enter into any free-press treaty that would "shrink American practice one jot." American journalists preferred agreements with a few nations consistent with American beliefs rather than agreeing "with all the nations of the world on any pact or treaty that would change our traditional conception of the independence of the press."[106]

Although concerned about the press's intransigence, Benton had more to worry about at the moment than the unwillingness of American journalists to compromise their principles. Diplomatic reality had caught up with him, and Benton discovered that his dream of bilateral free-press agreements might be impossible to achieve if for no other reason than the proposal lacked support within the State Department. One assistant, Joseph Jones, fed Benton's discontent by saying, "Bilateral agreements are not going to get anywhere at all unless they are given higher status and higher priority in the Department's program." Jones added, "We ought to stop talking about bilateral agreements unless we are going to do something more about them than we are doing at present."[107] Other avenues still open for achieving the same goal included a return to negotiating multilateral conventions through the United Nations, development of cultural conventions to deal with the importation of certain American media products, or reversion to freedom of information clauses in treaties of friendship, navigation, and commerce and in trade agreements.[108]

This newfound pessimism was more of an overreaction based on Benton's unfamiliarity and impatience with the slowness of diplomatic negotiations and the cumbersome nature of State Department operations than an accurate perception of reality. His new adviser on free-press issues, Lloyd Free, soon told Benton forthrightly: "Six months ago bilateral agreements were nowhere at all. Four months ago ... the only 'progress' consisted in one speech, ... delivered by you—a speech which had not been cleared within the Department and which represented nothing but a pious hope insofar as Departmental policy was concerned." Since then, Under Secretary of State Dean Acheson had "officially admitted that the negotiation of bilateral agreements is under consideration," and the department had sanctioned negotiations of free-press accords with Greece, Turkey, and Australia. Thus, "a pious hope" had become departmental policy. "This is not exactly 'getting nowhere on the bilateral agreements'. It is progress— maddeningly slow in the nature of things, but solid."[109]

But Benton needed to lower his expectations, Free said. No results were possible "until we can get this ponderous State Department machine geared up and headed in the right direction—which is a matter of gradual indoctrination of a hundred or two key people in the Department." In fact, "in judging 'progress', you had better realize that it will take five, ten, twenty, or thirty years to make a freedom of information dent on this stubborn, sick world." And in order for any real progress to be made,

Benton needed to launch an intensive research project. Bilateral treaties on freedom of information were possible only if the negotiators knew what they were talking about, and the department had no base for intelligent discussions. For instance, Free explained, the department needed to know about the information structures in foreign countries before trying to make treaties affecting those systems. Barriers to freedom of information around the world must be known and their political and economic causes understood. "Then you have to figure out what you can give the other country to induce it to 'open up'." Even then, more preparatory work was necessary.[110]

Before Benton could draft bilateral agreements acceptable to the American government as a whole, he had "to know about *American* restrictions on the importation of information" because "your agreement must not infringe these, at least unwittingly." Domestic limitations included tariffs on books and films; the Alien Agents Registration Act, which kept individuals of certain political persuasions out of the United States; copyright regulations; provisions in international telecommunications conventions; restrictive film distribution practices; and clauses in contracts between American and British book publishers. And, Free added, "You also have to find out what American news, radio, film and publishing agencies want from the particular country with whom you are about to negotiate." Although Free had little of this information on hand, he still thought that bilateral treaties held promise, and he worked to bolster Benton's sagging spirit.[111] Benton, impressed by his aide's analysis of the situation, wanted to know how to get the massive research project under way given the tight departmental budget. He asked, "Can't we call on the ASNE to live up to their words and hopes, and tackle some of this research? Or call on the AP and the UP to finance some of this?"[112] The record shows no full-scale cooperative effort on the research project, nor is the record clear as to whether these agencies were even approached for assistance.

A few months later, Free reported changes in the status of freedom of information at the United Nations that affected the outlook for bilateral treaties. The United Nations–sponsored conference on freedom of information, scheduled for early 1948, had "an agenda satisfactory beyond expectations from the U.S. point of view. There has thus been created a focal point for freedom of information matters in the eyes of the world." The question now was whether to pursue the bilateral agreements; when approached, most governments would respond that they were waiting for the results of the United Nations conference before making a commitment on freedom of information. If the United States maintained the bilateral treaty initiative, Free warned, "We will be accused of attempting to by-pass the U.N. in an area in which it has taken jurisdiction, so to speak, and where the U.N. cannot as yet be proved ineffectual." Efforts to negotiate solely with nations receiving American aid under the Marshall Plan and the Truman Doctrine could also backfire because "we will be accused of using our economic power to coerce them in the interests of 'American cultural imperialism.' "[113]

Free proposed splitting the freedom of information question into two segments. The first would focus on the problem of the gathering and international transmission of news by American correspondents in foreign countries; this part would be handled through a multilateral convention proposed at the United Nations conference. The second segment would center on the problems encountered by other countries importing processed American information products, such as newspapers, books, periodicals, and films; this part could be handled through commercial conventions, treaties of friendship, commerce, and navigation, and trade agreements. This approach to freedom of information differed from that of bilateral treaties, but Free saw the research necessary to make this two-pronged effort successful as identical to that needed for the bilateral treaties. In fact, State Department support would be even more important with this new plan. "The American press is agitating for freedom of information with growing vigor. Book, periodical and film circles are increasingly exercised," Free noted. "It is time that the Department of State attacked this problem vigorously and adequately."[114]

The Free proposal became the American government's approach for freedom of information topics in the United Nations conference of 1948. American journalists were reassured that the change in tactics did not alter the basic goals of the crusade and that problems brought to light by the Finnegan draft treaty were covered adequately by this alternate approach.[115] The Finnegan draft treaty itself, although formally shelved, was said to have influenced the free-press section included in a treaty of friendship, commerce, and navigation signed with Italy in 1948.[116] The free-press language in the Italian treaty, however, differed only minutely and inconsequentially from standard language on freedom of the press included in all draft treaties of friendship, commerce, and navigation as of 1946.[117] The Finnegan proposal also became the starting point for a draft convention on news gathering introduced by American delegates at the United Nations conference.

As the leaders of major American journalistic organizations developed agendas for worldwide freedom of the press, the working journalists of the United States joined 110 representatives of reporters' unions from fifteen countries in Copenhagen, Denmark, to create the International Organization of Journalists (IOJ). Participating in the 1946 session was Milton Murray, president of the American Newspaper Guild, who was elected an international vice president. Although the IOJ supported worldwide freedom of the press, the organization's rhetoric was quite different from that of American editors and news agency heads. Every working journalist, the group's resolution on freedom of the press said, must "assist by every means in his power the development of international friendship and understanding." To implement this responsibility, the IOJ executive committee planned to examine various professional codes in order to develop an acceptable way to punish a journalist who was "deliberately and knowingly spreading ... false information designed to poison the good relations between countries and peoples."[118]

Adding to the impending controversy, the IOJ free-press resolution continued, "Press freedom can never be fully assured while newspapers, news agencies and broadcasting systems are solely in the hands of individuals or private monopolies with no responsibility to the people."[119] Although both these points became major issues in the free-press debate, in 1946, Murray apparently had few qualms about either statement. The American Newspaper Guild brought an obviously different perspective to international free-press discussions. Ever since the Guild's stormy beginning during the Roosevelt administration's efforts to force the newspaper industry to write an industrial code under the National Industrial Recovery Act, the union had been dominated by activists and advocates. Guild members were liberals who believed in affirmative action on causes that they deemed appropriate. In supporting the IOJ resolution, Guild members simply acted on their beliefs.[120]

Even so, American journalists were unable to accept every point suggested by their colleagues abroad. Some European journalists, Murray said, wanted an international code of ethics to punish writers if their work contributed to disharmony among nations. The Guild constitution forbade punishing writers for anything they wrote, Murray argued; IOJ insistence on such language would mean the loss of American support. IOJ members dropped the offensive section. Perhaps even more distressing for American newspaper editors and press association chiefs than the free-press resolution was the fact that working journalists, as members of the IOJ, now had access to the floor of the United Nations, something denied to other free-press advocates in the United States. As an international organization, the IOJ won permission from the United Nations to have nonvoting observers at appropriate meetings and to have an IOJ voice heard directly on international press issues. The views of other American journalists interested in worldwide freedom of information were filtered through the State Department before being presented to the United Nations.[121]

State Department officials quickly noticed the new international organization. Increasingly aware of the threat posed to American institutions by Soviet ideology, departmental leaders thought that the official IOJ resolution on freedom of the press was "about ninety percent out of the Communist copy-book." The section dealing with the ownership of media, for instance, presented particular problems. Murray had argued successfully during debates for the insertion of "solely" in the text in order to mitigate the condemnation of privately owned media systems. The Russians, in telling their people about the resolution, however, "omit the word 'solely' and say that the representatives of 25,000 working American journalists admit that they are not free." Conference results, departmental representatives agreed, showed the dangers that could arise when amateurs became involved in international issues. Although Murray was strongly anticommunist, he was "unsophisticated in foreign relations and apparently in dealing with Russians in international conferences."[122]

The IOJ conference also worried State Department personnel because its debates and resolutions revealed that the Russians were working on a counteroffensive to the American freedom of information campaign. Also, the Soviets were skillfully exploiting the hard feelings between American newspaper labor and management. Departmental representatives recognized that although "owners and publishers are the strongest backers of the freedom of information campaign in the United States," the Guild "has never spoken on freedom of information at home, nor have its views been solicited." The union could probably be persuaded to cooperate with the department, but diplomatic planners knew that as its price, the Guild would want the State Department to do something "about the attitude of the American owners and publishers that the American press can do no wrong."[123]

By the time of the second IOJ convention in 1947, Murray had decided that the organization was communist dominated, and he denounced the group as such before the assembled delegates.[124] He also introduced an "American resolution on freedom of the press," calling for "free access to news, freedom to publish news, and treaties establishing free flow of news." IOJ delegates unanimously adopted Murray's resolution, which was very much in line with the official American position on international freedom of the press.[125] Murray returned from the meeting in Prague, Czechoslovakia, advocating Guild withdrawal from the organization,[126] a move that occurred in 1948. The American press—management and labor—now was united on the international free-press issue. Just what, if anything, the State Department did to facilitate this cooperation is unclear. A united stand was vital, however, because the American press faced increasing challenges to its ability to function abroad, and a divided house at home could have been disastrous.

JOURNALISTS AND DIPLOMATS WORK TOGETHER

The international free-press movement forced American journalists and the State Department into a close working relationship. As news-gathering operations became increasingly complicated in the postwar world, the press and the State Department soon cooperated to expedite the collection and dissemination of news around the globe. Problems were most severe within Soviet bloc nations, where the Russians regularly erected major impediments to American correspondents' operations. The State Department, entangled in ever worsening relations with Moscow, worked to tear down as many obstacles as possible—often at the persistent urgings of the press and always in the full knowledge of the power that the press could exert to obtain its demands. Perhaps the most important of numerous such episodes came after Secretary of State Byrnes agreed to the Soviets' request to hold the 1947 Council of Foreign Ministers meeting in Moscow.

Scheduling a Council of Foreign Ministers session in Moscow amazed American journalists. The move was more surprising coming from Secretary Byrnes, for he had vociferously protested the secrecy shrouding international sessions at other sites until he finally won some degree of openness.[127] The secretary's persistence may have been the reason that Soviet Foreign Minister Molotov agreed to open the Paris Peace Conference of 1946 to the press, although the Russian diplomat said an open conference was the only way to ensure a fair presentation of his country's views.[128] A Byrnes-Molotov confrontation over whether the Russian press would print a Byrnes speech also contributed to the secretary of state's growing belief that the Soviets were learning something of the value of full news coverage, if not of a free press.[129]

The determining factor in the decision to hold the Council of Foreign Ministers meeting in Moscow, however, was Molotov's assurances that the press "would receive the same freedoms and facilities" to cover the Moscow session as correspondents had enjoyed at sessions in New York and Paris. Speaking for the newspaper industry, *Editor & Publisher* doubted the Soviet promise, which would entail "a complete about face in Russian policy." To fulfill Molotov's promises, the Soviets would have to admit all correspondents without exception, completely eliminate censorship, permit news from other parts of the world to enter Russia unrestricted, expand facilities to accommodate press and radio correspondents, and allow freedom of movement. "If the Russians live up to Molotov's commitment . . . to what quirk of party line reasoning are we indebted for this change of mind?" Always suspicious of Soviet motives, the trade journal suggested that Byrnes "get detailed acceptance of these conditions for free press, free speech and free communications at the Big Four meeting."[130]

Negotiations with the Soviets over press representation at the Moscow meeting were not easy. Early sessions featured reassurances of freedom for correspondents to report but raised questions about how many American reporters could attend the conference. The Soviets promised to accommodate one hundred Americans, diplomats and correspondents. Although the official American delegation would be somewhat under that number,[131] by early January sixty-one United States correspondents had requested permission to cover the sessions. Press spokesmen expected the number of correspondents requesting visas to enter the Soviet Union to reach at least one hundred. With journalists anticipating Soviet chicanery, trouble obviously loomed.[132] With the State Department estimating a correspondents corps of fifty and the Soviet government unwilling to give even a tentative number of correspondents that would be admitted, trouble was inevitable. Further complicating matters, the Soviets would not say how many correspondents they would admit until they knew the exact sizes of official delegations. Diplomatic delegations had the first call on available housing, the Russians explained; correspondents would get any leftover rooms. Questions also remained about whether the Soviets planned to allow live broadcasting during the conference and about whether freedom to report extended to stories on nonconference matters.[133]

As the conference neared, Secretary of State George C. Marshall led the negotiations with the Soviets over the number of American correspondents that could cover the session. The Russians thought fifteen to twenty correspondents, besides the handful stationed in Moscow, was sufficient. The Soviet ambassador's response to Marshall's questions about "whether the size of our Delegation had any direct bearing on the number of correspondents who could go to Moscow or whether there was some other reason why his Government objected to the larger number" of correspondents was unclear. Bluntly phrased, the State Department wanted to know if a smaller official delegation meant more room for correspondents. The Russians would not answer.[134] A later conversation with Soviet diplomats produced a firm request to restrict the number of correspondents attending the conference to fifteen to twenty, chiefly because of limited accommodations. The Soviet spokesman added that since most of the council sessions would be closed to the public, the Russian government did not think that a larger number of correspondents was necessary.[135]

Acutely aware of the storms of protest that would descend on his office from American journalists omitted from the list of twenty, Marshall ordered the American ambassador in Moscow to protest the limitation. The protest, Marshall said, should stress that because of the large number of American newspapers that wanted to be represented in Moscow confining the list to the small number proposed would be very difficult.[136] The limit of twenty stayed in place, however, and Marshall astutely gave the task of picking the twenty correspondents to win visas from the seventy-plus journalists who had applied to representatives of the press.[137] The State Department was not out of trouble with the press yet, however, for the correspondents recommended that fifty news organizations be allowed to send correspondents to Moscow—if the American public was to be properly informed. The department also received "emphatic representations from associations of correspondents and leading newspapers" about the inadequate size of the press delegation. Journalists held the department responsible for the sorry situation because of Byrnes's premature acceptance of Molotov's assurances. To obtain at least fifteen more visas, Secretary Marshall authorized Ambassador Walter Bedell Smith to tell the Soviets that the department planned to reduce the size of the official American delegation by ten.[138]

Ultimately, Smith proposed reducing the official American delegation by five and giving up several rooms at a Moscow hotel designated for the American delegation, which he considered as insufficiently secure anyway, in exchange for fifteen to twenty more press visas. In advising Secretary Marshall of his proposal, Smith reminded the secretary to brief the journalists planning to cover the conference about the censorship situation awaiting them. For, although the Soviets promised no censorship on conference news, the Soviet government understood that American correspondents were more interested in what went on behind the iron curtain than in conference matters, "and has not slightest intention of relaxing general censorship. Our press people should be placed on notice so they will not come here with any illusions."[139]

Thirty-six American correspondents finally won visas to attend the conference, a number considered somewhat better than the initial twenty. Journalists voiced some cynicism about the total ultimately admitted by the Russians, however, for the additional visas allowed a representative from the *Daily Worker* of New York, who was thirty-fifth on the list, to attend.[140] Despite their desire to attend the Moscow conference, American journalists viewed Secretary of State Marshall's effort to reduce the size of the official delegation in order to win more press visas as inappropriate, preferring the British stand that the official delegation size and the number of press representatives were not interrelated. On the other hand, reporters considered Ambassador Smith's manipulation of housing space as "a good indication of our own government's belief in telling the story of these conferences as fully as possible to the people of the world."[141] Although problems existed in getting American correspondents into the Soviet Union to cover the conference, the Soviets kept their word about censorship. Copy labeled "CFM" and dealing with the conference itself was cleared rapidly and uncensored.[142] Ambassador Smith's warnings about nonconference-related stories also proved true. These latter stories, including one about department store prices, which most correspondents agreed was unrelated to the sessions, went through regular Soviet censorship.[143]

CENSORSHIP PROBLEMS APPEAR IN THE SOVIET UNION

American news correspondents were surprised when the Soviets kept their word about clearing Council of Foreign Ministers copy uncensored because beginning in 1946, the year before the Moscow session, the United States had started to take an increasingly harder line against the Soviet Union. With this change in American policy came a concomitant increase in harassment of American correspondents stationed in the Soviet capital. United States diplomats repeatedly intervened in censorship matters, usually without success, as the Russians introduced a new censorship organization, Glavlit, short for the Main Administration for Literature and Publishing, an arm of the Soviet Council of Ministers. Glavlit instituted one procedure that terrified correspondents everywhere: blind censorship, meaning that reporters usually had no way of knowing whether their dispatches were cut, rewritten, or sent at all. At times, censors even stopped routine messages to employers, as when Glavlit killed a message in which a correspondent requested that his byline be removed from future published dispatches because he could no longer be responsible for the truthfulness of news stories sent in his name.[144]

To circumvent this censorship, American diplomats allowed correspondents to use departmental facilities to send messages regarding censorship to their home offices. For instance, Henry Shapiro of the United Press's Moscow bureau used embassy facilities to tell his supervisors that the "censors now are anonymous invisible unapproachable. Foreign correspondents never been so disconsolate but no official protest yet made since there still is some hope relaxation."[145] The remote possibility for relaxation of the restrictions rested on the newness of the censorship system. Correspondents hoped that many of the problems were organizational in nature rather than due to a Soviet determination to restrict the free flow of information. The censorship procedures stayed in place, however, and they led to significant questions regarding the reliability of news from correspondents stationed in the Soviet Union.

The dangers of misinformation reaching the American people under this censorship system were so great that George F. Kennan, chargé in the Soviet Union, who had already advised the State Department about the dangers of accommodating the Russians,[146] protested that publishing copy sent under such conditions was "highly unsatisfactory and risky, if not quite unacceptable, . . . particularly at a moment when so much harm could be done by distorted or mutilated texts." Prompting Kennan's immediate concern was a report from one correspondent that of twenty-four telegrams delivered for censorship and transmission, only ten had reached their destination. One story was cut from two hundred words to fifty-one words. The Glavlit system, Kennan warned, allowed Soviet censors to distort any story filed by an American correspondent "without knowledge of either correspondent himself or of his home office." The Russians would not hesitate to use this power, Kennan implied, if some benefit accrued to the Soviet leadership. The only alternative, Kennan said, was for the department to contact the correspondents' employers, advise them of the situation, and determine the procedures that the correspondents should follow in filing their stories.[147] Journalists were equally concerned about the situation; Brooks Atkinson, correspondent for The New York Times, told his managing editor that he considered the Times Moscow bureau virtually useless. Even worse, Atkinson feared the censorship system would become more rigid in time.[148]

Washington bureau chiefs for the press associations, duly notified, told departmental officials that they felt that to protect themselves and the public the new censorship system must be publicized. Readers must know "they can place no . . . confidence in what they read from Moscow." The bureau chiefs agreed to postpone publicizing the new system until American diplomats in Moscow could discuss the subject with Soviet officials. In that conversation, the embassy spokesman was to underline that, although the State Department knew that censorship was a prerogative of a sovereign government, the department felt "very strongly . . . that when censorship is used it should be exercised to minimum and not maximum extent and inconvenience correspondents as little as possible." A correspondent must be able to discuss deletions with a censor and to withdraw the dispatch "if he feels deletions change its tenor." American diplomats also were to remind the Russians that Soviet reporters stationed in the United States encountered no such restrictions and that the United States government believed that in the long run, good relations between nations demanded "as much freedom as possible for our respective peoples to receive objective reports of news events in friendly countries through their own experienced correspondents."[149] Kennan's attempt to relay the government's position to Soviet official Andrei Vishinsky ended in a harangue from Vishinsky about the correctness of the Russian press policy. "I did not pursue this argument," Kennan reported, "but merely said that I thought we had enough troubles these days without adding superfluous ones and that I very much hoped that the very near future would see some change."[150]

A slight possibility for modifying the censorship system existed, so Kennan suggested that the correspondents wait before detailing the restrictions to their readers. In fact, Kennan hoped to pressure the Soviets into changing the system if they did not undertake alterations voluntarily. He cited a successful move by the Germans to break blind censorship some years before when the German government threatened that German newspapers would receive their news about Russia exclusively from the German Foreign Office until the Russians "desisted from this procedure." Or, perhaps, American correspondents could remain in the Soviet capital but not file any news at all. This would displease the Russians, who also would be hesitant to expel all the correspondents at once. "They might therefore prefer to make concessions," Kennan said.[151] Concessions of sorts came, as the Soviets told British officials that correspondents "would in the future be able to see copies of their censored despatches before they were actually sent." Ambassador Smith suggested caution in terming this a relaxation of censorship, preferring to take a wait-and-see approach before correspondents told their principals of a permanent change in Soviet policy.[152]

Such a pause was appropriate. The United Press correspondent soon informed his supervisors that Glavlit now telephoned reporters to tell them of deletions and killed stories. Under the new regulations, reporters could see their dispatches before transmission but were unable to discuss story changes with the censors. "We don't know who censors are nor how to reach them." This was a "slight improvement in blind censorship," but the new procedures made "no material improvement in situation."[153] Censorship problems continued for American press correspondents in Moscow. By late 1948, Russian censorship patterns intensified once more. Now, American diplomats suggested that news from the Soviet capital be publicly identified as censored. Ambassador Smith thought that publishing dispatches without such labels was "unfair to the American public and to the American correspondents in Moscow, if not downright dishonest."[154] The department decided against suggesting the labeling of stories from the Soviet Union because officials felt the headings would not change the reading public's attitude toward the news so marked. The department also thought that the "correspondents themselves will probably object to use of these slugs for fear of giving the impression that they are not doing their best to get the news out."[155]

Newspaper organizations, such as the Associated Press Managing Editors Association, regularly debated the reliability of news from Russia, but without resolution.[156] Further complicating an already complex problem, news organizations felt that maintaining a presence in Moscow was too important to jeopardize by repeated published complaints about Soviet censorship. The safety of correspondents in the Soviet capital also became a critical factor, especially as general harassment of American correspondents stationed in Moscow became commonplace. The United States Embassy heard complaints about the disappearance of Russians employed by news agencies, about the fear of Russians to talk to American reporters, about Soviet police following correspondents, and about threatened and actual expulsions of American reporters. Usually, the diplomats could do little to help correspondents caught up in such difficulties.[157] On a subtler level, Soviet officials practiced harassment by refusing to grant reentry visas to American correspondents leaving the Soviet Union on vacation. Officials also denied requests from correspondents for permission to travel anywhere in the Soviet Union other than Leningrad. And officials closed the one special facility granted to American reporters, a private entrance to the press section of the Foreign Office.[158] Soviet officials even accused one correspondent of spying and expelled him from the country for his alleged misdeeds. Ambassador Smith denied all allegations against the correspondent, claiming that the journalist was simply doing his job, but Smith was unable to win the reporter's reinstatement.[159]

Because of these difficulties, American news organizations placed increased reliance on stories written by correspondents who had recently returned from Moscow. But when these reporters wrote something critical of the Soviet Union, censorship imposed on journalists still in Russia increased.[160] Ambassador Smith viewed the Russian behavior as part of an intentional effort by the Soviets to reduce American news representation in Moscow to two reporters, one for the Associated Press and one for the United Press.[161] Smith's assessment may have been somewhat limited, for the Soviets apparently wanted a certain type of American correspondent assigned to Russia. Wire service affiliation was not necessarily the criterion for acceptability since the Soviets regularly attacked news agency correspondents such as Henry Shapiro of the United Press—chiefly because Shapiro could speak Russian. That language facility made Shapiro more dangerous than other reporters.[162]

Broadcasters initially escaped the Russian clampdown, for they usually got their scripts back from Glavlit censors in time to read them over the air. Consequently, the radio correspondents' first response to increased censorship was to overwrite the scripts submitted for review in order to have enough copy left after censorship to fill the allocated broadcast time.[163] Radio correspondents were vulnerable in one respect, however, for they had no transmission facilities of their own to use in sending their reports out of Moscow. Radio reports were sent back to the United States via Russian-owned shortwave transmitters. By October 1946, Soviet officials informed correspondents for CBS, NBC, and ABC that, due to a rearrangement of radio programming over the state-owned facilities, "no time was available for broadcasts by foreign correspondents." Consequently, American use of the shortwave facilities of Moscow radio to transmit news reports to the United States was terminated.[164]

The American press quickly complained about the curtailment, with *The New York Times* reporting that United States network news transmissions only filled about thirty minutes of time a day. Such a short broadcast period certainly could not be much of a drain on the facilities of a nation known to be second only to Great Britain in the size and quality of its shortwave operations. The newspaper suggested that the cessation of broadcasts was more likely due to the Soviet feeling that censors "could effectively control written word while could not control inflection broadcaster's voice." The State Department authorized American officials in Moscow to talk with the Russian Foreign Office about the new policy, adding that the diplomats might wait to see if a telegram sent directly to Premier Joseph Stalin by CBS Vice President Edward R. Murrow had any effect.[165] Soviet response to the Murrow telegram stressed that the Russians were not imposing any new censorship but were simply reinstituting prewar practices. Then, radio correspondents sent their dispatches out of the Soviet Union by telegram because they did not have access to voice transmission facilities. The Soviets were not prohibiting network correspondents from sending news abroad, Stalin said; the broadcasters could revert to prewar practices if they wished.[166]

Ambassador Smith was not optimistic about obtaining the restoration of broadcasting facilities.[167] The issue had been "kept alive by correspondents and ourselves for over six weeks," without denting the Soviet position. To Smith, this intransigence meant that the censorship decision had been made at the highest levels and that additional protests were useless. American diplomats and journalists had no good arguments for regaining access to the facilities either. Broadcasters did not even have a reciprocity argument to use because Russia had no radio correspondents in America. The correspondents' case was further weakened because they could still function under the revised policy, although on a drastically altered basis. The new policy made Soviet censorship more effective against broadcasters' attempts to use vocal inflections to send hidden messages in their transmissions, Smith said. The policy also meshed with a Soviet desire to "keep radio Moscow as pristine oracle of the faithful both with respect to Soviet as well as foreign audiences." When American broadcasters' transmissions from Moscow went out over normal shortwave frequencies, any Soviet citizen with a shortwave receiver could hear them.[168] CBS ordered its correspondent, Richard C. Hottelet, the only correspondent in Moscow who worked solely for a broadcasting outlet, to Berlin to await instructions.[169]

FREE-PRESS PROBLEMS ARISE IN FRIENDLY COUNTRIES

Censorship problems clearly bothered American news organizations in the years immediately after World War II, but censorship was not the only problem that the American media faced on the foreign horizon. Threats to the dream of exporting the American free-press system to the rest of the world loomed large on all sides. American journalists expected problems with the communist bloc, but difficulties arose within allied countries as well. In England, for instance, a parliamentary debate about the control and ownership of the British press ultimately led to the establishment of a Royal Commission on the Press to investigate the status of the press and to recommend changes.[170] This was particularly frightening to American journalists because the English press system was the one most similar to the American system, and journalists in the United States had expected English allies in the free-press crusade. Adding to the fears of American press representatives was the Hutchins Commission on Freedom of the Press, a privately sponsored investigation of the American press system occurring about the same time as the British probe.[171] Although American journalists knew that none of the criticisms of the press developed by the Hutchins investigation would gain the force of law in the United States, the existence of the investigation, and the virtual certainty that commission members would write a critical report, sullied the reputation of American media just when that image was most important. To make matters worse, the first published report of the American investigatory commission focused on international communications problems and suggested a covenant to govern the gathering and dissemination of news with enforcement by an independent agency housed within the United Nations as a remedy for perceived difficulties. Journalists considered the proposal an invasion of long-held American press beliefs and said that, if adopted, the proposal surely would put the press of the world under governmental control.[172]

American journalists found events in France, another expected ally in the free-press crusade, equally distressing. For example, American journalists considered plans for France's new constitution and other laws restrictive, despite the fact that the French saw the proposals as perfectly acceptable.[173] United States broadcasters also anticipated a growing challenge to the American system of commercial radio if a state-controlled radio system developed in France rather than one based on the American commercial format;[174] they also feared that the state-owned British Broadcasting Corporation sought to spread its influence and format throughout the world, further threatening the American system.[175] And American advertising agencies worried about whether they were doing enough to secure America's share of the world market and to build a constructive international economic policy in which American business would prosper.[176]

Although these concerns seem parochial, the issues they raised were quite real to the American information industry. Media representatives in the United States had great difficulty separating what was good for the free-press crusade as a whole from what was good for the media of the United States individually. Indeed, journalists often saw the two as identical, and the two points of view remained linked until the needs of the country, ever more involved with a burgeoning cold war, drove a wedge between representatives of the press over the issue of the medium's responsibility to support national policy over individual self-interest in times of crisis.

NOTES

1. Jerry Walker, "United Nations Call Invites Freedom of Information Plan," *E&P*, February 17, 1945, p. 54.
2. Ibid.
3. "International Court for Press Is Suggested," *E&P*, April 14, 1945, p. 22.
4. "Press Prepares Blanket Coverage at San Francisco," *E&P*, April 21, 1945, p. 7.
5. Jerry Walker, "On to San Francisco with Press Crusade!" *E&P*, March 17, 1945, p. 8.
6. "United Nations Conference: Proposed Procedure Regarding Press, Radio, and Motion Pictures," *Department of State Bulletin*, March 18, 1945, p. 435.
7. "Credo for San Francisco," *E&P*, April 21, 1945, p. 44.
8. Robert U. Brown, "1,800 in Press-Radio Corps As Conference Curtain Rises," *E&P*, April 28, 1945, p. 7.

9. "Accrediting Problem," *E&P*, May 5, 1945, p. 40. The trade journal did not want to bar such correspondents completely but suggested giving them lower-grade credentials that would limit their access to news and facilities.

10. Raymond McConnell, Jr., "Idea of Press Freedom Gains Slowly at S.F.," *E&P*, May 19, 1945, p. 34.

11. Minutes of the Sixth Meeting of the United States Delegation, April 10, 1945, *FR: 1945*, I:227-28.

12. Minutes of the Fourteenth Meeting of the United States Delegation, April 24, 1945, Ibid., p. 378.

13. Minutes of the Twenty-Third Meeting of the United States Delegation, April 30, 1945, Ibid., p. 489.

14. Minutes of the Thirty-Eighth Meeting of the United States Delegation, May 14, 1945, Ibid., p. 711.

15. Minutes of the Sixty-Fifth Meeting of the United States Delegation, June 6, 1945, Ibid., p. 1172.

16. Brown, "1,800 in Press-Radio Corps," p. 7.

17. "Free Information," *E&P*, April 28, 1945, p. 46.

18. Minutes of the Sixth Meeting of the United States Delegation, April 10, 1945, *FR: 1945*, I:233.

19. Minutes of the Forty-First Meeting of the United States Delegation, May 16, 1945, Ibid., p. 752.

20. Minutes of the Forty-Third Meeting (Executive Session) of the United States Delegation (B), May 17, 1945, Ibid., pp. 777–78.

21. Minutes of the Fifty-First Meeting of the United States Delegation, May 23, 1945, Ibid., p. 852.

22. "United Nations Conference on International Organization: Provisions on Human Rights, Statement by Secretary Stettinius," *Department of State Bulletin*, May 20, 1945, p. 929.

23. "'Fundamental Freedoms'," *E&P*, June 30, 1945, p. 38.

24. Frank M. Garcia, "Free Access to News Sources Asked by U.S. at Rio Parley," *E&P*, September 15, 1945, p. 9.

25. Jerry Walker, "Telecommunications Accord Eases Flow of Information," *E&P*, December 8, 1945, p. 7.

26. Kent Cooper to Harry S. Truman, September 4, 1945, Truman Papers, OF 630.

27. Ibid.

28. Harry S. Truman to Kent Cooper, September 7, 1945, Ibid.

29. Wayne Morse to Harry S. Truman, August 21, 1945, Ibid.

30. Harry S. Truman to Wayne Morse, August 27, 1945, Ibid.

31. "World Press Freedom," *E&P*, January 5, 1946, p. 42.

32. "Baillie, ASNE Exhort UNO On Free Press," *E&P*, January 12, 1946, p. 69.

33. Seymour Berkson, "Berkson Proposes Program for World Press Freedom," *E&P*, March 23, 1946, p. 9.

34. "Freedom Guaranteed in 47 Constitutions," *E&P*, May 31, 1947, pp. 58–61.

35. "Bogged Down," *E&P*, January 19, 1946, p. 40.

36. Terms of Reference of Commission on Human Rights: Freedom of Information, Draft, January 30, 1946, RG 84, NA, Records of the United States Mission to the United Nations, Box 33, Document 21.

37. "Forceful U.S. Stand on Free Press Urged," *E&P*, March 2, 1946, p. 28.

38. "Cooper Regrets Delay in UNO Press Action," *E&P*, February 16, 1946, p. 18.
39. Robert Bunnelle, "Press Freedom Faces UNO Test in May," *E&P*, February 23, 1946, p. 72.
40. "Freedom of Information," *E&P*, March 23, 1946, p. 42.
41. Bunnelle, "Press Freedom Faces UNO Test in May," p. 72.
42. "Free Press Before UN in Sept.; Dulles Urges Special Committee," *E&P*, March 23, 1946, p. 76.
43. GAOR, 1st session, 7th plenary meeting, January 14, 1946, pp. 108–9.
44. Ibid., pp. 109–10.
45. "Freedom of Information in American Policy and Practice," p. 35.
46. Memorandum of Meeting of the Department's Committee on Freedom of Information by D. H. Popper, Division of International Organization Affairs, July 3, 1946, RG 353, NA, Box 97, File 13.2: Freedom of Information Committee, 1946, a. background material.
47. GAOR, 1st session, General Committee, Annex 12, p. 59.
48. Freedom of Information Committee, Minutes of August 13, 1946, RG 353, NA, Box 98, File 13.2: Freedom of Information Committee, 1946: e. FOI Minutes/1–18.
49. "World Press Conference," *E&P*, April 27, 1946, p. 78.
50. Freedom of Information Committee, Minutes of August 6, 1946, RG 353, NA, Box 98, File 13.2: Freedom of Information Committee, 1946: e. FOI Minutes/1–18.
51. Wilbur Forrest, Report of the Committee on World Freedom of Information, April 19, 1946, *Problems of Journalism—1946*, p. 124. Seventy American press association correspondents serving in fifty-four nations, dominions, or dependencies provided the data on the status of freedom of the press in their areas. The study itself is found in "Report on World Press Freedom," *E&P*, April 13, 1946, pp. 7, 82, 84.
52. Forrest, *Problems of Journalism—1946*, p. 127.
53. Ibid., p. 128.
54. "UN Group Receives 5 Freedom Proposals," *E&P*, May 4, 1946, p. 15.
55. "U.S. Proposes Special Body on Freedom of Information," *E&P*, May 11, 1946, p. 7.
56. William Reed, "UN Debate Bares Dissent on American Freedom Ideas," *E&P*, May 18, 1946, pp. 7–8.
57. "Clash of Ideas Faces Freedom Commission," *E&P*, May 25, 1946, p. 57. The proposal for an expert commission was altered several times before gaining United Nations approval. Each time that forces supporting governmental appointees for the subcommission gained ascendancy, *Editor & Publisher* decried the danger that nations wielding such power created for American values. *See*, e.g., "U.S. Freedoms Idea Vetoed by UN Group," *E&P*, June 22, 1946, p. 54.
58. William Reed, "UN Debate Points Up Basic Press Clashes," *E&P*, June 8, 1946, p. 8.
59. Memorandum from Walter Kotschnig, Adviser to the United States Delegation, to John C. Ross, Deputy Director, Office of Special Political Affairs, July 24, 1946, RG 84, NA, Records of the United States Mission to the United Nations, Box 88, File: Public Information.

60. UNESCO Constitution, art. 1, sec. 2.
61. Report of the Barrett Committee with Regard to UNESCO and Mass Media, Freedom of Information Committee, October 2, 1946, RG 353, NA, Box 98, File d: FOI Documents 9–12.
62. Sidney Hyman, *The Lives of William Benton*, Chicago, University of Chicago Press, 1969, pp. 336–38.
63. UNESCO Constitution, Preamble.
64. S. J. Monchak, "Benton Advisers Open Talks to Draft Free Press Policy," *E&P*, April 6, 1946, p. 7.
65. Ibid., pp. 7, 68.
66. "UNESCO," *E&P*, April 6, 1946, p. 38.
67. Stephen J. Monchak, "U.S. Mass Media Report Asks Freedoms for World," *E&P*, September 28, 1946, p. 9.
68. "U.S. Drafts Press Policy; Will Present It to UNESCO," *E&P*, July 20, 1946, p. 12.
69. Walter Kotschnig, Adviser to the United States Delegation to the United Nations, to Maurine Mulliner, Special Assistant to the United States Representative on the Economic and Social Council, June 11, 1946, RG 84, NA, Records of the United States Mission to the United Nations, Box 88, File: Public Information.
70. "U.S. Drafts Press Policy; Will Present It to UNESCO," p. 12.
71. "Program for UNESCO," *E&P*, September 28, 1946, p. 44.
72. UNESCO Proceedings, 1st session, Sub-Commission on Mass Communication, 2nd meeting, December 2, 1946, p. 157.
73. Ibid., Report of the Sub-Commission on Mass Communication, pp. 225, 227.
74. Memorandum Submitted to the Economic and Social Council and the Commission on Human Rights of the United Nations by the Standing Committee on World Freedom of Information of the American Society of Newspaper Editors, Freedom of Information Committee, September 30, 1946, RG 353, NA, Box 97, File d: FOI Documents.
75. Robert R. Burton, International Broadcasting Division, to John Howe, Special Assistant to William Benton, July 24, 1946, RG 59, NA, Box 4983, 811.91/7-2446.
76. Wilbur Forrest to William Benton, September 13, 1946, Ibid., Records of the Assistant Secretary of State for Public Affairs, Box 7, File: ASNE.
77. "Freedom of Information," *E&P*, October 26, 1946, p. 46.
78. Freedom of Information Committee, Minutes of October 3, 1946, RG 353, NA, Box 98, File: FOI Minutes 1–18.
79. Memorandum on Concept of Freedom of Information, Freedom of Information Committee, September 12, 1946, Ibid., Box 97, File d: FOI Documents.
80. Freedom of Information Committee, Minutes of July 16, 1946, Ibid., Box 98, File: FOI Minutes 1–18.
81. Freedom of Information Committee, Minutes of September 10, 1946, Ibid.
82. Spruille Braden, Assistant Secretary of State, to William Benton, November 11, 1946, RG 59, NA, Box 2308, FW501.PA/10-746.
83. The British had already complained that British journalists in the United States did not receive the same treatment as American correspondents in Great Britain. Through the British equivalent of *Editor & Publisher—World's Press*

News—English journalists said that although British officials devoted time to American correspondents, American officials did not reciprocate and that American officials often excluded correspondents from other nations from press conferences even though the British admitted accredited reporters from all nations to sessions held by British leaders. *See* Richard A. Johnson, Third Secretary of Embassy, London, to the Secretary of State, July 12, 1945, Ibid., Box 5873, 841.91211/7-1245; Ibid., August 24, 1945, 841.91211/8-2445.

Paul Miller, assistant general manager of the Associated Press and head of its Washington Bureau, disputed the British claims, printing segments of an interview with President Truman in which the president reaffirmed his belief in and practice of opening his news conferences to correspondents from various countries. After responding to every British claim, Miller noted that if the English journalists sincerely wanted strict equality among correspondents, they would open the press facilities at the House of Commons to foreign reporters. Although Miller did not say so, all accredited foreign correspondents had access to the press galleries in Congress. *See* Paul Miller, "Truman Wants Equal Access for Newsmen," *E&P*, August 25, 1945, p. 13.

84. Freedom of Information Committee, Minutes of October 22, 1946, RG 353, NA, Box 98, File: FOI Minutes 1–18.
85. Memorandum by the Legal Adviser, November 25, 1946, RG 59, NA, Box 2253, 501.BD Freedom of Information/11-2546.
86. Ibid.
87. *See,* generally, "Freedom of Information in American Policy and Practice" and "American Policy toward Freedom of Information."
88. A Freedom of Information Program, Memorandum by William Benton, September 16, 1946, RG 353, NA, Box 97, File: FOI Documents 1-8/2.
89. "UN and Free Information," *E&P*, November 30, 1946, p. 36.
90. "Berkson, Hoyt Review Press Freedom Status," *E&P*, December 7, 1946, p. 74.
91. U.S., Congress, House, 79th Congress, 1st sess., November 1, 1945, *Congressional Record*, 91:10283.
92. "Free Press Abroad," *E&P*, September 1, 1945, p. 40.
93. "Freedom of Information in American Policy and Practice," p. 28.
94. Ibid., p. 29.
95. *See,* e.g., "Russians Still Pose Problems of Censorship," *E&P*, June 29, 1946, p. 58; Walter Bedell Smith, American Ambassador in the Soviet Union, to the Secretary of State, July 3, 1946, RG 59, NA, Box 4988, 811.91261/7-346.

In June 1946, President Truman notified Congress that "satisfactory arrangements were in effect to permit the American press and radio correspondents to report on UNRRA programs without censorship in all UNRRA receiving countries except Russia." The presidential notification was quickly followed by a statement from Assistant Secretary of State Will Clayton noting that "although the free interchange of information between peoples and countries of the world is essential to the creation of a secure peace," the legislation's provisions actually would "achieve the opposite effect and would seriously complicate US relations with the Soviet Union." *See* Policy Statements on Freedom of Information, October 4, 1946, RG 353, NA, Box 97, File 13.2: Freedom of Information Committee, 1946, a. background material. Most journalists agreed with Clayton.

96. Lloyd Free, Special Assistant to the Director, Office of International Information and Cultural Affairs, to Howland Sargeant, Deputy Assistant Secretary of State for Public Affairs, October 23, 1947, RG 43, NA, Box 5, File: Freedom of Information.
97. Freedom of Information Committee, Minutes of July 16, 1946, RG 353, NA, Box 98, File: FOI Minutes 1–18.
98. A Freedom of Information Program, Benton memorandum.
99. Ibid.
100. American press organizations were not alone in submitting proposals for international freedom of information. Among the other organizations contributing to the growing pile of suggestions on Benton's desk were the Committee on Human Rights of the Commission to Study the Organization of Peace, an affiliate of the American Association for the United Nations; the Inter American Juridical Committee; the American Federation of Labor; and the American Law Institute. See Compilation of Freedom of Information Clauses Appearing in Various Drafted Bills of Rights, etc., Freedom of Information Committee, August 22, 1946, RG 353, NA, Box 97, File d: FOI Documents.
101. Most of the work preparing the treaty was done by Finnegan's assistant, Warren Pierce. The vigor with which Pierce pursued his assignment amazed State Department officials; the Chicago newsman talked with

    key movie people in Hollywood; to a number of U.S. managing editors, including Forrest and other ASNE people; to Cooper and Baillie. He is now going down to Palm Beach for an informal session with Sumner Wells [sic]. . . . He then proposes to come to Washington to talk with Bill Benton and Dean Acheson. He has also had Quincy Wright at the University of Chicago at work drafting model international agreements. And he hopes to see Mrs. Roosevelt.

    Of concern to State Department personnel, however, was a rather heretical view held by Pierce. Bilateral treaties, Pierce thought, posed "many complications" in negotiation. Pierce had said that "there might be advantages in the approach to this problem by private individuals rather than 'through Government'." See John Howe to Lloyd Free, February 24, 1947, RG 43, NA, Box 4, File: Freedom of Information.
102. "Freedom Treaty Draft Submitted to Editors," *E&P*, December 14, 1946, p. 14.
103. "Treaty Draft on World Free Press Submitted," *E&P*, April 19, 1947, p. 17.
104. "Draft Treaty," *E&P*, April 19, 1947, p. 62.
105. "Treaty Draft on World Free Press Submitted," p. 17.
106. "State Department Receives Composite Freedom Plan," *E&P*, September 13, 1947, p. 12.
107. Joseph Jones to William Benton, June 24, 1947, RG 43, NA, Box 5, File: Lloyd Free.
108. William Benton to Members of the Staff Committee Concerning Agreements on Freedom of Information, Memorandum on an Alternative Plan to Bilateral Agreements, August 29, 1947, Ibid., Box 4, File: Freedom of Information.
109. Lloyd Free to William Benton, Memorandum Regarding Progress on Bilateral Agreements, June 30, 1947, Ibid. Benton's speech was given before the Inland Daily Press Association meeting in Chicago, in February 1947. See "Benton Outlines Plan for Treaties," *E&P*, February 15, 1947, pp. 10, 62.

110. Ibid.

111. Ibid. (emphasis in original).

112. William Benton to Lloyd Free, July 14, 1947, Ibid., Box 5, File: Lloyd Free.

113. Lloyd Free to William Benton, Memorandum Regarding Bilateral Agreements on Freedom of Information—An Alternative Approach, August 14, 1947, Ibid., Box 4, File: Freedom of Information.

114. Ibid.

115. " 'Not By-Passing UN'," *E&P*, September 13, 1947, p. 12.

116. "Finnegan Draft Used in Treaty with Italy," *E&P*, February 7, 1948, p. 11.

117. Freedom of Information Committee, Statement Currently Included in All Draft Treaties of Friendship, Commerce, and Navigation, undated, RG 353, NA, Box 97, File d: FOI Documents 1-8/2.

118. "ANG Joins New World Organization," *Guild Reporter*, June 28, 1946, p. 7.

119. Ibid.

120. *See* Daniel J. Leab, *A Union of Individuals: The Formation of the American Newspaper Guild*, New York, Columbia University Press, 1970.

121. "World Journalists Ask Role as UN Observers," *E&P*, June 29, 1946, p. 24. This IOJ role greatly concerned *Editor & Publisher*, which complained that no other journalistic organization was sufficiently interested to try to counter IOJ influence with the United Nations. *See*, e.g., "The Russian IOJ," *E&P*, June 28, 1947, p. 42; "Where Is the U.S. Press?" *E&P*, August 16, 1947, p. 32.

122. Freedom of Information Committee, Problems of Freedom of Information and the Press, October 17, 1946, RG 353, NA, Box 97, File d: FOI Documents.

123. Ibid.

124. "Murray Charges IOJ Now Is under Russ Domination," *Guild Reporter*, June 13, 1947, p. 5.

125. "U.S. Resolution Adopted by IOJ," *E&P*, June 14, 1947, p. 9.

126. "ANG May Split with IOJ, Called 'Debating Society'," *Guild Reporter*, July 25, 1947, p. 7.

127. James F. Byrnes, *Speaking Frankly*, New York, Harper & Row, 1947, pp. 248–53.

128. "Press Freedom Gains Are Scored in Paris," *E&P*, August 3, 1946, p. 9; "Molotov's Surprise," *E&P*, August 3, 1946, p. 46.

129. "Byrnes, Molotov Clash on Free Press Ideas," *E&P*, August 10, 1946, p. 8; "Byrnes and Molotov," *E&P*, August 10, 1946, p. 44; "U.S., Russian Press Tilt over 'Freedom'," *E&P*, August 17, 1946, p. 13.

130. "We're Skeptical," *E&P*, December 14, 1946, p. 48.

131. Memorandum of Conversation with V. A. Tarassenko, Soviet Counselor, and L. I. Pavlov, Third Secretary, Soviet Embassy, by Llewellyn E. Thompson, Chief, Division of Eastern European Affairs, January 10, 1947, RG 59, NA, Box 3837, 740.00119 COUNCIL/1-2047.

132. "What about Moscow?" *E&P*, January 18, 1947, p. 38.

133. Walter Bedell Smith, American Ambassador in the Soviet Union, to the Secretary of State, January 20, 1947, RG 59, NA, Box 3837, 740.00119 COUNCIL/1-2047.

134. Memorandum of Conversation between Secretary of State Marshall and Mr. Novikov, Soviet Ambassador, by H. Freeman Matthews, Director, Office of European Affairs, January 28, 1947, Ibid., 740.00119 COUNCIL/1-2847.

135. Memorandum of Conversation with V. A. Tarassenko, Counselor, Soviet Embassy, by Llewellyn E. Thompson, Chief, Division of Eastern European Affairs, February 6, 1947, Ibid., 740.00119 COUNCIL/2-647.
136. Secretary of State Marshall to the American Embassy, Moscow, February 6, 1947, Ibid., 740.00119 COUNCIL/1-3147.
137. W. L. Clayton, Under Secretary of State, to Thomas McCabe, President, Scott Paper Company, February 26, 1947, Ibid., Box 3838, 740.00119 COUNCIL/2-1247.
138. Secretary of State Marshall to Walter B. Smith, American Ambassador in the Soviet Union, February 13, 1947, Ibid., 740.00119 COUNCIL/2-1347.
139. Walter Bedell Smith, American Ambassador in the Soviet Union, to the Secretary of State, February 16, 1947, Ibid., Box 4989, 811.91261/2-1647.
140. "Moscow Free Press," Newsweek, March 31, 1947, p. 63.
141. "36 to Moscow," E&P, March 8, 1947, p. 44.
142. "Moscow Parley News Expedited by Soviets," E&P, March 15, 1947, p. 8; Eddy Gilmore, "Russians Keep Pledge; Newsmen Kept Awake," E&P, March 22, 1947, p. 8.
143. "Moscow Free Press," p. 63; Gilmore, "Russians Keep Pledge," p. 8.
144. George F. Kennan, Chargé in the Soviet Union, to the Secretary of State, March 4, 1946, FR: 1946, VI:711.
145. George F. Kennan, Chargé in the Soviet Union, to the Secretary of State, March 4, 1946, RG 59, NA, Box 4988, 811.91261/3-446.
146. See John Lewis Gaddis, The United States and the Origins of the Cold War, 1941–1947, New York, Columbia University Press, 1972, pp. 302–4.
147. George F. Kennan, Chargé in the Soviet Union, to the Secretary of State, March 6, 1946, RG 59, NA, Box 4988, 811.91261/3-646.
148. George F. Kennan, Chargé in the Soviet Union, to the Secretary of State, March 6, 1946, Ibid., 811.91261/3-646.
149. Secretary of State James F. Byrnes to the American Embassy, Moscow, March 13, 1946, Ibid., 811.91261/3-646.
150. George F. Kennan, Chargé in the Soviet Union, to the Secretary of State, March 19, 1946, FR: 1946, VI:718.
151. Ibid., p. 719.
152. Walter Bedell Smith, Appointed Ambassador to the Soviet Union, to the Secretary of State, March 30, 1946, Ibid., p. 728.
153. Walter Bedell Smith, Ambassador in the Soviet Union, to the Secretary of State, April 2, 1946, RG 59, NA, Box 4988, 811.91261/4-246.
154. Walter Bedell Smith, American Ambassador in the Soviet Union, to the Secretary of State, December 2, 1948, Ibid., Box 6498, 861.918/12-248.
155. Lloyd Free, Office of International Information, to Morrill Cody, Public Affairs Overseas Program Staff, July 28, 1949, Ibid., 861.918/7-2849.
156. See, e.g., Foreign News, The APME Redbook 1948, New York, Associated Press, 1949, pp. 64–67; Foreign News, The APME Redbook 1951, New York, Associated Press, 1951, pp. 23–24; Performance Report, Ibid., pp. 207–8; Foreign News, The APME Redbook 1952, New York, Associated Press, 1952, pp. 120–24.
157. Walter Bedell Smith, American Ambassador in the Soviet Union, to the Secretary of State, February 5, 1948, RG 59, NA, Box 4989, 811.91261/2-548;

Foy D. Kohler, Chargé in the Soviet Union, to the Secretary of State, February 10, 1949, Ibid., Confidential Box 441, 811.91261/2-1049; Walter Bedell Smith, American Ambassador in the Soviet Union, to the Secretary of State, April 15, 1948, Ibid., 811.91261/4-1548.

158. Foy D. Kohler, Chargé in the Soviet Union, to the Secretary of State, July 1, 1949, Ibid., Box 6498, 861.918/7-149. Associated Press reporter Eddy Gilmore was in a particularly delicate situation, for he had married a Russian woman. If he left the country, most likely he would not be allowed to reenter and thus would effectively abandon his family. See Ibid., Confidential Box 441, 811.91261/5-749.

159. Walter Bedell Smith, American Ambassador in the Soviet Union, to the Secretary of State, April 4, 1948, Ibid., Box 4989, 811.91261/4-1548.

160. Elbridge Durbrow, Counselor of Embassy at Moscow, to the Secretary of State, October 21, 1946, Ibid., Box 4988, 811.91261/10-2146. Walter Cronkite, a correspondent for United Press stationed in Moscow, made the comparison between increased censorship and the publication of adverse information in American papers. A later shutdown of American radio newscasts from the Soviet capital was linked, at least temporarily, to the publication of an unfavorable book about Russia by a former CBS correspondent. See "Networks Await Moscow Ban Ruling," *Broadcasting*, November 18, 1946, p. 18.

161. The International News Service was in disfavor because William Randolph Hearst owned the agency. At that agency's request, American diplomats repeatedly sought permission for an International News Service correspondent to take up residence in Moscow. Soviet officials continually denied the request. See Barry Faris, Editor in Chief, International News Service, to the Secretary of State, December 14, 1946, RG 59, NA, Box 4988, 811.91261/12-1446.

162. Alan G. Kirk, American Ambassador in the Soviet Union, to the Secretary of State, September 15, 1949, Ibid., Box 4990, 811.91261/9-1549.

163. George F. Kennan, Chargé in the Soviet Union, to the Secretary of State, March 17, 1946, Ibid., Box 4988, 811.91261/3-1746.

164. Walter Bedell Smith, American Ambassador in the Soviet Union, to the Secretary of State, October 9, 1946, *FR: 1946*, VI:790.

165. Dean Acheson, Acting Secretary of State, to the American Embassy, Moscow, November 8, 1946, RG 59, NA, Box 4988, 811.91261/11-846.

166. Walter Bedell Smith, American Ambassador in the Soviet Union, to the Secretary of State, November 22, 1946, Ibid., Box 4716, 811.42700(R)/11-2246.

167. Walter Bedell Smith, American Ambassador in the Soviet Union, to the Secretary of State, November 19, 1946, Ibid., 811.42700(R)/11-1946.

168. Walter Bedell Smith, American Ambassador in the Soviet Union, to the Secretary of State, November 23, 1946, Ibid., 811.42700(R)/11-2346.

169. "State Dept. May Act in Russian Ban," *Broadcasting*, November 25, 1946, p. 86. The correspondents for other broadcasting outlets also worked for newspapers.

170. See, e.g., Dorsey Gassaway Fisher, First Secretary of Embassy, London, to the Secretary of State, November 1, 1946, RG 84, WNRC, Box 82 London Conference, File 891 A–B, 1946; "British, U.S. Press Probes," *E&P*, November 2, 1946, p. 38; "Hutchins Book Guides Royal Press Inquiry," *E&P*, July

19, 1947, pp. 8, 56; "Watching English Commission Investigating the Press," *American Newspaper Publishers Association B Bulletin*, September 10, 1947, p. 93.

171. *See* Margaret A. Blanchard, "The Hutchins Commission, the Press and the Responsibility Concept," *Journalism Monographs* 49 (May 1977). Roger A. Simpson, a University of Washington journalism professor, argues that the Hutchins Commission's ideas about the social responsibility of the press "invited troubles from other nations, more zealous even than the Hutchins Commission about ensuring press responsibility through government controls." *See* Roger A. Simpson, "The Hutchins Commission at Geneva: Social Responsibility in the United Nations Crucible," abstract of unpublished paper, *Clio among the Media*, June 1984, p. 23.

    Conservative critics of the Hutchins Commission noted that the commission had probably polluted the international free-press debate, and opponents of the American system of freedom of the press often quoted from the commission's conclusions to criticize American proposals. But, then, opponents of the American system eagerly used any criticism of the American media in arguments against the United States's proposals. As newer books of media criticism superseded the Hutchins Commission report, the report receded into the background as a weapon to be used by opponents. When the opposition used studies such as the one conducted by the Hutchins Commission to argue against American proposals, United States representatives simply retorted that the very existence of such criticism proved that freedom of the press existed in the United States and showed the American press's willingness to consider possible improvements.

172. *See* White and Leigh, *Peoples Speaking to Peoples*; Philip Schuyler, "UN Covenant Advocated on Free Flow of News," *E&P*, March 30, 1946, pp. 7, 70; "Press Association Chiefs' Comments," *E&P*, March 30, 1946, p. 7; "Leigh-White Report," *E&P*, March 30, 1946, p. 42; "UN Reporters Judge Proposal for Covenant," *E&P*, April 6, 1946, pp. 7, 68; "Knight Assails Plan in Leigh-White Report," *E&P*, April 20, 1946, p. 120.

173. *See,* e.g., "France's 'Free Press'," *E&P*, March 2, 1946, p. 42; "French Press," *E&P*, April 27, 1946, p. 78; David Perlman, "French Editors Favor Press Control Clause," *E&P*, May 11, 1946, p. 20; "Press Bill Announced by French Govt.," *E&P*, July 26, 1947, p. 59; George Langelaan, "French Press Statute Checks Hidden Control," *E&P*, August 9, 1947, p. 68.

174. Sol Taishoff, "State-Controlled Radio Seen in France," *Broadcasting*, August 27, 1945, p. 17.

175. *See,* e.g., "Haley's [*sic*] Radio Comet," *Broadcasting*, September 3, 1945, p. 46; "Straws in the Air," *Broadcasting*, November 19, 1945, p. 56; "Busy as a BBC?" *Broadcasting*, December 17, 1945, p. 54; "Britannia Waves the Rules," *Broadcasting*, July 15, 1946, p. 52; "Watch Canada," *Broadcasting*, August 5, 1946, p. 50; "Hi, Neighbor," *Broadcasting*, February 24, 1947, p. 50.

176. *See,* e.g., "Agencies Move to Regain Foreign Billings in '46," *Advertising Age*, February 25, 1946, Section 2, pp. 1, 8–9; "U.S. Falling Down on Export Ad Job, Parton Declares," *Advertising Age*, October 21, 1946, pp. 42–43; "European Market Being Lost, Export Admen Are Warned," *Advertising Age*, December 2, 1946, p. 24.

CHAPTER 3

The Crusade Becomes Involved in Propaganda Wars

Cooperation between press organizations and the federal government was acceptable when the goal was establishing international freedom of the press. When the government asked American journalists to help launch a postwar information program, however, a full-fledged debate erupted over the possible effect that involvement with a government-sponsored information program might have on the reputation of the news supplied by American news organizations. Specifically, some press leaders contended that any connection with a government information service carried such tremendous potential for tainting the news agencies' product as propaganda that the agencies must oppose the request at all costs. The most drastic reaction from the press would be to destroy the government's information program and, possibly, in the process, irreparably harm the working relationship with the government that was necessary to fulfill the dreams of journalists seeking international freedom of the press.

During World War II, the Associated Press (AP), United Press (UP), and International News Service (INS) all provided their news free to the Department of State for use by the Office of War Information (OWI) and the Office of Inter-American Affairs (OIAA) in overseas broadcasts. Simply doing their patriotic duty, the news agency leaders later said of this era of press-government cooperation. But as the war ended, so, too—in the minds of many press leaders—did the need for the government to send information abroad. At war's end, private news organizations wanted to expand overseas, and a government information program endangered those plans. The possibility that potential clients would label news agency news as propaganda if the government used the same news for official broadcasts topped the agency chiefs' list of reasons for refusing to support the government's program. A second reason was the fear that government news programming would take potential clients away from the commercial agencies. Journalists and government leaders who wanted the press to aid the information program stressed the importance of the programming if the United States— now living in the shadow of the atomic bomb—was to preserve peace.

Arguments about the essential relationship between information and peace were quite familiar to press association leaders, who had been making identical statements since the end of World War I. The arguments presented by press association leaders, however, carefully excluded the government from the news dissemination process. Thus, the stage was set for an argument that persisted throughout the postwar years. Should the United States government have an information program at all? And what responsibility, if any, did American press organizations have to help that information program? As the sense of emergency imparted by the cold war deepened, the question became whether the relationship between the American press agencies and the government information program should change in any way.

THE GOVERNMENT BEGINS
AN INFORMATION PROGRAM

The struggle between the press associations and the government information program began with two seemingly unrelated events in 1945. In April, the Associated Press board of directors gave Executive Director Kent Cooper a $1 million-a-year fund "to make the AP a global institution."[1] In August, President Harry S. Truman announced that the Office of War Information and parts of the Office of Inter-American Affairs, the government's two major wartime propaganda operations, were going out of business. In a statement filled with contradictions, the president said that the nation henceforth planned to rely on private organizations as "the primary means of informing foreign peoples about this country." Although other nations planned to continue "extensive and growing information programs," the president contended that the United States' only informational goal was "to see to it that other peoples receive a full and fair picture of American life and of the aims and policies of the United States Government."[2] The immediate question was whether private enterprise could or would provide the kind of information necessary for the world to draw an accurate picture of American life. The president's statement left enough room for the federal government to decide that question negatively and thus to continue an information program of some kind. Truman even told the State Department to determine the best way to accomplish his goal of informing the world about American life and intentions.

OWI personnel had anticipated the president's termination of government information services at the end of hostilities, and they began negotiations with the State Department in early 1944 to ensure continuation of radio and other news work.[3] In 1945, negotiators concluded that if the United States was "not to be at a hopeless disadvantage," the nation must maintain an international information program after the war. Reports forecast that the British, French, and Russians planned to conduct extensive information programs during the postwar period. Thus, in order for Americans to rule their own destinies after the war, they must realize the importance of modern communications in international diplomacy. In fact, State Department planners emphasized that peace depended on assuring "an understanding by peoples of other countries of the essential facts about the American people, their character, their purposes, and particularly the objectives of their foreign policy." Planners noted that private channels of communication, where available, would play a key part in this postwar plan. When such private channels existed, the government's role would be limited to "promoting the cheapness, the equality, the speed, and universality of communications facilities." Where private communications operations were not available, as in sections of the world where requests for service would not make private service financially sound or where information available for transmission was too slight to merit full service, the government must "supplement the activities conducted by private companies and persons in order that the level of information required by the national interest should be maintained."[4]

With advocates of a continuing government information program finding a home in the State Department, the termination of the wartime information services set in motion a significant conflict over the way in which news of America would reach other peoples. Although American news agencies wanted to preempt the field for free enterprise, veterans of the wartime information programs believed that, in the past, commercial and competitive influences had forced free enterprise to send an inaccurate picture of America abroad. These wartime information specialists believed that the private news agencies would fail to meet the challenge again.[5] Complicating the advocacy of a government information agency, however, was the government's attachment to international freedom of the press and the real possibility that a government-sponsored information program was in basic conflict with that ideal. Still, the State Department did not intend to let the information program disappear completely.

The ideal solution to the developing dilemma was an accommodation between the government's need for an information program and the press's need for international expansion and freedom of information. The government could help to develop international communications facilities and to attain free-press guarantees in treaties and other international accords; the press could respond by helping to provide the needed information about America abroad.[6] This proposal, however, did not consider the fact that some American journalists saw government information operations as the equivalent of government propaganda operations. Some press leaders reluctantly accepted the need for propaganda in wartime, but propaganda was an unnecessary obstacle to the expansion of the American press system throughout the world in peacetime. And the very existence of government propaganda cast doubts on the purity of news organization dispatches, just as the existence of foreign propaganda operations had tainted the products of foreign news agencies in the past.

One of Assistant Secretary of State William Benton's main tasks, then, was convincing the American press—and the Congress—that the United States was not launching a propaganda drive. Instead, Benton argued that the information program proposed by the Department of State would distribute truthful data, not propaganda, about America abroad and that the department had no intention of competing with the commercial news agencies. As Benton explained to the House Foreign Affairs Committee, the government's role in dispensing information would be "facilitative and supplementary." First, the government would help private agencies involved in the international exchange of information. On the secondary, supplemental level, the government would "help present a truer picture of American life and American policy in those areas important to our policy where private interchange is inadequate, or where misunderstandings and misapprehensions exist about the United States and its policies."[7]

Specifically, the government's information program, as housed in the Office of International Information and Cultural Affairs (OIC) at the State Department, would distribute information items including complete texts of presidential and other important addresses and major policy statements. The program would also transmit background information designed to help foreign editors understand important American policies and issues. Commercial agencies had long ago decided that neither category of information was commercially viable for private transmission. Thus, the government service would supplement the private news agencies rather than compete with them. The main problem with the program, Benton said, was American paranoia over the word propaganda, which "has bad connotations to many Americans. That's because they associate it with lies and half-truths, told with a hidden purpose." But the United States information program would be different: "Our aim will be to present a well-rounded picture of America and American foreign policy." The program would not "select or distort the facts in order to give a completely favorable picture. The best propaganda in the world is truth."[8]

But the press associations of America remembered that the OWI had used their news dispatches to create the equivalent of a free international information service during the war. Besides, the government was meddling in the press associations' business in other ways. For instance, State Department planners wanted the news agencies to adopt the multiple-address format for sending news reports abroad. This form of transmission involved sending Morse code news dispatches over radio for simultaneous reception at several locations, and department planners considered the method ideal for getting the American news services into areas where conventional delivery of information was impossible.[9] The multiple-address system, though highly efficient and geared to reach every corner of the globe, meant fundamental changes in the news services' operations. By providing identical news to everyone in a certain area, the format upset the exclusive contract principle that served as the basis of press association operations. Other potential problems were easier pirating of news by newspapers and radio stations that had not paid for the service, more complicated bookkeeping, and lower profits.[10] Preservation of property right in news had long been an important item on the American journalists' free-press agenda, and the multiple-address format threatened that principle as well. American correspondents abroad had already experienced the theft of their news stories before publication. For instance, correspondents for *The New York Times* and *Newsweek* complained that a French intelligence agency transcribed stories that the journalists had filed for transmission to the United States. Copies of these news stories allegedly were to circulate solely among top government officials, but the stories often appeared in Paris newspapers before they were published in the American newspapers for which they had been written.[11] Understandably, creating additional opportunities for the misappropriation of news stories was unappealing to the news services.

Adding to the conflict between the government's planned information service and the private news agencies objecting to the program was the criticism of the quality of news transmitted abroad by the American press associations that was inherent in the government's proposal. State Department officials recognized that the American agencies never had considered exporting news about the United States as one of their major functions. And while the department couched its criticisms of the news about the United States that did appear in publications abroad in terms of "the inadequacy of news selection even where foreign newspapers subscribe to the American services,"[12] the sting was still present. The proposed government information program clearly implied that American news agencies were not sending a representative picture of the United States to the world and that the news agencies preferred to sell highly profitable and popular news of murder, sex, and Hollywood rather than offering less commercially appealing background pieces on the reasons behind labor unrest or racial problems. The proud news agencies did not appreciate such implications—especially when the critics of the agency heads contended that these particular press leaders refused to face the reality that facilities for correcting distortions abroad simply did not exist. Thus, the problem of accurate news dissemination in the foreign fields became much more complex. Some journalists also believed that the news agencies must exercise greater care in selecting news for transmission abroad than for circulation in the United States. At the same time, these journalists said, the government must supplement commercial news sent overseas to correct misperceptions of American life that arose from the interaction between American news values and foreign cultural values.[13]

Strong as such criticisms were, Benton did not publicize some-of his most telling points against the news agencies' stand. One argument focused on the willingness of the Associated Press to accept government help during World War II in Turkey and on the readiness of the United Press to accept government assistance in China and South Africa during the same years.[14] Now that the government needed a favor in return, the news agencies seemed to have conveniently forgotten that governmental aid. In fact, the department regularly provided assistance to journalists on all levels—even helping some of its strongest critics to travel abroad. For instance, diplomats eased the way for Colonel Robert McCormick of the *Chicago Tribune*, a member of the Associated Press board of directors and staunch supporter of Cooper, to travel throughout South America.[15] The State Department also helped Roy W. Howard of the Scripps-Howard Newspapers, former general manager of United Press and a leading opponent of the government information program, to travel to China.[16] In each instance, the journalist involved inserted himself into American foreign policy matters by pointedly stating his opinions on issues, which, at times, were at odds with policy as enunciated by the State Department. Although American diplomats on the scene reported the journalists' comments back to Washington, D.C., the diplomats made no attempts to interfere with the press visitors' free speech. Department representatives tried to reestablish a diplomatic equilibrium after the journalists left the foreign country.

American diplomats also expected that journalists from the United States would leave foreign countries with numerous confidential documents tucked in their luggage. A perfect example of this came with a Dutch-sponsored visit for United States correspondents to Indonesia in 1949. Consular authorities in Bombay, India, later had the gory task of collecting the confidential papers that thirteen journalists took with them from Indonesia after the reporters had died in an airplane crash.[17] Despite several bad experiences with journalists who had been helped by the department, Benton's advisers suggested that the department continue to provide as much assistance as possible to representatives of the press without linking such aid to the controversy over the information program. The advisers hoped that "at some time it should become apparent to AP and UP that we have done them many favors throughout the world and have not been trying to encroach upon their interests." Then, perhaps, the Associated Press and United Press would cooperate with the government information program.[18]

Benton also kept to himself criticisms from several American representatives abroad that stressed the poor quality of reporting of important news events being done by the press associations. For instance, Leo J. Margolin, public information chief for Europe, United Nations Relief and Rehabilitation Administration (UNRRA), complained to Benton, "the three press associations are up to their old tricks again, but this time with more vigor because they are in keen competition among themselves and with such foreign agencies as Reuters." Among the problems presented was the news agencies' failure to report significant news. According to Margolin, Americans' news philosophy had been "picked up in the county courthouses of the U.S.A." This approach to news basically meant that "tain't no story less at least 100 AMG [American Military Government] workers are arrested for blackmarketeering.' " The coverage of significant events was so poor that Margolin did not think a supplemental job by the government would be sufficient to correct misperceptions. "In their rush to sell their wares to the press of Europe, the press associations have done an excellent sales job, but it's been based on the fact that one press association can supply the Swedish, Danish, Italian or Greek papers with better and more scandal stories than the other."[19]

Reports from overseas posts that the American news agencies had no immediate plans to provide news to some of the more remote areas of the world were also kept more or less confidential. The delay in extending commercial service throughout the world was caused by the inability of newspapers in these areas to pay the costs involved in news transmission.[20] This reluctance of the private news services to provide information to commercially unprofitable areas of the world obviously boosted the argument for a government information program.

The proposed government information program had numerous facets: exchange of scholars; maintenance of information libraries abroad; distribution of official texts of speeches and documents; provision of photographs and filmstrips for noncommercial use; publication of the Russian-language magazine *Amerika*; circulation of documentary films about American life for noncommercial showings; distribution of background information and feature stories about life in America; placement of information officers in overseas missions; and development of a peacetime international shortwave radio outlet through the wartime Voice of America (VOA) facilities.[21] Press organizations actually objected only to the last item on the list—the development of an international shortwave radio voice—and then only to the transmission of news stories as part of its programming. Disregarding possible objections and problems, planners of the new government information program asked the wire services to continue supplying news to the State Department beyond the agreed-on December 31, 1945, termination date so that the department could maintain two so-called emergency services. One of the services was the department's shortwave broadcasts in various foreign languages; the other was its providing news to newspapers and radio stations in occupied areas.[22]

ASSOCIATED PRESS WITHDRAWS ITS SERVICE FROM GOVERNMENT USE

Not only did the Associated Press refuse to comply with the government's request, but the agency severed all connections with the State Department in mid-January 1946. The announcement by the news cooperative's board of directors was clearly grounded in Cooper's lifelong struggle against foreign news agencies with governmental connections. The official statement said that "government cannot engage in newscasting without creating the fear of propaganda which necessarily would reflect upon the objectivity of the news services from which such newscasts are prepared." Echoing another Cooper belief, the board added, news "disseminated by non-governmental news agencies is essential to the highest development of mankind and to the perpetuation of peace between nations." Government was not totally precluded from international information activities by the Associated Press board, but the permissible range of governmental operations was severely limited. Establishing and maintaining libraries around the world might be appropriate, and, of course, activities to advance international press freedom were highly acceptable. In other areas, however, the government's information program invaded a sphere reserved for private enterprise. The United Press soon served notice of its intentions to stop supplying the State Department's information needs as well, although Hugh Baillie agreed to hold his action in abeyance briefly until he heard Benton's arguments. The International News Service also delayed making a decision, refusing to take what General Manager Seymour Berkson called "precipitate action."[23]

Although the United Press also stopped serving the State Department's information program, the chief target of Benton's efforts to regain news service was the Associated Press, the oldest, largest, and most powerful American news agency. Never one to mince words, Benton told board president Robert McLean, publisher of the Philadelphia *Evening Bulletin*, that the Associated Press's decision had created "an obstacle to the conduct of American foreign policy." Shortwave broadcasting was "essential to the vital interests of the American people," yet the news agency, without even talking to State Department personnel involved, had removed a major source of the news necessary for these transmissions. Cooper and Benton agreed on one point, Benton told McLean—the peace of the world depended on understanding between peoples of the world. Yet, Benton believed that in order for the United States to be understood by other peoples, the government must supplement wire service activity because many areas of the world, such as several Balkan countries, much of the Near East, parts of Southeast Asia, and the Soviet Union, were beyond the reach of commercial agencies. In these areas, news of America was available only through shortwave broadcasts. By depriving government shortwave broadcasts of Associated Press news, "your decision will contribute to the misunderstanding of America abroad. To the extent that it does, it jeopardizes American interests, American security and the cause of peace itself."[24]

The best way to protect American interests abroad, Benton believed, was to give all people throughout the world true information about the United States. The strength of his belief blinded Benton to the very real fears of the press association leaders that any news supplied to a government-run information program by the press associations would be slanted before broadcast. Even if the department wanted to slant the news, which it did not intend to do, Benton contended that too many people—including the Congress and the press itself—supervised the information program for purposeful distortion of news to occur. The Associated Press's action, by implication, however, damaged the government information program's reputation and impugned the objectivity of news associations still serving the State Department. The self-righteous nature of the Associated Press's criticisms also grated on Benton's nerves because the news agency was not completely free of governmental entanglements. For example, the Associated Press intended to honor contracts with the British Broadcasting Corporation, the state-owned radio system in Great Britain, and with Tass, the Russian news agency, among others. Surely, Benton said, the matter of governmental involvement in information programs was so complicated that the Associated Press should thoroughly investigate the situation before making accusations or far-reaching decisions.[25]

Abandoning sections of the world unreachable by commercial services was the farthest thing from the mind of the Associated Press board, McLean protested, indicating that attempts to question the board's patriotism were not appreciated. After all, McLean said, the board had authorized government distribution of Associated Press news in most of the areas that Benton mentioned, "but this was evidently not satisfactory to the Department."[26] Although appreciating the Associated Press's efforts to cooperate, Benton thought the news service's proposal to make its file available to the government information program near the remote areas served was impractical because the staff and mechanical facilities needed to process the news were all in the United States. Once again he protested that the department's main objective was "to break down the barriers to the free flow of news and to foster its interchange between peoples." The government information program's objectives were limited, and the program would not interfere with private enterprise, Benton said, as he urged the Associated Press board to become familiar with the department's goals.[27]

Emotions ran high within the press community over the commercial agencies' moves. Howard, a leader in the interwar free-press movement, was upset about the way his longtime friend, Benton, had reacted to Howard's opposition to government news dissemination. Benton had accused Howard of opposing the plan solely because of commercial considerations. Howard contended that commercial interests were "the smallest factor" in his opposition to the government's plan to distribute news internationally. Rather, Howard's main concern was his belief that any news dissemination by the State Department "will inevitably be regarded as propaganda. Even if it were lily white, which it will never be, if it presented both sides of every situation it attempts to cover, which it will never do, it would still, by reason of its source, be propaganda in the eyes of the world." Benton's reaction to press criticism of the government's proposed information program showed "an almost complete lack of understanding of international press association journalism, its history and operating technique." Howard said that he was forced to believe that Benton's plan would "wreck one of our great national assets ... the world-wide acceptance of the objectivity and freedom from propaganda of the news reports of the American press associations."[28]

Strongly supporting the government's information program was Ralph McGill, editor of the *Atlanta Constitution* and one of the three men sent around the world in the quest for international freedom of the press by the American Society of Newspaper Editors in 1945. McGill thought that the fears expressed by the news agencies about a government information program tainting the reputation of the agencies' product were hypocritical. After all, American news organizations provided the copy used by government-owned radio stations in Britain, France, and Russia to broadcast "American news to the world with whatever interpretation they care to put on it." The situation greatly upset McGill, who said, "personally, I am a little sick of Hugh Baillie and Kent Cooper acting as if God had appointed them special protectors of a free press. It is a sanctimonious smug attitude which might make a silent giant of this country when every other giant and pigmy in the world is broadcasting its own interpretation of American news events and policies."[29]

Carl W. Ackerman, dean of Columbia University's Graduate School of Journalism—another member of the ASNE missionary team of 1945 and a close friend of Cooper—was as strongly opposed to the government's information program as McGill was in favor of it. The best contribution that the American government could make toward the establishment of international freedom of the press, Ackerman believed, was to abandon "the international propaganda business." If the government persisted in international propaganda, "we automatically bomb out of existence our ideal of freedom of news; an ideal to which our press is dedicated, not for selfish newspaper reasons" but because of a belief in the importance of free and impartial information to the cause of peace. Freedom of international news and "subsidized governmental propaganda are incompatible," Ackerman stressed.[30]

The third member of the round-the-world team, Wilbur Forrest, assistant editor of the *New York Herald Tribune* and chairman of the ASNE world freedom of information committee, sought a middle ground. As he told Benton, "I am backing the need of American information abroad up to the hilt. On the other hand, I do share the fears of the agencies that any government news—and I emphasize the word news—processed by government employees will carry the inference in foreign minds that it reflects government policy by commission and even omission." To avoid this danger, Forrest suggested that the information program transmit agency dispatches verbatim and give the originating agency credit for the information. This proposal would eliminate governmental editing of the news. "Personally," Forrest wrote Benton, "I do not see what argument could be made against this," for the plan was a "common sense solution, unless the A.P. and U.P. are out to wreck the whole information program. . . . which I do not believe they are—yet."[31]

Other editors involved in the international free-press movement, although a little less vehement, were just as positive about their interpretations of the news agencies' decisions. Richard J. Finnegan of the *Chicago Times*, who would soon draft the composite international free-press treaty, supported Benton's position. Finnegan believed that the news agencies, as commercial enterprises, should sell their news to anyone who wanted to buy it, including the United States government. After all, "the State Department can be trusted with reports quite as much as commercial broadcasters selling merchandise." Taking a different view, Erwin Canham, editor of the *Christian Science Monitor* and an emerging leader of the international free-press crusade, congratulated the Associated Press for its stand on principle. On the other hand, Nelson Poynter of the *St. Petersburg Times*, who wrote one of the first articles spurring the press on to international activity, supported the government's efforts "to fill in gaps of information which private agencies leave in the foreign field." Furthermore, Poynter said he feared the government's buying the news associations' products less than he feared "the second-rate government news service which otherwise will develop to fill a vacuum in foreign information."[32]

Although the Associated Press board gave little indication of reversing its position on the primary issue of providing the news agency's full wire service report to the department's information program, Benton did win on two minor points. The Associated Press agreed to continue supplying news for use in the department's daily bulletin sent to personnel overseas[33]—after receiving guarantees that embassy personnel, "chosen among other things for their ability to handle classified material," would not inadvertently disseminate the information contained therein.[34] And board president McLean promised that the news agency would examine its contracts with foreign agencies and governments with the goal of renegotiating any agreements not in compliance with the policy that the wire service had imposed on its own government.[35] Pursuant to instructions, Associated Press management began exploring the ramifications of its contract with Tass, the Soviet news agency, by asking the Associated Press correspondent in Moscow just what services Tass provided. For instance, did Tass notify Associated Press reporters of important breaking news events before other correspondents found out about the stories? After discovering that Tass provided little help to its correspondents, the Associated Press warned the Soviet agency that the contract might be terminated unless Tass contributed more to the allegedly reciprocal arrangement. The only concessions that the Associated Press won from the Soviet agency, however, involved sporadic advance notification on breaking news stories and limited access to the Russian news agency's library. Interestingly, instructions for the Associated Press–Tass negotiations and responses of the Soviet officials involved went to and from Moscow via State Department communications facilities, thus allowing American diplomats to know the exact status of contract terms at all times.[36]

Ultimately convinced that Tass was upholding the terms of the contract—although minimally—the Associated Press left the agreement in effect. After doing so, Associated Press leaders exacerbated the irritation of critics of the Tass arrangement by negotiating several short-term contracts with news agencies behind the iron curtain. As C. D. Jackson, vice president of Time, Inc., explained, the contracts required that the government-operated agencies in Czechoslovakia, Poland, Hungary, Rumania, and Yugoslavia, as well as in the Soviet Union, "not change the facts or the meaning of what they receive." Associated Press correspondents in these countries were to make sure that the agencies obeyed the terms of the contracts. Jackson doubted the observers' effectiveness, however, commenting, "Such inspection is difficult; it requires a great deal of time and diligence; often misrepresentation is accomplished by selection and emphasis, rather than distortion of facts." Surely, Jackson said, Associated Press leaders must now realize "the Communist agencies operate on the theory that theirs is a propaganda job and a service to the state, and their aim is not the objective presentation of the news which is the goal of the true American newspaper." Consequently, "the ethical question is raised: Should the wire services sell news reports when they know those reports are going to be twisted to misrepresent American life?" The wire service responded by contending that by selling news to the communist agencies, the Associated Press added to the total amount of information available to the people behind the iron curtain—that "by sending the report there is always the chance that some favorable news may trickle through."[37] The chance of news favorable to the United States trickling into Eastern Europe was not sufficient for the State Department, where planners wanted to force a torrent of news over the iron curtain by way of Voice of America transmitters. State Department personnel, led by Benton, were not ready to abandon that plan despite news agency objections.

Proposals and counterproposals flew back and forth during the weeks before the Associated Press meeting in April 1946, but all suggestions to dissolve the impasse called for considerable compromise by the Associated Press. Campaigners for the restoration of Associated Press service to the government information program included *Editor & Publisher*, the newspaper trade publication, which observed that the charge of propaganda would be more likely if a government newscast was "without benefit of all reliable news services than if it does have access to them." Since the press could not eliminate the government news operation, journalists must make the program as good as possible because "a mediocre operation would certainly be suspect around the world."[38]

Formal termination of United Press service to the State Department came on February 16, 1946. The reason for halting the service, which Baillie termed a wartime measure, was the United Press's history of noninvolvement with government news operations. To behave differently now, Baillie explained, would violate almost forty years of agency practice.[39] Positive news for the government information program came from Berkson, general manager of the International News Service, who pledged the continued availability of his agency's news on a day-to-day basis until American commercial agencies could compete throughout the world. The State Department, Berkson stressed, must never doubt that the news services' ultimate goal was free international competition, but temporary postwar conditions impeded rapid movement in that direction. Despite the current physical and political problems hindering worldwide activity by press associations, Berkson found "a real receptivity among all freedom-loving peoples throughout the world for the impartial and unbiased news services developed by the three great American press associations." The reliability of American news was the foundation of this trust. "Anything which would cast a shadow of doubt across the path of objectivity followed by the press associations might destroy or weaken that receptivity." Thus, although the government needed to transmit news to some areas of the world now, the government must abandon its information program as quickly as possible and leave the work to the private agencies. In fact, Berkson said, if the government established the necessary physical facilities to send news into the remote sections of the world, the government should then make that equipment available for press association use in order to speedily return international news dissemination to the private sector.[40]

Everything that Berkson said was true, but his letter to Benton omitted an important fact about commercial news agency operation. To stay in business, a commercial agency had to break even financially, if not make a profit. Providing news to many of the remoter areas of the world was a losing proposition financially. Most likely, the fiscal realities would never change because the volume of business necessary to make money simply was unavailable from these regions of the globe. Only the federal government could withstand the losses connected with providing news to these areas of the world and still stay in business. In light of financial realities, some individuals seeking to promote commercial news agency service throughout the world suggested that the government might subsidize the highly independent press agencies' efforts to serve important areas of the world.[41] The impracticality of a subsidy was so blatant that the notion never got beyond the suggestion stage.[42] Another point Berkson omitted was the existence of governmental barriers to expansion by American news agencies. For instance, when the Russian government forbade American agencies to sell their product in the Soviet Union, the only way left for Soviet citizens to receive unexpurgated information about America was via shortwave radio. Finally, the INS chief overlooked one other important issue that had already surfaced in this debate. The quality of news about America sent abroad by the United States' commercial news agencies was far too unrepresentative, shallow, and sensational to suit the planners of the government information program. This deficiency forced departmental planners to supplement news of America sent overseas by commercial news organizations.

Benton was too busy trying to clarify major misconceptions about the government's program to argue about some of these issues. His main difficulty centered on the news organizations' perception of the government information program as a news service that competed with the private agencies. " 'News distribution' or 'news service' connotes the delivery of news to intermediates for publication in their own papers or on their own radio stations," Benton wrote former United Press chief Karl Bickel. Although 15 to 20 percent of the total shortwave government programming consisted of spot news and although the newscasts definitely published the news, the transmission did not technically distribute the news, Benton argued. "This isn't an exercise in semantics; for applying these words to our news broadcasts at once raises the bogey of government competition with private enterprise, and that muddies up the thinking of a lot of commentators."[43]

He pursued the same point with Howard: "Certainly, the furnishing of background information about our system of electing to public office, or about rural education, soil erosion, public health or other phases of American life cannot be considered 'news dissemination' just because it is made available to newspaper and magazine feature writers and editorial writers." The distribution of full texts of official statements and documents might be news dissemination, Benton admitted, "but we have to undertake this activity only because the press associations have not in the past considered them newsworthy enough to carry in full."[44] Benton dismissed charges that governmental shortwave newscasts would diminish the value of the news agencies' product on the foreign market, reminding newspaper publishers that their previous fears that news broadcast over the radio would adversely affect newspaper circulations had been proven groundless. Instead, "a news story on the air sharpens the listener's interest in reading about it in his newspaper. There is no reason why the foreign shortwave listener should react differently."[45]

Arguing with increasing stridency, Benton pictured Associated Press leaders as mired in the past and as unable to recognize that "the task of informing the world about the United States is not only a matter of expansion of an existing business. It is an entirely new job, needing an entirely new viewpoint which involves deep and sympathetic understanding of the direct relation of such work to the cause of peace."[46] In an attempt to emphasize the predicament that the wire services' actions had created for the government information program, Benton painted a bleak picture of the international information scene. Information distribution by foreign governments was a fact of postwar life. That fact forced the United States government to tell America's story in conjunction with the commercial news services or, if forced to withdraw from the field, to let other nations tell America's story. No third alternative existed. Withdrawal from the information scene, Benton told the American Society of Newspaper Editors, would be similar to unilateral military disarmament and was totally unacceptable. Given the current situation, the United States had a unique opportunity to "set the worldwide standards of honesty and impartiality in the dissemination of the needed information by governments." But now State Department personnel must design an information program capable of winning the support of the all-important wire services. To achieve this end, Benton asked the ASNE to appoint a special committee to investigate the information program in order to determine whether the program constituted the danger that the wire services' executives feared.[47]

Benton won an ASNE committee investigation—after organization members engaged in a long and heated debate over the correctness of both the State Department and the wire services' positions.[48] He also won an unflagging defense of the Associated Press's stance and a rousing attack on the subversive nature of the goverment's demands on the news agency from Cooper during the news cooperative's annual meeting. The Associated Press, Cooper maintained, had not acted precipitously in withdrawing its news service from the government. The agreement with the government called for the news agency to provide news until the war's end; the Associated Press exceeded those requirements by extending the service until mid-January 1945. What the Associated Press refused to do was to indefinitely continue providing news until Congress authorized the planned government information agency. Cooper countered charges that the Associated Press served other governments and government-related news organizations while refusing to help its own government by noting that the agency sold its news services to such foreign organizations "for information only but not for use in propaganda."[49]

Addressing questions raised about the Tass contract in particular, Cooper said that agreement "specifically bars Tass from retransmitting AP news outside of Russia. AP news therefore is not involved in Russian international propaganda." Other government-related agencies overseas did purchase Associated Press news, but such connections with government-run media were not the Associated Press's fault. If the world was not dominated by state-controlled broadcasting operations and other news operations, the number of government-related customers would not be so high. News sold to these foreign outlets was for domestic use only, with an added contractual restriction requiring that the Associated Press news file be used only in the native language of the particular country in which the purchasing agency was headquartered. Despite its connections with government-controlled operations abroad, Cooper contended that Associated Press compliance with the government's request to use its news for international broadcasts would "make more difficult or disrupt the efforts of the Associated Press in its exchange of news on a world basis." Newspapers in foreign lands would refuse to purchase news from agencies "which cooperate with any government in disseminating propaganda." If the Associated Press cooperated with the State Department, Cooper believed that the news agency would ultimately have to ask the American government to make up the difference between the agency's income received while serving the United States government and what that income would have been had the agency been able to compete freely on the international market without any such encumbrances. If the American government made those substantial payments, the government would, in the process, become "the heaviest financial backer of the news organization." Thus, the Associated Press would become a kept organization, in the manner of the European agencies before World War II.[50]

Benton, of course, denied any nefarious motivations and contended that he had entered the department "in a role where I could be potentially helpful to the cause of promoting worldwide freedom of the press which has been so eloquently advocated by Mr. Cooper." Rather than receiving any help on the controversial issues that necessarily impinged on that topic, Benton found his motives questioned and the government's international information program, which he considered vital to world peace and mutual understanding, endangered. Pointed suggestions from Cooper that the government could better occupy its time by reducing the costs of international news transmission showed Cooper's basic lack of knowledge about governmental accomplishments thus far. Decisions conceived in such ignorance substantially affected the information program and other State Department efforts, Benton said, simply because of the prestige of the Associated Press. Because of the organization's reputation, the Associated Press ought to be more careful in making judgments.[51] Such charges and countercharges characterized the relationship between Benton and the Associated Press hierarchy for the remainder of his term. The rhetoric escalated, but the dispute came no closer to settlement before Benton left office.

One reason for Benton's repeated efforts to settle the Associated Press matter in favor of the State Department's position was the impact that the controversy had on plans to create the Office of International Information and Cultural Affairs. For example, withdrawal of Associated Press and United Press news files from the information program delayed congressional action on the legislation because of possibly higher costs involved if the government itself had to gather news for transmission.[52] The announcement that International News Service and Reuters promised to provide news for

State Department use quieted that fear among congressmen and pushed the information program proposal along toward a vote.[53] While Benton was trying to secure a steady flow of news for international broadcasting, he also was trying to establish a permanent framework for such transmissions. For once, eager representatives of American private enterprise seeking to expand into overseas markets failed to greet him. In fact, the seven United States firms involved in international shortwave broadcasting before or during the war all declared that international programming was commercially unfeasible for private enterprise after the war,[54] much to the dismay of the trade publication *Broadcasting*, which considered the stance traitorous to "a free American Plan radio system."[55]

ASNE BACKS GOVERNMENT INFORMATION PROGRAM

The State Department's plans for international news broadcasts soon won powerful support within the press community, as the American Society of Newspaper Editors committee, chaired by N. R. Howard, editor of the *Cleveland News* and first vice president of the society, reported that committee members had approved the United States government's plans to tell the country's story throughout the world. The ASNE committee findings rested on extensive meetings with State Department representatives and press groups, including wire service leaders. In an early session, Benton made a controversial request when he asked the committee not to use the word propaganda when referring to the government's program unless committee members "discovered distortion, untruth, or hidden purpose in the activity." Benton based his request on his belief that the term propaganda had an "evil connotation resting on the will to distort, mislead, or hide the objective truth." When committee investigations did not reveal such problems in the information program, members reported that they were inclined to grant Benton's request although some media representatives interviewed by the committee strongly disagreed with Benton's interpretation.[56]

At the time of the ASNE investigation, the State Department information program employed 1,276 persons in the United States and 1,895 persons abroad; 372 of the latter employees were Americans. The main news-related operations were: transmission of short newscasts over the Voice of America; distribution of background information, texts of speeches, and similar materials through embassy and consular staffs; and circulation of the wireless news bulletin sent to foreign outposts for the information of staff members. Some of the latter publications saw limited distribution among foreign press representatives as well. News items for the broadcasts came from data originated by New York and Washington, D.C., newspapers, from news services such as International News Service, Reuters, and Aneta, and from information prepared by government departments. Programming also included excerpts from editorials taken from newspapers and magazines around the country.[57]

News agency executives disputed government claims about the effectiveness of the information program and raised familiar arguments about the audience's "normal distrust of governmentally-disseminated and branded information." In response, government personnel reiterated the equally familiar argument about commercial news agencies ignoring vast portions of the world. Of necessity, State Department personnel said, "the private news flow must be miscellaneous and without national purpose" and, thus, "may accomplish 'disservice' to the American interests without fully realizing it." Supporting the government's claims about the effectiveness of OIC programming was an informal survey conducted by INS General Manager Berkson. In the opinion of Berkson's correspondents in Berlin, Frankfurt, Vienna, Madrid, and Rome, "large numbers in those countries listened to the Voice of America broadcasts with some regularity," although with "some evidences of listener skepticism and governmental irritation (notably in Spain)."[58]

A collection of comments from government overseas outposts about the suitability of news agency copy revealed two major complaints. In the opinion of diplomats, the commercial news services did not present foreign audiences with a clear picture of the American way of life. Nor did the commercial services carry enough textual material to present the official American position on important issues to foreign peoples. The news agencies responded that American newspapers undoubtedly did not offer very clear accounts of the life-styles of the British, Chinese, or Russians and "hardly considered it their function" to do so. News agencies did not exist to provide complete texts of official statements, for, as their leaders said, they found little use of such reports that had been carried in other countries, "indicating no great interest by press and broadcasters there." OIC representatives showed little inclination to reopen the Associated Press–United Press controversy, telling the ASNE committee that the government "operation has survived the loss." Associated Press and United Press leaders, however, still were fighting the battle because they feared any government news dissemination would be "regarded by peoples of the world as propaganda in its full cynical form." ASNE committee members found that press association leaders were "equally positive that the tested trust of people everywhere in the factual integrity and lack of nationalistic purpose of the private American press service gives these the only and the traditional opportunity to set the U.S. squarely, with rugged objectivity, before the rest of the world."[59]

Showing surprising insensitivity to the magnitude of the growing problems with the Soviet Union and the impending cold war, Cooper appealed to the ASNE committee to "keep the AP out of world politics as it has been kept out of national politics." If the ASNE committee did that, "the AP's strength will defend us all. Don't drag the AP into any contest between this country and Russia." Cooper added that he believed that some day the Russian people would demand unbiased news from private agencies. The press associations did not present a united front to the ASNE committee, though. Berkson, whose agency was supplying the government information program with news subject to a thirty-day cancellation clause, took the position that soon dominated press circles, noting that his agency found "some merit in considering the emergency confronting the U.S. government and in recognizing that it may have special needs of a temporary emergency nature which we have a moral obligation to meet." Ultimately, the ASNE committee decided that "honest differences of opinion existed among the news agencies," and members found no basis to criticize anyone for a position in which he or she truly believed.[60]

The committee as a whole backed the State Department's information program, concluding that "the present uncertainties in international relations justify an effort by the United States government to make its activities and its policies clear to the people of the world through the agency set up in the State Department." Committee members also recognized "the dangers inherent in government dissemination of news" and suggested that the ASNE review the program periodically. Supporting the government's position was not easy for the committee, as Oveta Culp Hobby, executive editor of the *Houston Post*, explained:

> I cannot recall a problem about which I have had as many conflicting responses . . . I am compelled to the conclusion that words are weapons in the contest of ideologies. . . . I have arrived at the conclusion that we must use the potentially powerful supplement of self-portrayal and interpretation. I abhor the necessity for it and despise the doing, but if such a program can be effective—or even partly so—it may be a partial peace insurance.[61]

The idea of words serving as a weapon in the cold war of ideologies rapidly won adherents.

Mrs. Hobby's comments were included in the ASNE committee report in December 1946—just about the time that Richard Finnegan was working on his draft treaty on international freedom of the press. The juxtaposition of events led to a challenging question: If words were weapons in a war of ideologies, could any government allow complete freedom of expression? For the moment, the relationship between the government information program and the continuation of the free-press crusade was obscured. Benton, who had asked for the ASNE study as a calculated risk, expressed delight over the committee report. He believed that committee members had sought the program's vulnerable points and had subjected it to "aggressive criticism"[62] and that their report might have destroyed departmental plans completely. Fortunately, Benton's gamble paid off. He later admitted that "the unexpected and surprisingly favorable ASNE report" changed national press attitude toward the information program and helped push OIC legislation through Congress.[63]

KENT COOPER CONTINUES TO BATTLE
THE INFORMATION PROGRAM

The battle over American government involvement in a propaganda campaign, however, was far from over. Cooper continued to throw every possible roadblock in the program's way. He tried, for instance, to stop a State Department survey of the use of United States news agency material by newspapers abroad. The department had asked the news agencies for the information directly, but the Associated Press and the United Press had refused to answer the request. When no information was forthcoming, the department sought the data from United States diplomatic posts abroad. Cooper intemperately demanded the immediate recall of the survey, but Associated Press board chairman McLean forced him to back down.[64] The survey was not being conducted with ulterior motives, Benton maintained. The department's main goal was to ensure that the government's information effort did not compete with commercial agency contracts already in place.[65]

Cooper's repeated charges that the OIC was engaging in international propaganda attracted the attention of departmental planners, who suggested that Benton publicly agree with Cooper that "international propaganda is a bad thing," especially the kind of propaganda "now being vigorously practised against the U.S." In fact, Benton should say that the United States wanted to eliminate all propaganda, "just as it wants to eliminate war as an instrument of national policy." But just as America had to maintain its military force "until other nations agree to eliminate theirs and to renounce war," the United States had to "rely on governmental information activities to combat political warfare in the form of international propaganda now being carried on against it." In addition, Benton should stress that his statement was made "on the assumption that truth will win in the end, if truth can be heard (which is where the Department's freedom of information campaign comes in)." If private agencies "would and could" provide the necessary information to the world, the government would abandon its project; the agencies, however, had proven themselves unable to do the necessary job. Consequently, the government's activities were essential and did not "constitute 'international propaganda' but rather the shield of truth against the poisoned spear of international propaganda and 'international libel.'"[66] Cooper probably lacked total support from his board of directors in his campaign to kill the international information program, State Department officials counseled Benton. His forced retreat from protesting the department's collection of information about wire service contracts abroad stood as proof of the possible division within the Associated Press. Because of the conceivable schism, Benton should try to separate criticism of Cooper as an individual from criticism of the Associated Press as an organization, thus trying to "drive a further wedge between Cooper and the ASNE."[67]

Although an opportunity to act on departmental suggestions did not arise, Cooper and Benton engaged in verbal combat once more in 1947. Again, the Associated Press executive took the initiative, this time as Cooper addressed the Inland Daily Press Association in Chicago. Congress had just authorized "dissemination of propaganda disguised as news" and established a government news agency for that purpose, Cooper disdainfully told his audience. Although American commercial news agencies did not view the government agency as a competitor, Cooper saw the State Department program as injuring the news agencies "in a presently nebulous sort of way. For the American press is unanimously sponsoring world-wide news exchange through each of its news agencies. To gain support of its proposal the government propaganda department publicly charged that it was necessary for it to disseminate news because of deficiencies in the scope of the news agencies' activities."[68] How could the agencies hope to fulfill their free-press goals if tagged with such a label?

The only way to promote international freedom of the press and international understanding among nations, Cooper maintained, was through a free, nongovernmental exchange of news. Yet, the American government wanted to retrogress, to try governmental propaganda, a form of information dissemination so fully discredited in recent years. The avowed goal of the State Department's program was to save the Soviet people and the world from communism, Cooper said, yet "in all the history of foreign propaganda, there is no record that any people at any time ever overthrew their government because foreign propaganda against their leaders was fed them." Official State Department rationale for the information program emphasized the need for American transmissions to counter Russian propaganda efforts. Suggestions that Americans must copy the Soviets in anything astonished Cooper, who added that propaganda repeatedly had shown itself as unsuccessful. He saw no need to continue this disastrous course when, for the first time, the alternative of the free competition for news existed.[69]

Focusing only on his criticisms of the State Department information program, Cooper again neglected to mention the department's role in advocating the international freedom of the press so ardently sought by the press associations. Benton quickly brought this omission to the attention of the American media. The government's work in the area of international freedom of the press "has received little public recognition or discussion," but "at no previous time has the United States undertaken so vigorous an effort in behalf of international freedom of information as it has begun in recent months." As proof of the department's good-faith efforts in this area, Benton pointed to work at the United Nations and UNESCO and to attempts to draft bilateral treaties guaranteeing freedom of information. Benton shared Cooper's "millennial hope" for international freedom of the press, but he thought the Associated Press chief must face the facts of life. "We would be less than candid with ourselves—indeed we would be living in a world of gossamer dreams—if either of us felt we had progressed very far toward our goal." Actually, "the world is in worse shape now with respect to freedom of information than it was in 1919" when Cooper made the first appeal for action. Estimates revealed that 75 percent of the world's population was "living today under some degree of censorship. In some important areas this censorship, and the deliberately fostered distortions that accompany it, are more virulent than ever before." Due to this censorship, the United States, Benton continued, was "grossly, shockingly and *dangerously* misunderstood by the peoples of many important countries."[70]

Benton and Cooper agreed that the government should advance international freedom of information and "encourage the activities of private, competitive agencies in the communications field." Their disagreement centered on what other action, if any, was appropriate for the government to take. Benton accused Cooper of desiring a return to the "status quo ante bellum," which Benton considered an unrealistic dream based on an incorrect reading of contemporary events. Benton argued instead that "we should never again be caught so helpless; that the government must act to fill the information gaps that are now so glaring." The government's role was to provide the facts, "openly and candidly and steadily in those areas and via those media not open to private channels or not profitable to them." When the commercial agencies were able to serve a certain area, obviously the government should withdraw from that field, but until that time, government information activities abroad were absolutely essential. Benton accused Cooper of prejudging the information program "by raising associations of dishonesty, malice and evil intent" and, thus, displaying traits that would merit dismissal if they were found in any reporter in Cooper's employ. To disprove charges that the information program was propagandistic, Benton pointed to the ASNE committee report. Benton labeled Cooper's assertion that if the United States abandoned its information program other nations would follow suit as "incredibly unrealistic," asking Cooper if he could "imagine Russia abandoning its propaganda if you are successful in your campaign to kill off the State Department's information activities?" Benton hoped to prove Cooper wrong in his evaluation of the effectiveness of the government's information program as well. If the information program did not "promote the interests of both the United States and the rest of the world," Benton said, "then we are in a very bad way indeed and neither the

Associated Press nor the State Department's information program has much long range reason for existence."[71]

The battle between the Associated Press and the State Department's information program continued, but without Benton, who left office on September 30, 1947. His replacement as assistant secretary of state for public affairs, career diplomat George V. Allen, also wanted news from the Associated Press and the United Press for the government's information program. Stories from the New York newspapers, International News Service, Reuters, Aneta, Transradio, and State Department resources formed the core of the news used in Voice of America broadcasts. Those sources were not enough, however, for without the Associated Press service, many key stories were unavailable, other stories could not be sufficiently verified for use, and feature stories on American life-styles were usually unattainable. Overseas coverage was incomplete as well because information program staff members had to double-check Reuters copy for possible errors and bias and because International News Service coverage, although termed excellent, was limited. The two missing news agencies were the main sources of both spot news from abroad and domestic news for American newspapers, and the United States information program had no access to such stories. Making matters worse, Allen was told by information program staff members that "occasionally we find our rivals in Moscow making good use of AP and UP by selective treatment of stories which we are unable to counter because the AP and UP available to them is not available to us."[72]

Because of these difficulties, Allen wanted to make the connection between press association cooperation with the State Department's information program and the department's international free-press efforts explicit. Despite the information program's being so circumscribed by the news agencies, Allen said, the primary aim of American foreign policy was "the preservation of democracy and the American way of life. This aim includes, notably, preservation of freedom of the press and of the American system of private enterprise and initiative as typified by the AP." Because the information program was "fighting, every day, to preserve and extend the very principles which the Associated Press so excellently exemplifies," Allen thought that the Associated Press should "help in every proper way to make our efforts as effective as possible." In fact, the press association should be part of a State Department team promoting the national welfare, Allen said, noting that the department regularly helped Associated Press employees—a service that would continue "regardless of the decision by the Associated Press to let us have its news." He said he cited examples of State Department assistance to Associated Press employees "merely as evidence of the advantage of cooperation to achieve the ends which both government and private industry so earnestly desire." Despite his pointed words, Allen told Arthur Hays Sulzberger, publisher of The New York Times, that he had "no desire to prolong a controversy in which feelings have unfortunately been exacerbated." But "my duty as a public servant requires me to report my findings in this matter as genuinely and honestly as I can."[73]

ASNE DEBATES FOCUS ON THE WIRE SERVICES' ATTITUDES

Allen took his message to the April 1948 meeting of the American Society of Newspaper Editors,[74] but he was speaking to a group of converts. A report by Hamilton Owens, editor of the *Baltimore Sun* and head of the ASNE committee keeping track of the United States information program in the wake of the Associated Press pullout of 1946, revealed just how strongly the ASNE supported the governmental effort. The information program fell on hard times in 1947, Owens reported, with its budget almost eliminated by Congress, its employees dismissed, its offices closed, and its chief, Benton, resigning. But in 1948, Congress, newly impressed with the need for an information service, passed, almost unanimously, the Smith-Mundt Act, which established an information program operating as the Office of Information and Cultural Exchange (OIE). Because of the growing tenseness in East-West relations, brought on in part by the fall of Czechoslovakia and the Berlin blockade, the government information program needed the news agencies' spot news reports even more now, Owens said. Those countries that generally opposed the United States were "exceedingly adept at twisting the news to serve their own ends. If the Russian broadcasters get the story first, they have time to distort it to suit their own purposes before we can get in with the accurate version. The truth has a hard time catching up with a lie." Consequently, Owens's committee believed that "without any permanent sacrifice of principle ... the press associations can and should put their respective reports at the service of the OIE." Committee members did not suggest a permanent arrangement, "but rather one which will endure as long as the present crisis lasts."[75]

The heated debate over a resolution calling on the wire services to help the information program had a decidedly anti–Associated Press tenor. In fact, the news agency's only real defender was John S. Knight of Knight Newspapers, a past ASNE president, and a member of the Associated Press board of directors. Knight, who stressed that he was speaking as an individual and not as a representative of the news agency, had long opposed the wire services providing copy to the government's information service. He still believed asking "these news services to turn over their full reports which the State Department can use with coloration or shading or in any manner that they see fit" would be a mistake. Instead, Knight sought a compromise that the news cooperative's board might accept. He pledged his support for a motion expressing the hope that the wire services would send factual news summaries to the OIE, which the State Department broadcasters would then label as to their source and use unedited—basically Forrest's proposal of two years earlier. Contending that all governmental transmissions were essentially propaganda, Knight explained that restricted use of wire service news summaries could ensure that the peoples of the world were getting accurate news.[76]

Knight's proposal to send news summaries to the State Department seemed insufficient to Paul Block, Jr., publisher of the *Toledo Blade*, who felt that providing anything less than the full services of the news agencies would impede the government's information efforts. A wide range of wire service news was vital for accurate Voice of America newscasts, said ASNE First Vice President Canham, who had just returned from serving as an American delegate to the United Nations Conference on Freedom of Information in Geneva. Although Canham had once congratulated the Associated Press for its stand on principle in cutting off its news service to the State Department, he now realized that the Voice of America was "regarded as a powerful adversary by the Eastern European countries." Unfortunately, however, the VOA suffered from a "great many factual lapses," due primarily, Canham believed, to an inadequate supply of news. "Personally," he added, "I would like to see the Voice of America have at its disposal the widest possible statement of facts, so that what it disseminates will have the largest probability of containing powerful, effective, impressive, honest information."[77]

The ASNE debate brought out two longtime issues in the argument over using Associated Press copy for government information purposes. First, Knight raised the problem of the news agency's commercial interests by pointing out that in 1947 the cooperative's foreign operations reported a $400,000 deficit. The Associated Press's board of directors was not considering curtailing the overseas operations to balance the budget, but Knight worried lest the State Department's news programming would increase the wire service's deficit by providing news free to persons who would otherwise purchase the service. Second, the quality of Associated Press reports was the concern of Lloyd M. Felmly, editor of the *Newark News*, who described the reaction of an editor visiting from Copenhagen, Denmark, to the variety of news that the wire service provided to an American publication. The news that the Dane reported purchasing from the Associated Press for his newspaper "was awful." The Danish file featured news about Hollywood and sensational divorces—"anything but candid views that the Voice of America wants to furnish on these broadcasts. I think unless we consider that that goes to the substance of the whole argument we are lost. It is a point that the Associated Press has been ducking for a long time."[78]

ASNE members caught up in the heat of debate were cautioned repeatedly to remember, however, that any resolution they adopted probably would have no influence on the leadership of either the Associated

Press or the United Press. Consequently, Oxie Reichler, editor of the *Yonkers Herald-Statesman*, said he thought that debating the issue again was somewhat ridiculous. He added, "It does strike me worthy of thinking at this moment that the United States Government has a right to take my son, but my Associated Press news item cannot be taken." Former ASNE president Forrest agreed on the futility of additional discussion, commenting that he had abstained from debate because, after several years of fighting the same battle, he was tired. ASNE members could not tell the news agencies how to answer the State Department's request; all members could do was to express "a pious wish" that the agencies would cooperate "in the present crisis."[79] The resolution ultimately adopted was a vague expression of hope that the two news services would "furnish factual and adequate news summaries" for use by the State Department's international information program for "as long as the crisis lasts" and "for the purpose of disseminating truth throughout the world."[80] Although disappointed that ASNE members were unwilling to call unequivocally for the Associated Press and United Press to provide the State Department with news, *Editor & Publisher* expressed satisfaction over the editors' finally deciding to tell the news agencies that the "world situation—already growing tense—warranted such measures."[81]

For whatever reason, the Associated Press's denial of its daily news file to the State Department's international information soon was up for discussion again—quietly, within the department and the news cooperative. Cooper and Allen agreed to "avoid any further public airing on this subject and to reach an amicable arrangement," although Allen warned that his tolerance was limited because intense propaganda campaigns against the United States used Associated Press news as their foundations. The British Broadcasting Corporation, Radio Paris, and other national radio operations also based portions of their newscasts on Associated Press dispatches. "To put it flatly, AP news is available to practically every official government information program in the world except the information program of the Government of the United States." American information officers were not even able "to correct misrepresentation of AP news by foreign governments, due to the fact that the AP file is not available to us."[82] Cooper once more disputed the idea that the Associated Press's sale of news to other governments' information outlets was a sufficient reason for the news service to cooperate with the United States government's propaganda program. Agreements with agencies such as Tass were news exchange agreements permitting use of the news only in the native language of the country to which it was sold. "There might be an analogy," he said, "if the State Department asked for availability of Associated Press news in exchange for news (which it does not collect!) for use in the English language only in the United States. Instead of that it asks for it to use in all languages in all international broadcasts, including those in Eastern Europe," where Cooper had just been negotiating contracts.[83]

Cooper, however, was bending a bit. Although Cooper saw "no chance of any agreement for the AP to sell the AP service to the Voice of America on a financial basis," perhaps the Voice of America could use Associated Press news after that news had appeared in New York or other newspapers. Information program personnel could also call the Associated Press for additional information on major stories for broadcasts.[84] Cooper planned to impose no charge for Associated Press copy procured this way, nor did he want the Voice of America to credit the Associated Press as the source of the information. State Department staff members saw this proposal as a breakthrough of sorts. "Acceptance of the proposal would give a good deal more than we have now, allow us to use all facts in AP stories, and be in accord with our present 'Gentleman's' agreement with UP—which would then probably continue indefinitely." Under the proposed arrangement, the Associated Press could continue to develop international markets without being stigmatized for refusing to help the government information program at home or being labeled as a propaganda tool of the government for providing such assistance abroad. "Mr. Cooper believes that they are proposing enough to be of considerable assistance to VOA without being detrimental to AP," staff members concluded. Allen wanted the full Associated Press service with no strings attached, but he agreed to accept "the arrangement suggested and to say nothing about it unless asked."[85]

McLean, president of the news cooperative's board of directors, reiterated the Associated Press's stand when he visited Secretary of State Dean Acheson at the State Department in April 1949. The Associated Press had no objection to departmental use of wire service news after publication, basically meaning after the property right or commercial value had expired. Installation of direct service to the department, however, was impossible. Acheson protested about the several hours' delay in obtaining the news that such an approach entailed, but McLean responded that any other accommodation would "involve the AP in a propaganda operation" and would be highly unacceptable.[86]

The American Society of Newspaper Editors was even less willing to tolerate the Associated Press's attitude in 1949 than at earlier sessions. The impartiality of the wire services was to be greatly cherished, J. Russell Wiggins, managing editor of the *Washington Post* and chairman of the committee on State Department dissemination of news and opinion, told ASNE members, but the State Department's information program was trustworthy. In addition, given the current world situation, there was more reason to take any risks involved. Indeed, if "western civilization is worth a struggle, its wars, either cold or hot, will bring forth honest conscientious objectors, who dislike the measures essential to survival. The hard facts of life, however, coerce most of us into a realist's choice between the lesser and the greater risk." Thus, Wiggins said, the committee was convinced "that it is wiser to give up something of our way of life for a short time than it is to risk giving up all of it for all time."[87] In the resolutions debate, Wiggins favored a motion to recognize that the information program was "an integral part of America's foreign policy, and to let the world and the American people know that this Society is not satisfied with an appeal to the world to support our foreign policy which rests solely upon our economic assets and our national resources and our military power."[88]

Opposing efforts to pressure the news agencies into submission was Ackerman, longtime foe of a State Department information program. The news agencies had a right to refuse to sell their news reports to the government, he argued, and the ASNE should respect the agencies' decisions. Asking editors to coerce the press associations into changing their minds was "the beginning of thought control." The growing antagonism between newspapers and the wire services led Edward Lindsay, editor of the *Decatur* (Illinois) *Herald and Review*, to suggest that the newspapers of the country, as the originators of most of the news transmitted by the news agencies, accept the responsibility of supplying information to the State Department's program rather than hounding the uncooperative news agencies into action. The editors, however, decided to call on "all newspapers and news agencies" to supply the necessary raw materials for dissemination abroad. The decisive argument probably was Wiggins's suggestion that the wire service leaders reexamine their reasons for supplying the Office of War Information with news during World War II. Then, wire service leaders cooperated with the government because they thought the crisis facing the nation was so great "as to make it advisable for the press of America to take any risk of impairment of their absolute independence in the emergency called for." To Wiggins, the present crisis was different "only in degree."[89]

During the ASNE debate, organization president Canham suggested that the impasse between the Associated Press and the United States information program was "gradually working itself out" and that "an informal working arrangement" existed among the parties. He implied that the situation, if left alone, would resolve itself.[90] Apparently this informal resolution occurred, for the conflict between the State Department and the two news agencies disappeared from view as the dangers posed by the cold war became more apparent. Indicators of cold war problems had been building over the years. Winston Churchill had proclaimed that an iron curtain was falling over Eastern Europe in March 1946. President Truman had announced his Truman Doctrine, designed to prevent a communist takeover of Greece and Turkey, in March 1947. George F. Kennan had enunciated his proposal for the containment of communism in July 1947. Final congressional authorization for the European Recovery Program, popularly known as the Marshall Plan, had come in spring 1948. And actions by the Soviets in early 1948 had set the stage for the Berlin blockade.

Cooper fought his battle against the United States information program with these events as a background. During late 1947 and early 1948, for instance, proponents of the information program testifying on Capitol Hill included Secretary of State George C. Marshall, General Dwight D. Eisenhower, and General Walter Bedell Smith, who was American ambassador in the Soviet Union. In opposition, said one contemporary observer, "was chiefly Kent Cooper, who now seemed to want free world news only for the press associations, and a hard-shell congressional opposition."[91] For his part, Cooper maintained that the prevalence of military men in high policy-making positions denied him the opportunity to fight the information program adequately. "The army always had considered war propaganda a prime necessity in an over-all military campaign," Cooper said, "so the hand of the military was exerted in peacetime to establish propaganda for a peacetime type of psychological warfare."[92] Regardless of Cooper's beliefs about the influence of the military in creating the information program, the rush of current events was the determining factor. Coinciding with these events, the Soviets launched a virulent anti-American propaganda campaign on several fronts, virtually ensuring the passage of the United States government's information program.

Consequently, Americans recognized, for the first time in the country's history, that a peacetime propaganda operation was absolutely essential. Gone were Benton's pious requests of the ASNE investigating team in 1946 that they not label his information campaign as propaganda unless committee members found something deceitful within the program. By 1948, everyone knew that the State Department wanted to engage in propaganda, and the term was dealt with openly. After the start of the United Nations police action in Korea in 1950, State Department planners conceded that the original intention of the information program—that of putting "a full and fair picture of America" before the world—was simply no longer adequate. Instead, the government's campaign was seen as moving away from the factual description of the nation to focusing more on "the exposition of what America stands for and the assurance to our allies of American strength and determination."[93] Americans had taken a major step since the closing days of World War II when many observers saw in their fellow countrymen a peculiar allergy to propaganda. This reaction led to rapid and unwise dissolution of wartime information programs, thus wasting the resources and techniques developed during World War II for telling other nations about the United States.[94]

Although some scholars had argued that America was built on propaganda ranging from the Declaration of Independence,[95] to the spreading of American religion and free enterprise around the world, to the ever-present advertisement, American experiences with government propaganda in the twentieth century were uniformly unhappy. George Creel and his Committee on Public Information built a strong case for defeating the Germans in World War I, but he established no foundation for keeping the United States in world affairs to help build the peace. Similarly, Elmer Davis and the

Office of War Information functioned during World War II under a cloud of mistrust and suspicion. The American problem with propaganda rested

> in the democratic thesis ... [that] facts provide the basis for free judgment and decision; "propaganda" betrays the democratic principle. The latter has no essential preoccupation with truth; it is the guerrilla warfare of communication, it creeps up on your blind side saying one thing and meaning another; clothed in friendliness and good intentions like a bad fairy, it seduces you into taking a bite from the beautiful poisoned apple. In a world in which propaganda has increasingly overshadowed diplomacy as an instrument for influencing the course of international events, Americans remain uneasy in making concessions to its use, even as an instrument of defense. Indeed, it is possible that more Americans approve of the use of the atom bomb in defensive warfare than approve the use of propaganda to forestall war.[96]

Many people, including numerous journalists, however, recognized the difference between good American propaganda designed to promote "a way of life that we consider good" and bad propaganda,[97] or psychological warfare, which, according to one practitioner, attacked the enemy's morale, leading to his early surrender and thus saving American lives.[98] To circumvent the American aversion to bad or black propaganda, some advocates of good or white propaganda proposed international agreements that would forbid "psychological aggressions." Under these accords, nations would agree to outlaw certain practices including attempts to discredit other nations in the eyes of their people; attempts to create divisions among the peoples of signatory nations; attempts to discredit "the structure and philosophy of government, or the social or economic way of life of the people of any other signatory nation"; or attempts to create "prejudice, hate and discrimination ... against any racial, social, economic, political or religious group anywhere in the world."[99]

American acceptance of propaganda measures grew in direct proportion to increased Soviet attempts to win the so-called war of words in Europe and elsewhere and in geometric proportion to American fears of the spread of communism. Soon Americans believed that, since public opinion was "a powerful instrument of national policy," the United States must mold public opinion abroad effectively. As Lester Markel, Sunday editor of *The New York Times*, explained, European communists saw the United States "as a hotbed of reaction and capitalist exploitation." Even within democratic circles, "the pre-war caricature of Americans persists—a portrait of a naive, aggressive and vulgar people." Although the United States was preferred throughout Western Europe, the choice was negative, "resting more on fear of Russian Communism than on admiration and respect for the American way of life." Markel firmly believed that Americans must see the propaganda task ahead as one of selling the goodness of the United States to the rest of the world: "For what is advertising but propaganda intended to win friends and influence people to buy a particular product?" No longer could Americans self-righteously hold themselves above the propaganda fray, Markel contended, adding, of course, that American propaganda would be truthful because false propaganda was doomed to failure.[100]

SOVIETS LAUNCH AN ANTIWARMONGERING CAMPAIGN AT THE UNITED NATIONS

Helping American journalists accept the notion that a United States propaganda program was essential was the Soviets' decision to make a frontal attack on the American press a key part of their anti-American propaganda campaign. This effort to discredit the American press eventually appeared at the United Nations, where the Russians promoted resolutions condemning warmongering and the spreading of false information by various media of information, particularly certain American publications. The campaign coincided, in part, with other Soviet actions against American reporters such as the institution of Glavlit censorship rules, the cessation of voice broadcasting from Moscow by American radio correspondents, and the attempts to limit the number of American correspondents covering the Council of Foreign Ministers meeting in Moscow in early 1947.[101]

Soviet journalists and lecturers attacked the capitalist press with vigor, spurred on by the American campaign to open the world to the prying eyes of Western reporters and by growing American propaganda efforts aimed at Eastern bloc nations. The campaign had multiple purposes, for the Russians were attempting to discredit news from Western sources and to justify the barriers that they had erected to full coverage of events by Western correspondents. For instance, readers of *Pravda* were told that news from the West could not be trusted because highly paid journalists in those countries "voluntarily distorted the facts, lied, and slandered" at the behest of "capitalist publishers and monopolists." Despite this background, *Pravda* complained, these same Americans had the gall to campaign for international freedom of the press, under the cover of which they were actually launching "an unbridled campaign" against the Soviet press, which was the only really free press in the world.[102]

The Russian people should not be deceived, one lecturer said, because America's vaunted freedom of the press was nonexistent—at least for the common man. Referring to the costs of starting a newspaper in the United States, the lecturer proclaimed, "even Americans say that no one can start to publish a paper unless he has 15 to 20 million dollars in the bank." Thus, "the great majority of newspapers belong to a few large owners such as Hearst, Patterson, McCormick." Because so few people owned American

newspapers and because the individuals who did own ou:lets had firm
opinions about the structure of the world, the American press served as "an
industrial enterprise for the manufacture of public opinion." Even if
American journalists escaped the pressure to shape public opinion to suit the
needs of their employers, the reporters' work was still not morally up-
lifting because of the "pursuit of sensationalism" inherent in American
journalism.[103]

Compounding lectures and newspaper and magazine articles were
highly publicized performances of a play, "The Russian Question" by
Konstantin Simonov, which depicted the dilemma of an American reporter
who wanted to write fair stories about the Soviet Union for his newspaper in
the United States. This "smear campaign" obviously was designed to
discredit the American press, and American diplomats stationed in Moscow
had little hope of the attacks ending soon.[104] The Russians thought that
their attitude toward the American press was highly reasonable. After all, "a
part of the American correspondents have an ill mood toward us," Prime
Minister Joseph Stalin explained, pointing to an error in a dispatch from
Russia by an American correspondent. How could he possibly trust
American correspondents when they sent false news items back to the
United States?[105] Had the Russians not tried to be conciliatory to the
American correspondents at the Council of Foreign Ministers meeting in
Moscow? But those efforts had failed. Journalists in Moscow for the sessions
had sufficient opportunities to report the council debate "truthfully and
fully," but many correspondents used these opportunities to portray the
session "in tendentiously murky light" by purposely distorting information
and "by representing matters as if Soviet Union were responsible for all
difficulties and failures." To the Soviets, such "poisoning of international
atmosphere, dissemination of suspicion and hatred among peoples, spreading of pernicious slander and incitement to war" were among the "most
treacherous attacks upon humanity." These perversions of the truth deserved to be discussed at the United Nations, and the Soviets intended to
ensure that the issue was fully aired before the international organization.[106]

Soviet complaints against the American press rested on the assumption
that capitalism alone corrupted the press's coverage of the Soviet Union. The
Russians paid little or no attention to a possible connection between press
coverage of events and planning by the United States government. Although
no evidence seems to exist to indicate such an actual connection, State
Department personnel did discuss the possibility of using the American
press to advance certain diplomatic goals during these years. For instance,
Elbridge Durbrow, chargé in the Soviet Union, suggested that the State
Department translate Russian newspaper and magazine articles for distribution to the American media so that the press could present an accurate
picture of Soviet life to its readers. Such a program also should remind the
press of past Soviet actions that might have been forgotten. One reason for

this endeavor, according to Durbrow, was that, at times, the American press missed the significance of certain events in the Soviet Union. With the proper guidance, American journalists would overlook fewer opportunities to explain the "realities of Soviet life, past and future policies, aims and tactics." With information about the Russians reported objectively, American public reaction to Soviet policies and tactics should be "less subject to propaganda influences and emotional extremes."[107]

American diplomats also were willing to suggest that correspondents discreetly contact exiled Eastern Europeans whose stories might be helpful to American interests and detrimental to those of the Soviets. The case of one Hungarian refugee highlighted the connection between the American media, State Department policy, and the government information program. In this instance, the American Legation in Vienna, Austria, was told that an interview with this individual was "of great potential usefulness" for the department's information program—"if it could be picked up from US press within next 10 days." The legation was to arrange the contact with an appropriate journalist so that the story could be written, printed, and thus be made available for use over the Voice of America.[108] Conversely, diplomats complained that available commentary from United States media often hurt the American propaganda effort. For example, during the Berlin crisis, diplomats wanted "commentators, who tend to cries of alarm, handwringing jitters, or to giving the impression that all is confusion here in Washington" to calm down. If "more assured and confident material" was available in the domestic press and on the radio, that copy "could be directly picked up for our use abroad." But hysterical commentary was definitely of no use.[109]

The Soviets preferred to concentrate on the alleged efforts of the American government to provoke a new war and United States media encouragement of such attempts. The Russians saw incitements to war in American support of noncommunist forces in Greece, Turkey, and China, in escalating calls for the United States to remain militarily alert, and in the beginnings of the Western alliance system. Growing increasingly fearful, the Russians took their complaints to the United Nations, where Soviet efforts to win United Nations denunciation of international warmongering began in the fall of 1947 when Soviet Deputy Foreign Minister Andrei Y. Vishinsky asked the General Assembly to condemn "the ever-increasing propaganda for a new war" that was appearing in certain countries. The Soviet Union was particularly concerned about warmongering within the United States because the American press and the presses of its allies, such as Turkey, had been waging "a furious campaign designed to prepare world public opinion for a new war." The campaign used newspaper, magazines, radio, and motion pictures to justify an armaments race and the "expansionist schemes" of the United States. The problems that this campaign posed for the Soviet Union were tremendous, Vishinsky explained, as newspapers and magazines "cry day after day in every possible key about a new war and systematically pursue this baneful psychological campaign to mould the public opinion of their countries." War publicists in America claimed only to be protecting the United States from the predatory aims of the Soviet Union, Vishinsky said, but his country was far too busy "devoting its energies to rehabilitating the regions ravaged and devastated by war, to the restoration and further development of its national economy" to plan another war.[110]

Not only was the American military and industrial machine conspiring against the Soviet Union, so, too, Vishinsky said, was the American press. The entire press, "at the behest of its masters, is agitating fiercely in favour of launching a new war, is disseminating all manner of insinuations and falsehoods appropriately devised to arouse hatred of the Soviet Union and other new democratic eastern European nations." Publications such as the *New York Herald Tribune* and "several other similar organs, principally of the Hearst Press, systematically reproduce all kinds of provocative articles, and drum into the minds of their readers the necessity 'of military action if Europe collapses or if it falls under the control of the Soviet Union.'" Despite the concerted efforts of the American press, Vishinsky said he believed that the American people were opposed to a new war. The American people, however, had no way to counter such scurrilous commentary. Because of these blatant efforts by and in the United States to violate the peace, Vishinsky sought a United Nations resolution that would condemn "criminal propaganda for a new war, carried on by reactionary circles in a number of countries and, in particular, in the United States of America, Turkey and Greece, by the dissemination of all types of fabrications through the Press, radio, cinema, and public speeches, containing open appeals for aggression against the peace-loving democratic countries." The Soviets wanted the United Nations to label this propaganda as a violation of the organization's charter and to call on all member nations to "prohibit, on pain of criminal penalties, the carrying on of war propaganda in any form, and to take measures with a view to the prevention and suppression of war propaganda as anti-social activity endangering the vital interests and well-being of the peace-loving nations."[111]

United States Ambassador to the United Nations Warren R. Austin replied that the Soviet proposal, far from seeking to advance the well-being of peace-loving nations, sought to impose suppression and censorship on the world. He urged that the United Nations reject the resolution outright. The resolution diverted attention from the real causes of war and sought to restrict freedom of speech, which was one of the fundamental freedoms protected by the United Nations Charter. The resolution was particularly offensive to Americans, who considered freedom of speech "as the sill under the whole house without which the house would fall." The Soviet resolution, if passed, "would put shackles on the brain of man as well as a gag in his mouth," Austin proclaimed. In addition, the ambassador said that the

Soviet representative had misread American public opinion. Granted, some Americans did speak as Vishinsky reported but "to present such artificially selected items as a genuine criterion of public opinion, particularly when they represent, not the utterances of a responsible government, but one of a small minority in a community where the vast majority are against war" was "distorted and misleading."[112]

Protecting the rights of that minority to speak was a primary goal of the United Nations, Austin maintained, for "only if all sides of the great issues can be heard and freely discussed can we hope to crystallize and organize public opinion into positive action here in the United Nations." Austin made no attempt to deny the existence of international problems: "Intemperate talk and provocative expression on all sides point to causes, deep-seated and significant. To attempt to suppress talk reflecting this anxiety is futile. Talk is a symptom. We must get at the causes, such as distress, despair, hunger, and ill health." Never, however, would the United States consider the cause of unrest to be either freedom of speech or freedom of the press, and America opposed all efforts to curtail these freedoms on the mistaken grounds that to do so would cool the world's tensions.[113]

As the debate over warmongering proceeded, a representative from Yugoslavia, Vladislav Ribnikar, introduced a companion measure to prevent the dissemination of false statements harmful to good relations among nations. The modern information media, which tended to abuse their freedom rather than use it to promote peace, were the targets of the Yugoslav resolution. In fact, Ribnikar charged that "a tendentious Press was dividing the world of today into several camps and attempting to raise insuperable barriers between the new popular democracies and the rest of the world." He further alleged that this press was responsible for erecting what was popularly termed the iron curtain to separate Russia from the rest of the world. Even though he advocated United Nations action against press organs spreading false reports, the Yugoslav stressed that he was not suggesting the establishment of international censorship. Rather, Ribnikar sought to hold persons responsible for statements that "might be harmful to good relations between the nations and which might constitute incitement to war."[114]

The United States had opposed similar proposals years earlier during League of Nations debates, and American opposition continued at all levels of the United Nations. After years of fighting efforts to define and punish false news dissemination, the American delegation refused to accept any proposal to limit freedom of discussion now, Eleanor Roosevelt told the General Assembly's Third Committee. "Admittedly things were sometimes said by certain persons in the United States which would have been better left unsaid," but abuse was inevitable in a country that guaranteed 140 million people the constitutional right of freedom of speech.[115] Speaking perhaps from the experience gained during her husband's White House years, Mrs. Roosevelt added that even she could not defend everything various American press outlets said: "However, much as I hate what some of our press has said in the past at times, I would defend their right to say it. And I would feel that it was up to the people to choose between different views. The right of people to speak is essential."[116]

Governments could handle media representatives who made such extreme comments in two ways, Mrs. Roosevelt said—"one being to imprison them and the other to discuss matters with them freely and bring them to a more sensible way of thinking." The United States preferred the second approach, a choice that nations having a "system of total control of the organs of public opinion might find it difficult to understand." Despite American traditions of freedom of speech, the United States found the Yugoslav proposal interesting, Mrs. Roosevelt said, because certain countries in the world were "conducting a campaign of systematic disparagement against the United States and other democratic nations having the same fundamental beliefs." Americans "did not mind being criticized for everybody had the right to criticize and every Government was subject to criticism," but Americans disliked incorrect criticism. "Peoples reading only a controlled Press were kept in systematic ignorance of the truth," she said. "It was in such ignorance that the threat to international peace and security really lay."[117] Consequently, the United States opposed the false-news resolution.

Many members of the United Nations had problems rejecting the Yugoslav proposal outright, though. The resolution was so artfully phrased that many European delegates, fresh from the trauma of war and propaganda accompanying that experience, had to accept its basic premise. As Raymond Offroy of France perceptively explained, disapproval of the resolution "might be construed by the public as indicating total indifference on the part of the United Nations, or as a refusal to face the problem." Offroy, in acknowledging "that the principle of responsibility was an essential corollary to that of liberty," voiced a point of view that gained favor among United Nations delegates over the years. In this particular debate, because delegates could not agree on a definition of false news, Offroy suggested referring the matter to the upcoming United Nations Conference on Freedom of Information. At that conference, the topic could be considered in conjunction with a French proposal calling for the creation of a mandatory right of reply designed to allow nations wronged in the press of other nations to rebut misinformation.[118]

Debate over the Yugoslav resolution to restrict the dissemination of false news foreshadowed future United Nations debates over the freedom of the press on the one hand and the responsibility of the press on the other. The United States remained a staunch supporter of freedom of the press without any imposed standard of responsibility, but other nations found the idea that freedom of the press forced certain affirmative responsibilities on journalists attractive. The Russian delegation was, of course, at the forefront of those nations advocating the creation of responsibilities for journalists. Such standards would not restrict freedom of expression, Valerian Zorin told the Third Committee; rather, "they could only enhance its educative role in the spheres of politics and morals."[119]

The Soviet argument touched a certain responsive chord in every representative of any nation who had ever complained about inaccurate reporting of his homeland abroad. Perhaps even delegates from the United States found parts of the Eastern bloc argument attractive, although American diplomats assuredly would have denied interest in a proposal to enforce journalistic responsibility—despite their constant concern about the quality of news about America being disseminated abroad. The fact that the proposal came from representatives of nations with highly controlled presses seemed immaterial to most debate participants; the principle had a life of its own. Even when arguing against the false-news resolution, delegates of many nations talked as if they thought that the press of the world should behave more responsibly. L.J.C. Beaufort of the Netherlands, for instance, thought that the Yugoslav resolution contained significant problems, that its language reflected the world's press situation solely from the communist perspective, and that the best way to combat false information was through "an open-door policy under which all nations would open wide their frontiers to everyone." But Beaufort also saw the resolution as symptomatic of the growing divisiveness in the world, a situation that could be ameliorated only by bridging the gap between nations. "A first step," he noted, "could be taken by refraining from disseminating unsound information and by refraining from insinuations and insults."[120]

Few representatives wished to adopt the Soviet press system, which was based on special laws that required the press to "defend democratic rights."[121] But the Western view of freedom of the press also presented problems. Under the latter system, Ernest Davies of the United Kingdom explained, governments "were in no way responsible for the writings of irresponsible journalists." No one wanted to hold governments responsible for press content or to restrain freedom of the press, maintained Enrique V. Corominas, representative of Argentina, another country experiencing difficulty with journalists. Instead, the aim of the resolution was to change the way in which journalists worked. "That was feasible and necessary because it corresponded to the expectations of the peoples of the world," he said. "There was only one right, and that was the right to tell the truth, not the right to spread lies."[122]

Both the warmongering and dissemination of false information proposals caused numerous difficulties for American diplomats at the United Nations. The problems arose not because of indecision over the preferred American response to the measures, for United States representatives knew from the beginning the only appropriate reaction to the resolutions. Rather, the problems regarding the warmongering resolution arose when American allies, such as Australia, Canada, and France, began to talk about amending the communist-sponsored proposal to make the resolution acceptable to Western nations and thus to avoid opposing the Soviets on everything during the session.[123] The allies also felt that they could not reject a resolution to outlaw warmongering and hoped to develop a resolution on "peacemongering" as a substitute[124] because most delegates would be unable to explain votes against a resolution opposing pro-war propaganda back home.[125] As a representative of one allied country, Justice Terje Wold of the Norwegian delegation, told his American counterparts, the "war of nerves" with the Soviet Union generally frightened Scandinavians. Wold added that he knew the warmongering resolution "had been placed on the agenda simply and purely for propaganda reasons, and that was all the Soviets desired or hoped to get out of it." But, the Norwegian added, the resolution "was having the effect which the authors intended."[126] American diplomats protested that attempts to compromise with the Soviets on the warmongering resolution "attacked a fundamental principle on which the United States could not compromise." Furthermore, the Americans considered that the warmongering resolution was "an attack on the United States, therefore the United States could not yield anywhere along the line."[127]

Regardless of the American stance, the allied view prevailed as an amended warmongering resolution condemned all forms of propaganda "designed or likely to provoke or encourage any threat to the peace, breach of the peace, or act of aggression" in all countries. The resolution also requested that member governments, within individual constitutional limitations, "promote, by all means of publicity and propaganda available to them, friendly relations among nations" and "encourage the dissemination of all information designed to give expression to the undoubted desire of all peoples for peace."[128] A milder view of the resolution to prevent the dissemination of false reports also prevailed, with the French compromise inviting member nations to study "such measures as might with advantage be taken on the national plane to combat, within the limits of constitutional procedures, the diffusion of false or distorted reports likely to injure friendly relations between States." Study results would be sent to the United Nations Conference on Freedom of Information.[129]

Part of the American difficulty with the motion governing the dissemination of false information centered on the number of different press systems in the world. In almost every country except the United States, the imposition of various positive responsibilities on the press was the norm rather than the exception.[130] Eastern bloc proposals for the prevention of warmongering and dissemination of false information differed only in degree insofar as the imposition of specific, affirmative tasks on the press for the advancement of world peace was concerned. Among the responsibilities of the press in this area, according to the Soviets, were "to expose war-mongers," "to struggle against the remnants of fascism," and "to expose propaganda inciting to racial and national hatred." As State Department officials said, "While the individual charges have been recognized by most delegations as flimsy and often even spurious, and the USSR remedy has always been rejected, the issues as a whole have been treated seriously because they have been placed in the context of 'peace or war'."[131] Ensuring a fair hearing for the American system of the press would be most difficult.

Communist bloc arguments against warmongering extended to the November 1947 sessions of UNESCO as well. In those meetings, the Polish delegate, M. Stephan Wierblowski, demanded that UNESCO move against individuals and nations that were actively promoting a new war. Opponents of the proposal declared that the subject was political and thus not within UNESCO's province, adding that the specialized agency must not duplicate work already done by the United Nations. The Polish delegate responded that the UNESCO charter placed the matter in the organization's hands: "In declaring that wars begin in the minds of men and that it is in the minds of men that the defences of peace must be constructed, we are bound to conclude that those who are supposed to fashion the minds of men have a graver responsibility than that resting upon the representatives of the Governments which adopted the resolution of the United Nations."[132] In promoting his resolution, Wierblowski came closer to attacking the American free-press crusade than had his Eastern bloc colleagues in the United Nations. Information promoting a new war, he proclaimed, was being distributed by "powerful weapons of propaganda and information, or rather misinformation." Keeping that in mind, "we are asked, under the pretext of the free flow of information, to open our doors to false news supplied by agencies so powerful that our own could not compete with them." In addition, "we are supposed to open our doors without there being any real reciprocity, because to-day our material and technical resources could not hope to oppose that other power." Exchange of information was one matter, Wierblowski said, "but we do not want what will really be a monopoly, although hypocrites euphemistically call it freedom."[133]

The Polish resolution, argued Benton, now American delegate to UNESCO, tempted the organization to "stumble into the pitfalls of repression, censorship and restriction." This fate must not befall as important an organization as UNESCO: "We must not let ourselves be drawn into a public expression that advocates legal action to control the things men think and say." But Benton thought that UNESCO could legitimately ask educators, scholars, scientists, artists, writers, and journalists to promote peace.[134] The resolution passed by UNESCO followed Benton's lead and called on these specialists "to denounce the pernicious idea that war is inevitable; to act as the mouthpiece of the conscience of the nations, refusing collective suicide; to combat, by every means in their power, surrender to fear and every form of thought or action which may threaten a just and lasting peace."[135] State Department planners viewed the Polish proposal as "bitterly anti-American" and as demanding careful action to avoid turning the UNESCO session into "a long, drawn-out propaganda battle between Poland and the United States." Again the problem with allies surfaced as the French and British sought a compromise acceptable to the Poles. Fortunately for the Americans, the Polish delegates themselves "became increasingly stubborn and in the final plenary were altogether intransigent, thus irritating almost all those who at the beginning of the Conference were in a mood to credit their good will."[136] In this way, then, the United States escaped another attempt to have American media labeled as warmongers.

Future debates on warmongering found American delegates pointing to "the lack of freedom of expression in Eastern Europe and the complete regimentation of public opinion by government (party) controls, with the attendant danger to peace and security." This attempt to focus on the restrictive press practices of the communist nations worked well because United States representatives quickly discovered that the Soviet bloc was "very sensitive to factual descriptions of the extent to which party machinery and governmental controls operate to prevent freedom of expression" and was "very much on the defensive when attempting to refute such criticism." Diplomats also attacked the warmongering and false-information issues by arguing that "most of the so-called war-mongering on the part of the press in democratic states is the proper and inevitable reaction of a free press to aggression and threats of aggression, in keeping with its moral responsibility to inform the people of any threats to their freedom." Thus, the obvious remedy to warmongering in the American press was a cessation of communist threats to peace.[137]

American press performance regarding the reporting of cold war news became quite controversial because of the warmongering debates. For instance, Curtis D. MacDougall, a practicing journalist turned college professor, charged that the American press "as a whole is not helping us to find a peaceful way out of the present tense international situation." Rather, MacDougall told a University of Colorado audience, "the majority of American newspapers and radio commentators are in the vanguard of those who are rapidly convincing the majority of the American people that war is the only solution."[138] Leaders of the establishment press quickly defended journalistic behavior. For example, Canham said, "The net effect of the American press attitude toward the world crisis is first, to keep the American people alert to the dangers and responsibilities of the situation, and second, to warn the Russians that the United States must be reckoned with if they intend to push their policy of expansion much farther." Differences did exist between American press coverage of the Soviet threat and coverage of the crisis in the European press, Canham said. "The tone of the American press—as of the American Congress and of military leadership—is considerably more violent than the western European press and governments. They are too weary and alarmed to permit such luxuries." Forrest joined Canham in condemning MacDougall's comments. "We all hope and pray that there will be no war," Forrest said, "but belligerent talk does not originate with American newspapers. It originates with the Russians themselves and the newspapers report the news."[139]

THE STATE DEPARTMENT PLANS VOA BROADCASTS

As American diplomats denied that the United States media were inciting another war or spreading false information throughout the world, the nation began its first peacetime propaganda effort. The United States information program was multifaceted and reached into many countries, but the Voice of America took the battle into the Soviet homeland, which, many observers believed, was the direct cause of the Russian outcry against warmongering. From the beginning, the State Department designed Voice programming to circumvent the Soviet blockade of news. Government officials believed that without such transmissions Russian citizens had no chance to hear unbiased news. As American Ambassador Averell Harriman explained, "the Russian press selects sentences out of texts which give completely false meanings." In order to successfully counter Soviet practices and to refute Soviet misrepresentations of American life, departmental personnel carefully monitored Russian press and radio outlets.[140] As the Voice broadcasts were planned, government officials discussed how the Russian government would react to the intrusion of uncensored news behind the iron curtain. Ambassador Harriman believed that although Soviet leaders obviously would not welcome the American broadcasts in the Russian language, the Russian leaders would say or do little about the transmissions because the Russians themselves had been broadcasting in English for years. Retaliation might include attempts to jam American transmissions, a possibility Harriman incorrectly downplayed on the assumption that Soviet jamming "would be an admission to its own people that it feared outside ideas and intensify public curiosity over American broadcasts."[141]

Planning for Voice of America broadcasts into the Soviet Union was so painstaking that transmissions did not begin until February 1947.[142] Even then, the broadcasts endured a considerable shakedown period. The choice of news presented was particularly tricky, Ambassador Smith reported. News about a threatened strike by high school teachers was undesirable for the newscasts because the Russian people lacked sufficient understanding to realize that the people involved would "sooner or later solve this problem in a fair and democratic way." Likewise, a story about a lynching was inadvisable. Tass would cover a grisly story in detail, Smith said. Voice of America coverage should wait until reporters could give a more comprehensive story stating that the American public had been aroused, that newspapers were demanding action, and that federal officers had made the arrests ordered by the president. Americans must not try to hide their problems from the Russians, Smith counseled, nor should the Voice of America "indulge guilt complex which so frequently seems to afflict American mind by making point of our faults." The Voice should put the nation's problems in perspective and emphasize what Americans were doing to solve those problems. "If we cannot present American news in such a way and still be honest, then we have no business broadcasting to Russians at all."[143] Whether news broadcasts of this nature constituted the truthful picture of America with all its faults that Benton promised to disseminate via the State Department's information program is debatable. But the Voice of America beamed this selective perception of America to the Soviet Union.

As Soviet propaganda efforts heated up toward the end of 1947, so did efforts to obtain additional funding for Voice of America programming[144] and so too, apparently, did Soviet concern over the effectiveness of the Voice. Ambassador Smith, for instance, reported that Soviet leaders were seriously considering jamming the VOA's frequencies.[145] Jamming became a problem in the spring of 1948, but Smith advised the United States government to "postpone any action until the interference becomes obnoxious enough to seriously interfere with the intelligibility of the broadcasts." If the jamming became more of a problem, Smith suggested "the fullest possible publicity be given to all the world including the Soviet Union." American options in case of continued jamming were limited. Retaliatory jamming of Radio Moscow signals was inadvisable, "in view of the unfavorable effect it would have on world opinion regarding the unequivocal traditional American stand on freedom of information."[146]

After more than a year of jamming, the situation deteriorated further, with reports in April 1949 noting that Soviet jamming completely obscured the frequencies used by the Voice of America.[147] Attempts to counter the jamming included increasing the number of scheduled Voice transmissions in the Russian language, combining efforts with the British to overpower the Russian transmitters, and protesting the jamming to the International Telecommunications Union.[148] Some observers thought that the new onslaught of Soviet jamming was motivated by a desire to keep the Soviet people from learning about the "phenomenal success" of the Berlin airlift and of the "Soviet diplomatic surrender on Berlin." Chargé Foy D. Kohler proposed another hypothesis—that the jamming might be a part of a long-range Soviet "drive for air mastery," which the Russian leadership considered as vital to their "drive for world mastery."[149] To some media observers in America, Soviet efforts to stop the Voice of America obviously meant that the programming was accomplishing its purpose.[150] Even *Broadcasting* magazine, which ardently opposed international broadcasting by the American government, admitted that, apparently, the Voice of America was reaching an audience in Russia. But the broadcast industry trade journal could not bring itself to endorse Voice transmissions and instead suggested another study of the issue.[151]

Since efforts to block American radio transmissions were hard to reconcile with the alleged interest of Soviet leadership in friendship among the peoples of the world,[152] the new American ambassador in the Soviet Union, Alan G. Kirk, was to tell Stalin directly that objections to the broadcasts' content should be handled through diplomatic channels rather than by jamming signals in violation of international communications conventions. Stalin gave no response other than to refer the matter to his government for study.[153] The difficulties continued into 1950, when Voice of America transmissions were only 15 to 20 percent effective due to Russian interference. Additional measures to counter Russian jamming were tried, including use of even more powerful equipment, employment of massed transmitters of the United States and other countries to overpower the Russian jamming efforts, rebroadcasts of programs at different times to elude the jamming, and alterations in wavelengths used to send the programs.[154]

The Soviet anti-American campaign was not in operation for long before State Department personnel realized that the Russians were actually waging psychological warfare against the United States, an activity that some American diplomats had termed obsolete at the end of World War II.[155] Initially, the American information program tried to stay above the fray, responding in an evenhanded, nonantagonistic way to constant Soviet criticisms. As of December 1946, though, the Office of International Information and Cultural Affairs began to answer Soviet propaganda more directly. Assistant Secretary of State Benton told Secretary of State Marshall that the American responses could become even sharper if Marshall wished, perhaps going beyond the refutation of Soviet charges against the United States to attacking Soviet policies themselves. Actions along the latter lines, Benton admitted, would move the United States into the realm of psychological warfare. The OIC was operating "on the assumption that overt techniques of psychological warfare against the Soviet Union should be avoided—for as long as possible."[156] Benton, however, did not dismiss American involvement in psychological warfare outright. With the increasing tensions between the United States and the Soviet Union, psychological warfare was obviously a weapon to use. The questions were when to use that weapon, to what degree, and how publicly.

From the beginning, government workers saw the information program as part of the nation's security apparatus.[157] In fact, some State Department planners even saw the freedom of information crusade as "directly connected with U.S. psychological warfare—as a softening up weapon (like bombing) which opens the way for propaganda assault troops. If the openings breeched [sic] by our freedom of information campaign are not fully exploited, our work will have been largely wasted."[158] Any possible connections between the crusade for worldwide freedom of the press and psychological warfare were for in-house consumption only, however. In 1947, State Department personnel still pursued a nonpolitical goal in their advocacy of international freedom of information. The double standard faced by members of the State Department here was somewhat analogous to that displayed during the battle for wire service copy for use by the Voice of America. Everyone knew that the press associations had pushed the State Department into the international freedom of information campaign, yet the two leading press associations refused to help the government begin its information program. Almost as if by unspoken agreement, the connection between the two efforts, although alluded to, was never used to coerce the wire services into submission. So, too, was the fact that the nation was on the brink of a psychological warfare campaign against the Soviets segregated from activities such as the international free-press crusade. That a truthful information program could turn into propaganda and then into psychological warfare was recognized by all involved in planning and debating the information program, just as planners realized that the freedom of information campaign was more than an altruistic campaign by the United States government—and more than a noble cause for the wire services. These connections, though, were seldom mentioned outside of secure surroundings.

The connection between psychological warfare and public opinion was made in closed governmental circles. For years, Americans contended that if the world had free access to information about the United States the peoples of the world would understand and trust their country and its motives. The argument extended the free marketplace of ideas concept to the international stage. Americans repeatedly said that they were willing to have American ideas meet in free combat with ideas from other nations, for they were secure in the knowledge that the American views would triumph. Now, an American victory in the free interplay of ideas no longer seemed so sure. The Soviet propaganda campaign wanted "not merely to undermine the prestige of the United States and the effectiveness of its national policy but . . . to weaken and divide foreign opinion to a point where effective opposition to Soviet aspirations is no longer attainable by political, economic or military means." Making matters even worse, the United States government was not "employing coordinated psychological measures to counter this propaganda campaign or to further the attainment of its national objectives." Faced with these realities, a special committee from the State, War, and Navy departments decided that "the present world situation requires the United States to develop and utilize strong and concerted measures designed to produce psychological situations and effects favorable to the attainment of U.S. national objectives."[159]

No longer was the free formation of opinion by the rest of the world sufficient. To meet the challenge of the day, the government must "initiate and develop ... specific plans and programs designed to influence foreign opinion in a direction favorable to U.S. interests."[160] Adding to the difficulties for proponents of domestic and international freedom of information was the fact that government planners believed the American public was not receiving the necessary information from the nation's media to build support for measures promoting national security. Perhaps, the security planners suggested, the activities of the American information media should "be coordinated with national policy" and become "an auxiliary to the achievement of national objectives."[161] Using information as an arm of national policy was a difficult notion for Americans to accept. The very idea raised "a series of questions—freedom of opinion and of the press, propaganda, censorship, government interference with the judgments of citizens—any one of which is enough to put public feeling into a fighting mood," a consultant on information policies told the State Department in 1948.[162]

Americans did not realize that the actual means of communication themselves were neutral. Rather, Americans accepted the communications system of the United States, which was built on physical facilities that could be used in many ways, as the only way in which mass media could be structured and operated. Thus, the idea that identical physical facilities could be used by the government to promote certain political and social goals in addition to being used by private enterprise was beyond the grasp of most Americans. The American view of the existing communications system as the ideal presented numerous problems to governmental planners. Modern communications were easily manipulated, and even though manipulation occurred regularly in America for advertising or entertainment purposes, the manipulation of media to influence other peoples to adopt favorable attitudes toward the United States was culturally unacceptable. Despite this attitude, conditions soon forced the United States government to realize "that the purposes and the methods by which the channels of mass communication are domestically operated are not necessarily a guide to what the American Government should be authorized to do if it is to communicate with foreign audiences in the name of the American people."[163]

Thus, divided needs and goals permeated the ranks of Americans advocating international freedom of information. The press associations were disaffected to some degree because of the constant pressure from the Department of State for their news files for use in the international information program. A widening rift was developing between members of ASNE and the press associations that supposedly served them because of the stiffnecked refusal of the Associated Press and the United Press to acknowledge the importance of telling America's story abroad. And within the State Department, officials wished that the domestic media would be more helpful in the propaganda war that was raging throughout the world. Just as these feelings were coming to light, the American crusade for worldwide freedom of information had its most favorable hearing within the United Nations. For the moment, then, the various parties in the festering disagreement put their differences aside and sallied forth to do battle with representatives from countries that believed that cooperation between a nation's press system and its international information activities was entirely appropriate. Despite all the problems recently encountered, American participants in free-press debates gave no hint of the discord brought on by the government's entrance into the propaganda wars as they worked for the adoption of the full American system of the press by the rest of the world.

NOTES

1. Jerry Walker, "$1,000,000 a Year Voted for Cooper's Global AP Aim," *E&P*, April 21, 1945, p. 15.
2. "Termination of O.W.I. and Disposition of Certain Functions of O.I.A.A.," Statement by the President, *Department of State Bulletin*, September 2, 1945, p. 306.
3. Memorandum of Conversation between Representatives of the Office of War Information and Representatives of the State Department, February 4, 1944, Stettinius Papers, Box 724, File: Memoranda of Conversation, L–A, General and Misc.
4. United States Government International Information Service after the War, Unsigned Secretary's Staff Committee Report, August 13, 1945, Byrnes Papers, File 588.
5. Warburg, *Unwritten Treaty*, p. 137; Frederick Lewis Allen, "Must We Tell the World?" *Harper's Magazine*, December 1945, pp. 553–59.
6. Warburg, *Unwritten Treaty*, p. 145.
7. William Benton, Statement before the House Foreign Affairs Committee, October 16, 1945, RG 59, NA, Box 448, 111.12 Benton, Wm./10-1645.
8. "Our International Information Policy," Transcript of a Radio Broadcast, *Department of State Bulletin*, December 16, 1945, pp. 949–50.
9. Arthur W. MacMahon, *Memorandum on the Postwar International Information Program of the United States*, Department of State Publication, Washington, D.C., Government Printing Office, 1945, pp. 102, xvi–xvii.
10. White and Leigh, *Peoples Speaking to Peoples*, p. 36.
11. Jefferson Caffery, American Ambassador in France, to the Secretary of State, June 17, 1946, RG 59, NA, Box 4987, 811.91251/6-1746.
12. MacMahon, memorandum, pp. 17–18.
13. C. D. Jackson, "Assignment for the Press," in Lester Markel et al., *Public Opinion and Foreign Policy*, New York, Published for the Council on Foreign Relations by Harper & Row, 1949, p. 182. Jackson was vice president of Time, Inc.
14. Ferdinand Kuhn, Jr., Director, Interim International Information Service, to William Benton, January 22, 1946, RG 59, NA, Box 5871, 841.911/1-2246.
15. *See*, e.g., John F. Simmons, American Embassy, Quito, Ecuador, to the Secretary of State, February 23, 1949, Ibid., Box 4985, 811.91210/2-2349;

Raymond G. Leddy, Second Secretary of Embassy, Caracas, Venezuela, to the Secretary of State, February 18, 1949, Ibid., Box 4396, 810.79611/2-1849; Garth P. James, Assistant Public Affairs Officer, American Embassy, Santiago, Chile, to Morrill Cody, Chief, American Republics Area, Public Affairs Overseas Program Staff, March 2, 1949, Ibid., Box 4985, 811.91210/3-249; Sheldon Thomas, Public Affairs Officer, American Embassy, Rio de Janeiro, Brazil, to Morrill Cody, March 9, 1949, Ibid., 811.91210/3-949; George T. Colman, American Consul, Belém, Pará, Brazil, to the Secretary of State, March 10, 1949, Ibid., 811.91210/3-1049.

16. J. Leighton Stuart, American Ambassador in China, to the Secretary of State, February 15, 1947, Ibid., Confidential Box 441, 811.91293/2-1547.

17. Charles A. Livengood, American Consul General, Batavia, Java, Indonesia, to the Secretary of State, July 5, 1949, Ibid., Box 4987, 811.91256D/7-549; Charles A. Livengood to the Secretary of State, July 19, 1949, Ibid., 811.91256D/7-1949; Clare H. Timberlake, Consul General, Bombay, India, to the Secretary of State, July 19, 1949, Ibid., Confidential Box 441, 811.91256D/7-1949. For the press's version of the trip and the deaths, see "Plane Disaster Kills 13 U.S. Correspondents," E&P, July 16, 1949, pp. 7, 54; "Journalistic Disaster," E&P, July 16, 1949, p. 32.

18. G. Stewart Brown, Office of International Information and Cultural Affairs, to William T. Stone, OIC, December 11, 1946, Ibid., Records of the Assistant Secretary of State for Public Affairs, Box 15, December 1946. Throughout the years under study, State Department officials helped press agency representatives through such diverse actions as playing paymaster for correspondents stationed in Moscow to trying to help the Associated Press and the United Press enter the Indian market.

19. Leo J. Margolin, Public Information Chief for Europe, United Nations Relief and Rehabilitation Administration, to William Benton, December 24, 1945, Ibid., Box 4479, 811.20200(D)/12-2445.

20. Charles W. Yost, Chargé at Bangkok, Thailand, to the Secretary of State, January 30, 1946, Ibid., Box 4483, 811.20200(D)/1-3046; Seymour Berkson, General Manager, International News Service, to William Benton, September 10, 1946, Ibid., Box 4993, 811.91294/9-1046. Berkson was discussing the high costs of servicing Japan and Korea.

21. "AP Board to Hear Benton; U.P. Studies His Arguments," E&P, January 26, 1946, p. 7.

22. J. Noel Macy, Assistant Chief, International Information Division, to Kent Cooper, November 21, 1945, RG 59, NA, Box 4983, 811.91200/11-2145.

23. "AP Stops Service of News for State Department Use," E&P, January 19, 1946, p. 11.

24. William Benton to Robert McLean, President, Associated Press Board of Directors, January 16, 1946, RG 59, NA, Records of the Assistant Secretary of State for Public Affairs, Box 7, File: Associated Press #1.

The problem of getting news of America to remote corners of the world plagued the information program. Lester Markel, Sunday editor of The New York Times, suggested that the government information program and the news agencies agree on classifying the world into black, white, and gray zones. The black areas, such as those behind the iron curtain, were not open to commercial news services and would be served by the government. The white areas, such as western Europe, would be the province of the commercial agencies. The gray areas, including certain portions of Europe where the communist threat was the greatest, would be served by both. *See* Lester Markel, "Opinion—A Neglected Instrument," in *Public Opinion and Foreign Policy*, pp. 36–37. The proposal, which resembled the old international news agency cartel's approach to dividing up the world, was not adopted.

25. William Benton to Robert McLean, Ibid.
26. "McLean's Reply to Benton," *E&P*, January 19, 1946, p. 40a.
27. William Benton to Robert McLean, January 18, 1946, RG 59, NA, Records of the Assistant Secretary of State for Public Affairs, Box 7, File: Associated Press #1.
28. Roy Howard to William Benton, January 17, 1946, Ibid., File: Associated Press #2. Karl Bickel, former president of United Press, also accused Benton of not knowing anything about press associations and added that Benton's failure to know either Kent Cooper or Hugh Baillie personally added to the problems Benton had encountered. *See* Karl Bickel to William Benton, January 25, 1946, Ibid.

    Benton hoped that the number of former wire service staffers involved in the information program would show the press association chiefs that the program was being handled by individuals in whom they "should have confidence." *See* William Benton to William T. Stone, Office of International Communication and Cultural Affairs, January 20, 1946, Ibid., Box 14, File: January 1946. Bickel quickly disabused Benton of that idea by saying that any journalists who worked for a propaganda agency would need "a lot of honest journalistic delousing" before they could win the trust of any reputable news agency or newspaper. *See* Bickel to Benton, January 25, 1946, Ibid.
29. Ralph McGill to Henry Luce, January 18, 1946, RG 59, NA, Box 4481, 811.20200(D)/1-1846. McGill wanted Luce to write an editorial in *Time* protesting the Associated Press action and sent a copy of the letter to the State Department.
30. "Ackerman: Requests President to Stop Propaganda," *E&P*, January 26, 1946, pp. 63–64.
31. Wilbur Forrest to William Benton, January 29, 1946, RG 59, NA, Box 4711, 811.42700-R/1-2946.
32. "Editors Express Views in E&P Survey," *E&P*, January 26, 1946, pp. 8, 66.
33. William Benton to Secretary of State James F. Byrnes, February 22, 1946, RG 59, NA, Records of the Assistant Secretary of State for Public Affairs, Box 14, File: February 1946.
34. J. Noel Macy, Acting Chief, International Press and Publications Division, Department of State, to Lloyd Stratton, Associated Press, February 11, 1946, Ibid.
35. Robert McLean to Secretary of State James F. Byrnes, January 28, 1946, Ibid., File: January 1946.
36. *See*, e.g., Secretary of State James F. Byrnes to the American Embassy, Moscow, March 22, 1946, RG 59, NA, Box 4988, 811.91261/3-2246; George F. Kennan, Chargé in the Soviet Union, to the Secretary of State, March 25, 1946, Ibid., 811.91261/3-2546; Walter Bedell Smith, American Ambassador in the

Soviet Union, to the Secretary of State, April 11, 1946, Ibid., 811.91261/4-1146; Dean Acheson, Acting Secretary of State, to the American Embassy, Moscow, August 2, 1946, Ibid., 811.91261/8-246; Elbridge Durbrow, Counselor of Embassy at Moscow, to the Secretary of State, August 7, 1946, Ibid., 811.91261/8-746.

37. Jackson, "Assignment for the Press," pp. 183–84.

38. "What Happens Now?" *E&P*, February 2, 1946, p. 38.

39. "U.P. Stops Service to U.S. on Feb. 16," *E&P*, February 2, 1946, p. 10.

40. Seymour Berkson to William Benton, February 5, 1946, RG 59, NA, Records of the Assistant Secretary of State of Public Affairs, Box 7, File: Associated Press #1. Benton later told Secretary of State James Byrnes that Berkson, an old friend, had consulted with Benton on the letter and that the International News Service chief intended "to continue to supply INS service to the Department." The letter was "largely written to the trade" and was to remain in Berkson's files unless and until Berkson needed to quote from it to protect his job. *See* William Benton to the Secretary of State, February 13, 1946, RG 59, NA, Box 4484, 811.20200(D)/2-1346.

41. Markel, "Opinion—A Neglected Instrument," p. 42; John D. Hickerson, Office of European Affairs, to Howland Sargeant, Office of the Assistant Secretary, January 13, 1948, RG 59, NA, Confidential Box 441, 811.91274/1-1348.

42. Even if a subsidy arrangement could tempt the press agencies, which was doubtful, the arrangements likely would be criticized publicly by influential members of the American press. At one point during the European Recovery Program, for instance, government officials attempted to help American newspapers and magazines that were circulating copies in Europe to exchange assets tied up in frozen foreign currencies for usable American dollars. When the *Chicago Tribune* found out about the program, the newspaper denounced the plan as a governmental subsidy, a payoff to publications for supporting the Marshall Plan. Everyone involved denied any connection between the two events, but journalists knew that government support for any press operation abroad would quickly become public knowledge. The guaranteed exposure of such activities would definitely sully the publications' reputations. *See* "Edwards Says Record Proves Subsidy Story," *E&P*, June 12, 1948, p. 6; "ECA Press 'Subsidy' Called 'Lie' by Macy," *E&P*, June 5, 1948, p. 8; "Subsidy Plan?" *E&P*, June 5, 1948, p. 38.

43. William Benton to Karl Bickel, February 12, 1946, RG 59, NA, Records of the Assistant Secretary of State for Public Affairs, Box 7, File: Associated Press #2.

44. William Benton to Roy Howard, February 16, 1946, RG 59, NA, Box 4485, 811.20200(D)/2-1646.

45. William Benton, "Shortwave Broadcasting and the News," *Journalism Quarterly* 23 (June 1946):159.

46. William Benton, "The American Press Associations: An Opportunity and Responsibility," Address Delivered before the New York Newspaperwomen's Club, *Department of State Bulletin*, April 7, 1946, p. 575.

47. William Benton, Assistant Secretary of State, Address, April 18, 1946, *Problems of Journalism—1946*, pp. 45, 51.

48. Resolutions Debate, April 20, 1946, Ibid., pp. 188–205.

49. "Kent Cooper's Report on State Dept. Stand," *E&P*, April 27, 1946, p. 120.
50. Ibid. Benton told Arthur Hays Sulzberger, publisher of *The New York Times* and member of the news cooperative's board of directors, that the government had no intention of reimbursing the news agency for losses and wanted only to become one of 2,600-plus Associated Press customers. "As for the theory that foreign peoples or editors might suspect the AP as being tainted because the government is one of its 2,600 customers, and despite the daily evidence that *both* the AP file and the government broadcasts are not in fact propaganda, it seems to me the AP is straining at a gnat or confessing the inability of its salesmen to get straight a very simple point that is borne out constantly by the product they sell." *See* William Benton to Arthur Hays Sulzberger, May 17, 1946, RG 59, NA, Records of the Assistant Secretary of State for Public Affairs, Box 14, File: June 1946 (emphasis in original).
51. William Benton to Robert McLean, April 24, 1946, RG 59, NA, Records of the Assistant Secretary of State for Public Affairs, Box 7, File: Associated Press #1.
52. "Vote Delayed for More Data on OIC Plan," *E&P*, March 16, 1946, p. 72.
53. "U.S. Newscasts Continue with INS, Reuters," *E&P*, March 30, 1946, p. 70.
54. Memorandum from William Benton to the Secretary of State Regarding the Organization of International Broadcasting by the United States, November 13, 1946, RG 59, NA, Records of the Assistant Secretary of State for Public Affairs, Box 1, File: IBD—Radio Foundation.
55. "Unclear Thinking," *Broadcasting*, July 22, 1946, p. 52.
56. "Government News Service Justified, ASNE Unit Says," *E&P*, December 14, 1946, pp. 80, 78. Other members were George Cornish, managing editor, *New York Herald Tribune*; Oveta Culp Hobby, executive editor, *Houston Post*; Edwin L. James, managing editor, *The New York Times*; Ben M. McKelway, associate editor, *Washington Star*; Hamilton Owens, editor, *Baltimore Sun*; Ben Reese, managing editor, *St. Louis Post-Dispatch*; and Gideon Seymour, executive editor, Cowles Newspapers, Minneapolis, Minn.
57. Ibid., p. 78.
58. Ibid.
59. Ibid.
60. Ibid., p. 80.
61. Ibid.
62. William Benton to Spruille Braden, Assistant Secretary of State, December 31, 1946, RG 59, NA, Box 4509, 811.20200(D)/1-1547.
63. William Benton to Secretary of State George C. Marshall, Memorandum Explaining Current Favorable Press Reaction to OIC, June 13, 1947, Benton Papers, Box 375, Folder 16.
64. Unsigned Memorandum to Dean Acheson, Acting Secretary of State, April 8, 1947, RG 59, NA, Confidential Box 434, FW 111.018/4-447.
65. William Benton to Robert McLean, April 14, 1947, Ibid., Records of the Assistant Secretary of State for Public Affairs, Box 4, File: S.
66. Lloyd Free, Special Assistant to the Director, Office of International Information and Cultural Affairs, to William T. Stone and G. Stewart Brown, OIC, April 10, 1947, Ibid., Box 10, File: Kent Cooper.
67. William T. Stone, Office of International Information and Cultural Affairs, to William Benton, April 10, 1947, Ibid.
68. "Text of Kent Cooper's Address at Chicago," *E&P*, May 31, 1947, p. 47.
69. Ibid., pp. 49, 48.

70. "Benton Answers Attack by Cooper," *E&P*, June 21, 1947, p. 68 (emphasis in original).
71. Ibid.
72. Jesse M. MacKnight, Special Assistant, Office of the Assistant Secretary of State for Public Affairs, to George V. Allen, April 12, 1948, RG 59, NA, Records of the Assistant Secretary of State for Public Affairs, Box 7, File: Associated Press #2.
73. George V. Allen to Arthur Hays Sulzberger, April 13, 1948, Ibid.
74. George V. Allen, Address, April 15, 1948, *Problems of Journalism—1948*, pp. 43–50.
75. Committee Report, April 15, 1948, Ibid., pp. 41–42.
76. Resolutions Debate, April 17, 1948, Ibid., p. 252.
77. Ibid., pp. 257, 259–60.
78. Ibid., pp. 253, 257.
79. Ibid., pp. 262, 266–67.
80. Resolutions Adopted, Ibid., p. 296.
81. "ASNE Resolutions," *E&P*, April 24, 1948, p. 66.
82. George V. Allen to Kent Cooper, May 26, 1948, RG 59, NA, Records of the Assistant Secretary of State for Public Affairs, Box 7, File: Associated Press #2.
83. Kent Cooper to George V. Allen, May 27, 1948, Ibid.
84. Lloyd A. Lehrbas, Director, Office of International Information, to George V. Allen, June 3, 1948, Ibid.
85. Lloyd A. Lehrbas, Director, Office of International Information, to Howland Sargeant, Special Assistant to the Assistant Secretary of State, December 20, 1948, Ibid. The memorandum noted that the State Department had reached a similar agreement with Hugh Baillie of the United Press, which allowed the departmental information program access to United Press news stories after publication.
86. Memorandum of Conversation by George V. Allen, April 15, 1949, Ibid.
87. J. Russell Wiggins, Report of Committee on State Department Dissemination of News and Opinion, April 21, 1949, *Problems of Journalism—1949*, p. 34.
88. Resolutions Debate, April 23, 1949, Ibid., p. 149.
89. Ibid., pp. 150, 152, 159, 158.
90. Ibid., p. 155.
91. Brucker, *Freedom of Information*, p. 217.
92. Cooper, *The Right to Know*, p. 251.
93. Under Secretary's Meeting, Foreign Information Policy Objectives in a Transition Period—Draft, August 22, 1950, SDR.
94. Charles A. Siepmann, "Propaganda and Information in International Affairs," *Yale Law Journal* 55 (August 1946):1260–61.
95. H. M. Spitzer, "Presenting America in American Propaganda," *Public Opinion Quarterly* 11 (Summer 1947):213.
96. Ralph Block, "Propaganda and the Free Society," *Public Opinion Quarterly* 12 (Winter 1948):678–80.
97. Arthur Hays Sulzberger to William Benton, May 23, 1946, RG 59, NA, Records of the Assistant Secretary of State for Public Affairs, Box 14, File: June 1946.
98. John A. Pollard, "Words Are Cheaper Than Blood," *Public Opinion Quarterly* 9 (Fall 1945):285.
99. Warburg, *Unwritten Treaty*, pp. 157–58.

100. Markel "Opinion—A Neglected Instrument," pp. 5, 10, 12, 18.
101. Feeding the Soviet campaign was a spate of books by American critics of the United States press system, each of which was liberally quoted to support Russian accusations. Books often cited by Soviet critics included George Seldes, *Freedom of the Press*, Indianapolis, Ind., Bobbs-Merrill, 1935; Morris Ernst, *The First Freedom*, New York, Macmillan, 1946; and Upton Sinclair, *The Brass Check*, Pasadena, Calif., Published by the Author, 1920. See Chargé in the Soviet Union to the Secretary of State, October 15, 1947, RG 59, NA, Box 4995, 811.917 AMERICA/10-1547. The criticism leveled by these authors was strong, but each hoped for correction within the system and not for its overthrow. See Margaret A. Blanchard, "Press Criticism and National Reform Movements: The Progressive Era and the New Deal," *Journalism History* 5 (Summer 1978):33–37, 54–55.
102. Walter Bedell Smith, American Ambassador in the Soviet Union, to the Secretary of State, July 9, 1946, RG 59, NA, Box 4499, 811.20200(D)/7-946.
103. W. A. Crawford, Second Secretary of Embassy at Moscow, to the Secretary of State, May 3, 1947, Ibid., Box 6493, 861.9111/5-347.
104. Elbridge Durbrow, Counselor of Embassy at Moscow, to the Secretary of State, May 8, 1947, Ibid., Box 6492, 861.911/5-847.
105. "Stalin Tells Stassen: People Distrust Press," *E&P*, April 19, 1947, p. 24. The Soviet prime minister was interviewed by Harold Stassen, former governor of Minnesota.
106. Elbridge Durbrow, Counselor of Embassy at Moscow, to the Secretary of State, June 6, 1947, RG 59, NA, Box 4983, 811.9111/6-547.
107. Elbridge Durbrow, Chargé in the Soviet Union, to the Secretary of State, June 10, 1947, *FR: 1947*, IV:568–69.
108. Robert A. Lovett, Acting Secretary of State, to American Legation, Vienna, Austria, April 7, 1948, RG 59, NA, Confidential Box 428, 811.42700(R)/3-2548.
109. Frederick Oechsner, Adviser to Director of Office of International Information and Educational Exchange, to George V. Allen, July 20, 1948, Ibid., Box 4524, 811.20200(D)/7-2048.
110. GAOR, 2nd session, 84th plenary meeting, September 18, 1947, pp. 92–93.
111. Ibid., pp. 99–100, 105–6.
112. "U.S. Rejects Resolutions Limiting Free Flow of Information," Remarks Made by Warren R. Austin before the First Committee (Political and Security) of the United Nations, *Department of State Bulletin*, November 2, 1947, pp. 869–70.
113. Ibid., pp. 870, 873. *Editor & Publisher* expressed delight over Vishinsky's criticisms because of the "tribute" he paid to the "power and influence of a free American press." The trade journal saw the Soviet diplomat's comments as "a futile smoke screen attack attempting to hide official Soviet fear of the truth that is being printed daily in our press." See "Vishnisky's [*sic*] Tribute," *E&P*, September 27, 1947, p. 42.
114. GAOR, Third Committee, 2nd session, 68th meeting, October 24, 1947, pp. 126–27.
115. Ibid., p. 129.
116. "U.S. Rejects Resolutions Limiting Free Flow of Information," Statement by

Eleanor Roosevelt, United States Representative to the General Assembly before the Third Committee (Social, Humanitarian, and Cultural Questions), *Department of State Bulletin*, November 2, 1947, pp. 874–75.

117. GAOR, Third Committee, 2nd session, 68th meeting, October 24, 1947, p. 129.

118. Ibid., pp. 130–31.

119. Ibid., 69th meeting, October 25, 1947, p. 138.

120. Ibid., 71st meeting, October 28, 1947, p. 145.

121. Ibid., p. 149.

122. Ibid., 70th meeting, October 28, 1947, pp. 141, 143.

123. G. Hayden Raynor, United States Delegation Staff of Advisers, to Warren R. Austin, United States Representative at the United Nations, October 19, 1947, *FR: 1947*, I:86.

124. Summary of Negotiations in the General Assembly on the Soviet War Propaganda Proposal, United States Delegation Handbook, March 5, 1948, RG 84, NA, Records of the United States Mission to the United Nations, Box 164, Position Papers: Conference on Freedom of Information.

125. Minutes of the Twenty-Fourth Meeting of the United States Delegation, October 21, 1947, *FR: 1947*, I:89.

126. Memorandum of Conversation with Justice Wold, Norwegian Delegation, by Hayden Raynor, United States Delegation, United States Mission to the United Nations, October 17, 1947, US/A/C.1/368, SDR.

127. Minutes of the Twenty-Fourth Meeting of the United States Delegation, *FR: 1947*, I:87.

128. GAOR, 2nd session, Resolution 110 (II). *See* Appendix A for the text of this resolution.

129. GAOR, 2nd session, 115th plenary meeting, November 15, 1947, pp. 957–58. *See* Appendix B for the text of this resolution. The United States supported the French proposal after learning that America would stand alone in opposition. *See* Issues Concerning Freedom of Information (Including the Yugoslav Proposal on Slanderous Dissemination) before the Third Committee of the General Assembly, 1947, March 2, 1948, United States Delegation Handbook, RG 84, NA, Records of the United States Mission to the United Nations, Box 164, Position Papers: Conference on Freedom of Information.

130. United States Position on General Assembly Resolutions on War Mongering and Slanderous Information, United States Delegation Handbook, March 5, 1948, RG 84, NA, Records of the United States Mission to the United Nations, Box 164, Position Papers: Conference on Freedom of Information.

131. War-Mongering and False Reports Harmful to Friendly Relations between States (Possible Issues for the General Assembly), August 12, 1948, Lot 71A5255, Box 488, 403.3 Warmongering, SDR.

132. UNESCO Proceedings, 2nd session, 11th plenary meeting, November 26, 1947, p. 128.

133. Ibid., 7th plenary meeting, November 11, 1947, p. 99.

134. Ibid., 11th plenary meeting, pp. 130–31.

135. Ibid., Resolutions, "Solemn Appeal against the Idea That War Is Inevitable," p. 63. *See* Appendix C for the text of this resolution.

136. Negotiations on the Polish War Mongering Resolution, Second Session of the

UNESCO General Conference, Mexico City, November–December 1947, United States Delegation Handbook, RG 84, NA, Records of the United States Mission to the United Nations, Box 164, Position Papers: Conference on Freedom of Information.

137. War-Mongering and False Reports Harmful to Friendly Relations Between States (Possible Issues for the General Assembly).

138. J. Harley Murray, "MacDougall Lashes Press on War Hysteria," *E&P*, May 8, 1948, p. 68.

139. "Editors Deny U.S. Press Fosters War Hysteria," *E&P*, May 15, 1948, p. 10. A scholarly study of American newspaper coverage of the cold war decided that publications handled the topic with restraint. *See* George E. Simmons, "The 'Cold War' in Large-City Dailies of the United States," *Journalism Quarterly* 25 (December 1948):354–59, 400. On the other hand, press critic George Seldes argued that American newspapers did not adequately inform the American people about cold war conditions. *See* George Seldes, *The People Don't Know: The American Press and the Cold War*, New York: Gaer Associates, 1949.

140. Averell Harriman, American Ambassador in the Soviet Union, to the Secretary of State, November 21, 1945, *FR: 1945*, V:920.

141. Averell Harriman, American Ambassador in the Soviet Union, to the Secretary of State, January 20, 1946, *FR: 1946*, VI:678.

142. Besides concern about news items to be broadcast, great attention was paid to such points as the choice of announcers, musical selections, and dramatic readings for the broadcasts. The goal was to create a quality broadcast worth the Russians' effort to listen. *See*, e.g., Averell Harriman, American Ambassador in the Soviet Union, to the Secretary of State, December 21, 1945, RG 59, NA, Box 4479, 811.20200(D)/12-2145; George F. Kennan, Chargé in the Soviet Union, to the Secretary of State, February 1, 1946, Ibid., Box 4483, 811.20200(D)/2-146; Walter Bedell Smith, American Ambassador in the Soviet Union, to the Secretary of State, February 18, 1947, *FR: 1947*, IV:533–34.

143. Walter Bedell Smith, American Ambassador in the Soviet Union, to the Secretary of State, February 27, 1947, RG 59, NA, Box 4717, 811.42700(R)/2-2747.

144. *See*, e.g., Joe Sitrick, "Expect New Plea for 'Voice' Funds," *Broadcasting*, October 20, 1947, p. 82; "Increase for 'Voice' Looms; Smith Seeks 5 Million Extra," *Broadcasting*, November 17, 1947, p. 20. Increased funding for Voice of America programming in 1947 was an abrupt change from the congressional stance of 1946, when the State Department's information program, including the Voice of America, was almost eliminated. The change in position was applauded by *Editor & Publisher* but severely criticized by *Broadcasting*. *See* " 'Voice of America'," *E&P*, January 31, 1948, p. 34; "Are There Ears to Hear?" *Broadcasting*, January 26, 1948, p. 48.

145. Ambassador Smith also reported that the American broadcasts were far more worrisome to the Russians than programming carried by the British Broadcasting Corporation because Voice news "generally reported factually with a minimum of barbed anti-Soviet items which nevertheless usually are effective and hit the mark while British broadcasts are too British and too full offensive items." *See* Walter Bedell Smith, American Ambassador in the Soviet Union, to the Secretary of State, October 31, 1947, *FR: 1947*, IV:604.

146. Walter Bedell Smith, American Ambassador in the Soviet Union, to the Secretary of State, April 20, 1948, *FR: 1948*, IV:832.

147. Foy D. Kohler, Chargé in the Soviet Union, to the Secretary of State, April 26, 1949, *FR: 1949*, V:609.

148. "'Voice' Jamming: Protest Filed through ITU," *Broadcasting*, May 9, 1949, p. 32; "U.S. Protests Soviet Jamming of Voice of America," *Department of State Bulletin*, May 15, 1949, p. 638.

149. Foy D. Kohler, Chargé in the Soviet Union, to the Secretary of State, May 17, 1949, *FR: 1949*, V:613–14.

150. "'Jamming' the Voice," *E&P*, May 14, 1949, p. 40.

151. "Jam-ski Session," *Broadcasting*, May 9, 1949, p. 42.

152. The Secretary of State to the Embassy in the Soviet Union, August 3, 1949, *FR: 1949*, V:638.

153. Alan G. Kirk, American Ambassador in the Soviet Union, to the Secretary of State, August 16, 1949, Ibid., p. 647.

154. Editorial Note, *FR: 1950*, IV:1074–75.

155. William Benton to the Secretary of State, February 6, 1946, RG 59, NA, Box 4711, 811.42700-R/2-646.

156. William Benton to the Secretary of State, March 7, 1947, Ibid., Box 4510, 811.20200(D)/3-747.

157. William Benton to Major General George J. Richards, Budget Officer, War Department, March 24, 1947, Ibid., Records of the Assistant Secretary of State for Public Affairs, Box 15, File: March 1947.

158. Lloyd Free, Special Assistant to the Director, Office of International Information and Cultural Affairs, to William Benton and William Stone, Director, Office of International Information and Cultural Affairs, March 13, 1947, RG 43, NA, Box 5, File: Lloyd Free.

159. Psychological Warfare, Concepts, and Organization, State, War, Navy Coordinating Committee (SWNCC), November 3, 1947, SWNCC 304, NA, pp. 64–66.

160. Ibid., p. 67.

161. Draft letter to the President from the Secretary of Defense, October 25, 1947, in SWNCC 304, Ibid. SWNCC planners recognized the difference between white psychological warfare, carried out by legitimate information sources, and black psychological warfare, carried out by covert measures to disrupt the enemy and to give aid and comfort to individuals opposing him. *See* SWNCC 304/1, December 10, 1946, in SWNCC 304, Ibid. Responsibility for black psychological warfare went to the newly created Central Intelligence Agency. State Department planners then were to decide the extent of its responsibilities for white psychological warfare. *See* George V. Allen to Robert A. Lovett, Under Secretary of State, September 2, 1948, RG 59, NA, Confidential Box 406, 811.20200(D)/9-248.

162. "Government Publicity and Information," Study by William Reitzel, Yale Institute of International Studies, January 2, 1948, Ibid., Box 4520, 811.20200(D)/1-248, p. 2.

163. Ibid., pp. 3–4. To put the best possible face on the American propaganda campaign, officials sold the program to the media and the nation as a campaign of truth. President Truman introduced the concept at a meeting of the

American Society of Newspaper Editors in 1950, and its principles were put into effect by Assistant Secretary of State for Public Affairs Edward W. Barrett, a former *Newsweek* executive, who had helped to design the United States position on mass communications introduced to UNESCO. *See* Harry S. Truman, Address, April 20, 1950, *Problems of Journalism—1950*, pp. 48–53; Edward W. Barrett, *Truth Is Our Weapon*, New York, Funk & Wagnalls, 1953. Kent Cooper thought truthful propaganda was a fundamental contradiction in terms. *See* Cooper, *The Right to Know*, p. 243.

CHAPTER 4

The Crusade Reaches Its Apex on the International Front

For months the American crusade for worldwide freedom of information was so bogged down at the United Nations that United States press leaders and State Department officials thought that diplomats within the international organization never would consider the issue. Consequently, they sought other ways, such as bilateral treaties, to attain the guarantees so ardently desired. Soon, however, delegates within the United Nations began discussing freedom of information and laying the groundwork for placing the American dream before an international conference devoted solely to that topic. Before the conference occurred, however, delegates had to establish an appropriate bureaucracy to plan the sessions.

Creation of the Subcommission on Freedom of Information and of the Press was the first step toward that conference. In the United Nations hierarchy, the subcommission fell under the Human Rights Commission, which was a permanent subsidiary of the Economic and Social Council. As an organ of the Human Rights Commission, the subcommission would establish the conference's agenda and lay the other necessary groundwork for convening the specialized session. Even as the subcommission was being formed, however, debates indicated the concerns that delegates from around the world had about the American ideal. If, for instance, the goal of international freedom of the press was to secure a more thorough knowledge of other peoples, some members of the Human Rights Commission contended that correspondents must promote that goal through responsible reporting. A press left free to interpret the world's events without externally imposed guidance most likely would hinder mutual understanding, the Indian delegate on the Human Rights Commission maintained. International press coverage had not promoted better understanding among the various nations of the world, Hansa Mehta said, for through the world's journalists, Indians saw America in terms of "gangsters in Chicago and film stars in Hollywood." The same press told Americans of India "as a land of mystery, fabulous splendor, elephants and snakes." Neither portrayal was accurate and neither advanced international understanding, which allegedly was the goal of efforts to protect freedom of the press throughout the world.[1]

Human Rights Commission members considered several ideas designed to ensure that the press played its rightful, responsible role in society. Some delegates, for instance, suggested that the subcommission write an international statute to govern journalists' behavior and establish an international press organization with the power to enforce the statute.[2] Both suggestions were reminiscent of proposals that the United States had opposed strongly when they were presented to the League of Nations. Eventually, subcommission members were instructed "to examine what rights, obligations, and practices should be included in the concept of freedom of information."[3]

THE HUMAN RIGHTS COMMISSION
DESIGNS A FREE-PRESS SUBCOMMISSION

One way to ensure that the subcommission took the proper attitude toward encouraging the world's journalists to act responsibly was to control the makeup of the body. Consequently, one of the earliest free-press battles within the United Nations centered on the membership of the subcommission and the relationship between those members and their home governments. The Americans wanted the subcommission to be an independent body of experts who could look at the problem of international freedom of information free from governmental influences. In this way, argued the Americans, subcommission members could "create world plans, above the interests of any particular power." The Russians wanted subcommission members to be representatives of governments. This latter approach was vital, the Soviets said, if the United Nations wanted the governments involved to implement the subcommission's recommendations. As representatives of governments, subcommission members could obligate their governments to abide by decisions made during discussions.[4] Ultimately, a compromise called for a subcommission composed of independent experts appointed by governments, with members' actions not binding on their home governments. The other side of this compromise was, of course, that home governments allegedly would not influence the actions of the subcommission's members. In reality, this decision brought government interests into free-press discussions. Much to the dismay of American journalists, subcommittee appointees epitomized the variety of approaches to freedom of information taken by governments. Members from the Soviet bloc generally represented official propaganda agencies; members from the West were fairly free of governmental influence; other delegates had some connection with government information programs. This combination placed the ideal of a subcommission free from governmental influence beyond reach and tainted most discussions of freedom of information with the various biases represented.[5]

The question of reconciling freedom of the press with its responsible exercise dominated the first session of the Subcommission on Freedom of Information and of the Press. Zechariah Chafee, Jr., a Harvard law professor and internationally recognized scholar on First Amendment issues, was the United States' representative on the subcommission; on his shoulders rested the responsibility for perpetuating the free-press crusade within the United Nations. Chafee's credentials as an advocate of First Amendment rights saved his nomination from opposition by professional journalists, who normally would have questioned placing such an important task in the hands of an academic.[6] Chafee's assignment was likely to bring him into conflict with American journalists, however, because his task was to combine the disparate views on freedom of the press advocated by professional journalists, intellectuals, and State Department diplomats into one position that the United States could support and that would win backing from other nations as well.

Many observers believed that the first segment of Chafee's constituency—the professionals—epitomized American journalism if only because the world evaluated American freedom of the press in terms of the performance of United States correspondents. These professionals, led by individuals such as Kent Cooper, believed that removing "all obstacles to the flow of information and the independent publication of newspapers" was the only answer to all press-related problems. To them, freedom of the press meant "freedom from such special interests as business organizations, labor unions and political lobbies, freedom from governmental control beyond the laws of libel, and freedom from the regulation of the journalistic profession beyond moral pressures." The intellectual position, stated in *Peoples Speaking to Peoples*, a publication of the Hutchins Commission on Freedom of the Press, included a call for the creation of correspondents' organizations throughout the world armed "with strict self-administered codes of ethics" to upgrade professional performance. The State Department view, expressed in the report of the National Commission for UNESCO, stressed concern over the quality of international communication and called for "serious study of the means by which mass media may be of more positive and creative service to the cause of international understanding."[7]

Even though two out of three of these stances seemed to advocate imposing certain responsibilities on journalists to ensure their positive contributions to international peace, all the views placed the United States at the liberal end of the spectrum concerning freedom of the press. The Russians, who supported strict injunctions on the press to enforce responsible journalism, were at the other extreme. Between the two superpowers were the other nations of the world, which regarded American campaigns for freedom of information that ignored the problem of press abuses with great suspicion. The smaller nations also feared that the American definition of freedom of the press meant "freedom for the invasion of powerful wire services, freedom for the cartellization of international news agencies, freedom to run the individual correspondent of the small newspaper out of business."[8] Optimism was at an all-time low as Chafee and representatives of eleven other countries sat down for the first subcommission meeting in May 1947. The challenge was to find enough commonality among all practices of freedom of information—American and others—to provide the foundation for an international guarantee. But any guarantee so produced obviously would have trouble meeting American standards.

Difficulties within the subcommission were apparent immediately as members differed over whether they should determine the rights, obligations, and practices inherent within the concept of freedom of the press by looking at the dangers that freedom of the press presented or the advantages that that freedom offered. Or, perhaps, delegates should not discuss freedom of the press at all. Perhaps debate should focus on the broader phrase freedom of information.[9] As G. J. van Heuven Goedhart of the Netherlands argued, freedom of information centered on "the free flow of news from its sources to the different means of distributing the news to the public, while freedom of the press referred to the dissemination of news from the distributing organizations to the public." Further differentiating between the two, he said that freedom of information concerned the operations of news agencies and other news-gathering and transmitting agencies, while "freedom of the press was considered a right of the citizen to freely express his views." Despite the fact that the conference was to deal with freedom of information, van Heuven Goedhart believed that freedom of the press also must be discussed.[10]

Unable to agree on this issue, subcommission members moved on to their most immediate assignment—planning the agenda for the United Nations Conference on Freedom of Information scheduled for Geneva in Spring 1948. Again the relationships between delegates' home governments and the press of those countries played a key role in decision making. For example, in writing the agenda item on the right of correspondents to enter other countries to gather news, an argument developed over semantics as delegates focused on whether conferees should discuss bona fide or accredited correspondents. Chafee thought accredited was a neutral term since that criteria "could be judged by clear evidence" while bona fide carried "a moral judgment." J. M. Lomakin of the Soviet Union wanted to abandon bona fide in favor of "words such as honesty, reliability and respectability," arguing that to earn permanent accreditation to a country a correspondent "must be of good moral character and reliable." Other characteristics of this paragon of reporters, according to P. H. Chang of China, included objectivity and a proper attitude. A foreign correspondent should be "a well-balanced, fair individual with a sense of fair play, and man of responsibility."[11]

American efforts to guarantee a correspondent's right to enter foreign countries, to have access to news sources, and to freely transmit copy from abroad clashed with the ideas of delegates who were interested in protecting their countries' national sovereignty and who were worried about the influence of foreign correspondents. André Géraud of France, for example, wanted the Geneva conference to consider whether governments should treat correspondents working for media in their own countries differently from foreigners working as journalists in other countries. "No one would quarrel with the right of a correspondent working in his own country who started a campaign to change his form of government," Géraud said. "But it is difficult to conceive that the same right should be accorded a foreign correspondent working in countries in which he is not a citizen. It would be a charge of dynamite at the heart of a nation." Chang had similar concerns about granting foreign correspondents unlimited freedom. Likening a foreign correspondent to an executioner unrestrained by judges or courts, he said that China favored freedom of the press but that the Chinese also wanted "to supervise whether it is news, gossip or lies that are printed, and check on the right of the press to make this decision."[12]

Almost every item proposed by the United States or its allies for the conference agenda brought an argument from the Russians or their Eastern European allies against including the point for discussion at Geneva and vice versa. Debate over an item to protect reporters abroad found Chafee stressing that foreign correspondents were "ambassadors of thought" who deserved a degree of protection similar to that provided diplomats. If nations granted such privileges, Lomakin countered, news personnel must make concessions in the area of responsibility. Czechoslovakia's Lev Sychrava also thought that provisions protecting correspondents heightened the need for reporters to be individuals of good faith, who would not misuse their privileges. Some items for the Geneva conference agenda were proposed quickly, protested quickly, and, generally, adopted quickly, despite Soviet objections. Lomakin wanted to delete an item calling for the eventual elimination of censorship of correspondents' copy because "censorship was usually the result of the unreliability of correspondents." Chafee short-circuited that Soviet protest by noting that he was not proposing the total abolishment of censorship but was simply advocating the installation of informed censorship under which journalists knew forbidden topics before they filed their stories. In addition, a correspondent should be told if his story had been censored to "prevent him for making the same mistake again."[13] The Chafee proposal, of course, was an implicit condemnation of Soviet censorship practices.

Lomakin also protested calls for the conference to examine the inequitable distribution of communications facilities around the world; he claimed that rebuilding newspaper plants or newsprint manufacturing capacity would detract from efforts to rebuild homes, hospitals, and schools.[14] The European nations, however, were greatly concerned about scarcities in equipment, newsprint, and other supplies necessary for operating the mass media—and for different reasons. Géraud of France, for instance, protested that the disparities in materials among nations were so great that "freedom of information is in danger of being synonymous with a monopoly of information in favor of those who are best supplied. It could result in a sort of mass media imperialism." Van Heuven Goedhart, chairing the subcommission, agreed that the lack of resources posed a grave danger to freedom of information in Europe. "The situation with regard to the available amount of newsprint is so desperate, that it, in fact, completely frustrates freedom of information, however beautifully phrased it may be."[15] Obviously, inequities in material wealth must be discussed at any international conference designed to promote the cause of international freedom of information.

The problem of dissemination of false news surfaced in debates over the agenda for the Geneva conference as well. Lomakin wanted the conference to study the problem of false reports "which confuse the broad masses of people and tend to aggravate relations between countries and interfere with the strengthening of confidence, mutual understanding and the establishment of a lasting peace." The Russian representative also suggested that the subcommission decide what the role of the press should be in peacetime, arguing that "since the war, some newspapers in a number of countries had worked to promote misunderstanding and distrust among friendly nations instead of creating goodwill among the Allies." If the subcommission planned to recommend certain privileges for the press, Lomakin said, members first must determine the "tasks of the press," which went far beyond the mere reporting of information. His list of affirmative obligations for the press reached into the political, economic, and social realms, stating that journalists had the responsibility

> (a) to struggle for international peace and security; (b) to develop friendly relations among nations based on respect for the principle of independence, equal rights, and self-determination of peoples; (c) to organize the struggle for democratic principles, for the unmasking of the remnants of Fascism and for the extirpation of Fascist ideology in all its forms; (d) to co-operate in solving problems of an economic, social, cultural or humanitarian character, and to encourage respect for human rights and for fundamental freedoms for all without distinction as to race, sex, language or religion; (e) along with the development of freedom of information, to organize an effective campaign against organs of the press and information which are inciting the peoples to war and aggression and a decisive and unremitting unmasking of war mongers.[16]

Placing any responsibilities on the press disturbed Christian A. R. Christensen of Norway. Adoption of the Soviet list, Christensen said, meant that "the press would thus become a weapon of the state." Granted, the struggle for international peace was vital, "but it was a greater one to seek the truth." Although truthful reporting might, at times, hinder international peace, Christensen believed that fair and honest reporting generally assisted international understanding.[17] Even thinking that the press had an affirmative responsibility to support governmental policy offended Archibald MacKenzie of the United Kingdom, who believed "the press's only responsibility is to tell the truth."[18] After additional debate, delegates adopted a softer, more positive, amended version of the Russian proposal, calling on the press "to tell the truth without prejudice," "to spread knowledge without malicious intent," "to facilitate the solution of the economic, social and humanitarian problems of the world as a whole through the free interchange of information," "to help promote respect for human rights and fundamental freedoms for all," and "to help maintain international peace and security through international understanding and co-operation."[19] To the Americans, however, calling on the press to abide by any standards other than internal norms was highly distressing.

American diplomats and press representatives had encountered a variety of proposals to impose standards of responsibility on journalists over the years. The latest lesson came during subcommission debates over the agenda for the Geneva conference. The French, for instance, suggested a conference agenda that called for the adoption of measures to protect the world from abuses of freedom of information by standardizing libel laws, applying a universal right of reply law, and circulating official denials of erroneous news accounts.[20] Primary American goals for the Geneva conference were familiar—freedom from censorship, equality of access to news sources and transmission facilities, ease of travel for correspondents, and preferential treatment of news dispatches by cable companies. Attaining these goals without some concessions from the American delegation, however, was unlikely. In return for assenting to the United States' proposals, other nations might reasonably expect American journalists to accept a code of ethics enforced by sanctions, an international right of reply law, effective measures to prevent the spreading of false news, and the establishment of a body to investigate violations of press freedom.[21]

Although the State Department viewed the conference agenda that emerged from the subcommission debates as "satisfactory beyond expectations," the agenda contained some problems. For instance, an American call for the progressive elimination of censorship was "now hedged about with qualifying conditions regarding national security, public order, etc." In addition, subcommission members had inserted attempts to create a distinction between foreign and domestic correspondents, as well as item calling for the creation of a foreign correspondents' corps with self-disciplinary powers in leading news centers of the world. Chafee initiated the latter item over vigorous objections from Llyod Free, a key State Department planner on freedom of information matters. Free feared that any effort to force correspondents to engage in self-discipline would be more acceptable to nations favoring the imposition of affirmative obligations on the press than to Americans, that host countries would use such a process to prevent American journalists from transmitting unfavorable news about the host country, and that host governments would cite unfavorable decisions by the correspondents' organizations as the basis for expelling reporters or for not readmitting them. While the agenda was generally acceptable, Free warned American journalists not to expect quick acceptance of American free-press ideas at the Geneva conference. The agenda debate had "strongly confirmed the fact that most of the countries of the world do not see eye-to-eye with America on freedom of information. Their position, rather, is somewhere in between the extremes of the U.S. view, on the one hand, and the Russian, on the other." That position allowed these nations to agree that freedom of the press was good, while stressing various affirmative obligations for the press and showing "much less distrust of governmental power as a means of implementing these obligations."[22]

Conference agenda proposals survived reviews by the Social Committee of the Economic and Social Council, the council itself, and the General Assembly without major alterations. But delegates within these other bodies added some points that led to substantial debates in Geneva. The Americans won approval for inclusion of language calling for the elimination of peacetime censorship, for example, while the French succeeded in adding a proposal for creation of an international identity card for professional journalists. An Indian request for the conference to seek ways to protect small domestic news agencies from the overpowering competition of foreign news-gathering organizations ran into strong opposition from United States delegate Leroy D. Stinebower. Obviously keeping in mind the expansionist goals of American news agencies, Stinebower protested that support for domestic agencies could turn into discrimination against foreign agencies.[23] A revised version of the Indian amendment to the agenda was finally approved.[24]

Delegates also added a Lebanese-sponsored amendment to the agenda that called for imposing an affirmative responsibility on journalists "to combat any ideologies whose nature could endanger" basic rights and freedoms. The proposal was introduced in an effort to counter Soviet attempts to condemn fascists and warmongers.[25] Although debate participants viewed this statement as requiring journalistic opposition to communism as well as opposition to any recurrence of fascism, the statement still required journalists to do more than simply report the news. The Soviets wanted journalists to assume a positive responsibility to advance enumerated political, economic, and social goals. The Lebanese proposal made the responsibilities of journalists even more specific. With the insertion of this notion into the conference agenda, the international free marketplace of ideas envisioned by American press leaders before and during World War II receded farther into the background, greatly upsetting American journalists.[26]

THE SUBCOMMISSION PLANS AN INTERNATIONAL CONFERENCE

The Geneva conference was still some months away when the subcommission convened for its second session with several important conference-related matters pending. For example, the subcommission still had not defined freedom of information or established a list of rights, obligations, and practices encompassed therein. And the subcommission also was to draft freedom of information clauses for both the International Declaration on Human Rights and the Covenant on Human Rights. Each item was controversial, but Article 17 of the draft Covenant on Human Rights provoked the most anguish among American journalists. As developed by the Commission on Human Rights, that article included a clause that allowed the imposition of restrictions on freedom of the press for

> matters which must remain secret in the interests of national safety; publications intended or likely to incite persons to alter by violence the system of Government, or to promote disorder or crime; obscene publications; (publications aimed at the suppression of human rights and fundamental freedoms); publications injurious to the independence of the judiciary or the fair conduct of legal proceedings; and expressions or publications which libel or slander the reputations of other persons.

Exact phraseology of the article was left to the subcommission, but the general direction that the section must take was clear.[27] The Declaration of Human Rights would not have the force of law but would serve as a moral statement of ideals for member nations to follow. The Covenant on Human Rights, however, would bind all member nations signing it. National and state laws must conform to the covenant's provisions, and the United Nations would create a mechanism to deal with violations.[28]

As soon as the subcommission reconvened in January 1948, the limitations clause in the draft covenant attracted significant attention. Arguments clustered around the question of whether the limitations listed should be specific or general, which served as camouflage for the real question of how free the press should be to operate around the world. Terming the road to specific limitations "perilous," José Mora of Uruguay expressed the fear that "to travel along it might be to nullify declarations of freedom." Any limitations cited in the covenant must be carefully defined, Géraud of France believed. Otherwise, governments would interpret the covenant's limitations, and governmental interpretation likely would lead to harsher restrictions than originally intended.[29] On the other hand, the Soviet Union's Lomakin viewed specific, wide-ranging limitations on the liberty of the press as absolutely essential. The Russian representative argued that because "the world had just emerged from a terrible war, the objectives and scope of the press had changed." Consequently, the United Nations must limit the ability of the press to be used "as a vehicle of war propaganda and exhortation to revenge."[30]

Now, the question became one of how to write a covenant article that permitted the narrowest possible interpretation. Most delegates, for instance, agreed that governments must be allowed to keep some information confidential. But what information? And how confidential? Delegates decided that the term national safety as found in the Human Rights Commission's draft was too broad, and they favored national military defense as a more limited phrase. Likewise, a statement permitting governments to restrict "publications intended or likely to incite persons to alter by violence the system of government" was considered too broad. Here, George V. Ferguson of Canada argued that the clause would allow bureaucrats to suppress any objectionable publication. The restriction would be especially oppressive in France, Géraud said, because "under the French Constitution it was the duty of every citizen to resist by force any government which proved itself tyrannical." Mora of Uruguay argued that governments should "permit all publications, so that they might know if any groups were plotting to overthrow the system of government." In fact, movements that did not publish their ideas were the most dangerous. The subcommission agreed that some restriction on language designed to incite the overthrow of the government was necessary, but members delayed drafting the exact wording.[31]

Similar discussions focused on the other restrictions. At each point, delegates cited the supposed power of the covenant as a reason to include or exclude the proposed limitation. The awesome power of a document that could override national laws and constitutions made the careful consideration of the list of restrictions on the activities of the press essential. According to some subcommission members, if a desired limitation was not on the document's final list and a signatory government wanted to impose that restriction, the covenant would bar such action. Some critics of the limitations provision also contended that if the covenant contained a restriction on press freedom that a signatory government did not wish to impose, that government would be helpless to withstand the measure. Thus, finding a series of limitations on the press agreeable to all nations—which was almost an impossible task anyway—grew harder as delegates became convinced that national sovereignty fell before the document.[32] Complicating the limitations debate even more was the growing rivalry between the Soviet Union and the United States. If the American representative accepted a particular point, the Russian delegate almost certainly rejected the provision, and vice versa. Debate became an exercise in futility, but subcommission members continued to pursue the impossible goal of writing a limitations clause acceptable to all countries having all varieties of freedom of the press.

After long debate, the subcommission agreed on a draft Article 17 for the Covenant on Human Rights guaranteeing that "every person shall have the right to freedom of thought and expression without interference by governmental action: this right shall include freedom to hold opinions, to seek, receive and impart information and ideas, regardless of frontiers, either orally, by written or printed matter, in the form of art, or by legally operated visual or auditory devices." Such rights carried duties and responsibilities, the subcommission said, and "penalties, liabilities or restrictions limiting this right may therefore be imposed for causes which have been clearly defined by law." The subcommission said restrictions on press freedom were acceptable under the following circumstances: if the vital interests of the state were at stake; if communications might incite hearers or readers to alter the system of government by violence; if the message urged persons to commit crimes; if the communication was obscene; if the information was likely to impede the fair conduct of legal proceedings; if the message infringed a legal copyright; and if the comment was libelous. Nations could institute a right of reply law, if they so desired. The covenant outlawed prior censorship of print media, radio, newsreels. The article also called for measures "to promote the freedom of information through the elimination of political, economic, technical and other obstacles which are likely to hinder the free flow of information."[33]

American journalists were highly critical of the draft covenant article. *Editor & Publisher*, for instance, denounced the covenant article as a "trickily written" statement that "will do more towards suppressing the existing free press in America than it will liberate the press of eastern Europe now under the shackles of the Soviet concept." Although the American Newspaper Guild did not join *Editor & Publisher* in terming the covenant article an "anathema to a free press,"[34] the Guild's executive board decided that the limitations clause went "far beyond the acceptable bounds in permitting improper curbs upon a free press." A Guild resolution picked the covenant's list of permissible restrictions apart one by one, saying, for example, that the article's bar against the incitement to overthrow an existing government "could have been used in the days of the American Revolution to silence the voice of Patrick Henry."[35]

Chafee tried to allay the critics' fears by stressing that the covenant could not force a government to pass any laws curbing press freedom against the government's will. All the covenant paragraph said was "that a nation will not be violating its promise to protect freedom of expression if its lawmakers decide that some publications within the listed types are so objectionable that they ought to be penalized by a well defined law." In fact, the paragraph accurately reflected journalistic life in the United States, where legal restrictions against libel and obscenity were common as were special limits on freedom of speech in times of war. "It might be very pleasant for the press to obtain absolute freedom through the Covenant, but this is crying for the moon," Chafee said. The best that American journalists could hope for, given the realities of life within the United Nations, was an assurance of freedom of information "qualified by some permissive exceptions." Furthermore, the proposed article contained safeguards "against tyrannical interpretation of the specific limitations" by requiring that any restrictions be imposed by lawfully enacted statute. This language meant that legislators elected by the people had to write any nation's list of limitations. All in all, Chafee termed the covenant draft reasonable.[36]

American journalists were not too sure about Chafee's assessment, however, and they unenthusiastically awaited the Geneva Conference on Freedom of Information, where the covenant draft would be among the items to be debated. The conference agenda offered both opportunities and dangers to American journalists and diplomats charged with forwarding United States proposals for worldwide freedom of information. Debates would look at the fundamental principles "to which the press, radio and films, as media of information, should have regard in performing their basic functions of gathering, transmitting and disseminating news and information without fetters" such as:

> (a) To tell the truth without prejudice and to spread knowledge without malicious intent; (b) To facilitate the solution of the economic, social and humanitarian problems of the world as a whole through the free interchange of information bearing on such problems; (c) To help promote respect for human rights and fundamental freedoms for all, without distinction as to race, sex, language, or religion; (d) To help maintain international peace and security through understanding and co-operation between peoples.

Specifically, conference delegates were to find ways to promote the gathering and dissemination of information, to ensure that all people received accurate and comprehensive information, to establish continuing machinery to promote freedom of information, to create ways for one country to share information about itself with other countries, and to write agreements that would put these measures into effect.[37]

When the proposal for an international press conference was first presented in 1946, American journalists thought the meeting might promote worldwide freedom of the press. In the year and a half since the adoption of the proposal, however, the world situation had worsened considerably, with Czechoslovakia falling under communist domination just six weeks before the conference convened. Negotiating international free-press accords in such circumstances would not be easy, said *Editor & Publisher*, as the trade journal expressed doubts as to whether the timing of the early 1948 meeting was "propitious."[38] State Department planners also held little hope for the conference because, among other things, peacetime restrictions on the free flow of information had become more pronounced. As the conference opening neared, the prospect for attaining world freedom of information was considered bleaker than ever.[39] Furthermore, Soviet attacks on the United States press had fashioned "an atmosphere in which calm discussion seems almost impossible." The Soviet propaganda attacks, which some observers saw as timed to undermine the conference, probably would also create problems with middle-of-the-road nations, which considered American views on freedom of information too liberal. Thus, the latter countries would probably be willing to accept "restrictions on freedom of information which are greater than the U.S. is willing to allow."[40]

THE UNITED STATES FACES CHARGES OF CULTURAL IMPERIALISM

The American free-press system obviously was the prime target for many conference delegations other than those representing the Soviet bloc. Charges that cultural imperialism lurked within American efforts to export the nation's First Amendment values, which already had been heard, echoed throughout the conference. American delegates believed that those fears were groundless, but these apprehensions had "swept the world in recent months, fanned on by Communist propaganda based on anti-U.S. nationalism." State Department planners realized that concern about the dangers posed by American culture had gained an international foothold because "a world whose communication facilities were shattered by the war looks with apprehension at U.S. preponderance in terms both of facilities and 'know-how.'" Consequently, "other nations fear a flood of American material which they believe may engulf their own cultures. They look with trepidation at American comic-strips and films and are apprehensive lest their own people be turned into 'gum-chewing Americans'."[41]

For instance, the Swedish representative of King Features, a major American distributor of comic strips and other syndicated materials, reported that the communists were campaigning against American comic strips because "the comics are being published by newspapers everywhere and nearly all comics constantly give glimpses of American everyday life and of American ideals." The number of children and young people reading the American comic strips allegedly worried the communists because the strips introduced the youths to noncommunist ideas and showed a United States in which people lived good lives, had successful careers, and owned houses and

automobiles—all concepts that the communists wished to hide from potential converts. The communist attack was not the only onslaught facing
American comic strips abroad, however, for political and press leaders in
Sweden also were questioning the continued use of American comic strips
by Swedish publications. One recurring criticism of American comics was
that they stressed crime, violence, and sensationalistic stories and drawings.
Teachers, lawyers, social workers, and parents in Sweden debated whether
these values were appropriate for their children to adopt.[42] Interestingly,
while such debates were occurring abroad, similar groups in America were
raising the same questions about the impact of comic strips and comic books
on young people in the United States. These American groups were
campaigning for restrictive legislation in various states to stop the flow of the
more objectionable material.[43] Ignoring the fact that identical concerns were
being voiced on both sides of the Atlantic, the State Department was ready
to protest when France considered limiting the percentage of foreign comics
that French publications could use or possibly excluding foreign comics
from France completely. Assistant Secretary of State George V. Allen
reported that the proposal violated the basic principles of freedom of
information and said that the American view "has been informally but
cogently communicated to the French Government. Our Embassy is
keeping a close watch on the matter."[44]

Even greater evidence of the effect American media could have on a
country if given free reign was apparent daily in Germany and Japan. In
those countries, the United States military governments saw the remodeling
of the press systems of the two defeated enemies in the image of the American
press system as part of their reconstruction tasks. Journalists serving in the
American military ran the newspapers and radio stations in Germany and
Japan for a time and then trained nationals who were untainted by the wartime regimes to run newspapers, news agencies, and broadcasting facilities.
Visiting journalists from the United States encouraged native reporters to
employ American techniques in dealing with public officials; numerous
Japanese and German journalists visited the United States for training sessions at the American Press Institute and several universities around the
country; Japanese and German journalists established professional organizations modeled after the American Society of Newspaper Editors and other
United States groups. The goal of these various efforts obviously was to
create a press system in Germany and Japan that emulated press operations
in the United States. The reason for the goal was equally plain—as
American journalists had been saying in every possible forum for years—
freedom of the press as practiced in the United States was the only way to
save the world from another war. If American occupation forces could
convert the press operations in the two major enemy powers of World War
II to freedom of the press, American style, then the Americans could use
their successes as blueprints for makeovers in other parts of the world. To

countries becoming increasingly dependent on the United States for economic reconstruction and military protection, the fear that mandatory changes in their press systems might be part of the price tag for such assistance was great. Most nations had press systems quite different from that of the United States. These countries were proud of their press systems and, certainly, did not want their systems made into carbon copies of the American press—especially since many nations so ardently disliked United States journalistic practices.[45]

Apprehension over American cultural imperialism was also likely to arise when the discussion turned to the overpowering nature of American news agencies. State Department planners believed that delegates could fend off this accusation by pointing out that the American concept of freedom of information stressed a "two-way flow of information between the various countries of the world. It must be made clear that we seek a situation where peoples can speak to peoples and not just America speak to the rest of the world." Still another manifestation of this fear of American cultural imperialism might show itself through the consideration of ways to protect developing national news agencies from the domination of American wire services. This infant-industries argument was appealing to many delegations because the dissemination of information was considered "vital to the preservation of national cultures." Although department advisers offered no advance position on the domestic news agencies issue, planners told American delegates to be sympathetic while insisting "that the end result must not be 'cultural isolationism' on a nationalistic basis."[46]

Calls by American delegates for international freedom to gather and transmit news also attracted criticism because some nations resented the United States' demanding permission for American correspondents to enter foreign countries on an unrestricted basis while America refused to allow all foreign reporters to enter the United States freely. The problem here rested with United States immigration laws that barred persons with criminal records, certain diseases, or, more importantly, holding membership in subversive organizations from entering the country. The restrictions prohibited communist reporters from entering the United States unless they worked for Tass, thus gaining admittance as representatives of the Russian government, or were assigned to cover the United Nations.

The United States position on international freedom of the press had been significantly weakened by several incidents in late 1947 and early 1948 relating to the admission of communist correspondents. In September 1947, for instance, Pierre Courtade, foreign political editor of *L'Humanité*, the Paris communist daily, sought permission to enter the United States to cover United Nations sessions. After much delay and in response to a special plea from the secretary-general, the Justice Department finally agreed to grant Courtade a limited visa to stay in the United States for the duration of the United Nations meeting. The visa restricted his travel to the vicinity of the

United Nations and prohibited his involvement in "extracurricular, subversive, or propaganda activities, or agitation against the U.S." during his stay. The latter point apparently restricted Courtade's writing to topics relating solely to the United Nations meetings. When French Foreign Minister Georges Bidault announced plans to visit Washington, D.C., to discuss the Marshall Plan, Courtade wanted to accompany him. Only after the direct intervention of Bidault did American officials allow Courtade to leave the confines of New York City. His problem, Courtade said, in a comment that his American colleagues who had tried to cover the Council of Foreign Ministers sessions in Moscow earlier in 1947 must have understood, was "to cover the United Nations, without offending the United States."[47]

Editor & Publisher clearly saw the anomaly in the United States' position and commented, "For some strange reason our State Department which has been actively engaged in the campaign for worldwide freedom of information has done an about-face and attempts to emulate the totalitarian countries in their treatment of the press."[48] To the State Department's credit, however, the problem apparently rested in the Justice Department, where the Federal Bureau of Investigation vigorously protested allowing known communists to travel freely in the United States. State Department officials attempted to win permission for Courtade to accompany Bidault to Washington,[49] despite the feeling among some diplomats that Courtade wanted "to make a martyr of himself and would prefer to say that he was not permitted to travel to Washington."[50]

American officials compounded the errors of the Courtade case a few months later when immigration officials interned two correspondents accredited to the United Nations on Ellis Island. Only the direct intervention of United Nations Secretary-General Trygve Lie won the release of Nicholas Kyriazidis, correspondent for the Greek newspaper *Demokritis*, and Syed Hasan, correspondent for the Indian publication *People's Age*. United States officials, in explaining the arrests, said Kyriazidis had lost his status as an accredited correspondent when the newspaper that he represented closed. Without newspaper employment, Kyriazidis was simply a communist who was inadmissible to the United States. Hasan had entered the United States on a student visa and later picked up the newspaper employment; he was arrested for failure to maintain his status as a student. The arrests, said State Department officials, stemmed from a communications failure between the State Department and the United Nations, which was to have informed American officials of the men's status as accredited correspondents. Such official notification would have prevented the arrests.[51]

State Department officials questioned whether Kyriazidis could remain in this country as a correspondent because, in the department's view, the Greek was not a bona fide journalist. The definition of a bona fide journalist, a topic of liberal declamation by American representatives at the United

Nations, now meant an individual working full time for a newspaper and receiving the bulk of his income from newspaper employment. Thus, even with United Nations accreditation, under such terms Kyriazidis would have been ineligible to remain in the United States.[52] The department also defended its actions by stating that the headquarters agreement, which called for unquestioned admission of correspondents to cover the United Nations once United Nations officials had requested accreditation, had not gone into effect at the time of the arrests.[53] State Department defenses were generally ignored as journalists roundly criticized the jailing of the two reporters. The Standing Committee of United Nations Correspondents, whose members were permanently assigned to the international organization, led the protests. Endorsing that organization's resolution was the Foreign Press Association, representing members of the world's press assigned to New York, which stressed that its members would take any measures necessary to protect the rights of foreign correspondents stationed in the United States.[54]

Again, American demands for extensive freedom for United States correspondents abroad seemed hypocritical in light of the treatment accorded representatives of some foreign publications in the United States. State Department officials apparently acknowledged this inconsistency when they discussed the possibility of Kyriazidis seeking reaccreditation as a United Nations correspondent. Lacking any evidence that the Greek posed a danger to the security of the United States, the department probably should allow him to remain in America, officials said. Any attempt to deport Kyriazidis raised the prospects "of another *cause celebre* in the press and another clash with the United Nations on the question of whether we are abiding by the terms of the Headquarters Agreement." In addition, "such a conflict would be particularly unfortunate on the eve of the United Nations Conference on Freedom of Information, where the United States Delegation will be contending for freedom to travel, observe and report."[55]

Despite this background and despite the realization of the likelihood of criticism in Geneva, the suggested delegate response to such comments was inadequate and circular in reasoning, perhaps reflecting the basic weakness of the American position. American delegates to the international conference were to stress that communist reporters were not kept out of the United States because they were reporters but that their entry was barred because they were communists. No communists could enter the United States, so the United States was erecting no specific discrimination against correspondents. Consequently, the United States did indeed follow the practice it requested of other nations; all the United States wanted was equal treatment for reporters and other individuals in matters of entering and residing in foreign countries.[56]

American delegates knew that considerable embarrassment was also likely when the discussion turned to the international supply of newsprint, for the United States consumed more than 60 percent of the world's newsprint production and published huge newspapers in comparison to newspapers available in other parts of the world, where two- and four-page publications were the norm in postwar publishing.[57] Members of the United Nations already had pointed out the intimate relationship between the newsprint supply and freedom of the press, with more than one delegate suggesting that American publications should share their newsprint with nations unable to purchase enough of the precious commodity. As Brigadier General Carlos P. Rómulo of the Philippines told the General Assembly, the newsprint shortage reached into the heart of freedom of the press almost everywhere and required immediate solution. In referring to the forthcoming international press conference, Rómulo said he hoped that the American delegates would be willing to discuss and compromise on the newsprint issue: "Any world plan requires individual nations to make sacrifices." Other nations had showed their willingness to compromise on vital issues when they had helped to set up the United Nations in the hopes of creating a foundation for international peace. Now, accommodation was necessary to establish the basis for worldwide freedom of information.[58]

Usually supportive of efforts to develop freedom of the press internationally, *Editor & Publisher* was unwilling to call for American newspapers to share their newsprint with other countries. The nation's economy depended on advertising, the trade journal argued, and newspapers were a vital outlet for advertising. Any plan to give American newsprint to other countries would decrease the size of United States newspapers, meaning that the amount of advertising in each issue would be cut and that the American economy could go downhill once again.[59] This rationale was undermined less than a year before the Geneva conference when UNESCO released a study of newsprint availability in twelve countries. Among the study's findings were bits of damning evidence about American newsprint consumption. Before World War II, international newsprint production was 8.2 million tons annually, with the United States consuming 45 percent of the total. War reduced the total international production to 6.8 million tons in 1946, with the United States consuming 65 percent of the total. In 1946, each American citizen received the equivalent of fifty-nine pounds of newsprint annually; each British subject obtained the equivalent of fifteen and one-half pounds of newsprint a year. Newspapers in Peru, Canada, and Argentina published twenty pages a day; in the Philippines, the average daily newspaper size was twenty-four pages; in Great Britain and France, the average size of a daily newspaper was four pages.[60]

This situation resulted from the loss of newsprint production facilities during the war and from currency shortages that led the major manufacturers, Canada and the Scandinavian countries, to seek sound markets— meaning American newspapers. Although these inequities of supply and demand led to the imposition of rationing of available newsprint supplies in some countries and although rationing often led to government involvement in press activities,[61] American newspaper leaders generally were unmoved by the world's newsprint problem. If this argument was raised at Geneva, departmental planners suggested that American delegates stress the United States' support for practical measures to develop additional newsprint supplies rather than endorsing any efforts to reallocate existing supplies.[62]

Delegates also knew that several dangers awaited them within the conference agenda. The Soviets were expected to advocate the enumeration of certain tasks for the media, and, State Department advisers feared, without positive American leadership, middle-of-the-road nations, which would constitute a majority at the conference, might seek an undesirable compromise position. Departmental advisers continually warned that these nations defined freedom of information far more narrowly than Americans and thought about the press in terms of responsibility rather than of freedom. These nations, "genuinely concerned about the problems of peace, war mongering and fascism," were apt to seek governmental intervention to reach desired ends. American diplomats had been caught off guard at the United Nations when traditionally strong allies such as Canada and Australia had successfully advocated a compromise on the Soviet war-mongering resolution, much to the consternation of the United States. Greater care and preparation were necessary at Geneva, for merely restating the classic American theory of freedom of information would not win many converts. The United States must offer other delegations something positive if it did not want to find itself, "along with the U.S.S.R., in a state of lonely grandeur, while the great majority of the delegations adopt 'compromises' which, in fact, compromise freedom of information itself."[63]

All in all, the American delegation must seek positive corrective measures for problems consistent with the total goal of freedom of information. Department advisers warned that the United States delegation must try to put the Soviets on the defensive—a position frequently occupied by the Americans in the past. According to departmental advisers, the best strategy for delegates to follow here involved detailing the kind of world that the United States wanted to create—one in which democracy and peace would triumph. "The requisite of democracy is an informed citizenry; and of peace, international understanding. To both, freedom of information is a keystone. The right of the public to receive information—their right to be fully informed—must be protected and promoted." Consequently, the ideal delegate response to Eastern bloc charges of warmongering and criticisms about the dissemination of false information was endorsing "a multiplicity of unfettered sources of information available to members of the public." American delegates also expected to hear demands for mandatory codes of ethics and for international organizations to supervise the behavior of journalists. Many European nations considered such codes and enforcement procedures as vital to freedom of information, but American delegates planned to support only voluntary codes and enforcement procedures administered by journalists themselves.[64]

THE AMERICAN DELEGATION
TO GENEVA TAKES SHAPE

Each nation attending the Conference on Freedom of Information sent five delegates and five alternates to Geneva. Selecting the five individuals to represent the United States was not easy. The State Department encountered difficulty in finding persons who could win support from the press and who would be able to survive the turbulent diplomatic situation awaiting them. After William Benton, former assistant secretary of state for public affairs and now chairman of the board of Encyclopaedia Britannica, was named delegation chairman, he repeatedly expressed concern to department officials about finding top-quality American delegates who could compete with the outstanding talent expected from the Soviet bloc.[65] Benton believed that no delegation would win unanimous backing from American journalists, if only because the American press was "naive in this field" and failed to understand either the importance of the conference or the complexity of agenda issues. Even the most carefully selected delegation likely would be "attacked by powerful newspaper or other representatives with complaints, adjurations, demands, etc." Since newspaper leaders had great influence with Congress, Benton warned that not only was this area "potentially very hot indeed" but that it was "loaded with powerful vested interests. No chairman and no group of ten Delegates, and no policy or set of policies, can prove popular with more than a part of the constituency."[66]

As if to underline the divisions within the press, Hugh Baillie, president of United Press (UP), one of the agencies that had refused to continue supplying news to the government information program only two years earlier, told Benton that if the delegation was to include a representative of the wire services, Baillie wanted to help select that individual. After all, Baillie said, the wire services had different approaches to international freedom of the press.[67] Baillie ultimately showed up at Geneva on his own initiative and served as a consultant to the American delegation. He and his executive assistant were the only wire service representatives at the conference. The Associated Press (AP) turned down an invitation to send a representative for fear that the representative would be asked to comment on policy matters that were reserved for the news service's board of directors.[68] While Benton wanted a delegation capable of winning the respect of the American press, State Department planners worried about anticipated attacks on American media monopolies and wanted some delegates "whose annual incomes were not in the five or six figure range."[69]

In the end, the American delegation met both needs. Erwin D. Canham, editor of the *Christian Science Monitor* and first vice president of the American Society of Newspaper Editors (ASNE), served as vice chairman. Other delegates were Chafee; Sevellon L. Brown, editor and publisher of the Providence *Journal* and *Bulletin* and founder of the American Press

Institute; and Harry Martin, president of the American Newspaper Guild. Martin's selection was clearly the most troublesome; his appointment was held up by allegations that the Guild leader had communist leanings. The accusation was based on contributions Martin had made in the late 1930s to an organization labeled as a communist-front organization in 1948. Martin's appointment to the delegation came directly from President Harry S. Truman after numerous appeals on the Guild leader's behalf.[70] State Department planners were pleased with Martin's appointment. In addition to providing the working journalist's perspective, a Newspaper Guild representative on the delegation would offset the expected influence of the International Organization of Journalists (IOJ), which was now considered to be communist dominated.[71]

DELEGATES DEBATE A
NEWS-GATHERING CONVENTION

The topic facing the Conference on Freedom of Information that was of greatest interest to American news agencies and other journalists working overseas dealt with the international gathering and transmission of news.[72] The American delegation was ready to satisfy the demands of this important constituency by introducing a draft convention designed to relax procedures for entry, residency, and travel for accredited news personnel and to protect correspondents from unwarranted expulsion from a host country. American representatives also planned to try to ensure equality of access to both official and private sources of news for foreign and domestic correspondents. And delegates were prepared to advocate replacing existing censorship operations with a system that required copy to be altered in the presence of the reporter if such curtailment of the freedom to report was deemed necessary in peacetime.[73]

What seemed to be perfectly reasonable proposals in light of American practices, however, appeared as anything but reasonable to a variety of delegations at the conference. The British, for instance, disapproved of the American plans because the Americans wanted the proposed news-gathering convention to apply to colonial territories. The British also were unhappy about a call for nondiscriminatory press cable transmission rates within countries. The British communications system favored the commonwealth's own correspondents, a practice that United Kingdom diplomats wanted to protect.[74] P. C. Chang, the chief Chinese delegate, thought that the news-gathering convention's clause calling for free entry of correspondents might backfire on the Americans. For instance, he asked, would the United States Senate ratify the convention once senators discovered that the document "would enable Soviet correspondents to overrun Latin America, to speak of only one part of the world"? The draft treaty's phraseology created problems for United States correspondents operating in China as well, Chang contended, because the Chinese government allowed American reporters more freedom than it permitted correspondents from other countries. If a news-gathering convention required equal treatment of all correspondents, then American reporters would find their freedom circumscribed in China.[75]

When debate over the news-gathering convention reached the floor at the conference itself, delegates wanted to go off in numerous directions to reach the same alleged end of guaranteeing the freedom of correspondents to gather and transmit news. For instance, Geraud Jouve, a French delegate, believed that the first step toward achieving the guarantee was establishing a system for distributing professional press cards to correspondents. The cards would simplify the bearer's entry into other countries and protect reporters carrying them from unreasonable expulsion. In opposing the French proposal, J. E. Jay of the United Kingdom protested that the conference would bog down in deciding who would issue the press cards.[76]

To Julian Przybos of Poland, guaranteeing equality of access to journalists regardless of race, sex, language, religion, or nationality seemed absurd in the face of contemporary practices. Everyone knew, for example, that reporters from the Arab world did not have the same rights as French journalists in France. And in the United States, "the coloured population, although theoretically on an equal footing, did not have free access to sources of information, and were not able to attend public meetings attended by white people." While the conference could not interfere in the domestic policies of various nations, Przybos thought that current practices made proposals for equality of treatment impossible to implement and thus worthless to consider. While admitting that discrimination did create problems, Brown of the United States responded that the conference would make more progress if delegates restricted their discussions to the international exchange of news and avoided comments on the domestic policies of other countries. Agreeing, S. A. Jawad of Pakistan said that delegates should avoid going off on tangents, for the conference could not solve the domestic problems of participating states. Instead, delegates must seek agreement on broad principles and leave the details of implementation to signatory nations.[77]

Soviet bloc members took the debate in predictable directions. Eugen Klinger of Czechoslovakia protested that the news-gathering proposal was phrased in indefinite terms and that the convention's provisions completely neglected the responsibilities that journalists must fulfill "while enjoying exceptional facilities." The Hungarian delegate, Edmond Ferenczi, added that he was unable to support any proposal to grant correspondents unrestricted freedom after having read a Swiss newspaper story about American plans to establish "clandestine movements in certain European countries and supply them with funds" with the goal of overthrowing the governments in power. If the United States planned to engage in such subversive activities, other nations would have difficulty viewing American proposals for freedom for reporters to travel as "purely platonic." His country, for instance, would exercise caution as far as United States correspondents were concerned while "such schemes were being encouraged."[78] And if governments were to grant foreign correspondents unlimited freedom, governments, then, reasonably could ask that the reporters adhere to United Nations resolutions against the dissemination of false information and propaganda encouraging a new war, Yugoslavian delegate Stevan Dedijer contended.[79]

What about provisions in the draft news-gathering convention that called on countries to admit foreign correspondents "in a manner consistent with their respective laws and procedures"? Dedijer asked. To him, the phrasing was not much of an improvement on the existing situation. In defending the American wording, Brown accused the Yugoslav of taking the statement out of context. The proposal's language, Brown argued, clearly forbade "discrimination against representatives of the Press." But, the Polish delegate asked, did the language not also mean that "certain foreign journalists would continue to be refused admission into certain countries"? And, asked the Hungarian delegate, had not the United States itself been guilty of such discriminatory practices in the past?[80]

Coming to the rescue was Jay of the United Kingdom, who reminded members of the Soviet bloc, who usually were strong advocates of national sovereignty, that "every nation retained the right to refuse anybody entry into its territory. That was not a measure directed against the press, but a measure adopted in the interests of the country concerned." The essential principle involved, Brown added, was not a request for new freedoms but a plea for immigration laws to apply to journalists as they did to other citizens.[81] As expected, the restrictive immigration laws of the United States were long belabored by representatives of the communist nations in an effort to show American hypocrisy in seeking the free admission of American correspondents to all nations of the world while barring journalists from Eastern bloc nations and reporters from other countries who were members of the Communist party from America. The criticisms had been anticipated, for American diplomats knew their vulnerability on the point.[82]

The reliability of news sent by American correspondents from Eastern bloc nations also was of concern to representatives from those nations. Dedijer, for instance, pointed to stories in the New York *World Telegram* that reported alleged Yugoslavian preparations to attack Italy. The stories even invented a speech by Marshal Josip Broz Tito "alleging that Yugoslavia was ready to attack the American fleet in the Adriatic with atomic bombs." Surely, Dedijer said, the committee did not plan to assist the work of correspondents who were warmongers. Supporting his Eastern bloc colleague was Ferenczi, who protested against a story in the New York *Daily*

News that proclaimed "Murder is national policy in Hungary" and detailed the executions of "a handful of men who had thousands of murders on their conscience." Surely, Ferenczi said, the committee did not plan to help correspondents who spread false information. The United States proposal, Brown replied, would help all correspondents—reporters who dispatched false stories as well as reporters who transmitted true stories—in the belief that readers would accept the true stories and reject the false stories. Only if all views were allowed to leave a country could the self-righting process of the marketplace of ideas work, he explained.[83]

Rather than attempting to stop Eastern bloc comments during debates over the news-gathering convention, delegates tended to allow the communists to bring up their timeworn arguments until the committee was ready to move on to other points. Once committee members disposed of most of the more flagrant Eastern bloc objections, members began work on the constructive details of the news-gathering convention. One of the first topics discussed called on governments to "permit the widest possible access to news sources, private and official, for all foreign press correspondents on the same bases as for national correspondents."[84] The American delegation had difficulty with this suggestion because its members wondered how governments could guarantee access to private sources of news and whether such a request was wise. American journalists wanted something more limited than this broad access; all they sought was the ability to compete equally with other journalists for official information.[85] Conference delegates, however, adopted language designed to ensure the reporter's ability to talk freely with private citizens, thus trying to institute a form of contact with a country's residents that some nations forbade.[86]

A United States proposal to have correspondents' copy transmitted "without censorship, editing or delay" was also considered vital to the dissemination of international information. The provision limited the acceptable grounds for censorship to "regulations relating directly to the maintenance of national military security" and said that if censorship was imposed, that review must be informed censorship.[87] After numerous protests from Soviet bloc nations that the United States and other Western allies practiced censorship of one sort or another and numerous proclamations by Western nations that censorship was destructive of freedom of information and international understanding, delegates adopted the American proposal made more specific by French amendments.[88] The Soviets, of course, practiced blind censorship through their Glavlit censorship agency, and no one expected the Russians to change their censorship practices, much less sign an international news-gathering treaty.

Jay introduced a British proposal for additional protection for foreign correspondents. The new language stressed the principle "that while foreign press correspondents must conform to the laws in force in the countries in which they were operating, they should not be expelled on account of their professional functions." A journalist should be so protected even if he criticized the government, Jay said, because "criticism was incidental," and protecting a journalist's right to comment on those in power was considered important in Great Britain. To show how different the practice was in other countries, Jay referred to the recent communist takeover in Czechoslovakia, during which government spokesmen had informed correspondents that only officially supplied information could be regarded as true. Because of the threat implicit in such a statement, Jay warned conferees to make sure that the news-gathering convention contained nothing that "would permit a correspondent to be dealt with as a spy if he took a line unpopular with the Government." Delegates approved a proposal designed to protect a journalist from arbitrary expulsion based on the content of his work for inclusion in the proposed news-gathering treaty.[89]

The Draft Convention on the Gathering and International Transmission of News, as approved by the conference, defined a foreign correspondent as an individual who was "regularly engaged in the collection and reporting of news (including opinion) to the general public" and identified as being so employed on his passport or similar internationally accepted document. Any nation signing the convention agreed to "expedite, in a manner consistent with their respective laws and procedures," the entry, residence, and movement both of the foreign correspondent himself and his necessary professional equipment. Signatories also promised to "impose no special discriminatory or unusual restrictions on such ingress or egress, nor upon the transit through or residence in their territories of such correspondents." Nations participating in the accord were to "permit and encourage the widest possible access to news, official and non-official, for all foreign correspondents on the same basis as for national correspondents" and were not to discriminate among foreign correspondents in granting such access.[90]

News material produced by the foreign correspondents was to leave the territory of contracting states "without censorship, editing or delay" except for situations "relating directly to the maintenance of national military security." Censorship for reasons of national military security, when in force, would apply equally to all foreign correspondents. In accordance with American arguments, the convention said that if peacetime censorship was established, the rules under which it operated must be clearly announced to reporters in advance and that reporters must participate in the review process. Reporters were "not to be expelled on account of any lawful exercise of their right to seek, receive or impart information or opinion." And journalists were to have access to facilities necessary for international transmission of news "on the same basis and at the same rates applicable to all other users of such facilities for similar purposes." Nothing in the convention abrogated laws regulating obscenity or national security matters.[91]

United States delegation chairman Benton expressed his delight with the conference's approval of the draft convention on news gathering. Benton firmly believed that the accord would "increase the volume, the diversity, and the accuracy of information available to the peoples of the world." Although the convention dealt only with the mechanical aspects of news gathering and transmission and would directly affect just a few thousand people, "its deeper effect will be felt by tens of millions" because foreign correspondents were " 'the Ambassadors of the Mind'. The more fully they are able to report, the better they will advance the understanding of men everywhere, and thus the better they will build the defenses of peace in the minds of men."[92] Adoption of the news-gathering convention was an unmitigated victory for the American interests, for the convention contained almost every point so ardently sought by United States advocates of worldwide freedom of information.

THE UNITED KINGDOM OFFERS A CONVENTION ON FREEDOM OF INFORMATION

Other proposals facing the conference were somewhat harder to bring into line with avowed American interests. The United Kingdom, for example, presented a draft convention on freedom of information that was so broadly written that American delegates refused to support it. The British proposal essentially was an effort to define freedom of information and to secure that freedom for individuals living within the territories of signatories. The draft guaranteed the right of individuals to "impart and receive information and opinions ... without governmental interference," which was acceptable to the Americans. But then the draft listed a variety of permissible restrictions on freedom of information including protection of data for national security reasons, regulation of obscene or blasphemous expressions, and barring of language intended to incite individuals to alter the existing system of government by violence.[93] For an American delegation strongly opposed to any listing of specific restrictions on freedom of information, the British itemization was totally unacceptable. The American delegation, however, was unable to dissuade the British from introducing their proposed convention. Thus, in an attempt to undercut support for the disagreeable document, members of the United States delegation planned to introduce a forceful resolution supporting the concept of freedom of information. This American proposal endorsed the basic ideas found in the first part of the British document but omitted the limitations listed in the second article of the draft convention. The Americans hoped that this resolution would supplant the British draft convention and would serve as the only statement necessary to guarantee freedom of information to people throughout the world.[94]

The American resolution termed freedom of information a fundamental right of the people, "the touchstone of all the freedoms to which the United Nations is dedicated, without which world peace cannot well be preserved." The resolution guaranteed everyone "the right to freedom of thought and expression," including the "freedom to hold opinions without interference; and to seek, receive and impart information and ideas by any means regardless of frontiers." The resolution also recognized the right of news personnel to gather information and said "the full exercise of these rights requires recognition of the rights of others, and protection by law of the freedoms, general welfare, and security of all." As a concession to delegates seeking to impose standards on the press, the American freedom of information resolution affirmed the "moral obligation of the press to seek the truth and report the facts." By fulfilling this moral obligation, reporters contributed "to the solution of the world's problems through the free interchange of information bearing on them, promoting respect for human rights and fundamental freedoms without arbitrary discrimination, and helping maintain international peace and security." The proper way to ensure appropriate professional performance, however, was by the pressure of public opinion and not by the creation of international rules and regulations.[95]

In supporting the American resolution, Canham spoke of the "profound conviction of those of us like myself who are members of the American newspaper profession that freedom of information does not belong to the press. It is not a possession of the press, it is not a right of newspapers, it is a right of the people." The people had the right to be informed, to consult different sources of news and opinion, to think for themselves, to make up their own minds, to function as "active, voting, thinking citizen[s] in a free democracy."[96] Despite Canham's eloquence and the adoption of his resolution, the British convention on freedom of information was warmly received by conferees.

The goal of the British convention, explained Ernest Davies of the United Kingdom, was to "guarantee freedom of expression and the unimpeded flow of information." The first article repeated what was commonly agreed to regarding "the free procurement and dissemination of information." The second article "listed the formal limitations demanded for the welfare or security of society" that were "clearly defined in statutory form." Although drafters of the United Kingdom convention wished to avoid "extraneous limitations, serving ideological aims," such proposals were likely as long as members of the Soviet bloc participated in the debate. Leo Mattes, a Yugoslavian delegate, fulfilled this role by introducing an amendment to the list of limitations that would outlaw the dissemination of false information and material leading to the incitement of a new war. In arguing against Mattes's suggestion, Davies responded that while all nations opposed warmongering, many countries also opposed "granting governments powers to restrict the freedom of information by censoring any information or opinions which they might wish to interpret as Fascist. The people of an educated, intelligent democracy should be able to decide for themselves what to reject as Fascist opinions."[97] Delegates rebuffed efforts to include traditional Soviet bloc provisions within the list of limitations in the United Kingdom convention, although delegates adopted a modified version of the proposal on false information. This proposal, backed by numerous American allies, supported General Assembly resolutions against false information and warmongering adopted in 1947. It also called on journalists "to serve the aims of friendship, understanding and peace by accomplishing their task in a spirit of accuracy, fairness and responsibility."[98]

During debates over the list of limitations for the British convention, Walter M. Kotschnig, chief of the State Department's division of international organization affairs, revealed the exasperation of the United States delegation regarding the continual arguments about restricting the freedom of the press. Rather than developing a convention promoting freedom of information, Kotschnig charged, delegates were "formulating an ever-lengthening list of restrictions," which might lead to a document "unacceptable, not only to those who had no desire to assume extra international obligations at this moment, but also to governments who had sent delegations to the Conference in the earnest hope that a workable agreement would be reached." He suggested, unsuccessfully, that the list of permissible restrictions be drastically shortened.[99]

One controversial amendment to the United Kingdom convention came from the representative of India who suggested language allowing countries to erect a wall of protectionism around developing national news agencies "until such time as such news agencies are fully developed" and to "prevent agreements in restraint of the free flow of information or the cartelisation in regard to information."[100] The Indian amendment was to be added to Article 3 of the original British proposal, which referred to "the right of any Contracting State to take measures which it deems necessary in order to bring its balance of payments into equilibrium."[101] That article, Davies said when objecting to the Indian perversion of it, was "prompted by difficulties involved in the shortage of newsprint." The British put no political connotations in the language and saw the provision as "restricted to questions of press materials and not to the free movement of journalists."[102] The Indian amendment obviously had a different goal, with G. S. Bhalja, the Indian delegate, arguing that the proposal simply recognized the inherent right of each country to develop news agencies to serve its native population.[103] Despite Indian practices that seemed to indicate a desire to exclude American news agencies from the Asian subcontinent, Bhalja denied that his proposal was "a cover for discrimination against foreign press correspondents." His country simply intended "to bring the development of Indian information agencies up to the standard of those of other countries."[104]

American delegates opposed the Indian amendment, arguing the obvious impropriety of a conference designed to tear down barriers to freedom of information sanctioning the creation "in some countries of single news agencies with some forms of government subsidy or support in the way of lower transmission rates." The end result of such practices would be multiple monopolies throughout the world, Brown said, noting that "in the news field such practices are particularly dangerous and must be used, if at all, with great care for fear that a news monopoly will result under which only one version of the news may reach a people." Although sympathizing with the Indian desire to build a stronger national news agency, Brown added that Indian newspapers should be "served directly by more than one version of the news, as we insist upon doing in the United States."[105] P. C. Chaudhuri of India countered that American practice was irrelevant to India and that the conference must "assist these national agencies covering domestic news and all matters relating to the life of the country, a sphere in which they were more impartial than foreign agencies." The Indian proposal won support from Jacques Kayser of France, who noted that the Indian suggestion did not interfere with the work of foreign correspondents in a country and added that protection of developing news agencies was logical and right. The Lebanese delegate, Jamil Mikaoui, also backed the Indian proposal, announcing, in the process, that the Lebanese government planned to start just such an agency to serve its domestic press.[106] Delegates adopted the Indian amendment, which obviously appealed to countries with underdeveloped information systems, despite American objections.[107]

The American delegation abstained from voting on the United Kingdom convention because of "domestic differences in interpretation and legal practice," Benton said.[108] Conference delegates adopted the convention without support from the United States. In final form, the British convention contained another proposal by the Indian delegation that drew significant debate when the Indian representative added similar language to the draft article for the Covenant on Human Rights. This second Indian proposal allowed governments to punish persons for "the systematic diffusion of deliberately false or distorted reports which undermine friendly relations between peoples or States." The British convention also contained a westernized list of affirmative tasks for journalists. The convention called on a contracting state to "encourage the establishment and functioning within its territory of one or more non-official organizations of persons employed in the dissemination of information to the public, in order to promote the observance by such persons of high standards of professional conduct." Enforcing these standards through nonofficial organizations of professionals made the idea slightly more palatable to the Americans but establishing standards by which journalists would be judged was still objectionable. The proposed responsibilities of journalists in the British convention were: reporting "facts without prejudice and in their proper context"; aiding "the solution of the economic, social and humanitarian problems of the world as a whole and the free interchange of information bearing on such problems"; promoting "respect for human rights and fundamental freedoms without discrimination"; helping "maintain international peace and security"; and counteracting "the persistent spreading of false or distorted reports which promoted hatred or prejudice against States, persons or groups of different race, language, religion or philosophical conviction."[109]

THE FRENCH PROPOSE AN INTERNATIONAL RIGHT OF CORRECTION

In a measure aimed directly at meeting complaints about the spread of false news, the French—traditional advocates of combining press freedom and press responsibility—proposed a draft convention that called for the creation of an international right of correction. Although United Nations resolutions encouraged promoting friendly relations among nations and combating the dissemination of false news designed to upset those relations, the French proposal recognized the unlikelihood of international penalties "for the publication of false reports whatever may be their danger." Consequently, according to the French, an international right of correction was the only way "to give all those directly affected by what they consider to be a false report spread by an organ of information the right to obtain the publication by that same organ of corrections or replies." The proposal called for the injured government to request the publication of its version of the story. If the offending medium denied the government's request, the injured government could appeal to an international body empowered to hear complaints. If that organization found the complaint justified, that body could publish the official response.[110]

The French proposal was based on a system in effect in France for 125 years and already used in many other nations. The right of reply within these countries was designed primarily to lower the number of libel suits brought against media outlets by providing offended parties with ways to place their sides of the story before the public. The domestic right of reply laws gave some protection to home governments but were not meant to defuse international misunderstandings. Under existing international law, the only way that nations assailed in false news stories could obtain redress was through the voluntary cooperation of the medium involved. A mandatory international right of correction would make this protection available to all.[111]

American delegates worried about whether an international right of reply would turn the State Department into a propaganda agency for other countries, but the delegation, composed almost entirely of journalists, agreed that the measure imposed no responsibilities directly on the press.[112] In fact, many American newspapers considered publication of corrections as a part of responsible journalism, so the measure was not far removed from United States custom either. Because of the limited impact that the measure would have on the American press and the familiarity of the underlying precept, United States delegates were urged to support the French proposal—if only because other nations were likely to back the idea in significant numbers. If United States delegates found the French proposal objectionable in any of its particulars, State Department advisers suggested that rather than opposing the entire measure, delegates try to amend the draft convention to satisfy American concerns.[113]

In fact, the United States had proposed a right of reply within its draft convention on the international gathering and transmission of news. The American provision called for offended nations to send responses to the government of the nation in which the incorrect statement was published. The home government would then make the offended government's views available to news agencies for publication within that nation.[114] The right of reply proposed by the United States did not require the publication of a correction by the offending medium nor did the American proposal authorize an appeal beyond the government of the offending state. In contrast, the French proposal was mandatory and carried the right of appeal to an international organization. The French believed that the American approach was too narrow. The Americans continued to support the more limited proposal despite opposition,[115] in the hope that the French, who had already modified their draft convention under prodding from the United States, would agree to additional changes.[116]

French delegates, who had already given up their proposals for an international professional card,[117] were reluctant to agree to more alterations, but additional changes were made on their right of reply proposal. For instance, the French agreed for the replies to be sent to signatory nations for distribution, but they still wanted an international appeals route. Representatives of Eastern bloc nations, displeased with some amendments to the French proposal, argued inconsistently that without a compulsive mechanism the right of reply was meaningless in countries such as the United States, where no national news agency existed to disseminate corrected information; that the entire proposal interfered with national sovereignty; and that false information must be stopped before initial circulation and not after publication.[118] Opposition to the measure also came from the British, who feared governmental abuse of any right of correction. Since governments did not always have the correct perceptions of events, who would correct the governments' versions? The British believed that only a free press truly could correct inaccurate statements, and Davies argued that any legislatively imposed right of reply would only reduce the ability of the free press to function satisfactorily.[119]

United States representative Canham disagreed with most of the objections raised against either the amended French convention or the more limited American proposal for a right of correction. Perhaps, Canham said, a right of correction would even increase the diversity of available news by circulating more information from different sources.[120] Other problems still faced the proposed right of correction, however. For instance, delegates wondered if the right of reply should be restricted solely to news stories or whether nations should have the right to respond to the expression of opinions by foreign correspondents.[121] And should the right of reply be limited only to news reports prepared by foreign correspondents or should incorrect statements made by reporters within their home countries about another country also be open for reply under the convention?[122]

After debate, the draft convention instituting an international right of reply, as approved by the conference, applied solely to news reports "transmitted from one country to another country by foreign correspondents or by news agencies and disseminated abroad." Any news reports considered as false or distorted by a signatory nation could be the subject of a communiqué from the nation disputing the circulated information. The signatory government housing the offending medium was to make the text of the communiqué available to that nation's press without comment or evaluation. If a signatory nation did not distribute the communiqué within a reasonable period, the secretary-general of the United Nations was to be notified, and he was to publicize that failure.[123] Even though the American delegation found many of its points included in the amended French convention, the document still was broader than the Americans wanted. The ideal right of correction, in the opinion of the United States delegation, was available only when the objectionable material was written by a foreign correspondent stationed in the offended country. The adopted version made the right of correction available to any nation complaining about a report transmitted from any country to any other country. The only criterion for activating the right of correction was that the offensive material was written by a foreign correspondent. After delegates approved the French convention, United States delegation chairman Benton said that his colleagues preferred to have the right of reply incorporated within the United States draft convention on the international gathering and dissemination of news rather than in a separate convention on the subject. The American delegation, rebuffed in efforts to achieve such a goal in Geneva, vowed to renew attempts to achieve consolidation when the United Nations considered the documents.[124]

THE COVENANT ON HUMAN RIGHTS ATTRACTS DEBATE

The last major document to emerge from the conference was the proposed text of Article 17 of the Covenant on Human Rights. Discussion of this article by the Subcommission on Freedom of Information and of the Press raised significant concerns among State Department and press circles because the text featured a list of restrictions that a government could levy on the press—including imposition of secrecy on matters of national security; limitations on the right to publish material designed to incite civil insurrection; and restrictions on obscenity, libel, and material that might disrupt the fair conduct of judicial proceedings.[125] American delegation goals for modifying the proposed language for the covenant provision were mixed. One aim, of course, was to replace the itemized restrictions with broader, more permissive language. American opposition to the specific limitations, however, was not based solely on the country's affection for freedom of expression. One State Department concern was that the language forbade "a number of legitimate restrictions on freedom of expression which now exist by law in the U.S." This list included "prohibitions against publishing the details of the execution of crimes, communications of certain types with foreign governments (the Logan Act), certain provisions of the Securities and Exchange Act, the Pure Food and Drug Act, and the Hatch Act." In order to safeguard these legal measures, the Americans were to insist on a general limitations clause.[126]

American delegates also found themselves in the awkward position of needing to protect the right to censor news reports dealing with "national or international control of atomic energy" and "matters relating directly to national military security."[127] The media-dominated American delegation overrode suggestions by staff members that the covenant article include some specific restrictions. Delegates favored, instead, the general language given as the minimum acceptable to the State Department: "The right to freedom of expression may be limited only for causes which have been clearly defined by law and which are based on recognition of the rights of others or on protection of the welfare, security and freedom of all." In making that decision, delegation members rejected a statement allowing special restrictions for "matters relating directly to national military security" on the grounds that proposing such language would give the impression that the delegation favored censorship.[128] State Department officials accepted the delegation's stance.[129]

Debate on the proposed article for the human rights covenant took many familiar twists. The Soviet bloc, for instance, wanted the list of permissible restrictions to contain prohibitions against the dissemination of false news and warmongering. Western delegates disagreed with the Soviet suggestions,[130] but a majority of the so-called Western allies also disagreed with the American proposal for a general limitations clause. For instance, W.V.J. Evans of the United Kingdom said that the general language proposed by the Americans "would justify any existing practice, or any which a State might find it convenient to introduce, in order to render freedom of expression illusory." Most nations believed that drawing up a specific list of internationally acceptable restrictions was far better than leaving the matter in the hands of governments that could not be trusted to act in the best interests of a free press. Fernand Terrou of France objected to the American proposal because it "omitted the fundamental issue of the duties and responsibilities which were an essential part of the right to freedom of expression."[131]

During the covenant debate, American free-press precepts were constantly attacked by friends and foes alike. Arguments soon swirled around how much freedom individuals should have to criticize their governments before the comments were subject to suppression as inciting the overthrow of those governments. Chafee argued for the American clear and present danger standard as the minimum acceptable rule because of the importance of striking "a balance between the right of the people to criticise their rulers and the interests and responsibility of governments." Evans, the delegate from the United Kingdom, protested—unsuccessfully—that "the person who published seditious expressions or made seditious speeches was equally guilty whether his speech or publication had the desired effect or not."[132] A British suggestion to bar expressions not aimed at overthrowing the government or inciting criminal actions but designed to promote public disorder also drew Chafee's disapproval. Such language, Chafee successfully argued, might lead to actions against strikers who were trying to clarify their position and, hence, was too dangerous for inclusion in the draft covenant.[133]

Perhaps the most controversial amendment to the list of specific limitations for the covenant came from the Indian delegation. This time, that nation's representative picked up the Eastern bloc's interest in preventing the dissemination of false information and suggested an amendment based on the General Assembly's resolution on the subject. Under the Indian proposal, nations could punish "the diffusion of false or distorted reports intended or likely to injure friendly relations between peoples and states."[134] Chafee argued that the provision was inappropriate to add to the existing list of limitations because the restrictions already enumerated were well established and codified in many countries. The Indian amendment, on the other hand, "was dangerously general in scope and would be open to abuse," and the proposal actually "would restrict freedom of expression in many countries." In addition, "the question of false or distorted reports likely to injure friendly relations between States arose from political problems and could not be decided by tribunals."[135] The United States delegation was defeated on this issue in committee and considered that this vote was the "only important setback for us among scores or even hundreds of complex issues here." Although American delegates felt "more strongly" on the Indian amendment than any other issue before the conference, they were reluctant to pursue the subject in the final days of the session. To raise the point again, Benton said, would precipitate another full-fledged debate on the warmongering and false-news issues and possibly dilute American victories.[136]

Thus, the American delegation voted against the draft of Article 17. Delegation chairman Benton explained that the Americans believed the proposed language "emphasized possible limitations and restrictions on freedom rather than freedom itself. The draft of Article 17 as it has emerged gives far more latitude for repression of the press than the United States can possibly countenance within its own territory." The Indian amendment, calling for restrictions on false or distorted reports that might undermine the good relations among nations, was of particular concern to the Americans, he said. The United States agreed that such reports deserved universal condemnation, "but to enforce repression by law is a step we cannot take and cannot support." Leading American newspapers shared that view, commenting that "legislation of this kind strikes at the very foundations of the free press, and turns over to governments authority to sit in judgment on the correctness of news reports and to decide what constitutes 'friendly' and 'unfriendly' reporting."[137] *Editor & Publisher* joined the chorus of opposition, noting that the language of the Indian amendment "would condone all the journalistic malpractices behind the Iron Curtain." The trade journal urged American newspapers to oppose the amendment.[138] Although the American delegation opposed the covenant article as written, Benton pledged that the United States would work to revise the offensive language. The American goal would be to write an article to "safeguard freedom of information and at the same time recognize the relation of responsibility to freedom."[139]

American protests were unsuccessful, as delegates added the Indian proposal, amended to make the language refer to the "systematic" diffusion of "deliberately" false or distorted reports, to the list of restrictions in the covenant.[140] The draft article for the Covenant on Human Rights allowed imposition of penalties for eight violations of the outer bounds of freedom of expression, including endangerment of national safety, incitement to overthrow the government or to commit criminal acts, and "the systematic diffusion of deliberately false or distorted reports which undermine friendly relations between peoples and States."[141]

THE AMERICAN DELEGATION DEFENDS THE FREE-PRESS CONCEPT

Other United States concepts of freedom of the press were carefully scrutinized during additional debates at the Geneva conference. For instance, many delegates wanted to consider "restrictions imposed by governments on persons or groups wishing to receive and disseminate information, ideas and opinions."[142] Despite this phraseology, the discussion quickly turned into a series of denunciations of nongovernmental restrictions on freedom of information—meaning big-business domination of news dissemination channels as found in America. That discussion led to arguments over the need for nations to shield themselves against such invasions of national sovereignty. These debates once again allowed the Soviets to use comments by American critics of United States press operations to substantiate Russian charges against American newspapers, much the same way the Soviets had used similar material during debates within other United Nations bodies. The Russian techniques thoroughly infuriated American representatives and, to a certain extent, put them on the defensive.

For instance, Lomakin, the Russian delegate, stressed that the press in America "was controlled by a very small number of newspaper proprietors who could, and did, exercise a continuous censorship."[143] His colleague from Poland, Witold Konopka, noted that Benton himself had admitted "that the United States press was not free from defects, which it was hoped would be remedied eventually." Konopka considered Benton's "pious hopes" for improvement of the American press inadequate because the defects of that institution included "the increasing denial to millions of the right of expression." The Polish delegate then pointed to findings along these lines in A Free and Responsible Press, a controversial publication by the Hutchins Commission on Freedom of the Press issued in 1947. This commission, he said, believed that "the progressive concentration not only of newspapers but of all media of information, in the hands of a few newspaper proprietors, both at national and local levels, enabled those proprietors to determine what facts, versions of facts and opinions should reach the public."[144]

Citing the same source—and other, similar documents—Nicolae Moraru of Rumania termed the American press "moribund" and expressed concern over the "pernicious influence" exerted by advertisers, "who alone rendered possible the production of bulky American newspapers at very low prices." From information garnered from American press critics, Moraru concluded that "public opinion in the United States of America was entirely at the mercy of a small band of unscrupulous newspaper owners and advertisers who did not hesitate to distort news at will for their own ends."[145] The Czechoslovak delegate, Alfred F. Biheller, challenged American claims to a multiplicity of voices from which its citizens chose information. Specifically, he asked whether a reader in the United States could "really be said to have freedom of choice in a country where the monopoly of all media of information was in the hands of a few commercial interests."[146] Soviet bloc nations contrasted this advertiser-restricted press system in the United States with the free Soviet press system in which the government financed the organs of communication and made them available to a variety of groups within the population.

Strangely enough, the primary defender of the business interests of American journalism was a man who usually was on the other side of the bargaining table—Harry Martin, president of the American Newspaper Guild. According to Martin, Eastern bloc representatives based their accusations against the press in the United States on "statements out of context, half truths, false judgments ... culled from the United States press." In fact, these statements "were in themselves a proof that the press in the United States was free." The favorite targets of communist critics—the conservative Hearst, Scripps-Howard, and Patterson-McCormick newspaper groups—only owned a total of 37 newspapers out of 1,700 daily papers in the country. To individuals who attributed excessive power to these three chains, the Guild president noted that Franklin Roosevelt successfully had defied the united opposition of these chains by winning reelection in 1940 and 1944. If someone wanted to see a controlled press in operation, Martin suggested inspecting the Soviet press.[147]

When delegates decided to write a positive statement calling on governments to promote actively the dissemination and reception of information, the expected criticism of American domination of the raw materials and facilities for communication finally surfaced. Most of the world, still suffering from the aftermath of war, endured shortages in newsprint and printing equipment as well as radio equipment. Currency problems and more urgent needs for available money in the affected countries made allocating funds to solve these material shortages almost impossible. Another problem stemmed from the fact that few nations in the world had news agencies strong enough to gather and disseminate information within their own boundaries much less throughout the world. In each instance, the United States had more than enough of everything—but it was unwilling to share any resources other than American news agencies.

American reluctance to promote freedom of information through sharing the country's material wealth perturbed such a staunch ally as Great Britain. Shortages in newsprint throughout the world led to much smaller newspapers, much higher prices, and cuts in the amount of news available. In the United States, J. Murray Watson, the British delegate, said, newsprint consumption had increased greatly while production had decreased. "How many people read the lengthy supplements to United States papers? The paper on which they were printed would be of great value to hard-pressed countries like the United Kingdom." But the Briton had no solution for the problem other than an "appeal to the good-will of those who possessed an abundance of news-print" to help make "the free distribution of information in all countries suffering from shortages" possible. S. A. Brelvi of India suggested something a little stronger. He proposed that delegates call on the highly developed countries to help the lesser-developed countries by equitably distributing "the supplies of physical facilities and technical equipment for the dissemination of information between all countries throughout the world," establishing a "system of priority for under-developed countries," and creating a way "to combat tendencies to monopolise the world supplies of news-print."[148]

Martin sympathized with the problems of India and other countries facing material shortages. Following departmental instructions, he stressed that "the United States did not want only to disseminate its own news but believed that there should be a free two-way flow of information between countries." The problem, however, was an impersonal one dealing with currency flow. American media outlets were simply not responsible for the imbalance of resources. In fact, the abundance of newsprint available in the United States was due primarily to the desire of certain countries "to export news-print in order to obtain vital dollars." Even though the United States wanted to improve economic conditions worldwide, Martin said that America could not "insist that other countries should consider news-print a priority over other vital materials." Such an attempt "would constitute a violation of United States policy of not interfering in other countries' domestic affairs."[149] Although American delegates were reluctant to accept a moral responsibility to supply raw materials to the world, delegation members understood the importance of newsprint to freedom of information and suggested exploring the problem with American publishers.[150]

American planners also had anticipated the delegation's vulnerability in any discussion of other nations' abilities to cover news within their own countries,[151] and, once again, their estimate was correct. Some conference leaders even feared that the fate of the entire proceeding hinged on the attitude of lesser-developed countries and that the issue of developing national news agencies was the key to winning these nations' support. The head of the Chinese delegation put the problem bluntly when he said: "The poor countries are being asked to give in these Conventions and the rich countries are not proposing to give us anything."[152]

How to balance the needs of countries such as China to establish and protect national news agencies with the opposition of American news agencies to such protectionism formed the core of the dilemma facing the United States delegation. Some American press critics saw the creation of government-subsidized news agencies as tantamount to establishing new monopoly agencies that would be just a step away from the "government-operated news-propaganda agencies" of the pre–World War II era.[153] Faced with such a complicated situation and with the possible fate of the conference at stake, the only answer available to the United States delegation seemed to be acknowledging that "any country which did not wish a foreign news agency to disseminate local news directly to local papers in its territory could pass a law getting them out." But the American delegates also stressed "that there should not be a United Nations mandate to encourage any government to do so."[154]

Despite American concerns, the conference adopted a Chinese resolution that recommended that a foreign news agency "operating within the territory of a country where national news agencies are under-developed, while it should enjoy full freedom as regards the international transmission of news, should refrain from releasing, at the locality of its operation, news concerning the country's domestic affairs."[155] Taken at face value, American press agency spokesmen protested, the statement "would prevent a Shanghai editor from using AP or U.P. reports from Peking, or a Zurich editor from using dispatches from Berne." American delegation consultants from the wire services—United Press president Baillie and his executive assistant, Robert Frey—met with the Chinese delegate to work out a compromise.[156] The result was an amendment that allowed foreign news agencies to transmit domestic news to other points within the foreign country if the agency had permission from the national agencies involved.[157]

The question of how to implement the various actions of the conference was constantly debated. Considerable support existed for the creation of an international court of journalists empowered to hear complaints about the transgressions and mistreatment of journalists. Development of an enforceable worldwide code of ethics also found advocates among various nations. Delegates found agreement on such measures impossible, however, and referred the topics to the Subcommission on Freedom of Information and of the Press for additional consideration. United States planners put great trust in developing the subcommission into a viable body, and they recommended making it a permanent organ of the United Nations and enlarging its terms of reference so that the subcommission could deal with problems relating to the international flow of news. Even if, for some reason, the subcommission did not develop as anticipated, referring matters to it still would be better than creating additional international organizations, according to State Department planners.[158] Conference delegates agreed and recommended a substantially increased role for the Subcommission on Freedom of Information and of the Press.

THE AMERICAN DELEGATION
PRAISES CONFERENCE RESULTS

American delegates were greatly pleased with conference results, especially given the gloom that surrounded the beginning of the conference. In fact, the delegation reported that "in the face of the difficulties, the record of constructive achievement of this Conference seems to us remarkable." The American delegation had voted against only one and had abstained from voting on only three of the forty-five proposals debated by the conference. With the exception of the Covenant on Human Rights, "every proposal which in advance of the Conference the United States Delegation thought it desirable for the Conference to adopt was adopted by a very large majority." In addition, "more than a score of proposals and amendments which would have served to cripple freedom of expression were decisively defeated."[159]

Before the conference, the delegation had worried about how the middle group of states, which had a "latent willingness to impose restrictions on freedom," would react to American ideas. This bloc drew allies from the Far East, Near East, and Latin America, with a potential combined voting strength that meant "we were far more alone, and far more in danger of being alone, than our constituency at home realized." Previous experiences with these nations on freedom of information questions had shown that these states "would not quickly embrace our ideas of press freedom," for they "had ideas of their own which they wanted us to adopt."[160] Preconference jitters were unfounded, for the middle states were unable to block American efforts at Geneva. The primary reason for the American supremacy at the conference, the delegation said, was "a decided change in the general political attitudes of most of the nations of the Western World during the last few months." Although the nontotalitarian nations still believed that "compromise and adjustment with the Soviet bloc are desirable and indeed essential in some fields," these nations were beginning to realize "that in areas involving deep-seated differences in fundamental principles, present attempts at compromise are not only useless but can be extremely dangerous."[161]

The growing intransigence of the Soviet bloc, which clearly showed unwillingness and inability to move toward greater freedom, helped to change this attitude also. Just six weeks after the fall of Czechoslovakia, American diplomats found "a keener realization of what the extinction of liberty means in those parts of the world which have fallen under communist control." And finally, the delegation reported that other nations of the world now believed that "the United States means to help the Western nations protect their own freedom and independence through such measures as the European Recovery Program."[162] Thus, after months of buffeting by communist propaganda, the United States was able to "seize and hold the initiative in the ideological field" for the first time at the Geneva conference.[163]

The Soviets apparently had contributed to their own defeat at the conference by not sending a delegation composed of leading propagandists, theoreticians, or parliamentarians. The Soviets offered no new ideas, presented no major resolutions, and often seemed to take a back seat to spokesmen of the satellite nations during debates.[164] The more optimistic among the American representatives at Geneva saw support for the American position at the conference as providing a broad basis for "the establishment of closer economic and political relations with Western Europe and other parts of the world which are under pressure from the Russians."[165] Career diplomat John Carter Vincent, American minister to Switzerland and alternate delegate to the conference, tried to keep these victories in perspective. He reported that he believed most of the agreement on American positions came from "fear of USSR and appreciation of our financial assistance" rather than from "full concurrence in our ideas on freedom of information."[166] But Vincent's voice of moderation was lost in the welter of congratulatory comments.

The fight was not over, however; delegates told the State Department to pay more attention to "the power of ideas" and to "exert moral leadership" in a world well aware of America's "economic power but not its spiritual force." From the concerns voiced by some nations at Geneva, United States delegates knew that Americans must clearly state "that we do not seek to monopolize news gathering by our agencies of communication" but that America preferred to see "the development of strong organs of information by all countries of the world." Other peoples must learn that "we seek to promote freedom of information in order to extend and implement the right of everyone everywhere to be fully informed in the interests of democracy and international understanding."[167] One way to show American interest in practicing freedom of information, Kotschnig said, was to allow foreign correspondents freer entry into the United States, even if they were communists—"it being understood of course that we cannot take unnecessary security risks." Also, the president or the secretary of state could make a public statement that "while commending the U.S. press for its independence and initiative, might include an appeal to the press to remain calm during these times of stress. This might be one way of meeting the accusation that the U.S. government is doing nothing whatsoever to curb the excesses of admittedly irresponsible journalists."[168] Neither of Kotschnig's suggestions won approval. The freer admission of correspondents allegedly rested in the hands of the Department of Justice, beyond State Department control. The inherent criticism of press behavior embodied in the second suggestion made the idea too sensitive from a public relations standpoint for the department to implement.

One reason for the failure of a suggestion calling for more responsible press reporting of cold war issues was the delegates' expressed belief that the struggle for worldwide freedom of information was no longer solely an international issue. A great deal of work remained to be done to enlist the American press in this crusade. After he had accepted the chairmanship of the American delegation, Benton stressed that "the first problem for the State Department and for our own Delegation was not the Russians, or even the wavering countries which worry more about press responsibility than about press freedom. Our first problem was and is the American press." United States journalists claimed that domestic and international freedom of the press was important to them, but "on few crusades do they show greater naivete." American editors and publishers "appeal for the projection internationally of the same freedom they enjoy at home; but they deplore the necessity of governmental action to accomplish this result."[169]

Efforts to win additional support for the products of the Geneva conference among American journalists began before those sessions ended. Canham, vice chairman of the United States delegation, was to become president of the American Society of Newspaper Editors at the society's annual meeting in late April. Even though Canham would miss the final week of the Geneva conference, State Department planners believed that his presence at the ASNE session was "vitally important." Consequently, they made special arrangements to fly Canham home for the annual meeting, partially in the hopes that Canham would make a complimentary address about State Department efforts on behalf of freedom of information when he arrived home.[170] Canham delivered just the kind of speech State Department officials hoped for; he told his colleagues how hard the State Department had worked to advance free-press issues at Geneva: "The position papers and statements of policy prepared by the State Department before our delegation was formed followed exactly the lines on which we as newspaper men would agree." To those members who doubted that the State Department could be so helpful, Canham said, "I have the documents to prove every word I say."[171]

The conference, Canham said, accomplished several things. For the first time, United States representatives "got the jump on the Eastern group and held the offensive throughout the Conference." Conference resolutions, written in large part by American delegates, established the basic principles of freedom of information. For example, the draft treaty on international gathering and transmission of news, based primarily on work done by ASNE member Richard J. Finnegan, "establishes and codifies important rights for the foreign correspondent and his copy" for the first time. And, finally, the conference allowed journalists from around the world to make important contacts with one another, laying the foundation for working journalists to cooperate to expand freedom of the press.[172]

ASNE members must not, however, ignore the problems uncovered in Geneva, Canham warned. The Indian amendment to the draft article for the Covenant on Human Rights, which allowed legal penalties for publishing false information, was one such problem. The American delegation fought that proposal but failed to stop its passage. Even if the United Nations should include the Indian provision in the covenant, "our liberties are and will be in no danger. Much as we dislike the Indian amendment, it could never be used against us or any other country." The list of permissible restrictions was just that—a list of allowable restrictions, Canham explained, and no one could force the United States to adopt any of them. But, "as a matter of fact, the United States right now and during most of its history has imposed limitations in most of these areas and nobody has complained that press freedom was destroyed thereby." In addition, if the covenant article went into effect, the specific enumeration of restrictions on freedom of the press could open information now protected by United States law, such as stock market data, and could free the American press from limitations imposed by the Taft-Hartley Act, the Federal Communications Commission, and the Federal Trade Commission.[173]

Members of the American press should not fear the French right of reply convention either, Canham said. "There is no compulsion involved, and nobody can force an editor to print anything he does not choose to print. But a legitimate reply is given some circulation." The greatest lesson learned from the conference, Canham said, was that "the status of the press must be lifted up in other countries, as this Society has helped to lift up the status of the press here." Journalists overseas wanted to talk with Americans about their mutual profession, and all parties could learn from one another. But American journalists must seize the leadership of this new movement.[174]

Brown also warned his colleagues against abandoning the start made at Geneva. The conference had convinced him that international action on information issues was inevitable and that American journalists could no longer safely ignore that point. In fact, Brown felt international participation should help to ward off government intrusions in the freedom of the press and would help journalists around the world. Early problems surrounding efforts by the United Nations on freedom of information issues were due primarily to the fact that "we publishers never took a single step to guard our interests," Brown said. "We simply cannot afford to stay out of this game. It is not of our choice. It is forced upon us by the power of government all over the world." With such an international responsibility ahead, American journalists must be careful lest they prove the fears of other nations about American cultural imperialism correct. If they did nothing else, journalists must try to "further internationalize the news direction of our agency reports outside the United States" because the feeling in many small countries "that all their news is handled with an American slant is too strong to be disregarded." Regardless of whether American journalists wanted to be involved in international issues, Brown noted that they were involved, and those journalists must not only recognize that fact but act on it.[175]

NOTES

1. William Reed, "UN Debate Revives 'Responsibility' Issue," *E&P*, February 1, 1947, p. 76.
2. ECOR, 4th session, 68th meeting, March 14, 1947, p. 104.
3. E/AC.7/12, 4th Session, March 23, 1947, *Draft Resolutions on Human Rights and on the International Conference on the Freedom of the Press*, p. 2.
4. William Reed, "UN Group on Press Freedom Set to Function in April," *E&P*, February 15, 1947, p. 10.
5. Members of the first subcommission were: George V. Ferguson, Canada, editor of the *Montreal Daily Star* and a journalist for more than twenty years; P. H. Chang, China, an educator who had served as a government spokesman between 1943 and 1946 and who was serving as director of the Chinese News Service in New York; Lev Sychrava, Czechoslovakia, the subcommission's vice chairman, editor-in-chief of the Prague *Narodni osvabozeni* and a journalist for twenty-plus years; André Géraud, France, a journalist and author who specialized in diplomatic issues and diplomatic history; G. J. van Heuven

Goedhart, the Netherlands, the subcommission's chairman, chief editor of *Het Parool*; Christian A. R. Christensen, Norway, editor-in-chief of the Oslo *Verdens Gang* and a journalist for more than twenty years; Salvador López, the Philippines, who had some journalistic background but had spent most of the 1940s in some governmental capacity such as press relations officer with the American military and, as of 1946, adviser to the Philippine Mission to the United Nations; J. M. Lomakin, Union of Soviet Socialist Republics, who served as an editor for Tass in New York in 1939 but had spent the 1940s in the diplomatic corps; A.R.K. MacKenzie, United Kingdom, first secretary and public relations officer for the United Kingdom's delegation at the United Nations; Zechariah Chafee, Jr., United States, law professor and expert on the First Amendment; Roberto Fontaina, Uruguay, who had some early radio experience but had spent the 1940s in the diplomatic service. See *Yearbook of the United Nations, 1947–48*, pp. 1048–93; Jane Bedell, "Building a Bridge," *New Republic*, June 9, 1947, p. 32.

Just how seriously other nations' representatives took their alleged independence from their governments is unknown, but Chafee firmly believed in his freedom from government instruction. As the State Department's freedom of information expert Lloyd Free reported, Chafee had "frequently ignored the Department's views. Some of the matters he initiated or endorsed, will almost certainly have to be opposed by the U.S. in ECOSOC and in the Conference on Freedom of Information." In spite of such problems, Free believed that Chafee's approach had "almost single-handedly created an illusion which undoubtedly influenced the Sub-Commission's proceedings, that the Sub-Commission was, indeed, a group of genuinely independent experts meeting in a spirit of unusual friendliness and cooperation." *See* Lloyd Free to William Benton and William T. Stone, Director, Office of International Information and Cultural Affairs, June 13, 1947, RG 43, NA, Box 4, File: Freedom of Information.

6. Lloyd Free, Special Assistant to the Director, Office of International Information and Cultural Affairs, to William Benton and William T. Stone, Director, OIC, March 7, 1947, RG 43, NA, Box 5, File: Lloyd Free. Roger Simpson argues that Chafee's membership on the subcommission allowed him to air the controversial ideas on press responsibility formulated by the Hutchins Commission on Freedom of the Press, eventually polluting the international crusade with these criticisms of American press performance and suggestions for reform. *See* Simpson, "The Hutchins Commission at Geneva: Social Responsibility in the United Nations Crucible."

Lloyd Free seemed to agree, at least in part, with that assessment. Free believed that one of Chafee's shortcomings as a subcommission member was that "his basic approach to the international aspects of freedom of information is colored by the domestic situation on freedom of the press in the U.S. Feeling that in America freedom is guaranteed, he tends to look on the chief problem as one of responsibility, not fully realizing that on the world stage the primary need is freedom, not obligation." *See* Lloyd Free to William Benton and William T. Stone, Director, Office of International Information and Cultural Affairs, June 13, 1947, RG 43, NA, Box 4, File: Freedom of Information.

7. William Reed, "U.S. at One Extreme in Responsibility Issue," *E&P*, April 26, 1947, p. 108.

8. Ibid., p. 111.

9. Kent Cooper decried the change in terminology, suggesting that the term freedom of the press "was distasteful to those politicians who hated the press in general and certain newspapers in particular. They would have nothing to do with anything first sponsored by newspapers that benefited the people through the press alone." Additional problems occurred when broadcasters and motion picture personnel sought freedom to disseminate their products as well. Cooper then suggested that the term "the right to know" was broad enough to cover all interested media. United Nations representatives rejected his proposal, leaving the accepted term as freedom of information. "By mid-century," Cooper said, "the original suggestion regarding 'freedom of the press' had been tossed about, cluttered up with qualifying phrases and battered into a form almost unrecognizable." See Cooper, *The Right to Know*, pp. 183–84.

10. E/CN.4/Sub.1/SR.2, 1st session, May 19, 1947, p. 5.

11. E/CN.4/Sub.1/SR.8, 1st session, May 22, 1947, pp. 6–7, 9.

12. William Reed, "Economic Factors Included on Agenda of UN Parley," *E&P*, June 7, 1947, pp. 7, 99.

13. E/CN.4/Sub.1/SR.9, 1st session, May 23, 1947, pp. 2, 6.

14. E/CN.4/Sub.1/SR.10, 1st session, May 23, 1947, p. 6.

15. Reed, "Economic Factors Included on Agenda of UN Parley," pp. 100, 99.

16. E/CN.4/Sub.1/SR.12, 1st session, May 26, 1947, pp. 2, 6–7.

17. E/CN.4/Sub.1/SR.14, 1st session, May 27, 1947, p. 3.

18. William Reed, "Censorship, Propaganda on Freedom Parley Agenda," *E&P*, May 31, 1947, p. 7.

19. E/CN.4/Sub.1/SR.14, 1st session, May 27, 1947, p. 2.

20. "French Delegate's Proposed Agenda," *E&P*, May 31, 1947, p. 63.

21. Reed, "Censorship, Propaganda on Freedom Parley Agenda," p. 8.

22. Lloyd Free, Special Assistant to the Director, Office of International Information and Cultural Affairs, to William Benton, June 13, 1947, RG 43, NA, Box 4, File: Freedom of Information. The agenda, based largely on a draft that Chafee proposed, called for facilitating the gathering and international transmission of news and for measures ensuring all persons access to "accurate, comprehensive and representative information." See E/CN.4/Sub.1/9, 1st session, May 16, 1947, *Draft Agenda for the Conference on Freedom of Information Proposed by Zechariah Chafee*.

23. E/AC.7/SR.18, 5th session, August 4, 1947, pp. 3–5.

24. E/AC.7/SR.20, 5th session, August 7, 1947, p. 2.

25. ECOR, 5th session, 118th meeting, August 15, 1947, p. 255.

26. William Reed, "UN Sessions Alter Free Press Concepts," *E&P*, December 13, 1947, p. 50; William Reed, "Europe Abets Growth of New Press Ideas," *E&P*, December 20, 1947, pp. 52–53.

27. ECOR, 2nd session, E/600, *Report of the Commission on Human Rights*, December 17, 1947, p. 34.

28. Zechariah Chafee, Jr., "Expert Explains Work of UN Press Group," *E&P*, January 17, 1948, p. 20.

29. E/CN.4/Sub.1/SR.26, 2nd session, January 20, 1948, p. 3.
30. E/CN.4/Sub.1/SR.27, 2nd session, January 20, 1948, p. 4.
31. E/CN.4/Sub.1/SR.29, 2nd session, January 21, 1948, pp. 5–7.
32. The covenant, if ratified by the United States Senate, would have the status of a treaty and as such, under a United States Supreme Court decision, *Missouri* v. *Holland*, 252 U.S. 416 (1920), an act of Congress could implement its provisions. Laws passed under the covenant's provisions would be superior to state laws and state constitutions. See John B. Whitton, "The United Nations Conference on Freedom of Information and the Movement against International Propaganda," *American Journal of International Law* 43 (January 1949):73–87. Some critics feared that the covenant's articles would also override United States constitutional provisions to the contrary. For a fuller discussion of this argument, *see* Chapter 6.
33. E/CN.4/80, February 6, 1948, *Report of the Second Session of the Sub-Commission on Freedom of Information and of the Press*, pp. 4–5.
34. "UN and Free Press," *E&P*, February 7, 1948, p. 42.
35. "IEB Unable to Give Unqualified OK," *Guild Reporter*, February 13, 1948, p. 9.
36. Zechariah Chafee, Jr., "Covenant Protects Fundamental Rights," *E&P*, March 6, 1948, p. 32.
37. ECOR, E/441, *Report of the Sub-Commission on Freedom of Information and of the Press to the Economic and Social Council and to the Commission on Human Rights*, June 5, 1947, pp. 12–16.
38. "Geneva Conference," *E&P*, March 13, 1948, p. 42.
39. Report of the United States Delegates to the United Nations Conference on Freedom of Information [hereinafter cited as Delegation Report], May 7, 1948, Benton Papers, Box 480, 528C, p. 1.
40. James Hendrick, Acting Associate Chief, Division of International Organization Affairs, to Charles E. Bohlen, Special Assistant to the Secretary of State, March 22, 1948, RG 43, NA, Box 5, File: Freedom of Information.
41. United States Delegation Annotated Agenda for the United Nations Conference on Freedom of Information [hereinafter cited as Annotated Agenda], March 4, 1948, Benton Papers, Box 250, Folder 2, p. 9.
42. John A. Brogan, Jr., Vice President and Director of Foreign Sales, King Features Syndicate, to George V. Allen, March 2, 1949, RG 59, NA, Box 6174, 851.918/3-249.
43. *See*, e.g., "Comics Cleanup," *E&P*, July 10, 1948, p. 34; "Comics' Censors Endanger Freedom and Grassroots Press Is Involved," *Publishers' Auxiliary*, November 6, 1948, p. 4; "Censorship of Comics," *E&P*, December 18, 1948, p. 36; "Rochester Censors," *E&P*, January 8, 1949, p. 42; "Comics," *E&P*, May 21, 1949, p. 36; "Comic Censors," *E&P*, February 23, 1952, p. 34.
44. George V. Allen to John A. Brogan, Jr., February 15, 1949, RG 59, NA, Box 6174, 851.918/2-1549.
45. For discussions of the American efforts in Germany and Japan, *see* "Japanese Editors Base Code of Ethics on ASNE Canons," *ASNE Bulletin*, August 1, 1946, p. 4; William L. Tisdel, "We Do Have a Policy in Germany: Democratic Press Is Set Up to Shape Public Opinion," *Guild Reporter*, October 10, 1947, p. 4; Lafe F. Allen, "Effect of Allied Occupation on the Press of Japan,"

Journalism Quarterly 24 (December 1947):323–31; "Martin Gives German Editors Taste of U.S. Press Conference," *Guild Reporter*, April 23, 1948, p. 1; Jack Meehan, "Clay Tells Press to Hammer at Official Secrecy," *E&P*, May 8, 1948, p. 65; Wayne Jordan, "Germany's Cultural Heritage Impedes Free Press Program," *Journalism Quarterly* 25 (June 1948):163–69; William S. Kirkpatrick, "Showing German Editors a Free Press at Work," *Journalism Quarterly* 26 (March 1949):29–35; Werner Friedman, "The New German Press," *Nieman Reports*, April 1949, pp. 8–10; Robert P. Martin, "The Japanese Press (Post-MacArthur)," *Nieman Reports*, April 1952, pp. 3–5; Earl F. Ziemke, *The U.S. Army in the Occupation of Germany, 1944–1946*, Washington, D.C., Center of Military History, 1975, pp. 367–79.

46. Annotated Agenda, pp. 24, 26.

47. "U.S. Invokes 1918 Law to Limit Red Writers," *E&P*, October 4, 1947, p. 8.

48. "Two U.S. Errors," *E&P*, October 4, 1947, p. 36.

49. W. J. McWilliams, Executive Officer, Office of Departmental Administration, to Norman Armour, Assistant Secretary of State, September 30, 1947, RG 59, NA, Box 2137, 501.AK/9-2947.

50. Memorandum of Telephone Conversation between Walter Kotschnig, Chief, Division of International Organization Affairs, and Thomas F. Power, Jr., Deputy Secretary General, September 27, 1947, RG 84, NA, Records of the United States Mission to the United Nations, Box 108, IO: P&I correspondents.

51. "Mixup on UN Reporters Laid to Lack of Liaison," *E&P*, December 27, 1947, p. 52.

52. "State Dept. Clarifies Policy on UN Writers," *E&P*, January 3, 1948, p. 6.

53. Robert A. Lovett, Acting Secretary of State, to the United States Delegation to the United Nations, December 31, 1947, RG 59, NA, Box 2137, 501.AK/12-2347.

54. Arthur Gunderson, "US and UN in Diplomatic Tiff over Arrest of 2 'Red' Correspondents," *Guild Reporter*, January 9, 1948, p. 6.

55. D. H. Popper, Division of International Organization Affairs, to Dean Rusk and Durward Sandifer, Office of United Nations Affairs, February 19, 1948, RG 84, NA, Records of the United States Mission to the United Nations, Box 108, IO: P&I correspondents (emphasis in original).

56. Annotated Agenda, pp. 11–12.

57. Ibid., p. 25.

58. William Reed, "World Newsprint Pool Suggested as UN Topic," *E&P*, November 30, 1946, p. 7.

59. "Newsprint and Information," *E&P*, December 7, 1946, p. 44.

60. "Newsprint-Freedom Link Made in Report," *E&P*, August 9, 1947, p. 10.

61. Ibid.

62. Annotated Agenda, p. 25.

63. Ibid., pp. 6, 8.

64. Ibid., pp. 9, 31.

65. William Benton to Jack Hickerson, Director of Office of European Affairs, February 18, 1948, RG 43, NA, Box 4, File: Freedom of Information.

66. William Benton to Robert Lovett, Under Secretary of State, January 19, 1948, Ibid.

67. Hugh Baillie to William Benton, January 28, 1948, Ibid., Box 1, File: U.S. Delegation (1).

68. William Benton to Robert Lovett, March 11, 1948, Ibid., Box 4, File: Freedom of Information.

69. Walter Kotschnig, Chief, Division of International Organization Affairs, to William Benton, February 9, 1948, Ibid.

70. "Martin to Attend Geneva World Press Parley as White House Spikes State Department Ban," *Guild Reporter*, March 12, 1948, p. 1.

71. Howland Sargeant, Deputy Assistant Secretary of State for Public Affairs, to Robert Lovett, Under Secretary of State, December 23, 1947, RG 43, NA, Box 1, File: U.S. Delegation (1). IOJ influence was negligible, but Martin's contributions to the American delegation were substantial.

    The five alternate delegates were Walter A. Graebner, European director, Time-Life International; Oveta Culp Hobby, executive vice president, *Houston Post*; Frank McCarthy, European manager, The Motion Picture Association of America; Howard K. Smith, chief European correspondent, Columbia Broadcasting System; and John Carter Vincent, United States Minister in Switzerland. *See* United States Delegation, United Nations Conference on Freedom of Information, March 29, 1948, Benton Papers, Box 480.

    This carefully crafted delegation won praise, on the one hand, for the way in which members showed how, "when it came to defense of the democratic way of free speech, domestic differences in the newspaper family vanished and publisher, editor and Guild official were as one." *See* "Toward a Free Press at Geneva," *Quill*, July 1948, p. 2. The delegation was criticized, on the other hand, because "it was overwhelmingly executive in function and conservative in principles." *See* Howard K. Smith, "Need More Working Press at Geneva Conference," *Nieman Reports*, January 1949, p. 15.

72. Proposed Agenda for Conference on Freedom of Information, May 14, 1947, RG 84, NA, Records of the United States Mission to the United Nations, Box 164, Position Book on Conference of Freedom of Information and Sub-Commission on Freedom of Information and of the Press.

73. E/CONF.6/41, March 27, 1948, *Draft Convention on the Gathering and International Transmission of News. Proposal Submitted by the United States.*

74. Minutes of the United States Delegation Meeting, March 25, 1948, RG 43, NA, Box 2, File: US Del Documents.

75. Memorandum of Conversation with Dr. P. C. Chang by W. M. Kotschnig, Chief, Division of International Organization Affairs, March 27, 1948, Ibid., Box 1, File: Memoranda of Conversations 1–8.

76. E/CONF.6/C.2/SR/3, March 25, 1948, pp. 2–3.

77. E/CONF.6/C.2/SR/4, March 27, 1948, pp. 2, 4, 6–7.

78. Ibid., pp. 8, 7.

79. E/CONF.6/C.2/SR/5, March 29, 1948, p. 3.

80. Ibid., pp. 3–5.

81. Ibid., pp. 5–6, 9.

82. The issue of barring communist reporters from America had been the topic of numerous anguished telegrams between the United States delegation and the State Department. Delegation members believed that the government's position

had caused delegates great embarrassment during debates, and they sought permission to announce that the department had altered the rules regarding admissibility of aliens. *See* William Benton and George Washington to Robert Lovett, Under Secretary of State, April 9, 1948, RG 43, NA, Box 1, File: Delfi Telegrams (Outgoing).

Finding little support for this request within the State Department, press representatives on the delegation sought to circumvent governmental intransigence by prompting the American Society of Newspaper Editors to pass a resolution calling for free admission of all bona fide correspondents regardless of political affiliation. State Department officials thought that such a resolution would be counterproductive because the proposal might force Congress to deprive the attorney general of his discretionary powers to admit correspondents. They also doubted the wisdom of seeking a blanket admissions policy. *See* George V. Allen to William Benton, April 17, 1948, RG 59, NA, Box 2254, 501.BD Freedom of Information/4-1748.

Complicating the American delegation's efforts to promote free entrance of correspondents abroad was the unwillingness of United States government officials to grant A. B. Magil, correspondent for the *Daily Worker* in New York City, permission to leave the country to cover the Geneva conference. Only after numerous protests and pleas from delegation members in Geneva and American journalists at home was the exit visa granted—against the government's better judgment. *See* Howland Sargeant, Deputy Assistant Secretary of State for Public Affairs, to William Benton, Ibid., 501.BD Freedom of Information/4-148.

83. E/CONF.6/C.2/SR/7, March 30, 1948, pp. 4, 6.

84. E/CONF.6/C.2/5, March 27, 1948, *Proposal by the French Delegation Concerning Point (d) of Paragraph 3 of the Agenda of Committee II*, p. 1.

85. Minutes of the United States Delegation Meeting, March 16, 1948, RG 43, NA, Box 2, File: US Del Documents.

86. E/CONF.6/C.2/SR/8, March 30, 1948, p. 11.

87. E/CONF.6/C.2/13, March 30, 1948, *Proposal by the United States Delegation Concerning Item 4(a) of the Agenda*, p. 1.

88. E/CONF.6/C.2/SR/12, April 1, 1948, pp. 10–11.

89. E/CONF.6/C.2/SR/13, April 2, 1948, pp. 2, 5–6, 11. The delegate from Czechoslovakia claimed that correspondents were only asked to confirm information with the government to prevent the transmission of stories based solely on hearsay. *See* Ibid., p. 7.

90. Draft Convention on Gathering and International Transmission of News, *Yearbook on Human Rights for 1948*, Lake Success, N.Y., United Nations, 1950, p. 498, *See* Appendix D for the convention's text.

An earlier version called for the right of correspondents to travel freely throughout signatory nations. State Department planners objected to this language because of the limitations placed on the travel of communist correspondents in the United States. *See* Harley Notter, Office of United Nations Affairs, to Dean Rusk and Durward Sandifer, Office of United Nations Affairs, February 17, 1948, RG 59, NA, Box 2253, 501.BD Freedom of Information/2-1748.

91. Ibid., p. 499.
92. William Benton, Address on the Convention on the Gathering and Transmission of News, April 19, 1948, RG 43, NA, Box 2, File: US Del Documents.
93. E/CONF.6/C.1/3, March 31, 1948, *Draft Resolution Presented by the United Kingdom on the Adoption of an International Convention on Freedom of Information*, pp. 2–3.
94. Walter Kotschnig, Chief, Division of International Organization Affairs, to Durward Sandifer, Office of United Nations Affairs, March 1, 1948, RG 84, NA, Records of the United States Mission to the United Nations, Box 88, File: Public Info: Confs 1946–48.
95. Resolution Proposed by the United States Delegation to the Conference of the United Nations on Freedom of Information, March 24, 1948, RG 43, NA, Box 2, File: US Del Documents.
96. Erwin Canham, Address, April 1, 1948, Ibid.
97. E/CONF.6/C.1/SR/19, April 6, 1948, pp. 2, 4–5.
98. Resolution No. 2, Final Act of the Conference on Freedom of Information, *Yearbook on Human Rights for 1948*, p. 505. Through this approach, the democracies of the world were credited with usurping "the warmongering resolution which long has been used as a noisy weapon for their embarrassment by the Soviet bloc." *See* Marguerite Johnston, "Democracies Head Off 'Warmonger' Measure," *E&P*, April 10, 1948, p. 11.
99. E/CONF.6/C.4/SR/18, April 12, 1948, p. 10.
100. E/CONF.6/C.1/9/Rev.1, April 5, 1948, *Indian Amendments to the United Kingdom Draft Convention on Freedom of Information*, p. 1.
101. E/CONF.6/C.1/3, March 31, 1948, *Draft Resolution Presented by the United Kingdom on the Adoption of an International Convention on Freedom of Information*, p. 3.
102. E/CONF.6/C.1/SR/20, April 6, 1948, p. 5.
103. E/CONF.6/C.1/SR/20.Corr.1, April 17, 1948, p. 1.
104. E/CONF.6/C.1/SR/20, April 6, 1948, p. 7. The Indian government had erected barriers to Associated Press and United Press penetration of that country and had encouraged the formation of a national press trust designed to provide news with an Indian slant for Indian media outlets. *See*, e.g., W. L. Thorp, for the Acting Secretary of State, to George R. Merrell, American Commissioner, New Delhi, India, May 27, 1946, RG 59, NA, Box 4986, 811.91245/5-2746; George R. Merrell, Chargé in India, to the Secretary of State, March 25, 1947, Ibid., Box 4512, 811.20200(D)/3-2547; Memorandum of Conversation by J. S. Sparks, Middle East and Indian Affairs, September 10, 1947, Ibid., Box 4986, 811.91245/9-1047; Howard Donovan, Chargé in India, to the Secretary of State, December 12, 1947, Ibid., Box 4519, 811.20200(D)/12-1247.
105. Sevellon L. Brown, Excerpts from Speech, April 7, 1948, RG 43, NA, Box 2, File: US Del Documents.
106. E/CONF.6/C.2/SR/16, April 7, 1948, pp. 5–7.
107. E/CONF.6/C.1/SR/20, April 6, 1948, p. 8.
108. Benton, address, April 19, 1948.
109. Draft Convention on Freedom of Information, *Yearbook on Human Rights for 1948*, p. 502. *See* Appendix E for the convention's text.
110. E/CONF.6/42, March 30, 1948, *Draft Convention Concerning the Right of*

Correction, the Establishment of an International Press Organ and an International Press Card, Submitted by the French Delegation, pp. 1–2.

111. E/CONF.6/12, February 27, 1948, *The Right of Reply—A Memorandum Prepared by the Secretary-General.*

112. Zechariah Chafee suggested the possibility of requiring the press to publish corrections, but his fellow delegates rejected the idea. *See* Minutes of the United States Delegation Meeting, March 15, 1948, RG 43, NA, Box 2, File: US Del Documents.

113. Allan Dawson, Chief, Division of Brazilian Affairs, to the Delegates, Memorandum Regarding Attitudes toward the French Convention on Right of Correction, International Press Organ, and International Press Card, April 3, 1948, RG 43, NA, Box 2, File: US Del Documents.

114. E/CONF.6/41, *Draft Convention on the Gathering and International Transmission of News. Proposal Submitted by the United States Delegation*, p. 4.

115. Minutes of the United States Delegation Meeting, April 10, 1948, RG 43, NA, Box 2, File: US Del Documents.

116. Minutes of the United States Delegation Meeting, April 12, 1948, Ibid.

117. These cards, similar to press cards issued by the French national government, guaranteed their bearers unspecified special privileges and required their bearers to submit to international supervision to maintain their status as accredited correspondents. American objections to the proposal included the fact that international press cards created a system based on special privilege, which was exactly the opposite of the American goal of equality among all foreign correspondents. *See* E/CONF.6/C.2/SR/14, April 5, 1948. Conference delegates referred the press card proposal to the Subcommission on Freedom of Information and of the Press for study. *See* E/CONF.6/C.2/SR/21, April 13, 1948, pp. 7–14.

118. E/CONF.6/C.1/SR/25, April 12, 1948, pp. 6–7.

119. E/CONF.6/C.1/SR/26, April 12, 1948, p. 4.

120. Ibid., p. 9.

121. E/CONF.6/C.1/SR/27, April 13, 1948, p. 5.

122. E/CONF.6/C.1/SR/28, April 14, 1948, p. 4.

123. Draft Convention Concerning the Institution of an International Right of Correction, *Yearbook on Human Rights for 1948*, p. 500. *See* Appendix F for the convention's text.

124. Benton, address, April 19, 1948. The Americans thought that the French had agreed with this consolidation proposal only to be faced with an abrupt change of attitude by their allies, due in part to American opposition to other favorite French proposals, including the international identity card for journalists. *See* Statement on French Attitude toward U.S. Convention Prepared by Walter M. Kotschnig, Chief, Division of International Organization Affairs, April 17, 1948, RG 43, NA, Box 2, File: US Del Documents.

125. E/CN.4/Sub.1/36, 2nd session, January 10, 1948, *Draft Articles for a Covenant and Declaration of Human Rights*, p. 2.

126. Howland P. Sargeant, Special Assistant to the Assistant Secretary of State for Public Affairs, to Robert Lovett, Under Secretary of State, March 6, 1948, RG 43, NA, Box 2, File: US Del File.

127. Minutes of the United States Delegation Meeting, March 29, 1948, Ibid.

128. William Benton to Howland P. Sargeant, March 30, 1948, Ibid., Box 1, File: Delfi Telegrams (Outgoing).

129. Robert Lovett, Under Secretary of State, to William Benton, March 31, 1948, RG 59, NA, Box 2253, 501.BD Freedom of Information/3-3148.

130. E/CONF.6/C.4/SR/4, April 2, 1948, pp. 2–9.

131. E/CONF.6/C.4/SR/5, April 3, 1948, pp. 7–8.

132. E/CONF.6/C.4/SR/6, April 5, 1948, pp. 9, 7.

133. E/CONF.6/C.4/SR/8, April 6, 1948, pp. 2–3.

134. E/CONF.6/C.4/7, March 31, 1948, *Amendments to United Kingdom Proposals on Items B and F of the Agenda*, p. 1.

135. E/CONF.6/C.4/SR/18, April 12, 1948, p. 5.

136. William Benton to George V. Allen, April 20, 1948, RG 43, NA, Box 1, File: Delfi Telegrams (Outgoing).

137. William Benton, Statement on the Proposed Draft of Article 17 of the Covenant on Human Rights, April 19, 1948, Benton Papers, Box 480, File 528.

138. "Limiting the Press," *E&P*, April 17, 1948, p. 74.

139. Benton, Statement on the Proposed Draft of Article 17 of the Covenant on Human Rights.

140. Delegates included a similar amendment, also proposed by India, in the draft British Convention on Freedom of Information over United States objections. *See* Draft Convention on Freedom of Information, *Yearbook on Human Rights for 1948*, p. 502.

141. Draft Covenant on Human Rights, *Yearbook on Human Rights for 1948*, p. 503. *See* Appendix H for the draft covenant article's text. Appendix G gives the text of the draft article for the International Declaration of Rights, the nonbinding accord, which Americans viewed as somewhat similar to the American Bill of Rights.

142. E/CONF.6/C.3/SR/3, March 25, 1948, p. 4.

143. Ibid., p. 7.

144. E/CONF.6/C.3/SR/4, March 27, 1948, p. 5. Benton's comments about American press faults came amid his denunciation of Soviet efforts to advance warmongering and false-news resolutions. The American delegate noted that although the United States press was not perfect, it was far better than the press of other nations, where governments systematically distorted the truth. *See* E/CONF.6/C.1/SR/3, March 25, 1948, p. 5. *See* Blanchard, "The Hutchins Commission, the Press and the Responsibility Concept," for a discussion of the Hutchins Commission findings and a look at the societal setting behind the criticisms.

145. E/CONF.6/C.3/SR/4, March 27, 1948, p. 11. After the conference, Chafee termed the Hutchins Commission report, *A Free and Responsible Press*, Chicago, University of Chicago Press, 1947, and Morris Ernst, *The First Freedom*, New York, Macmillan, 1946, another favorite source of the communist bloc criticism of the American press, as "reputable" books. Eastern bloc delegates quoted the books out of context, he said, adding that if multiple copies of the publications had been flown to Geneva for distribution "among delegations who would be led astray by quotations out of context," the American delegates might have been able to fight the Soviet bloc criticisms more effectively. *See* Zechariah Chafee, General Observations on the Conference, p. 4 in Confidential Report to Secretary of State George C. Marshall by

William Benton [hereinafter cited as Confidential Report], undated, Truman Papers, File: United Nations.

146. E/CONF.6/C.3/SR/5, March 29, 1948, p. 4.

147. E/CONF.6/C.3/SR/6, March 29, 1948, pp. 2–3. Martin's response to Soviet bloc criticism was unusual from the American delegation, for delegation members had decided not to respond to propaganda ploys in the hope their restraint would reduce the effectiveness of Eastern bloc efforts. Martin's attack on the Soviet press—especially his reading of the laws establishing the Glavlit censorship system—silenced the Soviets on the issue of business domination of American media for a while. See Confidential Report, p. 31. See also "Harry Martin's Own Story," Guild Reporter, April 9, 1948, p. 3.

148. E/CONF.6/C.3/SR/10, April 3, 1948, p. 3.

149. Ibid., p. 4.

150. Minutes of the United States Delegation Meeting, March 21, 1948, RG 43, NA, Box 2, File: US Del Documents. The American delegation was relieved when conference delegates did not pursue the newsprint or other issues relating to technical facilities because of America's vulnerability on them. The problem was acute, and Benton did not believe freedom of information throughout the world was possible while such shortages existed. See Confidential Report, pp. 27–28.

151. Walter M. Kotschnig, Chief, Division of International Organization Affairs, to Durward V. Sandifer, United Nations Affairs, March 1, 1948, RG 84, NA, Records of the United States Mission to the United Nations, Box 88, Public Info: Confs 1946–48.

152. Memorandum of Conversation with John P. Humphrey, Secretary of the Conference, by Erwin Canham, March 30, 1948, RG 43, NA, Box 1, File: Memoranda of Conversations 1–8.

153. "National News Agencies," E&P, April 10, 1948, p. 42.

154. Minutes of United States Delegation Meeting, April 7, 1948, RG 43, NA, Box 2, File: US Del Documents.

155. Resolution No. 19, Final Act of the Conference on Freedom of Information, Yearbook of Human Rights for 1948, p. 508.

156. Marguerite Johnston, "U.S. Views Prevail in Geneva Measures," E&P, April 17, 1948, p. 137.

157. Resolution No. 19, Final Act of the Conference on Freedom of Information, Yearbook of Human Rights for 1948, p. 508. The American delegation felt that China had a good point to make here but that Chang did not push the conference hard enough to achieve sounder results. See Confidential Report, p. 15.

158. Continuing Machinery to Promote the International Flow of Information, March 3, 1948, RG 84, NA, Records of the United States Mission to the United Nations, Box 164, United States Delegation Handbook, Position Papers: Conference on Freedom of Information.

159. Delegation Report, p. 2.

160. Confidential Report, p. 5. The middle group of nations feared American cultural imperialism, especially since their communications facilities had been devastated by the war or were underdeveloped, and they believed American journalists were "too-blythe" in accepting the possibility of another war, one that would not be fought in America. "They are well aware that the Soviet press

and propaganda share the blame for the present tension; but they also believe ways should be found to stimulate in our U.S. press 'a greater sense of responsibility'." *See* Ibid., pp. 5–6.

161. Delegation Report, p. 2.
162. Ibid., p. 3.
163. Confidential Report, p. 1.
164. Ibid., pp. 8–11. Despite the shortcomings of the Eastern bloc representatives, the Americans did have to combat some early efforts at compromise. *See* Ibid., pp. 19–23.
165. Walter Kotschnig, Observations of Mr. Kotschnig for Inclusion in Confidential Report, April 22, 1948, 400.48 FOI Conference, SDR, p. 2.
166. John Carter Vincent, American Minister in Switzerland, to the Secretary of State, April 7, 1948, RG 59, NA, Box 2254, 501.BD Freedom of Information/4-748.
167. Delegation Report, p. 9.
168. Observations of Mr. Kotschnig for Inclusion in Confidential Report, p. 7.
169. Confidential Report, p. 3.
170. Howland P. Sargeant, Special Assistant to the Assistant Secretary of State for Public Affairs, to John Peurifoy, Assistant Secretary of State, February 25, 1948, RG 43, NA, Box 1, File: US Delegation (2).
171. Erwin D. Canham, Address, April 16, 1948, *Problems of Journalism—1948*, pp. 155–56.
172. Ibid., p. 156.
173. Ibid., pp. 154–55.
174. Ibid., pp. 156–57.
175. Sevellon Brown, "Sevellon Brown to U.S. Press: 'Don't Highhat Task of World Freedom'," *E&P*, April 17, 1948, p. 26.

Later assessments of the Geneva conference were quite dismal. Hugh Baillie, writing in 1959, for instance, termed the conference "a disappointment," noting, "we soon found we could vote down the Russian bloc ... but we could not handle opposition from nations we had thought were on our side." The three conventions, Baillie said, were "shipped to the United Nations in New York, where they still moulder in some pigeonhole. They have become so loaded with amendments that they would probably damage the cause of Freedom of Information if they were adopted. So let 'em wither. It was a good try." *See* Hugh Baillie, *High Tension*, New York, Harper & Row, 1959, pp. 286–87.

One historian of the United Press termed the Geneva documents "the longest step forward ever taken by an international body toward establishing a method that would protect and encourage a freer flow of international news." The conventions were amended, "but the net result was real progress toward elimination of the old official news-agency system." *See* Joe Alex Morris, *Deadline Every Minute: The Story of the United Press*, p. 311.

CHAPTER 5

The Crusade Encounters Opposition at the United Nations

Even as American journalists encouraged their colleagues on to greater heights of enthusiasm for international freedom of information, the luster of the American victories in Geneva was wearing off. American delegates returned from the Geneva Conference on Freedom of Information confident of rapid United Nations action on international freedom of information accords. Such optimism was unwarranted, given the realities of the situation. Conferees had erected the first roadblock themselves by asking the secretary-general was also to determine whether any nations had proposals participating in the Geneva sessions on the conference documents. The secretary-general was also to determine whether any nation had proposals for other draft conventions based on the conference's actions. Deadline for submission of such material was July 5, 1948. United Nations consideration of suggestions and comments would begin in August 1948 at the Economic and Social Council committee level. Conference delegates hoped for a perfunctory review by United Nations committees, with approved documents being transmitted to the General Assembly quickly. By the end of 1948, American delegates hoped to see the conventions opened for signature.[1]

Even if the conferees had not asked the United Nations secretariat to participate in the ratification process, the involvement of the international organization's grinding bureaucracy was necessary anyway. The Geneva conference documents came from the hearts and souls of journalists, and four proposals likely to stir heated debate were:

- The Draft Convention on the Gathering and International Transmission of News, referred to as the news-gathering convention. The proposal, largely written by the United States, was designed to aid foreign correspondents in entering and leaving other nations, in obtaining news in those countries, and in transmitting that information back to their home news organizations without interference.

209

- The Draft Convention Concerning the Institution of an International Right of Correction, known also as the right of reply convention. This accord was presented by the French and was designed to establish a procedure whereby nations that felt incorrectly represented in news stories could provide a corrected version of the facts for possible publication in the offending country. The United States voted for this convention, although the American delegates said that they preferred to see the right of reply incorporated within the news-gathering convention.
- The Draft Convention on Freedom of Information. This treaty proposal, written by the British, was designed to guarantee the rights of freedom of information to individuals residing in signatory nations. The most controversial section of this draft was its article listing limitations that a nation could impose legally on the operation of the press. The United States abstained from voting on this accord in Geneva.
- Article 17 of the draft Covenant on Human Rights. The original language for this article was written by the Subcommission on Freedom of Information and of the Press. The controversial section of this proposal also dealt with the limitations that a nation could impose legally on the operation of the press. The United States voted against this article at Geneva.

No government would accept any of these proposals without amending them to protect their national interests. The United States proved no exception; the State Department even considered introducing amendments to the United States draft convention on international news gathering to make the document sanction governmental restrictions on the entry of certain correspondents and on the ability of some journalists to travel freely throughout a signatory nation—if the reporters could "endanger the public safety."[2] The proposed change would permit American restrictions against the admission of communist correspondents to remain in place despite the ratification of a news-gathering convention that allegedly guaranteed freedom of entry. The Americans also planned to pursue efforts to incorporate the French draft convention calling for an international right of reply within the United States news-gathering convention. In support of the latter proposal, State Department personnel argued that the special protection provided by the right of correction convention "should be extended only to States which are willing to facilitate the entry, movement, and operations of foreign correspondents in the interests of a freer flow of information between the countries of the world."[3]

Debates on the Geneva documents began in the Human Rights Committee, an ad hoc committee of the Economic and Social Council. After that committee finished with the documents, the Economic and Social Council itself would debate the accords before passing them on to the General Assembly for final action. Before the General Assembly acted, however, its

Third Committee, a standing committee designed to look at social, human-itarian, and cultural issues, would debate the documents. The accords clearly had a long road ahead of them. As debates started on the lowest level of the committee structure, delegates publicly proclaimed their desire to avoid long arguments that would simply reiterate points made in earlier debates. Despite their pledges, no delegate planned to curtail the fullness of his or her comments in the interest of speeding the documents on to the next level of the United Nations. Alexei Pavlov of the Soviet Union was more honest than his colleages in announcing his intentions. The Russians, who needed to rebound from their losses at the Conference on Freedom of Information, promised that no document would escape their exhaustive examination. Pavlov was defeated on his call for a general debate over the documents adopted in Geneva, but the committee decided to discuss each draft convention individually, thus effectively abandoning its plans to limit comments and opening the way for extensive deliberations. The Soviets exploited this opportunity to the fullest. Although the Russians and their allies broke no new ground in objecting to the drafts, they dominated the early sessions. Soviet bloc delegates deemed all three conventions unaccept-able because none of the accords prohibited warmongering or the dissemina-tion of false news, because the treaties interfered in the domestic affairs of signatory states, because the proposals contained permissive language about whether signatories with colonial possessions must extend the conventions' provisions to their colonies, and because the documents denied correspon-dents assigned to cover United Nations activities in the United States the freedoms demanded for journalists elsewhere.[4]

DELEGATES ATTEMPT TO LIMIT THE SCOPE OF THE NEWS-GATHERING CONVENTION

Initial debate on the news-gathering convention revealed tendencies from almost every delegation to limit the scope of the Geneva accords; this trend would only increase as United Nations consideration of the documents continued. For instance, W.V.J. Evans of the United Kingdom wanted to make sure that the privileges guaranteed by the news-gathering convention would be valid solely within signatory states.[5] Eastern bloc delegates, most likely anticipating their home countries' unwillingness to accede to the news-gathering convention, protested that if the benefits offered in the convention were so important, the guarantees must be available to all journalists anywhere—regardless of whether the foreign correspondent's home country had signed the accord. Delegates in favor of limiting the application of the guarantees stressed the international principle of recipro-city, the core of most treaty agreements. These delegates saw no reason to change tradition for this accord.[6] Delegates realized that correspondents from nonsignatory nations would benefit by working in a nation agreeing to the news-gathering convention. Once a country signed the document, the convention's provisions extended to all foreign correspondents within that nation's boundaries, regardless of whether the correspondent's home government had ratified the convention.[7] Efforts to remove this possible loophole continued in succeeding debates.

Another proposal by the Americans, French, and British called for the opening of all news sources to all correspondents equally—"so far as possible." Walter M. Kotschnig, the American delegate on the Human Rights Committee, explained that under existing practices, most countries reserved the right to exclude foreign correspondents from press conferences on certain sensitive topics.[8] The proposal simply legitimized that practice. As if to compensate for the insertion of this and other possible limitations on the convention's scope, committee members showed some tendencies to broaden the convention by making its provisions apply to correspondents of all news agencies, whether privately, publicly, or governmentally owned.[9]

Such changes, agreed to early in the debates over the news-gathering convention, took the concept of international freedom of the press as envisioned by American journalists into dramatically new directions. Rather than creating a world in which reporters of commercial agencies would be free to roam around at will gathering and transmitting information, the United States convention now might limit a correspondent's freedom of action to those countries that formally agreed to the terms of a specific document. And, under the provisions of the revised document, signatory governments could exclude foreign correspondents from certain news events, if government officials felt that the exclusion served the national interest. Additional important changes in the conventions were likely as the diplomats gathered at the United Nations sought even more ways to safeguard national interests from the guarantees provided in the news-gathering convention.

A discussion of permissible regulations on foreign correspondents provided no solace to Americans interested in international freedom of the press. The United States representatives on the committee defended the language in the convention that allowed restrictions such as censorship in peacetime for reasons of national military security—if the reporters knew the censorship rules. Without provisions for peacetime censorship, Lloyd Free, an American delegate, told the committee, numerous countries might be unable to ratify the final document. Included in that number apparently was the United States, which needed to protect atomic energy information. Adding the word military made the provision palatable to the United States because of the term's limiting nature.[10]

Other delegates did not necessarily agree with the American interpretation. For instance, the Canadian delegate, L.A.D. Stephens, argued that "the way to prevent news from circulating about defence projects of a secret nature was to deny access to them and not by means of censorship." Even though Stephens's statement was obviously true, the comment ignored the aggressiveness of the American press in seeking information and American fears that the propensity of officials to leak information to the media would lead to the dissemination of military information that should be held in strictest confidence. Consequently, specific legal prohibitions probably were the only recourse for Americans trying to keep certain information confidential. The debate, however, went farther than the Americans desired, for the committee decided to drop the word military from the convention clause, thus allowing contracting states to enact laws necessary for the protection of national security, which was a far broader concept than national military security.[11] An additional amendment, suggested by Mexico, allowed contracting states to pass necessary legislation to preserve both national security and public order, another widening of the scope of possible restrictive legislation.[12]

In an effort to regain some of the momentum for press freedom being lost in United Nations debates, the American delegation attempted to add provisions to the convention that would protect nationals of other countries employed by foreign news agencies. The proposal encountered objections from a variety of delegates who did not want the draft convention to interfere with the rights of countries to deal with their own citizens.[13] Although the protection would be very valuable to American news agencies, Kotschnig defended the amendment as one designed to help smaller countries with financial problems that kept them from sending their own nationals abroad as correspondents. By protecting foreigners employed by these smaller agencies, the news-gathering convention would promote the free flow of information throughout the world.[14] The importance of this provision to American news agencies remained unspoken, but United States news agencies increasingly employed residents of foreign countries to augment the coverage provided by American citizens in various nations. As the cold war intensified, the wire services even came to depend on nationals of Eastern bloc countries for news of those nations.

Pavlov objected to giving nationals of a country employed by a foreign news agency special privileges unavailable to their fellow countrymen who worked for national newspapers and contended that the proposal posed monumental problems. Foreign correspondents in Poland, for instance, enjoyed exemption from taxation, priority in transmitting news, and easy access to governmental officials, Juliusz Katz-Suchy, the representative from that country, said. Whether Poland wanted to extend such privileges to Poles working for foreign agencies was another matter.[15]

The goal of the proposal was not to create a privileged category of correspondents, the American delegate responded once again, but to promote the free flow of news throughout the world. Protecting nationals who worked for foreign news agencies accomplished that end. In fact, Kotschnig stressed, delegates who argued against the provision actually opposed the greater worldwide understanding that such internationalizing of news agencies offered. After all, local employees "possessed special qualifications for interpreting events in their own countries" unavailable to foreigners reporting the news. Eastern bloc representatives refuted the American contention by claiming that the potential problems involved in creating a double standard for native reporters who worked for foreign employers clearly outweighed any possible benefits.[16] Delegates defeated an attempt by the Mexican government to present the United States proposal in reverse. The Mexican proposal would have guaranteed the right of any country to force a foreign news agency to hire a certain number of the host country's nationals. The coercive nature of the provision, delegates decided, would force international news agencies to hire foreign nationals regardless of whether they wanted to do so and, hence, according to Free, violated the principles of freedom of information.[17]

When he lost on the issue of extending the news-gathering convention's protections to nationals employed by a foreign news agency, the Soviet delegate sought another way to amend the United States convention. Surely, Pavlov argued, the news-gathering convention protected only factual data. The convention clearly should exclude "inventions or false information." But the convention protected both news and opinion. And how could one determine if an opinion was factual? Under the Soviet proposal, Pavlov explained, "a correspondent would be free to express an opinion or even to exaggerate the facts, but his remarks would have to be based on facts or events which had actually taken place." The problem with this proposal, Kotschnig responded, was that someone must decide if a report was truthful, meaning, in most cases, the state concerned. Since no one had a reliable standard by which to judge the truthfulness of reports, Kotschnig did not think that governments should be given such a responsibility. Carried to a ridiculous extreme, the Soviet proposal could prohibit speculative stories about political matters or even bar commentary on international sporting events.[18]

One issue of great concern to many European nations was whether the news-gathering convention required signatories to admit a correspondent from another signatory nation regardless of nationality or previous record. Perceiving a concern about admitting former Nazis behind such questions, Pavlov suggested allowing a nation to exclude such an individual even if he or she was legitimately employed as a foreign correspondent. "For collaborators and traitors to be able to fulfil the task of foreign correspondents would constitute an injury to states," he argued, and prevention of this possibility was crucial. Delegates defeated the Russian suggestion.[19]

Despite the voicing of concerns to the contrary, admission of former Nazis employed as correspondents into countries against the wishes of the nations involved was unlikely. An amendment to the news-gathering convention proposed by the British, French, and Americans allowed a contracting state to routinely exclude certain correspondents in accordance with national laws and immigration policies. Although Soviet bloc nations protested that the proposal was discriminatory, supporters of the amendment responded that the provision simply protected national sovereignty, a concept usually endorsed by the Eastern bloc nations. Likewise, proponents used national sovereignty to defend language that would allow host countries to limit the activities of correspondents admitted to a country solely to report on United Nations activities occurring in the host country. Without the restrictive phrasing, Raymond Offroy of France warned, host governments might be unwilling to allow certain correspondents to enter their boundaries to cover United Nations activities at all. The provision allowed host governments to limit the topics that the foreign correspondent could cover to United Nations functions and to restrict the journalist's freedom of travel in the host country. Soviet protests against the proposals were met with recitations of Russian policies toward correspondents attending the Moscow Council of Foreign Ministers conference in 1947, which were almost identical to the limitations suggested by the committee.[20] American restrictions on the activities of communist journalist Pierre Courtade fell in the same category.

CONCERN ABOUT CHANGES IN
NEWS-GATHERING DRAFT APPEARS

Debates over the news-gathering convention took longer than expected, filling some ten days of the Human Rights Committee's time. Committee members never had the opportunity to discuss the other two Geneva documents—the British freedom of information convention or the French right of reply convention. In fact, debates on the news-gathering convention took so long in the Human Rights Committee that the Economic and Social Council itself had no time to debate any of the documents. Thus, the council sent all three Geneva conventions to the General Assembly without a recommendation for action—a move that some press observers saw as a victory for the Soviets.[21] As a result of this action, the General Assembly would likely return all three conventions to the Economic and Social Council with instructions for the council to inspect the documents very closely. Then, the Soviets could claim another victory in the effort to keep the documents bottled up. The "complicated organizational setup" of the United Nations and Russian adroitness at parliamentary maneuvering meant, in the eyes of some journalistic observers, certain failure on freedom of information issues. *Editor & Publisher* noted two areas in which the Russians allegedly had triumphed: the change in the news-gathering convention clause from permitting censorship for national military security reasons only to allowing censorship on the grounds of national security, "which can mean almost anything in the terminology of the Iron Curtain countries," and the downward revision of guarantees calling for the widest possible access to official news sources to language requiring access to official news sources "so far as possible." According to the trade journal, the Russians were "bending every effort to limit freedom of information throughout the world rather than expand it."[22]

Erwin D. Canham, president of the American Society of Newspaper Editors (ASNE) and vice chairman of the United States delegation at the Geneva conference, also believed that the Soviets had won significant changes in the news-gathering convention because "middle ground nations, which should know better, fell away from our cause." Changes that Canham labeled as dangerous to the American concept of freedom of the press were the dropping of the word military from the section of the convention giving the grounds for peacetime censorship and the opening of news sources equally to all "so far as possible." The ASNE president worried lest the text had been "watered down to the point of being meaningless." Some of these changes might have slipped through because the American delegation charged with defending the convention contained no journalists. This lack of press representation was not the department's fault, however, for the State Department had tried to place journalists on the delegation. Another such failure to cooperate must be avoided. From now on, Canham said, the department and the press must work together to convince so-called allies of the correctness of the United States draft convention and to keep these countries in line: "We must keep a close watch on the situation, otherwise our own handiwork is being turned against us."[23] And William Benton, former assistant secretary of state for public affairs and chairman of the United States delegation at Geneva, also expressed concern over the changes made in the news-gathering convention. In fact, Benton thought that enough nations of the world supported the American idea of freedom of the press that if the United Nations refused to revert to the language of the news-gathering convention written at the Geneva conference, the United States should promote the convention as a bilateral treaty.[24]

Despite these observations about the overwhelming power of the Soviet bloc, delegates routinely had defeated Russian amendments to the news-gathering convention. Proposals to restrict press freedom for reasons of national security and public order actually were introduced by countries "in which political conditions were normally unstable."[25] The American delegation itself had strongly supported restricting access to sources of news. Even *Editor & Publisher* had labeled China, Australia, and New Zealand as being as guilty as the Eastern European nations in blocking attempts to enact freedom of information guarantees endorsed at Geneva.[26] In fact, the Soviets themselves failed to find any Russian victories within the Human Rights Committee's deliberations. The Soviets considered the news-gathering convention that emerged from the committee as far less satisfactory than "the already unsatisfactory draft originally proposed by the Conference."[27] The lesson most apparent from the first round of discussions on the Geneva conventions at the United Nations was that the American free-press crusade would encounter problems from friend and foe alike. The Soviets and their allies were obstructionist and would subject the press of the United States to regular and predictable attacks, but the objectionable votes did not come solely from that small group of nations. The reality of the situation made *Editor & Publisher*'s call to "get on with the job for the benefit of the rest of the world"[28] unlikely to win many adherents.

Even though journalists were concerned over the condition that the draft convention was in and over the influence exerted by the Soviets in shaping that draft, they could not afford to forget that the battle over the news-gathering convention would be renewed at the General Assembly session of September 1948. Regardless of what members of the press said, the news-gathering treaty had survived attempts to significantly alter its provisions in the Human Rights Committee. The draft still faced numerous challenges in the General Assembly—especially since the Economic and Social Council had not debated the committee draft before transmitting it to the General Assembly.

Exemplifying the complexity of the opposition facing the American effort was a conversation with Raúl Noriega, a member of the Mexican delegation, in which Noriega told two United States representatives that the Mexican government viewed the news-gathering convention as "a one-way affair, designed almost exclusively to assist United States information agencies." To quiet Mexican fears of the United States convention, Noriega demanded American support for amendments that would guarantee the right of nations "to restrict the *domestic* dissemination of news to their own nationals" and "to protect their general laws requiring foreign enterprises of all kinds to employ varying percentages of natives."[29] Delegates at the Geneva conference had supported a government's ability to determine who distributed news to a country's citizens when they adopted a resolution proposed by China. Members of the Human Rights Committee had rejected a proposal that would have required foreign news agencies to hire nationals of other countries when working in their homelands. Both ideas indicated strong resistance from an allegedly friendly, noncommunist country to the possibility of American infiltration of that country via the United States' large news agencies.

Both hopes and fears for the Geneva documents appeared futile as the General Assembly session progressed. The Soviets and their Eastern bloc allies filled debate time in the General Assembly by resurrecting their 1947 attack on American media for warmongering. In the General Assembly's Third Committee, delegates struggled over Article 17 of the draft human rights covenant. Neither discussion covered any new ground. Article 17, as approved by the Geneva Conference on Freedom of Information, also had gone to the General Assembly without additional change.[30] As the General

Assembly session moved into late November, press observers realized that delegates would be unable to consider any of the three Geneva conventions before the end of the session, especially since two of the accords had not even been debated within a lower United Nations body.

Actually, reasoned *Editor & Publisher*, a delay might be beneficial, for, in the trade journal's eyes, the whole range of United Nations priorities was questionable. Economic and Social Council deliberations over free-press issues had been conducted "in an atmosphere of international antagonism [that] almost scuttled the freedom of information ship." Only by passing the news-gathering convention on to the General Assembly could the council save the issue. After receiving the free-press package, however, the assembly found "itself in the same atmosphere with interminable debates and wrangling over the Berlin question, Palestine, atomic bombs, etc." Even if the assembly managed to find time to debate the Geneva conventions, *Editor & Publisher* reasoned, "it is a safe bet the conventions would meet with the same hopelessness." This atmosphere made press watchfulness even more imperative. And since many smaller nations were as ardently opposed to complete freedom of information as the Soviets, American journalists also had to worry about possible conspiracies among such nations to enact conventions that "would be wholly unacceptable to us and prove to be actually restrictive of information." Still unwilling to recognize the possible futility of the United Nations effort, *Editor & Publisher* noted that some delegations were talking about calling a special conference in 1949 to deal solely with the freedom of information issue. Perhaps, the trade journal said, a conference not otherwise distracted could accomplish something positive on the freedom of information front.[31]

A coalition of nations including the United States suggested a resolution for a specialized conference in late November 1948.[32] Although the Third Committee of the General Assembly approved the proposal,[33] no special conference met. Instead, the conventions were referred to the next meeting of the Third Committee, which convened in April 1949. Delegations to this particular session included many individuals with journalistic backgrounds, making the committee composition similar to that of the Geneva conference. The American spokesperson at the session was a man in whom the American press community placed great trust—Erwin D. Canham, editor of the *Christian Science Monitor*, who had noted the absence of a press voice at the 1948 United Nations debates.[34]

PLANNING FOR DEBATES ON NEWS-GATHERING ACCORD

The Americans expected a stiff fight on each Geneva convention and planned to campaign to delete objectionable amendments attached during earlier United Nations debates. They also wanted to strengthen existing language in drafts in order to achieve documents more in line with American ideals. Regarding the United States convention on the international gathering and transmission of news, American delegates planned to insist that the word military be reinserted between national and security in the section that allowed peacetime censorship of news. Success here probably rested on winning support from the Latin American countries, which had supported the deletion of military in earlier debates. The Human Rights Committee also had authorized the derogation of responsibilities under the treaty in times of war or other public emergency. Because of this change, American delegates planned to argue that since nations could impose censorship in times of public emergency, they could "safely agree" to limit censorship under normal conditions to matters impinging on "national military security." The new phraseology also was designed to please the British, who feared that the news-gathering convention would prevent them from halting communications that appeared to endanger national security or to be "contrary to public decency." When this was combined with other minor changes, the State Department believed that the United Kingdom's delegation would offer no more objections to the news-gathering convention.[35]

Satisfying British concerns in committee was essential because, if the issue came to a vote in the General Assembly, "the United Kingdom would be successful in watering down the limitations on censorship desired by the United States." If the altered text prohibited censorship except on the grounds of national military security, the British would agree that the language permitted the occasional interception of "dangerous messages" by government employees. Although the American delegation would accept that interpretation, the Americans also wanted to eliminate the section of the amended convention allowing censorship if threats to the public order occurred. The Americans had not objected strenuously to this language in the Human Rights Committee as a concession to the British, who threatened to protest on another matter if the Americans opposed this point. The disagreement with the British now was settled; the next step was deleting the public order phrasing from the news-gathering convention. After all, said State Department planners, "the Convention has nothing to do with the domestic dissemination of information. It deals primarily with outgoing news material and it is difficult to see how information leaving the country can endanger public order." If necessary, however, the language could remain in the document, as long as everyone clearly understood that the provision could not be used to censor news material leaving a country.[36]

Continued resistance to attempts by the Soviet bloc, China, or Latin American countries to exclude nationals of a country employed by a foreign news agency from the protections offered by the convention was advisable, the State Department said. But, if necessary, the American delegation could agree to language exempting "nationals of a Contracting State, in their personal capacities, from the rights granted by the convention as against that State, provided the text makes it clear that the rights of foreign information agencies for whom they work are not affected thereby." The United States delegation also could make some concessions to the Chinese and Latin American delegations on the issue of protecting underdeveloped news agencies and the compulsory hiring of nationals of host countries by foreign news agencies—if necessary. Since both suggestions would be difficult to defeat if they came to a vote, the delegation could agree to, "though not formally to propose," language stating specifically that the convention applied solely to news transmitted abroad and that its provisions did not contravene laws requiring foreign businesses to hire a certain percentage of nationals in order to operate in a host country.[37]

United States delegates were not prepared to compromise on one issue. The news-gathering convention must include language that restricted the ability of states to exclude correspondents because of their prior work as correspondents. As now phrased, government officials could refuse to admit any journalist for any reason, particularly if "they feared that once admitted the correspondent might transmit news distasteful to the government." The American delegates also were to resist attempts to delete the term contracting state from the convention. The Soviets would argue that the language injected discrimination into the document. The Americans must counter that the principle involved was reciprocity: "The Soviet bloc should not be allowed to benefit from the Convention without undertaking the obligations it lays down." According to the State Department, a nation's ratification of the convention provided complete protection for its reporters and, in any case, refusal to sign left existing privileges for foreign correspondents intact. The convention simply gave "new assurances and guarantees for existing rights."[38]

Discussion of the second Geneva accord, the British draft convention on freedom of information, was also expected in April 1949. The United States delegation had abstained from voting on this document at Geneva because of its list of limitations permissible for governments to impose on the press. Since the Geneva conference, however, discussions with the British had led to promises that the draft would be substantially revised to eliminate the most distasteful provisions. The State Department decided that the United States delegation must rely on the British promise because the United Kingdom could "obtain majority support for the present unacceptable draft, should it decide to press forward despite US opposition. In view of the general political situation, and the drive the US is waging on the broad front of human rights, it is desirable that, if possible, agreement be reached with the UK on this convention in order to avoid an open split." At the very least, the United States delegation was to obtain a more general limitations clause. If the necessary changes were not made, the United States delegation must abstain from voting on the freedom of information convention once again.[39]

State Department planners felt that American delegates must fight the so-called Indian amendment to the British convention, which allowed governments to punish the press for disseminating false or distorted news. The United States feared that allowing governments "to arrogate unto themselves the power to determine what is true and what is false, what is friendly and what unfriendly—a power which could be effectively exercised only through censorship or suppression—might well mark the end of the free press." The chances of defeating the Indian amendment or indeed of removing the specific limitations list were not good, advisers said. Since the United States had been defeated several times on the issue of a general limitations clause, the only possible way to avoid the inclusion of specific limitations rested with winning the British delegation—"the most vigorous advocate of specific limitations—away from this approach." An American appeal to the United Kingdom resulted in a suggested modification, stating freedom of the press carried certain responsibilities and could

> therefore be subject to certain penalties, liabilities, and restrictions provided by law and necessary: in the interest of national security; for the prevention of disorder or crime; for the protection of public health or morals; for the protection of the rights of other persons; for preventing the disclosure of information received in confidence; or for maintaining the fair administration of justice.

Although the State Department termed the revised language "a notable improvement," the new version still left "a good deal to be desired." If the British insisted on maintaining this language, the United States delegation could accept the new version of the restrictions clause—if the British agreed to add public safety to the list of permissible regulations. The delegation also was to seek deletion of provisions permitting regulation of the press to prevent crime and public disorder and protecting information received in confidence from disclosure.[40]

The United Kingdom draft convention also listed responsibilities for journalists such as reporting facts without prejudice, and the United States delegation was to seek alteration of that provision, arguing that "the sole primary obligation of information personnel is to seek the truth and report the facts, and that the other highly desirable objectives listed in the Conference draft will flow from the honest performance of this primary obligation." The point was critical, the State Department warned, since the Soviets wanted "to secure recognition of the theory that organs of information must be assigned affirmative 'tasks', such as promoting peace and security, combatting fascism and racial hatred, etc., else freedom loses its pragmatic significance from the social point of view." Modifying the word duty, which introduced the responsibilities of the press, with the word moral also was desirable.[41]

One additional problem in the United Kingdom draft convention on freedom of information was the Indian amendment protecting a government's right to shield developing national news agencies from incursions by large international news services. Here, the State Department told delegates to argue "that national news agencies are not 'fully developed' until they enjoy a complete monopoly," but planners were doubtful about winning adherents. Both the Indians and the Chinese, strong supporters of the protective provision, would fight to retain the existing language. If the debate swung in favor of the supporters of the amendment, United States delegates must seek a clause permitting "affirmative assistance to national news agencies, but not such negative assistance as restrictive measures designed to hamper competing foreign news agencies." Failing that, the Americans should try to restrict government assistance to a country's news agencies "to the extent required to enable them to compete with equal opportunity within its own territory with foreign news agencies."[42]

Debate on the third Geneva document, the French draft convention instituting an international right of reply, should be noncontroversial, State Department advisers predicted. The United States delegation had eliminated most of the difficulties contained within the French proposal in Geneva, where the French had modified the proposal along lines more acceptable to the Americans. The main goal for United States delegates regarding this convention during the United Nations debate was to incorporate its provisions within the American draft convention on international gathering and transmission of news. The amalgamation was important because State Department advisers believed the United States Senate was more likely to approve an international right of correction "if it were embodied in a more general convention providing rights and privileges for the press."[43] Thus, the United States delegation was ready to fight for international freedom of information within the Third Committee of the General Assembly. The delegation's platform as prepared by the State Department almost could have been written by the editorial writer for *Editor & Publisher* or by a leading international free-press advocate within the American Society of Newspaper Editors. Both the press and the government expected the main foe of American proposals to be the Soviet bloc delegates; unexpected opponents were delegations from numerous smaller nations. The hectic debates once again clearly revealed how few supporters the American ideal of freedom of the press had around the world.

SMALLER NATIONS ATTACK AMERICAN PROPOSALS

Debate on the United States draft convention on the gathering and international transmission of news topped the agenda at the Third Committee session. The initial challenge to the convention came not from the Soviets but from representatives of the smaller, so-called middle-of-the-road nations still concerned about the status of their nationals employed by foreign news agencies. The news-gathering convention that had emerged from the Economic and Social Council by way of the Human Rights Committee offered guarantees to information agency correspondents. The question, then, was whether the provisions applied only to foreigners working for foreign news agencies within another country or to nationals employed by a foreign agency within the employee's own home country as well. Canham, representing the United States, said that he had always considered the language as covering both nationals and foreigners employed by a foreign information agency, an interpretation immediately disputed by the representative from India. P. C. Chang, the Chinese delegate, supported the Indian objections, pointing out that the original convention language, as prepared in Geneva, referred specifically to a foreign correspondent and defined a foreign correspondent as someone who held a valid passport. The precision of the draft's initial language indicated the delegates' intention to exclude nationals employed by foreign information agencies from the provision's protections.[44] In fact, every statement within the Geneva document referred to facilitating the entry, transit, and exit of foreign correspondents. Of course, the Third Committee could change the meaning of the language, but Chang's protest carried an implicit warning against such tampering.[45] Any protection for nationals employed by foreign news agencies must be carefully weighed because of the broad principles involved, the Chinese delegate stressed.[46]

Ernest Davies of the United Kingdom registered surprise over Chang's comments. "The word 'foreign' as applied to a correspondent implied that a person was the correspondent of a foreign agency or newspaper, and not himself a foreigner," Davies argued. "That was surely the only correct and fair interpretation possible" because no one either at the Geneva conference or at the Economic and Social Council session had intended to "discriminate in any way between the nationals of a State and foreigners; nothing had occurred since then to militate in favour of such discrimination." Canham added that neither the conference nor the council drafts had contemplated giving the foreign head of a news agency bureau in a foreign country any protection denied to his employees who might be nationals of that country. "To deprive nationals of such protection would greatly diminish the value of the convention; such an interpretation could not be entertained."[47] Although not part of his argument before the United Nations, Canham knew that about 50 percent of the correspondents employed by American news agencies and newspapers abroad were nationals of the countries in which they worked. Thus, the interests of these American news organizations in the debate were great.[48]

But the United States encountered adamant opposition to protecting nationals of a host country under the provisions of a convention written to safeguard the rights of foreign correspondents. Noriega, the Mexican delegate, even suggested adding language to the news-gathering convention that specifically said that "no Contracting State shall be obliged to consider any of its own nationals as foreign correspondents under the terms of this convention." Without such language, Ana Figueroa of Chile noted, nationals employed as foreign correspondents "would virtually be placed outside the laws of their own country." Simply because the nationals worked for a foreign agency, they could "engage with impunity in activities harmful to that Government." The Chilean delegation opposed the provision. And Karim Azkoul, the Lebanese delegate, considered the point so important that the future of the draft convention hinged on solving the problem. Arguments that including the protection violated national security were lost on Davies, who noted that the draft convention said that correspondents were subject to the laws of the host countries. "It would be most unfortunate," the United Kingdom's delegate said, if the committee failed "to adopt a text stating clearly and unambiguously that foreign correspondents were all those persons, regardless of nationality, who were employed by a foreign information agency and engaged in transmitting news to it."[49]

Failure to protect nationals employed by foreign news agencies on an equal basis with foreigners employed by the same agencies ran "counter to the United Nations' whole aim of raising the level of information," Canham warned, echoing the arguments of American delegates at earlier debates. If the difficulties perceived by the representatives from China, Chile, Mexico, and other countries were really so important, safeguards were necessary to protect signatory nations. But any protections must be carefully worded and inserted in an appropriate point in the draft; neither condition was met by the current proposals. The American points were quickly discarded by Chang, who noted that few countries sent correspondents abroad. The convention's provisions affected most nations only by requiring them to grant special privileges to a few nationals employed by foreign news-gathering agencies and, thus, were unfair.[50]

Arguments grew repetitious, and delegates ultimately approved language including both nationals and foreigners under the umbrella of protections given the foreign correspondent. Important principles were at stake. One point, of course, was the need for foreign agencies to hire nationals of particular countries to supplement the foreign agency's ability to gather news in those countries. Accompanying that argument was the valid point that natives of a country, when employed by foreign news agencies, brought a particular depth and expertise to the reporting of events that foreign reporters were unable to provide. Running counter to these arguments, however, was the problem that certain countries said they faced if they were forced to grant special privileges to a small group of nationals employed by foreign news agencies. Finally, nationals employed by foreign news agencies were historically more susceptible to pressures from their home governments than were foreigners sent in by the same agencies. The right of nations to exert such pressure was an important, although generally unspoken, part of the debate. Underlying all the comments, pro and con, was the realization that the protections sought would primarily benefit the Associated Press (AP), the United Press (UP), and the International News Service (INS) of the United States and Reuters of Great Britain. With these additional protections, the big commercial agencies could increase their stranglehold on the news of the world, making the development of domestic agencies even more difficult.

The question of how to identify foreign correspondents grew naturally from the debate over which correspondents the news-gathering convention protected. One issue centered on whether holding a passport that identified the bearer as a correspondent was sufficient to merit the convention's protections or whether a correspondent needed other papers classifying him as a reporter entitled to the document's privileges. If correspondents must carry documents from employers certifying them as reporters, problems immediately arose for free-lance journalists who roamed the world on their own initiative seeking stories to sell any available market. Delegates refused to require additional identification for foreign correspondents at this point,[51] but the question reappeared, bringing additional threats to the American concept of freedom for correspondents to function without interference.

Since delegates repeatedly had refused to create an agency that would firmly control correspondents' behavior, the Soviet bloc decided that reporters covered by the convention should be required to distribute reliable information. Thus, Jan Drohojowski of Poland sought to amend the convention to ensure the availability of not only full information, as promised, but of trustworthy information as well. The change was vital, Drohojowski said, because of the tendency of the world's press "to publish extremely unreliable and distorted information." A daily reading of the American press underlined the unreliability of journalists and highlighted the reasons for mandating responsible reporting, Stevan Dedijer of Yugoslavia added. Again, Dedijer said, American press critics had condemned their own newspapers in a new book that revealed that fewer than 1,800 individuals owned newspapers in the United States and thus were able to impose their opinions on millions of American readers. Compounding the problems caused by this lack of diversity in media ownership in America, according to the Yugoslav, was a recent call for American newspapers to unite in support of national foreign policy. How could such policies go uncensured, Dedijer seemed to be asking.[52] All the communist bloc delegates wanted, said Frantisek Vrba, the representative from Czechoslovakia, was for information protected under the terms of the convention not only to be true but to "serve the ends of peace" as well. After all, a convention granting such freedom "without at the same time imposing certain obligations and ensuring truthful reporting would be meaningless."[53]

Supporting the Eastern bloc effort to impose a sense of greater responsibility on reporters was the Peruvian delegation, which suggested allowing only the circulation of authentic opinion.[54] Western delegates generally opposed the imposition of such standards because of the difficulties involved in defining the necessary criteria neutrally. Definitions of reliable and authentic information varied from one country to another. The question, for some, came down to whether governments should tolerate a little war propaganda and false information as part of a free flow of information or impose restrictions to stop all possible distribution of objectionable material. Imposition of restrictions, even for the noblest of reasons, most noncommunist nations argued, compromised freedom of the press and, hence, was unacceptable. Members of the Third Committee decided that allowing the press to disseminate all kinds of information and relying on the people to choose among available data was a far better practice. Delegates defeated the Peruvian proposal by a vote of thirty-two to eight, with four abstentions.[55]

Defeated again on an issue closely related to their campaign against the dissemination of false information, the Soviet bloc moved once more to amend the draft convention to strip individuals with fascist backgrounds of all protection. Vehement arguments against this proposal surprised S. K. Tsarapkin, the Soviet delegate, who denounced his colleagues' refusal to take such actions as being "tantamount to a desire to rehabilitate those ideologies." In response, representatives of nations devastated by the fascists during World War II quickly pointed out that they had no sympathy with persons of such political persuasions but that their countries would find other ways than interfering with freedom of the press to restrict the actions of such individuals. Political abhorrence could not be allowed to define journalistic practice.[56] Exempting certain correspondents from the convention's provisions based on ideology was dangerous, most delegates agreed, and the term fascist was particularly hard to interpret.[57]

Other delegates were also reluctant to say that correspondents with fascist backgrounds were responsible for all of the problems surrounding news dissemination in the world. As Jamil M. Baroody, the delegate from Saudi Arabia, noted, his country had "suffered considerably at the hands of professedly democratic correspondents."[58] In fact, the Saudi delegate believed that the costs of freedom of information, as advocated by the United States, were simply too high for most countries to pay. Countries with underdeveloped news agencies could not allow distorted or false news to enter, especially if that news threatened their national existence.[59] The prevalence of such conditions around the world made the journalist's integrity, not his political persuasion, a more appropriate standard for judging foreign correspondents, argued B. Shiva Rao, the delegate from India, whose country also had suffered at the hands of journalists who, "irrespective of personal ideology, had transmitted distorted news."[60]

Saved once again from Soviet efforts at amendment, the news-gathering convention faced another challenge from Noriega, who observed that the ideas of any single country or small group of countries could not be allowed to dominate any international convention. Standards adopted should be acceptable "to the largest possible number of nations." In debating the conventions, delegates must remember "that most of the countries had only limited technical and economic facilities, or indeed no facilities at all, for the transmission of news, while other countries had substantial resources in that field." If they did nothing else, delegates must weigh the needs of journalists against the needs of a country and its people.[61] One way to accomplish this balancing, the Mexican delegate argued, was to require the institution of an international right of correction as part of the news-gathering convention.

MAKING PLANS TO ADD A RIGHT OF REPLY TO THE NEWS-GATHERING DRAFT

The United States delegation wanted the international right of correction incorporated within the news-gathering convention, but Noriega proposed inserting his amendment calling for such a right in what the Americans considered to be an inappropriate place. If successfully lodged where the Mexican delegate suggested, the right of correction would become mandatory and would be intimately tied to the privileges sought for foreign correspondents. And, in the American view, Noriega prefaced his amendment with highly unacceptable language, which said that information agencies and foreign correspondents had the duty "to report the facts, without discrimination, to promote respect for human rights and fundamental freedoms, to further international understanding and co-operation and to contribute to the maintenance of international peace and security." The Mexican proposal then added that information agencies and correspondents that would benefit from the convention must accept, distribute, and publish "any corrections requested by the Contracting State directly concerned and in whose territory the report requiring correction originated."[62]

Canham found Noriega's proposal one of substance, and he agreed that "the first duty of information agencies and foreign correspondents should be to report the facts." But, "it was useless to indicate any other obligations arising from that duty." Placing the right of correction within the heart of the guarantees to protect foreign correspondents and using coercive language to enforce that right worried the ASNE president. The Mexican amendment gave governments extensive powers to force foreign correspondents and information agencies to publish the corrections that the governments thought were necessary. "Such a practice would be dangerous, as under the guise of corrections Governments could demand the diffusion of certain news, which would help to intensify the already violent propaganda." A list of the obligations of correspondents was highly inappropriate for the operative sections of the convention, Davies of the United Kingdom added. Any mention of the obligations of correspondents in the news-gathering convention should be in the preamble, where they would serve as moral guides; even then, the references must be as general as possible.[63]

In rebutting arguments that the right of correction did not belong in the operative section of the convention as suggested by Noriega, delegates claimed that if the document guaranteed greater rights for correspondents, then forcing journalists to correct intentional and unintentional mistakes was critically important. Because of the correspondents' power, Baroody said, the right of correction must appear in each convention. The delegate from Ethiopia, Ato Haddis Almayehou, picked up this strain, which was intruding into United Nations free-press debates with greater frequency and which was becoming of great concern to American proponents of freedom of information. If governments must make concessions for the sake of freedom of information, Almayehou said, then so must correspondents and news agencies.[64]

Additional support for imposition of obligations on reporters came from Gilberto González Fernández, the delegate from Colombia, who noted that Latin American countries without the resources to disseminate news about themselves abroad depended on foreign agencies to perform this task. Sometimes "the prestige of those countries was damaged by false news transmitted by certain correspondents"; consequently, governments should be able to demand correction of such false news.[65] In fact, Latin American countries, which felt abused by both the American and European presses, considered the Mexican amendment important, said Ramón Zaydín, the delegate from Cuba. Only through the establishment of principles of performance and a right of correction would these countries have even the slightest chance of being accurately portrayed before the world.[66] Despite such support, the Mexican right of correction proposal encountered strong opposition from the Western nations, and Noriega agreed to defer the matter for the moment. But the issue would come up again.

Obviously, the smaller nations were gaining strength in the debates. Complaints against the performance of American news agencies now no longer came solely from the Soviet bloc, and this change had significant effects as the discussions continued. To deflect additional criticisms, Canham found himself apologizing to countries such as India and Saudi Arabia, which felt as if they had been misreported by United States correspondents. The American press continually strove for self-improvement, he said, but "with all its defects, it was vastly preferable to a controlled totalitarian Press; it had already contributed a great deal towards international understanding and peace and it was to be hoped that, under the convention, it would do still more in that direction."[67] But the attitude of the smaller nations worried observers within the American press, who found the Mexican attempt to make the right of correction compulsory dangerous and impossible to accept. As *Editor & Publisher* said, "What a field day for the propagandists! The Kremlin could force the press of the world to print its own version of every incident, under this provision. What Goebbels could have done with that one!" Although certain that the United States would never vote for such a provision, the language could be adopted despite American opposition. If that happened, the United Nations action would become in effect an international law "which would blight freedom of information for years to come." Although the activities of the American press would be unrestricted within the country's territorial boundaries, American efforts to report the news of the world would be seriously limited with passage of the Mexican amendment.[68]

American efforts to reinstate national military security as the only acceptable grounds for peacetime censorship were somewhat more successful, although the new clause allowed censorship for national defense reasons to circumvent linguistic problems in the Latin American countries.[69] In introducing the United States amendment, Canham stressed that the provision forbade countries from exerting control over news entering their territories but permitted regulation of internal news communications to remain in the hands of sovereign governments. He personally preferred no peacetime censorship, but without some mention of the problem in the convention, governments might establish far broader regulations than restrictions mandated by national defense considerations.[70]

Support for banning peacetime censorship except on grounds of national defense was relatively easy to find within the Third Committee. Many delegates proudly reiterated their countries' long opposition to such practices and added that they supported the proposal reluctantly because they preferred to see the complete outlawing of peacetime censorship. Soviet bloc delegates opposed the language altogether, arguing again that the suggested convention section interfered with the sovereign rights of individual states. As they launched another tirade against the controlled press of the United States, Soviet bloc representatives added that the section ignored the fact that some countries currently imposed censorship for economic and political reasons. In addition, charged Tsarapkin, the measure omitted language affecting American news agencies that deliberately employed persons who would send biased and untruthful reports from abroad. Thus, the eloquence of delegates' speeches supporting freedom of information had "a hollow sound."[71]

Other delegates doubted the efficacy of a peacetime censorship ban. For instance, Zaydín, the Cuban delegate, did not believe that the statement, if added to the convention, would prevent censorship in countries wishing to regulate the news. Consequently, he planned to vote against the provision.

Jacques Kayser, the French delegate, likewise believed that the provision's terminology was imprecise, saying that he could not favor the change until its terms were carefully and fully defined. On the other hand, the language was too specific for Renuka Ray, the Indian delegate, who stressed that, while India imposed no censorship, restrictions unrelated to military or defense security might be necessary on some occasions. The proposed amendment allowed governments no leeway for such action. The major challenge to the proposal came from delegates whose countries had no national military security or national defense issues to protect but who argued, with Victor M. Pérez Perozo, the Venezuelan delegate, that the key issue was "national security expressed in terms of internal stability." Other convention provisions allowed nations to enforce laws to protect national security and public order and to take appropriate, self-protective steps in time of war or other public emergency. Thus, a statement relating solely to national defense needs seemed superfluous.[72] Delegates refused to accept these arguments and finally amended the convention so that its provisions sanctioned peacetime censorship only for matters of national defense.

With the amendment, another problem surfaced. The news-gathering convention also called for informed censorship, meaning that the correspondent was to be told what the censor cut from the story and why. To Baroody this provision was tantamount to telling reporters national defense secrets. Displaying little confidence in the integrity of correspondents, he continued that in such a case, a journalist would find a way to notify his employer of the sensitive information; his employer, in turn, would publish the news, being "careful not to give the source of the information, which could always be offered as rumour."[73] What was a country's recourse if that happened? Disregarding the realities of contemporary news gathering that were contained in Baroody's objection, delegates approved the provision requiring notification of correspondents about material deleted from their copy.

DEBATE TURNS TO ADMISSION OF CORRESPONDENTS TO THE UNITED STATES

Soviet bloc opposition increased during discussion of a provision that would allow nations to grant conditional entrance to correspondents covering United Nations–related events. The provision was of great interest to the United States because its terms sanctioned the agreement struck with the United Nations that called for the unrestricted admission of correspondents to report United Nations activities, while leaving intact American immigration restrictions against the admission of communists. Under the United States–United Nations agreement, correspondents accredited to the United Nations—including communists—could enter the country to cover a particular meeting, but while in the United States, the government could restrict the reporters' travel to the immediate area of the United Nations. And the correspondents must leave the United States immediately after the session ended. Traditional immigration laws would apply to correspondents seeking general admission to the United States, meaning the exclusion of any individuals adhering to certain subversive ideologies.

Eleanor Roosevelt supported the provision in terms of the policies of various nations rather than by mentioning the concerns of the United States specifically, but Soviet bloc representatives saw her arguments as defending the objectionable American practices. The proposed provision, said A. S. Stepanenko, the representative from the Byelorussian Soviet Socialist Republic, would allow the United States government to use the convention to discriminate against certain newspaper correspondents. Making matters even worse in the eyes of the Soviet bloc, American efforts to justify their exclusionary immigration practices coincided with United States attempts to obtain inordinate privileges for their correspondents abroad. Rather than seeking to advance freedom of information, charged Tsarapkin, the United States was promoting a system of discrimination that placed certain correspondents "in an unfavourable situation in comparison with others who were granted extensive privileges under the convention." Inserting the suggested provision in the news-gathering convention would simply encourage additional discrimination. The earnestness of Mrs. Roosevelt's defense of her country's immigration laws failed to impress Stephan P. Demchenko of the Ukrainian Soviet Socialist Republic, who noted that when delegates discussed other articles of the convention "no importance had been attached to the need to conform to the laws and regulations of certain countries." He did not believe that the issue was rightfully raised here. If the treaty permitted American immigration laws to stand, the convention would allow the United States the right to exercise a policy of exclusion that the Americans systematically attempted to deny to other nations.[74]

Generally, explained Mrs. Roosevelt, the United States admitted all appropriately accredited journalists, granting them unlimited residence permits. And generally, correspondents entering the country to report on United Nations activities had the same privileges under the convention as any other foreign correspondent. At times, however, the country needed to regulate the activities of some correspondents for national security reasons. The convention article was an attempted compromise designed to ease the entry of correspondents who ordinarily would be excluded from the United States under its immigration laws. She refused to consider the measure as restrictive, arguing that its provisions "concerned only a very limited number of persons as all other correspondents accredited to the United Nations would enjoy to the full extent all the rights and safeguards laid down in the convention."[75]

Attempts to limit the admission of communist correspondents into the United States caused a deep division between the American press community and governmental representatives and created some dissension within governmental ranks as well. The Justice Department strongly supported excluding communist correspondents from the United States, and many congressmen backed the principle. To numerous journalists, however, barring communist reporters from the United States for any reason undermined the fundamental concept of international freedom of the press. Although the press position found some support within the State Department, the stance of the Department of Justice prevailed. Therefore, American delegates at various United Nations conferences found themselves advocating the somewhat contradictory right of the United States to exclude journalists from communist countries and communist correspondents from other nations. Thus, the Soviet bloc was correct in assessing the intent of the provision. Other nations unconcerned with this discrimination sanctioned the American practice.

As debate on the news-gathering convention progressed, the American delegation encountered one difficult issue after another. Such was the case when the discussion turned to merging the news-gathering convention and the French convention calling for the institution of an international right of correction. The American delegation desired the merger, but the debate surrounding the combination of the two drafts again revealed how small a portion of the world supported American ideas on freedom of the press. The French, who had refused American entreaties to combine the two documents in Geneva, now supported incorporating provisions that would create an international right of correction within the draft convention on news gathering. The French had come to see the right of correction as indispensable to the full implementation of the news-gathering convention. Adding the right of correction to a treaty that extended considerable privileges to reporters also appealed to the French belief in responsible journalism, for the merged treaties would establish "the responsibility of news agencies without limiting their freedom in any way." Finally, by agreeing to a right of reply, delegates would make "the first practical attempt to solve, on an international level, the problem of the dissemination of false and distorted reports."[76] Under the French proposal, the right of correction convention would become a separate section of the news-gathering treaty establishing the mechanics for correcting false news reports. The right of reply so guaranteed would be noncoercive. Offended parties simply would make corrections available for distribution, but the convention did not force the media of offending states to publish those corrections. Nor did the provisions offer any appeals route if a contracting party failed to fulfill its obligation other than sending the complaint to the secretary-general for public airing.[77]

The United States welcomed the French proposal, Mrs. Roosevelt said, because the anticipated merger of the two draft conventions "provided an answer to those who felt that the only effective way of correcting abuses by information agencies was to institute government controls—a view which was a denial of the very principle of freedom of information." But the Americans wanted to ensure that the right of correction did not give governments the power to compel information agencies to publish corrections. Even though the United States had been strongly criticized in stories distributed by foreign information agencies, Mrs. Roosevelt said that her government did not want to force foreign press outlets to publish American corrective communiqués, nor did the American government intend to allow other governments to issue orders to American news agencies. Since the French draft avoided these problems, the provision should win the support of delegates "who had insistently decried the evils of false or distorted reporting," Mrs. Roosevelt added. Combining the French and United States drafts meant that the right of correction would be available only to those countries agreeing to facilitate the work of foreign correspondents. The United States, she stressed, opposed extending the right of correction to any nation unwilling to assist foreign correspondents under the provisions of the news-gathering convention.[78]

Although many nations supported combining a journalist's freedom with a statement about the correspondent's responsibility to file factual reports, some delegates opposed merging the two conventions. For instance, Georg Andren, the Swedish delegate, thought that the right of correction as proposed could turn into a propaganda tool for some governments. A separate draft, one which addressed these problems far more particularly, was necessary, the Swede argued. H. Smitt Ingebretsen, the Norwegian delegate, agreed with his Scandinavian colleague that a combined convention might create problems regarding the compelled publication of propaganda. Norway remembered the imposition of a right of correction during the Nazi occupation, and Ingebretsen questioned "the right of any Government to ask another Government to transmit certain *communiqués* to its news agencies against its better judgment." Separate conventions provided essential protection against abuse.[79] Soviet bloc objections centered on the invasion of national sovereignty imposed by the right of correction. Despite the expression of various doubts about the wisdom of the amalgamation, Third Committee members decided to merge the two conventions.

American delegates viewed the combination of the two conventions as a significant victory, but they soon encountered a problem that State Department planners specifically had warned them to avoid. The original draft of the Geneva convention instituting a right of correction contained no provisions for resolution of disputes arising from implementation of the document. During the conference, delegates discussed briefly assigning jurisdiction over disagreements to the International Court of Justice. American planners feared that the suggestion would resurface during Third Committee discussions and instructed delegates to abstain from voting on any provisions granting compulsory jurisdiction over disputes to the international court.[80] The proposal to award jurisdiction over disputes to the International Court of Justice came from the Norwegian delegate, who noted that the United Kingdom's convention on freedom of information called for submitting controversies to the international court, thus making the court a logical destination for complaints stemming from the news-gathering convention as well. The United States, however, preferred the creation of a special committee authorized to investigate and publicize complaints, said Mrs. Roosevelt, rather than a direct appeals route to the International Court of Justice, which was designed to deal with larger problems than those involving alleged violations of these conventions.[81]

Among the delegates who welcomed compulsory appeals to the International Court of Justice was Roland Lebeau, the Belgian delegate, who noted that most disputes would involve legal interpretations of the convention and said that the court was best equipped to provide the necessary assistance. But automatic appeal to the International Court of Justice was unacceptable to many nations, the United Kingdom's Davies argued, as he took the lead in opposing the appeals formula. His government proposed making a court appeal the final option after other remedies—including review by committee and publicity from the secretary-general's office—had failed. This proposition, Davies thought, would be acceptable to most potential signatories. But the need for a system of appeal other than the International Court of Justice was lost on Abdur Rahim Khan, the delegate from Pakistan, who said that use of the international court was well established. If some countries objected to appeals going to the International Court of Justice, most likely some countries would object to any other appeals route as well.[82]

In addition, Azkoul, the Lebanese delegate, argued that establishing a new appeals route, which included creating a committee acceptable to all parties involved in the disagreement, could allow the guilty party to delay settling the dispute indefinitely. And because the court's sentence would be harsher than any committee's punishment, a guilty party might escape censure by circumventing the International Court of Justice. Faced with mounting criticism, Davies withdrew his support of a noncourt appeals route and noted that his country had always recognized the court's jurisdiction. He had advocated the noncourt proposal only to "enable as many States as possible to sign the convention."[83] Delegates adopted the Norwegian proposal for giving the International Court of Justice the responsibility for appeals resulting from the convention's implementation.[84]

But the discomfiture of the United States delegation over the allegedly noncontroversial task of merging the French right of reply convention and the American news-gathering convention was only just beginning. Noriega, the Mexican delegate, soon reintroduced an amendment that earlier had caused considerable concern among United States delegates and their dwindling circle of allies. The Mexican proposal read:

It is the duty of information agencies and foreign correspondents to report the facts, to promote respect for human rights and fundamental freedoms without discrimination, to further international understanding and co-operation and to contribute to the maintenance of international peace and security. To this end, information agencies and correspondents benefiting by this Convention shall be required to accept, distribute and publish any corrections requested by the government concerned.[85]

Concerted opposition from Western nations had led to the proposal's deferment during earlier debates. Now, however, the amendment, which stressed the Eastern bloc's notion of affirmative responsibilities for the press and made publication of corrections mandatory, appeared in the proper place; American delegates could not avoid discussing the proposal. To this language, Noriega was ready to add that contracting states could invoke the right of correction when their "prestige or dignity had been impaired by false or mendacious information."[86] Thus, another favorite topic of the Eastern bloc gained access to the floor without a Soviet ally broaching the subject.

EFFORTS BEGIN TO PROTECT NATIONAL PRESTIGE AND DIGNITY

If the news-gathering convention was designed to guarantee the same degree of freedom for the gathering and transmission of news internationally as existed in democratic countries, "why should States not be given the right of correction when their prestige or national dignity was injured?" Noriega asked. "Why should they not be granted guarantees similar to those accorded to individuals under ordinary law to enable them to defend themselves against slanderous attacks?" Perhaps the convention excluded such protections because those nations enjoying political and economic stability considered the national dignity of other nations of minor importance, or perhaps those stronger nations even planned to attack the weaker nations through international propaganda. Often victimized by hostile press campaigns that not only had wounded its prestige and national dignity but had led to serious political unrest, Mexico wanted to end the possibility of additional assaults by the mass media.[87]

The Mexican amendment was immediately criticized. For instance, Davies said that although he respected the reasons behind the Mexican amendment, he thought that the amendment would restrict the freedom of expression of the press and could lead to too many corrections. Fernand Terrou, the French delegate, also worried about the ramifications of the Mexican proposal. He understood how seriously attacks against national prestige could hurt a country, but he believed that restraint and discretion were essential in establishing an international right of correction—neither of which was present in the Mexican proposal. Mrs. Roosevelt joined the French and the British delegates in noting her understanding of Noriega's motives, but she, too, thought that the proposal expanded the right of correction undesirably. Any right of correction must be strictly limited, offering only two grounds on which the right was appropriate—"where the news dispatches transmitted were false or distorted" or "where they were likely to injure the relations of a Contracting State with other States." To Mrs. Roosevelt, these limitations encompassed false news reports that affected a country's national dignity "in such a way that its relations with another country were compromised."[88] Definition of terms created another problem in the Mexican proposal, according to G. J. van Heuven Goedhart of the Netherlands, who noted that "Mexico might have a clear and concrete idea of what constituted national prestige and dignity" but that his country did not. "If such a concept were included, the way might be opened to all kinds of complaints, the airing of which might have most undesirable consequences."[89]

Objections by the mainline democracies had little influence on the smaller nations. For example, Azkoul, the Lebanese delegate, had opposed the Mexican amendment when it was offered earlier, but now he supported the provision as part of a right of correction, primarily because its language protected countries that had been hurt by hostile press campaigns. And Juan R. Otaño Vilanova, the Argentine delegate, said that he enthusiastically endorsed the Mexican proposal, "which was designed to safeguard the national prestige and dignity of the States." Without a provision that required the publication of corrections, Otaño Vilanova said, corrections would only be heard on the diplomatic level. With such a restriction on the dissemination of corrected versions of the news, the people of the world might never truly understand one another.[90]

American ideas on freedom of information had been increasingly and pointedly criticized during free-press debates by delegates representing the smaller, basically nonaligned countries who were members of the United Nations. The American delegation was becoming somewhat accustomed to that phenomenon. Up until now, however, that criticism had not resulted in a major defeat for the Americans. For the first time, with the vote on the Mexican amendment, the United States delegation saw the possible ramifications of the voting strength of these smaller nations clearly. Representatives of the smaller states on the Third Committee—and within the United Nations—outnumbered representatives of the larger nations. Consequently, delegates adopted the Mexican amendment establishing responsibilities for journalists and calling for mandatory publication of replies by twenty votes to thirteen votes, with fifteen abstentions. Counted among the nations voting for the measure: Venezuela, Afghanistan, Argentina, Brazil, China, Cuba, Egypt, Guatemala, Haiti, Honduras, India, Iran, Lebanon, Mexico,

Nicaragua, Pakistan, Panama, Peru, Saudi Arabia, and Siam. The United States and its immediate allies—the United Kingdom, France, Belgium, Denmark, the Netherlands, Greece, Norway, Sweden, the Philippines, the Union of South Africa, Australia, and New Zealand voted against the amendment. The abstentions came primarily from Soviet bloc nations but also included Canada, Chile, Colombia, the Dominican Republic, Ecuador, Liberia, Syria, and Turkey.[91]

This vote actually foretold the future of the international free-press crusade. For the first time, an idea strongly opposed by the big three Western allies—the United States, the United Kingdom, and France—went down to defeat at the hands of smaller nations that were concerned about the treatment given their national reputations in the international media. Although these nations' objections had constituted minor annoyances during earlier debates, the primary focus of attention for both State Department planners and American journalists interested in freedom of information issues was on countering Soviet bloc moves that could destroy American free-press goals. But the Eastern bloc nations never marshaled enough votes to erect any real barriers to American aims. All that representatives of the Soviet bloc could do was talk about an issue until the other delegates tired of hearing their repetitive comments. The true danger to American ideals rested with the middle states—the smaller, nonaligned nations, some of which were just emerging as national entities in the wake of the destruction of colonial empires after World War II. These nations regularly offered amendments to the American news-gathering convention that "would infringe freedom of information just as seriously as any previous Soviet proposals." In fact, the proposals of the smaller nations were "more dangerous to the U.S. press and to any progress that has been made in the UN because they are not tarred with the Soviet brush, and advocates of press freedom, aside from the U.S. delegates, are not as quick to see the dangers."[92] Responding to such criticisms, Baroody, the Saudi Arabian, spoke for many of his colleagues when he said that, for the small countries of the world, the price of freedom of information was simply too high. "Those countries did not possess the necessary means for replying to slanderous attacks; their only arm was to be found in the proposed convention." Any measures that would strengthen the protections that the convention provided were deemed appropriate by these small countries.[93]

Inequality of resources in the news dissemination field played an important part in the decisions of some delegates to support proposals such as the ones put forward by Mexico. While some nations had powerful information agencies, others had very limited means, said Mrs. Figueroa, the Chilean delegate, thus placing some countries at a distinct disadvantage. Because the basic inequalities would continue for the foreseeable future, delegates must find a way "to ensure the accuracy and objectivity of the information they transmitted." If the accuracy of news reports improved, no abuse of the right of correction was likely.[94] The United States press would not tolerate such criticisms or such attempts to alter the crusade's path for long. Soon, American journalists began calling on the State Department to abandon the Geneva conventions if the documents could not be brought into line with American principles.[95]

Another Mexican amendment to the right of reply section of the news-gathering convention soon concerned the Americans as well. Here, Noriega suggested that contracting states "ensure that information agencies and correspondents accept and distribute through their customary channels" any corrections submitted by contracting states in whose territories the erroneous report originated.[96] In supporting this proposal, Noriega took aim at the monopoly that journalists thought that they had on freedom of the press. He stressed that his government knew the importance of safeguarding freedom of information and ensuring the complete independence of the press. Mexican officials thought, however, that "peoples were entitled to enjoy the advantages of freedom of information and that the latter should not be the prerogative of big information agencies."[97]

Adoption of the Mexican proposal, Mrs. Roosevelt warned, would keep some delegations that favored a right of correction from accepting the convention because the suggestion introduced an element of compulsion and considerably extended the right of correction. With this amendment, "correspondents and information agencies might be used by another State for propaganda purposes and the free distribution of information might thus be impaired." American delegates consistently supported a right of correction without an enforced obligation to disseminate corrections, but the Mexican proposal was quite another issue. Under no circumstances should a government be able to exercise control over correspondents or information agencies, Mrs. Roosevelt said. In fact, "the United States could not accept a convention which would turn correspondents and information agencies into the propaganda agents of another State."[98] On this matter, the United States position prevailed, and delegates defeated the Mexican effort to introduce an element of governmental supervision into the publication of replies.

The United States' worst defeat at the hands of the Third Committee awaited as delegates began considering Article 9 of the draft convention. This section itemized points excluded from the news-gathering convention's protections. By the time the Third Committee was finished with its initial debates on the section, the article authorized states to "make and enforce laws and public regulations for the protection of national security and public order"; "reserve to its nationals the right to establish and direct in its territory newspapers and radio-broadcasting and television organizations"; require "that a portion of the staff employed by foreign agencies operating in their territories shall be nationals of those States"; take "measures to help the establishment and development of independent domestic information agencies or to prohibit practices tending to create monopolies"; and prohibit "news material which is blasphemous or contrary to morals or decency."[99] Much of the debate over these points concentrated on the economic factors involved in communications industries and on the problems that most smaller countries encountered in competing with the larger nations in media-related activities. Much of the discussion also posed significant problems for Americans who were seeking to open the world to American news agencies.

Language allowing individual states to take self-protective action was necessary, Noriega argued, because of the problems recently encountered in the war and because of the imbalance of power in the information field. Without such provisions, Noriega said, nations could find themselves "at the mercy of foreign correspondents and information agencies." Too many countries already had endured situations in which "foreigners had been held to be above the law of the land," and any convention endorsed by the United Nations must not perpetuate those conditions. Kayser, the French delegate, agreed, saying that the news-gathering convention was designed to ensure freedom in the gathering and transmission of news. Theoretically, the information agencies of all signatories would have the same rights under the convention; "in practice, unhappily, the powerful information agencies would grow more powerful still, at the expense of agencies in less developed countries, unless the convention set up safeguards against that possibility." To avoid this result, Kayser said, delegates must make sure that nations that had "once lost their freedom of expression under enemy occupation did not lose it again under economic pressure." Such protection was essential since freedom of information "was a domain in which the genius of each nation could best express itself and could contribute most fully to international understanding."[100]

Fears about foreign domination of the news seemed a bit exaggerated to Davies, who hoped to settle the question without enacting too many limitations on freedom of information. But Noriega was adamant. National newspapers must not be sacrificed "under the pretext of safeguarding the freedom of information." Although his country stood "in the forefront of the struggle for freedom of information," Noriega stressed that "every country should be entitled and empowered to conduct that campaign as it deemed most appropriate." Canham strongly disagreed, contending that no country had a right to "effectively stifle all the operations of information agencies on an international plane." If Mexican suggestions that required the employment of a certain percentage of nationals by news agencies and regulated the activities of foreign correspondents within another nation went into effect, they would have just such a stifling effect.[101]

Mexico did not intend to establish a news monopoly of its own, Noriega replied, despite implications to that effect by the United States and the United Kingdom. The Mexican delegation simply wanted to prevent powerful foreign information monopolies from "engaging in ruinous competition with national information agencies to the extent of eliminating the latter completely." And how dare the United States representative criticize a Mexican law calling for the employment of a certain percentage of nationals by foreign businesses as an infringement on freedom of the press? Even the United States did not offer absolute freedom for radio and films, Noriega said. "That fact proved that in certain cases the Government had the right to establish regulations." Abdur Rahim Khan, the Pakistani delegate, also believed that the Mexican proposal presented no danger of a country barring foreign information agencies from its territory. The proposal, which seemed indispensable, simply stressed the need to consider the situation in each country. Added Mrs. Ray, the delegate from India, "Obviously, freedom of information could not be prejudicial to the right of peoples to have at their disposal the means of expression which was in keeping with their own national temperament."[102]

Tsarapkin, the Soviet delegate, observing this debate, apparently was fascinated by the small countries' efforts "to protect themselves against the floods of slander and false news circulated in the world by the monopolies." Despite the valiant efforts of the smaller countries, the Russian contended that nothing could curb the general thrust of the convention, which was to protect British and American monopolies. If the convention went into effect, he warned, information agencies from the United States and the United Kingdom would "become so powerful that they would come to play a decisive role in the national life of countries too weak to protect themselves against them. Foreign correspondents would be the masters not only in the field of information, but also in the field of domestic politics."[103]

When the discussion on Article 9 turned to regulations affecting the content of the news, attempts were made to delete provisions that would allow states to impose restrictions on the press in order to protect public order. Andrés Aramburu, the Peruvian representative, wanted to keep such language in the convention because his experience had convinced him that correspondents were, at times, "closely linked" to subversive organizations. Since many underdeveloped countries feared internal convulsion and therefore imposed restrictions for self-preservation, such countries would find it difficult to sign the convention "if their right to maintain public order were restricted by it."[104] The imposition of certain duties on journalists also picked up considerable support, for, as Almayehou, the Ethiopian delegate, said in reiterating a point made many times before, "rights entailed obligations."[105] Including the mention of the obligations of correspondents in this particular convention segment led the American delegation to refuse to vote for the entire article. No one could assume, Canham contended, that moral obligations would not lead to legal obligations, and while his delegation could support the use of moral suasion on journalists, the delegation could not approve any language that might lead to legal efforts to force correspondents to behave in a certain way.[106]

Throughout these arguments, committee members clearly perceived the incongruity between American opposition to several proposals that the smaller nations felt essential to the maintenance of their security and American support of measures designed to preserve United States security. In the end, the United States and the Soviets opposed Article 9. The Americans voted against the measure, the Russians abstained. Delegates adopted the article by a vote of twenty-seven to seventeen, with seven abstentions.[107]

Americans termed the vote on Article 9 the first major defeat of United States proposals in the Third Committee, and the State Department planned to ask for reconsideration of the article when the convention went before the General Assembly. Inclusion of the article would "make it impossible for the U.S. to support or sign the convention," even though the United States had initiated the document in Geneva. The chances of overturning the article, however, were slim, given the majority by which delegates had adopted the provision. Press observers believed that "all the fears and bitterness the so-called 'underdeveloped' countries feel for the large foreign news agencies were poured into the making of Article 9, a hodge-podge of reservations to the convention."[108] To Hugh Baillie, president of United Press, the adoption of Article 9 turned "what started out to be a Magna Carta for the press . . . into a police machine to discipline it."[109]

AMERICAN DELEGATES CONTINUE EFFORTS TO AMEND THE NEWS-GATHERING CONVENTION

United States delegates continued their efforts to amend the provision. American threats not to sign the convention if the Mexican provision establishing certain duties for correspondents remained as part of the enforceable language of the document quickly bore fruit. When the final language of the Draft Convention on the International Transmission of News and the Right of Correction emerged from a subcommittee, the offensive Mexican amendment was in the preamble to the right of correction segment of the convention. In that location, the Mexican proposal stood as a statement of principle rather than as an enforceable part of the draft. Other changes recognized that the professional responsibilities of correspondents and news agencies required them "to report facts without discrimination and in their proper context and thereby to promote respect for human rights and fundamental freedoms, to further international understanding and co-operation and to contribute to the maintenance of international peace and security."[110]

Professional ethics rather than governmental authority now mandated that "all correspondents and information agencies should follow the cus-tomary practice of transmitting through the same channels or of publishing, respectively, corrections of news dispatches transmitted or published by them which have been demonstrated to be false or distorted." Special efforts to ensure the dissemination of a corrective communiqué would be made when a contracting state protested the transmission by a foreign correspondent or information agency of "a news dispatch capable of injuring its relations with other States or its national prestige or dignity." Signatories agreed to send copies of the communiqué to the home office of the offending party without comment, but delegates refused to endorse enforced publication of corrections in the offending country.[111]

Supporting these changes was the representative from Mexico, who now claimed that his delegation's position had been misrepresented by the press, and as a result, Mexican proposals "had been regarded as repeated attempts to restrict freedom of information." Ignoring the fundamental incongruity between his initial proposals and his new stance on the news-gathering convention, Noriega noted that the news stories were inaccurate appraisals of his motives because "Mexico had never tried to restrict freedom of information or the lawful right of correspondents." His amendments simply had been "designed to safeguard the veracity of information within the framework of freedom due to it." Baroody, the Saudi Arabian delegate, disliked the convention revisions that Noriega now supported because "the guarantees for which the small nations had fought so energetically had in fact been deleted from the clauses of the proposed new articles." The Saudi Arabian also wanted to draft a convention that would be acceptable to the greatest number of countries, but he believed that moral obligations alone were insufficient to remedy the problems that existed between the smaller states and huge international news organizations. Baroody believed that Noriega had sacrificed the only possible solution to these problems in an effort to obtain the approval of the United States for an international document.[112]

The United States had indeed won a significant victory in the compromise draft forwarded to the General Assembly. American journalists could find segments of the convention to dislike, Canham admitted, but the document was the best one possible under the circumstances from the American perspective. He reminded his colleagues that regardless of the position taken by the United States on the document, the other nations of the world intended to have a convention. Consequently, the American delegates had made the accord as palatable to American interests as possible, for a bad treaty "could have been used against us." Only time would tell if the document emerging from the Third Committee was better than no convention at all. American journalists must be realistic about the free-press issue, he added, because American journalists were novices in the international arena. Only after they had urged the worldwide free-press crusade on the government had press leaders realized that their efforts might just as easily lead to restrictions of that freedom. Although some press spokesmen might think that the draft convention on international news gathering was too restrictive, Canham had no such fears, and he urged the United States to sign the document after its final approval by the General Assembly.[113]

But concern was rising within the press community. For instance, Earl J. Johnson, vice president and general news manager of the United Press, said that the question was still unsettled about "whether or not we have won this battle against restrictions." Restrictions had been included and excluded from the convention so many times during debates that only after a copy of the final version of the convention was available could press representatives make a valid analysis of its provisions.[114] *Editor & Publisher*, on the contrary, believed that the concessions made by a variety of nations to the United States' principles provided proof that "the international law that is being created in the treaties may well be the basis on which freedom-loving nations outside of the Iron Curtain can build for the future."[115]

But the trade journal's editorialist apparently had not analyzed the vote tallies on the draft convention carefully. Members of the Third Committee had approved the draft by a vote of twenty-seven to four, with twelve abstentions. Abstaining were Afghanistan, Argentina, Belgium, Burma, China, Egypt, Guatemala, India, Iran, Saudi Arabia, Siam, and Syria. Fifteen other delegates were absent at the time of voting. The trade journal's own reporter predicted that the abstaining countries probably would refuse to sign the treaty. Combined with the Soviet bloc nations, which voted against the convention, opposition to the draft came from countries representing half the world's population. "Even delegates voting for the treaty admitted they were not entirely happy with the results," the reporter added. "But all stated that the final document was the best that could have been achieved for the maximum number of countries without compromising the principles of broad press freedom."[116] Whether a treaty giving rise to so many misgivings could survive another round of debate, much less the test of time, was questionable at best.

General Assembly members devoted eleven hours to debating the Draft Convention on the International Transmission of News and the Right of Correction. Delegates realized that the convention was a compromise designed to avoid a deadlock rather than a full statement advocating any one group's particular views. The drafters hoped to ensure the freedom of the media to operate while at the same time protecting nations and peoples from the unrestrained exercise of that freedom. Debate within the General Assembly broke no new ground; once again, however, discussions showed how deep-seated the problems facing the United States' concept of freedom of the press throughout the world were.

Mrs. Figueroa, the delegate from Chile, for instance, believed that a "real conspiracy of silence" existed in the world to conceal bias in handling of the news. In some nations, in fact, information was a propaganda vehicle used "to spread the doctrines and ideologies of their governments throughout the world. The inhabitants of those countries knew nothing of what was happening beyond their frontiers and the outside world was ignorant of what happened in those countries." Elsewhere, news was simply another business, creating a situation in which "news was not intended to report the facts as they stood, but rather to ensure the largest possible profits." In still other areas, particularly in Western Europe, "journalism was characterized by a tendency to underestimate the younger peoples or the older but less-developed nations." In her view, providing "the world only that true, complete and free information which would facilitate the development of international co-operation by promoting mutual understanding among the peoples of the world" was almost impossible. Signing conventions pledging a freer flow of information would not solve the problem, Mrs. Figueroa contended, because the treaties contained insufficient safeguards for the younger, lesser-developed countries. To truly promote freedom of information, the framers of documents must be far more sensitive to the needs of countries other than their own.[117]

Charging that the news-gathering convention showed that some states had an abnormal understanding of democracy, Baroody claimed that the document's provisions threatened the independence of other people, a problem that some states were unwilling or unable to recognize. Physical occupation was not the only way for "a perverted democracy" to control foreign countries, the Saudi Arabian contended. Other proven methods included "propaganda, political pressure, the installation of puppet governments, economic domination and financial monopolies." Propaganda and political pressure had created the recent problems in Palestine, and the world's press had failed to spotlight the tactics of countries that had led "to the extermination of a large part of the Arab people." Any convention on the right of foreign correspondents to work, Baroody argued, must consider these problems.[118]

Disagreements prevalent within the Third Committee likewise appeared within the General Assembly. For instance, Hector McNeil, the delegate from the United Kingdom, agreed that some smaller nations had complained justly that foreign information agencies "had published false or distorted news concerning them" and that they did not have the means "to present their point of view to a wide public." But the solution to these problems, according to the Briton, rested in raising the sense of moral obligation among journalists rather than in forcing certain standards on reporters.[119] The French delegation, which had long favored making the relationship between the freedoms and the responsibilities of journalists explicit, endorsed the imposition of something greater than a moral obligation on reporters in return for special privileges. The United Nations, said Kayser, must protect "freedom of information, not only against its enemies, as was natural, but also against itself." Presenting a somewhat different perspective was Carlos P. Rómulo, the delegate from the Philippines, who stressed that the extremely difficult task facing foreign correspondents was the reason behind many of the disagreements about press performance heard in the United Nations. Delegates often overlooked the fact that journalists could not always avoid offending host governments. The Third Committee, although tempted to restrict the ability of correspondents to function, had, in the end, wisely avoided placing such limitations in the draft convention. The document that had emerged from committee, Rómulo continued, "recognized the full responsibility and all the rights and obligations which normally belonged to the Press. That would enable the Press to fulfil still more effectively its vast and important mission."[120]

Contrary to the insinuations of several speakers, the press of the United States asked no special privileges, Canham said. Indeed, "the Press asked for one sole right, that of gathering and distributing news in complete freedom. Freedom of the Press was a right that belonged to the people. The Press, on its side, had to report the news of the whole world as accurately and objectively as possible." At times, objective reporting displeased governments, he said, and, at times, objective reporting justifiably did not promote peace. The best example of the latter occurred when reporters sent dispatches from Germany just before World War II. As a result of such reporting, the world had been alerted to the dangers of nazism; consequently, "those journalists had worked for peace." Such was the value of a free press, Canham said, but the pre–World War II example also revealed the danger of trying to impose obligations on correspondents and of trying to establish a right of correction that required contracting nations to publish responses to allegedly false dispatches. Despite urgent and vocal calls for the imposition of standards of responsibility on the press, the committee had acted correctly in voting against a coercive document, he said.[121]

When the debates were over, the news-gathering convention, basically as approved by the Third Committee, passed thirty-three to six, with thirteen abstentions and seven absent. The six negative votes represented the Soviet bloc, the thirteen abstentions came from the same basic nonaligned bloc that had opposed the document in committee.[122] The news-gathering convention, as adopted by the General Assembly, pleased three members of the press who were delegates to the Geneva conference, although each had a somewhat different perception of just how the current convention compared with the draft written in Geneva.

To Harry Martin, president of the American Newspaper Guild, the revised document was "such a vast improvement over the earlier drafts emerging from Geneva that it takes on the nature of the miraculous." The convention would greatly aid foreign correspondents, Martin said, adding that the convention's right of reply provisions were similar to the American practice of giving "space for corrective purposes to those who think they have been mistreated in the newspaper columns." The latter measure carried no compulsion except for that "which already exists in America—the force of the editorial conscience in action." The treaty obviously would be ineffective in communist countries, but the convention was valuable anyway, Martin said, because freedom increased "every time ANY government, including our own, is willing to spell out still further the freedom of the press, and the mere writing of that freedom into an international treaty brings home once more to all men the true nature of the modern democracy as compared with modern totalitarianism." For countries "outside the ideological prison of Communism," Martin believed the treaty would represent "definite advancement along the path of free speech and their conversion to our way of journalistic life."[123]

Although Sevellon Brown, editor and publisher of the Providence *Journal* and *Bulletin* and another American delegate at Geneva, also found the convention acceptable, he did not think that it was much different from the document ratified in 1948. Press leaders in the United States must review the document carefully, he stressed, although he was confident that they would find that the convention avoided regulating correspondents while establishing provisions "that will greatly benefit our newspaper operations in the foreign field."[124]

As the Geneva delegate most closely involved in shaping the final convention draft, Canham found the debates within the United Nations interesting. Changes in the delegations' composition between the two meetings revealed themselves in "the natural desire of government to cling to power," which was revealed in "little changes of language, 'safeguarding' clauses, and amendments of ingenious import." Acceptance of even one-tenth of the proposed amendments would have changed the convention "into a dangerous mechanism of press control, instead of a charter of liberties." Also apparent in the debates were the significant misunderstandings "between the small group of nations which have had experience of genuine press freedom, and those which lean toward controls." Problems were especially visible within Latin American and Arab delegations, which "had a very serious 'have-not' attitude toward the American press associations and the United States Press in general. The Arabs, in particular, were imbued with a deep bitterness resulting from the Palestine dispute, in which they felt the American press had not fairly stated their case."[125] Consequently, the latter delegations sought to place restrictions within the convention.

Nevertheless, Canham believed the convention that ultimately emerged from the United Nations represented a significant achievement for the American press. Of course, journalists could argue that some countries might interpret the convention's language as limiting rather than advancing the freedom of the press. But "no treaty could have been drafted on this subject without language that could be abused," he said. "This treaty certainly does not make the news-gatherer's position any worse than it would be without a treaty." The right of reply imposed no compulsion on the American press other than "for a government to place a hand-out on a table in the press room of its foreign office." Even if American journalistic concerns about the convention were valid, the time had passed for United States journalists to leave the international arena, Canham said. "In good faith, the great majority of American newspaper voices demanded State Department action, and in good faith, the Department set to work. But when things began to happen, oddly enough, newspapermen began to lose interest." Now, American journalists must not renege on their commitment to international freedom of the press because such a change of heart would be "infanticide. We can be extremely grateful that we haven't got a far worse treaty on our hands. It may be a poor thing, but it's our own—the end-product of newspaper demands."[126]

DELEGATES TURN TO THE BRITISH CONVENTION

With the battle on the news-gathering convention apparently won, the United States delegation had dealt successfully with two of the three Geneva conventions—the United States proposal on the international gathering and the French proposal for an international right of reply. Now, American delegates faced even greater challenges as debates over the third Geneva accord—the United Kingdom's draft convention on freedom of information—began in the Third Committee. This last major Geneva conference convention attempted to protect the rights of individuals to freedom of information and listed acceptable legal restrictions on the press. The United States delegation had abstained from voting on the convention at Geneva, and, in the interim, the State Department had pressured the British to revise the convention significantly. Given the tenor of the discussions within the Third Committee supporting restrictive measures for the Convention on the International Transmission of News and the Right of Correction, however, attempts to modify the language of the third and final Geneva convention were likely to encounter significant opposition.

The British, indicating their willingness to accommodate American interests, began the discussion by suggesting a more general limitations statement, one that said that the exercise of freedom of information

> carries with it duties and responsibilities and may therefore be subject to certain penalties, liabilities and restrictions provided by law and necessary in the interest of national security, for the prevention of disorder or crime, for the protection of public safety, health or morals, for the protection of the rights of other persons, for preventing the disclosure of information received in confidence or for maintaining the authority and impartiality of the judiciary.[127]

Davies explained that the new phrasing stemmed from the belief that a compromise should be found between an elaborate listing of limitations and a condensed text that "might weaken the convention by its very brevity."[128]

The new clause was designed to be flexible enough to win as many signatures as possible.[129] The language was now "precise and explicit and would encourage a number of States to adhere to the convention which might not otherwise have been prepared to do so," Davies said.[130] Debate on the restrictions followed the pattern set at Geneva, with delegates either affirming their belief in the more generalized statement of permissible limitations because of the impossibility of listing every restriction agreeable to all or contending that the only way to protect freedom of the press was to enumerate a precise list of limitations to apply in all signatory states.[131]

Submission of the substitute limitations text by the United Kingdom astonished some delegates who thought that the limitations issue had been settled at Geneva.[132] In the end, however, Davies was the one who was surprised. So many changes were made in his substitute draft during the course of a brief Third Committee debate that he announced that he no longer sponsored the text and that his delegation planned to vote against the revised statement.[133] In fact, according to the session's rapporteur, Davies announced that his delegation regretted that it had failed to satisfy the needs of some of the delegations, which, by suggesting amendments to the British amendments, "had contributed to the creation of that monster" for which Davies was being held responsible.[134] The revised restrictions article, approved by a vote of eighteen votes to twelve, with twelve abstentions, permitted

> certain penalties, liabilities and restrictions clearly defined by law and necessary only in the interest of public order and national security; for the prevention of the diffusion of reports for racial, national or religious discrimination; for the prevention of disorder or crime; for the protection of public safety, health or morals; for the protection of the rights of other natural or legal persons; for preventing the disclosure of information received in confidence; for maintaining the fair administration of justice; for preventing the diffusion of false or distorted reports which undermine friendly relations between peoples or States; or for the removal of economic obstacles which may hamper the free dissemination of information.[135]

The split vote, with as many abstentions as votes in favor of the proposition, led to immediate calls for postponing additional debate. The committee had just finished long and arduous debates on the news-gathering convention, some delegates argued, and members did not have enough time left in the session to adequately consider the freedom of information convention. Nor did delegates have sufficient time to obtain instructions from their governments on certain controversial points. Consequently, some delegates began proposing that they delay final action on the freedom of information document until just before the fall 1949 meeting of the General Assembly, with the Third Committee coming into special session to consider the freedom of information convention.

Even though postponement of action was inevitable, delegates continued to propose additional controversial amendments to the freedom of information convention until the postponement became official. Noriega, the Mexican delegate, for instance, again brought up his proposal for a coercive right of reply provision, this time demanding that the freedom of information convention include a right of reply clause that would force offending information organs to publish any corrections provided. Once more, Canham argued that the suggested language would lead to government control of the press.[136] American delegates successfully fended off proposals for an international code of honor for journalists, joining with representatives from most of the democracies in a call for the establishment of "non-official organizations of persons employed in the dissemination of information to the public, in order to promote the observance by such persons of high standards of professional conduct." Although nonofficial, these organizations would be asked to promote an understanding of a correspondent's "moral obligation to report facts without prejudice and in their proper context and to make comments without malicious intent." This statement ultimately led to a list of westernized responsibilities for the press that called on reporters to contribute to the solution of the economic, social, and humanitarian problems of the world, promote respect for human rights, help to maintain international peace, counteract the spread of false reports, and combat war propaganda.[137] The committee also favored allowing nations to protect underdeveloped national information agencies over the objections of delegates from the United Kingdom and the United States, both of whom argued that such steps could create national news monopolies.[138]

Debates on the freedom of information convention revealed a new Soviet bloc tactic. Recognizing the problems that the smaller nations had with the news-gathering convention, the communist states began to exploit the cleavage between the United States and the United Kingdom and their large information-gathering operations on the one hand and the nations with underdeveloped news agencies on the other. The American approach to unsatisfactory convention provisions was always the same, said Stepanenko, the delegate from the Byelorussian Soviet Socialist Republic: If the committee did not rewrite its proposals, the United States would not sign the convention. Thus, "the United States made its accession to the convention subject to the Committee's adoption of an amendment which was contrary to the interests of small nations and which, if it were adopted, would hamper the development of information agencies in many countries."[139] The Polish delegate, Stefan Boratynski, also noted that the committee regularly set aside the views of smaller countries when those opinions opposed the position of the United States and the United Kingdom. Feeling as if some of the criticism was directed toward him, Noriega denied having bowed to pressure to vote a certain way on the news-gathering convention's provisions. Terming the General Assembly "one of the freest deliberative bodies known to history," Canham labeled any effort to imply that members had been intimidated into voting a certain way "highly improper."[140] These retorts failed to stop the accusations, as Srdja Prica, the Yugoslavian delegate, proved when he claimed that "the United States conception of freedom of information seemed radically opposed ... to that of all the small nations which were anxious to safeguard their independence and sovereignty."[141]

Demchenko, the Ukrainian delegate, tried to use this new strategy to prevent a postponement of the debate on the freedom of information convention until September. The real purpose for delaying consideration of the convention, he said, was to allow the United States time to "find a method of rallying those countries which had shown some reluctance to accept proposals for provisions encroaching upon their domestic legislation." The United States delegation needed some "breathing space" to develop a new plan, Demchenko charged. Not so, responded van Heuven Goedhart, the Dutch delegate, who had sponsored the motion for delay. The reason for the delay proposal was simply that the number of abstentions on some provisions of the convention exceeded the number of votes both for and against particular provisions. No document should be sent to the General Assembly with such uncertain support.[142]

After much debate over the efficacy of the move, the Third Committee voted to delay final action on the freedom of information convention until fall 1949 and to ask the General Assembly to withhold the news-gathering convention from signature until both documents were ready for distribution.[143] Canham was disappointed at the move, but he understood that many nations saw the news-gathering convention as providing privileges for the press while the freedom of information convention stated the obligations that the press must fulfill in order to qualify for the privileges. Thus, some nations were extremely reluctant to separate the two documents.[144]

The fate of the freedom of information convention worried Canham, who said that world conditions made him wonder whether amending the convention into a form acceptable to the United States, Great Britain, and their allies was possible. With amendments, delegates possibly could transform the freedom of information convention into "an innocuous document"[145] that would serve as "a noble declaration of principles." But without careful amendment, the convention "could be the basis of restrictive action, serving perhaps to nullify the advantages of the first convention, and even worse, to set up barriers and controls which do not exist."[146] Brown agreed, terming the British convention a declaration of international policy that was "fundamentally an avowal of the right of government to police press performance and of the obligation of the press to be 'responsible' according to governmental standards." The United States government must never adhere to such a document.[147]

Debates also showed Canham that American journalists, who had initiated the free-press crusade, might have to abandon programs requiring governmental action. The United Nations debates had made him realize that "our newspapers and information agencies are big, strong, rich, powerful. They are a tempting target. Everyone wants to get his story in the American press, nearly everyone feels he is misrepresented there." He was not, however, advocating abandoning international free-press efforts. Although he found "much resentment against these agencies on the part of foreign governments," he did not think that those feelings extended to the journalists of other countries. If the press had to forego governmentally sponsored accords, journalists could make progress through international cooperation on their own.[148]

When the Third Committee reconvened in September 1949 to finish drafting the freedom of information convention, prospects for a document that the United States could approve were dim. In fact, most observers believed that the convention would turn into "a Convention on limitations of Freedom of Information rather than a positive instrument designed to further Freedom of Information." Given such a likelihood, the United States was ready to suggest abandoning the United Kingdom convention and to ask, instead, that the United Nations guarantee freedom of information through the Covenant on Human Rights, which was being drafted at that time.[149] Mrs. Roosevelt put the idea before the Third Committee asking, also, that the draft convention on the International Transmission of News and Right of Correction be opened immediately for signature.[150] The idea of abandoning the work already done on the British convention annoyed many delegates, most of whom thought that the freedom of information convention was inextricably linked with the news-gathering convention. Most of the delegates who opposed discarding the freedom of information convention thought that including a statement on freedom of information within the Covenant on Human Rights was an excellent idea. In fact, the Geneva conference had prepared a draft covenant article on freedom of information. In order to preserve the freedom of information convention as well, delegates suggested that the General Assembly establish a special working committee with the sole responsibility of drafting an acceptable freedom of information convention.

The United Kingdom's delegate stressed that his country did not mean to abandon the convention altogether but only wanted to postpone its consideration until the Commission on Human Rights had defined the principles of freedom of information. Because delegates had perceived no movement toward reconciliation of divergent views in the months between the sessions of the Third Committee, he added, debating the convention again would be fruitless. In the end, the Third Committee agreed to defer action on the freedom of information convention until the Commission on Human Rights had described the necessary terms. The committee did not, however, agree to open the news-gathering convention for signature.[151] After minimal debate, the General Assembly agreed to the postponement requested by the Third Committee.[152]

American journalists were generally pleased with the delay, for they saw the freedom of information draft convention as a restrictive document rather than as one designed to promote freedom of information. The delay bought some time for American journalists interested in international free-press issues to educate their fellow journalists about the value of the news-gathering treaty, which now was effectively shelved,[153] and to work to liberalize the freedom of information convention. Journalists in the United States still hoped that United Nations action would advance their worldwide free-press goals. The debates over the news-gathering convention, however, revealed how significant the disagreements were on the nature of freedom of the press.

NOTES

1. Report on Freedom of Information and of the Press, *Yearbook of the United Nations, 1947–1948*, p. 589.
2. Lloyd Free, Office of International Information, to Erwin Canham, president, American Society of Newspaper Editors, June 10, 1948, RG 43, NA, Box 4, File: Freedom of Information.
3. Unsigned Instructions to the Acting United States Representative to the United Nations, July 6, 1948, RG 59, NA, Box 2254, 501.BD Freedom of Information/7-648.
4. E/AC.27/SR.13, 7th session, August 7, 1948, pp. 5–7, 9, 16.
5. E/AC.27/SR.14, 7th session, August 9, 1948, p. 8.
6. E/AC.27/SR.17, 7th session, August 11, 1948, p. 15.
7. E/AC.27/SR.24, 7th session, August 19, 1948, pp. 1–21.
8. E/AC.27/SR.16, 7th session, August 11, 1948, p. 23.
9. E/AC.27/SR.14, 7th session, August 9, 1948, p. 13.
10. E/AC.27/SR.18, 7th session, August 12, 1948, p. 4.
11. Ibid., pp. 5, 15.
12. E/AC.27/SR.22, 7th session, August 17, 1948, p. 6.
13. E/AC.27/SR.14, 7th session, August 9, 1948, pp. 16–18.
14. E/AC.27/SR.15, 7th session, August 10, 1948, p. 4.
15. Ibid., pp. 5–6.
16. Ibid., pp. 7–9.
17. E/AC.27/SR.22, 7th session, August 17, 1948, p. 13.
18. E/AC.25/SR.15, 7th session, August 10, 1948, pp. 16–19. Delegates defeated the Soviet proposal. *See* E/AC.27/SR.16, 7th session, August 11, 1948, p. 8.
19. E/AC.27/SR.16, 7th session, August 11, 1948, pp. 9–10, 18.
20. E/AC.27/SR.20, 7th session, August 14, 1948, pp. 8, 10–12. The section finally allowed a contracting state to refuse entry to any person for any reason. The United States felt that this language was too broad, preferring a provision grounded in immigration regulations or laws to protect national security. *See* ECOR, 7th session, 221st meeting, August 27, 1948, p. 763.

21. "Soviet Victory Seen on Information Pacts," *E&P*, August 21, 1948, p. 6.
22. "UN Conventions," *E&P*, August 21, 1948, p. 34.
23. Erwin D. Canham, "Dangerous Set-Back Abroad," *ASNE Bulletin*, November 1, 1948, p. 3.
24. "Benton Advises Treaties," *E&P*, October 9, 1948, p. 11.
25. ECOR, 7th session, 221st meeting, August 27, 1948, p. 752. The delegate from Colombia proposed the amendment in question; supporters included Russia, Poland, Byelorussia, France, Australia, Venezuela, Chile, and Peru. The amendment passed the Human Rights Committee by a vote of eight to seven with three abstentions. *See* Comment Paper on Draft Convention on the Gathering and International Transmission of News, March 25, 1949, RG 84, NA, Records of the United States Mission to the United Nations, Box 181, Background Book, 4th General Assembly 1949, Position Papers.
26. "UN Conventions," p. 34.
27. ECOR, 7th session, 221st meeting, August 27, 1948, p. 754.
28. "The U.S. Attitude," *E&P*, September 18, 1948, p. 38.
29. Memorandum of Conversation with Raúl Noriega of the Mexican Delegation and George Washington and Lloyd Free of the United States Delegation, October 14, 1948, RG 84, NA, Records of the United States Mission to the United Nations, Box 181, Position Papers 1949 (emphasis in original).
30. GAOR, Third Committee, 3rd session, 130th meeting, November 10, 1948, p. 428.
31. "Freedom Conventions," *E&P*, November 20, 1948, p. 42.
32. GAOR, Third Committee, 3rd Session, *Resolution Calling for a Second United Nations Conference on Freedom of Information* (A/C.3/374), November 27, 1948, p. 101. Cosponsors were Argentina, Bolivia, Brazil, China, Denmark, France, Mexico, Netherlands, the Philippines, and Sweden. At the Geneva conference, the American delegation considered the advisability of another conference on freedom of information but deemed another session unadvisable for at least five years. A second session should concentrate on technical rather than substantive matters, according to the United States delegation. *See* Benton Proposal, April 20, 1948, RG 43, NA, Box 2, File: US Del Documents.
33. Ibid., 179th meeting, December 7, 1948, p. 892.
34. Dean Rusk, Assistant Secretary of State for United Nations Affairs, to the Secretary of State, February 17, 1949, *FR: 1949*, II:4–5.
35. Comment Paper on Draft Convention on Gathering and International Transmission of News.
36. Ibid.
37. Ibid.
38. Ibid.
39. Comment Paper on Draft Convention on Freedom of Information, Undated, RG 84, NA, Records of the United States Mission to the United Nations, Box 181, Background Book, 4th General Assembly 1949, Position Papers.
40. Ibid.
41. Ibid.
42. Ibid. *Editor & Publisher* reported the British plans to revise the convention, adding that a British spokesman noted little press comment in the United Kingdom about the actions of the Geneva conference "because the discussions

so far have had an air of unreality to the British press, since it was felt that owing to the immense division between the Russian-Eastern European concept of press freedom and that of Western Europe and America, it was unlikely that anything very concrete could come of it." *See* "British Will Rewrite UN Press Convention," *E&P*, March 19, 1949, p. 6.

43. Comment Paper on Draft Convention Concerning the Institution of an International Right of Correction, February 28, 1949, RG 84, NA, Records of the United States Mission to the United Nations, Box 181, Background Book, 4th General Assembly 1949, Position Papers. The Americans were also to protect the rights of Congress by including a non–self-executing clause in the United Kingdom draft convention. The provision called on a signatory to adopt measures "in accordance with the provisions of this convention and in accordance with its constitutional processes," thus allowing Congress "to work out and to fit the provisions of the Convention into domestic legislation." *See* Position Paper on Non-Self-Executing Article for United Kingdom Convention on Freedom of Information, March 28, 1949, Ibid. And the United States delegation was also to seek the inclusion of a federal-state clause within the United Kingdom draft convention. The provision called on a signatory to adopt existing in the United States. *See* Position Paper on Federal-State Article for the United Kingdom Draft Convention on Freedom of Information, March 28, 1949, Ibid.

44. GAOR, Third Committee, 3rd Session, 182nd meeting, April 7, 1949, pp. 7–8.

45. Ibid., 183rd meeting, April 8, 1949, p. 15.

46. Ibid., 182nd meeting, April 7, 1949, p. 8.

47. Ibid., pp. 10–11.

48. Doris Willens, "Definitions Worked Out in Week's UN Debate," *E&P*, April 16, 1949, p. 6.

49. GAOR, Third Committee, 3rd Session, 183rd meeting, April 8, 1949, pp. 15–17.

50. Ibid., pp. 18, 21–22.

51. Ibid., 185th meeting, April 11, 1949, pp. 35–36, 38.

52. Ibid., 182nd meeting, April 7, 1949, pp. 6, 11. The Yugoslav quoted from two new books: Herbert Brucker, *Freedom of Information*, New York, Macmillan, 1949, and Lester Markel, ed., *Public Opinion and Foreign Policy*, New York, Published for the Council on Foreign Relations by Harper & Row, 1949. Markel was Sunday magazine editor of *The New York Times*.

53. Ibid., 186th meeting, April 13, 1949, pp. 42–43.

54. Ibid., *Recapitulation of Amendments to Article 1 of the Draft Convention on the Gathering and International Transmission of News* (A/C.3/419/Rev.1), April 9, 1949, p. 16.

55. Ibid., 187th meeting, April 13, 1949, p. 55.

56. Ibid., 188th meeting, April 14, 1949, pp. 57, 61, 63.

57. G. J. van Heuven Goedhart, the delegate from the Netherlands, noted that communist rhetoric labeled anyone who opposed the communist ideology as a fascist. In recent months, for instance, Soviet propaganda had labeled several wartime antifascist leaders in the Netherlands as fascists simply because they opposed Soviet goals. *See* GAOR, Third Committee, 3rd Session, 189th meeting, April 14, 1949, p. 67.

58. GAOR, Third Committee, 3rd Session, 188th meeting, April 14, 1949, p. 58.
59. Ibid., 192nd meeting, April 19, 1949, p. 100.
60. Ibid., 188th meeting, April 14, 1949, p. 60.
61. Ibid., 189th meeting, April 14, 1949, p. 69.
62. Ibid., p. 70.
63. Ibid., pp. 71, 76.
64. Ibid., pp. 76–77.
65. Ibid., p. 77.
66. Ibid., 190th meeting, April 18, 1949, p. 80. Irving Florman, United States Ambassador in Bolivia, confirmed the problems that Latin American nations had with American reporters in 1951. Writing in *The Quill*, the journal for Sigma Delta Chi, the society of professional journalists, Florman cited several instances in which American journalists had misquoted and misrepresented information that they had received in Latin American countries. He concluded by saying that such behavior was the main reason "why there is not as much enthusiasm in some quarters today for complete freedom of information, North American style, as there is among North American journalists." *See* Irving Florman, "U.S. Writers Stir Ill Will," *Quill*, July 1951, p. 19.
67. Ibid., 191st meeting, April 18, 1949, p. 97.
68. "UN Proposals," *E&P*, April 16, 1949, p. 32.
69. Samuel DePalma, expert on international affairs, to Senator Warren R. Austin, United States Representative to the United Nations, April 15, 1949, RG 84, NA, Records of the United States Mission to the United Nations, Box 108, Treaties: Public Information. The Latin American countries said national military security would refer only to army matters.
70. GAOR, Third Committee, 3rd Session, 191st meeting, April 18, 1949, pp. 87–88.
71. Ibid., pp. 90–91, 95.
72. Ibid., pp. 91–92, 95.
73. Ibid., 192nd meeting, April 19, 1949, pp. 99–100.
74. Ibid., 194th meeting, April 20, 1949, pp. 123–26.
75. Ibid., pp. 127–28.
76. Ibid., 195th meeting, April 20, 1949, p. 130.
77. Ibid., *France: Amendments to the Draft Convention on the Gathering and International Transmission of News* (A/C.3/425, Corr.1 and Corr.2), April 8, 1949, pp. 17–19.
78. Ibid., 195th meeting, April 20, 1949, pp. 130–31.
79. Ibid., pp. 131–32, 134 (emphasis in original).
80. Position Paper on Implementation Article for the Three Draft Conventions Dealing with Freedom of Information, March 28, 1949, RG 84, NA, Records of the United States Mission to the United Nations, Box 181, Background Book, 4th General Assembly 1949, Position Papers. Senate objections to references to the International Court of Justice were one reason for concern; another cause was the fear that countries not parties to the conventions might try to bring harassing actions against press organs before the court. Once the documents were universally accepted among United Nations members, then delegates could construct an appeals route within the United Nations, departmental planners said.

81. GAOR, Third Committee, 3rd Session, 195th meeting, April 20, 1949, pp. 136–37.
82. Ibid., pp. 138–42.
83. Ibid., p. 142.
84. The State Department decided against bringing this point up again at later debates. The United Kingdom, whose delegate had presented the American view in the Third Committee despite his own nation's preference for International Court of Justice jurisdiction, did not want to advance the cause again. The French representative, who had also backed the United States' position in spite of personal misgivings, refused to support the American effort again as well. Given the defections of allies, "it would be foolhardy to plunge into a move for reconsideration only to be defeated once more." *See* Samuel DePalma, United States Mission to the United Nations, to Durward Sandifer, United Nations Affairs, May 3, 1949, RG 59, NA, Box 2277, 501.BF/5-349.
85. GAOR, Third Committee, 3rd Session, *Recapitulation of Amendments to Articles 2 and 3 of the Draft Convention on the Gathering and International Transmission of News* (A/C.3/431 & Add.1), April 9, 1949, pp. 19–20.
86. Ibid., 196th meeting, April 21, 1949, p. 146.
87. Ibid., p. 147.
88. Ibid., pp. 147, 150, 148–49.
89. Ibid., 197th meeting, April 21, 1949, p. 152.
90. Ibid., 196th meeting, April 21, 1949, pp. 148, 150.
91. Ibid., 197th meeting, April 21, 1949, p. 157. Delegates also approved the additional Mexican amendment listing offenses to the national prestige or the dignity of a country among the items for which an official reply was appropriate. Delegates dropped language calling for the compulsory publication of corrections from the final draft convention that emerged from the Third Committee.
92. "UN Proposals," p. 32.
93. GAOR, Third Committee, 3rd Session, 198th meeting, April 22, 1949, p. 169.
94. Ibid., p. 172.
95. "UN Conventions," *E&P*, April 23, 1949, p. 66.
96. GAOR, Third Committee, 3rd Session, *Mexico: Additional Article for Insertion in the Draft Convention on the International Transmission of News and the Right of Correction* (A/C.3/470), April 22, 1949, p. 36.
97. Ibid., 198th meeting, April 22, 1949, p. 163.
98. Ibid., p. 165.
99. Ibid., *Report of Sub-Committee 5: Draft Convention on the International Transmission of News and the Right of Correction As Referred by the Third Committee to the Sub-Committee* (A/C.3/496), May 4, 1949, p. 63. The section also contained the prohibition on peacetime censorship except on grounds of national defense, the right of a contracting state to refuse admission of any particular person into its territory, and the Mexican statement on the duties of foreign correspondents.
100. Ibid., 200th meeting, April 25, 1949, pp. 183, 185.
101. Ibid., pp. 190, 187, 191.
102. Ibid., 201st meeting, April 25, 1949, pp. 193–95.
103. Ibid., pp. 199–200.

104. Ibid., 200th meeting, April 25, 1949, p. 186.
105. Ibid., 201st meeting, April 25, 1949, p. 196.
106. Ibid., 203rd meeting, April 26, 1949, p. 216.
107. Ibid., p. 218. *Voting for the article*: Dominican Republic, Ecuador, Egypt, Ethiopia, Guatemala, Haiti, Honduras, Iraq, Liberia, Mexico, Pakistan, Panama, Peru, Poland, Saudi Arabia, Siam, Ukrainian Soviet Socialist Republic, Yugoslavia, Afghanistan, Argentina, Burma, Byelorussian Soviet Socialist Republic, Chile, Colombia, Costa Rica, Cuba, and Czechoslovakia. *Voting against the article:* Lebanon, Netherlands, New Zealand, Norway, Philippines, Sweden, Syria, Turkey, Union of South Africa, United Kingdom, United States of America, Uruguay, Australia, Belgium, Brazil, Canada, and Denmark. *Abstaining:* France, India, Iran, Union of Soviet Socialist Republics, Venezuela, Yemen, and China.
108. Doris Willens, "UN Correspondents' Code Faces Battle in Assembly," *E&P*, April 30, 1949, p. 12.
109. "Boomerang, Says Hugh Baillie," *E&P*, April 30, 1949, p. 122.
110. GAOR, Third Committee, 3rd Session, *Colombia, France, Mexico, Peru, United Kingdom and United States of America: Joint Amendments to Articles IX, X, and XII of the Draft Convention on the International Transmission of News and the Right of Correction* (A/C.3/502), May 6, 1949, p. 78.
111. Ibid.
112. Ibid., 220th meeting, May 7, 1949, pp. 365, 368–69.
113. "Best Treaty That Could Be Worked Out—Canham," *E&P*, May 14, 1949, pp. 5–6.
114. "Clarification Is Needed, Says Johnson of U.P.," *E&P*, May 14, 1949, p. 6.
115. "UN Conventions," *E&P*, May 14, 1949, p. 40.
116. Doris Willens, "United Nations Completes First Information Treaty," *E&P*, May 14, 1949, p. 5.
117. GAOR, 3rd Session, 209th plenary meeting, May 13, 1949, pp. 363–64, 366. The Chilean delegate planned to vote for the convention, despite its shortcomings, because she considered the document to be a first step in a long process.
118. Ibid., 210th plenary meeting, May 13, 1949, pp. 372–73. Nevertheless, the Saudi delegation supported the text of the convention as developed by the Third Committee.
119. Ibid., p. 385.
120. Ibid., 209th plenary meeting, May 13, 1949, pp. 367, 371.
121. Ibid., 210th plenary meeting, May 13, 1949, p. 378.
122. Doris Willens, "Press Treaty Passes Final UN Hurdle," *E&P*, May 21, 1949, p. 6.
123. Harry Martin, "Acceptable Document," *E&P*, August 20, 1949, pp. 26–27 (emphasis in original).
124. Sevellon Brown, "The UN Convention," *E&P*, August 27, 1949, p. 30.
125. Erwin D. Canham, "International Freedom of Information," *Law and Contemporary Problems* 14 (Autumn 1949):594.
126. Erwin D. Canham, "Future Uncertainties of News-Gathering Treaty," *E&P*, September 3, 1949, p. 26.
127. GAOR, Third Committee, 3rd Session, *Recapitulation of Amendments to Article 2 of the Draft Convention on Freedom of Information—Proposed*

Substitute for Article 2 Presented by the United Kingdom Delegation (A/C.3/472), April 25, 1949, p. 39.

128. Ibid., 211th meeting, May 2, 1949, p. 294.
129. Ibid., 213th meeting, May 3, 1949, p. 309.
130. Ibid., 211th meeting, May 2, 1949, p. 294.
131. Ibid., 212th meeting, May 3, 1949, pp. 297–98.
132. Ibid., pp. 305–6.
133. Ibid., 213th meeting, May 3, 1949, p. 316.
134. Ibid., 214th meeting, May 4, 1949, pp. 317–18.
135. Ibid., 213th meeting, May 3, 1949, p. 316.
136. Ibid., 214th meeting, May 4, 1949, p. 323.
137. Ibid., 215th meeting, May 4, 1949, pp. 333–34.
138. Ibid., 217th meeting, May 5, 1949, p. 341.
139. Ibid., 210th meeting, May 2, 1949, p. 281.
140. Ibid., 211th meeting, May 2, 1949, p. 295.
141. Ibid., 212th meeting, May 3, 1949, p. 301.
142. Ibid., 217th meeting, May 5, 1949, p. 344.
143. GAOR, 3rd Session, 209th plenary meeting, May 13, 1949, pp. 357–58.
144. Canham, "International Freedom of Information," p. 597.
145. Canham, "Future Uncertainties of News-Gathering Treaty," p. 26.
146. Canham, "International Freedom of Information," p. 598.
147. Brown, "The UN Convention," p. 30.
148. Canham, "International Freedom of Information," p. 598. Canham made similar comments when discussing the free-press crusade in the ASNE official history. *See* Pitts, *Read All About It!* pp. 182–85.
149. Walter Kotschnig, Chief, Division of United Nations Economic and Social Affairs, to Dr. G. J. van Heuven Goedhart, Netherlands delegate, September 13, 1949, RG 84, NA, Records of the United States Mission to the United Nations, Box 92, Treaties: Public Info.
150. GAOR, Third Committee, 4th session, 233rd meeting, September 27, 1949, p. 2. Sponsoring the proposal to refer the matter to the Commission on Human Rights for inclusion in the Covenant on Human Rights were the United States, the United Kingdom, and the Netherlands.
151. Ibid., 234th meeting, September 27, 1949, pp. 7, 11.
152. GAOR, 4th Session, 232nd plenary meeting, October 20, 1949, p. 117.
153. "UN Treaty," *E&P*, October 8, 1949, p. 36.

CHAPTER 6

The Crusade Falls into Disfavor at the United Nations

From the American press's perspective, the major question resulting from the early United Nations debates on freedom of information issues was whether the United States could maintain control of the situation. The strength of the smaller nations that made no attempt to hide their dislike of American media obviously had increased during the debates over the news-gathering convention. Next on the agenda were two controversial issues: the freedom of information article for the human rights covenant and the revision of the British draft convention on freedom of information. American delegates correctly predicted numerous attacks on the American system of freedom of the press during consideration of each point.

The next round of debate was scheduled for the Commission on Human Rights, an organ of the Economic and Social Council. But even before the commission could begin discussing the human rights covenant, delegates had introduced thirty exemptions to the freedom of information article's guarantees—an ominous sign for American interests. If the document emerged from the commission in this form, Eleanor Roosevelt, the commission's chair, believed that the covenant would curb freedom of information rather than expand it or even protect the status quo. Hence, the United States delegation planned to encourage a simple covenant article[1] that called for guaranteeing everyone the right to enjoy "freedom of information and expression without governmental interference." Under the United States proposal, that freedom of information included the "freedom to hold opinions, to seek, receive and impart information and ideas, regardless of frontiers, either orally, in writing or in print, in the form of art, or through any other media." In order to be acceptable to the United States, any limitations on this freedom must be imposed by law and were allowable only "in the interest of national security, public order, safety, health or morals, or for the protection of the rights, reputation or freedoms of other persons."[2]

DEBATES BEGIN OVER THE CONTENT OF
FREEDOM OF INFORMATION PRINCIPLE

Despite signs that this interpretation of freedom of information would not be welcomed by most members of the human rights commission, the American delegation urged the adoption of this broad statement of general principle. Such language was necessary, argued James Simsarian, because freedom of information was in greater danger now than any time in the previous twenty years. "The systematic indoctrination of entire peoples with party dogma and propaganda, the denial of access to outside sources of information and the deliberate conditioning of peoples by controlled information services to hate and fear the outside world" created grave threats to world peace. Consequently, the human rights covenant provision must be framed broadly enough to guarantee individuals the right to receive information without governmental interference. Delegates quickly realized that the United States proposal promised to lead the United Nations into yet another debate over the comparative value of various press systems. And Pierre Ordonneau of France wondered aloud whether any freedom of information clause, no matter how beautifully or carefully framed, could ever garner enough support to win United Nations ratification. Three years of discussion on the topic by various United Nations bodies had been disappointing and inconclusive, he said. Other United Nations committees' efforts to draft whole conventions capable of winning substantial support had failed, and Ordonneau believed that the Commission on Human Rights would be equally unable to draft one article for an international covenant that would be satisfactory to all interested parties.[3]

The difficulties involved in framing the guarantee were immediately apparent. The United States, for instance, wanted the covenant's language to refer only to governmental interference in freedom of information, for extending the provision's reach to the "field of private infringements on freedom of information would create complications and give rise to many unpredictable situations." But Max Sörenson, the Danish representative, called for prohibiting infringements on freedom of information by private individuals as well, citing a recent printers' strike in his country, which had closed all newspapers other than party organs for more than two months, as an example of the practices that should be prohibited.[4] And M. Leroy-Beaulieu of France argued that while the suppression of freedom of information must be placed securely beyond governmental reach, at the same time, governments must be allowed to promote freedom of information.[5]

Mrs. Roosevelt rejected the French proposals. In speaking of governmental efforts to promote freedom of information, she wanted to know if the French delegation meant that "editors should be forced to publish everything submitted to them, regardless of the opinions expressed?" If so, the concept violated "the very principle of freedom of individual thought."[6] The United States delegation believed that any attempt to make the article reach beyond governmental interference would create "serious complications and difficulties." American refusal to accept French ideas for the covenant article displeased Ordonneau, who told Mrs. Roosevelt that Americans must realize that every freedom has two components: protecting the individual from the state and protecting the freedom itself "by the enforcement of the individual's respect for it." Eliminating the latter aspect significantly weakened any covenant guarantees.[7] Agreeing on the need to protect freedom of information from nongovernmental interference, Karim Azkoul, the Lebanese delegate, noted that "in many countries, private interference from groups of individuals was more likely to be feared than governmental interference."[8] Mrs. Roosevelt was forced to admit that although other kinds of interference existed, exposing or preventing such activities would be difficult. Thus, her delegation opposed any covenant language to prevent private interference in an individual's right to freedom of information.[9]

At times, even the simplest topics threatened to escalate into major problems. For instance, commission members became bogged down in a recurring argument about semantics. Were they writing a covenant article dealing with freedom of expression, or freedom of information, or freedom of opinion? To some delegates, freedom of expression encompassed the other freedoms; to other commission members, freedom of expression implied a right to dispense information, while freedom of information was a narrower, more passive freedom to receive data. The questions that these differences in perceptions raised were numerous. For instance, could a person receive information without forming an opinion based on that information? And did an individual have a right to share his opinions with others? While some nations supported the more limited notion of freedom of information, Mrs. Roosevelt said that the United States believed in guaranteeing the right to receive and to share information, for one right was incomplete without the other. J. Marguerite Bowie, the British representative, found arguments that the rights were mutually inclusive unconvincing. "In totalitarian countries, opinions were definitely controlled by careful restriction of the sources of information," she said. "Molestation might also occur before an opinion was formulated. Without some reference to freedom of thought or opinion as a necessary prerequisite to freedom of expression, there would be a definite gap in the covenant." Ordonneau, however, believed freedom of information was only one means of expression, thus making the various comments about the appropriate term unnecessary. But he bowed to the wishes of the majority and agreed to a more specific description of freedom of expression.[10]

Terminology was considered so important here because of the pending debate over the limitations clause for the covenant article. Would the limitations clause restrict receiving information, forming opinions, or expressing opinions—or all three? Ultimately, delegates agreed informally that any limitations placed in the covenant article would refer solely to the expression of opinions, for individuals must have the right to form opinions without interference.[11] The direction of the debate led H.F.E. Whitlam of Australia to state his belief that the task facing the commission would be difficult, if not impossible, to accomplish. Indeed, positions of various delegations were already crystallizing, and commission members were finding themselves even farther apart than before on key issues. Obviously, Whitlam said, the commission eventually must decide among proposals, and some members' ideas must be defeated. Because of the past difficulties encountered by United Nations bodies in writing any statement on freedom of information, the commission's role in writing a covenant article assumed greater importance.[12] Many delegates saw the covenant article as being their only possible chance to insert a statement on the conditions governing freedom of information in a United Nations document, and they intended to write a covenant article covering every possible contingency.

For instance, the Egyptian delegate, Abdel Meguid Ramadan, wanted to add language stating that "any offence committed through the press against the person of a sovereign or head of state of a foreign country and likely to impair the friendly relations existing between States shall also be liable to penality." Articles in the American press about the love life of Egyptian King Farouk apparently inspired this proposal. Although not mentioning this precipitant specifically, Ramadan said that the journalistic campaign against his nation showed "utter disregard for that international courtesy prevailing among countries." Since the United States did not recognize a right of reply, "every effort to have a correction published in the magazine or editorials which had published or spread the defamatory information had been useless." Although Ramadan said that he recognized "the liberal tradition of the United States press," he believed that when a professional attitude "threatened to impair friendly relations between two States it was necessary to add a provision to international law in order to prevent such abuses." Recalling the "tendentious information on Middle Eastern countries published by certain elements of the western Press" during the recent Palestinian crisis, Azkoul, the Lebanese representative, found the Egyptian proposal attractive. On the other hand, Carlos Valenzuela of Chile attacked the Egyptian proposal as endorsing the equivalent of censorship. In the modern world, nations must realize that "either the press was a government service, in which case the government was responsible for what was published, or the press was a free enterprise, and journals' contributions could in no way compromise relations between countries." Delegates could not endorse both interpretations.[13]

When the discussion turned to the duties and responsibilities encompassed within freedom of information, Mrs. Roosevelt's emphasis on the rights of individuals to freedom of information rather than on the duties and responsibilities that the privilege entailed was almost solitary. Even Miss Bowie of the United Kingdom advocated including certain penalties or restrictions on freedom of information within the covenant's provisions "because the freedoms in question, by virtue of their very nature, carried with them special duties and responsibilities." Ramadan, still irate about American media treatment of Egypt, agreed: "The idea of duty and responsibility should be expressed; that was all the more obvious when the current state of mind and tendencies of a certain section of the press were concerned." But the covenant article was no place for sermonizing, retorted Mauro Méndez of the Philippines, who was unable to find any "reason for supposing that journalists did not have a sense of their responsibility; on the contrary, it would seem that complete confidence could be placed in them." Even if journalists merited all the confidence that the Philippine delegate was willing to accord them, Charles Malik of Lebanon pointed out that the covenant was designed to recall that although freedom of the press was "precious," that freedom "might be a very dangerous thing." Practicing a profession that "consisted in seeking, receiving and imparting information and ideas carried with it special duties and responsibilities of such a nature that it was advisable to recall them in the draft covenant."[14]

Insertion of limitations on freedom of information in the interests of national security into the draft covenant article drew almost no comment from members of the Commission on Human Rights. Discussion of this particular provision apparently had been exhausted during debates on the news-gathering convention, where the Americans and other delegations had agreed that nations might impose restrictions on the gathering and transmission of news to protect national security. Allowing a nation to pass laws to restrict freedom of information to preserve public order likewise met with general approbation. Much of this debate had also occurred earlier, but some delegates still wondered if the term was too vague. For instance, Branko Jevremovic of Yugoslavia reminded his colleagues that "the fundamental aim of the United Nations was to keep the peace and ensure harmonious relations between peoples." Consequently, commission members must remember that freedom of information easily could be exploited. "If misused, it could even run counter to the fundamental aim of the Charter, namely, the maintenance of peace." To guard against abuse, Jevremovic contended that the covenant must state that the freedoms guaranteed were limited if they "endangered peace, collective security and the attainment of the fundamental aims of the Charter."[15]

To accomplish this end, Hansa Mehta, the Indian delegate, wanted to exclude "spreading deliberately false or distorted reports which undermine friendly relations between peoples and States" from the protections offered by the covenant article. Once again, with the introduction of the Indian proposal, the Soviet bloc's campaign to prevent the dissemination of false news entered United Nations discussions on the promotion of freedom of information. And the idea once more came from India, originator of the proposals at the Geneva conference so distasteful to the United States that American delegates voted against the draft article for the human rights covenant containing this language. Debate on the topic again was predictable. For instance, the United Kingdom's delegate sympathized with the Indian delegate while pointing out that the planned international right of correction addressed India's concerns more directly. But eliminating the clause dealing with the dissemination of false information would be costly to the Americans, Malik warned. Only if the Americans pledged to work on a comprehensive freedom of information convention would other delegates support the United States effort to delete the Indian amendment from the draft article for the covenant on human rights.[16]

Ultimately, delegates did agree to drop the specific recitation of limitations from the covenant article. Without apparent compromise by the United States, the covenant language adopted actually was quite similar to earlier American proposals. Now numbered Article 14, the freedom of information provision read:

1. Everyone shall have the right to hold opinions without interference.
2. Everyone shall have the right to freedom of expression; this right shall include freedom to seek, receive and impart information and ideas of all kinds, regardless of frontiers, either orally, in writing or in print, in the form of art, or through any other media of his choice.
3. The right to seek, receive and impart information and ideas carries with it special duties and responsibilities and may therefore be subject to certain penalties, liabilities and restrictions, but these shall be such only as are provided by law and are necessary for the protection of national security, public order, safety, health or morals, or of the rights, freedoms or reputations of others.[17]

With the drafting of this language, work effectively stopped on freedom of information provisions for the human rights covenant. The document covered topics as diverse as outlawing slavery, protecting individuals against arbitrary arrest, and prohibiting discrimination based on race, color, sex, language, religion, political opinion, national or social origin, property, or social status.[18] The covenant was shuttled from committee to committee for the next few years because of the inability of members of the United Nations to agree on various provisions, with the problems encountered not necessarily related to freedom of information topics. By 1952, the Commission on Human Rights again was working on the human rights covenant, this time under orders from the General Assembly to split that covenant into two documents, one dealing with civil and political rights and the other covering economic and social rights.[19]

AMERICAN JOURNALISTS REACT
TO COVENANT PROPOSALS

Apparently not recognizing that the freedom of information section of the proposed covenant was only one small portion of a highly controversial document, American journalists reacted strongly every time another United Nations body considered the covenant. Deliberations by the Commission on Human Rights in April and May 1950 brought mixed reactions. The Soviets were boycotting United Nations sessions over the refusal of the international body to expel representatives of Nationalist China, now occupying Taiwan, in favor of delegates from the Chinese mainland, now held by the Chinese communists. Because of the Soviet absence, the possibilities for a positive statement on freedom of information should have been much better. American journalists discovered, however, that "delegates from India, Egypt, Lebanon, Yugoslavia and other states had some serious grievances against the press of the Western democracies. This freedom, they felt, could not be unbridled liberty; it must be subject to certain curbs." Thus, in the view of *Editor & Publisher*, these nations had saddled the American press with a compromise covenant article that was unsatisfactory to everyone. In fact, approving these "so-called permitted restrictions" had raised concern within press circles because the American media opposed any United Nations accord that suggested that restrictions "could be imposed upon their overseas personnel." American arguments against the provisions had been useless because "a coalition of small powers" was able to overrule the United States. These nations hoped that the treaty "if and when it is written—will give them some defense against some of the less-popular practices of the powerful American press organs and wire services, which they feel have frequently given unfavorable and biased accounts of conditions abroad."[20]

With the *Editor & Publisher* stories about the dangers that international attitudes toward American press practices posed to negotiations within the United Nations, Erwin D. Canham felt compelled to speak out. As a former president of the American Society of Newspaper Editors (ASNE), Canham tried to allay his colleagues' fears about the covenant article. Realistically, any covenant article had to contain a limitations clause because "the United States, like every other nation, has always had to impose certain limitations on absolute freedom, even in the area of free speech." Few newspaper editors disagreed with the restrictions on freedom of the press existing in the United States, Canham said. The most common limitations in America included libel, slander, and copyright laws, postal regulations, and the ability of courts to protect themselves via the contempt power. Hinting at the overarching authority of the covenant article, Canham said that none of these commonly accepted protective provisions could stand without covenant approval. In fact, even laws regulating obscenity "could not be upheld if the

Covenant of Human Rights or any other treaty on internal freedom of information were ratified without an exceptions or limitations clause." Nothing in the limitations clause required the United States to impose any new restrictions on freedom of speech. Nor did anything in the clause "validate any future limitations which might otherwise be contrary to the American Constitution." The clause simply meant that the government could impose no limitations except those listed in the clause.[21]

Some critics focused on covenant language that protected national security information and pointed to Canham's strenuous efforts during debates over the news-gathering treaty to change a similar clause so that it covered only national military security. In making such an analogy, critics of the covenant attempted to show that the covenant provision was dangerous to the American press. Canham, however, saw no parallel. The covenant article referred to the freedoms exercised by individuals within a contracting state: "To say that internal restriction on absolute freedom of information inside the United States can be limited only to national military security or national defense would be to negate a number of present useful restrictions to which the most zealous newspapermen have never objected, and would not dream of objecting." While he believed that Article 14 offered no real challenge to the American system of freedom of information, Canham still worried about the implementation of the covenant article within the United States. Because he was not a lawyer, Canham suggested that a special ASNE committee study the provision. "We must be sure that we do not fail to discern and combat any actual threat to the standards of free information which we are dedicated to uphold and extend as our duty to the people and to free society."[22]

Members of the legal community soon complicated the discussion when the American Bar Association's (ABA) Committee for Peace and Law Through the United Nations called for "prompt and positive action by the press and allied agencies in protest against this assault on the freedom of information." Without a concerted and successful protest against the covenant's limitations, warned Cranston Williams, general manager of the American Newspaper Publishers Association (ANPA), state legislatures could use the human rights covenant "to fetter the press in any manner and by any method they chose upon a mere declaration of policy that the fetters were imposed for the protection of National security, public order, safety, health or morals, or of the rights, freedoms and reputations of others or any of such reasons."[23] ABA comments confirmed the suspicions of many editors and publishers about the effects "of such documents in our First Amendment guarantees: Treaties and conventions, once ratified by our Senate, become binding as law throughout the U.S. and even supersede the provisions of the Constitution." Thus, warned *Editor & Publisher*, usually a strong supporter of international free-press accords through the United Nations, editors must "be wary and alert as to what is being attempted in the name of freedom of the press but which might ultimately destroy that freedom."[24]

Intense domestic debate over the proposed Covenant on Human Rights article was only beginning. The American Newspaper Publishers Association, a group known for its conservative political leanings,[25] heretofore had abstained from the international free-press movement. Now, the ANPA became actively involved in the campaign against the United Nations document as its general counsel, Elisha Hanson, denounced Article 14, the freedom of information article, of the Covenant on Human Rights. The covenant article, Hanson proclaimed, "contains certain unctuous platitudes" guaranteeing numerous freedoms, but American journalists must not be deceived by enticing phrases. After all, liberty could not be imposed on people. "Only restraint can come about by imposition, and we do not want that in America, however altruistic may be the motives of those who espouse this proposed covenant."[26] Members of Sigma Delta Chi, an organization representing 19,000 professional journalists, also condemned Article 14, saying that the provision contained "a clear and apparent threat not only to the efforts to extend freedom of the press to other parts of the world but also to our own press freedom within our own shores."[27] In addition to condemning the covenant draft, the organization denounced "any in our government or representing us in the United Nations who, for the sake of compromise, would give approval to the language of the covenant."[28]

A special Sigma Delta Chi committee headed by Lyle Wilson, chief of the United Press bureau in Washington, D.C., noted that by 1950 the international crusade to promote freedom of information had become "a fixture on the calendars of foreign offices in virtually every country." Although now the object of great attention and declamation, the crusade's accomplishments rested more in the extensive records of United Nations debates than in "the actual pushing back of the frontiers of freedom of information." In fact, "the past year has seen a diminution rather than an increase in the extent of news freedom. Military needs, developed by the Cold War, have blanked out growing areas of information. The number of countries practicing censorship has not grown less." Danger lurked in additional debate at the United Nations because the member nations represented such disparate views on the subject. Rather than continuing the work on an international covenant, the Sigma Delta Chi committee said that journalists should revert to a notion popular before the Geneva conference in 1948 and promote bilateral treaties with countries having compatible ideas.[29]

The primary controversy over the freedom of information article in the Covenant on Human Rights focused on whether the article superseded American constitutional provisions protecting freedom of the press. Opponents of the United Nations covenant contended that the treaty clause in the Constitution placed international accords on a par with the Constitution itself. Almost everyone involved in the argument agreed that treaties were superior to state legislative and constitutional provisions to the contrary and that the United States Supreme Court had permitted Congress to enact legislation under the treaty power that otherwise would not be within congressional authority. No one knew the outer limits of the treaty power, however, for the United States Supreme Court had heard only one case testing the treaty provision—a 1920 action involving migratory birds.[30] The Supreme Court opinion in that case was broadly written, giving covenant opponents room to claim that all sorts of potential evils were possible after the human rights covenant was combined with the treaty power in the Constitution. Covenant opponents conveniently ignored express language in the international document that forbade any covenant provision from restricting rights already specifically granted within a signatory nation. And opponents also overlooked the growing willingness of American journalists to litigate free-press issues. Any hint that the covenant might impinge on First Amendment rights would lead to an immediate court challenge, which most likely would result in the necessary and desired limitation of the treaty power. Regardless of its intensity, the debate within the American press community over the alleged power of the covenant article was occurring in a vacuum. The General Assembly returned the 1950 draft to the Commission on Human Rights for additional work, and no one could guarantee when or if the commission would be able to write a draft that would gain sufficient support to pose the threat anticipated by some American journalists.[31]

Covenant critics also challenged the ability of the United States government "to enter into any such a binding international compact respecting human rights and freedoms."[32] Successfully limiting the American government's freedom of action in this manner could bar additional efforts on many fronts within the United Nations and possibly force the country to revert to a state of noninvolvement in international affairs similar to what had existed between the wars. Perhaps, with the growing threats posed by the cold war, some Americans, particularly some of the more conservative opponents of the Covenant on Human Rights, desired to return to simpler times. Hanson, the ANPA general counsel, exemplified the conservative viewpoint. After World War II, he would argue, the American government began participating in world affairs at an unprecedented level and started using its treaty-making power "for purposes that could not have been foreseen or even contemplated a few years ago." As a result, "the American people are today confronted with the question as to whether, in an attempt to give greater liberty to other peoples in the world, they will destroy their own."[33]

In Hanson's opinion, the government's error in diplomatic judgment that led to such expansive action on the international front was compounded in the area of international free-press issues. He was particularly concerned about proposals to restrict the dissemination of information that undermined the good relations between states or to ban the circulation of false news, either of which could destroy a free press—an institution Hanson had long defended with considerable vigor. If the proposal to ban the circulation of information that could injure the feelings of citizens of a state "had been in effect in 1933, not a word could have been printed in the American press regarding the policies of the Hitler government and the tyrannical methods used to enforce them." In 1950, the proposal meant that "not a word could be published in American newspapers about the Stalin government in Russia, the Peron government in Argentina, the Mao government in China or the Franco government in Spain." Thus, the Covenant on Human Rights represented "the ultimate in hostile action against the right of the American people to enjoy free speech and to have a free press."[34]

Fears about the alleged power of United Nations treaties to override United States laws found support in a single California lawsuit. In that case, a state judge cited language in the United Nations Charter that demanded the elimination of discrimination on the basis of race, sex, language, or religion, as the basis for overturning the state's Alien Land Law. After this decision, according to George Sokolsky, a columnist syndicated by William Randolph Hearst's King Features, only two avenues of protection from the United Nations incursion into the Bill of Rights guarantees remained. One, of course, was to disavow further interest in writing free-press accords and to refuse to agree to additional international documents. The second possibility focused on demanding the insertion of a non-self-executing clause in each United Nations document, something that the State Department had sought unsuccessfully in Geneva. Such a safeguarding provision at least would grant Congress control over any legislation necessary to implement international accords.[35] If upheld, Hanson said, the California case meant that the government could, through the treaty-making power, "abrogate our rights of free speech, to have a free press, to worship God according to our own beliefs, and all the other individual rights guaranteed by our forefathers 160 years ago."[36] For conservatives with Hanson's background, apprehensions about the excessive and malevolent power of a liberal president and Congress were nothing new. Hanson and many members of the newspaper community that he represented had chafed under liberal administrations for eighteen years; seeing sinister motives behind governmental actions was customary.

Conservative opponents of the Covenant on Human Rights were not likely to be swayed by legal arguments that opposed their point of view. But arguments defending the covenant and attempting to defuse the conservatives' fears were made anyway. For instance, supporters of the covenant pointed out that restrictions similar to the ones included in the covenant article were "practiced by all civilized nations of the world including the United States." A University of Virginia law professor argued that "at the worst, the draftsmen of the Covenant have done no more than enshrine considerations which have been repeatedly honored by the United States Supreme Court." The idea that the president and Senate could implement covenant provisions without restraint was ridiculous, he continued, because the Supreme Court was the final check under the constitutional system. A court that was showing a growing interest in First Amendment issues would not let attempts to abridge those freedoms slip by unnoticed. Turning to the constitutional argument, the law professor noted that no "responsible authority" had ever contended that "a treaty or an executive agreement could override a provision of the Federal Constitution. No decision of the Supreme Court may be found which holds that the treaty making power is free from any provision of the Bill of Rights." When looked at dispassionately, the California case simply reiterated "the proposition that a treaty of the United States is paramount to conflicting state laws. It has no relevance to a potential abridgement of any provisions of the Bill of Rights of the Federal Constitution." The argument against the covenant provision was "grossly cynical" because the provision's opponents assumed incorrectly "that our independent Supreme Court would interpret a provision relating to 'national security' in a treaty of the United States as authorization for an unreasonable executive or legislative assault upon the constitutionally established immunities of individual conduct from government interference."[37]

Logical arguments, though, swayed few people. The battle against the covenant heated up as Senator John W. Bricker (R-Ohio), who would propose a constitutional amendment limiting the treaty power, demanded that Congress stop American participation in discussions that "would legalize the most vicious restrictions of dictators both past and present." The "most shocking feature" of the proposed covenant, Bricker said, was that "it would authorize penalties to be placed on the press in order to protect the rights and freedoms of others." Citing the worst possible scenario, "American newspapers could be shut down in order to protect the rights of others" under the covenant's provisions.[38]

Zechariah Chafee attempted to rebut such contentions by pointing out that the much-feared limitations in Article 14 stemmed from repeated efforts by the Americans to write a general statement of restrictions rather than using the cafeteria-style list of limitations advocated by many other delegates. Representatives of the departments of State, Defense, and Justice had approved the language now in the covenant article. "Freedom-loving nations, therefore, put every phrase into Article 14," he added, wondering, were "the representatives of freedom-loving nations who wrote the whole of Article 14 so utterly base as to want to throttle freedom of the press while pretending to give it new strength?" If opponents of the article were to be believed, the provision's authors were "either consummate knaves or hopeless idiots." On the contrary, their goal was "to devise a formula which would express the principles laid down by our courts in a manner acceptable to other free peoples with different constitutions than ours." In addition, Chafee argued, the covenant was designed to ensure more freedom for countries where excessive restrictions existed and to prevent other nations from increasing suppression. Immediately bringing every signatory nation "up to the high level of fundamental human rights which fortunately has long prevailed in our land" would be "very pleasant"—but "obviously impossible."[39]

DEBATE RESUMES ON THE
FREEDOM OF INFORMATION CONVENTION

Arguments over the provisions of Article 14 of the draft human rights covenant were just a prelude to pending debates over the draft convention on freedom of information. Delegates had suspended work on this controversial document in 1949 after they had been unable to reach agreement on necessary definitions for the principles that the draft was to contain. Introduced at the Geneva conference by the British, the draft convention on freedom of information had been highly controversial from its inception. The United States had abstained from voting on the convention in Geneva as an indication of its opposition to the convention's restrictive provisions. Attempts by the British to soften the convention's provisions in 1949 were met with such hostility that the British disavowed further responsibility for the document. After a futile attempt to revise the document in 1949, the General Assembly postponed additional debate on the convention until the Commission on Human Rights completed writing the freedom of information article for the human rights covenant. The postponement had included the shelving of the American-backed convention on the international gathering and transmission of news and the right of correction, for delegates had argued that the conventions were two halves of one whole. When the postponement was suggested, delegates hoped that, because the provision planned for the human rights covenant covered many of the more controversial points included in the draft convention on freedom of information, the human rights commission would solve many of the outstanding problems for other United Nations bodies. The commission finished its work in August 1950, two months after the outbreak of the United Nations police action in Korea, and, as seen, the commission left some of the most controversial questions unresolved. Despite this fact, and regardless of the tenuous international situation, some delegates quickly began efforts to revive consideration of the draft convention on freedom of information.

Strangely enough, the fighting in Korea did not initiate another round of great rhetoric similar to the testimonials of World War II about how international freedom of information would have prevented another war. Nor did American journalists seek even more State Department involvement in efforts to develop worldwide freedom of the press as a counter to future wars. In fact, although the State Department still endorsed international freedom of the press, departmental planners, supported by American journalists, wanted to block efforts to revive the freedom of information convention. Considering the language of Article 14 of the draft human rights covenant as "basically satisfactory," departmental advisers hoped to convince other nations that no more work in the field was necessary. Influencing this decision was the belief that any draft convention on freedom of information probably would turn into a document "unacceptable to the United States and detrimental to this Government's efforts to promote world-wide acceptance of our concept of freedom of information." In fact, any convention "embodying ambiguities and restrictive provisions," such as the limits placed in the convention during previous debates, "would constitute a serious setback to the promotion of freedom of information by the United Nations whether or not the United States and a few like-minded countries adhered to it." Not only would the convention give official United Nations sanction to restrictive practices, but the document also threatened the successful implementation of the news-gathering convention that delegates had pigeonholed until completion of the freedom of information convention.[40]

American representatives successfully blocked an effort within the Economic and Social Council to bring the draft freedom of information convention back before the General Assembly. Debate on the motion revealed that many delegates, including Raúl Noriega of Mexico, designer of many controversial freedom of information proposals in earlier sessions, wanted to reconsider the convention.[41] The victory placed the American delegation in a difficult situation, however, because of the popularity of the freedom of information convention with delegations from France, India, the Middle East, and Latin America, "which are anxious to secure international recognition of their concept of the 'responsibility of the Press'." The only possible American response to these nations' arguments was that the State Department believed that the provisions in the draft human rights covenant article represented "the maximum degree of international agreement now obtainable on freedom of information principles which are consistent with the traditional democratic concept of this freedom."[42]

In fact, American delegates did not intend to kill the freedom of information convention; they merely wanted to postpone additional debate until the chances of writing an acceptable convention improved. If unable to win an indefinite postponement of debate, the State Department told American delegates to try to postpone consideration of the issue until the General Assembly adopted the human rights covenant. As a fallback position—if other nations persisted in pursuing work on the British draft convention—the Americans were to seek modifications in the freedom of information convention that included the elimination of several restrictive phrases and the incorporation of a non–self-executing clause. Without such changes, the department warned, the United States would find the document completely unacceptable.[43]

The challenge to the American position on the document increased as delegates from Lebanon, France, India, and Mexico continued their efforts to revive the convention in every available forum. An American-led coalition defeated each attempt, often by a narrow margin. State Department planners expected the disappointed delegations to retaliate by trying to block the opening of the news-gathering treaty for signature. In the event of that contingency, American delegates must insist that the two issues were unrelated. Given the changing atmosphere regarding freedom of information issues, United States representatives must not even suggest opening the news-gathering convention for signature "unless prior consultations indicate the likelihood of majority support."[44]

Recognizing that the American position on the freedom of information convention was essentially unpopular and that the Americans had won only reluctant support from other nations in previous debates, United States delegates at the United Nations planned to discuss the matter "rather casually with other delegations with no attempt to put pressure on them." When dealing with delegations from Western Europe, the British Commonwealth, and Scandinavia, American representatives expanded traditional arguments. Here, they stressed that the current tense international mood had so many governments preoccupied with national security considerations that those governments likely would support restrictive changes in the original text. Although such modifications might be valid in light of existing political conditions, American representatives warned that "it would be undesirable to establish them in an international convention and thus give them a kind of permanent status and respectability which at a later time may prove undesirable."[45] Several nations indicated their willingness to abandon the draft convention, but no delegation wanted to introduce the appropriate proposals. The United States might have to assume the burden of killing the convention itself, much to the State Department's discomfort.[46]

The French suggested another approach to the problem—establishing a special committee of experts to work solely on the freedom of information convention.[47] The timing of the French proposal was inauspicious for American journalists; efforts to revive the draft convention came soon after the American Bar Association warned about how the human rights covenant could abolish First Amendment rights. Some journalistic observers doubted that the United Nations would adopt a restrictive document, but with the freedom of information convention coming up for debate again, American editors and diplomats "ought to be on their toes." Once more, American journalists labeled the Soviets as the key enemy in the debates.[48] Once again, their assessment was wrong.

A SPECIAL COMMITTEE BEGINS
DEBATE ON THE CONVENTION

A special fifteen-nation committee was established to reexamine the British freedom of information convention and the objections to it. The General Assembly instructed the committee to draft an acceptable document, which then would go to a special international conference for approval. Committee members came from the United States, Great Britain, France, the Union of Soviet Socialist Republics, Cuba, Egypt, India, Lebanon, Mexico, the Netherlands, the Philippines, Ecuador, Pakistan, Saudi Arabia, and Yugoslavia.[49] The committee roster immediately showed how little support the American vision of freedom of the press had among its members. Other than Soviet bloc critics, participants included some of the most vociferous opponents of American news-gathering techniques in the United Nations, such as India, Mexico, and Saudi Arabia. And the French representative would be sure to sponsor his nation's peculiar blend of freedom and responsibility. Committee sessions promised to be rather taxing.

Perhaps the tone for the sessions of the special Committee on the Draft Convention on Freedom of Information was set when members elected Noriega of Mexico as chairman. No one individual had created quite so many problems for United States freedom of information proposals in recent years, and no one individual had suggested so many restrictive measures for incorporation in various documents. Yet Noriega was to supervise the writing of a document that was to command the approval of all. Underlining the difficulty of the assignment, Henri Laugier, assistant secretary-general for social affairs, reminded committee members that they were meeting "at a particularly critical moment in world history, for recourse had been had to armed force for the settlement of conflicts among nations which could and should be settled through negotiation, conciliation, compromise and mutual respect in accordance with the Charter and the aspirations of all mankind." No one expected another world war if the delegates failed to find a solution to the world's freedom of information problems. Nevertheless, Laugier said, "all men of goodwill would be gravely disappointed if the Committee failed to achieve agreement and compromise." As if to accent Laugier's statements and in an attempt to set a positive tone for discussions, Noriega asked the delegates to present constructive proposals that would establish a new basis for the committee's work rather than restating hackneyed arguments. The current world crisis made protecting freedom of information of supreme importance, he said, calling on members to discard their "legitimate preoccupation with the broader world problems" in order to draft an adequate convention.[50]

The problems of the world, however, could not be so easily avoided. In fact, the "conflict of ideas between totalitarianism and liberal democracy" already had polluted the world's communications channels, Manuel Braña, the Cuban delegate, said. Now, "propaganda directed against the peoples of small countries whose voice was not strong enough to be heard by the world was one of the problems with which the Committee would have to cope." But the totalitarian-democratic split did not concern Jamil M. Baroody of Saudi Arabia, who was more interested in the disparities between the power of the media of information in large, technically advanced countries and the power of the media in smaller nations. Countries with powerful information media gave more attention to opinion than to news, Baroody charged, and propaganda dominated information. Due to international tensions, the larger countries were becoming even more involved in propaganda, and "the genuine news" available to small countries was in even shorter supply. Indeed, Baroody continued, political indoctrination had replaced religious indoctrination in the modern world. "The change had taken place deliberately in a few countries and unconsciously in almost all the others," but the information media were "the natural instruments of that indoctrination." Journalists seeking successful careers found that "they must conform to the propaganda plan adopted consciously or unconsciously in their own country." Similar pressures were exerted on newspaper owners, "who must be the instruments of national propaganda or resign themselves to bankruptcy." Perhaps the solution to this predicament, Baroody said, was an international code of ethics to compel the responsible exercise of freedom of information.[51]

Supporting the Saudi Arabian's arguments was Azkoul, the Lebanese delegate. Only countries with highly developed information systems strongly endorsed absolute freedom of information, he said, while countries with lesser-developed systems, "not being in a position to make it known to the whole world what was really going on within their borders, feared that the information agencies might give a distorted picture of their institutions and way of living." Countries with well-developed information systems argued that a multiplicity of voices ensured the emergence of truth, but Azkoul doubted that statement's validity on an international basis. Journalists from different countries often did report on events in the same country, so, allegedly, their stories could be checked against each other for accuracy. But these reporters wrote in different languages and for media in distant countries, thus preventing any viable comparison of their work. To show that his fears were not groundless, Azkoul pointed out that history recorded instances in which "the fate of one country had depended on public opinion in another, more powerful country and where a false picture built up by tendentious reports might have the most unfortunate consequences." To protect the world from miscarriages of freedom of information, the committee must draft a convention carefully restricting the press's freedom. In doing so, Azkoul said, members must, of course, "take great care that the limitations authorized in the convention should not tempt countries hitherto free from them to introduce them into their legislation."[52]

French delegate Jacques Kayser found committee members' comments heartening, for he believed that the tense world situation made the freedom of information convention more important than ever. One imperative item for the convention, according to Kayser, was a list of specifically drawn limitations on freedom of information, which, "if defined with the utmost precision would make it easier for the journalists and agencies to avoid committing any abuses in the first place." Noriega was greatly satisfied with the calls from his colleagues for specific steps to preserve international freedom of information. He said that previous objections to the convention had focused on fears that the convention "might be violated or that its provisions might be used by unscrupulous Governments as an excuse for suppressing freedom of information." Such protestations were weak, he said, because accepting these arguments literally meant that "no national law could ever be adopted, since laws were constantly violated and evaded." The committee, however, could "do more constructive work if it had greater confidence in the good will and the good faith of the Governments which would be signatories to the convention."[53]

Realizing the struggle before him, the United States delegate, Carroll Binder, a former foreign correspondent serving as editorial page editor of the *Minneapolis Tribune*, stressed the philosophical underpinnings of the American view of freedom of information rather than its practical ramifications. Currently, he said, "freedom, which had been under constant relentless attack by totalitarian regimes, nazi, fascist and now communist, during much of the twentieth century, was again being assailed with every weapon of political intrigue, propaganda and even military force." The only valid question for the committee to consider was whether its efforts "would strengthen and protect the principle of freedom of information, or whether the document it produced would utilize the prestige of the United Nations to legitimize certain restrictive governmental practices which were not now internationally accepted." The United States believed that freedom of information was essential to a democratic society, that information was the key to informed decision making by the peoples of the world. Inadequate, incorrect, or false information warped this process and imperiled the democratic way of life. Basically, Americans thought that "freedom of information meant that every person should have access to all available facts, ideas and opinions regardless of source, and not only the information approved by his Government or any party."[54]

Abuses of freedom of information were possible, Binder admitted, but limitations on freedom of information "must evolve through long democratic experience, must safeguard the maximum of freedom for each person, must not be experimental in character, and must always be subject to public criticism and to review by impartial judicial authority." If limitations were necessary, he added, only restrictions imposed after publication were acceptable; no restraint of information prior to its dissemination was permissible. Americans saw no middle ground between a controlled press and a free press. Although compromise was essential in international relations, he vowed to make "a careful distinction" between "compromises relating to the way in which fundamental principles were to be executed and compromises on the principles themselves." The United States refused to sacrifice the basic principle of freedom of information. In fact, seeking a compromise simply to reach an agreement even among free nations was "more likely to restrict freedom than to promote it." Thus, writing a convention now that would be acceptable to the United States seemed impossible. After all, delegates had been debating the convention for three years, and Binder saw nothing that offered any hope of success for the special committee's deliberations. The United States preferred to "acknowledge that a temporary impasse had been reached and to await developments in connexion with the draft international covenant on human rights." To Binder, the committee's choice was clear—members could avoid taking any action that might further impair the spread of facts and ideas, or they could "seek escape through purely verbal agreements which might only serve to strengthen those whose actions were responsible for the grave threat to world peace."[55]

His colleagues in the American press considered Binder's position most difficult. Somehow, other nations had maneuvered the United States "into the unfortunate position of appearing to be against Freedom of Information while in fact it is all for it." Now, Binder must convince the other committee members that Americans truly believed in freedom of information while, at the same time, opposing suggestions that "are restrictive but which the other nations believe will strengthen the proposed treaty." The problem, again, was partly one of international semantics. Everyone talked about freedom of information, but no one defined the term identically. Binder would be fighting a "rear-guard action" if other nations pursued their points. Granted, the United States was under no compulsion to sign an unsatisfactory committee-produced document, but the convention's provisions "could be used by the signatory nations against our reporters and correspondents within their borders."[56]

As the debates within the special committee assigned the task of drafting an acceptable freedom of information convention began, so, too, did the recitations of the transgressions of the American news media. The Arab states labeled the United States media pro-Zionist for their coverage of the Palestine conflict. The Latin Americans disliked the way in which the North American press focused on their revolutions while ignoring their social, political, and economic growth. Asiatics thought that American journalists submitted false reports about their religious conflicts. The Yugoslavs complained that the American media had been duped by a Soviet propaganda campaign against Yugoslavia. And the Russians still accused the American monopolistic press of engaging in warmongering practices designed to destroy the Soviet Union.[57]

Introduction of convention provisions and debate on them followed predictable lines, but, once again, representatives of each point of view demanded committee time to try to win the votes of other delegates or at least to ensure that their arguments were heard for any potential propaganda value. For instance, S. K. Tsarapkin of the Soviet Union wanted the convention to call on "all States to take all steps necessary for the achievement of a press free from monopolistic control." Within Binder's comments about stopping work on the convention, Tsarapkin saw an effort "to afford full protection to trusts and monopolies under the control of United States and United Kingdom companies" while avoiding "imposing any responsibilities on them." The Soviet delegate also wanted to insert provisions forbidding the spread of fascist doctrine and warmongering propaganda by the media and to require the press to disseminate only truthful information.[58]

Soviet arguments always maintained that the press should be assigned a certain prescribed, positive role to play in world affairs. Binder worried about who would define the press's role if the Soviet theory gained the ascendancy. Such defining "could only be done, and in fact it was only being done, by governments which had assumed the power to control the press." Nothing could be farther removed from the true concept of freedom of the press. "The one great responsibility of the press was to seek the truth and to report its findings as comprehensively and objectively as possible. It could promote desirable social, economic and political ends only in so far as it succeeded in providing the general public with available facts and opinions," thus enabling the people to reach their own conclusions. If a government had the power to determine the truthfulness of information, its leaders could decide that South Korea had attacked North Korea instead of the reverse. The press in a country ruled by such a government would have to circulate the perversion "as a fact even in the face of conclusive evidence, accepted by the rest of the world, that the opposite was true." These tactics, Binder declared, "could deceive only those who were not in possession of all the facts." But some representatives, including Saudi Arabia's Baroody, believed that the possession of facts was simply not enough. Baroody believed that the Soviet position was far too narrow; he wanted protection against "the pernicious policies of certain 'perverted' democracies," which he considered to be "just as dangerous as fascism and nazism." Ignoring the American call for wide-open exchange of news, Baroody said that the committee must draft a complete list of obnoxious ideologies or write a precise preamble to "draw a clear distinction between propaganda and genuine information," granting protection to the latter while restricting the former.[59]

DELEGATES CONTINUE TO
ATTACK THE AMERICAN POSITION

Delegates used the various United Nations forums to peck away continually at the American stance on freedom of information. The smaller states, for example, consistently argued against American-backed provisions that they perceived to be designed to protect the highly developed information media of the larger nations at the expense of the media in underdeveloped countries. When this topic came up before the special committee drafting the freedom of information convention, Baroody pursued the argument, contending that the freedom of information problems of the larger and smaller nations were definitely dissimilar. Consequently, any freedom of information convention must make provisions for the media-related problems of the smaller countries. Binder tried to reassure the Saudi Arabian that the United States understood the special problems these countries faced in the information field. But, he added, the United States must not "be asked to abandon or renounce the values which it had evolved during many years of trial and error and which it felt morally bound to transmit to future generations. Experience had demonstrated that, through the proper use of information, the orderly evolution of the people towards a better life could be ensured." Baroody rejected Binder's comments, citing once again the abuse of his country "by the press of some Powers" and contending that the individuals who controlled media outlets must be made to understand their great responsibility to the people of the world.[60]

Nations—such as the United States—that argued for the absolute freedom of their media to determine their own destinies were unrealistic, according to Méndez of the Philippines. In fact, committee members should admit frankly that no system of government was perfect and that the information media were not totally free from "pressure and dictation" in democratic or totalitarian nations. If this was not the case, a freedom of information convention would be unnecessary. The Filipino's phrase "pressure and dictation" caught the attention of H.T.A. Overton, delegate from the United Kingdom, who protested that merely calling for freedom of the media from governmental influence implied that such governmental pressure existed, an assumption the Briton refused to accept. But, countered Méndez, private enterprises were "operated by human beings, who were, by their very nature, fallible. The democracies should not fall into the error of the totalitarian States by considering themselves and their institutions to be perfect." Méndez said that his proposal rested on reality rather than ideology; he found room for improvement everywhere.[61]

One improvement desperately needed, according to Tsarapkin, would require governments "to promote the dissemination of truthful and objective information." He was especially concerned, of course, about the press in the United States, which, influenced by the deepening cold war and the United Nations police action in Korea, "spoke only of war, war preparations and of the fighting which was going on in certain parts of the world; it analysed the military potential of the great Powers and examined the possible uses of the atomic weapon, listing the USSR cities which would have to be destroyed and the United States cities which would be threatened." By such reporting, the American press was "creating a war psychosis and literally poisoning the mind of the masses. The responsibility for such a situation lay with those who controlled information media, in particular the press, the radio, television and cinema." To be successful, any convention must directly address this problem, Tsarapkin said.[62]

Such blatancy by the Soviet Union drew little support from committee members. Noriega of Mexico, for instance, termed the Russian's suggestion "a request to Governments to exercise very strict censorship over all means of information." Naturally, Binder also opposed the Soviet proposal, claiming that the Russians wanted to restrict freedom of information "in the interest of totalitarian Governments." And Azkoul, the Lebanese delegate, criticized the Soviet comments because, if they were adopted, governments might cite the preservation of peace as an excuse for restricting freedom of information. The Soviet proposal won only one vote—its own—for passage.[63] The vote revealed that the Soviet Union had lost almost all of its influence on freedom of information issues.

American interests discovered just how much influence the United States could still exert on freedom of information issues when the discussion turned to Article 2 of the draft convention, the section containing the list of permissible restrictions that governments could impose on freedom of information. Realizing the potential divisiveness that awaited him when debate began on this article, Noriega insisted that "individual members would have to sacrifice their particular preferences and bear in mind the need for reaching general agreement." After all, he said, the General Assembly expected the committee to reach consensus and produce a convention draft. Members could not pursue petty personal causes and serve the greater good at the same time. The chances of self-sacrificial concessions by delegates were slim, however, as Binder led off the debate by condemning the notion of the convention's listing any specific limitations on freedom of information. Kayser of France followed by pleading for a combination of explicit freedoms with explicit responsibilities. So pronounced were the differences on the issue, Kayser said, that no compromise was possible—the committee must decide to adopt one point of view or the other in its entirety.[64] Given the makeup of the committee, the limitations inserted in the convention draft likely would be far more specific than the United States could ever accept.

Problems raised by the proposals for a specific restrictions clause were acute. State Department planners noted that if the United States itself decided to accept as limitations all those items that might be valid topics for laws in America or that were already covered by laws, American representatives would have to ask for the inclusion of twenty to thirty specific acceptable limitations on freedom of information. Even with such an expansive listing, departmental advisers found "no assurance that all essential governmental authority had been safeguarded in terms of the future." If the Americans proposed so many permissible exceptions to complete freedom of information, other nations surely would add innumerable additional protections that they considered essential for their governments to enact in order to protect their parts of the world. This would lead "to undesirable compromises of the 'log-rolling' variety, with the result that certain limitations are voted in which by themselves might not merit majority approval." Such concerns were met squarely by the reality that United Nations delegates repeatedly had defeated American attempts to write generalized language citing permissible governmental restrictions on freedom of the press—until the passage of Article 14 of the Covenant on Human Rights. Acceptance of more generalized language for that provision led State Department planners to hope for similar success when the time came to draft the restrictions clause of the freedom of information convention. The American success with the covenant language, unfortunately, proved to be more an aberration than a trend.[65]

Many delegates thought that the American generalized statement, which permitted only restrictions on freedom of information authorized by law, might be abused far more easily than an itemized list of limitations. For example, Azkoul of Lebanon suggested that delegates remember how Nazi Germany had established a long list of allegedly justifiable restrictions on information. No matter how detrimental such a law might be, the legislation would conform with provisions proposed by the United States. Consequently, the American concept of a generalized limitations provision was "dangerous, because it would open the way for every kind of abuse." Azkoul preferred a highly specific itemization of practices susceptible to legal limits, but the Lebanese delegate pledged to accept a shorter, more generalized list of activities subject to restriction. Although he realized that his shorter list of restrictions was likely to be more specific than those acceptable to the United States, Azkoul said that he hoped other nations would follow his example and also compromise.[66] Siding with the Lebanese delegate, F. A. Vallat of the United Kingdom said that his delegation believed that freedom of information "could best be protected if the limitations permissible to governments were defined in detail and with great precision." A loosely defined limitations clause likely would "give rise to the imposition of limitations which could not be reasonably justified."[67]

Among the most controversial limitations on freedom of information suggested for the convention were two generally associated with the Soviet bloc and lately advocated by the smaller nations. Under these proposals, nations could restrict the dissemination of data likely to offend the feelings of their peoples and to punish the spread of false information. When discussed by their new sponsors, the restrictions took on a double meaning, for they condemned the information practices of both Eastern and Western super-powers. For instance, Abdel Hamid Abdel-Ghani, the Egyptian delegate, supported restrictions on the dissemination of distorted news, commenting that three American magazines had carried articles recently "containing false and distorted information regarding Egypt, apparently based on the same source material and for the same motives." Even though none of the publications were "fostering a campaign directed against the interests of Egypt," a nation was justified in seeking protection from abuse. Agreeing with his Egyptian colleague, A. A. Farouq, the Pakistani delegate, likewise wanted a "safeguard against unwitting or deliberate offences which might arouse national sentiments." Referring to resentment "provoked among Moslem peoples by certain caricatures and distorted films dealing with the Prophet of Islam," Farouq noted that "the sensitiveness of the majority of the inhabitants of certain countries was well-known, particularly countries where great importance was attached to religious symbols." No improvement in relations among states would be possible "if attacks on national customs and beliefs were not banned in a convention on freedom of information."[68]

The larger, more-developed nations must realize, said Saudi Arabia's Baroody, that "the people of Asia had suffered unduly from the bad taste of highly developed countries." The problem rested more in the "search for sensationalism" than in "deliberate bad taste," but the "results had often been disastrous." In a possible reference to stories about the love life of Egyptian King Farouk, Baroody continued, "excessive curiosity about the intimate details of the private lives of notable personalities had in many cases gravely injured the sensibilities of small nations." The nations involved demanded that protection from these repeated affronts be built into the convention. While sympathetic to the problems of the smaller nations, Kayser of France pointed out that larger nations were also the targets of stories that offended their national sensitivities. The difficulty in correcting such problems rested in determining "whether a slight had been intentional or unintentional, or whether the country concerned was hypersensitive to criticism." And who, he asked, had the wisdom to establish and enforce the criteria for judging?[69]

Even the United States' national feelings had been attacked, Binder said. Since the beginning of the Korean conflict, he said, "the United States had suffered more than 46,000 casualties, killed, wounded or missing. Yet the press and radio of certain Member States had made the most shocking and slanderous statements about that great sacrifice," deeply wounding the American people. Despite this abuse, the American delegate agreed with his French colleague about the impossibility of drafting effective legislation to prevent recurrences of such abusive commentary. The only viable solution, Binder said, was to develop a greater sense of individual professional responsibility among journalists.[70] Committee members generally agreed that most journalistic problems could be solved if journalists simply would behave more responsibly. Binder, however, thought that the journalists must develop this responsibility on their own; representatives of some other nations felt that reporters would act more responsibly only under coercion.

Efforts to protect national sensitivities were far from selfish, according to R. S. Chhatari, the Pakistani delegate. In areas of the world where people were still very conservative religiously, journalistic use "of phrases or expressions which might wound their religious feelings would serve no useful purpose and would merely bring discredit on the journalists."[71] Many of the delegates' complaints about journalistic misbehavior seemed poorly conceived to Jorge Mantilla, the Ecuadorian delegate, who believed that many of the criticisms rested not so much on story content as on "lack of understanding of the true functions of modern journalism." All the journalist did was "to make the true facts known to the public," and because of that act, nations around the world immediately complained about irresponsible journalism. Saudi Arabia's Baroody doubted that a misunderstanding of the role of journalists in the world was a root cause of the problems caused by the press. Just as any other profession, journalism "had its quota of scoundrels." Since those who were scoundrels "were not readily identifiable," Baroody said, "there was no means of denying them access to the organs of the press." Although experience had shown "the need to urge journalists to exercise a sense of discernment," the only way to make correspondents behave responsibly was to require certain behavior before granting them the protections and rights guaranteed in the convention.[72]

Debate over a provision that would protect the sensitivities of nations and peoples continued, with no likely compromise in sight. Binder remained adamantly opposed to such a provision and was supported by the French delegate. Many smaller nations continued to criticize the American stance, noting, for instance, that the United States' generalized statement of acceptable limitations included the right of governments to enact laws protecting public morals. To Baroody, establishing a workable definition of public morals was just as difficult as explaining national dignity. After debate on the proposed American generalized statement of restrictions concluded, delegates defeated the generalized article by a vote of seven to six, with two abstentions. Binder himself voted against the American proposal, saying that amendments had changed the wording so significantly that the United States no longer supported the article. Fearing an impasse, Noriega once again called on the committee "to adopt a more flexible attitude in its work on the convention." Progress was impossible "if members adhered so rigidly to the instructions of their Governments that they were not prepared to reconcile divergent views and agree on compromise formulae likely to win acceptance by a majority." Little chance of compromise existed, however; the United States stood firm. Any draft convention on freedom of information produced by the special committee would lack United States support.[73]

Eventually, the delegates admitted their inability to develop a mutually acceptable new text for Article 2. Despite this realization, delegates also knew that the limitations article had to be written. Consequently, they reverted to the language adopted at the Geneva conference—phrasing that the

American delegation had implicitly rejected when members abstained from voting on the convention. Reversion to the earlier language displeased some committee members, for they knew that the language had not garnered any support beyond the confines of the Geneva conference. But perhaps the earlier language could at least guide later discussions. Committee members were constantly looking beyond their specialized sessions to an expected meeting of plenipotentiaries, or diplomats, with the full authority to commit their governments to the convention. These special emissaries might find the Geneva language helpful in revising the controversial article. In any event, circumventing the impasse created by debate over Article 2 was essential. By reverting to the old version of the article, delegates might begin moving again on the convention. The committee must continue working in order to fulfill its obligations to the General Assembly, Noriega repeatedly reminded delegates. If the special committee failed in its mission, the effect on world opinion would be "incalculable." Failure to adopt a convention on freedom of information also meant that the news-gathering convention, which included the right of reply section, would probably never be opened for signature and that the freedom of information article in the draft covenant on human rights would probably suffer a like fate. Petty squabbling must be put aside for the greater good, he again stressed.[74]

Committee members thus began working through the text of Article 2, as originally adopted in Geneva, making various alterations and amendments. Binder remained quiet during much of the debate; the United States would not support any version of the completed document. The American stance made little difference, however, for committee members adopted Article 2—a version that contained a specific itemization of permissible restrictions—by a vote of seven to two, with five abstentions. Voting against the article were the United States and the Union of Soviet Socialist Republics; abstaining were Cuba, Ecuador, the Netherlands, the United Kingdom, and Yugoslavia.[75] The draft, as adopted, read:

> The exercise of the freedoms referred to in Article 1 carries with it duties and responsibilities and may be subject to limitations clearly defined by law and applied in accordance with the law, but only necessary with regard to: (a) The protection of national security; (b) Expressions which incite persons to alter by violence the system of government or which promote disorder; (c) Expressions which incite persons to commit criminal acts; (d) Expressions which are obscene or which are dangerous for youth and expressed in publications intended for them; (e) Expressions which are injurious to the fair conduct of legal proceedings; (f) Expressions which infringe literary or artistic rights; (g) Expressions about other persons, natural or legal, which defame their reputations; (h) Legal obligations resulting from professional, contractual or other

legal relationships including disclosure of information received in confidence in a professional or official capacity; (i) The prevention of fraud.[76]

As a safeguard, Binder later proposed amending Article 2 so that "nothing in this convention may be interpreted as limiting or derogating from any of the rights and freedoms which may be guaranteed under the laws of any contracting state or any conventions to which it is a party." The amendment, he explained, would prevent the article's provisions from "automatically creating certain restrictions in a country where they did not now exist." The addition, altered slightly to limit its effectiveness solely to rights and freedoms "in connexion with freedom of information," was adopted.[77]

The remainder of the draft convention caused little debate. In his final comments, Binder proclaimed the United States' dislike of the entire document. The limitations clause was the most distasteful element of the convention because, in the American view, the proviso "was an open invitation to add other limitations." The American delegate also criticized the refusal of committee members to accept his proposal to make the document non–self-executing. On the latter point, Binder noted that "the United States could not consider becoming a party to such a convention, since to do so would upset its system of judicial safeguards of the freedoms in question." Few other delegates, of course, shared Binder's concerns. Noriega, pleased with the outcome of debates, found the compromise that he had so earnestly sought. Only the Soviet Union and the United States had registered repeated negative votes against the convention and usually for different reasons. Despite those delegates' disapproval of the proceedings, both delegates had participated in debates by offering articles and amendments, which Noriega considered positive signs. Kayser, speaking for the French delegation, also was pleased with the results, for the committee's work marked the first time in three years that anything substantive had been accomplished in the field of freedom of information at the United Nations.[78]

Binder considered other delegates' praise for the committee's accomplishments unmerited. The committee actually had refused to vote on the final completed draft, and members had decided to send two controversial amendments to Article 2—one referring to prohibitions on "matters likely to injure the feelings of the nationals of the State"[79] and the other on "false or distorted reports which undermine friendly relations between peoples or States" or "reports regarding racial, national or religious discrimination"[80]—on to the secretary-general's legal experts for evaluation. Binder criticized this approach, saying that the committee should resolve all doubts about the proposals itself. "If it believed that the amendments in question were useful and compatible with freedom of information, it should record that fact by a vote on them." To pass the decision on to someone else was highly irregular. Binder also failed to comprehend how the committee could "adopt a proposal which implied that the key article of the draft was not acceptable because it did not incorporate two amendments rejected by the Committee." In his view, such actions indicated that the committee was determined to have a convention at any cost.[81]

Kayser, undaunted by Binder's criticisms, said that referring the two amendments to a panel of international law experts was primarily a conciliatory move to show that "the ideas expressed by some members of the Committee were worthy of study in order to find a basis for agreement and thus better serve the cause of freedom of information." Accommodation was apparently beyond the ken of the American delegation, Baroody of Saudi Arabia charged; Binder's unwillingness to bend was seen as typical of the cavalier attitude that the United States had displayed toward the concerns of smaller nations throughout the debates. "The United States delegation wished to ignore the frequently expressed fears of small nations which did not have powerful media of information; it wished even to ignore the many incidents which justified those fears. The dignity and the feelings of states and peoples were at stake." If Baroody had his way, the United States would never forget exactly how the smaller nations felt about the American media. He pointedly informed Binder that the defeat of amendments proposed by the smaller nations in this special committee was inconsequential. In the committee, the smaller countries had formed a numerical minority, Baroody said. The concerns of the lesser-developed countries, however, deserved a fairer hearing because the smaller countries "actually represented populations which were greater in number than those represented by the majority." To the Saudi Arabian, that difference meant more than votes on a committee. And the fairer hearing he sought would come within the General Assembly.[82]

But the United States was not demanding that the convention be written to American specifications or threatening to veto the convention completely, Binder said. The Americans simply wanted a convention guaranteeing the fundamental freedom of information, and the document produced by the committee was grossly inadequate.[83] Despite Binder's objections, the committee voted to forward the two amendments for additional study. And, inadequate or not, the draft convention on freedom of information was sent on for consideration by other United Nations bodies.

AMERICAN JOURNALISTS REACT TO THE CONVENTION

American journalists greeted the draft convention with dismay and disdain, terming the document more likely "to reduce freedom of information than to increase it."[84] Stalwarts of the international free-press campaign such as Hugh Baillie, president of the United Press (UP), believed that the convention had "been captured by the enemies of freedom of the press and distorted into a monstrosity for control and regulation of the press." Such an unfortunate turn of events was not Binder's fault. In fact, Binder had performed excellently under very difficult circumstances, Baillie said, but, "if this matter is pursued toward a conclusion in other bodies of the United Nations, all who value a free press should make themselves heard" against ratification.[85]

After reading the draft convention on freedom of information, a portion of the American press wanted to boycott all additional discussions of freedom of information within the United Nations. Still others wanted the United States to withdraw completely from the United Nations.[86] Binder worried about his colleagues' reactions; he knew that "refusal of the United States to have anything to do with further attempts to draft conventions on freedom of information would not bring an end to such attempts at the U.N." In fact, the United States' withdrawal from discussions would actually help the delegates who wanted to restrict freedom of information because when present, the United States "exposes the true character of the proposals and sets the powerful case for freedom." Thus, "it would be the greatest folly to leave the field free to foes of freedom."[87]

Journalists calling for withdrawal from additional free-press discussions were upset about the tendencies toward restriction revealed in the United Nations debates and were also deeply hurt by the incessant criticisms of the American press system during those debates. Many Latin Americans, for instance, long considered by North Americans as supporters of a free-press system, had allied themselves with the Asians and Middle Easterners in condemning the American press. For some, Binder said, the change of heart was due to feelings that "their revolutions are falsely exaggerated in the American press. Some dislike the way we have reported their financial difficulties, believing that their prospects of obtaining loans, credits, or gifts from the United States are thereby prejudiced."[88] Disregarding the feelings of the rest of the world would be the greatest mistake that American journalists could make now, Binder said, noting that, personally, he believed some of the criticisms had "considerable justification." All American media, he continued, have not "exercised their responsibilities as fairly, intelligently and honestly as they should."[89]

In fact, argued Alan Barth, a member of the American Newspaper Guild, "no one familiar with the American press can very well pretend that its freedom doesn't provide a cover for some pretty serious excesses, banalities, outright untruths and offenses against decency and good taste," but these behavior patterns were insufficient to warrant the kind of suppression proposed within the United Nations.[90] Perhaps American readership patterns were a major cause of the press's problem, Herbert

Brucker, editor of the *Hartford Courant*, suggested. As a nation of headline readers, "we tend to pass by items, particularly from distant parts, that do not have a shock value. This does lead to sensationalism and at times to a distorted view of what is happening in these foreign lands."[91]

Regardless of the cause of the discontent, American journalists searched for ways to defuse the growing distrust of American media. Barth favored simply admitting outright that "the free press is a fallible, often fumbling institution. Its freedom ought to be exercised with greater responsibility. But it is indispensable to a free world."[92] Brucker, on the other hand, preferred gauging the situation somewhat more carefully. The problems encountered at the United Nations had forced him to the conclusion that "the Anglo-Saxon theory of the free press in its pure and native form will not capture the world." A form of that tradition might be triumphant, he added—if American journalists recognized that the press's success at home "made us just a bit too smug for our own good" and if press leaders developed "an acute sensitivity to the need for improvement." With changes, the American concept of the press had a better chance to win the world.[93]

Keeping American journalists in the campaign long enough to win the necessary behavioral changes would be difficult. Binder, who firmly believed that the United States must remain active in the international freedom of information arena, took his appeal to the American Society of Newspaper Editors. There he asked fellow members to remember that "we are godparents of the international approach to problems of freedom of information. We may not like the way in which the child has grown. We may strongly object to its present wayward disposition. Some may wish we had never sponsored it. We cannot deny that it is our baby." The ASNE began the free-press crusade because "our country was fighting a war which we hoped would make the world safer for our way of life. We assumed, as Americans are wont to assume, that what we find good would be found good by the rest of the world if only ways could be found to share our blessings." International agreements seemed the most logical way to spread the American free-press system abroad, so ASNE members asked the State Department for help. Remembering the movement's history was essential so that any journalists who objected to "my or the State Department's endeavors in the United Nations in connection with freedom of information issues may realize that neither I nor the State Department fathered the baby for which some have developed such a strong dislike." Instead, he was working with American diplomats "to prevent the child from becoming a grave menace to all that we hold dear and, so far as possible, to re-convert it into the liberating force which it was intended to be."[94]

Although the free-press movement had begun auspiciously with the world tour by three ASNE members, the crusade foundered in the wake of international events such as the partitioning of Palestine, the cold war between the Soviet Union and the United States, and the Korean crisis. Even so, the challenges facing international freedom of the press would be less overpowering if they originated merely with communist nations, Binder said. Then, the battle would be with only half a dozen or so members of the United Nations instead of with the majority of the organization's members. And the Soviet arguments were easier to counter. "But the painful truth is that many non-communist governments think they have much to gain and nothing to lose by placing fetters upon the kind of freedom practiced in the United States." These nations had enough votes in the United Nations "to make their suspicions and animosities a grave menace to the values and practices we cherish." Also, these nations viewed American efforts to promote international freedom of the press as primarily designed to increase the domination of American and British news agencies throughout the world. "They regard our media of information as agencies of 'cultural imperialism' against which they must protect themselves lest they become vassals of the United States or dominated by its culture which they do not esteem at all highly."[95]

Indeed, the rising tide of nationalism sweeping the world after the crumbling of former colonial empires held the free-press movement captive, according to Gilbert W. Stewart, Jr., a former journalist, who was serving as press adviser to the United States Mission to the United Nations. These peoples, "as they achieve greater degrees of political, economic and cultural independence, [want] to do things themselves, even though they do them badly." They desperately wanted to exclude all outsiders and deeply resented any outsiders beyond their control. The underdeveloped countries were highly sensitive to all forms of imperialism, including the cultural imperialism allegedly practiced by major international news media. This resentment focused on three factors: most of their news about the world came from sources controlled by other countries; their own way of life was transmitted to the rest of the world by foreigners; and they never could correct "misrepresentations" of news events in their countries distributed by others.[96] Using the forum provided by the United Nations, the smaller nations sought restitution from the United States press for perceived mistreatment in any form possible—including the adoption of restrictive conventions.

Complicating the issue, Binder said, was expert Soviet propaganda that exploited the fears of Arab, Asiatic, and Latin American countries seeking the restrictions on freedom of information. These countries were fearful of "becoming involved in the propaganda battle of the cold war and a shooting war if one should develop." These middle-of-the-road nations considered the American struggle with Russia a great power rivalry that they wished to avoid.[97] Despite the problems and the rather gloomy outlook for an American victory, Binder urged his colleagues to continue the crusade that they had started.

Giving impetus to Binder's arguments was an event that riveted the attention of American journalists on Prague, Czechoslovakia, for two years. In 1951, the Czechoslovak government arrested William N. Oatis, an American citizen and chief of the Associated Press bureau in Prague, and charged him with participating in activities hostile to the nation, gathering and disseminating information that the government considered secret, and spreading malicious stories about Czechoslovakia. The charges sounded suspiciously similar to language in various restrictive clauses of the freedom of information convention and human rights covenant. At the moment, *Editor & Publisher* saw the similarity as a reason to continue the United Nations fight in an effort to deprive totalitarian states of any shred of international approval for such despicable acts.[98]

The State Department supported Binder's position within the special freedom of information committee. Ernest E. Gross, acting United States representative to the United Nations, officially informed Secretary-General Trygve Lie that the American government found the freedom of information convention as written by the special committee "not consistent with long established and deeply cherished principles of freedom of speech and freedom of the press" practiced in America. Consequently, the United States would not support the convention during debates before various United Nations bodies and would oppose a call for a special international conference to ratify the document.[99] Although anticipating that the United States would ultimately be defeated in its efforts to block the freedom of information convention, *Editor & Publisher* still praised the State Department's stand and called for "commendation from the press of America for its forthright support of the principles of freedom of information."[100]

The Social Committee, an ad hoc committee of the Economic and Social Council, discussed the draft convention on freedom of information in August 1951. Its members focused on the wisdom of calling a meeting of plenipotentiaries to put the document into final form for signature. Favorite topics for debate reappeared once more as Social Committee members repeated points already heard within special committee sessions. Social Committee members, however, sensitive to the deep divisions among nations and reflecting a slightly different composition as well, refused to convene the requested special conference for final action on the freedom of information convention.[101] The only other positive result of the Social Committee meetings from the American standpoint was passage of a resolution, a direct outgrowth of Oatis's imprisonment in Czechoslovakia, calling for nations to protect the rights of foreign correspondents to gather and transmit news. Delegates adopted the resolution by a vote of thirteen to three, with the three negative votes coming from Czechoslovakia, Poland, and the Union of Soviet Socialist Republics.[102]

As the Social Committee considered the special committee's report on the freedom of information convention, the American Bar Association unloaded another salvo against all international freedom of information agreements. Writing in June 1951, Hanson, general counsel for the American Newspaper Publishers Association, claimed that the human rights covenant would sanction actions such as those taken by Juan Perón in Argentina in March 1951, when, after years of persecution, he shut down *La Prensa*, one of the hemisphere's leading newspapers. Furthermore, Hanson feared that governments could warp treaty language so that its provisions could be interpreted as approving recent Spanish actions demanding that correspondents pledge to publish corrections for any errors in stories in return for a visa to enter that country.[103] And in August 1951, the ABA again warned that, under a possible interpretation of the treaty power in the United States Constitution, American adoption of the freedom of the information convention could force the imposition of restrictions listed in the convention on the press in the United States.[104]

Comments from bar association members and the prominence given them caused much consternation among convention supporters. Chafee, as chairman of the ABA's section on international and comparative law, disputed the claims made by Hanson and other ABA members. As an early architect of American freedom of information policy, Chafee was especially concerned when the legal doubts spread to the news-gathering convention, which the General Assembly had already approved. According to critics, the news-gathering convention would legalize the judicial travesty known as the Oatis trial and hinder efforts to win his release. These same critics claimed that convention language broadened the power of both the Congress and the president to legislate on information-related matters traditionally considered beyond their reach. None of these fears was valid regarding the news-gathering convention, Chafee said, for the document's protections applied only to foreign correspondents and would not affect the relationship between reporters in the United States and the American government. Nor would the news-gathering convention change Oatis's legal situation. American journalists enjoyed exactly the same protection in foreign countries as any other American traveling abroad, and conditions would not change regardless of whether the news-gathering convention was ratified. Although Chafee insisted that the press had "nothing to fear from the Convention, and much to hope" from the document's adoption, he won few converts.[105]

ASNE MEMBERS DEBATE CONTINUING THE FREE-PRESS CRUSADE

Legal arguments against the news-gathering convention won numerous adherents within journalistic groups, as a faction within the American Society of Newspaper Editors began calling for the total abandonment of the international freedom of information effort, including the news-gathering treaty. Despite this change of attitude, the society must not apologize for its early efforts in the field, said opposition leader JS Gray, editor of the *Monroe* (Michigan) *Evening News.* "No defense is needed for the completely worthy motives which prompted us in the early postwar period to favor effort on the diplomatic front seeking broader commitments between nations to free news channels of government controls, restrictions and coercions; and to safeguard those engaged in the gathering and transmission of news." Likewise, "no defense can be adequate . . . to explain a failure on our part NOW to record our ringing denunciation of the perversion of these principles in UN councils."[106]

Defending the news-gathering convention was Canham, who helped frame the draft that suddenly had become so controversial. To Canham, current concerns were primarily political, and "the arguments against the treaty are grossly exaggerated and distorted" and even "demagogic." The idea that adoption of the news-gathering convention sanctioned espionage trials of journalists was particularly offensive. "The treaty contains no provision about prosecution of foreign newspaper correspondents for espionage, which was the crime charged against Mr. Oatis." Any government could charge any newspaper correspondent truly or falsely with espionage, and the convention neither permitted nor barred such actions.[107]

In fact, Canham said, American journalists knew quite well that the United States would never sign a treaty that "prevented us from trying foreigners in our midst for espionage or for committing other serious crimes, and it would be folly to give up the right of enforcing other criminal laws." Arguments about the convention's granting anyone authority over domestic news gathering were absurd, Canham said, adding, "let us not invent dangers where they do not exist." Despite the sincerity of Canham's comments, even the former ASNE president did not believe that the news-gathering convention would be signed and ratified, especially since most of the delegates regarded the document "as a major concession to the United States and American newspapers and agencies." Actually, Canham had lost confidence in advancing international freedom of information through treaties and diplomacy. Now, the best hope for international freedom of information rested on interpersonal relations among journalists themselves.[108]

While this argument raged within the newspaper community, the State Department was planning for the anticipated discussion of the draft convention on freedom of information in the General Assembly in early 1952. The United States delegation intended to encourage an indefinite postponement of discussion on the convention. The primary American objection to finishing work on the draft was well known—any convention written under existing circumstances "would emerge in a form unacceptable to the United States and detrimental to this Government's efforts to promote worldwide acceptance of our concept of freedom of information."

Not only that, but such a document would be "a serious setback to the promotion of freedom of information by the United Nations whether or not the United States and a few like-minded countries adhered to it, because it would place a United Nations stamp of approval on a number of restrictive practices which, though current in many countries, do not now enjoy international sanction."[109]

When formal instructions on the freedom of information convention went out to the United States delegation at the United Nations in late 1951, delegates were told to stress that the United States found "no indication that the press in any free nation favors this Convention." In fact, journalists in several countries actually were fighting "similar restrictions which have been enacted, or are being considered for enactment, in the laws of their countries," and the prestige of the United Nations must not be perverted into sanctioning such limitations. The delegation must oppose calling a special meeting of plenipotentiaries to work on the convention as well. If outvoted, as was likely, American delegates then were to seek a broadening of the conference agenda to allow the introduction of a new, more liberal document.[110]

The dilemma facing the American government was obvious. Although the government would welcome a convention that advanced and protected freedom of speech and of the press internationally, the United States opposed the existing text. A main point of contention was the assumption that seemed "to underlie much of the present text, namely that the pressing task of the moment is to define ways and means by which governments may curb the reporting of news which they consider undesirable." In the State Department's view, any proposal that might impose additional limits on the availability of information throughout the world would "be singularly inappropriate at this time when governmental restrictions on the flow of news threaten increasingly to deprive the public of the information which it needs to form conclusions on the many vital problems affecting world peace."[111]

Continued concern about growing international tendencies to restrict freedom of information led the State Department to convene an extraordinary meeting with several leading journalists in October 1952. World attitudes on free-press issues had deteriorated significantly over the years, and departmental officials sought suggestions from professional journalists on appropriate future actions. Press leaders attending the special session in New York included Canham; Robert L. Frey, of the United Press, who had served as an adviser at the Geneva conference; Lester Markel, Sunday editor of *The New York Times* and founder of the International Press Institute; Williams, ANPA general manager; and Frank Starzel, who had become general manager of the Associated Press on Kent Cooper's retirement in 1948.[112]

To convene such a stellar group of American journalists, the State

Department had argued successfully that departmental planners considered increased restrictions on freedom of information "one of the foremost threats to free journalism today." Such actions by foreign powers could limit both the amount of information reaching the United States and its accuracy. This, then, would "warp the attitudes of our people toward foreign problems" and threaten "the accuracy of the basic foreign policy decisions of the people and of the Government." The invitation also stressed that the department thought that the reasons other countries gave for supporting their restraints on freedom of information were "evidence of deep-seated conditions which will give rise to other actions restricting the press even if we are successful in side-tracking the restrictionist convention in the General Assembly." Consequently, both the attitudes of foreign governments and pending information proposals needed "the most careful scrutiny by the best minds among the American information media in order that there may be a wider awareness of the problem and a wider effort—both within and outside the U.S. Government—to stem the restrictionist tide."[113]

When the experts' discussion turned to the freedom of information convention, Walter M. Kotschnig, director of the office of United Nations economic and social affairs, reported that the State Department believed that the convention had "grown into such a monster that there is just nothing that we can do but to oppose it with everything we have." Press representatives concurred with Canham, who believed that freedom of information was an area in which international legislation was impossible "now or in any visible future."[114] In fact, the journalists agreed that the American delegation to the United Nations must abandon international accords as the solution to world free-press problems and, instead, stress new points in debates, including positive American contributions to the development of freedom of information. These positive contributions, according to the journalists, involved official and private efforts "to promote the exchange of journalists, or to arrange for visits of journalists, newspaper editors and owners, et cetera to the United States."[115] Journalists attending the New York meeting also sought to convert State Department officials to their belief "that the press in most countries was much less 'restrictionist' than their governments and that by and large the press did not agree with the kind of restrictions which governments attempted to write into such conventions."[116] Regardless of the accuracy of the journalists' evaluation, the diplomats left the meeting elated because, as Kotschnig reported, "for once the United States Government and the United States mass media appeared to be really at one on the major issues of policy."[117]

One major issue of free-press policy that remained of great concern to both press and diplomats was the news-gathering and right of reply convention, which had been pigeonholed since 1949. American delegates had tried—unsuccessfully—to free the news-gathering convention and to open the document for signature several times. Instructions transmitted to American representatives at the United Nations in late 1951, in preparation for General Assembly sessions of early 1952, approved another attempt at opening the news-gathering convention for ratification. Although the State Department had acquiesced to the requests of other nations to postpone opening the convention for signature until the completion of the freedom of information convention, American diplomats had never considered the two documents as interdependent. In early 1952, they emphasized this separateness by noting, "With the increase in political tensions and the growth of totalitarian regimes following the war, the operations of foreign correspondents and news agencies have been increasingly subjected to restrictions and harassment, with a resulting curtailment in the international flow of news." The Oatis case illustrated the problem in the extreme. The news-gathering convention, which was designed "to provide an international norm for the treatment of foreign correspondents and an agreed limit on peacetime censorship of news despatches," could alleviate some problems encountered regularly by correspondents. And, with the convention's provision for a right of correction, "which has proved acceptable to a majority of governments," the convention would "meet a need which has been loudly proclaimed by those states which have not yet managed to develop strong news agencies."[118]

The possibility of opening the news-gathering treaty for signature was not warmly greeted in American journalistic quarters. Doubts about possible effects of the treaty were rampant. Despite early commentaries praising the news-gathering convention by Geneva conference delegates Canham, Sevellon Brown, and Harry Martin, Editor & Publisher now warned that the document under consideration by the United Nations was not the same convention as drafted in Geneva. On its face, the statement was indeed true, but the revision, guided by Canham in 1949, had been praised at the time. In 1951, the trade journal changed its mind, arguing "that the treaty would be absolutely ineffective, would accomplish nothing in promoting the free international transmission of news. A few sections of it are so liable to double interpretation that it would not change the status quo in any country that signed it." Even worse, nations without censorship systems now could establish censorship in peacetime "for reasons of 'national defense' under the authorization of this treaty." Consequently, Editor & Publisher advocated leaving the document on the shelf where it had languished since 1949.[119]

Once again, however, press organizations had anticipated action by the United Nations, and the bureaucratic structure of the international organization barely moved. The General Assembly session of February 1952 postponed consideration of the issue until the fall because preparatory discussions in its Third Committee bogged down in debates about the Oatis case.[120] By mid-1952, the State Department joined members of the press in changing its opinion of the news-gathering convention. In debates before the

Social Committee of the Economic and Social Council, for instance, Kotschnig said that the United States government was convinced that world conditions made multilateral conventions on journalistic topics impossible. If the United States participated in any international accords on freedom of information at all, the American government favored reverting to the earlier idea of bilateral agreements. Such limited agreements with "countries with analogous ideas and of a similar level of development" could be expanded as circumstances required. One reason for the change of heart, Kotschnig explained, was the inclusion of the right of correction within the news-gathering convention. Once strongly supportive of merging the two documents, the American government's position had been undermined by the increasing propaganda campaigns of the cold war as well as by the growing uncertainties about the impact that the convention might have on national law—uncertainties that had been fed so successfully by ABA and other critics of all proposed free-press accords. The State Department now believed that such a convention "would impose on governments a moral, if not a legal, obligation to ensure that their national press published corrections which might easily be contrary to the truth and designed for propaganda purposes only and even to adopt legislative measures for coercing their information organs."[121]

The decision to withdraw American support from the news-gathering convention was made after much careful deliberation, Kotschnig told the news executives gathered in October 1952. Departmental advisers did not believe that the Americans could win enough support to open the news-gathering convention for signature in the first place. Even if the votes could be found to remove the news-gathering accord from the shelf, the department worried about the increasing domestic criticism of clauses that instituted a right of correction, which were an integral part of the treaty. The new State Department position on the right of correction contradicted earlier statements about how similar the right of reply was to American practices of running corrections for stories containing errors and about the noncoercive nature of the correction provisions. Now, the department feared that those same right of reply provisions could be used to export propaganda by countries that were clever enough to manipulate the convention's terms into a perversion of its drafters' intent.[122]

As Kotschnig told the assembled news executives, "The more we look at this right of correction, the more we see what is happening in the various countries, the more we are afraid that this right of correction could be abused by various governments." Under this provision, governments could use the State Department "as another channel for their propaganda, because what the right of correction really means is that if someone says that a news item was wrong, was not true, then the government of the contracting state can demand that the foreign office—which would be our State Department—make available a reply." This did not mean that the press had to print the correction, but "we would be saddled with continuous hand-outs from Russia, Poland, and so forth." In addition to such new concerns, the State Department believed that by opposing the opening of the news-gathering convention for signature, the United States strengthened its overall position: "We can simply say this is not the climate for conventions. You can't legislate in that field. If we made an exception in this case, our position on the others would be weakened. By taking this overall position that we don't want any conventions in this field, we think that our position opposing the other conventions is strong." News executives present at the 1952 session offered no objections to the department's plans, thus effectively ending the main thrust of the free-press crusade at the United Nations.[123]

Third Committee members discussed the freedom of information convention again in fall 1952, but once more a United Nations body was unable to make any progress on a freedom of information topic. Debates reiterated issues by now quite familiar to international freedom of information discussions. The one move made by the United Nations in the area of freedom of information concerned the joint convention on international news gathering and the right of correction. France, the author of the Geneva document from which the right of correction segment of the merged convention stemmed, proposed severing the international right of reply provisions from the news-gathering convention. The United States successfully stymied the French attempt to separate the two conventions in the Social Committee of the Economic and Social Council and opposed the French effort to develop a separate right of correction convention in the General Assembly as well. State Department planners believed that separation of the draft right of reply convention from the news-gathering convention was dangerous because many nations would adopt the former convention, which imposed certain obligations on the information media, while ignoring the latter accord, which granted certain protections to foreign correspondents.[124] Arguments that the American delegates pursued within the General Assembly stressed the idea that a right of correction convention alone would not contribute "to the affirmative concept of freedom of information, but would only encourage propaganda and cross propaganda through attempts to correct news stories which, in the opinion of one government, were not accurate and would tend to put even more governmental pressure on news media." If the nations of the world perceived the need for an international right of correction, American delegates argued that the best way to institute such a practice was through bilateral treaties or through normal diplomatic channels.[125]

United States opposition notwithstanding, the General Assembly voted, twenty-five to twenty-two, to send the right of correction convention out for signature as a separate document. The news-gathering convention remained shelved. Included among the nations voting against separating the two documents were the Soviet bloc nations and the United States.[126] With this vote and in light of the abysmal record of the United Nations on freedom of information topics, *Editor & Publisher* decided, "If the delegates of the United Nations cannot agree on doing something constructive to foster the growth of free press freedom throughout the world, then they ought to refrain from doing anything."[127]

NOTES

1. "Freedom of Information," *E&P*, January 7, 1950, p. 32.
2. E/CN.4/433/Rev.2, *Draft International Covenant on Human Rights: Revised Text of the United States Proposal for Article 17*, April 20, 1950.
3. E/CN.4/SR.160, 6th Session, April 19, 1950, pp. 9, 11.
4. Ibid., pp. 10, 12.
5. E/CN.4/SR.161, 6th Session, April 19, 1950, p. 18.
6. Ibid., p. 19.
7. E/CN.4/SR.162, 6th Session, April 20, 1950, pp. 5, 13.
8. E/CN.4/SR.163, 6th Session, April 20, 1950, p. 11.
9. E/CN.4/SR.165, 6th Session, April 21, 1950, p. 5. In some United Nations debates on the subject, private interference in an individual's right to freedom of information had been interpreted to mean the interference of private enterprise—in particular large American news agencies or newspaper chains—in the flow of information.
10. E/CN.4/SR.164, 6th Session, April 21, 1950, pp. 3, 8, 5.
11. Ibid., p. 12.
12. E/CN.4/SR.163, 6th Session, April 20, 1950, pp. 3–4.
13. Ibid., pp. 5, 11, 9.
14. E/CN.4/SR.165, 6th Session, April 21, 1950, pp. 15–16.
15. E/CN.4/SR.166, 6th Session, April 24, 1950, pp. 7, 11.
16. E/CN.4/SR.167, 6th Session, April 24, 1950, pp. 4, 8–9.
17. Draft First International Covenant on Human Rights, *Yearbook on Human Rights for 1950*, New York, United Nations, 1951, p. 460. The restrictions article proposed by the United States read: "The right to seek, receive and impart information and ideas shall be subject only to such limitations as are provided by law and necessary in the interest of national security, public order, safety, health or morals, or for the protection of the rights, reputation or freedoms of other persons." See E/CN.4/433/Rev.2, 6th Session, *Revised Text of the United States Proposal for Article 17*, April 20, 1950.
18. Ibid., pp. 458–63.
19. *The Yearbook of the United Nations: 1952*, Lake Success, N.Y., United Nations Department of Public Information, 1953, p. 447. Among the bodies discussing the covenant: the Commission on Human Rights, the Social Committee of the Economic and Social Council, the Economic and Social Council, the Third Committee of the General Assembly, and the General Assembly itself. Each time, the document went back to the Commission on Human Rights for additional work.
20. "'Compromise' Drawn on Covenant Art. 17," *E&P*, April 29, 1950, p. 132.

21. Erwin Canham, Report, April 20, 1950, *Problems of Journalism—1950*, pp. 43–45.
22. Ibid., pp. 45–46.
23. "Bar Group Says UN Treaties Threaten Press," *E&P*, November 4, 1950, p. 26.
    The Bar report said:
    For what standard of free speech would we be fighting for under the banner of the United Nations—the standard of the covenant or the standard of the constitution of the United States? Which standard shall we teach and advocate for the world?
    The question seems to be deeper than all that. Is this part of the persistent demand for a dominant state? Freedom of speech and information simply cannot be permitted in such a state. Examples around us confirm that beyond all question.
    These definitions (of free speech and press) if agreed to by us are a legal and moral admission that the definition of our founding fathers is a miserable mistake.
    Quoted in "SDX Opposes UN Proposal on Press; Cites Alternative," *Quill*, January 1951, p. 12.
24. "Bar Report," *E&P*, November 11, 1950, p. 38.
25. *See*, e.g., Margaret A. Blanchard, "Freedom of the Press and the Newspaper Code: June 1933–February 1934," *Journalism Quarterly* 54 (Spring 1977): 40–49.
26. "Covenant Imposes Restraint, Hanson Says," *E&P*, November 18, 1950, p. 6.
27. Robert U. Brown, "Sigma Delta Chi Condemns Language of UN Covenant," *E&P*, November 18, 1950, p. 7.
28. "SDX Opposes UN Proposal on Press, Cites Alternative," p. 12.
29. Ibid.
30. *Missouri* v. *Holland*, 252 U.S. 416 (1920).
31. Malcolm Bauer, "Article 14 of the Covenant on Human Rights: Is It Constitutional?" *Nieman Reports*, April 1951, p. 17.
32. Ibid., p. 20.
33. Elisha Hanson, "Tyranny by Covenant," *Quill*, July 1951, p. 12.
34. Ibid., p. 14.
35. George E. Sokolsky, "Could United Nations Treaty Nullify U.S. Law? Test Case Says Yes," *Quill*, July 1951, p. 17.
36. Hanson, "Tyranny by Covenant," p. 12.
37. Neill H. Alford, "He Sees No U.N. Threat to Bill of Rights," *Quill*, July 1951, pp. 15–16.
38. "Senator Bricker Charges: UN Treaty Imperils Press Freedom," *E&P*, July 28, 1951, p. 10.
39. "Professor Chafee Defends: Freedom Lovers Wrote Each Phrase," E&P, July 28, 1951, pp. 11, 60. *See also* Zechariah Chafee, Jr., "Legal Problems of Freedom of Information in the United Nations," *Law and Contemporary Problems* 14 (Autumn 1949): 545–83.
40. Position Paper Prepared in the Department of State, September 2, 1950, *FR: 1950*, II:526.
41. ECOR, 11th session, 404th meeting, August 9, 1950, pp. 257–61.
42. Position Paper Prepared in the Department of State, p. 527.

43. Ibid., p. 528.
44. Ibid., p. 529.
45. United States Delegation Working Paper, October 18, 1950, *FR: 1950*, II: 530–31.
46. Minutes of the Thirty-fifth Meeting of the United States Delegation to the General Assembly, November 8, 1950, *FR: 1950*, II: 532.
47. Kathleen Teltsch, "Information Treaty Up for Debate Again," *E&P*, November 18, 1950, p. 6.
48. "UN Treaty," *E&P*, November 25, 1950, p. 36.
49. Kathleen Teltsch, "Small Nations' Plan for Info Parley Gains," *E&P*, December 2, 1950, p. 27.
50. A/AC.42/SR.1, January 15, 1951, pp. 4, 7.
51. A/AC.42/SR.2, January 16, 1951, pp. 3–5.
52. Ibid., pp. 6–7.
53. A/AC.42/SR.3, January 17, 1951, pp. 11–12, 14.
54. Ibid., pp. 5–6.
55. Ibid., pp. 6–10.
56. Robert U. Brown, "Shop Talk at Thirty," *E&P*, January 20, 1951, p. 64.
57. Kathleen Teltsch, "UN Efforts to Draw Up Freedom of Information Treaty Snarled by Maneuvers to Write in Curbs," *Guild Reporter*, January 26, 1951, p. 2.
58. A/AC.42/SR.6, January 19, 1951, pp. 4–5. Another Soviet delegate later criticized the American press for advocating rearmament and preparation for war. The Yugoslav delegate, representing a nation that once strongly supported the Russian warmongering campaign, ruefully asked how the Soviet propaganda campaign against Yugoslavia fell outside the parameters of warmongering. *See* A/AC.42/SR.7, January 19, 1951, pp. 8, 12.
59. A/AC.42/SR.7, January 19, 1951, pp. 4–6, 2.
60. A/AC.42/SR.9, January 22, 1951, pp. 5–6, 8.
61. A/AC.42/SR.11, January 23, 1951, pp. 2–4.
62. A/AC.42/SR.12, January 24, 1951, pp. 2–3.
63. Ibid., pp. 4, 6, 9, 16.
64. A/AC.42/SR.13, January 26, 1951, pp. 2–7.
65. Background Paper on Draft Convention on Freedom of Information, Confidential Background Book, Freedom of Information, Fifth Session, General Assembly 1950, SD/A/C.3/115/Rev.2, SDR, p. 3.
66. A/AC.42/SR.13, January 26, 1951, pp. 11–13.
67. A/AC.42/SR.14, January 26, 1951, p. 2.
68. Ibid., pp. 4–5. Binder tried to soothe the Egyptian's feelings by explaining that American magazines often went to press weeks before actual distribution of the issues in question and that several editors might feature the same story because of newsworthiness rather than an intentional attempt to abuse a particular country. *See* Ibid., p. 6. The Pakistani's reference apparently was to an American motion picture about Fatima, the daughter of Mohammed.
69. Ibid., pp. 9, 12.
70. Ibid., p. 12.
71. A/AC.42/SR.15, January 29, 1951, p. 7.
72. A/AC.42/SR.19, January 31, 1951, p. 11.

73. A/AC.42/SR.17, January 30, 1951, pp. 5, 8–9. Erwin Canham worried lest Binder was fighting a losing battle against representatives from Latin America and the Middle East, where "there is a heightened feeling of nationalism and a deep resentment at the way in which national affairs have been treated by the American press." He called on journalists throughout the country to support Binder "in the uphill job he faces at Lake Success in making clear to other governments the position which is so fundamental to us." *See* Erwin D. Canham, "The Problem at Lake Success," *ASNE Bulletin*, February 1, 1951, p. 1.

74. A/AC.42/SR.19, January 31, 1951, p. 2.

75. Ibid., p. 14.

76. A/AC.42/L.27, *Text of Paragraph 1 of Article 2 Adopted at the 19th Meeting of the Committee on the Draft Convention on Freedom of Information on 31 January 1951*, February 1, 1951.

77. A/AC.42/SR.23, February 2, 1951, pp. 10–11. The suggested change came from the Lebanese delegate.

78. A/AC.42/SR.25, February 5, 1951, pp. 3–5, 7–8.

79. A/AC.42/L.18/Rev.1, *Egypt, India, Pakistan, Saudi Arabia: Amendment to Article 2 of the Draft Convention on Freedom of Information*, January 23, 1951.

80. A/AC.42/L.22, *Yugoslavia: Amendment to Article 2 of the Draft Convention on Freedom of Information Proposed by the United Nations Conference on Freedom of Information*, January 25, 1951.

81. A/AC.42/SR.25, February 5, 1951, pp. 9–11.

82. Ibid., pp. 11–13.

83. Ibid., p. 14.

84. "UN Convention," *E&P*, February 10, 1951, p. 40.

85. "Baillie Calls Treaty Regulatory 'Monstrosity'," *E&P*, February 10, 1951, p. 67.

86. Carroll Binder, "The Shadow of Global Censorship," *Saturday Review of Literature*, March 24, 1951, p. 35.

87. Carroll Binder, "A Clarification and Reply," *ASNE Bulletin*, March 1, 1951, p. 3.

88. Binder, "The Shadow of Global Censorship," p. 8.

89. Carroll Binder, Report, April 21, 1951, *Problems of Journalism—1951*, p. 192.

90. Alan Barth, "Washington Roundup," *Guild Reporter*, April 13, 1951, p. 8.

91. Herbert Brucker, "Storing Up Trouble," *Saturday Review of Literature*, May 26, 1951, p. 22.

92. Barth, "Washington Roundup," p. 8.

93. Brucker, "Storing Up Trouble," pp. 22–23.

94. Binder, Report, *Problems of Journalism—1951*, pp. 188–89.

95. Ibid., pp. 189–90, 192.

96. Gilbert W. Stewart, Jr., "World Threat to Free Press," *Quill*, July 1951, p. 6.

97. Binder, Report, *Problems of Journalism—1951*, pp. 194–95.

98. "Stay with It," *E&P*, May 5, 1951, p. 34. *See* Chapter 8 for more details on the Oatis incident.

99. "U.S. Voices Objection to Information Treaty," *E&P*, June 30, 1951, p. 53.

100. "Draft Convention," *E&P*, June 30, 1951, p. 36.

101. "UN Drops Parley Plan for Info Pact," *E&P*, August 25, 1951, p. 59. Both the

United States and the Union of Soviet Socialist Republics voted against the special session.

102. E/AC.7/SR.204, 13th session, August 16, 1951, p. 13.

103. Elisha Hanson, "Freedom of the Press: Is It Threatened in the United Nations?" *American Bar Association Journal* 37 (June 1951): 417–20, 477–78.

104. Frank E. Holman, "The Convention on Freedom of Information: A Threat to Freedom of Speech in America," *American Bar Association Journal* 37 (August 1951): 567–70, 635. Fears about the extent to which the treaty power infringed on constitutional guarantees led the American Bar Association to propose a constitutional amendment that would cancel the effectiveness of any treaty provision contrary to existing constitutional language. *See* William H. Fitzpatrick, "News-Gathering Treaty Called Threat to Constitutional Rights," *ASNE Bulletin*, June 1, 1952, pp. 6, 8.

105. "Chafee Refutes Opinion Given on UN Treaty," *E&P*, March 1, 1952, p. 11.

106. JS Gray, "Is News-Gathering Treaty a Menace? 'Mocks Traditions to Which Society Is Committed'," *ASNE Bulletin*, April 1, 1952, p. 3 (emphasis in original).

107. Erwin D. Canham, "Is News-Gathering Treaty a Menace? 'Arguments Against It Exaggerated and Distorted'," *ASNE Bulletin*, April 1, 1952, p. 3.

108. Ibid., p. 4.

109. Department of State Instruction to the United States Delegation to the Sixth Regular Session of the General Assembly, October 10, 1951, *FR: 1951*, II: 792.

110. Ibid., p. 794.

111. Ibid., p. 793.

112. Transcript, Consultative Conference on Freedom of Information Composed of Press, Radio, and Motion Picture Representatives [hereinafter cited as Transcript, Consultative Conference on Freedom of Information], October 1, 1952, 402.3.1952 FOI Consultative Group, SDR, p. 1. Carroll Binder, United States delegate at the special committee sessions to write the freedom of information convention and member of the Subcommission on Freedom of Information and of the Press, was invited to the conference but was unable to attend.

113. Gilbert W. Stewart, Jr., United States Mission to the United Nations, to James Green, Office of United Nations Economic and Social Affairs, September 11, 1952, 402.3.1952 FOI Consultative Group, SDR.

114. Transcript, Consultative Conference on Freedom of Information, p. 35.

115. Walter Kotschnig, Director, Office of United Nations Economic and Social Affairs, to James Simsarian, United States Delegate to the United Nations, October 6, 1952, 402.3.1952 FOI Consultative Group, SDR.

116. Walter Kotschnig, Director, Office of United Nations Economic and Social Affairs, to James Simsarian, United States Delegate to the United Nations, October 8, 1952, 402.3.1952 FOI Consultative Group, SDR.

117. Kotschnig to Simsarian, October 6, 1952.

118. Department of State Instruction to the United States Delegation, pp. 795–96.

119. "News Treaty," *E&P*, September 22, 1951, p. 38.

120. Editorial Note, *FR: 1951*, II: 820–21.

121. E/AC.7/SR.215, 14th session, June 17, 1952, pp. 6–7.

122. Transcript, Consultative Conference on Freedom of Information, pp. 40–41.

123. Ibid., pp. 41–42.

124. Ibid., p. 45.
125. Draft Position Paper on Freedom of Information, Seventh Regular Session of the General Assembly, September 15, 1952, 402.3.1952 FOI Consultative Group, SDR, p. 6.
126. Kathleen Teltsch, "UN Asks Signatures on Correction Treaty," *E&P*, December 20, 1952, p. 8.
127. "UN Treaties," *E&P*, November 15, 1952, p. 38.

CHAPTER 7

The Crusade's Last Chance at the United Nations

The last remaining hope for the free-press crusade within the United Nations resided with the Subcommission on Freedom of Information and of the Press, the body of experts in which American delegates to the Geneva conference placed so much hope. Delegates to the Geneva conference had recommended extending the subcommission's life and giving that body the responsibility for studying and recommending action on free-press issues. The United States delegation had wanted to grant the subcommission additional authority over freedom of information matters. American diplomats at the United Nations even hoped to elevate the subcommission to full, permanent commission status under the Economic and Social Council, to create an expert staff for the new commission within the secretariat, and to establish a schedule calling for the new commission to meet twice a year.[1]

Instead, the United Nations simply renewed the subcommission's charter along much the same lines as its initial grant in 1947. Except for retaining the subcommission's expert status rather than having its members serve as representatives of their home governments, American proposals for the rechartered subcommission disappeared. The subcommission maintained its subsidiary role within the United Nations organization, with its meeting times subject to approval by the Economic and Social Council and other supervisory bodies and its staff support pulled from workers also assigned to other tasks. Rechartered shortly after the 1948 Geneva conference, the second Subcommission on Freedom of Information and of the Press drew its members from the United States, United Kingdom, France, China, the Soviet Union, Lebanon, Egypt, Yugoslavia, India, the Philippines, Chile, and Uruguay.[2] Members convened for the first time in May 1949. As the debates progressed, the subcommission's composition revealed that any hopes for that group to make substantial progress on freedom of information topics along the lines desired by the United States were sadly misplaced. Among the subcommission's members were some of the most vociferous critics of the American press system in the United Nations.

Controversy even preceded the sessions. Days before the first meeting, Karim Azkoul of Lebanon announced plans to seek subcommission support for underdeveloped countries that wanted to build national information agencies, an ambition first revealed at Geneva. In fact, Azkoul even wanted American financial help in establishing these agencies through President Harry S. Truman's Point IV program of technical assistance to developing nations. Although Azkoul planned to promote his program, he promised to wait for a "favorable" atmosphere within the subcommission before introducing the proposal.[3]

MEMBERS TRY TO ESTABLISH THE SUBCOMMISSION'S AGENDA

Whether Azkoul would ever find such a climate within the subcommission was extremely doubtful. Delegates could barely agree on items for the official agenda; achieving consensus on controversial proposals probably would be impossible. One of the subcommission's initial tasks was to establish a list of priorities for study and debate. This agenda setting effort clearly revealed the personal interests of many delegates. For instance, Carroll Binder, the American delegate, thought that the most important item for subcommission discussion was determining who supplied the world's news and evaluating how satisfactory that news was. André Géraud of France believed that implementing the Geneva conventions was the subcommission's most important task, while Devadas Gandhi of India wanted to discuss promoting freedom of information and reducing the number of obstacles to it.[4] Vasily M. Zonov of the Soviet Union, of course, insisted on emphasizing the kind of news distributed throughout the world, still contending that the news must promote peace and be free of warmongering propaganda.[5] The issues were the same as in previous United Nations debates; in fact, so too were some of the participants.

Material shortages, including the adequacy of the world's newsprint supply—discussed briefly at Geneva—were of paramount importance to Francis Williams, the United Kingdom's delegate. The limited international supply of newsprint had forced newspapers in his country to cut their sizes, making it difficult for publications to give the people the news necessary for them to survive in an increasingly complex world. Great Britain rationed newsprint, with the formula based on the percentage of newsprint consumed in 1938. This procedure helped some newspapers, but the formula kept new publications, which might be more interested in highlighting the "new philosophies, new ideas and movements" of the postwar world, from starting.[6] Gandhi brought up the now standard complaints about the poor distribution of the world's newsprint supplies. The realignment of newsprint distribution was a key to removing obstacles to international freedom of information. Obviously, he said, in criticizing what he perceived to be the wasteful use of newsprint by United States media, American publications must make sacrifices to help other countries suffering from severe shortages of newsprint.[7]

Another limitation on the world's access to information, Azkoul of Lebanon said, was the nonexistence of news agencies in many of the lesser-developed countries. Technical assistance to counter this imbalance was just as important, he implied, as finding more newsprint to allow the more developed countries to increase the size of their publications.[8] So, Azkoul introduced his promised resolution asking the Economic and Social Council to "pay special attention to the encouragement and development of national information agencies in countries where these are under-developed." In this way, these agencies could "be strengthened and the flow of information accordingly increased with a view to improving understand-ing between peoples and developing friendly relations among nations."[9] Binder expressed confusion over Azkoul's suggestion about promoting national news agencies. Although sympathizing with the desire to develop better facilities to allow the people of the world to receive more information, if the proposal meant using government funds to develop national informa-tion agencies in fifty-nine countries, Binder opposed it. Private enterprise was a far better way to develop news agencies, he said, pointing with pride to American news agencies, which were "developed by the efforts, risks and sacrifices" of individuals or organizations using private funds "without regard to profits to provide news." He simply could not recommend using Point IV monies, which would come from American taxpayers, to create official news services in each country of the world.[10]

Binder's objections were peculiarly American and did not apply to the problems facing underdeveloped nations, Williams pointed out. Aid for news agencies in underdeveloped countries was essential, although he did not know the most expeditious way to provide the needed assistance. Conse-quently, Williams suggested further study rather than expressing immediate support for the development of national news agencies.[11] But additional research was unnecessary, Azkoul protested. In fact, the situation was so critical that the opportunity to establish any national agencies might be lost if United Nations support hinged on the outcome of lengthy deliberations. Perhaps his terminology had been imprecise. In using the term national information agencies, Azkoul said he actually meant aiding insufficiently developed private agencies rather than creating governmental institutions, which might be more easily opposed. Binder's unwillingness to use Amer-ican funds to develop news agencies abroad caught the attention of Roberto Fontaina of Uruguay, who thought that the American's attitude was somewhat hypocritical. Noting the burgeoning United States information program that was spreading news about America far and wide, Fontaina pointed out that the United States could undertake such a program by using its own resources. Governments of the underdeveloped countries were largely dependent on foreign information agencies for the circulation of news about themselves and the world. Underdeveloped countries should be able to have their own information agencies to promote adequate distribution of their own news, Fontaina maintained.[12]

Trying to extricate himself from this controversy, Binder claimed that the imprecision of Azkoul's proposal had caused his comments, saying he thought that the Lebanese delegate wanted the United States to fund government-run information programs. Even so, and although Congress had not yet approved the Point IV legislation, Binder did not see the legislation as encompassing the financing of private news agencies. As a counterproposal, he suggested that underdeveloped countries build their news organizations by sending their journalists to the United States for college training and on-the-job experience with American news agencies.[13] The controversy over providing support for national news agencies ended the first brief session of the Subcommission on Freedom of Information and of the Press in 1949. Even though the delegates had spent most of their time on developing an agenda for future meetings, the national news agency idea caught the attention of American journalists. Once again, they denounced the proposal as a sure way to create propaganda agencies throughout the world similar to the government-connected news agencies that existed before World War II.[14]

The State Department was happier with the results of this subcommission session than the press was; given the nations with membership on the subcommission, the United States position had survived without serious challenge. The work program adopted—studying the adequacy of news available to peoples of the world, the obstacles to the flow of news, and the governmental regulations affecting the free dissemination of news—was promising. Another encouraging sign was the participation of UNESCO representatives in the sessions, indicating the possibility of future cooperation between the two bodies on free-press issues. In fact, UNESCO had agreed to research economic and professional obstacles to the free flow of news and to make suggestions on how to raise the professional competence of journalists. The State Department saw only "one minor drawback" in the subcommission's relationship with UNESCO, noting "the unwillingness of UNESCO to deal with anything of a political nature" could limit that body's effectiveness in dealing with freedom of information topics. But evaluation of that potential handicap awaited further developments.[15]

Just how the various superior bodies at the United Nations felt about the subcommission's accomplishments during its 1949 session is more difficult to assess. Discussion in the Social Committee of the Economic and Social Council revealed some displeasure over the subcommission's few concrete accomplishments. For instance, Jacques Kayser of France noted that the subcommission had had some twenty items on its agenda and had considered only four of those points. This led Kayser to wonder if the group's assigned tasks would ever be completed.[16] Zonov of the Soviet Union, who had served on the subcommission, likewise complained about the subcommission's becoming bogged down in procedural matters rather than examining the substantive problems that specifically were called to its attention by the Economic and Social Council.[17] Such petty criticisms offended Azkoul, another subcommission member serving on the Social Committee, who said that repeated rejections of subcommission work would give subcommission members the "mistaken" impression "that the Committee wished to restrain somewhat the Sub-Commission's activities."[18]

The full Economic and Social Council was no kinder in reviewing the fruits of the subcommission's labors. Zonov, as a member of that council as well, noted that the delegates most likely would be disappointed with the official report of the subcommission's recent session. One reason for Zonov's disapproval, of course, was the subcommission's failure to deal with the issue of warmongering propaganda. Kayser, too, was still disappointed and noted that he had several reservations about the subcommission's approach to its work. However, the French delegate was willing to provide additional monetary and staff support for the subcommission in the hopes that, with such assistance, its next session would be far more productive.[19]

THE SUBCOMMISSION WRITES A CODE OF ETHICS

Whether the subcommission would live up to the expectations of its superiors in the United Nations was unclear in May 1950 when the subcommission met in Montevideo, Uruguay. In an attempt to find some work that would produce the visible results demanded by other United Nations organs, Fontaina of Uruguay, the subcommission's new chairman, suggested that members explore agenda items that would arouse no sharp political confrontations, including "the preparation of concrete and positive proposals to raise professional standards through an international code of ethics for journalists and an international court of honour or other methods."[20] Binder did not think that the preparation of a code of ethics was such a noncontroversial subject, and he soundly criticized the idea that the subcommission should write a code simply because the task allegedly skirted political differences. Writing a code merely to provide the subcommission with something tangible to display to superior United Nations committees also displeased the American. Binder's point of view, however, did not win many adherents. Far more popular was the notion advanced by Fontaina, Mahmoud Azmi of Egypt, and others that the subcommission must complete some project during the current session in order to secure Economic and Social Council support for future meetings. A code of ethics, Azmi said, might be the key to winning council favor.[21]

Clearly, "the unethical conduct of journalists was a serious obstacle to freedom of information and of the press," which had as its goal the distribution of complete and accurate information. "Furthermore, many newspapers wantonly printed distorted information," and because of this, many governments were unwilling to support freedom of information for fear that "they might be sanctioning a distortion of the true facts." In the past, United Nations attempts to solve journalistic problems had become mired down in political considerations and had failed. Perhaps a code of ethics drafted by a body of experts—the subcommission—could succeed where efforts by individuals concerned with the political ramifications of free-press problems could not. A code of ethics promised to fill an even more important need, Fontaina said, arguing that if journalists followed such a code, governments no longer would need to impose restrictions, "for the members of the profession would impose their own rules." Sensing that his fellow members might be too optimistic about the ramifications of a code of ethics, Melchor Aquino of the Philippines noted that the most serious ethical problems arose from political issues; thus, a professional code of honor had to venture into this controversial area. Despite the potential for controversial debate, Aquino acknowledged that "departures from professional ethics were largely responsible for the present international tension." A code of ethics might be a good idea.[22]

Binder tried to derail the code bandwagon by suggesting that rather than wasting their time by writing a code of ethics that was likely to be disavowed by professional journalists, subcommission members should attack obstacles to the free flow of information. Delegates should not become sidetracked when millions of people were kept in ignorance about events beyond the borders of their own countries. Turning to one particular problem, he noted that "true security could not exist in a world in which the free flow of information was hampered" by such practices as the jamming of radio signals. Interference with radio reception was a limited, solvable problem. Attempting to promote a compromise, Azmi proposed investigating the obstacles to the dissemination of information as part of the code preparation process. But the delegates must not delay drafting the code in order to work on these other problems, Azmi warned. For even after the code of ethics was written, its provisions would not go into effect immediately. The subcommission planned to submit its version of the code to a conference of professional journalists convened especially to make any necessary revisions in the document before it was adopted as the worldwide standard.[23]

When the debate moved from discussions of an international code of ethics to other freedom of information topics, the existence of the cold war dominated discussion—much to the dismay of some delegates. Cold war overtones were most apparent in Binder's efforts to obtain a subcommission resolution that would condemn governmental jamming of radio broadcasts sent across international boundaries, a move obviously in the interests of the burgeoning United States information program. The chances of securing the passage of such a resolution increased greatly when the Russian representative left the session to protest the fact that the Chinese Nationalists held the subcommission seat that the Soviets thought belonged to the mainland government. Thus, Binder freely criticized the Soviet Union for keeping news transmitted by the Voice of America and the British Broadcasting Corporation from Russian citizens. Soviet behavior, he said, was obviously "a threat to the maintenance of international peace and security" and deserved official reproach.[24] Although some delegates tried to recast Binder's resolution in more general terms to avoid a direct attack on the Soviet Union, the proposal adopted by the subcommission specifically cited Russian broadcasting agencies as responsible for interfering with the freedom of Soviet citizens to receive radio signals originating in other countries.[25] The Soviet policy of jamming foreign radio signals was so well known, the delegates finally agreed, that not naming the Russians in the resolution would limit the statement's credibility.

But some delegates saw the American proposal condemning radio jamming as an attempt to entrap the subcommission in cold war politics. Stevan Dedijer of Yugoslavia was one delegate voicing such a belief, and he refused to support Binder's measure. Fontaina disagreed with Dedijer's interpretation of the resolution, claiming that the subcommission was "fighting for the fullest possible freedom of information and of the press" rather than promoting any particular ideology. Subcommission members, however, exhibited mixed feelings about participating in the campaign against communism. Despite Binder's statement that the United States would be equally opposed to the jamming of radio signals by any member of the United Nations regardless of that nation's political persuasion, Azkoul of Lebanon wanted a strong United Nations proclamation "that totalitarian regimes constituted the greatest obstacle to the exercise of human rights and freedom of information." Géraud, on the other hand, saw Binder as demanding subcommission sanction of Western propaganda, and he refused to cast France's vote for the proposal.[26]

The subcommission was meeting just a month before the start of the United Nations involvement in the Korean conflict, and unsettled world conditions intruded regularly into discussions supposedly designed to promote the highest degree of freedom of information possible. For instance, various United Nations pacts on freedom of information and human rights contained language allowing nations to abrogate the agreements in time of war or national emergency. By 1950, too many countries had conveniently found themselves facing states of emergency necessitating restrictions on freedom of information to please Azkoul. The Lebanese delegate asked the subcommission for a resolution declaring "that a state of emergency should not be used as a pretext for ruthless censorship and that no Government should limit freedom of information beyond the strict exigencies of the situation." Without such subcommission support, journalists facing state-of-emergency restrictions had no United Nations statement to use in fighting the regulations.[27] Thus, Azkoul wanted the subcommission to ask the General Assembly to adopt a resolution recommending that when members were compelled to declare a state of emergency, "no measures shall be taken to limit freedom of information and of the press except to the extent strictly required by the situation."[28] Although Fontaina recognized the likelihood that some nations would charge that the United Nations was meddling in their domestic affairs if the international organization moved too far into this area, the subcommission chairman agreed that the statement was necessary.[29] Other subcommission members voiced similar concerns about possible invasion of national sovereignty, but since the proposal essentially called for moral persuasion rather than active intervention, delegates ultimately adopted it.

Leaving cold-war related topics behind, subcommission members returned to the controversial issue of an international code of ethics. Binder wondered why subcommission members thought that they could enumerate professional standards when such attempts in the past by professional journalists in various parts of the world had failed repeatedly. But subcommission members remained undaunted, and they began considering a draft code prepared by the delegates from Lebanon, Egypt, and China. The main headings of the code revealed the interests of the drafters. Journalists were "to tell the truth without malice or prejudice"; "to use only honest methods in gathering, transmitting and disseminating information"; "to have regard for professional dignity, responsibility and discretion"; "to work for the solution of economic, social and humanitarian problems and to help promote respect for fundamental human rights"; and "to help maintain international peace and security."[30] Code cosponsor Azkoul saw the document as solving numerous journalistic problems. Ultimately, the code would "eliminate governmental restrictions imposed on journalists because of abuses of rights and privileges which might be committed by a very small minority of newspaper men." More immediately, the code should protect the press and encourage journalists to resist pressures placed on them. Finally, the code should shield "the people of the world against abuse by journalists of the universal right to freedom of information" and help "in the preservation and dissemination of truth."[31]

Looking at the code, P. H. Chang of China pinpointed one significant problem of modern journalism not mentioned in its provisions—the reporter's lack of background knowledge about the events being covered. A viable code, he thought, must stress the journalist's responsibility to provide accurate background information on the events being reported. Most of the "mistakes, misunderstandings and fallacious ideas" for which journalists were responsible were due, at least in part, to the reporters' failure to place events in their proper contexts. If journalists themselves were ignorant of the historical background, "their comments could only be superficial and their accuracy and impartiality could not be relied on." Chang spoke from personal experience when he complained about reporters' lack of background information on important news events. Foreign journalists, he said, were largely responsible for the impression held in many parts of the world that China's fall to the communists "was the result of the incompetence and corruption of the Nationalist Government, and that the communist rebels were not communists, but agrarian reformers." Chang did not think that "foreign journalists had deliberately given that false impression; their mistake had arisen from lack of information and their failure to understand that poverty had always existed in China." Nor did the foreign correspondents know that this poverty had been complicated by "the Japanese aggression and the intervention of the USSR, and not the measures taken by the Government."[32] To avoid future misreporting based on such a lack of knowledge, the code should require that journalists be fully informed about the events they were assigned to cover.

Binder found Chang's all-encompassing criticisms unfair because they condemned many correspondents who possessed just the qualifications that Chang demanded. Chang responded that he had not meant that all foreign correspondents in China had committed such errors, adding that reporters who misinterpreted events "had acted out of ignorance, and not out of malice." Despite the reason for their transgressions, the problem of uninformed reporting still existed, Chang said, and any code of ethics that hoped to promote objectivity and accuracy must require the adequate training of foreign correspondents. But, Binder argued, no code provision could make journalists infallible, and "nothing could prevent them from making erroneous predictions or misinterpreting events." Perhaps not, Chang countered, but "journalists would commit fewer errors if they had a more thorough knowledge of historical and other background."[33]

Aquino, the delegate from the Philippines, continued the battle against the proposed educational provision. He agreed that journalists should be as well prepared as possible, but professional training was unrelated to professional honor. The best approach to the problem of poorly trained journalists, the Filipino thought, lay in separating the concerns into two categories—one dealing with the professional training of journalists and the other with their functioning on the job. Azkoul of Lebanon disagreed somewhat with Aquino, noting that if potential journalists understood "that the profession conferred obligations as well as privileges, any conscientious person desiring to enter it should be careful to acquire the necessary ability and be in a position to assume those responsibilities." A journalist, Azkoul said, should know foreign languages, history, geography, ethnology, and the general culture of his or her assignment area. And before accepting a foreign assignment, the reporter should study the issues of particular importance in that part of the world. But if a journalist must master everything cited, Philip Jordan of the United Kingdom protested, the reporter "would have to be virtually omniscient." Moreover, Jordan could not see how any journalist could find enough time to learn all of the information necessary to function on the level suggested.[34]

After hearing this additional criticism of his proposal, Chang said that he was sorry that his suggestion had attracted so much negative comment. His main goal had been to show that "honesty and impartiality were not always sufficient to ensure the presentation of accurate information." Although Binder sympathized with Chang about the problems he had encountered in China, he stressed that "what was regrettable was the event itself, not the fact that it had been reported." Based on personal experiences as a foreign correspondent and an editor, Binder believed that editors tried to assign reporters to particular areas "on the basis of their special knowledge."[35] Despite Chang's unwillingness to accept the consensus, delegates agreed that his standards for journalism education were more appropriate for a handbook of instructions for journalists than for an international code of ethics.

THE UNITED STATES DELEGATE OPPOSES CODE PROVISIONS

As the debate progressed, most subcommission members revealed a deep belief in the efficacy of an international code of ethics. Binder, as an almost solitary opponent to the code, remained unconvinced that a code of ethics was "desirable or achievable." The professional philosophies motivating journalists throughout the world were so different that writing a universally acceptable code would be impossible. In fact, so much of the proposed document was "alien to professional thinking" in the United States that Binder planned to abstain from most discussions of the code.[36] At another time and under other circumstances, such strenuous objections by the American delegate might have led to proposals to placate the Americans. Here, however, subcommission delegates barely noted the American opposition and went ahead with their work on the draft code of ethics regardless of Binder's comments.

Some of the topics arising during code debates were familiar to American journalists. The code, for instance, referred to journalists as "members of the information professions,"[37] a point that had been long argued in the United States. Jordan, the British delegate, objected to terming journalism a profession because the word implied a restricted occupation that could be entered only after completing certain educational requirements and licensing by some external organization. Joining the United Kingdom's delegate in objecting to such terminology, Binder noted that American journalists strongly opposed all licensing proposals because the American press "considered as dangerous any tendency to establish bodies with authority to judge fitness to engage in newspaper work." In addition, licensing organizations almost inevitably wound up "under the direct or indirect control of the State and that, in corporate states or totalitarian regimes, the organization of professionals led to restrictions and malpractices which were repugnant to those who cherished free institutions." But terming journalism a profession rather than a trade "need not necessarily lead to the disastrous consequences which had occurred in totalitarian regimes," Chang responded. "The essential difference was that those who looked upon journalism as a trade were willing to accept any person who reported with a reasonable degree of honesty. In China, however, journalists were also expected to fulfill the important function of guiding public opinion." In addition, he said, designating journalists as members of a profession tended "to increase their dignity and emphasize their grave responsibilities as powerful influences in the lives and welfare of humanity."[38]

The United States also objected to language that imposed numerous affirmative responsibilities on correspondents. Previous freedom of information proposals had "made it clear that the only moral obligation of journalists was to report facts without prejudice and in their proper context and to make comments without malicious intent," Binder said.[39] The proposed code, however, required reporters to do much more than report the truth. Under the code's provisions a journalist was to help solve the world's economic, social, and humanitarian problems "through the free interchange of information bearing on such problems." Journalists were also to promote respect for human rights and fundamental freedoms, to work to maintain international peace, and "to counteract the spreading of intentionally false or distorted reports which promote hatred or prejudice against States, persons or groups of different race, colour, sex, language, religion, political or other opinion, national or social origin, property, birth or other status."[40] After reading the list of requirements for reporters, Binder warned, "newspapermen of the United States and of a number of other countries would be utterly unable to accept such a concept of their mission."[41]

Debates on the code of ethics also raised numerous questions about longtime journalistic practices. For instance, journalists traditionally distinguished between presenting fact and offering opinion. If the code required the presentation of truthful information, how would its provisions treat editorialists? On another level, the requirement that correspondents be forced to report truthful information raised the question of how thorough reporters must be in checking the validity of their notes. Many delegates could tell horror stories about how twisted information about their countries circled the world because reporters had failed to verify facts. On the other hand, "journalists could not be compelled to check the credentials of every person who held a press conference when their essential duty was simply to report the statements made to them, regardless of their content," Jordan said. How, then, could journalists verify information to the satisfaction of all delegates? Regardless of possible problems in implementing this provision, delegates accepted a code passage reading, "Every item of information, whenever open to doubt, shall be checked and no fact distorted or essential fact suppressed."[42]

Code debates also raised the question of whether journalists should agree to perform "only tasks compatible" with their professional integrity and dignity. Jordan thought the provision "would in practice lead to anarchy and starvation. The essence of the contract between employer and employee was the acceptance by the employee of the obligation to perform assigned tasks." But Dedijer, the Yugoslav, believed that "a journalist had the right to reject an assignment and to accept the consequences of his action. The code of ethics should promote a sense of personal dignity and pride in standards of work"—even, apparently, if unemployment was the consequence. While the code allowed journalists to refuse assignments "contravening the aims and principles set forth in the code of ethics," Azkoul, the Lebanese delegate, said the provision was not intended to allow a journalist to refuse assignments "regarded as being beneath his dignity."[43] Subcommission members accepted Azkoul's explanation, and the language stayed in the code.

Even though Binder saw much of the code as restrictive, one provision did expand existing American practices. This section established an international newsman's privilege, which allowed reporters to keep the identities of their sources of information confidential when necessary. Both the British and the American delegates were wary of the proposal, noting that only priests and physicians enjoyed such protection in their countries. Delegates from the two nations argued that reporters in America and Great Britain found that journalistic tradition was sufficient to protect the identities of confidential sources. Despite the preference of both Binder and Jordan for continuing this informal practice, subcommission members voted to include a reporter's privilege protection in the code.[44]

Discussions became no easier for the Americans. The segment of the code calling for journalists "to work for the solution of economic, social and humanitarian problems and to help promote respect for fundamental rights"[45] earned Binder's condemnation as the most objectionable section of the entire document. Journalists reported "facts as they were rather than as they ought to be," he argued. That concept guided most American journalists, and "none of them, no matter how great his love of peace and his desire to promote friendly relations among nations, would accept the obligations" presented in the code. Géraud of France agreed, calling for the rejection of the entire section because "instead of ensuring freedom of information, it imposed the duty of disseminating propaganda." Although freedom of information might help the world to reach the objectives listed, "journalists should not be given instructions which in fact limited that freedom." While admitting that the French and American objections had some validity, Azkoul urged his fellow delegates to recognize that the press and the other information media were "among the greatest forces which might work in favour of either war or peace." In fact, "journalists were actually more powerful than governments since they influenced public opinion while governments could act only with the support of public opinion." This particular code section took note of the press's power by stressing the "ideals which the entire world was anxious to defend." The section should be retained "with the sole reservation that journalists, in fulfilling their functions as indicated, should always remain faithful to the truth."[46]

Debates about a journalist's role in promoting positive goals spilled over into the discussion of the last section of the code, which said journalists should help to preserve international peace and security.[47] Binder, claiming to be as "anxious as anyone to see peace, justice, freedom and security for all," said journalists should not "turn the news into propaganda for those ideals." Although "the public must be given accurate facts," calling on correspondents to promote international peace and security posed a grave threat to journalistic truthfulness.[48] Ultimately, subcommission members dropped both controversial sections of the draft code.

Delegates refused, however, to abandon the code itself, despite Binder's denunciation of the document as "a radical departure from the standards cherished by American journalists" and as a program designed to create "an inferior and dangerous type of journalism." Throughout the debates, Binder denied that national pride sparked his opposition to practices that varied from American traditions. He continually stressed his belief that journalists should follow "a voluntary sense of responsibility," with no one telling them how to slant the news.[49] Thus, he firmly repudiated all attempts to codify time-honored journalistic practices.

General dislike of American practices also surfaced when Gandhi, the Indian delegate, suggested modeling the international code after either the Canons of Journalism of the American Society of Newspaper Editors (ASNE) or the Journalist's Creed, written by early international journalism pioneer Walter Williams, a former dean of the school of journalism at the University of Missouri. Faced with significant criticism over his choice of role models, Gandhi defensively said that he mentioned the American documents "not in an effort to extol American journalism" but because he was limited to English sources for examples. Other delegates must introduce similar documents in different languages, Gandhi said. In any event, subcommission members ought to show less concern about the source of code models than for their actual content. The code that the delegates produced "would bear the *imprimatur* of the United Nations and would therefore be likely to commend itself to the profession generally." Hence,

Gandhi said, the subcommission's code "should be of permanent value, regardless of any temporary course of world events."[50]

Basing the code of ethics on timeless principles distressed Azkoul, however, for the Lebanese delegate was convinced that separating the code's provisions "from the imperative needs of the contemporary world" would limit the document's effectiveness, ultimately making it "a dead letter." At the very least, Azkoul said, the document must refer to the journalist's role in preserving peace.[51] Gandhi's approach to the code "took no account whatever of current realities; it might just as well have been written in the 18th century or two hundred years hence." Regardless of the value of timeless language, Azkoul reminded subcommission members of the very real danger that failure to include points considered important by other United Nations bodies could lead the Economic and Social Council and the General Assembly to doubt the value of the subcommission's efforts.[52]

Although members of the subcommission were experts in the field of journalism, Azkoul maintained that the subcommission still must adhere to the goals set forth in the United Nations Charter, which emphasized the promotion of peace. The United Kingdom's Jordan objected to Azkoul's efforts to reaffirm the principles of the United Nations Charter within the code of ethics. The subcommission's task, he said, was not to please other United Nations bodies but to draft a code of ethics that would be acceptable to journalists worldwide. If subcommission members deviated from that goal, they would "merely prolong their work and put another weapon into the hands of the enemies of freedom."[53]

Again declaring himself firmly in favor of peace and the purposes of the United Nations, Binder announced his opposition to inserting Azkoul's call for peace in the code of ethics. Although acknowledging Azkoul's good intentions and recognizing that language in the code promoting peace would not harm the press, Binder noted that the American delegation to the Geneva conference had voted for a similar proposal. Those delegates had not foreseen how the Soviet propaganda machine would use that resolution to launch "a cynical campaign to persuade the peoples of the world that it alone desired peace and that certain other countries wanted war." Binder was afraid a subcommission-drafted code would furnish "more grist for the mill of Soviet propaganda." Despite his refusal to accept language calling on journalists to promote international peace, the United States had not abandoned its efforts to win world peace, nor had he sacrificed his plans to pursue that end personally. But the provision simply did not belong in a code of ethics where governments could abuse its language.[54]

Jordan also found Azkoul's proposal irrelevant to a code of professional ethics. The code's main goal was to "urge journalists to try to publish accurate and objective news corresponding to fact. Journalists were not, however, professionally obligated to concern themselves with the maintenance of peace." Delegates all knew that peace did not depend on freedom of information alone; "besides, it was common knowledge that certain Governments invoked that freedom to justify the pressure which they exerted in the publication of news." The subcommission must not "insert in the code mysterious definitions which would merely play into the hands of totalitarian regimes."[55]

Although he lived in a country that regularly felt the sting of Soviet propaganda, Dedijer said that Yugoslavia still wanted the draft code to call on journalists to promote international peace. Even though governments had exploited similar language for propaganda purposes, "yet it was an incontestable fact that the peoples of the world wanted peace, and that their collective desire for peace was the principal factor in the prevention of another war." The code must "take into account that fervent wish of all mankind." If Binder's fears about the perversion of United Nations calls for peace into propaganda campaigns were carried to their logical conclusion, the United Nations must admit its mistake in advocating world peace initially and "abstain from any further exhortations of that kind," Azkoul argued. Obviously the United Nations would never abandon its peace initiative, and the subcommission must not give up the cause either. "Moreover," he said, "it should not be impossible to counteract injurious propaganda by equally effective propaganda serving a better purpose." Despite the Lebanese delegate's best efforts, the attempt to have the code call on journalists to promote world peace was decisively defeated, seven to three, with one abstention.[56]

Finally, delegates adopted the draft code by a vote of eight to one, with two abstentions. Dedijer voted against the code. Binder and Jordan abstained. With the draft code behind them, delegates attempted to consider another controversial topic—the establishment of an international court of honor to enforce code provisions. Binder, who personally opposed the court, strongly recommended against even opening debate on the topic. The subcommission session was almost over, he argued, and delegates would have no time to adequately discuss the merits of the controversial proposal. Binder won this point, and delegates postponed consideration of a court of honor.[57]

The next item was no less controversial, for delegates began debating the merits of calling a special international conference of journalists to approve the draft code of ethics. Before scheduling the meeting, however, the subcommission had to circulate copies of the draft code to professional organizations throughout the world. Here, the subcommission cast aside its much vaunted independence from governments and decided not only to transmit the draft code to governments but to ask the governments to relay the code to appropriate professional organizations within each country. Subcommission members planned to use comments from the professional groups as guidelines for revising the code at their next session. Then, the delegates would plan the international conference.[58]

A YUGOSLAVIAN ATTEMPT TO PREVENT
MISTREATMENT OF CORRESPONDENTS

Having failed to stop the code of ethics, anticommunist interests brightened considerably when Dedijer introduced a resolution condemning the "mistreatment and discriminatory treatment of a correspondent on account of the country whose press he represents." The resolution termed such actions "an infringement both of freedom of information and the principle of equal rights of nations,"[59] and the Yugoslav wanted the secretary-general to collect information on this problem for possible future action by the United Nations. The reason for the request, he said, was the mistreatment of a correspondent for Tanjug, the Yugoslav state news agency, in Czechoslovakia, where authorities had subjected the reporter "to shocking mistreatment, prevented him from working and finally were holding him as a virtual prisoner." The correspondent "had been refused access to official press conferences, forbidden to attend public meetings or to send news published in Prague to Yugoslavia, his movements had been severely restricted and he had finally been placed under police surveillance." The Yugoslav agency eventually had recalled its employee, but the Czechoslovak government now refused to allow him to leave the country. The Yugoslav agency's latest information indicated that the journalist "might be brought to trial as a further pretext for the Czechoslovak authorities to slander Yugoslavia."[60]

The reason for this treatment mystified Dedijer, who claimed that the Czech correspondent in Belgrade "had been offered every facility in his work and had been granted an exit visa for his return to Prague without difficulty." As a socialist state, Dedijer said, Yugoslavia "found it inadmissible that correspondents should be subjected to mistreatment and prevented from performing their important functions." When another socialist state, Czechoslovakia, behaved in this manner, the act became even more reprehensible.[61] After making his statement, which obviously grew out of the widening rift between Yugoslavia and other communist nations closely aligned with the Soviet Union, Dedijer withdrew his resolution from the floor.

Other members of the subcommission, however, refused to allow Dedijer to withdraw the resolution. Western delegates saw within the proposal a way to vent their frustrations over restrictions imposed on news gathering in communist states. The United Kingdom liked the resolution, Jordan said; British correspondents "had been forced to leave the USSR because they could not work under the conditions imposed by the Soviet authorities." The situation was just as bad in Eastern Europe, where British correspondents depended on "nationals who lived in constant fear of discovery and punishment by State authorities" for information. This further restricted both the quantity and quality of information received. Although the arrest of American correspondent William N. Oatis in Czechoslovakia was still a year away, Binder also supported Dedijer's proposal. The American delegate viewed the mistreatment of the Yugoslav correspondent in Czechoslovakia as typical of the way in which totalitarian governments responded to reporters. Few American journalists remained in Eastern Europe or the Soviet Union, he said, and Russian harassment of correspondents had "virtually stopped the flow of information from that part of the world." Similar problems existed in China where the new communist authorities "refused access to correspondents unless they were nationals of countries enjoying diplomatic relations with the new Communist Government."[62] The Chinese restrictions obviously excluded journalists from the United States and other Western nations because their governments had refused to recognize the regime on the mainland.

Complaints about the treatment of correspondents by the communist Chinese naturally caught the attention of Chang, who cited additional examples of violations of freedom of the press on the mainland. Chang saw the Dedijer proposal as complementing Binder's earlier resolution condemning the jamming of radio signals entering a country. In fact, he suggested sending the Yugoslav resolution to the Economic and Social Council for transmission to the General Assembly with a recommendation that all members "refrain from such violations of freedom of information." Dismayed over the tenor of debate, Dedijer criticized efforts to abandon discussions of the mistreatment of correspondents in favor of attempts "to decide the problem of the co-existence of two different social systems." Chang denied any such motivations, commenting that "the case cited by Mr. Dedijer exemplified a practice which should not be tolerated; it concerned wide geographical areas, and the Sub-Commission could not disregard it."[63] Despite the Yugoslav's objections, the subcommission decided to consider action on Dedijer's proposal. Chang was to redraft and reintroduce the resolution, thus allowing Dedijer to dissociate himself from the motion that he had initiated.

The Dedijer-Chang resolution was one of the few propaganda coups scored by Western interests at the Montevideo meetings, although viewing efforts to promote international freedom of information in terms of propaganda advances seems to be a basic contradiction in terms. To assume that subcommission members believed that anything concrete would come from their sessions, however, strains credulity. American interests, so confident of success at the beginning of the crusade for worldwide freedom of information, had suffered repeated setbacks. Consequently, minor victories such as the Dedijer-Chang resolution were easily blown out of proportion. Now, in the waning days of the 1950 session of the Subcommission on Freedom of Information and of the Press, the American position once again faced attack at a highly vulnerable point—the admission of foreign correspondents and their families to the United States.

The old problem of the free entrance of reporters with communist connections into the United States surfaced on two fronts. Azmi wanted all discussions about the entry, travel, and residence of correspondents in foreign countries to include debate about permitting the correspondents' families to accompany them on assignment. For instance, Azmi said, American officials had refused admittance to the wife of a journalist because of her Russian birth. This action indicated that "an atmosphere of fear bordering on hysteria prevailed in the United States, and the attitude behind that environment impeded the free flow of information. Binder professed ignorance of the case in question and asked for details, assuring the Egyptian that although "officials granting entry permits had occasionally been less liberal than might have been warranted," American journalists were trying to soften the bureaucrats' approach.[64]

Pursuing the same basic problem, Azkoul, the Lebanese delegate, asked about restrictions encountered by certain correspondents who wanted their families with them while they covered United Nations sessions in New York City. Without an amicable settlement of this problem, he said, some journalists might face the choice of "of having to undergo long periods of separation from their families or of being forced to give up their professional activities." But the agreement between the United States and the United Nations regarding the admission of journalists considered correspondents as professionals, not as diplomats, Binder said, and it made no provision for reporters' families to accompany them. The United States position here was appropriate since these correspondents were considered to be on temporary visits. To Binder, the resolution was not even worth voting on. The right of families to stay together might not be part of the United States-United Nations agreement, Azkoul retorted, but the Universal Declaration of Human Rights guaranteed that right. "If the United States Government was afraid that, under cover of his profession a journalist might engage in activities which it did not wish to tolerate, it would be more humane automatically to refuse to accredit him rather than to accredit him and later refuse to allow his family to join him."[65]

The problem of families accompanying some correspondents, however, was not as simple or as humanitarian as the Lebanese delegate suggested. Foreign correspondents crossed American territory to reach the United Nations and lived within the United States while working. Consequently, the American government could establish standards for their admission, Fontaina, the subcommission's chairman, explained. While sympathetic to Azkoul's concern, Jordan, the United Kingdom's delegate, saw the relationship between the United States and the United Nations as a special, sensitive one. Their agreement required the United States to admit all journalists accredited to the United Nations into its territory. Thus, the visitors bypassed normal security screenings long recognized as falling within national prerogatives. "Journalists accredited to the United Nations could not be compared to journalists who went to any other foreign country," Jordan said. "Moreover, since any person admitted to the United States had the right to move freely anywhere in that country, it was quite natural that the United States Government should seek to provide safeguards in connexion with journalists who in principle were accredited only to the United Nations." Despite Jordan's and Fontaina's explanations, subcommission members adopted Azkoul's resolution asking the United Nations to investigate the matter.[66]

Another resolution raised an issue that usually created problems for Americans—the distribution of newsprint. This time, however, the newsprint resolution dealt with the worldwide shortage of the vital raw material in a slightly different manner and omitted the traditional criticism of American newsprint consumption. Because of the international shortage of newsprint, nation after nation had set up regulations governing the distribution of newsprint. Some of the quota systems were equitable, while others were obviously biased toward publications supporting the individuals who operated the allocation program, thereby creating a form of indirect censorship. Economic problems were forcing governments to intervene in the sale and purchase of newsprint, either "by limiting the amount of foreign currency allocated for its importation, or by rationing it among the various publications, or even by confiscating it," said Chile's Alfredo Silva Carvallo. Such actions "constituted a definite danger, since State intervention might easily take the form of arbitrary measures and become discriminatory," and subcommission members must support equitable, independent allocation programs. Subcommission members warmly received the resolution, for delegates meeting in Uruguay were quite aware of the way in which Juan Perón was manipulating the newsprint supply for nearby Argentine newspapers in an attempt to strangle some of the continent's most prestigious publications. Newspapers contending with such governmental intervention needed encouragement in their struggles against tyranny, said both Binder and Jordan, who joined other delegates in supporting the Chilean proposal.[67]

Regardless of other measures adopted at the Montevideo meetings, American journalistic reaction to the subcommission's sessions centered on the draft code of ethics. The code, Binder explained, was a product of the times, in that it forced individuals and nations interested in freedom of information to "devote most of their efforts to protecting such freedom as still exists from those who would curtail or destroy it." One reason why code proposals created so many problems for American journalists was that the provisions were just one part of a constant assault on freedom of information that permitted "little effective effort to widen the area of freedom and lower existing barriers to the free flow of information." Further complicating the situation was the disquieting fact that the greatest challenge to freedom of the press now came from "regimes which purport to follow a 'middle' course between totalitarianism and democracy." In fact, those nations that saw themselves as pursuing peace by requiring the information media to perform in a certain way were "a greater danger to freedom than the totalitarians. Of the two the second is the more insidious and dangerous encroachment because it looks so plausible to the unwary and puts those who resist it in a bad light in the eyes of the unthinking."[68]

Any individual or nation opposing the latter view of the press encountered considerable difficulty during subcommission sessions and escaped the meetings being labeled an obstructionist by many delegates, said Binder, who was speaking from experience. Since the supporters of such allegedly noble motives "always professed to be seeking implementation of UN objectives and implied that those opposing their indoctrinating principles are against peace it was not easy to deal with this type of encroachment on freedom." In fact, Binder saw little hope for altering the outlook of most delegates, and, without changes, the subcommission was more likely to inhibit freedom of the press than to promote that freedom.[69] Frank Starzel, general manager of the Associated Press (AP), was equally concerned about the effect of the proposed code. Although Starzel believed that "no one could seriously disagree with the apparent meaning of the proposed code," he also felt that the document's provisions "could be described as a collection of pious platitudes" that could serve as "the entering wedge by which governments gain control of public information." American journalists should "make no mistake and be not deluded. Fine-sounding phrases hide cunning and insidious intent. Whenever any government starts tampering with the free flow of information, it is time for the people to beware. The most sinister purposes can be and always are clothed in innocent or alluring phrases." One consolation emerging from the debates, however, was the fact that the Americans were not alone in opposing the code. "The American, British and Filipino delegates opposed the draft of the code in virtually every detail, but were always outvoted," Starzel noted. "This is an interesting manifestation of a trend which might have serious consequences."[70]

UNITED NATIONS MEMBERS QUESTION THE SUBCOMMISSION'S WORTH

American journalists were not alone in their growing disapproval of the activities of the subcommission either, as soon became apparent when superior United Nations bodies reviewed the subcommission's actions. The Social Committee, a subsidiary of the Economic and Social Council, was one of those bodies that indicated displeasure with the subcommission's performance. Kayser of France, for instance, noted that the 1950 subcommission session matched the body's disappointing record in 1949. Members broke no new ground, made no significant advances, and adopted no resolutions suitable to their status as experts in the field. In fact, "an objective perusal of the draft resolutions failed to indicate that the shadow of a solution of the general problem of freedom of information was in sight," Kayser said. "They could boast of only one positive element, namely, that they enunciated certain generally accepted principles." Diplomatic representatives at the United Nations could have performed just as well. Why, then, Kayser wanted to know, did the United Nations need a special technical subcommission on freedom of the press? The subcommission had been created "to give technical advice and to produce practical solutions, not to turn out pious maxims," and it was obviously not fulfilling its mission.[71] Thus, the campaign against the subcommission, which had surfaced briefly after the body's 1949 session, began anew.

The Economic and Social Council had established the Subcommission on Freedom of Information and of the Press as a continuing organization at the request of the 1948 Geneva conference. Delegates had supported reauthorization of the subcommission, B. C. Ballard, the Australian delegate on the Social Committee, said, in the hopes that it would build on the work done by the Geneva conference and provide the United Nations with useful data that would help to remove obstacles to freedom of information. But his government now wanted to indicate "its serious disappointment" over the subcommission's achievements. Even more to the point, the Australian viewed the problems of the subcommission as typical of the larger problems that surrounded all freedom of information projects within the United Nations. Lengthy discussions about freedom of information over the last few years had shown the fruitlessness of reverting "to subjects which had already been fully debated. It had long since become apparent that, even when there was no basic ideological disagreement, the limit of agreement on principles had already been reached." In turning his attention to specific measures taken by the subcommission, Ballard said that the subcommission's resolution asking governments to limit restrictive measures taken against freedom of information in times of emergency was "a pious exhortation," which "could easily be twisted by an authoritarian government to justify itself in muzzling freedom of expression." On another issue, he said that he believed the matter of entry visas for families of correspondents was best left to representatives of governments to debate and decide. If the subcommission continued to exist, the Australian added, its members should concentrate solely on limited technical questions unlikely to be contaminated by ideological differences.[72]

Although the American government firmly believed in advancing freedom of information, Walter M. Kotschnig, the United States delegate to the Social Committee, echoed the concerns of his colleagues about the value of the work done by the Subcommission on Freedom of Information and of the Press. According to Kotschnig, the United States government believed that the subcommission had not met the challenge before it "to awaken the conscience of the world to the necessity for unfettered dissemination of true information." Despite the subcommission's work, recent studies by the Associated Press showed that barriers to freedom of the press around the world were increasing at an alarming rate. But "the more freedom of information was discussed, the more restrictions were imposed upon it by governments." The recent subcommission session gave no indication that its members "had grasped the seriousness of the situation" or that they had discussed any measures to counter such problems. The subcommission's resolution against governmental jamming of radio signals was useful, Kotschnig said, but more than balancing that positive accomplishment, the subcommission "spent an inordinate amount of time on the question of an international code of ethics without giving due preliminary consideration to the possible attitude of governments to such a code." The United States government, Kotschnig said, also wanted the subcommission to "apply itself in a more direct and practical manner to the technical aspects of the problem with which it was most competent to deal, and particularly to the removal of obstacles to freedom of information."[73]

The contradictory nature of their criticisms seemed lost on Social Committee delegates. Most subcommission members firmly believed that they had attacked obstacles to freedom of information. The inability to have families along on foreign assignments interfered with the ability of correspondents to devote their full attention to the job. The call for governmental self-restraint in restricting freedom of information in times of emergency tried to bring the moral force of the United Nations into the struggle to promote the widest possible latitude for freedom of expression, especially in times of national crisis. And, above all, the delegates had designed the code of ethics specifically to remove obstacles to freedom of the press. Subcommission members supporting the code believed that governments had been forced to create barriers to freedom of information in order to protect themselves from irresponsible journalists. Comments about the reactions of governments to the draft code missed the main point of the subcommission's deliberations—the responses of governments were immaterial. As a body of experts, the subcommission saw its audience as the world's journalists rather than the world's governments. An international code of ethics, drafted by the experts of the subcommission rather than by the diplomats of other United Nations bodies, was a direct attempt to change the way in which journalists functioned in order to remove major obstacles to freedom of the press throughout the world.

Subcommission members had recognized the stalemate within the United Nations on freedom of information topics and had deliberately addressed different subjects in an attempt to make progress. Part of the discontent of the Social Committee members reviewing the subcommission report was probably inevitable because in creating a body of experts drawn from such a highly individualistic profession as journalism, the United Nations virtually had ensured unexpected results. In any event, representatives of the Western democracies, whose views generally had been defeated, did not appreciate the subcommission members' attempts to break new ground at the expense of Western press systems. Representatives of the Soviet bloc likewise disapproved of the subcommission's work because it was not restrictive enough. Thus, the subcommission was caught in a totally untenable situation.

The Belgian representative, Frederic Blondeel, was somewhat more understanding of the subcommission's problems than several other delegates. He noted that if the subcommission had become too absorbed in debating general questions, its members were only following precedents set by the Economic and Social Council, the Conference on Freedom of Information, and the General Assembly. The United Nations, in general, had found discussions of freedom of information subjects basically unmanageable.[74] The Chilean delegate, Carlos Valenzuela, also believed that the subcommission was not entirely responsible for its shortcomings. "Since the General Assembly and the Council had begun to concern themselves with the question of freedom of information, strict censorship had continued in the totalitarian countries, and there were signs that it was about to be introduced in others." Such events were far "more important than a thousand sub-commissions resolutions, and a solution to the fundamental problem involved was beyond the scope of experts." In fact, expectations that the United Nations would make any progress on freedom of information topics were unrealistic given existing world conditions, Valenzuela added. "One day it might be found that general disappointment of hopes of world peace had compromised all the activities of the United Nations, and that the vapid resolutions in the Sub-Commission's report were a manifestation of the widespread repercussions of that disillusionment."[75]

Disillusionment, however, was not the only cause of the subcommission's difficulties. The position held by freedom of information in the hierarchy of values supported by the United Nations had slipped noticeably by mid-July 1950, two weeks after the North Koreans invaded the South. Blondeel of Belgium bluntly outlined the new status of freedom of information when he said that the subcommission erred in considering that "freedom of information was the most fundamental of the freedoms defended by the United Nations. The most fundamental of these freedoms was that of States, which sometimes unfortunately encroached on other freedoms." References to the supremacy of freedom of information now were superfluous.[76]

Similar questions developed when the Third Committee of the General Assembly debated the subcommission's report in October 1950. By this time, the Economic and Social Council had decided not to call the subcommission into session in 1951, and Azmi of Egypt, the next subcommission chairman, appeared before the Third Committee to protest the council's decision. Refusing to schedule a subcommission session for 1951,

Azmi contended, discounted the important work done by the delegates in Montevideo in drafting the code of ethics. Criticisms of the code angered the Egyptian, who wondered how anyone could "underestimate the importance of that document which aimed at striking a happy medium between the freedoms and duties of journalists—in other words, at safeguarding the freedom of information while preventing any abuses." The subcommission still had a great deal of important work to do, especially in creating an international court for journalists to enforce code provisions, Azmi said, pleading for permission to meet in 1951.[77] In addition, under the terms of the subcommission's charter, that body only had three years in which to prove itself worthy of continued existence. If the subcommission could not meet for one of the three years, he said, its members would have difficulty convincing United Nations delegates to renew the subcommission's charter in 1952.[78]

But displeasure at the subcommission's performance was not the only reason for skipping the 1951 session, Kayser of France said. The secretary-general had requested fewer meetings of independent commissions and subcommissions in 1951 because of administrative and budgetary constraints. The Subcommission on Freedom of Information and of the Press simply was one organ that the Economic and Social Council thought could miss a session without damaging the ongoing work of the United Nations. Nor were the problems with the 1951 subcommission session solely financial, according to Eleanor Roosevelt. The subcommission had numerous tasks yet to accomplish, but the secretariat was unable to process the information necessary to make meetings in 1951 productive. Complicating preparations for a subcommission session, added G.H.R. Rogers, the United Kingdom's delegate, was the secretariat's move into permanent headquarters in early 1951, which rendered servicing numerous special meetings almost impossible.[79]

Raúl Noriega of Mexico, who soon would head a special committee to draft a freedom of information convention, thought that these arguments concealed the delegates' real motivation for not calling the subcommission into session in 1951—which was a loss of interest in freedom of information. "Three years previously it had often been said that freedom of information was the cornerstone of all the freedoms; in the brief ensuing period, the cornerstone seemed to have come down to the size of a brick," he said, appealing to the committee to give freedom of information the importance that the subject deserved. The pleas worked; Third Committee members returned the matter of a 1951 subcommission session to the Economic and Social Council for reconsideration. But the Third Committee sent no instructions along with the referral; Third Committee members planned to accept any Economic and Social Council decision after council members had debated the issue once again.[80] In a hierarchical organization such as the United Nations, the Third Committee's failure to attach instructions to its request to the Economic and Social Council put the action in the category of diplomatic buck-passing.

The subcommission's reprieve was predictably short-lived; by December 1950, when the Economic and Social Council resumed debate on calling a subcommission session for 1951, the outlook for positive action was gloomy. Citing economics and the pending meetings of the special committee assigned to draft the freedom of information convention as reasons against convening the subcommission, opponents of a 1951 subcommission session quickly gained supremacy. The poor record of the 1950 session weighed heavily in the decision-making process as well. Some of the subcommission's problems in 1950 were due to lack of sufficient preparation for the meetings, Kotschnig said. Pursuing a line a reasoning far from the 1948 American ideal of a United Nations commission on freedom of information that would meet twice a year, Kotschnig contended that by delaying the next subcommission meeting until 1952 officials could gather enough information to allow for sound decision making. An East-West alliance of the United States and the Soviet Union in addition to their respective allies defeated efforts to call the subcommission into session in 1951 by a vote of ten to eight. Nations wanting the subcommission to convene were Chile, Denmark, France, India, Iran, Mexico, Pakistan, and Peru.[81] The issue, however, was far from settled.

DEBATES OVER MOVING FREEDOM OF INFORMATION QUESTIONS TO UNESCO START

Attacks on the subcommission were only just beginning; soon an effort began to dissolve the subcommission completely and to transfer its duties to UNESCO. Apparently, United Nations delegates suddenly had discovered that UNESCO duplicated many of the activities of the Subcommission on Freedom of Information and of the Press. Redundancy was inefficient and costly; thus, putting UNESCO in charge of all communications-related issues appeared attractive. But were all the subcommission's tasks replicated by UNESCO? If gaps occurred, should the subcommission be kept alive to fill them? D. R. Roper, the delegate from the United Kingdom, preferred abolishing the subcommission entirely, terming "its demise . . . a gain." In fact, UNESCO was "admirably suited to deal with the very kind of problem which the Council had been sending to the Sub-Commission. Indeed it had been constituted to solve such problems. It was independent and therefore in a better position to concentrate on the technical aspects of those problems." Kayser of France also opposed renewing the subcommission's charter in 1952. But how would the United Nations deal with freedom of information problems after the subcommission's dissolution? Surely the United Nations would not abandon the field totally—regardless of how well UNESCO filled the void. Or would it?[82] Such queries touched off debate over the roles of the two organizations and over whether two bodies dealing with the same subject were necessary.

Overlapping between UNESCO and the subcommission did not worry Silva Carvallo of Chile, who believed the two organizations were sufficiently different in character to allow them to coexist. The subcommission, a technical body of experts in journalism, served as a watchdog to protect freedom of information. UNESCO, however, dealt with cultural questions, collected information, and prepared technical studies for use by the subcommission and other bodies. Even though the subcommission had accomplished "little on the practical plane," the subcommission was not entirely to blame. "When countries placed obstacles in the way of freedom of information, the United Nations frequently refrained for diplomatic reasons from denouncing them by name, and the Sub-Commission was therefore unable to take action." Silva Carvallo thought that precipitous action against the subcommission "would be rather unfortunate, at a time when freedom of information was under fire from all sides."[83] If the United Nations still believed in its 1946 resolution that termed freedom of information the "touchstone of all the freedoms," Silva Carvallo could not understand how the international organization could destroy the subcommission.[84] The ability of the subcommission to deal with political questions made that body rather important, Sir Ramaswami Mudaliar of India contended. For instance, UNESCO could never have protested the jamming of radio signals, looked at obstacles to freedom of the press, or considered drafting a code of ethics. UNESCO gathered information and did not act, Mudaliar said; missing that critical distinction could cause significant problems for the future of freedom of information within the United Nations.[85]

Soviet bloc delegates thought that debates over where to house freedom of information activities were absurd; as Oldrich Kaiser, the Czechoslovak delegate, said, both the United Nations and UNESCO "had failed in the task which had been entrusted to them." By this he meant, of course, the organizations' failure to act against warmongering and the dissemination of false information, thereby missing the point of the debate that was swirling around him.[86] But Kaiser was not alone in purposefully ignoring the main point of the debate. United Nations delegates were trying to decide whether the freedom of information question had become so politicized that the world organization could no longer handle the subject. More basically, had freedom of information itself become expendable in a world in which a United Nations police action now raged in the Far East and where a cold war threatened almost daily to turn into a nuclear holocaust? Or, still more fundamentally, could the world afford the kind of freedom of information that American newspaper editors had dreamed of in the glory days after their World War II victories? These questions were far too controversial to discuss; the issue was best handled obliquely by talking about duplication of services, economy, and efficiency.

The American participant in the debates was in a particularly delicate position. The United States had introduced the entire issue of international freedom of information to the world in the first place; now what did the Americans want to do with the topic? Freedom of information certainly was "the touchstone of all other freedoms to whose defence the United Nations was devoted," United States delegate Kotschnig affirmed. But "the United States delegation was not yet convinced as to what methods would best enable the cause of freedom of information to prevail. The only conclusion it had reached was that the efforts made in that field by UNESCO and the United Nations had not achieved the results expected," perhaps because "the terms of reference of those organizations had not been defined clearly enough."[87] So, rather than facing the problem head-on, the United States sided with those nations that preferred to study the possible overlap between the two organizations and to decide later what to do about freedom of information issues within the United Nations.

Despite such Social Committee debates, the Economic and Social Council undoubtedly would be asked again for a subcommission meeting in 1951. Enrique Bernstein, the Chilean delegate, wanted the council to reverse the Social Committee's action and allow the subcommission to meet in 1951 because "in the current state of international tension, such an organization composed of independent journalists could do even more useful work in counteracting the dissemination of false and distorted information and ensuring an adequate supply of accurate information to the peoples of the world." The Chilean delegation believed that "freedom of information was of vital importance in the campaign to secure respect for fundamental human rights throughout the world" and thought that the subcommission should have a chance to prove its worth.[88]

Refusing to schedule a subcommission session for 1951 was reexamined carefully once more because of the Third Committee's request. Defending the council's earlier decision to cancel the 1951 session, Kotschnig, the American representative, pointed out that the Third Committee had not ordered the council to do anything. Not only were all the previous arguments against a 1951 subcommission session still valid, but, he said, the United States believed that forcing a premature meeting of the subcommission would harm the cause of freedom of information. To avoid a potentially divisive and embarrassing vote on the issue, Economic and Social Council members postponed a final decision on convening the subcommission in 1951 until its summer session.[89] The vote to postpone making any decision effectively decided the question negatively, for organizing a subcommission meeting in the few remaining months of 1951 would be impossible logistically.

In the meantime, the Economic and Social Council created a special ad hoc committee designed to increase the council's operating efficiency and to weed out superfluous appendages. A prime target was the Subcommission on Freedom of Information and the Press. Action against the subcommission would not upset the United States, Isador Lubin, the American representative on the ad hoc committee, told other members, for America was dissatisfied with the subcommission's "negative approach" to freedom of information problems. Future cooperation with UNESCO or other United Nations organs might help "to establish a clear-cut and practicable programme of work in the light of the technical and political factors which, equally with economic factors, might obstruct freedom of information and the press." UNESCO could handle the technical aspects of freedom of information problems, G. T. Corley Smith of the United Kingdom suggested, and if any extraordinary issue arose, the Economic and Social Council could always establish a special emergency committee to deal with the matter.[90] Following additional debate, Corley Smith proposed that the subcommission meet once more before dissolution, after which the Economic and Social Council would distribute the subcommission's work among other United Nations bodies. Ad hoc committee members accepted the suggestion, thus dooming the Subcommission on Freedom of Information and of the Press.[91]

What, then, would be the role of UNESCO in promoting freedom of information? The United States had some definite ideas, Lubin said. In fact, his government refused to "accept the idea that UNESCO's activities in the field of freedom of information and of the press should be confined to the purely technical aspects." Such limits were arbitrary, rigid, and unnecessary. The American government simply "could not accept the idea that an organization set up to disseminate information should not act when political obstacles hindered such dissemination. UNESCO was quite as much concerned with the nature of the information to be disseminated as with the practical means of disseminating it." While UNESCO's main work focused on removing technical obstacles to the worldwide circulation of educational, scientific, and cultural materials, Lubin continued, UNESCO also should "combat the effects of any harmful propaganda and attempt to stamp out any form of discrimination liable to hinder man's cultural development. Activities of that kind necessarily had political aspects," and the United States saw no reason for UNESCO to shy away from such functions.[92] Although delegates would discuss the issue of transferring freedom of information concerns to UNESCO again, the ad hoc committee established the groundwork for blurring the distinction between the technical and political aspects of the freedom of information question and for moving the entire topic to the jurisdiction of UNESCO.

THE SUBCOMMISSION CONVENES
FOR ITS FINAL SESSION

When the subcommission reconvened for its final session in March 1952, its members were decidedly downcast. The conditions under which foreign correspondents worked had become increasingly oppressive, Azmi, its new chairman, reported, but because of the decisions of superior United Nations bodies, the subcommission would have little opportunity to find ways to ameliorate the problems. The primary question before subcommission members was how to use the limited time remaining to promote freedom of information. Binder, again representing the United States, once more pressed for a study of the adequacy of news available to the peoples of the world and of the obstacles to the free flow of information. Other members wanted to continue discussion of the draft code of ethics, but Binder protested that the subcommission never would "succeed in drafting a code that would satisfy both the countries favouring a government-controlled press used as a medium of official propaganda and countries which preferred a free press." If the subcommission pursued the code of ethics, members would make no permanent contribution to freedom of information. If, on the other hand, members looked into the problems relating to the free flow of news, Binder said the subcommission could leave a lasting imprint. But, Binder was told, such a study of the obstacles to the dissemination of news was impossible. The Economic and Social Council's instructions were specific, and they permitted the subcommission to deal only with the draft code of ethics and with allocating its remaining work among other United Nations bodies.[93]

If delegates must discuss the draft code of ethics again, Binder wanted the subcommission to revise the work done in 1950. He sought "a simple and concise code, avoiding the ambiguous and vague terms which had tended to creep in at Montevideo." Also, he argued against sending the draft code to governments, as the Montevideo session had recommended, proposing instead that the code go directly to professional organizations and that it be accompanied by a request from the subcommission asking for voluntary adherence to the code.[94]

Any discussion of a draft code of ethics in 1952 would be quite different from the debates of 1950 because the Soviet delegate was once again present. The Russian boycott over the presence of Nationalist China in the United Nations was over, and Zonov reclaimed his seat on the subcommission. Binder's desire for a simple, concise code was more than offset by Zonov's pleas for a far more explicit document. Zonov campaigned for specific language listing basic obligations that should be imposed on every journalist. The provisions restated the traditional Soviet suggestions requiring reporters to fight to maintain international peace and security, to promote friendly relations among peoples, and to "combat the spread of nazism and fascism and oppose all types of discrimination on grounds of race, religion and sex." This language was vital, Zonov said, because in a world in which Atlantic treaty nations were being "crushed by the burdens brought by the increase in armaments" and were "openly preparing for war," journalists must work harder "to eliminate the causes of friction and promote the maintenance of international peace." To Zonov, a code of ethics that did not require journalists to fight for peace "would not deserve the name."[95]

Even if, by some miracle, Binder and Zonov could be convinced to agree on a document, additional discussion of the draft code of ethics might be useless, Azkoul of Lebanon said. Journalists throughout the world had inspected the draft during the months between subcommission sessions, and some of their comments "expressed doubts about the practical usefulness of the code, while others had gone so far as to affirm that it was entirely unnecessary." The strongest reservations had come from British and American news organizations; without the support of these two leaders in the field, finishing a code might not be worth the effort. Azkoul refused, however, to see sinister motivations behind the objections. At times, "the most scrupulous and honest of men did not like their moral obligation to be transformed into a material obligation and did not like to account for the way in which they had done their duty. That did not in any way mean that they had no ideal or refused to live up to it." Subcommission members must realize that some journalists, "while adhering strictly to the rules of their profession, preferred to maintain absolute independence and to remain accountable for their actions to their associations or to public opinion and not to any national or international body."[96]

The American Society of Newspaper Editors was one of a handful of press-related organizations answering the United Nations request for reactions to the proposed code. The ASNE response followed the pattern perceived by Azkoul; society leaders decided, not unexpectedly, that the proposed code was an unsatisfactory statement of journalistic principles. The ASNE board of directors did not believe that "a universally acceptable code" could be written "in existing circumstances" and opposed calling an international conference to discuss the issue. The society had its own code of ethics, the Canons of Journalism, whose principles ASNE leaders would be pleased to see internationalized. But, they added, "we recognize, however, that there are many countries which take a different view of the rights and duties of the press. We do not believe that the principles we cherish can be advanced by compromises of the sort implicit in certain provisions of the proposed draft code." In conclusion, the ASNE said, since its members did not believe American principles would win international acceptance and since "American newspapermen would not accept a code which encroaches upon freedom of information or thinks of the newspaperman as an indoctrinator," the organization believed further work on the code would be "a waste of time and effort."[97]

Responses from American journalists disappointed the Lebanese delegate, who believed that if American and British press organizations had agreed "to subject themselves to criticism from other press organizations, even if less well-equipped and less powerful, they would have rendered a great service to the cause of freedom of information." Anglo-American support could have removed various obstacles encountered by the press in other countries, but, Azkoul said, assistance from journalists in those two countries was not forthcoming. Now the subcommission must determine its next step. Although American and British reactions dimmed prospects for a code of ethics to win wide support, he suggested that the delegates continue their work. The greatest fear voiced about the code focused on the danger of governments' perverting its provisions into instruments of suppression. Azkoul responded that the draft came from representatives of the profession, not from representatives of governments, a fact supposedly known to members of the press worldwide. The subcommission must make sure that correspondents knew that journalists meeting in a special international conference would write the final code provisions and not diplomats at the United Nations. And journalists must also understand, that, if adopted, the code "would be the property of the professionals, not of the United Nations or of governments."[98]

Azkoul recognized the fundamental disagreements between the Soviets and the Americans on the code, but he refused to see the two positions as mutually exclusive. Attempting to smooth over differences, Azkoul suggested making a clear distinction "between the basic duties of information personnel, resulting from the very nature of their functions, the complementary obligations deriving from the social role of the profession, and, finally, the moral duties, international in character, which did not concern journalists alone." Binder's belief that reporters should only be asked to report the truth was the basic mission of the press, the Lebanese delegate said. Zonov's emphasis on journalists' working to promote peace and mutual understanding among men was a moral duty of reporters as individuals, which had "nothing to do with their professional code and could not be imposed from without."[99] No journalist, Azkoul continued, "should be a missionary, save of his own free will; all that could be required of journalists was that they should be honest reporters."[100] If the draft code separated the professional from the personal obligations of journalists, then, perhaps, the code would win wider acceptance.

Binder appreciated Azkoul's efforts to separate professional and personal responsibilities of journalists: "A journalist, as an individual, might well try to further international peace; but he could not be forced to become a propagandist for any ideology whatsoever in the course of his work. That was not the way to further international peace." In fact, in "democratic countries, honest and conscientious journalists sought above all to find the truth." But, "if the international code of ethics tried to force them to distort or conceal the truth in the name of any ideology, however noble, they would find the code unacceptable."[101] Binder even objected to asking journalists to support the ideals of the United Nations. Such urgings, the American editor contended, were just another example of the Soviet government's continual attempts "to use the United Nations to spread and enforce their view that the regimented journalist should be an instrument of the state rather than a reporter of events, loyal to the truth as he saw it and to his readers' interests." Even though everyone favored peace, Binder contended that a statement supporting that view would be "out of place in a binding code of ethics which would allow the state to define what constituted a threat to peace."[102]

American objections to the code were wearing thin on other delegates by this time. If subcommission members just ignored the negative reactions of the Anglo-American press, they would find a great deal of international press support for a code, Moni Moulik, the Indian delegate, contended. In fact, most newly formed national and international press organizations considered drafting a code of ethics as one of their first responsibilities, thus proving that journalists of the world thought that ethical standards were indeed important. Governments had not imposed these codes of ethics on journalists in various countries, Moulik stressed, nor had governments even urged the adoption of codes. With such professional self-awareness emerging around the world, the subcommission must settle its outstanding differences on the code quickly in order to provide the necessary international standard.[103] Other members of the subcommission agreed that opposition from the British and American press was not an insurmountable barrier to writing an acceptable press code. Most subcommission members saw these negative comments as coming from powerful organizations that were more than capable of protecting themselves if the unrealistic dangers predicted in their responses actually came to pass. Thus, delegates wanted to continue working on the code.

Azmi found the criticisms of the code by American journalists far harsher and more unjustified than the British journalists' comments. The reasons for the American stance were unclear to the Egyptian: "A country in which philanthropy was practised on so large a scale, and which had so many foundations engaged in social and cultural work, should have been more ready to welcome the benevolent impulse which had led the United Nations to propose a moral discipline to be freely accepted by a profession which was the traditional guardian of freedom of information."[104] Why American journalists were unable to properly judge the beneficence of the subcommission's motives mystified Azmi, but American parochial reactions must not halt a salutary international movement.

DEBATE AGAIN CENTERS ON A CODE OF ETHICS

In fact, the subcommission had to act on the code, even if members decided simply to abandon the project. Delegates were told again that, as an agency of the Economic and Social Council, the subcommission had to do that body's will—and the council wanted a completed draft code of ethics. So subcommission members became locked in yet another replay of debates on freedom of information that had occurred within far too many United Nations bodies. Prior debates had featured disagreements between the

Soviets and the Americans on whether to use the draft code to impose obligations on the press. The smaller countries spent their time trying to build ways to protect themselves from the media of larger nations into the code. And, after hours of debate, the smaller nations seemed to prevail while the United States and the Soviet Union remained deadlocked. The pattern held true once more, with the majority of delegates repeatedly defeating ideas suggested by both Soviet and American representatives.

After American attempts to moderate the code had been defeated at almost every turn, Azkoul suggested a new conclusion for the draft designed to assuage American fears. The Lebanese delegate's amendment stated that "no provision of this code may be interpreted as authorizing governments to intervene in any manner whatsoever to ensure that the personnel of the press and of other media of information comply with the moral obligations set forth herein." This language, Azkoul said, ought to calm professional organizations that were apprehensive about the ability of governments to twist the code into a means of suppression.[105] The language obviously was intended to blunt some of Binder's concerns, but the American delegate continued to stress the futility of trying to impose a code of ethics on journalists. In response to statements that pointed to the basically uncontested existence of codes of behavior in other professions, Binder found such examples inapplicable. Although doctors and lawyers were "subject to very strict professional rules, generally approved by the public authorities," the extension of such rules to journalists—"who were more jealous of their independence than anyone else"—would be impossible. Rather than imposing a professional code of ethics on journalists, "it would be wiser to disseminate the draft very widely and leave each professional association free to decide whether to adopt it."[106]

Binder found himself supporting another losing cause when the debates turned to calling an international conference of professional journalists to adopt the code. Throughout the discussions, delegates had stressed the professional nature of the code and had emphasized how professional journalists would draft the final language. Yet when the discussion turned to the mechanics of calling the conference, the United Nations suddenly had a role to play in the process. Since the Economic and Social Council had instructed the subcommission to complete work on the code, surely the council should review the draft, some subcommission members said. And how could an international meeting be staged without the aid of the United Nations bureaucracy? But if the subcommission took either step, Binder contended that governmental intervention would contaminate an already dubious code. The mechanics of the suggestion for United Nations involvement also presented problems. For instance, Binder wanted to know how the United Nations could call such an international professional conference. "To whom would its invitations be addressed and what criteria would it apply in appointing participants since at present the Secretariat did not even have a complete list of the information enterprises and professional associations concerned?" Furthermore, if the United Nations financed the conference, "it might seek to influence the discussions."[107]

In fact, Binder felt that the United Nations was already overly committed financially and could not afford to underwrite the conference. In addition, he said, the time for the meeting was poor, given existing international tensions. Many problems awaited an international conference, Moulik, the Indian delegate, agreed. If a twelve-member subcommission could not agree on a draft code, expecting a conference of some 150 people to come to a consensus was unrealistic. The possibility of problems did not mean that subcommission members should scuttle the session, however; "whatever happened, even an unsatisfactory code was not entirely devoid of value."[108]

One reason for Binder's opposition to the draft code was the voting pattern on its provisions reflected within the subcommission. Few sections had passed without numerous abstentions, leading the American delegate to believe that no subcommission member strongly supported the document. Silva Carvallo of Chile, however, thought that Binder "attached too much importance to the relatively high number of abstentions in the voting on the different articles of the code." Members whose amendments had been rejected logically would "abstain from voting on a text which they would have drafted differently," but the differences "were more apparent than real." When the journalists of the world came together to debate the code, settling any remaining difficulties would be easy. Binder was unable to agree with his colleagues; to him, the high number of abstentions proved that "the different ideas of journalism held in different countries were irreconcilable." Rather than being indications of hurt feelings over rejected amendments, the abstentions "clearly showed a lack of enthusiasm for the code." In fact, Binder planned to "vote against such a futile draft" if he had the opportunity to serve either in the General Assembly or on the Economic and Social Council. Calling an international conference would only exacerbate differences rather than ameliorate them. Binder believed that the code's only value was as an artifact that reflected its times. The document should be studied in journalism schools and viewed as "the maximum which the journalists of the time had been able to achieve." But the code would never be widely accepted, especially in the United States.[109]

Most subcommission members disagreed vehemently with Binder's assessment. If professional journalists could only work on the draft code, subcommission members felt sure that most journalists would welcome its provisions. But before the world's journalists could meet, the subcommission had to plan the necessary conference. To circumvent Binder's arguments about the political contamination involved if the United Nations itself organized the conference, Azkoul suggested asking the secretary-general to establish an ad hoc committee of press experts to make the necessary arrangements. Subcommission refusal to proceed with conference plans "would encourage intervention by some intergovernmental body, such as the Economic and Social Council or the General Assembly." The failure of any code-writing conference to materialize would undoubtedly have a disturbing influence on public opinion, but, he contended, anticipating the failure of the conference and therefore refusing to convene the session at all was almost the equivalent of dooming the conference to failure. The subcommission had to make a good faith effort to complete its work.[110]

For once, Zonov agreed with Binder. He also opposed sending the draft code to a special conference but for different reasons. The Russian believed that any code produced by an international gathering of journalists would be just as unsatisfactory as the one written by the subcommission. Only if the United Nations itself became involved in the code-writing process did the Soviet delegate think that a code acceptable to his country could be drafted.[111] And, of course, if the Soviets found the code acceptable, the Americans would not, and vice versa. Regardless of the protests from the two superpowers, subcommission members adopted the draft code of ethics that the majority of them had written.

Debate over the future work of the United Nations on freedom of information topics also revealed the great gulf between the perceptions of the United States and other subcommission members on the world's information needs. Binder's list of suggestions for the future stressed increasing the amount of news available to the people of the world by removing obstacles to correspondents operating in foreign countries and lowering national barriers to the exchange of information.[112] Admirable though the American list might be, Salvador P. López of the Philippines believed that Binder's suggestions were slanted toward the difficulties that confronted journalists from countries in which the information media were highly developed. Censorship and other infringements were politically motivated and "were merely the result of current international tension. They could only be removed if international relations improved, whereas the purely physical obstacles were by far the most important for the under-developed countries." The latter nations needed printing presses, radio equipment, newsprint—in short, everything necessary to establish an in-formation industry—"and had no means of obtaining them." To López, for instance, getting news to the people of India, "who had neither newspapers nor radios," was more important than providing American citizens "with even fuller news."[113]

Rather than pursuing that point, Binder turned to another criticism of the United States—one condemning the nation's seeming withdrawal from the international information scene. Stressing that he had not consulted his government before making comments that were critical of United Nations efforts on freedom of information topics, Binder said that his remarks did reflect the disillusionment of American journalists over "the meagre results of the Sub-Commission's work." That discontent was real and was becoming ever more widespread, he warned, and such feelings were "creating an atmosphere of hostility to all the work the United Nations had done in that field." The American Bar Association recently had denounced the newsgathering convention as a threat to the constitutional liberties of the American people and had "requested the public authorities to reject it categorically." The same attitude was developing within the American Society of Newspaper Editors, originally one of the strongest supporters of international free-press action. Binder himself still supported international action to promote freedom of information, but he admitted that when asked by his government about the advisability of continuing the subcommission's charter, he had suggested its termination.[114] The United Nations still had work to do in the field of international freedom of information, but he believed that future efforts must be far more constructive than the code of ethics, which might cause an American withdrawal from continued discussions.

In addition, Binder opposed a subcommission effort to create a special office within the United Nations to deal with information-related problems. Experience had shown that both the subcommission and special committees on information questions created by the United Nations "served only as forums for the expression of profound differences." Since a constructive discussion of "lowering the barriers to the flow of information between the peoples" seemed impossible, Binder refused to support any effort to rejuvenate the subcommission or to create a special organ within the secretariat to consider information problems.[115] As if to prove Binder's contention about the inability of any organization within the United Nations to deal successfully with information-related questions, the proposal to set up an independent committee of experts to investigate abuses was almost immediately criticized by subcommission member on the basis of the body's potential membership. The five-member body suggested by André Géraud of France drew protests from Moulik, the Indian delegate, who complained that "the Sub-Commission's debates had shown that members from the under-developed countries were more interested in the problems of freedom of information than those from the major Powers. Any new body would probably include members from the United States of America, the USSR and France, so that the smaller Powers would inevitably be in a minority." Therefore, membership must be large enough "to give equitable geographical representation to members who were interested not only in the general subject but also in specific problems of newsprint shortage, technical assistance and the supply of equipment."[116]

Thus, the subcommission's final session ended, with its members still locked in the disagreements that had marred its work from its beginning. Binder saw the subcommission's failure as symptomatic "of the deep differences which beset the contemporary world." With the world divided over issues such as totalitarianism and democracy, any United Nations debate almost naturally would be caught up in the battle for ideological supremacy. Some nations, preferring not to take sides in this great struggle, would "try to divert such a subcommission to less challenging endeavors." In accepting the subcommission assignment in 1949, Binder had hoped to "convince people who distrust or detest freedom of information and of the press that there are greater dangers to their well-being in governmental controls than in freedom, even when freedom is abused." But his dream was beyond reach in a burgeoning cold war. Rather than providing a plan for international freedom of information, the subcommission simply "called attention to the profound differences existing among the 60 members of the UN in freedom of information matters."[117]

THE FINAL CAMPAIGN AGAINST
UNITED NATIONS INVOLVEMENT BEGINS

The campaign against additional United Nations involvement in freedom of information issues continued as the Social Committee of the Economic and Social Council debated the subcommission's final report. During these discussions, Kayser of France cited some awesome statistics. Nine different organs within the United Nations had debated freedom of information topics since the Geneva conference in 1948, with a total of thirty-three sessions devoted in whole or in part to the subject. Freedom of information took up more than 600 hours of discussion by other organs devoting their time exclusively to the topic. The United Nations had circulated seven questionnaires to governments, prepared about 100 working papers, and printed millions of pages of documents on freedom of information topics. The total cost to the United Nations for this work probably exceeded $100,000—with little to show for the time and expense. Considering the United Nations investment, the organization faced a fundamental decision, Kayser said. "If freedom of information was an important problem, then one must find out what was wrong and remedy the situation; if it was considered a secondary problem, one should have the courage to give it up and once and for all put an end to a debate deemed to be frustrating and fruitless."[118]

The French delegation, Kayser said, "believing that the dissemination of accurate news might contribute to the relaxation of tension, would like to see the United Nations finally join in the fight for truth and peace although the obstacles to freedom were now greater than ever on account of politics, diplomacy, economic systems and the financial situation." Rather than abandoning the issue altogether or asking UNESCO to deal with freedom of information matters, Kayser picked up the idea of Géraud, his countryman who had served on the subcommission, and suggested the establishment of a special five-member committee to investigate the obstacles to international freedom of information and to propose ways to overcome these barriers.[119]

Debates over the future of freedom of information work within the United Nations continued, without the support of the effort's previous driving force, the United States. In fact, Azmi of Egypt, the subcommission's chairman, saw the deterioration of the freedom of information movement solely in terms of the two great powers who were "currently engaging in a 'cold war' and the fear and suspicion engendered had resulted in changing their original positive attitude to a negative one."[120] Protests to the contrary from the representatives of the United States and the Soviet Union simply confirmed his opinions, Azmi said.[121] López of the Philippines agreed that the United Nations had encountered problems and numerous disagreements during its discussions on freedom of information, but, he argued, "waiting until peace prevailed throughout the world before attacking the problem of freedom of information" would be very dangerous. "In reality, freedom of information was essential to the establishment of a lasting peace."[122]

Seeking a compromise, Robert Feneaux of Belgium suggested that the United Nations change its approach to freedom of information questions. Rather than seeking philosophical solutions to free-press problems, direct action on slightly less controversial topics might be more appropriate. The list for possible action was substantial: securing an adequate supply of newsprint, writing an international statute to protect journalists, helping underdeveloped countries improve their media, and training journalists satisfactorily. A concrete approach might yet crown United Nations efforts to promote freedom of information with positive results, he said. Another reason for United Nations paralysis on freedom of information topics, said C.A.G. Meade, the representative of Great Britain, was the way in which the subcommission was organized. Here, the United Nations itself was responsible for the subcommission's problem; Meade did not think that the United Nations could name a body of experts, such as the subcommission, and reasonably expect that its members would be free from governmental influence. Inevitably, some members spoke on their own, and others voiced governmental positions; the mixture doomed debate. The best approach to freedom of information questions in the future, Meade felt, was to break those questions into smaller units for study.[123]

Defending the United States position was not easy, but Kotschnig, the United States representative on the Social Committee, made the attempt. While he agreed that "freedom of information, the touchstone of all freedoms, was seriously threatened in the modern world," Kotschnig refused to accept the responsibility for the problems encountered in developing a United Nations–sanctioned plan to secure that freedom. Although unwilling to grant the subcommission additional life or to back the creation of a panel of experts to investigate the world's information problems, Kotschnig said the United States could support the appointment of one man, a rapporteur, who would be instructed to draft a concise report on the status of international freedom of information. The report would, of course, be accompanied by recommendations for action. Regardless of what his colleagues at the United Nations thought of the American position, Kotschnig said, "the Government, the press and the people of the United States of America would continue to fight for freedom of information and to uphold the right of all to think and express themselves freely, without any outside interference."[124]

Although the United States pledged to continue the fight for international freedom of information, by 1952 the American approach, which was approved by both the government and the press, was quite different from that of earlier years. While Binder faced persistent frustration within the subcommission on a variety of freedom of information topics and especially on the proposed code of ethics, American diplomats successfully sidetracked the code of ethics by capitalizing on the general discontent of superior United Nations bodies with the subcommission's work. By mid-June, American diplomats notched a considerable victory when the Economic and Social Council adopted a resolution saying that additional work on the draft code of ethics "should be undertaken by professional workers in the media of information without governmental interference, national or international." The resolution asked the secretary-general to distribute copies of the draft code to all national and international organizations interested in the topic and to inform those groups "that, if they think it desirable, the United Nations might co-operate with them in organizing an international conference for the purpose of drawing up an international code of ethics."[125]

With the Economic and Social Council's resolution in hand, Kotschnig told the October 1952 meeting of leading journalists he hoped the code of ethics was dead in the United Nations. The resolution passed by the council endorsed the American position on the code, even though delegates amended the proposal to mention United Nations willingness to help organize an international conference if professional organizations desired such a session. "Frankly," Kotschnig said, "we very much hope that the various press and other agencies, mass media agencies, will make it quite clear that they do not want to have such a conference under the auspices of the United Nations."[126]

American diplomats were pleased with changes in the status of the Subcommission on Freedom of Information and of the Press as well. As Kotschnig explained, after having been "saddled" with a subcommission that met several times over four years "and which produced next to nothing," the United States and its allies managed "to get that subcommission killed." In the face of a great deal of pressure for maintaining a United Nations presence in freedom of information activities, the United States, by using "a good deal of time and I am afraid a fair amount of arm-twisting," obtained a resolution appointing a single rapporteur to investigate the status of international freedom of information. As Kotschnig said, "in exchange for a subcommission, which is quite uncontrollable and quite useless as we see it, we proposed—we had to propose something, we just couldn't say nothing—we proposed the appointment of a rapporteur on freedom of information." This one man would work with the secretariat for a year to prepare "a substantive report covering major contemporary problems and developments in the field of freedom of information" as well as recommendations for practical actions "to surmount those obstacles to the fuller enjoyment of freedom of information which can be surmounted at the present time." With the acceptance of the rapporteur, Kotschnig said, "we are safe for the time being" from the subcommission and other United Nations free-press activities.[127]

Gone was any acknowledgment of American parentage of the subcommission notion; of American support for the subcommission's becoming the continuing machinery within the United Nations that would deal successfully with international problems relating to freedom of information; of the 1948 idea that the subcommission should be granted commission status, a staff, and should meet twice a year to deal with free-press matters. Instead, in 1952, said Erwin D. Canham, who chaired the consultative session, the subcommission now was viewed as "futile, dangerous, expensive." As a body that achieved nothing, the subcommission provided "a forum at which restrictive proposals could be made with some prestige. It was basically a device for airing this whole subject, I believe, in an unhelpful and unconstructive manner." Ideally, the press preferred to "wash this subcommission business all up. Realistically, there is not much hope" of accomplishing that end, Canham said. But the subcommission "has now been reduced from a continuing commission meeting at periodic intervals to one man drafting a report. That would seem to be some progress."[128]

In the end, various United Nations bodies up through the General Assembly accepted this American perception of progress on freedom of information topics, thus giving the Americans a final victory on this most controversial subject. A rapporteur was to study and write a report on obstacles to international freedom of the press. The secretariat would refer the code of ethics to professional groups for additional consideration. In addition, the United Nations would continue to explore the possibilities of UNESCO's becoming the primary home for all international freedom of information questions.[129] Despite the formality of the study, the decision to move freedom of information questions to UNESCO effectively had been made already. With the expiration of the subcommission's charter and with repeated hostile debates on freedom of information topics occupying valuable committee time within the United Nations, the international organization was more than ready to move on to other subjects. As the United States withdrew its support for additional United Nations efforts in the field, a leading force behind the organization's continued presence in freedom of information matters disappeared. Just what the United States hoped to gain from moving free-press discussions to UNESCO, an independent, specialized, and autonomous agency, joined to the United Nations only through agreements to coordinate efforts on certain topics, is unclear. But even a simple change of venue might bring welcome relief from the direction that freedom of information debates had taken at the United Nations.

In the years since its founding, UNESCO had tried to increase the availability of various kinds of information around the world by conducting regular studies of technical and other difficulties impairing communication. Because its activities—trying to reduce international tensions through educational, social, and cultural activities—were so different from the growing political emphasis of the work of the United Nations, UNESCO's efforts relating to freedom of information avoided some of the problems that plagued free-press discussions within the United Nations. In fact, UNESCO's constitution gave the organization specific responsibilities to fulfill in the area of international communications while the United Nations Charter failed to mention freedom of information. Under terms of its charter, UNESCO was to "collaborate in the work of advancing the mutual knowledge and understanding of peoples, through all the means of mass communication and to that end recommend such international agreements as may be necessary to promote the free flow of ideas by word and image." The organization was also to initiate "methods of international co-operation calculated to give the people of all countries access to the printed and published materials produced by any of them."[130]

To promote these ends, UNESCO was to be a clearinghouse "for the collection, analysis, dissemination and exchange of information and experiences in the techniques, uses and effects of the press, film, radio and allied media, in the fields of education, science and culture, in collaboration with international, regional and national institutions and research centres and with individual experts." UNESCO also was to survey the condition of technical facilities for press, film, and radio outlets worldwide, with particular emphasis on conditions in East Asia, Africa, and Europe. If asked, UNESCO organized commissions of experts to help war-devastated countries rehabilitate their communications facilities. The director-general of UNESCO also supervised work aimed at reducing obstacles to the free flow of information, but this work was limited to basically nonpress items, including the promotion of the exchange of educational, scientific, and cultural materials; the study of the effects of postal rates and customs duties and the impact of copyright regulations; and the evaluation of problems caused by the poor distribution of radio frequencies and shortages of raw materials. Until the early 1950s, UNESCO's involvement with the press focused primarily on the gathering of information for use by the Subcommission on Freedom of Information and of the Press. UNESCO left much of the direct contact with press-oriented organizations to the subcommission, concentrating instead on cooperation with regional economic commissions and specialized bodies such as the International Telecommunications Union, which were on the periphery of the subcommission's interests. Occasionally, UNESCO submitted special reports to the Economic and Social Council on items such as the shortage of newsprint and on journalism education.[131]

Leaders of the two bodies saw the organizations' work as separate. The subcommission emphasized solving problems "involved in the dissemination of information, e.g., such as those created by legal or political barriers to the free flow of information or by the dissemination of false or distorted reports," said a report prepared jointly by the director-general of UNESCO and the secretary-general of the United Nations. UNESCO, on the other hand, was concerned "with the quality, and quantity of news reaching the public by means of press, radio and film, and with the reduction of obstacles to the international circulation of educational, scientific and cultural materials of all kinds."[132] UNESCO, however, did deal with several topics that had caused problems when they were discussed at the United Nations. For instance, UNESCO was studying the possibility of an international convention designed to ease the movement between countries of "persons engaged in educational, scientific or cultural pursuits," including teachers, students, researchers, museum personnel, librarians, writers, and artists.[133] When the United Nations tried to ease the travel of news correspondents, it ran into a good deal of difficulty. Observers could not predict how UNESCO would fare in turning its attention to informational problems.

A brief review of several UNESCO debates would have provided little comfort to Americans who were seeking a friendlier home for freedom of information efforts. Although prolonged tirades against the United States communications system may have been less obvious at UNESCO meetings, the difference may have been due to the limited scope of UNESCO's commission rather than to satisfaction with the American media. Undercurrents of discontent were apparent. At the 1946 UNESCO session, for instance, delegates had discussed the possibility of writing a journalistic code of honor to govern professional practices.[134] At the 1947 UNESCO session, J. B. Priestley, British delegate and author, attacked United States proposals for removal of obstacles to communication, charging that the United States wanted to use UNESCO to spread its culture throughout the world by creating a massive communications network for use by American news agencies.[135] The same 1947 UNESCO sessions found the communist bloc raising the issue of the alleged warmongering tendencies of the American press and complaining that despite having proof of American intentions, the nations of the world were still being asked, "under the pretext of the free flow of information," to allow foreign correspondents from the United States to freely enter all countries of the world.[136]

At the Geneva conference on freedom of information in 1948, Julian

Huxley, director-general of UNESCO, told delegates that "freedom of information did not consist simply in opening up access to more and more masses of information. A laissez-faire anarchy in the services of information was incompatible with the true nature of liberty and could only derive from a blindness to the real needs of the world."[137] Debates in 1949 were not much better from the American perspective. A proposal for UNESCO to seek ways to promote international understanding through radio broadcasts brought a critical allusion to the American broadcasting system from Sir James Shelley, New Zealand's delegate, who noted, "in some countries the radio was in the hands of private institutions, tolerant only of their own point of view, and whom no government would dare to touch."[138] And in 1951, UNESCO called for a special conference to deal with the continuing problem of newsprint availability and distribution. As the Belgian delegate, Jean de Spot, pointed out, although all UNESCO members recognized the need for an independent press, the shortage of newsprint "was a grave threat to the very existence of such a press." Not only was the existence of a free press threatened by the newsprint shortage, but so, too, was UNESCO's literacy campaign, Camille Lhérisson, the Haitian delegate, noted. Comments on the unavailability of newsprint, while not specifically aimed at American consumption patterns, put the United States delegate, Samuel DePalma, on the defensive. He stressed that America was importing less newsprint from Scandinavian countries and was not responsible for increased charges imposed by those nations.[139]

Thus, although UNESCO only occasionally had been caught up in issues that might make the United States or its press uneasy, its discussions still could be as threatening to the American system of freedom of the press as debates in the United Nations itself. After seven years of unpleasantness within the United Nations over freedom of information issues, however, moving the debate to an organization with somewhat less visibility was attractive. And by 1952, when support for the move to UNESCO grew appreciably, support for the international free-press movement had all but disappeared within the United States.

NOTES

1. Lloyd Free, Office of International Information, to Walter M. Kotschnig, United Nations Affairs, June 23, 1948, 400.48 FOI Conference, SDR.
2. Members of the subcommission were: Carroll Binder, United States, editorial editor of the *Minneapolis Tribune* and former foreign correspondent; Francis Williams, United Kingdom, special writer for the *London Observer* and former public relations adviser to Prime Minister Clement Attlee; Vasily M. Zonov, Soviet Union, with ten years of press-related experience; André Géraud, France, journalist and author specializing in diplomatic affairs; Alfredo Silva Carvallo, Chile, editor of the *Valparaiso La Union*; P. H. Chang, China,

director of the Chinese News Service for North America; Salvador P. López, Philippines, adviser on political affairs to the Philippine Mission to the United Nations; Devadas Gandhi, India, editor of the *New Delhi Hindustan Times* and president of the All-India Newspaper Editors Conference; Mahmoud Azmi, Egypt, owner of *Al Esteklal* and editor of several other newspapers; Stevan Dedijer, Yugoslavia, deputy director of Tanjug, the Yugoslav state news agency; Karim Azkoul, Lebanon, representative and acting representative on several United Nations bodies; Roberto Fontaina, Uruguay, holder of various diplomatic appointments. Chang, Géraud, López, and Fontaina held appointments on the previous subcommission. *See* "Press Subcommission Members Selected," *E&P*, April 16, 1949, p. 52.

3. Doris Willens, "Corps of UN Reporters in Trouble Spots Proposed," *E&P*, May 28, 1949, p. 8.
4. E/CN.4/Sub.1/SR.49, 3rd session, June 1, 1949, pp. 1–6.
5. E/CN.4/Sub.1/SR.50, 3rd session, June 2, 1949, pp. 1–3.
6. E/CN.4/Sub.1/SR.63, 3rd session, June 10, 1949, pp. 7–8.
7. E/CN.4/Sub.1/SR.65, 3rd session, June 13, 1949, p. 11.
8. E/CN.4/Sub.1/SR.64, 3rd session, June 13, 1949, p. 3.
9. E/CN.4/Sub.1/92, 3rd session, *Proposed Draft Resolution Concerning the Encouragement of National Information Agencies*, June 10, 1949.
10. E/CN.4/Sub.1/SR.66, 3rd session, June 14, 1949, p. 12.
11. Ibid.
12. E/CN.4/Sub.1/SR.67, 3rd session, June 14, 1949, pp. 2–3.
13. Ibid., pp. 3–4. American endorsement of technical assistance provided by the newspaper industry lasted through 1952, when the consultative group meeting in October 1952 suggested that additional efforts be made for exchanging and training journalists rather than agreeing to requests to help sponsor national news agencies in other countries. *See* Transcript, Consultative Conference on Freedom of Information, pp. 25–34.
14. "Subsidized News Agencies," *E&P*, June 18, 1949, p. 32.
15. Samuel DePalma, United Nations expert, to Durward Sandifer, United Nations Affairs, June 17, 1949, RG 59, NA, Box 2255, 501.BD Freedom of Information/6-2949.
16. E/AC.7/SR.96, 9th session, July 18, 1949, p. 17.
17. E/AC.7/SR.97, 9th session, July 19, 1949, p. 8.
18. E/AC.7/SR.98, 9th session, July 19, 1949, p. 11.
19. ECOR, 9th session, 314th meeting, July 28, 1949, pp. 461–62.
20. E/CN.4/Sub.1/SR.68, 4th session, May 15, 1950, p. 10.
21. E/CN.4/Sub.1/SR.69, 4th session, May 15, 1950, pp. 4–5.
22. Ibid., pp. 5–7.
23. Ibid., pp. 12–14.
24. E/CN.4/Sub.1/SR.71, 4th session, May 16, 1950, pp. 3–4.
25. ECOR, 11th Session, *Report of the Sub-Commission (fourth session) to the Economic and Social Council*, Supplement 5A, p. 2.
26. E/CN.4/Sub.1/SR.71, 4th session, May 16, 1950, pp. 13–14, 16.
27. E/CN.4/Sub.1/SR.72, 4th session, May 17, 1950, pp. 3–4.
28. E/CN.4/Sub.1/116, 4th session, *Draft Resolution Concerning the Limitation of Freedom of Information in a State of Emergency*, May 15, 1950.

29. E/CN.4/Sub.1/SR.72, 4th session, May 17, 1950, pp. 4–5.
30. E/CN.4/Sub.1/114, 4th session, *Draft of an International Code of Ethics*, May 15, 1950.
31. E/CN.4/Sub.1/SR.72, 4th session, May 17, 1950, p. 17.
32. E/CN.4/Sub.1/SR.73, 4th session, May 17, 1950, pp. 4–5.
33. Ibid., pp. 5–7.
34. Ibid., pp. 6–9.
35. Ibid., pp. 12–13.
36. E/CN.4/Sub.1/SR.74, 4th session, May 19, 1950, pp. 4–5.
37. E/CN.4/Sub.1/114, 4th session, *Draft of an International Code of Ethics*, May 15, 1950, p. 1.
38. E/CN.4/Sub.1/SR.74, 4th session, May 19, 1950, pp. 5–7.
39. Ibid., p. 11.
40. E/CN.4/Sub.1/114, 4th session, *Draft of an International Code of Ethics*, May 15, 1950, pp. 1–2.
41. E/CN.4/Sub.1/SR.74, 4th session, May 19, 1950, p. 11.
42. E/CN.4/Sub.1/SR.75, 4th session, May 19, 1950, pp. 14–15.
43. E/CN.4/Sub.1/SR.76, 4th session, May 20, 1950, pp. 13–14.
44. Ibid., pp. 15–17.
45. E/CN.4/Sub.1/114, 4th session, *Draft of an International Code of Ethics*, May 15, 1950, p. 4.
46. E/CN.4/Sub.1/SR.77, 4th session, May 22, 1950, pp. 10–12.
47. E/CN.4/Sub.1/114, 4th session, *Draft of an International Code of Ethics*, May 15, 1950, p. 4.
48. E/CN.4/Sub.1/SR.77, 4th session, May 22, 1950, p. 15.
49. E/CN.4/Sub.1/SR.78, 4th session, May 22, 1950, p. 6.
50. Ibid., p. 8 (emphasis in original).
51. Ibid., p. 7.
52. E/CN.4/Sub.1/SR.79, 4th session, May 23, 1950, p. 11.
53. Ibid., pp. 23, 19.
54. Ibid., pp. 13, 16–17, 23–24.
55. Ibid., pp. 13–14.
56. Ibid., pp. 20–22, 25.
57. E/CN.4/Sub.1/SR.80, 4th session, May 23, 1950, pp. 7–8, 10. The text of the code of ethics adopted in Montevideo is found in Appendix I.
58. E/CN.4/Sub.1/SR.81, 4th session, May 24, 1950, pp. 1–12.
59. E/CN.4/Sub.1/127, 4th session, *Draft Resolution Concerning Mistreatment and Discriminatory Treatment of Foreign Correspondents*, May 23, 1950.
60. E/CN.4/Sub.1/SR.82, 4th session, May 24, 1950, p. 9.
61. Ibid., pp. 9–10.
62. Ibid., pp. 11, 10–11.
63. Ibid., pp. 13–15.
64. E/CN.4/Sub.1/SR.70, 4th session, May 16, 1950, pp. 3–4.
65. E/CN.4/Sub.1/SR.83, 4th session, May 25, 1950, pp. 8–9. American journalists had similar complaints about the treatment of their families in Eastern bloc nations. The dilemma of some United States correspondents stationed in the Soviet Union was complicated by the fact that they had married Russian citizens who might never be granted permission to leave the country. *See* "An Open Letter to a Soviet Editor," *Guild Reporter*, October 26, 1951, p. 3.

66. Ibid., pp. 12, 11, 14.
67. E/CN.4/Sub.1/SR.85, 4th session, May 26, 1950, pp. 5–8.
68. Robert U. Brown, "Shop Talk at Thirty," *E&P*, July 1, 1950, p. 60.
69. Ibid.
70. Frank J. Starzel, "The Business of Informing the Public," *Nieman Reports*, October 1950, p. 5.
71. E/AC.7/SR.135, 11th session, July 12, 1950, p. 6.
72. Ibid., pp. 9–10.
73. Ibid., pp. 11–12. The Social Committee ultimately endorsed the subcommission's resolution against jamming of radio signals. In the resolution's final form, however, delegates dropped the reference to the Soviet Union, which Binder had fought so hard to include. Members of the Social Committee believed that a specific reference to the primary offender would be counterproductive, especially since the Soviets, who were boycotting United Nations sessions at the time, could not defend themselves. *See* E/AC.7/SR.136, 11th session, July 12, 1950; E/AC.7/SR.137, 11th session, July 14, 1950.
74. Ibid., p. 13.
75. E/AC.7/SR.136, 11th session, July 12, 1950, pp. 4–5.
76. Ibid., p. 11.
77. GAOR, Third Committee, 5th session, 276th meeting, October 3, 1950, p. 32.
78. Ibid., 277th meeting, October 3, 1950, p. 40.
79. Ibid., p. 41.
80. Ibid., p. 42.
81. ECOR, 11th session, 436th meeting, December 13, 1950, pp. 465–67.
82. E/AC.7/SR.179, 12th session, March 6, 1951, pp. 5, 7.
83. Ibid., p. 9.
84. E/AC.7/SR.180, 12th session, March 9, 1951, p. 4.
85. E/AC.7/SR.179, 12th session, March 6, 1951, p. 11.
86. E/AC.7/SR.180, 12th session, March 9, 1951, p. 11.
87. Ibid., p. 12.
88. ECOR, 12th session, 464th meeting, March 9, 1951, p. 230.
89. Ibid., 466th meeting, March 13, 1951, pp. 240, 243.
90. E/AC.34/SR.10, April 17, 1951, p. 13.
91. E/AC.34/SR.13, April 18, 1951, p. 8.
92. E/AC.34/SR.19, June 25, 1951, pp. 10–13.
93. E/CN.4/Sub.1/SR.87, 5th session, March 3, 1952, pp. 3–4, 10.
94. E/CN.4/Sub.1/SR.88, 5th session, March 4, 1952, p. 3.
95. E/CN.4/Sub.1/SR.89, 5th session, March 5, 1952, pp. 2–4.
96. Ibid., p. 5.
97. The United Nations had asked more than 400 organizations to comment on the draft code; fewer than fifty actually replied. Two other American groups—the National Conference of Editorial Writers and the American Council on Education in Journalism—responded; each strongly objected to the code's provisions. *See* E/CN.4/Sub.1/151/Add.1, 5th session, *Analysis of Comments of Information Enterprises and National and International Professional Associations on Draft International Code of Ethics*, February 6, 1952, pp. 9–10.
    The ASNE leaders did not tell the subcommission about the problems that the society had encountered in writing and enforcing its canons, both of which were considerable and both of which made the organization wary of becoming

involved in any attempts to impose ethical standards on its membership. This attitude logically carried over to attempts to impose ethical standards on the world's journalists. *See*, e.g., Pitts, *Read All About It!* pp. 3–7; Harvey Saalberg, "The Canons of Journalism: A 50-Year Perspective," *Journalism Quarterly* 50 (Winter 1973):731–34.

98. E/CN.4/Sub.1/SR.89, 5th session, March 5, 1952, pp. 6–7.
99. Ibid., p. 8.
100. E/CN.4/Sub.1/SR.92, 5th session, March 6, 1952, p. 5.
101. E/CN.4/Sub.1/SR.91, 5th session, March 6, 1952, p. 5.
102. E/CN.4/Sub.1/SR.92, 5th session, March 6, 1952, p. 4.
103. E/CN.4/Sub.1/SR.89, 5th session, March 5, 1952, pp. 9–10.
104. E/CN.4/Sub.1/SR.90, 5th session, March 5, 1952, p. 3.
105. E/CN.4/Sub.1/SR.100, 5th session, March 12, 1952, p. 2.
106. E/CN.4/Sub.1/SR.101, 5th session, March 13, 1952, p. 4. By the time that these debates were occurring, Sigma Delta Chi, the society of professional journalists, representing some 19,000 journalists in the United States, had proven Binder's statements about the impossibility of getting journalists to agree on a code of ethics. That organization began considering a code of ethics in 1947 in the wake of the Hutchins Commission on Freedom of the Press's criticism of American journalism. In 1948, a committee was established to frame such a code. In 1949, the code was presented at the organization's annual meeting and was tabled. In 1950, the code came up again and was once more tabled for further study. In 1951, the code came up one more time and was tabled indefinitely. Members decided that the organization's ritual, which stressed professional responsibility, and the ASNE Canons of Journalism provided all of the ethical guidance that journalists required. *See* "Convention Assails Press Curbs, Loose Practices in News Handling," *Quill*, Section Two, Sigma Delta Chi Section, December 1951, p. 7.

    When the code was discussed in 1949, comments stressed the difficulty that members would encounter in drawing the line between ethical and unethical journalistic behavior. Some members supported the adoption of a code without enforcement provisions, but the dominant feeling was that members wanted freedom of the press even for unethical publications. *See* "Dallas Host To Record Convention," *Quill*, December 1949, p. 6.

107. Ibid., p. 4.
108. Ibid., p. 5.
109. Ibid., pp. 6, 9–10.
110. Ibid., p. 8.
111. Ibid., p. 10.
112. E/CN.4/Sub.1/SR.102, 5th session, March 14, 1952, pp. 7–10.
113. E/CN.4/Sub.1/SR.103, 5th session, March 14, 1952, p. 10.
114. Ibid., p. 11.
115. E/CN.4/Sub.1/SR.108, 5th session, March 19, 1952, pp. 4–5. The subcommission voted, nine to two, to recommend, in principle, the establishment of a special freedom of information office.
116. E/CN.4/Sub.1/SR.110, 5th session, March 20, 1952, pp. 5–6.
117. Carroll Binder, "Failure of a Mission," *Nieman Reports*, October 1952, p. 12.
118. E/AC.7/SR.214, 14th session, June 4, 1952, pp. 3–4.

119. Ibid., pp. 4–5.
120. Ibid., p. 7.
121. E/AC.7/SR.216, 14th session, June 6, 1952, p. 8.
122. E/AC.7/SR.215, 14th session, June 5, 1952, p. 4.
123. Ibid., pp. 8–10.
124. Ibid., pp. 5–7.
125. ECOR, 14th session, *Freedom of Information:Resolutions of 12 and 13 June 1952* (E/2263), June 24, 1952, p. 1. The General Assembly adopted a similar resolution in December 1952.
126. Transcript, Consultative Conference on Freedom of Information, pp. 4–5.
127. Ibid., pp. 7–9.
128. Ibid., p. 11.
129. Freedom of Information, *Yearbook of the United Nations: 1952*, United Nations, New York, Department of Public Information, 1953, pp. 465–66, 475–79.
130. UNESCO Constitution, art. 1.
131. ECOR, 12th session, *Co-ordination of the Activities of the United Nations and UNESCO Relating to Freedom of Information: Report by the Secretary-General of the United Nations, Prepared in Collaboration with the Director-General of UNESCO* (E/1891), January 8, 1951, pp. 7–9, 12. *See also* René Maheu, "The Work of UNESCO in the Field Of Mass Communications," *Journalism Quarterly* 25 (June 1948):157–62; Ralph D. Casey, "UNESCO's Role in Advancing Education for Journalism," *Journalism Quarterly* 25 (December 1948):386–90; Julian Behrstock, "Free Flow of Information: UNESCO's World-Wide Program," *Journalism Quarterly* 26 (December 1949):453–59.
132. Ibid., p. 14.
133. E/CN.4/Sub.1/142, 5th session, *The Activities of UNESCO in the Field of Freedom of Information (1947–1951): Submitted by the Director-General of UNESCO*, June 14, 1951, p. 5.
134. UNESCO Proceedings, 1st session, Report of the Sub-Commission on Mass Communication, p. 227.
135. "Charges U.S. Wants to Control UNESCO," *E&P*, November 22, 1947, p. 52.
136. UNESCO Proceedings, 2nd session, 7th plenary meeting, November 11, 1947, p. 99.
137. E/CONF.6/C.1/SR/2, March 24, 1948, p. 4.
138. UNESCO Proceedings, 4th session, Programme and Budget Commission, 11th meeting, September 28, 1949, p. 307.
139. UNESCO Proceedings, 6th session, Programme Commission, 13th meeting, July 3, 1951, pp. 357–58.

CHAPTER 8

The Profession Abandons The Crusade

The debate within the United Nations had greatly disillusioned American journalists who initially had supported the international free-press crusade. Slowly, the less committed among them pulled away from the campaign, and as the United Nations wound up its work in the field, few backers of international accords remained within the profession. The debates, however, were not the only reason behind the American press's change of heart. Events at home and abroad impinged on news gathering with increasing regularity, causing fundamental revisions in the profession's view of several of the crusade's major tenets. Never really comfortable with its relationship with the government during the crusade, the rush of events destroyed the uncertain alliance between the press and the State Department.

Underlying most of the rhetoric in the international free-press campaign was an effort to protect American correspondents working in foreign countries. Generally, the protection centered on ensuring the individual's right to gather and disseminate information; on a more basic level, the guarantee also sought to safeguard the correspondent's personal safety. In the last few years of the crusade, American journalists saw foreign correspondents abused and ejected from various countries on sundry pretexts. Even worse, the late 1940s and early 1950s found one American correspondent murdered for doing his job and another thrown into a communist prison for the same reason. In neither of the latter two instances could the State Department provide much assistance to the reporters involved or to their worried employers.

AMERICAN CORRESPONDENTS ENDANGERED ABROAD

George Polk, Columbia Broadcasting System (CBS) correspondent in Greece, became a martyr to the free-press cause in May 1948. The journalist, described posthumously as a "courageous young reporter for United States newspapers and radio,"[1] probably was too devoted to reporting about a country torn by political conflict. One night, Polk left his hotel, apparently en route to a prearranged visit behind guerrilla lines. No one saw him alive again. Someone bound Polk's hands and feet, shot him once in the back of the head, and dumped his body in Salonika Bay. Several days later, his body washed ashore. Neither his wallet nor his watch was gone, so the motive behind the crime obviously was something other than robbery. Although Polk had contacts within both factions involved in the civil unrest in Greece, he was suspected of being sympathetic to the leftist guerrillas. Consequently, most observers saw his slaying as politically motivated. Speculation placed responsibility for his murder on both the right-wing faction because of his reporting and on the left-wing faction as an attempt to incriminate the right.

American journalists were incensed by Polk's murder and by the heavy-handed attempt at intimidation implicit in the slaying. The clear lesson from the killing was that "whoever murdered Polk did so as a warning to all newspapermen in Greece not to dig too deeply for the truth." Other journalists in Greece were in great danger "because newspapermen are traditionally difficult characters to intimidate"; additional murders might "make the warning more emphatic." If Polk's killers were not quickly apprehended and punished or if other journalists failed to continue Polk's work in Greece, *Editor & Publisher* feared that murder would "certainly be tried in other countries where political groups are afraid of the spotlight of world publicity."[2] The American Newspaper Guild, of which Polk was a member, agreed, declaring "no American news correspondent can be considered safe in carrying out his duties while the murder of George Polk remains unsolved, with its perpetrators unpunished. Neither can the American concepts of freedom of the press and free access to the news be guaranteed while the murder of Polk remains unsolved."[3] The entire episode raised serious questions about who was responsible for protecting correspondents throughout the world in order "to insure that the largest possible measure of truth reaches America." Furthermore, American journalists feared that "if investigation shows that Mr. Polk was murdered because he wrote and talked as he pleased, more has been lost than a trussed body in Salonika Bay. The American radio and press will have lost a singularly important freedom."[4]

Already concerned about the reaction of American journalists to the murder, the State Department soon faced a special committee of overseas writers, led by Walter Lippmann, asking about the status of the Greek investigation into the slaying. Lippmann emphasized that the American press believed the United States government must "take a strong line in this case to show its determination to protect American citizens who are carrying out the important task of reporting on events abroad." For now, the correspondents told the department, the press planned to follow the government's lead, but to preserve the press's interests in the case, the committee had obtained the services of General William Donovan, head of the wartime Overseas Special Services division, as legal counsel.[5] CBS added to the pressure on the State Department by sending two top correspondents to Greece to conduct a separate investigation.[6]

As a result of such press interest, the American government carefully followed the Greek investigation to ensure that the case was solved expeditiously. The State Department also was concerned about efforts to label Polk and his work as procommunist because, as Secretary of State George C. Marshall said, an "honest appraisal" of Polk's recent stories from Athens showed them "to be among fairest and most informed and objective emanating from Greece."[7] As proof of the government's intentions to ensure proper handling of the case, the American consul general in Salonika personally followed developments; two officers at the Athens Embassy were also assigned to the investigation. The British police mission in Greece participated in the investigation as well, and American correspondents had complete access to data in an attempt to secure press support for the results.[8] While basically satisfied with the manner in which Greek officials were handling the case, the United States government added the security officer for the American Aid Mission in Athens, a man with several years of experience with the Federal Bureau of Investigation, to the fact-finding team as well.[9] Individuals having communist connections ultimately were charged with committing the crime with the intent to implicate the rightists in Polk's murder[10]—and the case was closed.[11]

Murder was too heavy-handed for the Soviet Union and its Eastern bloc allies to attempt, even though they were equally intent on curbing the activities of meddlesome American correspondents. But the intimidation techniques that worked so well on Eastern bloc citizens were also successful when applied to obnoxious foreign correspondents. So, communists in Czechoslovakia arrested William N. Oatis, Associated Press (AP) bureau chief in Prague, on charges of espionage,[12] held him incommunicado for seventy days, tried and convicted him of espionage without access to United States Embassy officials or an adequate lawyer, and, on July 4, 1951, sentenced him to ten years in a Czechoslovak prison to be followed by expulsion from the country. Oatis was not sentenced to death, said the judge, because he had confessed to his crimes.[13]

Oatis's confession regurgitated traditional communist charges against the American press. Correspondents for other news agencies regularly sent stories to America based on their espionage activities, Oatis told the court. His employer, the Associated Press, was engaged in a highly competitive business and demanded similar copy. "My own espionage activity resulted from trying to check on stories that these other correspondents had produced in Prague," he said. The newspapers the Associated Press served in America "expect to get news and slanderous reports." Because of this, "I was under constant pressure" to produce such copy. Labeling himself "a man in the middle," Oatis said, "I am sorry I allowed myself to be used in

this way."[14] The confession failed to discourage Oatis's American supporters, who never doubted for a moment that some form of diabolical
communist coercion had forced Oatis's participation in a staged espionage
trial. "Like a ventriloquist's dummy, Oatis went through all the stiff
motions of 'confessing' to espionage," his colleagues said. To American
journalists, Oatis simply followed orders from his superiors in New York,
as expected; he pursued traditional news-gathering techniques, deliberately
misinterpreted by the Czechs as spying; and he visited foreign diplomats,
which was also part of his job.[15] Associated Press leaders labeled Oatis's trial
"a sham and a mockery of elemental justice." Evidence offered by the Czech
government proved only that Oatis was legitimately gathering news, based
on the American understanding of that profession's activities. The Associated Press vowed to work for the release of its employee, confident of the
support of "freedom-loving people everywhere" in the effort.[16] If the
communists planned to turn the Oatis case into a cause célèbre, the
Associated Press and its allies in the American newspaper community
planned to match them move for move.

Indeed, the Oatis case immediately became the premier issue within the
American journalistic community, for Oatis personified the reason behind
the international free-press crusade—that the gathering and dissemination of
news were not to be grounds for jailing a correspondent. Never once
throughout the campaign to win his release did an American journalist
overtly wonder if Oatis actually had engaged in espionage activities—despite
his confession. The very idea of a reporter for a reputable wire service
sharing his information with the American government was ridiculous, an
"anathema to everything AP and the American press stand for."[17] American
journalists sputtered and fumed that the Prague government could have
simply expelled Oatis. "But that might have been interpreted as a sign of
weakness. It serves their purpose more to apprehend him, try him and
convict him in a one-way court, so that they can proclaim to the world that
all newspapermen of the Western nations are spies." The communists also
hoped to intimidate correspondents by these actions; they most likely had
not anticipated the fervor with which the American press would work to
gain Oatis's release.[18]

American Newspaper Guild officials quickly denounced the kidnapping
of a fellow Guild member.[19] Directors of the American Society of Newspaper Editors (ASNE) sought to expedite Oatis's release. Retaliation was among
the alternatives considered, ASNE president Alexander F. Jones, executive
editor of the *Syracuse Herald-Journal*, said. Compensatory moves might
even go so far as to revoke the organization's long-advocated belief in equal
access to official news sources for all foreign correspondents in the United
States. If a communist nation jailed an American correspondent for espionage, the minimum American response must be denying Tass representatives
access to official sources of information, some ASNE leaders began saying.[20]

Promises of aid came from the American Newspaper Publishers Association (ANPA), which only recently had entered the international free-press arena. The Oatis case involved more than trying and convicting a journalist, according to the ANPA; the case "was actually one more effort on the part of communist countries to destroy forever a free press for a free people," and the ANPA pledged to fight on these grounds.[21] Sigma Delta Chi, the organization of professional journalists, also voiced concern over the jailing of a journalist—who was only doing his job—for espionage.[22]

Oatis's plight aroused the United States government as well. The State Department denounced Oatis's trial as a "kangaroo court staged before the kleig lights of propaganda" in an attempt to intimidate the world's free press. Even though Oatis had confessed, the Department of State said that Oatis only had admitted doing his job as journalist. The department responded immediately by banning travel by American citizens to Czechoslovakia,[23] with other forms of retaliation expected momentarily. United States delegates to the United Nations Economic and Social Council demanded action and obtained an official resolution that said the United Nations was extremely concerned about "the imposition of arbitrary personal restraints and the infliction of punishments" on correspondents "solely because of their attempts faithfully to perform their duties in gathering and transmitting news." The resolution also appealed "to governments to do all within their power to safeguard the right of correspondents freely and faithfully to gather and transmit news."[24] President Harry S. Truman canceled trade concessions with Czechoslovakia,[25] and when the new Czech ambassador presented his credentials, he received a series of presidential "tongue lashings" and was told that diplomatic relations between the two countries would improve only after Oatis's release. The diplomatic coolness continued as Secretary of State Dean Acheson reportedly refused to shake hands with the Czech envoy on his first formal call at the State Department. The Czech ambassador angrily responded to these snubs by telling all who asked that the Oatis case was closed.[26] Truman, however, considered the case still open and planned to end trade relations between the United States and Czechoslovakia.[27]

Despite the rhetoric and threats of retaliatory action, Oatis remained in prison. Associated Press officials, however, contended that the international spotlight focused on his case had saved the correspondent's life. Oatis clearly was a pawn in an important international chess game. Throughout his ordeal, Associated Press leaders reported to organization members that the American government was doing everything consistent with national interests to obtain the correspondent's release, but, as of September 1951, Oatis remained in jail.[28] To impatient journalists, the government's progress toward obtaining the reporter's release was agonizingly slow; Oatis had been in Czechoslovakian jails since April. By October 1951, economic sanctions appeared to be at least somewhat effective—the Czechoslovakian government began mentioning the possibility of negotiating Oatis's release.[29] But perhaps American journalists needed to exert additional pressure to procure speedier action. Perhaps, suggested Harry Martin, president of the American Newspaper Guild, various press organizations should set aside their historic animosities to pursue a common cause. At the State Department's suggestion, the idea was promptly dropped; the government wanted room to maneuver without the intense pressure that could be produced by the combined efforts of all of the nation's journalistic organizations.[30]

Oatis remained in prison throughout 1951 and 1952. In the spring of 1952, hope for his release rekindled briefly. Newspaper stories said that the Czechs wanted to trade Oatis for the possession of a $17 million steel mill that Czechoslovakia had already purchased, delivery of which had been held up by the American government. The State Department termed such reports as speculative and not worth discussing.[31] Although the government did hint that other actions were being considered, the press was clearly becoming restless. Oatis had been in prison for almost a year, including ten months of being held incommunicado. Enough was enough, said *Editor & Publisher*: "Whatever the price, Oatis must be freed as soon as possible. We have paid ransom to bandits before for the release of U.S. citizens." Such a practice was "distasteful and a sad commentary on the state of international diplomacy. But the precedent has been set, so let's make the best bargain we can and get it over with."[32]

After the Czech government used Oatis as a witness in the spy trial of his twelve supposed accomplices, some American journalists hoped that the correspondent, having served as an object lesson for the world's press, would be released.[33] Journalists had no factual basis for this hope, but the Czechs finally allowed the United States ambassador to visit Oatis in May 1952.[34] In October, another American embassy representative saw the jailed Associated Press correspondent.[35] By fall 1952, Oatis's predicament was almost lost in the hubbub of world affairs; Associated Press General Manager Frank Starzel had no new developments to report because "the Kremlin apparently has not decided what to do about Oatis." But Starzel remained satisfied that the United States was doing everything it could to obtain his release.[36]

The imprisonment of an American news agency employee behind the iron curtain greatly affected the news-gathering business. Czechoslovakia had expelled two Associated Press correspondents just before Oatis's arrest. Immediately after his arrest, employers pulled all American correspondents out of Czechoslovakia, leaving the Associated Press and other agencies dependent on Czech nationals for news from that country. The Associated Press Managing Editors Association deplored the news-gathering conditions in Czechoslovakia because "nationals are subject to severe reprisal for transmitting any news likely to prove objectionable to their governments."[37]

Obtaining reliable, on-the-spot news from behind the iron curtain was almost impossible under such conditions. Events surrounding Oatis's arrest also highlighted the question of the wire service's right to expose its correspondents to personal risk by assigning them to communist countries.[38] But if the reporters were not assigned to communist countries, how would the United States obtain information about what was going on in these countries? Associated Press leaders were on the horns of a dilemma. News gathering had suddenly become a dangerous profession, especially when practiced in parts of the world that were unsympathetic to American journalistic traditions.

The ability of the United States government to protect American journalists who insisted on going into areas that were particularly unsafe for them obviously was limited. Throughout the Oatis case, zealous votes of confidence in the government's diplomatic maneuvers to free the correspondent concealed underlying apprehensions about the ability of the government to act on Oatis's behalf. Again, the immediacy of journalism clashed with the slow and methodical nature of diplomacy. The press community, for instance, welcomed President Truman's remark in March 1952 that he hoped Oatis would be out of jail soon; journalists believed that the Oatis case had been "quiescent in government circles for too long."[39] Oatis, however, remained in a Czechoslovakian prison until 1953.[40]

TROUBLE LOOMS FOR A SOUTH AMERICAN NEWSPAPER

When combined with the Polk murder, the Oatis imprisonment made American journalists increasingly aware of the dangers of practicing their profession abroad. Both cases showed that the United States government apparently was unable to protect journalists at work abroad. Both instances made the international freedom of the press crusade seem somewhat shallow and meaningless. A third international incident—the closing of *La Prensa*, a leading South American daily, by Juan Perón—was the final blow to the free-press crusade for most North American journalists. If the government could not protect United States journalists working abroad, at least the government could pressure a supposedly friendly govenment into treating its domestic press more liberally. Once again, however, American journalists relied on the State Department for action, and once again, the journalists were disappointed.

Members of the press community were especially sensitive about the closing of *La Prensa*, for they believed that the newspaper extended North American journalistic practices into another part of the world. In fact, United States journalists had long cited Argentina's pre-Perón press as an example for other Latin American countries to follow; even the free-press guarantee in that nation's constitution closely resembled the United States Bill of Rights.[41] Perón's campaign against *La Prensa* began even before he became Argentina's president, and the North American press had worried about his intentions for years. Even so, Perón's campaign to silence this great independent newspaper took five years to bear fruit.[42]

As early as 1947, some ASNE members, concerned about the growing problems in Argentina, suggested a resolution supportive of *La Prensa* and its editor and publisher, Dr. Alberto Gainza Paz. The ASNE membership, unwilling to antagonize Perón directly, adopted a broad resolution supporting worldwide freedom of the press without naming any transgressor nations or persecuted newspapers by name.[43] None of the editors' inhibitions afflicted *Editor & Publisher*, however, as the trade journal consistently pictured the Argentine leader and his followers as mimicking the repressive tactics of Hitler and Mussolini. Press restrictions in Italy and Germany had caught the attention of only a few people; "now the world is aware of the procedure by which individual liberties are lost, but still it happens." North American newspaper leaders who ignored early warnings about Hitler now could "watch a dictator in action, see how a free press dies, and civil liberties end."[44]

While *Editor & Publisher* often inflated dangers to the press out of proportion to the actual problems, this time the trade journal's analysis was correct. Through periodic editorials, the journal kept readers' attention riveted on the drama transpiring in Buenos Aires. After a series of problems with newsprint supply and the imposition of special financial regulations, the final blow to *La Prensa* was a phony labor dispute in 1951 that was combined with the refusal of police to protect loyal employees trying to cross picket lines in order to work. With *La Prensa* under constant attack, *Editor & Publisher* optimistically believed that pressure from newspapers in neighboring countries would force Perón to reevaluate his actions; Perón, unfortunately, was immune to such pressures.[45] *La Prensa* finally ceased publication in January 1951. When the paper was silenced, journalists in the United States took the closing of *La Prensa* personally. Flags on newspaper offices around the country flew at half-staff as editors of North American publications vowed to keep the cause of *La Prensa* alive. One possibility remained for helping the stricken publication—sovereign nations, by exerting diplomatic and economic pressures on Perón, might be able to force the Argentine leader to return *La Prensa* to its former condition. But efforts to enlist the United States government in *La Prensa*'s cause were singularly unsuccessful.[46]

The State Department also had worried about freedom of the press in Argentina for several years. American representatives raised the issue of governmental pressure on various newspapers with Argentine leaders[47] but with little success. North American diplomats were especially concerned about the condition of the so-called independent press of Argentina, meaning newspapers that were still privately owned and resistant to government pressure. Although State Department officials listed *La Prensa* among these independent publications, diplomats found that the publication's editors, apparently bending to incessant pressures from the government, had toned down the newspaper's opposition to Perón. As departmental officials reported in 1949, *La Prensa* still "strongly resists tremendous Government pressure and won't touch Government propaganda, but its opposition is expressed mildly and 'reasonably.'"[48] Official American reaction to Perón's moves against the press varied greatly according to the ambassador on the scene. When Spruille Braden was in Buenos Aires, he actively defended the rights of both American and Argentine journalists and often voiced his concern about freedom of the press to Argentine officials. When George S. Messersmith took over, he was more supportive of Perón and more likely to overlook minor incursions into press freedom. By the time the final battle over *La Prensa* occurred in 1951, Ellsworth Bunker was ambassador, and a balance had been struck between the two extremes. However, American need for Perón's participation in a hemispheric solidarity movement was also greater, and support for freedom of the press was consequently less vocal.

No matter how much the United States press agitated, the State Department refused to publicly criticize Perón's treatment of *La Prensa*. The reason for this refusal was obvious: the nation's foreign policy needed Perón's support in South America much more than the government needed to protest the murder of one newspaper. By 1951, the United Nations police action in Korea was well under way, and Americans feared that the fighting in Asia was the introductory phase of World War III. Indeed, the United States was so concerned that the State Department sought to strengthen its alliances around the world. In one such effort, leaders of twenty-one American republics met to reaffirm their intentions to defend the hemisphere from hostile actions. Seeking a unanimous declaration, the United States needed Argentina's adherence, and the American desire for full participation freed Perón to act against *La Prensa*. As American journalists later said, Perón correctly "figured that the United States was too busy fighting communists and preparing to fight Russia to do much about him."[49] The *La Prensa* issue was particularly troublesome just before a scheduled meeting of foreign ministers from all the Americas. State Department officials, anxious for the session to be successful, advised President Truman to avoid any questions about the newspaper at an upcoming press conference. In fact, the State Department told the White House that "the President should not say anything that could be considered an attack on Peron, since this might split the hemisphere on the eve of the Foreign Ministers Meeting." If asked, Truman might "point out that the United States views on freedom of the press are well known and that we hope the present situation with regard to LA PRENSA in Argentina will be resolved in accordance with these principles."[50]

American diplomats attending the March 1951 foreign ministers meeting were under strict instructions not to broach the *La Prensa* issue themselves or to support another country's attempt to place that specific subject on the agenda. If any other Latin American nation introduced a general resolution favoring freedom of the press, the United States delegation could support the proposal, but delegates must avoid taking a position on the Perón–*La Prensa* struggle. In private conversations, American diplomats should stress that although the *La Prensa* question was "an internal Argentine problem to be resolved in Argentina," reactions from throughout the hemisphere "clearly show that the problem has international aspects." Thus, "we should state that when free institutions are attacked, the suppression of any part of them becomes a matter of concern to all who are fighting for their preservation." American representatives also could discuss "the detrimental effects of this affair on US-Argentine relations." But under no circumstances could the American delegation, for years the initiator of resolutions that condemned any nations violating freedom of the press by name, make any statement remotely critical of Perón's handling of this internal problem.[51]

The United States had fallen back to a position lately associated with the Soviets by contending that relations between a government and its press were internal matters, secure from interference by any other nation. If the United States delegation strayed from this new position, delegates "would in all probability strain US-Argentine relations to an extent which might wreck the whole Meeting and make hemispheric solidarity on security objectives impossible." State Department officials realized the damage that the nation's image as a defender of civil liberties would sustain if the delegation refused to support a general resolution on freedom of the press, which "all the world knows we believe in so firmly." But they were clearly willing to sacrifice that reputation for increased hemispheric security.[52] The *La Prensa* issue obviously was difficult for the State Department; perhaps because of this issue, American diplomats realized just how impossible a free-press campaign was in the midst of a cold war.

American journalists probably felt deserted by the government's change in attitude. During the previous five years, press reliance on the United States government as a strong ally on international free-press issues had increased. Close cooperation at the United Nations highlighted the relationship, as had the government's efforts to secure bilateral treaties promoting freedom of the press and to obtain admission of American correspondents into countries throughout the world to gather the news. On *La Prensa*, however, journalists found no support within the State Department. By nature suspicious of governmental intentions, journalists, too, realized that the free-press crusade was a cold war casualty.

Journalists in the United States, however, were far from silent on Perón's actions. The murder of *La Prensa* provided the perfect support for an argument advanced by Marquis Childs about the indivisibility of the liberty of the press throughout the world. "The death of that newspaper," he said, "was like a lightning flash revealing that the sky over this hemisphere, too, was darkened by the menace to freedom that has spread so far across Europe and Asia. There has come the realization that the bell that tolled for *La Prensa* conveyed a deep and solemn warning for all of us."[53] Harry Martin, president of the American Newspaper Guild agreed, commenting that American journalists, accustomed to Soviet suppression of the press, "still react with horror and surprise to the official rape of a great newspaper when it occurs in a non-Communist, supposedly civilized American nation."[54]

Roots of suppression even existed in the United States. American journalists saw the telltale signs of the Argentine pattern already visible in attempts at all levels of government in the United States to restrict access to information. Journalists also worried about various labor union actions against the press because strikes finally had killed *La Prensa*.[55] Consequently, journalists strongly believed in sharing their concerns with their audiences because those audiences would ultimately suffer from any press suppression in the United States. If journalists allowed the issue to die, "the American reader may shrug off *La Prensa's* fate. Argentina is far away and no visible threat to a nation which has big and urgent problems of security against world communism." But "freedom is whole and we either speak for it everywhere or fight a cold war in vain."[56] United States journalists were not alone in this great battle. Newspaper editorial pages in both North and South America strongly condemned Perón's action, proving once again that "when liberty is extinguished anywhere, a little bit of freedom dies everywhere. And if the press does not rise to protect its freedom, who will?"[57]

Fearful of worldwide repercussions, the American Society of Newspaper Editors asked Perón to review the *La Prensa* case personally. If the Argentine leader undertook such a review, ASNE President Dwight Young, editor of the *Dayton Journal Herald*, optimistically believed that Perón would promptly "clarify that situation with respect to the continuation of a free press in Argentina."[58] Perón, of course, ignored the ASNE appeal, and no one at the 1951 ASNE convention wanted to soft-pedal the organization's criticism of the Argentinean leader and his actions. The ASNE membership condemned the actions taken against *La Prensa* and Gainza Paz, adding, "furthermore, we believe that such reversion to the standards of the Dark Ages erects another barrier between Argentina and the United States, marking Argentina as callous to one of the supreme principles of Twentieth Century civilization."[59]

Condemnation of the suppression of *La Prensa* was well based in international law. For example, the Act of Chapultepec, which the Argentine government had signed in the closing days of World War II, contained nonbinding pledges that required signatories to protect and encourage freedom of the press in their respective homelands. Efforts to spotlight this earlier agreement brought complaints from the American government that such comparisons hampered the State Department efforts to discuss the entire subject with the Argentine government—out of the glare of publicity surrounding the foreign ministers' meeting and without intruding into Argentina's internal affairs. This complaint annoyed *Editor & Publisher*, which believed that press comment could "hamper only a pussy-footing diplomacy and that such vigorous and unanimous opinion should be an invaluable support to a vigorous and protesting government."[60]

Although *La Prensa* was lost,[61] the situation provided the United States press with a new, living symbol of freedom of the press. Gainza Paz, editor and publisher of *La Prensa*, whose family had owned and operated the newspaper throughout its seventy-five-year history, had fled Argentina before Perón's police could arrest him for violating state security. Within a year of the suppression of his newspaper, he had made several trips from Uruguay, his home in exile, to the United States to accept honorary degrees and to speak before various professional groups. Consequently, Gainza Paz became "a symbol of freedom in a world where freedom has rapidly disappeared in some areas including his own country." American journalists proclaimed themselves "glad that he is free to visit this country where freedom is appreciated and to receive the honors due him for his journalistic achievements."[62] Gainza Paz's appearances at North American journalistic meetings usually sparked renewed consideration of freedom of the press in the Western Hemisphere. One such session, for instance, led to a statement recognizing that "any threat to democracy in any place in the Western Hemisphere is of instant concern to the people of every one of the Republics." Thus, the suppression of *La Prensa* was "a threat to the freedoms of the peoples of the other 20 Republics."[63]

In a world filled with totalitarian governments on both the political right and the left, Gainza Paz stressed that journalists could find little difference between the two when it came to the suppression of newspapers. Winning the struggle between press and government, he explained, was crucial because the press was "an irreconcilable enemy of absolute governments, and an unconditional ally of freedom." A free press and a totalitarian state could not coexist—dictators quickly quieted an opposition press. Then, needing some means of communications to run the government, the dictator established a kept press. Modern dictators greatly feared accurate news, Gainza Paz said, because news allowed an oppressed people to "realize that many privileges, denied to them, are normal and usual among other peoples, close at hand or far away." If an enslaved people could only obtain the news, they could survive without editorial criticism of the regime in power, "but a people lacking free information, and getting their news distorted, directed and censored, are blind—destined to suffer all manner of indignities and tragedies." Gainza Paz and his staff on *La Prensa* had learned the importance of freedom of information from bitter experience: "We must bear in mind this eternal truth—when liberty is lost, it must be regained. When you have it, you must defend it."[64]

The Latin American publisher's message came to journalists in the United States at an ideal psychological time, for their dreams of creating a world in which all nations practiced and honored freedom of the press, American style, had foundered and failed. The United States press felt encircled by enemies and saw few individuals interested in or willing to help defend freedom of the press. Even the United States government, an ally in the United Nations adventure, had sacrificed the philosophical principle of freedom of the press to pragmatic diplomacy. Representatives of the United States press were regrouping after numerous setbacks at the United Nations when Gainza Paz arrived. Feeling vulnerable, friendless, and defenseless, American journalists realized that if no one else would help to promote freedom of the press at home and abroad, the press must carry on alone. For, as Gainza Paz made clear, "journalism can have no truce in its crusade for freedom of information and of opinion. By this crusade it will save itself and help to save the peoples who are oppressed today or who may be oppressed tomorrow. This is the time to discourage the false belief that all governments—even the worst dictatorships—will rise up as champions of liberty."[65] Journalists must undertake this quest alone, and American journalists were ready to launch their own private international free-press crusade.

AMERICAN JOURNALISTS CREATE INTERNATIONAL ORGANIZATIONS OF JOURNALISTS

Just how to conduct this private crusade, however, was unclear. After repeated encounters with hostile forces within the United Nations, American journalists no longer wanted any part of an organization that contained representatives of the Soviet bloc. Consequently, journalists believed that the membership of any new international organization must be restricted to noncommunists. And because American journalists wanted a community of interest, any new organization must seek members from areas of the world that provided the strongest support for American ideas on freedom of the press. Thus, the new organization must be closely tied to European journalism.[66] But how could American journalists become active on the perilous world scene? The only worldwide organization for journalists in existence was the International Organization of Journalists (IOJ), denounced as a communist front in 1948 by its American affiliate, the American Newspaper Guild. Realizing that a void could be harmful, Guild members quickly supported the establishment of another international organization for noncommunist journalism trade unions.[67] The Guild effort culminated in the creation of the International Federation of Journalists in 1952.

The new group's bylaws permitted any national trade union for working journalists to affiliate with the International Federation of Journalists—if the union was "dedicated to freedom of the press and giving their primary attention to collective bargaining in behalf of professional journalists who devote the majority of their time to the profession of journalism and derive from it most of their income."[68] Even before the first federation meeting, eighteen trade unions, primarily from Europe and North America, indicated their intentions to affiliate.[69] Organizational aims stressed safeguarding freedom of the press internationally, "including the collection and dissemination of information"; taking action "against threats to the rights and liberties of newsmen and of the newspaper industry"; and promoting relationships "among its member unions to insure goodwill and aid to traveling newsmen." Federation leaders also sought recognition from the United Nations so that the new group could represent free, working journalists before the international organization, when and if the need arose. No longer would the lone voice on the international journalism scene belong to the discredited IOJ.[70]

Members of the American Society of Newspaper Editors also believed that talking face-to-face with their counterparts in the free world was the only way to realize their dream of international press freedom. Although the ASNE had enthusiastically supported early United Nations action on freedom of information, many members had thought for quite some time that an international organization of journalists created by journalists and run by journalists for journalists was far more sensible than forcing both journalists and governments into some common cause via the United Nations. Erwin D. Canham, long a leader in the movement to internationalize freedom of the press, had advocated such a professionally oriented approach as early as 1948. Shortly after the Geneva conference, Canham spoke of having made useful contacts with publishers, editors, reporters, and union officials on other delegations that could lead to real progress on international freedom of the press. "With the newspaper men of many other countries, we can speak the common language of experience," Canham explained, something that was lacking in diplomatic conversations. American journalists could learn from European practitioners and vice versa. Even as Canham spoke, European journalists were creating an international organization for editors, and he urged ASNE members to participate in the group's establishment. Arguments with the Russians would be impossible in the new organization, he promised, because the goal of the founders was to create a completely Western association. ASNE participation was vital, he said, still speaking in terms of Americans guiding international free-press policy, for now was the time to "take the leadership of this movement." If the ASNE delayed action, the opportunity to sway organization members to the American system of press freedom might disappear.[71]

The International Federation of Newspaper Publishers and Editors, known as FIEJ after its French name, Fédération Internationale des Editeurs de Journaux, was the organization being established as Canham spoke in April 1948. The group's first meeting was held at the end of June 1948, and although no ASNE members made the trip to Paris, two American reporters on assignment abroad represented the editors' interests.[72] Unfortunately, European FIEJ members were more akin to American publishers than to American editors, a possibility Canham had anticipated because of differences in the organization of European and American newspapers.[73] Nevertheless, the ASNE decided, on Canham's recommendation, to affiliate with FIEJ for a year, if only to give the journalists of the world moral support from the United States in their fight against communism.[74] Canham continued to believe in the efficacy of international organizations, even though FIEJ was obviously not the place for ASNE efforts.[75]

Editors in the United States, however, still needed a way to meet with their editorial counterparts from other parts of the world to discuss problems peculiar to their jobs. Members of the International Federation of Journalists talked about contracts and collective bargaining. Members of the International Federation of Newspaper Publishers and Editors discussed ways to increase newsprint production. Editors, though, had nowhere to go to talk about the flow of news from one nation to another, or about the problems of training journalists, or about any of their other concerns. Soon, however, Lester Markel, Sunday editor of *The New York Times*, developed plans for the International Press Institute (IPI), which would be quite different from other international organizations in which United States journalists had participated. Americans, under the chairmanship of Markel, would create the organization, but ASNE members were told that "any such program cannot be carried through as a program of the American press alone. The doubts about us overseas, the fears of domination, extend also into the newspaper field. It is essential, therefore, that any project like this should be a joint effort and not a unilateral program of American editors."[76]

American efforts got the organization off to a good start. Financial backing from the Rockefeller Foundation and the Carnegie Endowment for International Peace in 1950 brought sixteen foreign editors to the United States to learn about American journalism firsthand and to discuss the possibility of an international press institute. Attention focused on the American Press Institute, housed at Columbia University, as a possible model for the international body. Markel hoped that the visitors would approve of the American initiative because he saw the International Press Institute as an instrument of world peace. To him, as to many of his journalistic colleagues, world peace depended on "understanding between peoples and peoples, rather than on understanding between leaders and leaders or between diplomats and diplomats." This understanding, though, was built on informed public opinion, and public opinion was not being adequately informed. "To bring about understanding between peoples and peoples, a fundamental step, it seems to me, is to bring about understanding between editors and editors," Markel said. But building this understanding was something that newspaper editors had to do for themselves, without government help.[77]

The visiting editors supported the creation of the International Press Institute.[78] Thus, the institute, which planned to focus on the editorial problems of journalism and which was labeled as a "project not of governments but of newspapers," began. Membership was limited to editorial directors of newspapers that were "devoted to the cause of freedom of the press."[79] The project, most journalists agreed, was admirable—so admirable in fact that the institute encountered few roadblocks in organizing.[80]

Despite the warm reception, Markel still worried. What if American journalists decided not to support the new organization? This potential pall had hung over every international effort ever launched by the American press; indeed, the record of journalistic support of such projects was not good. "Unless the American press plays its part in the Institute," Markel said, "unless the members of this Society give its active support, the full purpose cannot be achieved—and that would be a great pity for us and for the rest of the world." Although the International Press Institute was not an American organization, "the world looks to us for a degree of leadership—the kind of leadership which persuades rather than commands, which moves by reason rather than by emotion, which presents its own views with patience and considers other views with tolerance." Markel feared that some of his fellow editors had repudiated geographic isolationism while still believing that "we can shut ourselves off from the great currents that sweep the world. That is more dangerous even than physical isolationism, because we have entered upon a period in which ideas, more than arms, will determine the outcome."[81]

Regardless of his concerns, Markel made sure that Americans would be unable to dominate the new organization, no matter how great the support from United States journalists. The permanent director would be a European, and the permanent office would be in Europe as well. As the first meeting approached, membership consisted of 450 journalists from thirty-two countries, with more than 100 members from America. A total of 107 editors representing twenty-two nations gathered in Paris for the first institute meeting and named Markel chairman.[82]

Would worldwide freedom of the press fare any better because of the International Press Institute? Reliable answers rested in the future, but journalists, an impatient lot, sought predictions almost immediately. Thus,

The Quill, the official publication of Sigma Delta Chi, sought the views of Basil L. Walters, executive editor of Knight Newspapers, member of the institute's American committee, and a "singularly hard-headed newspaper-man," who long had been skeptical of international organizations for journalists. Walters, however, had changed his mind about such efforts after the Paris meeting: "It was amazing to hear newspaper people from all parts of the free world express the same ideals and many of the same thoughts about trends in journalism that I have heard at ASNE and Inland Daily Press meetings. While Americans spoke their share, it was not an American dominated meeting." Even more impressing to Walters was the lack of "starry-eyed talk of world unity. I have a hunch, however, that the seed for better world understanding that dropped incidentally as men with mutual interests discussed ways and means to improve themselves and their products will develop into great oaks as the years go by."[83] Markel was also pleased with the progress made in the Institute's first year of life,[84] but despite progress here, the state of international freedom of the press seemed dismal at the end of 1952.

FREEDOM OF THE PRESS DIMINISHES INTERNATIONALLY

American journalists were well informed about international press condi-tions during these years, for the new journalistic pastime was monitoring the status of freedom of the press at home and abroad. A few organizations, such as the Associated Press, formalized the process into annual, country-by-country tallies of press freedom during the late 1940s and early 1950s. Other groups, including the American Society of Newspaper Editors, had been monitoring free-press topics since the 1930s. Still others, such as the American Newspaper Publishers Association, participated more passively through group publications. The *ANPA Bulletin,* for instance, carried a regular feature, "It Can't Happen Here," in which the editor briefly noted instances in which foreign governments had infringed freedom of the press.

   Members of various press organizations stationed overseas provided the raw material for these worldwide surveys. *Editor & Publisher,* in starting a spurt of annual reports in 1946,[85] collated information from correspondents of the Associated Press, United Press, and International News Service. Each survey, regardless of the sponsoring organization, focused on similar topics. How much freedom of the press existed in the country? Did laws exist to curb press activities? Had the status of freedom of the press been adversely influenced by suspensions of publications, prosecutions of editors, or adoption of protective laws during the time period under study? Could the national press criticize the government? Could national press organs dis-seminate news freely within the country? Could foreign correspondents travel freely? Could correspondents send stories out of the country without having the information within them censored? The reports stated the amount of freedom of the press, measured by American standards, available to nationals of various countries and to foreign correspondents. The American-based evaluation guidelines were clear: Freedom of the press was limited if national laws unreasonably restricted press action; if public information was unavailable to the press; if problems existed in transmitting information within a country or in transmitting information out of the country; or if the government maintained any controls over raw materials such as newsprint, ink, or equipment needed for publication.

Horror stories revealing the problems that journalists faced abroad filled the reports. Iran imposed censorship by "maladministration," a technique that allowed journalists' cables to "frequently get 'lost'." In Uruguay, "cable companies are held responsible if they transmit any news held to be against the interest of the State." Although Finland might restore freedom of the press soon, until the government made that move, officials planned to guide the domestic press, and censors would continue to monitor telephone calls.[86] The editor of a Turkish newspaper destroyed in a political demonstration was convicted of "harming the dignity" of government leaders and sentenced to three and one-half months in jail. When Turkey imposed martial law, seven opposition newspapers suspended publication indefinitely. The minister of education in Spain announced his intention "to wait until the world returned to law and order" before restoring liberty of the press. In Venezuela, two news directors were jailed for publishing a letter attacking the government. The Roman Catholic Church ordered the staffs of two Italian newspapers excommunicated "for conducting a campaign against the Vatican" during a church trial.[87]

In addition, reporters in Portugal could be barred from practicing their profession if they published anything displeasing to the government. And, in Greece, the army and coalition cabinet disagreed on censorship policy. An army court, over the objections of the civilian prime minister, questioned an editor who had published an article critical of the military.[88] Citations were endless. Everywhere that American journalists looked, freedom of the press was in jeopardy. Everywhere stories of newspaper licensing, censorship of copy, imprisonment of journalists, and expulsions of foreign correspondents abounded. International working conditions progressively worsened. Each new report told of additional restrictions around the world until, in 1950, more than one-fourth of the world's population experienced censorship or some other restraint on freedom of the press.[89]

As the 1950s began, the periodic updates on freedom of information around the world started to include curtailments of freedom of the press within the United States as well.[90] The Freedom of Information Committee of the American Society of Newspaper Editors, taking its cue from changing domestic conditions, dropped the word world from its title and cut back on its activity relating to international freedom of information in favor of action on domestic problems. Soon the ASNE became preoccupied by local, state, and national infringements on freedom of information. Sigma Delta Chi likewise began focusing its efforts on internal free-press issues, as did the American Newspaper Publishers Association. As freedom of information problems appeared closer to home, American journalists became significantly more interested in the resolution of these problems. Now, perhaps, observers said, American reporters who encountered trouble in fulfilling their professional obligations would finally realize that freedom of the press was not merely something for other nations to worry about.[91] Trouble flared in Argentina, Czechoslovakia, Korea, and Washington, D.C., proving what journalists already knew—that the world was not filled with nations eager to support international freedom of information.

American journalists could no longer assume that anyone—including fellow Americans—appreciated the vital nature of freedom of the press. According to press spokesmen, some individuals in the United States who were trying to suppress, distort, or delay the distribution of information that should be made available to the American people by the press were actually flirting with totalitarianism. After all, "the totalitarian state shapes the thinking of the people by propaganda and by allowing the public only such information as will mold favorable attitudes toward those in control." To the dismay of some journalists, they found that "this very thing is being attempted at various levels in the United States today."[92] These concerns led American journalists to defend freedom of the press far more rigorously than ever. But despite increased professional vigilance, journalists still needed "to teach frequently indifferent readers that we are really fighting for them."[93]

As American journalists voiced concern about the fates of Polk and Oatis, worried about La Prensa, created the International Press Institute, and fretted over increasing barriers to freedom of the press at home and abroad, an even greater threat to international freedom of the press appeared on the horizon. The heroic figure of the American foreign correspondent, long cited as the reason for the international free-press crusade, was disappearing from the world scene. The dwindling number of foreign correspondents on the job stood in stark contrast to the much-proclaimed American belief that reporters from the United States must be at major world events in order to provide Americans with reliable news accounts. Reliable, in this sense, meant filtered through the American perspective, for, as time went on, American news agencies and newspapers grew less comfortable with perceptions of events from journalists of nationalities unfamiliar with the needs of American readers or whose stories might reflect governmental intimidation.

During World War II, many American journalists considered a foreign posting glamorous. But as the war ended, most of the 2,700 correspondents on duty around the world were quickly called home. The number of reporters remaining abroad dropped so significantly that much of the rhetoric at the United Nations about protecting American correspondents overseas seemed unnecessary. News from abroad was no less vital, however, but greater emphasis was placed on coverage by the major news services, which ironically put greater reliance on local employees in the countries covered. The shift in responsibility for providing foreign news gave increased importance to the unpopular attempt to protect nationals of foreign countries employed by international news agencies. By 1950, fewer than 300 American correspondents remained on station abroad. Rough figures gathered by Russell F. Anderson, editor of McGraw-Hill's *World News*, showed an American foreign correspondents' corps composed of 293 American citizens working full time, 210 nationals of the countries in which they worked full time, and 1,150 part-time employees, or stringers, who often worked for more than one international agency as well as for a news agency or newspaper in their home countries. Because these part-time people worked for several media outlets, the number of persons actually providing foreign news to Americans was probably even lower than the total showed.[94]

The few Americans working abroad raised significant questions about the adequacy of news available to the American public in a highly unstable world. The advent of the Korean conflict, for instance, surprised most Americans, few of whom "had the slightest idea that a major conflict was in the making, much less any understanding of the issues at stake," Anderson said. "The number of newsmen in Korea when war broke out, including part-time string correspondents, could be counted on the fingers of one hand." Shortly after the war began, American correspondents poured into Korea from other parts of the world. Within two weeks, 50 American journalists were in Korea; within a month, 150 reporters were covering the latest hotspot.[95] Korea was not the only story badly handled by American news agencies during these critical days. Most stories on the assassination of the prime minister of Pakistan in October 1951 came from New Delhi, hardly a neutral point for the transmission of stories about Pakistan. Part-time stringers, natives of Iran, wrote the initial stories about the assassination of the premier of that country in 1951. American correspondents from other locations arrived after the event.[96]

Only Britain, France, Italy, Germany, and Japan were regularly and sufficiently staffed by American reporters. A few other countries had a single American correspondent stationed in them; most nations had no American reporters within their borders at all. This sad state of affairs greatly affected the quality of news that Americans received from around the world, Anderson said. As if to underscore the complaint made by China's P. H. Chang in the Subcommission on Freedom of Information and of the Press, Anderson noted that reporters who traveled from one trouble spot to another often failed "to understand that the occurrence may be the climax of a situation that has been gradually developing for years." Not only were average Americans misled by such shallow reporting, but the United States government, which depended on the nation's press agencies to gather much of the raw data used in decision making, also ran into difficulties. "The sometimes unrealistic moves by the U.S. State Department, and foolish policy demands from the floor of Congress, are the telltale tip-offs as to just how important our foreign press coverage is in formulating official government opinion," Anderson said. "With this realization one begins to understand the dangers involved in depending on less than three hundred foreign correspondents to report intelligently what is going on in the world."[97]

Anderson was especially critical of the lack of American correspondents in Eastern European countries. When he conducted his survey in 1950, only five American correspondents were in Moscow; several Eastern bloc nations had expelled all American correspondents. Even worse, Anderson said, "U.S. news agencies put up very little fight against ouster orders. There is not much evidence that foreign editors are ready to battle, hook or crook, for their overseas news."[98] Alan J. Gould, executive editor of the Associated Press, hotly disputed Anderson's comments about the unwillingness of the news agencies to fight for the rights of agency correspondents to cover the news in Eastern Europe. "The Associated Press and other news organizations do not advocate calling out the Marines or dropping A-bombs when correspondents are expelled." Did any of Anderson's readers actually "believe The Associated Press should *try* to send another U.S. correspondent into Prague as long as Bill Oatis is in jail? Note the word *try*. A news agency cannot have a correspondent in Prague or Moscow or Warsaw simply because it wants one there." In order for a correspondent to work behind the iron curtain, the news agency first had to obtain an entry visa for that reporter. Several countries, including Poland, Bulgaria, and Rumania, "do not choose to admit A.P. correspondents," leaving the news agency no recourse. Anderson was unequivocal in his response: "Damn right I think the A.P. ought to try to get another man in! For my money the things we are fighting for in Korea are the same issues at stake in Czechoslovakia. If a patrol is sent out on the fighting front and fails to return we send out another and another." By such actions, he said, "victories are molded. Is it unreasonable then to hope that the press would battle for its rights the same way?"[99] Anderson's response fit the ideal that spawned the rhetoric at the United Nations; the reality involved was a different matter.

Reasons for the decreasing number of foreign correspondents were at least twofold. Increasing publishing costs forced newspaper owners to seek ways to economize. With newsprint and mechanical costs rising and advertising revenues holding steady, the news budget was the only place to cut. Editors, looking for soft spots in their budgets, were fairly certain that readers would not complain if expensive foreign coverage was reduced; with World War II over, American readers and listeners had reverted to their usual disinterest in foreign news. Most Americans want to be entertained, Anderson explained. "Most foreign news, by entertainment standards, is pretty heavy reading, and thus there is not the demand on the part of the public for more complete foreign coverage. And if the readers do not insist, the editors in turn do not make demands upon the news agencies."[100]

Editors encountered distinct problems with American readers who wanted no more dismal foreign news. Most newspaper managing editors could explain the problem of carrying foreign news succinctly: "Despite the rumblings of fresh trouble, people wanted to forget war and read other news. The story any cable editor heard was 'Keep it short' and 'Who cares about that when we can't even get our local news in the paper?'" Some observers, however, thought that the problems of the foreign news editor were decreasing in the early 1950s, for the argument against carrying international news "weakened with Korea, and Eisenhower's command in Europe. Foreign news is back on Page One."[101]

Even if such an optimistic statement about increased reader interest in foreign news happened to be true, traumatic domestic problems quickly forced interest in foreign affairs to a secondary level. Each new challenge pushed American journalists farther away from the ideals of the international free-press crusade. Each new battle led the United States press a little closer to the conclusion that the world's press must fight its own battles for a while. Journalists in the United States had enough problems at home to occupy their attention, for, suddenly, the ability of the domestic press to fulfill its historic role in American life was in doubt.

DOMESTIC RESTRICTIONS ON ACCESS TO OFFICIAL INFORMATION

One cornerstone of the international crusade was equal and open access to official government information. American journalists interpreted that principle to mean complete access to official government information, as a bar to almost all restrictions on the distribution of information. No matter what was going on in the world—war, rumors of wars, blockades, reconstruction programs, military alliances—American journalists believed that they should have full access to all information, with the possible exception of details about top secret weapons developments. Decisions to withhold diplomatic or military information from the public must be made by the press, United States journalists believed, not by the government. In fact, some critics charged that American journalists calculated the success of the free press's role in the democratic decision-making process in terms of the number of stories that appeared in print despite governmental entreaties to the contrary.[102] As the cold war intensified, the American government, always a reluctant participant in the campaign for total openness, changed its position. Journalists now found themselves facing a government increasingly protective of official information. Fighting to obtain access to information in Moscow soon became much less important than fighting for access to information in Washington, D.C.

Efforts to curtail the amount and nature of information released to the press were not well organized until late 1947, after the government had committed itself to an active policy for the containment of communism through the Truman Doctrine and other initiatives. Before then, journalists' problems in obtaining information were minimal. But, in October 1947, reporters discovered that President Truman's Security Advisory Board was considering ways for federal agencies to withhold information from the press and the public. Representatives of the press were irate. One section of the proposal even allowed a government agency to stamp as confidential any information that was "prejudicial to the interests or prestige of the nation, any governmental activity, or any individual; or would cause administrative embarrassment or difficulty."[103] Such power was foreign to the American system, journalists contended, and the program's implementation "would practically put our government on an equal footing with the totalitarians."[104]

The American Society of Newspaper Editors immediately opposed the classification program, which was initially designed to support the president's recent loyalty order. The ASNE claimed that the directive "could be used to deprive the public of information to which it is entitled" and that the order could erect a shield around government operations "behind which many evils could flourish without detection."[105] Shortly after this protest, government officials dropped the section of the proposal calling for protection of information that could be possibly embarrassing to the government,[106] and journalists took credit for saving the American people from the imposition of censorship.[107] President Truman, however, criticized newspaper leaders for overdramatizing the situation, claiming that he had not even seen the proposal that they had so vigorously condemned. The editors acted without reasonable justification, according to the president, and were just trying to frighten their fellow journalists and their countrymen.[108]

Even though the proposal was substantially modified, the government did not totally abandon the classification program. Instead, department heads sought to develop a standard, but voluntary, procedure for all government agencies to use in evaluating and classifying information. Strongly objecting, journalists said that the proposal permitted civilian agencies to use in peacetime the censorship provisions that were traditionally reserved for use by the military in wartime. Journalists generally conceded that valid reasons existed to conceal information coming from the Atomic Energy Commission (AEC) and the Defense Department—and possibly even some State Department data. Reporters, however, saw no rational reason for providing government agencies concerned solely with the civilian side of American life "with a method or excuse for withholding public information of any kind." Such a policy, they protested, "offers a perfect screen behind which public officials could hide with any piece of information for any reason, public, private or otherwise."[109]

Proposals for a classification program soon disappeared from view, and some agencies dealing regularly with top secret information attempted to reach informal understandings with the press about material that would be available for publication. For example, the Defense Department under James V. Forrestal started a reexamination of agency policies relating to the release of information, and David Lilienthal, chairman of the Atomic Energy Commission, agreed to work with the ASNE to find ways to help the press cover atomic energy stories.[110] Consequently, the two major government agencies that might, according to most journalists, have valid reasons for security regulations decided to approach the problem positively by trying to determine what information could be released. Press observers thought that this approach held promise, for a continuing consultation between press and governmental representatives might eliminate confrontations altogether.[111]

Journalists based their demands for the ready availability of security information on the profession's record of voluntary cooperation with the government during World War II. American journalists saw their decisions to publish or not to publish certain stories during the war years as grounded in enlightened patriotism. Press representatives felt that they had protected national security, and journalists were proud of their war record. If a voluntary censorship system had worked during the war years, they asked, why would a similar system not work during the cold war? In the current world situation, "editors and reporters will want to cooperate voluntarily in the protection of our national security" as they did during World War II, said *Editor & Publisher*. The government must give journalists an opportunity to prove their patriotism; after all, "American newspapermen are Americans first and newspapermen second."[112] Government planners, however, seemingly forgot World War II experiences during the early cold war. Military leaders, in particular, who had supervised a far more extensive censorship program at the battlefront than was in force domestically, believed that journalists behaved patriotically only if they were properly guided. These planners saw the hazards of the cold war as far greater than the dangers of World War II. Leaving the security of the world during the atomic age in the hands of journalists who voluntarily agreed to follow general guidelines for the self-censorship of vital information was simply out of the question. The reality of press-government relations in the United States during these years thus made many arguments for open availability of information presented within United Nations councils collapse under the weight of their own hypocrisy.

Arguments that national security measures interfered with the ability of the press to function in the United States were heard often. In March 1949, for instance, debate centered on a bill creating penalties for the publication of information about code-breaking. Punishing innocent reports dealing with such information turned the proposal into a "censorship bill, pure and simple," journalists protested. Besides imposing censorship at the source of information, the measure would keep editors "running to determine what is and what is not 'classified' when they obtain a story anywhere near bordering on it" and, thus, would "effectively bottle up information in government agencies that ought to be matters of public record."[113] In May 1949, journalists voiced concern over a statement from the House of Representatives appropriations committee claiming that witnesses supporting military appropriations requests were too specific when they testified before the committee while the press was too lax in imposing self-censorship of the details revealed through such statements. The result, according to the House committee, was the circulation of military secrets.[114] In June 1949, Secretary of Defense Louis Johnson instructed his public information officers to inspect any statements that military officers intended to make to the public and the press more carefully to guard against inadvertent disclosure of data dangerous to national security. Journalists challenged the move as an attempt to restrict the flow of information from department sources, and Johnson retracted the order.[115]

These battles were minor skirmishes compared to the conflict that erupted when President Truman finally installed his classification program in 1951. The basis of this conflict was a fundamental difference of opinion about the role of the press in American society. Faced with what was perceived to be an increasing communist threat at home and abroad, the government saw restricted access to information that might help the enemy as one solution to the government's growing concern for national security. The best method to control information, in the government's view, was to stamp material as top secret and to forbid government employees to give the data to journalists. Reporters, on the other hand, wondered whether a government preserved in this way was really worth saving. Again the argument surfaced that allowing government officials to limit information available for publication could permit an executive to conceal embarrassing or incriminating information. The reporters' awareness of this possibility heightened significantly as revelations about corruption within the Truman administration continued. Any government effort to restrict access to information for nebulous national security reasons might lead to a definition of national security that permitted the concealment of scandal. Consequently, journalists, naturally suspicious of government, were even more alert as the president announced an executive order extending the military's classification system to the entire executive branch.

In the months before the president revealed his program, executive department spokesmen sent the press conflicting messages about Truman's plans for classifying documents. For example, Secretary of Commerce Charles Sawyer, a former newspaper owner himself, urged journalists to adopt a voluntary censorship program. "Experienced men have told me that 96% of the information useful to our potential enemies comes not from spies but from the careful examination and collating of documents and official statements," he said. Journalists must help to reduce the amount of information available to potential enemies.[116] On the other hand, Attorney General J. Howard McGrath, speaking about the same time as Sawyer, categorically promised that President Truman planned "no Federal delimitation of freedom of the press in this cold war." Hidden within McGrath's fulsome praise of freedom of press, though, was the government's position, which the president soon enunciated. "The Government may and does release its own information," the attorney general said;[117] conversely, the government could decide not to release information, which was the goal of the classification system.

Censorship at the source was a main feature of the classification plan that the president announced in late September 1951. The order's provisions were to become effective in thirty days. The program covered all agencies handling security-related information, but the actions of journalists were not restricted. By implementing this plan, the president said that he hoped the American people would receive even more information about the government because, by standardizing classification procedures throughout the government, incorrectly restricted information would be freed for press use.[118] Press leaders found the president's announcement more oppressive than liberating, however, terming the proposal "the most drastic peacetime censorship ever attempted in this country." Civilian agencies lacked such powers in wartime, and journalists feared that "the magic words 'national defense' or 'national security' can be made to mean almost everything." To journalists, the future was bleak: "The public, and newspaper editors acting in its behalf, have a fight on their hands to keep Washington from becoming the 'blackout' capitol of the country under this order."[119]

Some American journalists knew of the president's plans before he announced the executive order. In fact, prior to the public disclosure of the classification plan, representatives of the American Society of Newspaper Editors expressed their concern to White House officials about allowing "the top officials of all Government agencies the discretion to determine how much and what of the public's business should be disclosed to the public."[120] Fear of press opposition to the plan did not dissuade Truman, however, and he made the proposed order public. As probably anticipated, early press reaction ran strongly against the executive order. Secretary of Commerce Sawyer dismissed the responses as emotional, stressing that the press "should be much more concerned with the fact that too much information is given out" rather than with the mistaken notion that too little information would be available under the executive order. Besides, Sawyer said, the order left regular relationships between government officials and journalists untouched: Government officials "should be freely investigated, talked about, commented on and should be reminded constantly to keep the public fully informed about how our government is run up to the point where it involves the nation's security, and up to that point there should be no censorship. Beyond that point the situation changes."[121]

National security considerations would dominate future relationships between the press and government.[122] Even though press groups made numerous protests about the executive order, they made no comparisons between the United States government's behavior and the standards of openness and freedom enunciated by American representatives at the Geneva Conference on Freedom of Information or at the United Nations. The news-gathering convention, now collecting dust at the United Nations, would not have barred the president's plan. As United States representatives had stated repeatedly, the news-gathering convention affected only foreign correspondents operating within another country; the document's provisions had no impact on domestic relationships between a government and its press. The United Kingdom's freedom of information convention, on the other hand, would have influenced the domestic actions of a government toward its press, for that convention guaranteed freedom of information to a nation's residents. The United States had consistently opposed the freedom of information document because of its limitations clause, and the convention remained trapped within the United Nations bureaucracy. Even if United Nations members had written an acceptable freedom of information pact and even if the United States had ratified the treaty—both unlikely circumstances—the convention's provisions allowing regulation of information on national security grounds never had been seriously contested. Journalists overlooked the international ramifications of the executive order as press organizations fought for what they considered to be a constitutionally guaranteed right to gather news. The sorry example that the United States was setting for other nations by such restrictive actions also was generally lost in the debate occasioned by the executive order.

JOURNALISTS' LOYALTY TO THE UNITED STATES BECOMES AN ISSUE

The access debate soon became mired in another sticky issue of the day—loyalty to the United States. President Truman brought the point up at an October 1951 news conference when he stated categorically that the nation's newspapers and slick magazines had disclosed 95 percent of the nation's secret information. The president referred reporters to a map published in *Fortune* magazine that detailed the locations of atomic energy plants as an example of material that never should have been released for publication in the first place, even though the Defense Department had apparently approved its publication. Regardless of such approval, Truman contended that patriotic editors would have stopped the map's release. The comment fascinated reporters, who returned to the subject several times during the news conference: "Do we understand you correctly that in the event a newspaper or magazine gets some information from, say, the Defense Department . . . that the primary responsibility for publishing it rests on the publishers?" Yes, indeed, said the president. The prohibition should extend to information released by Congress as well, he added, in complaining about congressional sources who divulged details about Russian atomic bomb tests that the executive branch wanted kept secret.[123]

By the time the conference ended, confusion was rampant. Press Secretary Joseph Short, trying to clarify the president's comments later, said that reporters who obtained information from sources qualified to determine the safety of releasing information could use any data thus received. If reporters got information from sources not authorized to release it, the journalists "should, as loyal Americans, exercise the most careful judgment in determining the safety of publishing such information."[124] Short's attempt to reassure American journalists failed. Truman's statements stood as "a question mark on the loyalty and patriotism of newspapers and magazines" simply because they published material from official sources such as the Defense Department. To journalistic observers, the president's comments that "editors should withhold information which might affect the security of the country even if the story is publicly available and released by a proper source" showed how confused he was about the subject. Perhaps the president had forgotten that representatives of foreign news agencies, including Tass, the Russian news agency, moved around the nation's capital freely and could easily obtain almost any government information. Consequently, critics said, Truman actually was saying "that some information should be kept from the American people while everyone else in the world may know about it."[125] Looking at the president's classification order, *Editor & Publisher* wondered "if the United States is not drifting slowly but surely from its pre-eminent position as the citadel of press freedom."[126]

Indeed, more than one journalist drew the comparison between the actions of the Truman administration and actions of totalitarian states in limiting access to information.[127] Members of Sigma Delta Chi demanded the immediate recall of the executive order because the order "duplicates in the name of national security the practices of totalitarian states which, as among their first steps, seized control of the channels of communication and information to the people which they later enslaved." Press Secretary Short, angrily responding to the Sigma Delta Chi resolution, said that no part of Truman's order affected "the channels of communication and information in this country and your effort to link the President's order with totalitarian systems is a detestable slander worthy only of the totalitarians themselves."[128]

Throughout the debates at the United Nations, American delegates had insisted that certain restrictive journalistic practices were typical only in totalitarian regimes. Among these actions were curbing access to official information, similar to the effect of the regulations imposed under President Truman's classification program, and limiting jobs within journalism solely to persons who were ideologically sound. In the late 1940s and early 1950s, American journalists themselves sacrificed the latter principle as they purged individuals with communist affiliations from newsrooms across the country. Some American journalists even questioned the right of communist news organs, such as the *Daily Worker*, to exist. By the end of the time period, some American journalists seriously challenged another foundation of the crusade—the openness of America to foreign correspondents from all countries—as they disputed the right of representatives of Tass to work in the United States.

American failure to protect communists holding jobs in the communications industry was not an aberration. In fact, Americans never willingly have shared freedom of expression with persons whose beliefs might alter their society. The history of suppression extends back to colonial days and includes actions against tory printers, supporters of Thomas Jefferson, abolitionists, southern sympathizers in the North during the Civil War, labor radicals, and pacifists. The international crusade for freedom of information should have sensitized American journalists to the needs of all to express themselves. If journalists truly believed, as they proclaimed, that freedom of the press was the international ideal—that the institution of freedom of the press in the Soviet Union would lead to the ouster of communism there—then granting communists in the United States more freedom should have hastened the communists' conversion to the American way. But American journalists failed to make this connection.

Instead, American journalists blamed the Soviet Union and its allies for the failure of the United States press's dream of winning the world to freedom of the press, American style. Coupled with this anger was the significant fear that communism could not be stopped peaceably—that soon the United States and the Union of Soviet Socialist Republics would face each other in one final, awful struggle to determine the fate of the world. Thus encumbered, all Americans faced the threat of internal communism. Most American journalists reacted to this communist threat as did their colleagues in other professions. The journalists were frightened and unwilling to grant the slightest freedom to communists for fear that any opening would lead to the end of all freedoms for all Americans. A few journalists argued that the First Amendment was weak indeed if its provisions could not protect the voices of a few communists, but support for the long-advocated marketplace of ideas was lost in the flood of events.

Taking action against communists in the newsroom clearly worried American journalists. If journalists were not careful, action against employees with communist affiliations could lead to firing employees because they belonged to the wrong political party or the wrong church or were the wrong color. Obviously such discriminatory actions on the whole were wrong, but communists were "a different breed" and merited only limited toleration.[129] "Members of the Communist Party have no place on free American newspapers or on our free radio," *Editor & Publisher* stressed. "They have demonstrated they are committed to certain views and, therefore, to certain actions dictated and governed by others. They are the first to cry 'bias' and 'prejudice' at others when in truth they are the most biased and prejudiced." As these comments illustrate, response to the communist threat varied. *Editor & Publisher* spoke for many journalists when it suggested ousting communists from newspaper and radio offices "before they start tainting the columns and air waves with the propaganda laid down in Moscow."[130] Publishers who demanded loyalty oaths from their reporters received considerable support,[131] as did broadcasters who believed that license holders must "ascertain that those who harbor views contrary to our form of government be denied access to our microphones."[132]

When news sources tried to deny access to information pending a reporter's signing of an anticommunist oath, however, press reaction was almost universally hostile. The responsibility for determining a reporter's loyalty rested with his or her employer and not with someone obligated to disseminate public information to the press. Any attempts by public officials to institute loyalty checks of reporters were almost immediately labeled as efforts to license the press and fought as violations of the First Amendment.[133] Basically, most journalists rejected a full-scale purge of news staffs, but they did endorse the philosophy of *The New York Times* as described by publisher Arthur Hays Sulzberger. "We would not knowingly employ any Communist, or any other kind of totalitarian, in our news or editorial departments," Sulzberger said, "for we have a deep-rooted prejudice for democracy and a deep-seated faith in our capacity to develop under a system of law."[134] But how employers were to determine if a current or potential employee had totalitarian tendencies remained a burning issue.

Questions about what to do about communists worried the American Newspaper Guild as well. The labor union had had problems with communist members early in its history, but by 1946, Guild leaders proudly proclaimed "the ANG was one of the first unions to wrest control from party liners." The victory came in 1941 when mail balloting for national officers permitted the entire membership to elect the union's leadership. Then, the membership elected a full slate of anticommunists to the union's International Executive Board, breaking "the hold of party liners on the Guild."[135] Alleged communists still held leadership positions in some of the largest Guild units, with officers in the New York and Los Angeles units becoming the targets of an anticommunist campaign in 1947. Communists had gained leadership positions in various Guild units, union president Milton Murray explained, because "commies are eager beavers; they do the jobs no one else wants to do, become prominent, and eventually dominate the organizations to which they affiliate."[136]

Even though communists held power, Murray believed that rank-and-file Guild members could drive them from office at any time; he also doubted that communist Guild members would ever gain control of American newspapers. Publishers, said the union president, had "the right to remove the communist from a position where he can control in any degree the editorial policy of the newspaper. They can transfer them to the night police beat, or some back desk some place where they will be perfectly harmless."[137] Personally, Murray leaned "toward the proposition that no communist should be allowed to be a member of the guild." The prohibition was possible despite Guild constitutional provisions against punishing a member for his political beliefs, Murray said, because the oath that every party member took pledging allegiance to Russia disqualified communists from union membership.[138]

By 1948, members had purged communists from most Guild unit leadership positions,[139] but Guild units still faced questions stemming from the firings of members who had admitted their communist connections. Guild contracts forbade retaliation for the political beliefs of members, but few members wanted to protest the firings of their colleagues. Most members apparently agreed that Communist party membership was a "just and sufficient" cause for dismissal.[140] Many Guild members argued that when a reporter joined the Communist party that reporter "surrendered a degree of freedom of action and independent judgment and became a party member under discipline, subject to party leadership and bound to the Communist party line." That action alone removed the journalist from Guild contract protections.[141] When an arbiter upheld the firings of two Los Angeles *Daily News* employees because someone had named them as communists before a congressional committee,[142] anticommunism had triumphed as the dominant philosophy of American journalists. Clearly, said *Editor & Publisher*, "newspapers dedicated to serving the American people, our way of life and our form of government cannot tolerate termites in their structure in the form of Communists who know no rules or principles excepting those which will achieve the subversive ends of their organization."[143]

The patriotic need to support the greater good of the nation and to maintain the purity of newspapers defeated the desire to protect the freedom to discuss communism and the toleration of communists within the American journalism community. This new mindset of American journalists logically led to the conclusion that representatives of the American press were fundamentally unqualified to negotiate international free-press issues with representatives of societies far different from their own. Normally highly perceptive individuals, American journalists now were unable to recognize the similarities between their actions and the actions of individuals that they so soundly condemned. For example, the purge of journalists with communist affiliations from newspapers in the United States and Czechoslovak removal of reporters with impure political beliefs from jobs on Czech newspapers after the 1948 takeover were not so far apart in terms of underlying motivations.[144] To journalists in the United States, the American actions were justified as examples of democratic self-preservation; the Czechoslovak moves constituted unmerited persecution of noncommunists.

American journalists showed ambivalence toward the continued existence of the *Daily Worker* as well. Early in the international free-press crusade, most members of the press would have agreed with Wilbur Forrest, then ASNE president and a leader in the worldwide freedom of information movement, who said that the nation's conservative newspapers would lead the protest against either the suppression or destruction of communist newspapers "for their slurs on the American way."[145] Affirmations that even communist publications enjoyed the protections of the First Amendment dot the era, but the communists' repeated claims to the guarantee quickly wore thin. In 1947, for instance, the *Worker* encountered difficulty obtaining syndicated comic strips. After the creators of one popular strip successfully demanded dropping the *Worker* from the subscriber list, other artists tried the same tactic. *Worker* management regarded the effort "to bar *Daily Worker* use of commercially marketed strips and features as a new attack on freedom of the press."[146] Noncommunist journalists worried when the *Worker*'s financial condition worsened in 1951. Although few American journalists would mourn the publication's passing, the noncommunist press believed that the newspaper's death would "be turned into good propaganda fodder by Commies all over the world," who would claim that the *Worker* had been "suppressed by capitalistic interests." In fact, "the way they distort things, they might even say it was suppressed by the government." Such comments were to be expected, though, because the "Commies will say almost anything to avoid admitting they couldn't face the economic facts of life in making their paper pay its own way."[147]

Would the establishment press allow nongovernment forces to suppress the communist journals? Members of the Detroit American Newspaper Guild unit protested a 1950 attempt to ban the sale of the *Daily Worker* in that city. Even though they opposed communism, the Guild members stressed that "the preservation of freedom within the United States is an essential defense against Communists throughout the world and in the United States." A newspaper such as the *Daily Worker* must never be suppressed, the Guild unit contended, because the publication's very existence was visible proof of American beliefs.[148] After a similar attempt to ban the sale of the *Daily Worker* in New York City, lawyers argued that efforts by newsstand owners to boycott the publication in lieu of a city ordinance that forbade sales of the newspaper violated the Bill of Rights.[149] *Editor & Publisher* simultaneously supported the *Worker*'s right to sell copies of the publication and termed newsdealers' concerns understandable "in these troublesome times." Hatred of the communist system, the trade journal counseled, must never, however, "cloud our vision in respect to our own Constitutional guarantees." Individual action against the *Daily Worker* was acceptable, but when an association of newsstand owners took concerted action, that organization could "attempt to do what our government in Washington does not feel it necessary to do"—close the *Daily Worker* down.[150] When the ban against sales of the communist publication became effective, the trade journal criticized the newsdealers' "short-sighted patriotism." No matter how admirable the newsdealers' motives, the newsdealers should not "decide what reading matter should be made available to citizens of a large city. The free press clause of the Constitution not only protects the right of a newspaper to print but it also encompasses the right of the people to read and be informed."[151]

One point that American journalists stressed in each instance was that private parties were trying to shut down the Communist party press when the federal government had not yet decided that such action against the publications was necessary. This stance led to the logical question: How would the press react if the government did close the *Daily Worker*? Fortunately, the press was never called on to test its belief in the First Amendment freedom of publication in light of drastic moves by the federal government. When the government did arrest individuals, including journalists, under the Smith Act for speech and press activities subversive to the nation's well-being, however, American journalists supported the action. Among the defendants in the first great trial of communist leaders in the United States, *Dennis v. United States*,[152] was John Gates, managing editor of the *Daily Worker*. Gates, journalists decided, was tried and convicted because "he was a member of a conspiracy advocating the overthrow of the government by force" and "not because he was editor of a daily paper." Even if other *Worker* writers and editors were tried and convicted on similar charges, editors predicted that would be no violation of the freedom of the press because the newspaper was still free to publish. If the newspaper was suspended "arbitrarily by action of the government," *Editor & Publisher* concluded, "it will be time enough to examine the free press aspects of the case."[153]

When the government indicted twenty-one additional communists, prosecuted in the case known as *Yates v. United States*,[154] circumstances had changed somewhat. Here, the indictment was for publishing and circulating books, magazines, and newspapers advocating the overthrow of the government. In fact, the indictment cited four publications, including the *Daily Worker*, by name.[155] Despite the direct mention of publishing activities, most journalists still saw freedom of the press as untouched by the prosecutions.[156]

Communist propaganda about the violations of freedom of the press inherent in the charges failed to mention "that the indictments are levelled specifically at a conspiracy against the United States," *Editor & Publisher* said. The Communist party was not just another political organization, not "a group of loyal Americans striving to influence United States action by peaceful means or a democratic method. This is a compact unit of subversives holding allegiance to a foreign power."[157] When the *Daily Worker* tried turning the prosecution of communist journalists into a free-press case, *Editor & Publisher* rejected the attempt, saying: "The free press guarantee in the Constitution does not make newspapermen immune from the laws of the land. They are expected to be law-abiding citizens the same as citizens in any other occupational or professional group." Journalists were just as susceptible to prosecution under the Smith Act as anyone else. "The editors and staff members around whom the Daily Worker is trying to wrap a freedom of the press issue have been arrested, are charged and will be tried as alleged members of such a conspiracy and not because they are or were newspapermen."[158] Although no one mentioned the parallel at the time, the charges on which William N. Oatis was convicted in Czechoslovakia were distressingly similar to the charges lodged against communist journalists in the United States. One major difference was that the communist journalists charged in the United States faced prosecution in their homeland; Oatis's prosecution occurred far from home.

ASNE TRIES TO BAR TASS CORRESPONDENTS FROM CONGRESSIONAL PRESS GALLERIES

One other example of the blurring of values caused by the cold war occurred when leaders of the American Society of Newspaper Editors turned that organization's long-held values upside down in order to campaign for the exclusion of Tass reporters from the Congressional Press Galleries in Washington, D.C. The controversy over whether Tass was a news agency or an intelligence-gathering arm of the Russian government first appeared in 1949, when *Editor & Publisher* directed its readers' attention to a libel suit pending in a British court. An English judge had dismissed an action brought against Tass by a Czech refugee after the Soviet ambassador had testified that Tass, as an official organ of the Soviet government, qualified for diplomatic immunity and could not be sued. Although Tass reporters carried diplomatic passports in America, they did not enjoy diplomatic immunity. Tass correspondents did, however, have the same freedom of movement and access to information as any other reporter in the United States. The London case "should be a tipoff to everyone dealing with Tass to be wary. The court said its representatives are not primarily newsmen but are Soviet agents."[159] Later that year, both Canada and Great Britain were investigating whether the relationship between Tass and the Russian government should lead to the revocation of any privileges granted to Tass employees based on their alleged roles as correspondents.[160]

In 1950, two United States government agencies excluded Tass representatives from certain news briefings. Michael J. McDermott, spokesman for the State Department, said that department officials, if they so desired, would talk to American journalists exclusively from then on. McDermott admitted that the new policy directly conflicted with the position that American delegates at the Geneva conference had taken in 1948 regarding equal access for all correspondents to official news sources. Although that question had been raised then, delegates received no cooperation at all from some countries. The State Department provided equal access to news so far as possible, McDermott said, "but there are times when Americans, as Americans, will hear what their officials have to say." No American reporter complained about this selective release of news.[161] The Department of Defense soon announced a similar policy.[162]

The problem of Tass representation within the Washington press corps stayed out of the spotlight for a few more months but then dominated the scene shortly after the arrest, trial, conviction, and imprisonment of Associated Press bureau chief Oatis in Prague on charges of espionage. Leading the campaign to exclude Tass correspondents from sources of official news—including the congressional galleries—was Alexander F. Jones, president of the American Society of Newspaper Editors, who entered the fray angry about both the Oatis case and the conditions under which American correspondents in Russia lived and worked. "So long as Bill Oatis is in jail and American reporters in Russian territory live like underground fugitives, the sight of Tass representatives walking into the White House will continue to be a red flag to me," he told the ASNE membership in 1951.[163]

As a first step toward regaining American control of its allegedly free press, Jones advocated stripping Tass representatives of all privileges in the United States until the Russians and their satellite peoples treated American press personnel better. Americans must not worry about curbing the freedom of the press through such actions, Jones maintained, for Tass was a propaganda bureau, not a news service, and, as such, it was not properly entitled to press privileges in the first place. The news stories produced by Tass reporters were more for the information of the Soviet government than for use by Russian newspapers, he said. And, even though Tass employees transmitted some of their copy out of the United States uncensored as did other foreign correspondents, they also sent confidential information out of the country via the diplomatic pouch.[164]

While lacking hard evidence to support his charges, a reporter for the Gannett Newspapers virtually labeled Tass reporters, including Mikhail Fedorov, head of the Washington bureau, as spies. Among the bits of evidence justifying the categorization was Fedorov's career as an aeronautical engineer before he abruptly switched professions. Despite this alleged proof of their duplicity, Tass representatives went everywhere that American reporters did in the capital and received every bit of news available to American reporters. For instance, a Tass reporter was seen vigorously taking notes at a press conference held by Lieutenant General Elwood R. Quesada to discuss the results of atomic bomb tests at Eniwetok.[165] Reporters from both Tass and the *Daily Worker* attended a press conference that President Truman declared off-the-record, which American journalists said meant that the Soviets would find out what the president had to say while American citizens would be kept in the dark.[166] A Tass reporter was taking notes "like mad" during General Alfred M. Gruenther's testimony before a congressional committee about NATO defense problems.[167] And a representative of the Russian agency was among foreign correspondents viewing atomic bomb tests at Bikini, courtesy of the United States government.[168]

The situation reached its current dimensions, Jones said, because the government feared that expelling Tass representatives or curtailing their activities would encourage the Russians to throw American wire service correspondents out of Moscow. Despite such a danger, American press toleration of Tass reporters was over, and Jones offered a four-point program designed to limit the Russian news agency's activities. First, the rules committees in both houses of Congress must tell the Standing Committee of Correspondents that individuals accredited to the press galleries could no longer represent a news agency supported by any government. Second, government officials must declare Tass representatives who carried diplomatic passports persona non grata and expel them. Third, the American government must notify Russia that any harsh or unreasonable treatment of American correspondents in Moscow in retaliation for these acts in the United States would be viewed as unfriendly actions. Finally, "American newspapers, which are really playing footsie with Communist control of this international press situation can get off their dead posteriors and start to fight."[169]

Jones's attack on Tass correspondents within the Congressional Press Galleries upset Markel, founder of the International Press Institute, who viewed the presence of Tass reporters in the congressional galleries as significant pro-American propaganda. During repeated trips abroad, "in discussions with 'neutralists' and pro-Communists, I have pointed with pride to what goes on here and I have said, 'Look, a representative of Tass can attend a Presidential news conference in the United States. That is how free we are and how little we are afraid.'"[170] Although Markel's argument had some validity, many journalists believed that, since Tass provided information to its home government, Tass was not a traditional news agency entitled to traditional protections. "We agree that we must not ape dictator methods and we must not do anything counter to the principles of freedom of the press," said *Editor & Publisher*, adding that no such problems arose by taking action against Tass.[171] All that the ASNE wanted the Standing Committee of Correspondents to do was to enforce its rules that clearly stated that reporters who worked for a government agency were ineligible for membership in the Congressional Press Galleries. A few years earlier, the standing committee had applied galleries' rules to exclude representatives of the United States information program who were trying to gather information to replace news denied them by the Associated Press and United Press.[172]

Standing committee members, however, unanimously refused to eject Tass reporters from the press galleries, commenting that they did not feel qualified "to move into the field of international diplomacy" by ruling on the relationship between Tass and the Russian government.[173] Traditionally, the standing committee simply accepted the credentials of foreign correspondents "when satisfied that they are bona fide representatives of the press of their countries."[174] The precedent rested on pre–World War II experiences when no reporters were excluded from the press galleries, even though practically every foreign news agency had some connection with its home government.

American editors urging correspondents to discriminate against the Russian journalists must remember the recent "squawking in this country about the proposed UN convention on the press on the grounds that it would license governments to toss out reporters who write unfriendly stories," Chalmers M. Roberts, a member of the Washington, D.C., guild unit, wrote in *The Guild Reporter*. Now, newspaper editors wanted American reporters to practice such discrimination, Roberts said; even though reporters might face repercussions from their employers because of their refusal to follow instructions, problems at home were preferable to retaliation abroad. Practically, the presence of Tass or *Daily Worker* reporters at some press conferences did restrict the availability of background news. "But every reporter worth his salt can edge around that and I feel it's a minor price to pay for the principle involved, to wit, that any newspaperman here from any other nation ought to be allowed to operate here as long as he's gathering news, regardless of what his country's policy is or how controlled his press." The government, not representatives of the press, must decide whether a foreign correspondent was actually qualified to be considered a correspondent or whether that reporter was really a government agent.[175]

The ASNE formed a special committee designed to convince the Standing Committee of Correspondents to reverse its decision, but the reporters held firm, much to the delight of former ASNE president Benjamin McKelway, editor of the *Washington Star*. McKelway, who as ASNE head led the fight to exclude representatives of the United States Information Service from the press galleries, said that he took "considerable satisfaction in the unanimous decision of the Standing Committee not to throw Tass out of the galleries." Because of the correspondents' decision, international freedom of the press would benefit significantly, for "as they said in their excellent statement, 'That the principles of a free press cannot be upheld by abridging them.' "[176]

Thus, out of three skirmishes between communism and the press in the United States, traditional American free-press values held firm in just one episode. And the heroes in the last instance were not the editors who had loudly advocated free-press guarantees for the world but the reporters who, in providing freedom of the press with one of its finest hours during the cold war, jeopardized their standing with their employers.[177] As the international free-press campaign was running out of steam at the United Nations, conditions within the United States raised increasingly pointed questions about whether the American press could maintain the crusade's moral leadership in the face of a deepening cold war. Perhaps all parties concerned were thankful that, for all practical purposes, the crusade was over.

NOTES

1. "Polk Slaying Climaxes Press Ordeal in Greece," *E&P*, May 22, 1948, p. 8.
2. "George Polk's Murder," *E&P*, June 26, 1948, p. 34.
3. "Convention Hits Delay in Probe of Polk Murder," *Guild Reporter*, July 9, 1948, p. 9.
4. "War's Radio Legacy," *Broadcasting*, May 31, 1948, p. 44.
5. Memorandum of Conversation with Committee of Overseas Writers by William Baxter, Division of Greek, Turkish, and Iranian Affairs, May 14, 1948, RG 59, NA, Box 4991, 811.91268/5-2448.
6. Davidson Taylor, Vice President and Director of Public Affairs, Columbia Broadcasting System, Inc., to Secretary of State George C. Marshall, May 18, 1948, Ibid., 811.91268/5-1848.
7. Secretary of State George C. Marshall to the American Embassy, Athens, Greece, May 20, 1948, Ibid., 811.91268/5-1948.
8. Robert A. Lovett, Under Secretary of State, to Senator Henry Cabot Lodge, May 26, 1948, Ibid., 811.91268/5-2148.
9. William Baxter, Division of Greek, Turkish, and Iranian Affairs, to Robert Lovett, Under Secretary of State, May 27, 1948, Ibid., 811.91268/5-2748.
10. Raleigh A. Gibson, American Consul General, Salonika, Greece, to the Secretary of State, October 17, 1948, Ibid., Box 4992, 811.91268/10-1748.
11. The only person convicted in the case was a communist who was charged with complicity in the death. In the late 1970s, arguments to reopen the case emerged on the basis that new evidence indicated that right-wing responsibility for the crime had been suppressed during the original investigation. *See* Yiannis P. Roubatis and Elias Vlanton, "Who Killed George Polk?" *More*, May 1977, pp. 12–24.
12. "Czechs to Try AP Writer at Early Date," *E&P*, June 30, 1951, p. 54.

13. "Communists Imprison 4 AP Men in Prague as 'Spies'," *E&P*, July 7, 1951, p. 7.

14. "Excerpts from the Proceedings," *Department of State Bulletin*, August 20, 1951, p. 288.

15. "The Kangaroo Court," *Time*, July 16, 1951, p. 54.

16. "Communists Imprison 4 AP Men in Prague as 'Spies'," p. 7.

17. "Trial of Oatis," *E&P*, July 14, 1951, p. 42. The idea of American correspondents aiding the United States government had been raised by a British newspaper in December 1950. The charge came out of a complicated interaction in which a British parliamentary source talked off-the-record with an American journalist. Through a few innocent telephone calls, a stateside reporter contacted the State Department for comment on the unexpected British plans. The State Department then asked the British about the possibility, the anonymity guaranteed to the source was somehow broken, and a progovernment newspaper, the *London Tribune*, suggested editorially that talking to American journalists was akin to conversing with American spies. See Raymond Daniell, "Diplomats Get Press Into 'Spy' Tempest," *E&P*, December 9, 1950, p. 10; "Correspondent 'Spies'," *E&P*, December 16, 1950, p. 34.

State Department officials had considered using American journalists as regular sources of information in 1946—when the idea was broached by a journalist. John Parkerson, manager of the Washington office of Press Wireless, Inc., suggested that reporters with foreign-assignment backgrounds could serve as informal, unpaid advisers to the department. Comment from within the department indicated that good ambassadors usually kept in close touch with American journalists in their areas anyway and depended on them "for a great deal of information and advice," without any formal arrangement. See John Parkerson, Manager, Washington Office, Press Wireless, Inc., to Francis Colt de Wolf, State Department, February 6, 1946, RG 59, NA, Box 4983, 811.91200/2-646; Selden Chapin, Director General, Office of Foreign Service, to Donald Russell, Assistant Secretary of State, February 20, 1946, Ibid., 811.91200/2-1246.

Most journalists accepted the fact that foreign correspondents had informal conferences with ambassadors, just as ambassadors had informal meetings with correspondents. Journalists did not equate these sessions with spying, however, and, if Oatis had such an arrangement with the United States ambassador in Czechoslovakia, the contacts were considered as just part of his job. Although American journalists did not question Oatis's possible connections with the United States government, they also failed to protest his arrest and trial vehemently enough to suit *Editor & Publisher*. The trade journal thought that journalists had reacted in this rather disgraceful manner in the mistaken belief that the communists lacked the nerve to convict Oatis. When Oatis was convicted, *Editor & Publisher* encouraged journalists to campaign unstintingly to obtain his release and to ensure that no such disaster ever befell another American journalist. See "Oatis Case," *E&P*, August 4, 1951, p. 32.

18. "Intimidation," *E&P*, June 30, 1951, p. 36. *See also*, "We Should Help Free Oatis from His Communistic Prison," *Publishers' Auxiliary*, August 2, 1952, p. 4.

19. "Czech Big Shot Spurns Guild's Demand for Release of Oatis, Jailed Newsman," *Guild Reporter*, July 13, 1951, pp. 1, 14.

20. "ASNE and the Oatis Case," *ASNE Bulletin*, August 1, 1951, p. 1.
21. "ANPA Resolution Condemns Oatis Conviction," *American Newspaper Publishers Association B Bulletin*, August 8, 1951, p. 123.
22. "SDX Council Takes Action on Oatis," *E&P*, August 25, 1951, p. 59.
23. "State Dept. Brands Oatis Trial Travesty," *E&P*, July 7, 1951, p. 8.
24. "ECOSOC Resolution Asks Protection of Correspondents' Rights," *Department of State Bulletin*, August 20, 1951, p. 289. The Oatis case was brought up before a variety of United Nations bodies in 1951 and 1952 including the Third Committee of the General Assembly and the Subcommission on Freedom of Information and of the Press. *See* "Ask UN Action," *E&P*, August 18, 1951, p. 8; "UN Council Hits Persecution of Correspondents," *E&P*, August 25, 1951, p. 59; "U.N. Can Act on Oatis Case, Lawyers Say," *E&P*, November 10, 1951, p. 42; "Oatis Case Brought Up Officially Again in UN," *E&P*, February 2, 1952, p. 8; "The Case of William N. Oatis," *E&P*, March 8, 1952, pp. 10, 71.
25. "ASNE, ANPA Directors Act in Oatis Case," *E&P*, August 4, 1951, p. 10.
26. "Czech Official Defies U.S. on Oatis Case," *E&P*, September 1, 1951, p. 13.
27. "Truman's Comment," *E&P*, September 1, 1951, p. 13; "Czech Trade Ban Appears Certain," *E&P*, September 1, 1951, p. 13.
28. Campbell Watson, "AP Editors Consider Oatis, Security Screen," *E&P*, September 29, 1951, p. 10.
29. "Progress on Oatis," *E&P*, October 6, 1951, p. 38.
30. "Guild Calls for Industry-wide Committee to Spur Moves for Release of Oatis," *Guild Reporter*, November 9, 1951, pp. 1–2. Guild president Harry Martin met with representatives of the State Department and with Frank Starzel, general manager of the Associated Press, about forming a Newspaper Committee to Free Oatis. After the session, Martin reported, "I, like Mr. Starzel, came away convinced that the State Department is really doing everything within its power to free Bill Oatis and that, for the moment at least, the appointment of any official committee on a national scale might complicate rather than facilitate the efforts that are being made." *See* "Martin Sees U.S. Acting to Free Oatis," *E&P*, November 24, 1951, p. 15.
31. "New Efforts Made to Free William Oatis," *E&P*, March 8, 1952, p. 10.
32. "Action on Oatis," *E&P*, March 8, 1952, p. 40.
33. "Reds Say Oatis Testifies in New Spy Trial," *E&P*, March 22, 1952, p. 62.
34. "Czechs Allow Oatis to Talk to U.S. Envoy," *E&P*, May 10, 1952, p. 13.
35. "Embassy Aide Visits Oatis in Prague Jail," *E&P*, October 11, 1952, p. 71.
36. Resolutions, *The APME Red Book 1952*, New York, The Associated Press, 1952, p. 225.
37. News Barriers, *The APME Red Book 1951*, New York, The Associated Press, 1951, pp. 34–35.
38. News Production, Ibid., p. 42.
39. "Action on Oatis," p. 40.
40. The Czechs released Oatis from prison on May 15, 1953, after President Dwight D. Eisenhower appealed directly to Czech President Antonin Zapotocky. The actual release may have been due in part to a lessening in East-West tensions brought on by the death of Stalin on March 5, 1953. *See* Ray Erwin, "Oatis Promises Full Story after He Reviews Record," *E&P*, May 23, 1953, pp. 9, 58–59.
41. The Argentine constitution said: "The federal Congress shall not enact laws

that restrict the liberty of the press or that establish federal jurisdiction over it."
See "Freedom Guaranteed in 47 Constitutions," *E&P*, May 31, 1947, p. 58.

42. *See*, e.g., Ernie Hill, "The Murder of La Prensa," *Quill*, June 1951, pp. 12–14;
Donald B. Easum, "'La Prensa' and Freedom of the Press in Argentina,"
Journalism Quarterly 28 (Spring 1951):229–37; Joseph F. Kane, "The
Totalitarian Pattern in Peron's Press Campaign," *Journalism Quarterly* 28
(Spring 1951):237–43.

43. Resolutions, April 19, 1947, *Problems of Journalism—1947*, pp. 211, 230.

44. "End of Freedom," *E&P*, April 12, 1947, p. 58.

45. *See*, e.g., "Argentina's Press," *E&P*, August 9, 1947, p. 40; "The Easiest Way,"
E&P, March 12, 1949, p. 38; "Freedom in Argentina," *E&P*, January 7, 1950, p.
32; "Best Endorsement," *E&P*, September 23, 1950, p. 30.

46. "End of La Prensa?" *E&P*, March 10, 1951, p. 50.

47. *See*, e.g., Memorandum of Conversation with Dr. Juan A. Bramuglia, Argentine Foreign Minister, by Paul C. Daniels, Director of the Office of American
Republic Affairs, December 9, 1948, *FR: 1948*, IX:304.

48. Thomas J. Maleady, Buenos Aires Embassy, to Henry Dearborn, Division of
River Plate Affairs, January 27, 1949, RG 59, NA, Box 5491, 835.91/1-2749.

49. Hill, "The Murder of La Prensa," p. 14.

50. Telephone Conversation between T. C. Mann, American Republic Affairs, and
Roger W. Tubby, Assistant Press Secretary, White House, March 1, 1951, RG
59, NA, Box 5868, 935.64/3-151.

51. Unsigned Position Paper—*LA PRENSA* Problem, March 13, 1951, Ibid., Box
5866, 935.61/3-1351.

52. Ibid.

53. Marquis Childs, "What Signs Threaten Free Press?" *Nieman Reports*, July
1951, p. 7.

54. "Martin Raps Dictators at Brussels Congress of Professional Workers," *Guild
Reporter*, April 27, 1951, p. 3.

55. Robert U. Brown, "Shop Talk at Thirty," *E&P*, February 3, 1951, p. 52.

56. "Shrinking Perimeter of Freedom," *Quill*, April 1951, p. 5.

57. Robert H. Estabrook, "Chairman's Corner," *Masthead*, Spring 1951, p. 1. This
issue of *The Masthead* also carried an analysis of editorial comment on the
death of *La Prensa*. *See* George E. Simmons, "La Prensa's Defense in the
United States," *Masthead*, Spring 1951, pp. 4–8.

58. "Young Sends ASNE Protest to Peron," *ASNE Bulletin*, April 1, 1951, p. 4.

59. Resolutions, April 21, 1951, *Problems of Journalism—1951*, p. 231.

60. "Chapultepec & La Prensa," *E&P*, March 17, 1951, p. 32.

61. Once the expropriation of *La Prensa* was completed, Perón turned the
newspaper over to the General Confederation of Labor, which soon used the
La Prensa nameplate to top a new, government-approved publication. *See*
"Hollow Shell," *E&P*, May 5, 1951, p. 34.

62. "Dr. Gainza Paz," *E&P*, September 8, 1951, p. 36.

63. "Fundamental Right of People Undermined," *E&P*, October 6, 1951, p. 10.

64. Alberto Gainza Paz, "Tyranny Can't Live with a Free Press," *Quill*, November
1951, pp. 7–8.

65. Alberto Gainza Paz, Speech, April 19, 1952, *Problems of Journalism—1952*, p.

280. Gainza Paz resumed publication of *La Prensa* in February 1956, after the fall of Juan Perón.

66. An exception to this desire to work with European press representatives centered on the involvement of United States journalists with the Inter-American Press Association, which drew members from North, South, and Central America. *See*, e.g., "Victory in Quito," *E&P*, July 30, 1949, p. 28; "Inter-American Press," *E&P*, August 19, 1950, p. 32; "Hemisphere Press Meet in New York," *E&P*, October 7, 1950, pp. 7, 10; "Important Conference," *E&P*, October 7, 1950, p. 42; "Conference Adopts Free Press Principles," *E&P*, October 14, 1950, p. 105; "Another Victory," *E&P*, October 13, 1951, p. 38; "A Free Press," *E&P*, October 20, 1951, p. 40; "Bold Step," *E&P*, October 18, 1952, p. 38; "Our 'Iron Curtains'," *E&P*, October 18, 1952, p. 38; Robert U. Brown, "IAPA Acts to Reinforce Hemisphere Press Freedom," *E&P*, October 18, 1952, pp. 7, 67.

67. Pat Frayne, "World Newsmen Congress Credit to Martin Says Frayne," *Guild Reporter*, November 9, 1951, p. 6.

68. G. Langelaan, "New Federation of Journalists' Unions Set Up," *E&P*, October 27, 1951, p. 48.

69. "13,000 Guild Members in World Labor Group," *E&P*, May 31, 1952, p. 10.

70. "Newsmen's Unions Set Up Free-World Organization at Brussels Conference," *Guild Reporter*, May 23, 1952, pp. 1–2.

71. Erwin D. Canham, Report on the Geneva Conference on Freedom of Information, April 16, 1948, *Problems of Journalism—1948*, pp. 156–57.

72. George Langelaan, "FIEJ—Publishers, Editors Form International Body," *E&P*, July 10, 1948, pp. 9, 64.

73. Erwin D. Canham, "President Urges Affiliation with International Federation," *ASNE Bulletin*, September 1, 1948, p. 1.

74. "Board Votes Year's Affiliation with International Federation," *ASNE Bulletin*, December 1, 1948, p. 1.

75. By 1950, the American FIEJ membership was being shared with the American Newspaper Publishers Association as the concerns discussed strayed from news-related topics. At times, members focused on free-press questions, but one of the most popular topics on the agenda was the availability and distribution of newsprint. *See*, e.g., "FIEJ Membership Is Taken by ASNE Jointly with ANPA," *ASNE Bulletin*, November 1, 1950, p. 1; G. Langelaan, "37 Attend Federation Congress in Holland," *E&P*, June 25, 1949, pp. 10, 24; G. Langelaan, "FIEJ Assails Newsprint Control by Government," *E&P*, May 27, 1950, pp. 11, 52; Doris Willens, "FIEJ Heeds U.S. Leaders in Shunning Gov't Controls," *E&P*, June 2, 1951, p. 9; G. Langelaan, "Japanese Publishers Accepted in FIEJ," *E&P*, June 21, 1952, p. 53.

The group also supported American freedom of information positions. *See* Doris Willens, "Information Treaty Opposed by FIEJ," *E&P*, May 26, 1951, p. 15; "FIEJ Freedom of Information Resolution Helpful to U.S. Position," *ASNE Bulletin*, September 1, 1951, p. 2.

76. Lester Markel, Special Committee Reports, April 20, 1950, *Problems of Journalism—1950*, p. 63.

77. "World Press Institute Considered by Editors," *E&P*, April 8, 1950, p. 26;

"ASNE Brings Foreign Editors to U.S.," *ASNE Bulletin*, September 1, 1950, pp. 1–2.

78. "Editors, Ending Tour, Will Confer with Committee," *ASNE Bulletin*, October 1, 1950, pp. 1–2; "500 Voted for Organization Work of International Press Institute Plan," *ASNE Bulletin*, November 1, 1950, p. 2.
79. "Institute May Open in Switzerland Soon," *E&P*, February 10, 1951, p. 65.
80. "International Institute," *E&P*, February 10, 1951, p. 40.
81. Lester Markel, Reports of Officers and Committees, April 19, 1951, *Problems of Journalism—1951*, pp. 25, 29.
82. G. Langelaan, "107 Editors of 22 Nations Attend Paris Press Meeting," *E&P*, May 24, 1952, p. 11. UNESCO had talked about creating an international press institute as well, but early proposals failed for financial reasons. *See* Robert W. Desmond, "Plans for International Press Institute Are Bright Spot in 1947 Picture," *Journalism Quarterly* 25 (March 1948):33–37; George Langelaan, "International Press Federation Call Issued," *E&P*, May 15, 1948, p. 34. Members of the Subcommission on Freedom of Information and of the Press also briefly considered establishing such an organization.
83. "Telling the Big Truth," *Quill*, July 1952, p. 4.
84. Lester Markel, "The International Press Institute Enables Editors to Speak to Editors," *Quill*, December 1952, pp. 5, 11. Markel wanted the institute to actively conduct research on problems that faced the world's newspaper community. The institute issued its first research report late in 1952. *See* "Improvement of Information," *Nieman Reports*, October 1952, pp. 47–48.
85. "Report on World Press Freedom," *E&P*, April 13, 1946, pp. 7, 82, 84.
86. Ibid., pp. 82, 84.
87. "Varied Restrictions Harassed Press in '46," *E&P*, December 28, 1946, p. 10.
88. "Barriers Are Still Up, AP Survey Discloses," *E&P*, February 7, 1948, p. 36.
89. "Freedom of Press Curbed during '48, Survey Shows," *E&P*, December 25, 1948, pp. 7, 40–41; "New Barriers to Press Shown in AP Survey," *E&P*, January 21, 1950, p. 54.
90. "Report on Freedom in Americas Made in Montevideo Meeting," *E&P*, October 20, 1951, p. 60.
91. "Report on Freedom of Information," *Quill*, January 1952, p. 10.
92. Ibid., p. 21.
93. "At Least the Free Press Is Alert," *Quill*, December 1952, p. 4.
94. Russell F. Anderson, "The Disappearing Foreign Correspondent," *Michigan Alumnus Quarterly Review* 57 (December 1950):1, 3. Anderson said that his figures were rough because each agency considered the exact number of foreign correspondents stationed abroad a trade secret, which no agency would release. He believed, however, that his survey methods made the totals fairly accurate.
95. Ibid., pp. 1–2. Anderson's tying of the poor quality of foreign news to the decreasing number of foreign correspondents was a theme of a 1947 article written by an academic, which did not garner as much attention as did Anderson's piece. *See* Max R. Grossman, "Some Contemporary Problems of Foreign Correspondence," *Journalism Quarterly* 24 (March 1947):37–42.
96. Russell F. Anderson, "News from Nowhere," *Saturday Review of Literature*, November 17, 1951, p. 10.
97. Anderson, "The Disappearing Foreign Correspondent," p. 4.
98. Ibid., p. 5.

99. Letters to the Editor on "News from Nowhere," *Saturday Review of Literature*, December 15, 1951, pp. 25–26 (emphasis in original).

100. Anderson, "The Disappearing Foreign Correspondent," p. 5.

101. "The Vanishing Foreign Correspondent," *Quill*, February 1951, p. 5.

102. American journalists believed in openly conducted diplomacy. Thus, if journalists revealed the details of secret negotiations, they saw freedom of the press as functioning well. For instance, the publication of details of proposed draft treaties with Finland, Italy, and the Balkan states by the *New York Herald Tribune* was praised by *Editor & Publisher*. Although the British Foreign Office protested that the publication could complicate future negotiations, American journalists easily dismissed the complaint because of lack of proof. The *London Star* considered the publication of the treaties as "the latest example of the gangster journalism which is too prevalent in Washington." See "Secret Treaties," *E&P*, July 27, 1946, p. 38.

103. James J. Butler, "Truman OK Unlikely on Tight Secrecy Rule," *E&P*, October 25, 1947, p. 13.

104. "Censorship Threat," *E&P*, October 25, 1947, p. 38.

105. "Protest to Washington," *ASNE Bulletin*, November 1, 1947, p. 3.

106. "Security Board Modifies 'Gag' on Documents," *Publishers' Auxiliary*, November 1, 1947, p. 5.

107. "Secrecy Modified," *E&P*, November 1, 1947, p. 36.

108. "President Hits ASNE Protest of Censorship," *The Publishers' Auxiliary*, November 15, 1947, p. 1.

109. "Washington News Gag," *E&P*, November 22, 1947, p. 34.

110. James J. Butler, "ASNE, Atomic Board Join in Security Study," *E&P*, December 6, 1947, p. 10.

111. "Security Regulations," *E&P*, December 6, 1947, p. 38. Forrestal carried his consultations farther than any other governmental official by talking with twenty-two Pentagon correspondents in an attempt to enlist the journalists' help in developing standards for the release of information. The Defense Department promised to stop leaks of classified information and to establish a unified policy on the release of technical material. In return, Forrestal asked the press to voluntarily refrain from publishing information that might be detrimental to national security. The reporters, after studying the problem, agreed that some Defense Department information probably must remain confidential, but they argued that keeping the information secret was the responsibility of the military and not of the press. To the reporters, any agreement between the press and the military to set up guidelines for the release and publication of information would inevitably curtail the freedom of the press, which must be preserved at all costs. See "Seek Plan to Guard Security Information," *E&P*, March 6, 1948, pp. 9, 68; "Media Security Advisors Suggested to Forrestal," *E&P*, April 3, 1948, pp. 12, 68; "Security Advisory Council Recommended," *American Newspaper Publishers Association B Bulletin*, April 2, 1948, pp. 73–78; Resolutions, April 17, 1948, *Problems of Journalism—1948*, pp. 233–44.

112. "Security Problem," *E&P*, April 3, 1948, p. 36.

113. "Security Bill," *E&P*, March 26, 1949, p. 30.

114. "Publicity Affecting National Security," *American Newspaper Publishers Association B Bulletin*, May 4, 1949, p. 74.

115. "Johnson Vetoes Rules Criticized as 'Gag'," *E&P*, June 11, 1949, p. 11.
116. "Sawyer Asks Voluntary Code on Technical Data," *E&P*, March 10, 1951, p. 8.
117. "Truman Spokesman Gives Pledge of 'No Censorship'," *E&P*, March 10, 1951, pp. 5–6.
118. James J. Butler, "'Voluntary' Security Rules Broaden Restricted Area," *E&P*, September 29, 1951, p. 11.
119. "Blackout," *E&P*, September 29, 1951, p. 38.
120. Walker Stone, "ASNE and the Directive," *ASNE Bulletin*, October 1, 1951, p. 3.
121. "President's Order 'Reasonable,' Commerce Secretary Declares," *Publishers' Auxiliary*, October 2, 1951, p. 5.
122. Arguments about press access to governmental information generally excluded demands for access to atomic energy developments. A perfect example of the journalism community's reluctance to divulge this information involved reporters and editors of the *Baltimore News-Post*, who were offered pictures of materials going into the atomic bomb. Rather than jumping at the scoop, reporters called the Federal Bureau of Investigation. For their patriotism, the journalists earned the commendation of J. Edgar Hoover; none of their professional peers criticized the journalists' actions. See "Baltimore Daily Praised for A-Bomb Coup," *E&P*, October 19, 1946, p. 12.

In fact, leaders of the Atomic Energy Commission and the American Society of Newspaper Editors campaigned hard to encourage journalists to explain atomic energy to their fellow Americans. The subject was so complicated and so shrouded in national security considerations that few reporters wanted to try writing about it. See, e.g., David E. Lilienthal, Speech, April 19, 1947, *Problems of Journalism—1947*, pp. 238–45; Gideon Seymour, Report of the Special Committee on Atomic Information, April 16, 1948, *Problems of Journalism—1948*, pp. 168–76.

The problem rested in reconciling the "practice of full and free dissemination of fact with the common-sense requirement that we do not put into a potential enemy's hands information which will help him to kill our young men, devastate our cities, and overthrow our nation," said Dr. Vannevar Bush, president of Carnegie Institution. Making that determination was difficult, but in the early years of atomic energy's existence, press and Atomic Energy Commission officials seemed to agree on the basic ends. See Program Presented by the Special Committee on Security Issues, April 16, 1948, *Problems of Journalism—1948*, p. 188. In fact, journalists were so cooperative in maintaining the necessary secrecy that scientists sometimes found themselves pleading for dissemination of information about atomic energy while the newspapers were "aiding and abetting the cause of secrecy." See "Secrecy Blamed for Retarding Atom Science," *E&P*, April 2, 1949, p. 28.

By 1951, however, ASNE members were being told that "while the press must recognize the necessity for some military secrecy, it also must constantly review and question the validity of AEC's decisions on what is to be withheld." See Freedom of Information Committee Report, April 21, 1951, *Problems of Journalism—1951*, p. 177.
123. "When Mr. Truman Sounded Off on Responsibilities of the Press," *E&P*, October 13, 1951, pp. 62–63.

124. "Statement by Short," *E&P*, October 13, 1951, p. 7.
125. "Offense and Defense," *E&P*, October 13, 1951, p. 38.
126. "A Free Press," *E&P*, October 20, 1951, p. 40.
127. The American Newspaper Publishers Association, for instance, used its *Bulletin* to carry, side-by-side, attempts by foreign governments that Americans considered totalitarian to restrict their presses and attempts by local, state, and national governments in the United States to use the same methods. *See* "Are Rights of People to Freedom of Information More Secure Here?" *American Newspaper Publishers Association B Bulletin*, November 28, 1951, pp. 185–88.
128. "False, Misleading Statements, Says White House Secretary," *Quill*, Sigma Delta Chi Section, January 1952, p. 2.
129. "What's to Do about 'Reds' Who Turn Up as Newsmen," *Publishers' Auxiliary*, August 5, 1950, p. 4.
130. "Kick Them Out," *E&P*, October 11, 1947, p. 42.
131. "Loyalty Oath Demanded by Hammond Publisher," *Guild Reporter*, January 28, 1949, p. 1. *Editor & Publisher* found the oath unobjectionable; after all, an employer established the standards that his employees must meet. *See* "U.S.A. or Communism," *E&P*, February 5, 1949, p. 36. The American Newspaper Guild unit at the Hammond newspaper denounced the suggested oath as an unwarranted implication that Guild members were communists. *See* "Hammond Rejects Publisher's Demand for Non-Commie Press Card Affidavit," *Guild Reporter*, February 11, 1949, p. 3.

Similar oaths for broadcasting employees were considered appropriate by various industry representatives because "the Kremlinites could not ignore radio or TV—the swiftest and most potent means of reaching the people." *See* "Loyalty vs. 'Liberalism'," *Broadcasting*, June 26, 1950, p. 38.
132. "Double-Talk in Red," *Broadcasting*, August 15, 1949, p. 38.
133. Detroit Police Commissioner Harry S. Toy tried to force all Detroit area reporters covering the police department to sign noncommunist affidavits before granting them press cards. After some initial uncertainty about a proper response, journalists ranging from the local unit of the Guild to editors of local newspapers to ASNE leaders denounced Toy's effort as an attempt to license the press. Toy later withdrew the proposal. *See* "Editors Split on Loyalty Oath Requirement for Police Pass," *E&P*, January 29, 1949, pp. 5, 50; "Detroit Says Phooey to Demand of Cop Boss for Press Card Loyalty Oath," *Guild Reporter*, January 28, 1949, pp. 1, 7; "Dear Mr. Toy," *ASNE Bulletin*, February 1, 1949, p. 2; "Drop 'Licensing' Move, Walters Urges Toy," *E&P*, February 5, 1949, p. 62; "Headline Harry Meets New Opposition on Press Card Loyalty Oath in Detroit," *Guild Reporter*, February 11, 1949, p. 3; "Toy Keeps Oath Order, Says It Protects Press," *E&P*, February 26, 1949, p. 64; "Toy Exempts 3 Papers from Press Card Oath," *E&P*, March 5, 1949, p. 50; "Canham Attacks Move to Bar Reds from News," *E&P*, March 19, 1949, p. 45; Basil L. Walters, Report of the World Freedom of Information Committee, April 21, 1949, *Problems of Journalism—1949*, pp. 38–39.

Journalists also opposed an attempt by the Defense Department to require reporters to complete a long loyalty questionnaire before receiving necessary clearances to enter military posts. The accreditation procedure, begun in 1948, was designed to provide reporters with credentials that would grant them immediate access to battlefields in case of war. Among the questions on the three-foot-long questionnaire: "Are there any unfavorable incidents in your life not mentioned above which you believe may reflect upon your loyalty to the U.S. Government or upon your ability to perform the duties which you will be called upon to undertake? If so, describe." The long questionnaire was quickly withdrawn and a short, one-page form substituted before journalists raised the licensing issue. Although journalists firmly believed that "loyal, patriotic Americans in government employ" would want "to prove their own loyalty and weed out the disloyal to protect the democratic structure in which we all survive or fall together," only a publisher or editor had the right to judge a reporter's loyalty. See "Does the Press Care?" E&P, December 4, 1948, p. 30. See also "Newsmen's Loyalty Check May Be Eased," E&P, October 23, 1948, p. 6; "Army Accreditation," E&P, October 23, 1948, p. 36; "U.S. Accrediting Plan," E&P, December 18, 1948, p. 36.

134. "Sulzberger Describes Press as Peace Factor," E&P, May 14, 1949, p. 71.
135. "Chips Are Down as CIO 'Tackles Internal Communistic Situation'," Guild Reporter, June 10, 1949, p. 2.
136. "Guild Head Specifies 2 Red-Controlled Units," E&P, March 22, 1947, p. 60.
137. "Testimony of Murray before the House Labor Committee," Guild Reporter, March 28, 1947, p. 6.
138. "Murray and Rodgers War on Reds in Guild," E&P, February 22, 1947, p. 10.
139. "N.Y. Guild Delegates Back Ryan, Boo Murray," E&P, March 22, 1947, p. 11; "New York RA Rebukes Murray, Votes Confidence in Officers," Guild Reporter, March 28, 1947, p. 6; "Statements on Murray Charges of 'Communism'," Guild Reporter, March 28, 1947, p. 6; "3 NY Units Take Individual Action over Murray Charges," Guild Reporter, April 11, 1947, p. 5; Milton Murray, "Points of Information," Guild Reporter, April 11, 1947, p. 7; "Murray Charges 'Secret Cabal'," Guild Reporter, June 27, 1947, pp. 2, 6; "McManus, Ryan Ousted as N.Y. Guild Leaders," E&P, December 27, 1947, p. 10; "New NY Officers Fail to Gain Control of Executive Committee," Guild Reporter, January 23, 1948, p. 7; "Guild Cleans House," E&P, July 17, 1948, p. 44.
140. "Washington Ponders Case of Reporter Fired for Communist Party Membership," Guild Reporter, June 11, 1948, p. 1.
141. "Locals Called on to Fight Firings Based Solely on Political Beliefs," Guild Reporter, July 9, 1948, p. 5.
142. "Arbiter Justifies Firing of 2 Named as Commies," E&P, August 16, 1952, p. 9.
143. "Two Decisions," E&P, August 23, 1952, p. 34.
144. Richard S. Clark, "Reds Grab Czechoslovakia after Gagging Press, Radio," E&P, February 28, 1948, p. 7; Robert E. Black, "Leftists Distorted Press Laws to Capture Czech Newspapers," Journalism Quarterly 26 (June 1949):181–85; "Czech Journalists," E&P, May 15, 1948, p. 40.
145. "Foreign News Plan Offered by Forrest," E&P, February 2, 1946, p. 13.
146. "Daily Worker Plans Fight to Retain Comics," E&P, December 13, 1947, p. 14.
147. "Daily Worker," E&P, November 3, 1951, p. 34.
148. George W. Parker, "'Battle of the Newsstands': 'Nuisance' Rule Avoids Test of Red Press Ban," E&P, August 5, 1950, p. 13.

149. "Daily Worker Seeks Writ against Proposed New York City Newsstand Ban," *American Newspaper Publishers Association Federal Laws Bulletin*, December 6, 1950, p. 246.
150. "The Commies Again," *E&P*, December 9, 1950, p. 42.
151. "Worker Ban," *E&P*, January 20, 1951, p. 34.
152. 341 U.S. 494 (1951).
153. "The Free Press," *E&P*, June 30, 1951, p. 36.
154. 354 U.S. 298 (1957).
155. "Text of Indictment," *E&P*, September 1, 1951, p. 7. The relevant part of the indictment read: "It was further a part of said conspiracy that said defendants and co-conspirators would publish and circulate and cause to be published and circulated, books, articles, magazines, and newspapers teaching and advocating the duty and necessity of overthrowing and destroying the Government of the United States by force and violence." The indictment continued,
   It was further a part of said conspiracy that said defendants and co-conspirators would write and cause to be written articles and directives in publications of the Communist Party of the United States of America, including but not limited to, Political Affairs, Morning Freiheit, Daily Worker, and The Worker, teaching and advocating the duty and necessity of overthrowing and destroying the Government of the United States by force and violence.
156. "Free Press Not Editor's Cloak, Replies Clarvoe," *E&P*, September 1, 1951, p. 55; Robert U. Brown, "Editors See No Press Threat in Communist Indictments," *E&P*, September 1, 1951, pp. 7, 54.
157. "No Free Press Threat," *E&P*, September 1, 1951, p. 34.
158. "No Free Press Case," *E&P*, September 27, 1952, p. 34.
159. "Soviet Agents," *E&P*, July 16, 1949, p. 32.
160. "Canada and England Probe Tass Privileges," *E&P*, December 3, 1949, p. 22.
161. James J. Butler, "State Department to Bar Foreign Press If It Pleases," *E&P*, November 18, 1950, p. 6.
162. "Press Selection Also Followed at Pentagon," *E&P*, November 25, 1950, p. 18.
163. Alexander F. Jones, "A Call for Courage," *ASNE Bulletin*, September 1, 1951, p. 2.
164. Ibid., p. 1.
165. Robert U. Brown, "Shop Talk at Thirty," *E&P*, September 8, 1951, p. 64.
166. "Keeping Secrets," *E&P*, December 22, 1951, p. 30.
167. "Tass Man Gets Something to Write Home About," *E&P*, March 29, 1952, p. 8.
168. Walter A. Shead, "Should America Toss Out Reds' Newspapermen?" *Publishers' Auxiliary*, September 15, 1951, p. 1.
169. Jones, "A Call for Courage," pp. 1–2. Expelling Tass reporters from the country would not put the agency out of business in the United States. The Russian news agency followed the somewhat universal practice of employing nationals of the country in which it was operating as correspondents. Hence, some American citizens would remain to carry on Tass's work even if the Soviet employees were deported.
170. "Editors (28 to 12) Endorse Barring Tass from Gallery," *E&P*, September 15, 1951, p. 11.

171. "Opinions on Tass," *E&P*, September 15, 1951, p. 34.
172. B. M. McKelway, "U.S. in Press Gallery Will Bear Watching," *E&P*, November 5, 1949, pp. 8, 51; "USIS Press Gallery Application Delayed," *E&P*, February 18, 1950, p. 10; "Press Gallery Places Denied to State Dept.," *E&P*, June 10, 1950, p. 28.
173. "Newsmen Vote Down Tass Ouster," *Guild Reporter*, September 28, 1951, p. 5.
174. "Tass Allowed to Keep Place in Press Gallery," *E&P*, September 29, 1951, p. 12.
175. Chalmers M. Roberts, "Washington Roundup," *Guild Reporter*, September 28, 1951, p. 8.
176. B. M. McKelway, "Should Tass Reporters Be Curbed? No," *ASNE Bulletin*, October 1, 1951, p. 2.
177. Standing Committee members acknowledged the importance of their vote to international press freedom:

> We subscribe to the aims of American journalistic leaders who have been working toward a freer exchange of information among the peoples and countries of the world. The committee believes that Russia's drastic restrictions on the movement and reporting by American correspondents in the Soviet Union and the similar cynical bonds on the free press throughout the Communist world constitute a long step backward to the dark ages of ignorance and intolerance.

Imitating such actions, they said, would retard rather than advance freedom of information. *See* "Tass Allowed to Keep Place in Press Gallery," p. 12.

Epilogue

As far as the United States was concerned, the crusade for international freedom of the press was over. Conceived as a dream during World War II, the campaign had turned into a nightmare due to postwar tensions and the concerns of the so-called underdeveloped nations. In putting the crusade to rest, most American journalists and diplomats undoubtedly believed that the campaign would stay buried. But these diplomats and journalists had forgotten that the crusade's antecedents stretched back to before World War I—in fact, unrest over an international communications structure dominated by the major nations began, perhaps, with the creation of the news cartel in the nineteenth century. Concern about the distribution of false news damaging to a nation's reputation had been voiced even before the turn of the century. With such a background, any belief that the rest of the world would join the Americans in abandoning interest in international freedom of information was simply unrealistic.

The freedom of information campaign, fairly quiescent for almost two decades after the United Nations endeavor, burst forth on the international scene once again in the 1970s. Debates occurred within UNESCO, and the crusade's sponsors were the third world nations that had so strenuously opposed the United States ideas in the earlier campaign. Now, these third world nations were setting the international free-press agenda, and their campaign advanced under the title of the New World Information Order. Among the program's precepts: establishment of an international code of ethics, licensing of journalists, more representative and balanced coverage of world events, and development of facilities in third world countries to allow them to report their own news to the rest of the world.

These points were, of course, raised in the United Nations debates of the late 1940s and early 1950s. In the earlier encounters, American representatives—despite evidence to the contrary—tended to see these issues as part of a worldwide communist conspiracy against the United States and all of its institutions, including its press. In the 1970s, many Americans still saw the campaign as a communist-inspired attempt to gain control of the world's communications system, despite the obvious influence of third world nations on the movement. By the 1980s, debates over this new proposal within UNESCO's forums became one reason behind government and press calls for the United States to pull out of that international organization.

Few people, it seems, had learned the lessons of the postwar free-press campaign. Few people had discovered that freedom of the press was culturally based and that no nation could impose its press system on another nation, just as no nation could impose its system of religion or government on another nation. Few people yet had grasped the futility of debates on the topic. Perhaps only a debate about imposing the religious system of one country on other countries would raise the emotional level of discussions as quickly as debates over exporting the press systems of the world to other parts of the globe. No one seemed to have learned the main point of the earlier United Nations debates—that as each nation must be allowed to develop its own religious system, each nation also must be allowed to develop its own press system. And the development of that press system basically is the responsibility of each nation, for help from another nation implicitly carries the desire to pass along the value system of the nation offering the assistance. Nor have the nations learned that, although there are indeed inequities in news coverage around the world, the chances of correcting those inequities are almost nonexistent. Debates over the adequacy and accuracy of news coverage are long standing, and despite long and heated debates explicating the needed changes, no substantial alterations have yet occurred. The press is an institution run by human beings to serve other human beings; as long as human beings are involved in this most human of institutions, problems will arise.

As for the American press, by the 1980s many of its members who reacted strongly to the third world nations' plans seem to have forgotten the attempts of American journalists of the postwar era to export American press values to the rest of the world. And the American press sometimes tends to forget its own foibles, such as those demonstrated by the domestic events of the early 1950s, which do not increase the credence of arguments supporting the American press system. With the postwar effort firmly in view, the campaign by the third world nations to mold the international communications network into a form more acceptable to those countries takes on a somewhat different perspective.

The fate of the New World Information Order may well be written in the past. Attempts by the League of Nations to deal with issues such as false news and the adequate dissemination of news failed. Efforts by the United Nations to deal with similar topics met a similar fate. In both sets of debates, the unwillingness of various nations to abandon their press systems in favor of programs advocated by others was the key to failure. Although the debates over the New World Information Order may wax rather hot indeed, the chances are good that this attempt to reshape the world's communications structure will meet the same fate as its predecessors.

Appendixes

APPENDIX A

Measures to Be Taken against Propaganda and the Inciters of a New War—1947

Whereas in the Charter of the United Nations the peoples express their determination to save succeeding generations from the scourge of war, which twice in our lifetime has brought untold sorrow to mankind, and to practice tolerance and live together in peace with one another as good neighbours, and

Whereas the Charter also calls for the promotion of universal respect for, and observance of, fundamental freedoms which include freedom of expression, all Members having pledged themselves in Article 56 to take joint and separate action for such observance of fundamental freedoms,

The General Assembly
1. *Condemns* all forms of propaganda, in whatsoever country conducted, which is either designed or likely to provoke or encourage any threat to the peace, breach of the peace, or act of aggression;
2. *Requests* the Government of each Member to take appropriate steps within its constitutional limits:

   (a) To promote, by all means of publicity and propaganda available to them, friendly relations among nations based upon the Purposes and Principles of the Charter;

   (b) To encourage the dissemination of all information designed to give expression to the undoubted desire of all peoples for peace;
3. *Directs* that this resolution be communicated to the forthcoming Conference on Freedom of Information.

—Resolution 110 (II), GAOR, 1947.

APPENDIX B

False or Distorted Reports—1947

The General Assembly
Considering that, under Article 1 of the Charter, Members are bound to develop friendly relations amongst themselves and to achieve international co-operation in promoting and encouraging respect for human rights and fundamental liberties;

Considering that to attain this end it is essential to facilitate and increase the diffusion in all countries of information calculated to strengthen mutual understanding and ensure friendly relations between the peoples;

Considering that substantial progress in this sphere can be achieved only if measures are taken to combat, within the limits of constitutional procedures, the publication of false or distorted reports likely to injure friendly relations between states;

Invites the Governments of States Members

1. To study such measures as might with advantage be taken on the national plane to combat, within the limits of constitutional procedures, the diffusion of false or distorted reports likely to injure friendly relations between States;
2. To submit reports on this subject to the Conference on Freedom of Information so as to provide the Conference with the data it requires to enable it to start its work immediately on a concrete basis;

Recommends to the Conference on Freedom of Information that it study, with a view to their co-ordination, the measures taken or advocated in this connexion by the various States. . . .

—Resolution 127 (II), GAOR, 1947.

APPENDIX C

Solemn Appeal against the Idea That War Is Inevitable—1947

A
The representatives of Education, Science and Culture, meeting together at Mexico City at the Unesco General Conference:
Aware of the responsibilities imposed upon them by the Constitution of

the Organization to further universal respect for justice, for the rule of law, for human rights, and the fundamental freedoms of the peoples of the world, without distinction of race, sex, language or religion;

Concerned at the dangers to peace resulting from currents of thought conducive to the idea that another war is inevitable;

Troubled by the indifference, resignation and even calm acceptance which such currents of thought meet in certain sections of public opinion;

Address a solemn appeal to all who are concerned for the dignity of Man and the future of civilization, particularly educationalists, scientists, artists, writers and journalists throughout the world;

Adjure them to denounce the pernicious idea that war is inevitable;

To act as the mouthpiece of the conscience of the nations, refusing collective suicide;

To combat, by every means in their power, surrender to fear and every form of thought or action which may threaten a just and lasting peace.

B

Whereas the General Conference of Unesco has adopted unanimously the resolution initiated by the French delegation appealing to educationalists, scholars, artists, writers and journalists throughout the world to combat, by every means in their power, surrender to fear and to every form of thought or action which may threaten a just and lasting peace, and

Whereas the General Assembly of the United Nations adopted unanimously the resolution of 3 November 1947, requesting the Government of each Member to take appropriate steps within its constitutional limits to promote by all means of publicity and propaganda available to them friendly relations among nations based upon the purposes and principles of the Charter of the United Nations, and to encourage the dissemination of all information designed to give expression to the undoubted desire of all peoples for peace.

The General Conference sees no need to consider further resolutions on this subject.

—Resolution 3, UNESCO Proceedings, 1947.

APPENDIX D

Draft Convention on the Gathering and International Transmission of News—1948

The Contracting States

Desiring to implement the right of their peoples to be fully informed,

Desiring to improve understanding between their peoples through the free flow of information and opinion,

Having resolved to conclude a Convention for this purpose,

Have agreed as follows:

Art. 1.

For the purposes of the present Convention, the following expressions are to be understood in the sense hereinafter defined.

A. *Information Agency.* A press, radio or film organization, whether public or private, created or organized under the applicable laws and regulations within the territories of a Contracting State, regularly engaged in the collection and dissemination of news (including opinion) to the public, including Press associations, news feature services, newspapers, periodicals, radio and television broadcasting organizations, and newsreel companies.

B. *Foreign Correspondent.* An individual employed by an information agency, or a national of a Contracting State, who in either case is regularly engaged in the collection and reporting of news (including opinion) to the general public, and who is the holder of a valid passport identifying him as a correspondent or of a similar document internationally accepted identifying him as such.

C. *News Material.* All news material, whether of information or opinion, and whether visual or auditory, for public dissemination.

Art. 2.

In order to encourage the freest possible movement of foreign correspondents in the performance of their functions, the Contracting States shall expedite, in a manner consistent with their respective laws and procedures, the administrative measures necessary for the entry, residence, movement and travel of foreign correspondents, together with their professional equipment, and shall impose no special discriminatory or unusual restrictions on such ingress or egress, nor upon the transit through or residence in their territories of such correspondents.

Art. 3.

The Contracting States shall permit and encourage the widest possible access to news, official and non-official, for all foreign correspondents on the same basis as for national correspondents and shall not discriminate among foreign correspondents as regards such access.

Art. 4.

The Contracting States shall permit egress from their territory of all news material of foreign correspondents and foreign information agencies without censorship, editing or delay; provided that each of the Contracting States may make and enforce regulations relating directly to the maintenance of national military security. Such regulations must, however, be communicated to foreign correspondents and apply equally to all foreign correspondents and foreign information agencies.

If the requirements of national military security should compel a Contracting State, in peace-time, to establish censorship for a certain period of time, it shall:

1. Establish in advance such categories of news material for the use of an information agency in another country as are subject to previous inspection and publish the directives of the censor announcing forbidden matters;

2. Carry out censorship as far as possible in the presence of the foreign correspondent;

3. Where censorship in the presence of the person concerned is not possible:

(a) Fix the time-limit allowed the censors for the return of news material;

(b) Require the return of news material submitted for censorship direct to the foreign correspondent or foreign information agency so that they may know at once what has been censored in their text and what use they may make of the censored information;

(c) Base the charge on the number of words composing a telegram after censorship;

(d) Return the total telegraph charges for telegrams submitted for censorship, the transmission of which has been delayed more than six hours.

Art. 5.

The Contracting States, while recognizing that foreign correspondents must conform to the laws in force in the countries in which they are operating, agree that foreign correspondents legally admitted into their territories shall not be expelled on account of any lawful exercise of their right to seek, receive or impart information or opinion.

Art. 6.

The Contracting States agree that foreign correspondents shall have access to all facilities generally and publicly used for the international transmission of news material and may transmit news material from one country to another on the same basis and at the same rates applicable to all other users of such facilities for similar purposes.

Art. 7.

Each of the Contracting States agrees to permit all news material of foreign correspondents and information agencies of the other Contracting States to enter its territory and reach information agencies operating therein on the same conditions as are accorded to any other foreign information agencies.

Art. 8.

Nothing herein contained shall be construed as depriving any Contracting State of its right to make and enforce regulations prohibiting obscene news material.

Art. 9.

The present Convention shall not apply to foreign correspondents who, while not otherwise admissible under article 2 into the territory of a Contracting State, are nevertheless admitted conditionally in accordance with an agreement between that Contracting State and the United Nations, or a specialized agency thereof, in order to cover its proceedings, or pursuant to a special arrangement made by the Contracting State in order to facilitate the entry of such correspondents.

Art. 10.

Nothing herein contained shall be interpreted as exempting foreign correspondents or foreign information agencies from public laws and regulations promulgated by any Contracting State for the protection of national security.

Art. 11.

The present Convention shall be ratified on behalf of the States signatory hereto in conformity with their respective constitutional procedures. The instruments of ratification shall be deposited with the Secretary-General of the United Nations, who shall notify all signatory and acceding States of each such deposit.

Art. 12.

The present Convention shall remain open for accession of all States which are not signatories. Instruments of accession shall be deposited with the Secretary-General of the United Nations, who shall notify all signatory and acceding States of each such deposit.

Art. 13.

The present Convention shall come into force as soon as two States have deposited their respective instruments of ratification or accession. The convention thereafter shall come into force with respect to each other State on the date of the deposit of its instrument of ratification or accession.

Art. 14.

(a) A State party to the present Convention may at the same time of its accession thereto or at any time thereafter by notification addressed to the Secretary-General of the United Nations declare that the present Convention shall extend to any of the territories for the international relations of which it is responsible, and the Convention shall extend to the territories named in the notification as from the thirtieth day after the date of receipt by the Secretary-General of the United Nations of the notification.

The respective Contracting States undertake to seek immediately the consent of the Governments of such territories to the application of the present Convention to such territories, and to accede forthwith on behalf of and in respect of each such territory, if and when its consent has been obtained.

(b) A State which has made a declaration under paragraph (a) above extending the present Convention may with the consent of the Government concerned at any time thereafter by notification to the Secretary-General of the United Nations declare that the Convention shall cease to extend to any territory named in the notification, and the Convention shall then cease to extend to such territory six months after the date of receipt by the Secretary-General of the United Nations of the notification.

Art. 15.

The present Convention shall remain in force indefinitely, but may be denounced by any Contracting State, by means of six months' notice in writing given to the Secretary-General of the United Nations, who shall transmit a copy of the notice to each of the other Contracting States. After the expiration of this period of six months, the Convention shall cease in its effect as regards the State which denounces it, but shall remain in force for the remaining Contracting States.

IN WITNESS WHEREOF, the Plenipotentiaries of the respective States, being duly authorized thereto, have signed the present Convention.

Done at ——— this ——— day of ——— 1948 in the ——— languages, each equally authentic, the original of which shall be deposited in the archives of the United Nations. The Secretary-General of the United Nations shall transmit certified copies thereof to all the signatory and acceding States.

—Yearbook on Human Rights for 1948, pp. 498–500.

APPENDIX E

Draft Convention on Freedom of Information—1948

The States Parties to this Convention

Considering that the free interchange of information and opinions, both in the national and in the international sphere, is a fundamental human right and essential in the cause of peace and for the achievement of political, social and economic progress, and

Desiring to co-operate fully with one another to promote the peace and welfare of mankind by this means,

Have accepted the following provisions:

Art. 1.

Subject to the provisions of articles 2, 4, 5, and 6 of this Convention,

(a) Each Contracting State shall secure to all its own nationals and to the nationals of every other Contracting State lawfully within its territory freedom to impart and receive information and opinions, orally, by written or printed matter, in the form of art, or by legally operated visual or auditory devices without governmental interference;

(b) No Contracting State shall regulate or control the use or availability of any of the means of communication referred to in the preceding paragraph, in any manner discriminating against any of its own nationals or of the nationals of any other Contracting State on political or personal grounds or on the basis of race, sex, language or religion;

(c) Each Contracting State shall secure to all its own nationals and to the nationals of every other Contracting State, freedom to transmit and listen to information and opinions within its territories and across its frontiers by any legally operated means without governmental interference;

(d) Each Contracting State shall permit the nationals of other Contracting States as much freedom to seek information as it grants to its own nationals;

(e) The Contracting States shall encourage and facilitate the interchange between their territories of those of their nationals engaged in the gathering of information and opinions for dissemination to the public and shall deal expeditiously with applications by such persons to enter their territories;

Art. 2.

1. The freedoms referred to in paragraphs (a), (c) and (d) of article 1 carry with them duties and responsibilities and may therefore be subject to necessary penalties, liabilities and restrictions clearly defined by law, but only with regard to:

(a) Matters which must remain secret in the interest of national safety;

(b) Expressions which incite persons to alter by violence the system of government or which promote disorder;

(c) Expressions which incite persons to commit criminal acts;

(d) Expressions which are obscene or which are dangerous for youth and expressed in publications intended for them;

(e) Expressions which are injurious to the fair conduct of legal proceedings;

(f) Expressions which infringe literary or artistic rights;

(g) Expressions about other persons, natural or legal, which defame their reputations or are otherwise injurious to them without benefiting the public;

(h) Legal obligations resulting from professional, contractual or other legal relationships including disclosure of information received in confidence in a professional or official capacity;

(i) The prevention of fraud;

(j) The systematic diffusion of deliberately false or distorted reports which undermine friendly relations between peoples or States.

2. A Contracting State may establish on reasonable terms a right of reply or a similar corrective measure.

Art. 3.

Each Contracting State shall encourage the establishment and functioning within its territory of one or more non-official organizations of persons employed in the dissemination of information to the public, in order to promote the observance by such persons of high standards of professional conduct, and in particular:

(a) To report facts without prejudice and in their proper context and to make comments without malicious intent;

(b) To facilitate the solution of the economic, social and humanitarian problems of the world as a whole and the free interchange of information bearing on such problems;

(c) To help promote respect for human rights and fundamental freedoms without discrimination;

(d) To help maintain international peace and security;

(e) To counteract the persistent spreading of false or distorted reports which promote hatred or prejudice against States, persons or groups of different race, language, religion or philosophical conviction.

Art. 4.

Nothing in the present Convention shall affect the right of any Contracting State to take measures which it deems necessary in order:

(a) To bring its balance of payments into equilibrium;

(b) To develop its national news enterprises until such time as such news enterprises are fully developed;

(c) To prevent agreements in restraint of the free flow of information or the cartelization in regard to information:

provided that such measures may not be used as a means of preventing the entry of nationals of other Contracting States who are engaged in the gathering of information and opinions for dissemination to the public.

Art. 5.

Nothing in the present Convention shall prevent a Contracting State from reserving under its legislation to its own nationals the right to edit newspaper or news periodicals produced within its territory.

Art. 6.

Nothing in the present Convention shall limit the discretion of any Contracting State to refuse entry into its territory to any particular persons, or to restrict the period of his residence thereon.

Art. 7.

As between the Contracting States which become parties to any general agreement on Human Rights sponsored by the United Nations and containing provisions relating to freedom of information, the present Convention shall be superseded by such agreement to the extent that the two instruments are inconsistent.

Art. 8.

In time of war or other public emergency a Contracting State may take measures derogating from its obligations under the present Convention to the extent strictly limited by the exigencies of the situation.

Any Contracting State availing itself of this right of derogation shall promptly inform the Secretary-General of the United Nations of the measures which its has thus adopted and of the reasons therefor. It shall also inform him as and when the measures cease to operate.

Art. 9.

Any dispute between any two or more Contracting States concerning the interpretation or application of the present Convention which is not settled by negotiations shall be referred to the International Court of Justice for decision unless the Contracting States agree to another mode of settlement.

Art. 10.

1. The present Convention shall be open for accession to every State invited to the United Nations Conference on Freedom of Information held at

Geneva in March and April 1948, and to every other State which the General Assembly of the United Nations shall, by resolution, declare to be eligible.
2. Accession shall be effected by the deposit of an instrument of accession with the Secretary-General of the United Nations.

Art. 11.

When any two of the States mentioned in article 10 have deposited their instruments of accession, the present Convention shall come into force between them on the thirtieth day after the date of the deposit of the second instrument of accession. It shall come into force for each State which accedes after that date on the thirtieth day after the deposit of its instrument of accession.

Art. 12.

Any Contracting State may denounce the present Convention by notification of denunciation to the Secretary-General of the United Nations. Denunciation shall take effect six months after the date of receipt of the Secretary-General of the United Nations of the notification of denunciation.

Art. 13.

(a) A State party to the present Convention may at the same time of its accession thereto or at any time thereafter by notification addressed to the Secretary-General of the United Nations declare that the present Convention shall extend to any of the territories for the international relations of which it is responsible, and the Convention shall extend to the territories named in the notification as from the thirtieth day after the date of receipt by the Secretary-General of the United Nations of the notification. The respective Contracting States undertake to seek immediately the consent of the Governments of such territories to the application of the present Convention to such territories, and to accede forthwith on behalf of and in respect of each such territory, if and when its consent has been obtained.

(b) A State which has made a declaration under paragraph (a) above extending the present Convention may with the consent of the Government concerned at any time thereafter by notification to the Secretary-General of the United Nations declare that the Convention shall cease to extend to any territory named in the notification, and the Convention shall then cease to extend to such territory six months after the date of receipt by the Secretary-General of the United Nations of the notification.

Art. 14.

The Secretary-General of the United Nations shall notify each of the States referred to in article 10 of the date of the deposit of every instrument of accession and of the date on which this Convention comes into force and of any information received by him in accordance with the provisions of article

11 and of every notification received by him in accordance with the provisions of articles 12 or 13.

—Yearbook on Human Rights for 1948, pp. 501–3.

APPENDIX F

Draft Convention Concerning the Institution of an International Right of Correction—1948

The Governments Parties to the present Convention,

Considering the danger to the maintenance of friendly relations between peoples and to the preservation of peace, presented by the publication of inaccurate reports;

Considering that at its second session, the General Assembly of the United Nations recommended the adoption of measures designed to promote friendly relations among nations and to combat the dissemination of false or distorted reports likely to injure the friendly relations between States;

Considering, however, that it does not at present appear possible or desirable to envisage the institution on the international level of a procedure for verifying the accuracy of a report such as might lead to the imposition of penalties for the publication of false or distorted reports;

Considering, moreover, that to prevent the publication of false or distorted news or to reduce its pernicious effects, it is above all necessary to sharpen the sense of responsibility of the various media of information and to promote the wide circulation of news;

That an effective means to this end is to give all those directly affected by a report which they consider false or distorted and which is spread by an organ of information the possibility of ensuring commensurate publicity for their corrections or replies; that the right of reply or correction had been embodied in the legislation of a large number of States and that its legitimacy is recognized in the draft of article 17 of the Covenant on Human Rights which the Sub-Commission on Freedom of Information and of the Press decided, at its second session, to recommend to the Commission on Human Rights; that failing the adoption, by all States, in their own legislation, of a like right available to foreign nationals under the same conditions as to their own nationals, it is particularly desirable to institute on the international level a right of correction; that it is necessary, however, in order to prevent any abuse, strictly to define the extent of the right of correction, and clearly to specify the conditions for its exercise;

Have adopted the following articles:

Art. 1.

In cases where a Contracting State alleges that news reports likely to injure its relations with other States transmitted from one country to another country by foreign correspondents or by news agencies and disseminated abroad, are false or distorted, it may submit its version of the facts (hereinafter called *communiqué*) to the Contracting States within whose territories such reports have been published in one or more newspapers or periodicals or disseminated by radio. Such *communiqué* may be issued only with respect to news reports and must be without comment or expression of opinion. As far as possible the *communiqué* should not contain a larger number of words than the news report objected to, and in no case more than double the number of words in the news report to be corrected. The *communiqué* must be accompanied by a verbatim text of the report as published or disseminated, and by evidence that the report objected to has been transmitted from one country to another by a foreign correspondent or by a news agency.

Art. 2.

1. Any Government of a Contracting State receiving such a *communiqué* shall, whatever be its opinion concerning the facts in quesion, make available to the news enterprises functioning in the territory where it exercises its authority the *communiqué* of the Government exercising the right of correction and, within five clear days from the date of receiving this *communiqué*, shall facilitate its dissemination through customary channels in accordance with its procedure for releasing news concerning international affairs.

2. In the event of the failure of any Contracting State to discharge its obligation under this article with respect to the *communiqués* of another Contracting State, the latter may discharge on the basis of reciprocity its obligation with respect to any *communiqués* thereafter submitted to it by the defaulting State.

Art. 3.

If any of the Contracting States to which this *communiqué* has been transmitted fails to fulfil, within the prescribed time-limit, the obligation laid down in the preceding article, the Government exercising the right of correction may submit the said *communiqué* to the Secretary-General of the United Nations who shall, within five clear days from the receipt thereof, give it appropriate publicity. This paragraph shall come into force as soon as the General Assembly of the United Nations has instructed its Secretary-General to perform this duty.

Art. 4.

Every Contracting State may, to the extent strictly limited by the exigencies of the situation, derogate from its obligations under the present convention.

(a) As long as a state of war or public emergency prevails in its own territory,

(b) As long as such a state prevails in the territory of one or other Contracting States, but only with regard to those States.

Art. 5.

Any dispute between any two or more Contracting States concerning the interpretation or application of the present Convention which is not settled by negotiations shall be referred to the International Court of Justice for decision unless the Contracting States agree to another mode of settlement.

Art. 6.

The present Convention shall be open for accession to every State invited to the United Nations Conference on Freedom of Information held at Geneva in March and April 1948, and to every other State which the General Assembly of the United Nations shall, by resolution, declare to be eligible.

Accession shall be effected by the deposit of an instrument of accession with the Secretary-General of the United Nations.

Art. 7.

When any two of the States mentioned in article 6 have deposited their instruments of accession, the present Convention shall come into force between them on the thirtieth day after the date of the deposit of the second instrument of accession. It shall come into force for each State which accedes after that date on the thirtieth day after the deposit of its instrument of accession.

Art. 8.

Any Contracting State may denounce the present Convention by notification of denunciation to the Secretary-General of the United Nations. Denunciation shall take effect six months after the date of receipt by the Secretary-General of the United Nations of the notification of denunciation.

Art. 9.

1. A State party to the present Convention may at the same time of its accession thereto or at any time thereafter by notification addressed to the Secretary-General of the United Nations declare that the present Convention shall extend to any of the territories for the international relations of

which it is responsible, and the Convention shall extend to the territories named in the notification as from the thirtieth day after the date of receipt by the Secretary-General of the United Nations of the notification. The respective Contracting States undertake to seek immediately the consent of the Governments of such territories to the application of the present Convention to such territories, and to accede forthwith on behalf of and in respect of each such territory, if and when its consent has been obtained.
2. A State which has made a declaration under paragraph 1 above extending the present Convention may with the consent of the Government concerned at any time thereafter by notification to the Secretary-General of the United Nations declare that the Convention shall cease to extend to any territory named in the notification, and the Convention shall then cease to extend to such territory six months after the date of receipt by the Secretary-General of the United Nations of the notification.

Art. 10.
The Secretary-General of the United Nations shall notify each of the States referred to in article 6 of the date of the deposit of every instrument of accession and of the date on which this Convention comes into force and of any information received by him in accordance with the provisions of article 5 and of every notification received by him in accordance with the provisions of articles 7 or 8.

—Yearbook on Human Rights for 1948, pp. 500–501.

APPENDIX G

Article for the Draft Declaration on Human Rights—1948

Everyone shall have the right to freedom of thought and expression; this right shall include freedom to hold opinions without interference and to seek, receive and impart information and ideas by any means regardless of frontiers.

—Yearbook on Human Rights for 1948, p. 503.

APPENDIX H

Article 17 for the Draft Covenant on Human Rights—1948

1. Every person shall have the right to freedom of thought and the right to freedom of expression without interference by governmental action; these rights shall include freedom to hold opinions, to seek, receive and impart information and ideas, regardless of frontiers, either orally, by written or printed matter, in the form of art, or by legally operated visual or auditory devices.

2. The right to freedom of expression carries with it duties and responsibilities and may, therefore, be subject to penalties, liabilities or restrictions clearly defined by law, but only with regard to:

(a) Matters which must remain secret in the interests of national safety;

(b) Expressions which incite persons to alter by violence the system of Government;

(c) Expressions which directly incite persons to commit criminal acts;

(d) Expressions which are obscene;

(e) Expressions injurious to the fair conduct of legal proceedings;

(f) Infringements of literary or artistic rights;

(g) Expressions about other persons natural or legal which defame their reputations or are otherwise injurious to them without benefiting the public;

(h) The systematic diffusion of deliberately false or distorted reports which undermine friendly relations between peoples and States;

A State may establish on reasonable terms a right of reply or a similar corrective remedy.

3. Measures shall be taken to promote the freedom of information through the elimination of political, economic, technical and other obstacles which are likely to hinder the free flow of information.

4. Nothing in this article shall be deemed to affect the right of any State to control the entry of persons into its territory or the period of their residence therein.

—Yearbook on Human Rights for 1948, p. 503.

APPENDIX I

Draft International
Code of Ethics—1950

Whereas freedom of information and of the press is vital to the peace of humanity and to the fundamental freedoms consecrated by the Charter of the United Nations and the Universal Declaration of Human Rights;

Whereas that freedom can best be safeguarded by the personnel of the press and of other media of information constantly maintaining and promoting, through their voluntary action, the spirit of responsibility in which they seek the truth and report facts or comment on them;

Therefore the following Code of Ethics is proclaimed as a standard of practice and professional conduct for all engaged in the gathering, transmission and dissemination of news and in commenting thereon.

Art. I.

All engaged in gathering, transmission and dissemination of news and in commenting thereon shall make the utmost endeavour to ensure that the information the public receives is factually accurate and objective. They shall check all items of information whose veracity is open to doubt. No fact shall be distorted or essential fact suppressed. They shall never publish, or in any way be party to the publishing of, information known to be false.

Art. II.

1. Personal interest shall not influence professional conduct. Whether for publication or suppression the acceptance of an inducement or bribe is one of the gravest professional offences.
2. Calumny, slander, libel, unfounded accusations and plagiarism are also serious professional offences.
3. Any published information which is found to be inaccurate shall be voluntarily and immediately rectified.
4. Rumour and unconfirmed news shall be identified and treated as such.

Art. III.

1. All engaged in the gathering, transmission and dissemination of news and in commenting thereon shall seek to maintain full public confidence in the integrity and dignity of their profession. They shall assign and accept only such tasks as are compatible with this integrity and dignity; and they shall guard against exploitation of their status.
2. Full responsibility shall be assumed for all information and comments

published. If responsibility is disclaimed, this shall be explicitly stated in advance.

3. The reputation of individuals shall be respected, and news regarding their private lives likely to harm their reputation shall not be published unless it is in the public interest, as distinguished from public curiosity, to do so. Charges against reputation or moral character shall not be made without opportunity for reply.

4. Discretion shall be observed about sources of information and matters revealed in confidence. Professional secrecy must be observed; and this privilege may always be invoked, taking the law of the country into account.

Art. IV.

All engaged in the gathering of information about countries other than their own, or in commenting on them, shall make the utmost endeavour to acquire the necessary background knowledge conducive to accurate and objective reporting and comment concerning such measures.

—Yearbook on Human Rights for 1950, p. 478.

Bibliographic Essay

Primary sources of information for this study are United States Department of State records housed at the National Archives in Washington, D.C., at the Washington National Records Center in Suitland, Maryland, and at the State Department itself; records of United Nations meetings and proposals published by the United Nations; several private paper collections; and professional publications representing various journalistic organizations.

The State Department records at the National Archives and at the Washington National Records Center are abundant, but they are filed under so many different headings and decimal classifications that digging out the pertinent material was a considerable challenge. Unfortunately, only State Department records through 1949 are available at the National Archives. Records for 1950–1952 still were housed in the Department of State when the research for this book was done, and most of the departmental records for United Nations issues are also kept at the Department of State. To obtain material still in the custody of the State Department, multiple Freedom of Information Act requests are necessary. Although these requests yielded valuable information, the data found through these Freedom of Information Act requests was discovered by State Department researchers rather than by the author, a factor that may have limited the breadth of the investigation.

United Nations records are numerous and full. The international organization mimeographed and distributed to depository libraries almost every document submitted to its various committees as well as the summary records of the meetings of various committees, commissions, subcommissions, and special conferences. Details about the debates are indeed full, but most of the reports are summary in form rather than verbatim accounts of what the speakers said. The accuracy of the comments is not in doubt, however, for after the summary records of a particular meeting were issued, participants in debates had ample opportunity to review the record and to submit corrections to their remarks, which the United Nations then mimeographed and distributed. Thus, although the phrasing may be awkward and the words may not exactly be those emanating from the mouths of the speakers, the positions stated and the information introduced into debates are correct.

Fleshing out some of the background of this story are papers from various manuscript collections around the country. William Benton's papers at the University of Chicago and documents from the Harry S. Truman Library in Independence, Missouri, are especially valuable. Also useful are items from the Edward R. Stettinius, Jr., collection at the University of Virginia, Charlottesville, Virginia, and the James F. Byrnes collection at Clemson University, Clemson, South Carolina. The George C. Marshall papers housed at the George C. Marshall Foundation in Lexington, Virginia, were closed to outside scholars at the time that this book was researched. The George V. Allen papers at the William R. Perkins Library, Duke

University, Durham, North Carolina, contained no pertinent information. No papers from leading journalistic participants in the campaign could be found.

Publications by various journalistic organizations provide the bulk of the information on press opinion about the free-press crusade. Because this is primarily a newspaper story, *Editor & Publisher*, the weekly newspaper trade journal, is particularly valuable. Not only did this journal campaign editorially for international freedom of the press, but its reporters covered many of the important debates for publication. Also of great importance are the publications of the American Society of Newspaper Editors—its *Bulletin* and its *Problems in Journalism* series, which contains the published proceedings of the organization's annual meetings. Through these publications it is possible to see the way in which the crusade developed and collapsed within the organization that supplied the campaign's most ardent supporters. Other journalistic publications providing helpful insights are *The Quill*, the monthly publication of the professional journalism organization, Sigma Delta Chi; *The Guild Reporter*, the official semiweekly publication of the American Newspaper Guild; *Nieman Reports*, the quarterly publication of the Nieman Fellows at Harvard; *The Publishers' Auxiliary*, the weekly publication serving the smaller newspapers of the United States; the *American Newspaper Publishers Association B Bulletin*, a primary publication of the American Newspaper Publishers Association; the *APME Red Book*, the yearly publication of the Associated Press Managing Editors Association, representing reports of the annual meetings; and *Journalism Quarterly*, the quarterly journal of college-level journalism educators. Requests for correspondence and other documents brought references to printed materials.

Once beyond these primary sources of information, data about the free-press crusade becomes harder to find. Kent Cooper gives his perspective on the campaign in two books, *Barriers Down* (New York, Holt, Rinehart and Winston, 1942), and *The Right to Know: An Exposition of the Evils of News Suppression and Propaganda* (New York, Farrar, Straus & Giroux, 1956). The former is devoted almost entirely to the Associated Press's effort to break the international news cartel; the latter contains a variety of criticisms of government propaganda operations and touches on the United Nations campaign in the context of how the once noble free-press crusade was perverted by its connection with government. Hugh Baillie, another participant in the crusade, deals with the free-press effort briefly and primarily through a discussion of the conventions prepared in Geneva in his autobiography, *High Tension* (New York, Harper & Row, 1959). A brief review of the American Society of Newspaper Editors' role in the international information campaign is found in Alice Fox Pitts, *Read All About It!* (Easton, Pa., American Society of Newspaper Editors, 1974). This latter publication, a general history of the ASNE, sees the campaign from a perspective of twenty-plus years, thus obscuring the idealism that led the organization into the crusade.

Other contemporaneous comments about the international free-press campaign can be found in Herbert Brucker, *Freedom of Information* (New York, Macmillan, 1949); Edward W. Barrett, *Truth Is Our Weapon* (New York, Funk & Wagnalls, 1953); James P. Warburg, *Unwritten Treaty* (Orlando, Fla., Harcourt Brace Jovanovich, 1946); Llewellyn White and Robert D. Leigh, *Peoples Speaking to Peoples* (Chicago, University of Chicago Press, 1946); and Sidney Hyman, *The Lives of William Benton* (Chicago, University of Chicago Press, 1969). Barrett was assistant secretary of state for public affairs in the early 1950s and an architect of the crusade for truth campaign. The White and Leigh book was a publication of the Hutchins Commission on Freedom of the Press. Warburg deals with problems raised by psychological warfare and advocates outlawing it.

Of the leading statesmen whose careers were touched by the campaign, only James F. Byrnes addresses freedom of information questions in his autobiography, *Speaking Frankly* (New York, Harper & Row, 1947), and even then, his comments deal primarily with opening various international meetings to the press. Dean Acheson discusses the problems involved in trying to make sure that the press reports important information in *Present at the Creation* (New York, Norton, 1969). The published Stettinius diaries—Edward R. Stettinius, Jr., *The Diaries of Edward R. Stettinius, Jr., 1943–1946*, edited by Thomas M. Campbell and George C. Herring (New York, New Viewpoints, 1975)—also focus primarily on the problems encountered with the press's desire to cover secret diplomatic negotiations.

General histories of the era ignore the free-press campaign. The crusade is mentioned in more specialized works, however, such as William H. Read, *America's Mass Media Merchants* (Baltimore, Johns Hopkins University Press, 1976). The historical motivations behind the 1940s effort are well explained in Emily S. Rosenberg, *Spreading the American Dream: American Economic and Cultural Expansion, 1890–1945*, (New York, Hill & Wang, 1982). And Oliver Boyd-Barrett, *The International News Agencies* (Beverly Hills, Calif., Sage, 1980), gives some background on the development of the international news agencies, which played such a key role in starting the crusade.

Works about the later New World Information Order controversy, such as Herbert I. Schiller's two works, *Communication and Cultural Domination* (White Plains, N.Y., International Arts and Science, 1976), and *Mass Communications and American Empire* (New York, Augustus M. Kelley, 1969), acknowledge the historical antecedents of the crusade but do not deal with the topic in any great detail. The same is true for Anthony Smith's *Geopolitics of Information: How Western Culture Dominates the World* (New York, Oxford University Press, 1980). Parallels between the press agency campaign for open access to the sources of news in the 1930s and the actions of press agencies in the 1970s are explored in Marlene Cuthbert, "Reaction to International News Agencies: 1930s and 1970s Compared," *Gazette*, 26 (1980):99–110.

Index

425